The Aztecs Under
Spanish Rule

The Aztecs Under Spanish Rule

A History of the Indians of the Valley of Mexico
1519–1810

CHARLES GIBSON

STANFORD UNIVERSITY PRESS
STANFORD CALIFORNIA

For A. K. G.

Stanford University Press
Stanford, California
© 1964 by the Board of Trustees of the
Leland Stanford Junior University
Printed in the United States of America
Cloth ISBN 0-8047-0196-2   Paper ISBN 0-8047-0912-2
Original printing 1964
Last figure below indicates year of this printing:
07   06   05   04   03   02

Preface

In recent years increasing attention has been given to the Indian peoples of America. For certain areas it is now possible to know the modern Indian civilization quite thoroughly and to discern at least the larger outlines of the past. The critical deficiencies of our understanding of Spanish America appear not where one might expect, in remote antiquity, for twentieth-century archaeology has made and continues to make enormous gains; they occur, paradoxically, where written documentation is most abundant, between the time of the first white contact and the twentieth century. It has therefore seemed to me that investigations of Indian history in the relatively recent past might be useful and worthwhile.

In an earlier book dealing with the Mexican province of Tlaxcala, I sought to examine some features of Indian history in the post-conquest years. One defect of that work was that it failed to carry the research beyond the sixteenth century, a limitation that surely had consequences in the conclusions reached. In dealing with the Valley of Mexico, I have tried to cover the whole of the colonial period. My first intention was to treat the nineteenth and twentieth centuries as well, but the complications of the colonial years persuaded me that these alone are adequate for one inquiry, and for better or for worse this work terminates at 1810.

Bibliographical commentary on sources has been reduced to a minimum, for the forthcoming Handbook of Middle American Indians will make such commentary superfluous. Subjects that may be regarded for the present as sufficiently understood and subjects that I know to be under investigation by others have likewise been dealt with only summarily; I have not, for example, treated the procedures of missionary conversion or technical demography or Indian arts with the attention that a uniform documentation *would require. My occasional trespasses on preserves already staked out by friends and colleagues are intended chiefly to call attention to their work, which will speedily supersede what I have to say.*

My study of this subject began in the fall of 1951 and continued to January 1963. Several important new items have appeared in recent months, but I have abided by my terminal date and refrained from incorporating them. I wish especially to mention, however, the new work of Woodrow Borah and Sherburne F. Cook, The Aboriginal Population of Central Mexcio on the Eve of Spanish Conquest, *which would otherwise receive well-merited citation in these pages.*

My indebtedness to the researches of Robert Ricard, François Chevalier, Silvio Zavala, Lesley B. Simpson, George Kubler, and the late Robert Barlow will be evident to all readers familiar with twentieth-century investigations of Mexican colonial history. My colleagues in the Ethnohistory sections of the Handbook of Middle American Indians—*Howard F. Cline, Henry B. Nicholson, John B. Glass, and Donald Robertson—have provided me with much general and particular information. Correspondence and personal discussions with José Miranda and Wigberto Jiménez Moreno in Mexico and with Pedro Carrasco, France Scholes, and Woodrow Borah in the United States have consistently enlarged my data and bibliography. Special aid on points of fact, bibliography, or presentation has been furnished by Bohumil Badura, Ernesto de la Torre, Jean-Pierre Berthe, Earl J. Pariseau, Robert Potash, Robert Knowlton, Donald Cooper, Jack Rounceville, Paula Bylsma, and Mary Anglim. The John Simon Guggenheim Memorial Foundation supported my archival studies in Mexico in 1952–53, and the Rockefeller Foundation furnished a grant in 1960–61 for further archival studies in Spain, France, Mexico, and the United States. The bibliographical work was accomplished in large part with the library resources of the State University of Iowa. My wife has contributed at all stages to the preparation of this book.*

C. G.

July 1, 1964

Contents

Illustrations

General orientation maps appear on pp. xi–xii.

MAPS

FIGURES

PLATES

Plates I – VIII follow page 178

Plates IX – XII follow page 274

Plates XIII – XVI follow page 370

Top map:

MEXICO

GULF OF MEXICO

0   100   200   300
Miles

• Zacatecas

• Panuco
• Calpa
• Guadalajara   • Guanajuato   • Tuxpan
• Zimapan

• Colima   Campeche •   *Yucatan*
Valley of   • Jalapa
• Mexico   • Veracruz
Michoacan
Tehuacan •

Tabasco

• Oaxaca   *Tehuantepec*
Acapulco •

Huatulco •   GUATEMALA   HONDURAS

PACIFIC OCEAN   Soconusco •
Sonsonate •   NICARAGUA

Bottom map:

• Misquiahuala

• Pachuca
• Tula   • Tulanzingo

Zumpango

• Otumba   • Apam

• Calpulalpan

• Texcoco

Mexico City

• Tlaxcala
Chalco Atenco •   • Tezmelucan
Iuca
• Lerma   *Ixtaccihuatl*
Metepec   Amecameca •   • Huejotzingo
Tenango   • Cholula
• Ocuilan   *Popocatepetl* • Puebla
• Malinalco   • Cuauhtinchan
• Oaxtepec   • Atlixco   • Tepeaca
• Cuernavaca   Tecamachalco •
• Cuauhtla
• Huacachula

Taxco   *Atenango River*   • Izucar

River
Nezapa   *Aroyac River*

0   10   20

Miles

Lake Zumpango

Lake Xaltocan

Lake Texcoco

Lake Xochimilco

Lake Chalco

Huehuetoca

Citlaltepec

Zumpango

Xaltocan

Tecama

Teotihuacan

Tepozotlan

Cuauhtitlan

Chiconauhtla

Acolman

Tepexpan

Tizayuca

Tequicistlan

Ecatepec

Chiauhtla

Tenayuca

Tlalnepantla

Texcoco

Azcapotzalco

Huexotla

Los Remedios (Tototepec)

Tacuba

Coatlichan

Tlatelolco

Tenochtitlan

Chimalhuacan Atenco

Chicoloapa

Tacubaya

Coatepec

Santa Fe

Dike of Nezahualcoyotl

Ixtapalapa

Mixcoac

Mexicalzingo

Coyoacan

Culhuacan

Ixtapaluca

Huitzilopochco

Xochimilco

Cuitlahuac

Chalco Atenco

Mixquic

0   5   10   15

Miles

Lake Level, 18ᵀᴴ Century

Lake Level, 1520

The Aztecs Under
Spanish Rule

CHAPTER I

The Valley of Mexico

Aztec civilization is best known for its extraordinary imperial achievement in the fifteenth and early sixteenth centuries, and for its sudden defeat at the hands of a Spanish army in 1519–21. This book examines the history of Aztec civilization following that defeat and the changes that took place in Indian life during the succeeding three centuries of subjugation to the power of the Spanish crown. Our geographical focus and limit will be the Valley of Mexico, for it was here that Aztec civilization flourished and here that the special features of post-conquest Aztec history may most appropriately be examined. It should be noted that the term "Aztec" has no very precise meaning. We use it in an inclusive sense, in reference to Indian peoples whose more particular tribal nomenclature will be analyzed in due course.

The Valley of Mexico is a tiny area in comparison with the total territory of the Aztec empire, but the intricacy of its colonial Indian history is not to be measured in terms of physical size. Situated near the southern edge of the Mexican *mesa central*, it extends approximately seventy-five miles in a north-south direction and forty miles from east to west. Technically it is not a valley but a basin, for it lacks a natural outlet. Volcanic eruptions beginning in the late Tertiary period gave it the form of an irregular elliptical depression surrounded by high mountains.[1] In the pre-Spanish period the mountainous perimeter was heavily forested,[2] the internal slopes were agricultural zones of high fertility, and the basin's central and lowest parts were large shallow lakes.

The surrounding mountains were never absolute obstacles to the movement of peoples, but in pre-Spanish times they did tend to circumscribe and confine the Valley's inhabitants and to differentiate them from the Indians of neighboring areas. This elevated rim, uninhabited and uncultivated, fixed a natural boundary for the gradual expansion and increasing use of land that occurred within the Valley at lower altitudes. It is probable that the encircling mountains impeded the dispersal of peoples, whereas the internal lakes attracted and held them. The locations of the earliest known human occupation—Tepexpan, Iztapan, El Arbolillo, Zacatenco, Ticoman—were lake-shore sites. The Valley's rivers, by contrast, seem to have attracted few settlers; they were precipitous streams, swollen to flood level in the wet summer season and reduced to dry *arroyos* in the winter.

It is tempting to ask what, besides lakes and mountains, engendered the long procession of Indian civilizations here, what sequences of "challenge and response" made this Valley the location of such highly developed native cultures. Perhaps the seasonal alternations of moisture and drought aroused the initiative of peoples whose survival was chiefly dependent on the lakes; and perhaps regional variations in soil, temperature, and conditions of humidity stimulated competitive adaptations, or facilitated the domination of one group over another, in a way that more uniform and less provocative surroundings could not have done. All such matters of course remain conjectural, and we must turn to the known facts of historical change. Although the various periods of change are not fully defined, present evidence favors the acceptance of four main stages: Ancient, Formative, Classic, and Post-Classic.[3]

A long interval of time still separates Ancient man, known from his remains at Tepexpan and his tools at Iztapan, and dated at about 10,000 B.C.,[4] from Formative or Pre-Classic man, who emerged at about 1500 B.C. The Formative period itself is relatively well understood. Its key archaeological locations are El Arbolillo, Zacatenco, Copilco, and Tlatilco. The period is known by its village sites near agricultural lands, and by its pottery, stone and bone tools, and terra-cotta figurines. Social stratification is indicated in the variety of appurtenances with which the dead were buried. The frequent remains of child burials suggest an age distribution not unlike that of colonial times. In the late Formative period, man discarded fewer bones than his predecessors and he terraced his hills, from which facts we infer that he relied less on hunting and responded to the pressures of population increase. His tools became more numerous and complicated, and he used a larger number of trade objects from outside the Valley. His ritual religion was expressed in the oval mound at Cuicuilco, a great ceremonial structure designed to serve the spiritual needs of a mass population.[5]

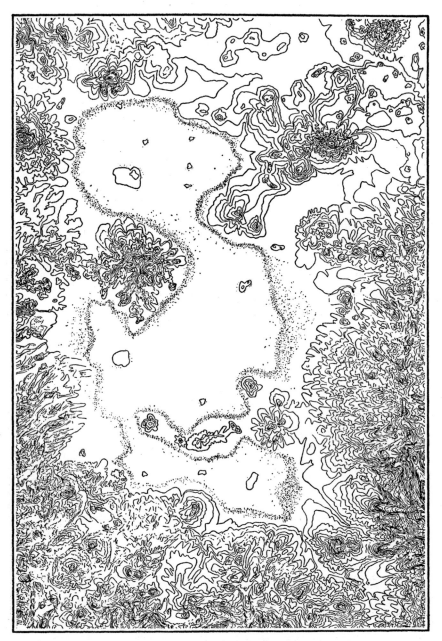

Map 1. Valley of Mexico elevations, showing the approximate lake level
of the conquest period.

These tendencies of the late Formative period achieved spectacular fulfillment in the Classic civilizations, which began in the first centuries of the Christian era and continued to about the year 900. The foremost monument of the Classic period is the Pyramid of the Sun at Teotihuacan, which is half a mile around at the base and several times the height of the Cuicuilco mound. It is part of an immense system of paving and building, with subsidiary mounds and temples, platforms, patios, and sculpture, the whole covering an area of some two thousand acres. Classic artifacts demonstrate a developed commerce and an enlarged pantheon. The theocratic society was highly organized and capable of regulating laborers in vast numbers. But for all its grandeur, the Classic period remains mysterious. Its social organization, government, and language are unknown. Most enigmatic of all is its collapse, which coincided with the decay of Classic civilization outside the Valley and cannot be attributed to any cause yet determined.[6]

In Valley of Mexico archaeology, the term "Post-Classic" refers to the approximately six centuries preceding the arrival of the Spaniards in 1519. This was a time of new immigration, by Tolteca, Chichimeca, Otomi, and "Aztec" peoples. The Tolteca, perhaps under Olmeca pressure, withdrew from the Valley to Tulanzingo and to their foremost capital, Tula. The Chichimeca established themselves at Tenayuca and Amecameca. The Otomi created a capital at Xaltocan. In a series of power shifts, the communities of Xaltocan, Culhuacan, and Azcapotzalco rose and fell as centers of authority. Tenochtitlan emerged in the fifteenth century as the capital of a newly conquered area extending to the Guatemalan border. The Post-Classic period was one of expanded urbanism, enlarged commerce, and intensified military activity.[7]

The chronology of pre-colonial history rests essentially upon the classification and interpretation of artifacts. Time sequences have been established by stylistic analysis, archaeological stratigraphy, and carbon dating; for the later period they depend on the written literature, which is derived from Aztec pictorial and oral sources, and which convincingly registers the competitions of late migrant peoples settling in a confined space.[8] In recent years students have devoted increasing attention to the natural history of the Valley in relation to this recorded human occupation. Their objective has been to discover not so much the results as the causes of civilization, and the primary questions relate to agricultural changes and the responses of successive populations to long-term variations in moisture and aridity.

In the Valley of Mexico, a long drought in the late Formative period is indicated by sites that fall beneath later water levels and by the high incidence of pine (as opposed to oak) pollen.[9] Aridity may have stimulated the adoption both of the aquatic gardens called *chinampas* and of systems of irrigation, possibly during the period of Teotihuacan I. This means that an extended agriculture may have furnished the economic base for Classic civilization. With increased humidity, permitting a further extension of agriculture, we have an appropriate prior condition for the large populations and the power struggles of Post-Classic times.[10]

In comparison with the late Formative, the Post-Classic was a period of abundant moisture, and of all Indian peoples those of late Post-Classic times made the most accomplished adaptation to their lakeside setting. They built dams, causeways, aqueducts, canals, irrigation works, terracing systems, and cities situated partly in the water and partly on land. Fish and water birds helped to provide them with one of the most balanced diets in all America, and chinampa agriculture rivaled Asiatic rice-paddy cultivation in its intensity. Canoes carried merchandise to and from the lakeside cities and towns. The island city of Tenochtitlan-Tlatelolco, originally confined to a small area of insular marshland, became a major urban site and the capital of the Aztec empire. Its avenues were canals; its supplies came by canoe and causeway and aqueduct. Its site was inauspicious, being only a few feet above water level, but in the early sixteenth century it was one of the great cities of the world.

The Valley's population in the early sixteenth century may be estimated at between one and three million, and its density at more than three hundred persons per square mile—a figure substantially higher than that of the Iberian peninsula then or now.[11] In all likelihood, the Spanish conquest took place at a time when the Aztecs were using all available resources, when the population of the Valley was larger than it had ever been, and before the advent of any spontaneous calamities such as those presumed to account for the downfall of Teotihuacan six hundred years earlier.[12]

With the Spanish conquest, the equilibrium of resources and population changed abruptly. The conquerors cut down huge quantities of timber for building material and fuel. Their plows cut more deeply into the earth than had the Indian digging sticks, and their cattle and sheep cropped the land bare. New irrigation systems and gristmills concentrated or redistributed the water flows. No one of the new developments was disastrous in itself, but the combined effect over the years was an accelerated depletion of agricultural land. In the rainy season, topsoil was washed to the Valley bottom. Erosion produced gulleys, and slopes that had once been capable of cultivation became barren.

Other American areas suffered in a similar way from Spanish exploitation. But in the Valley of Mexico the process was aggravated by an unusually heavy influx of Spanish colonists and by the program for controlling flood in Mexico City, which the Spaniards built on the old site of Tenochtitlan. To protect the city, new dams were built, old canals filled, and new ones constructed. Above all, in one of the largest engineering enterprises of pre-industrial society anywhere in the world, a drain consisting partly of tunnel and partly of open trench was cut through the northwestern wall of the Valley for the purpose of drawing water out toward the Río de Tula. This Desagüe, as it was called, was a prodigious operation, carried forward at a great cost in lives, labor, time, and money. It was completed, or virtually completed, only in the nineteenth century, with mechanized equipment.[18] In the colonial period the work was done by Indian laborers with hand tools. But so great was the initial effort that in 1608, only a year after the work had begun and for the first time in any historic period, water was flowing from the Valley on its way to the sea.

Other factors being equal, one might expect a decrease in population following so profound a disturbance in the relations between land and water. One finds, in fact, not simply a decrease but an extremely rapid and severe decline, followed by a partial recovery. Present evidence suggests that the low point was reached in the mid-seventeenth century. We may compute an Indian population of perhaps 1,500,000 in 1519, a drastic reduction to about 70,000 in the seventeenth century, and a rise to approximately 275,000 by the end of colonial times.

The chief cause for the decline of the Indian population in the post-conquest years was pestilence. New diseases were inadvertently introduced by Spaniards and against them the Indians possessed no immunity and no measures of control. The extreme decline after 1519 went far beyond any loss that could be explained by the deterioration of natural resources. Moreover, the population rise in the eighteenth century still failed to press closely upon the Valley's capacity to support human life. Population continued to increase in the nineteenth century, and it is still increasing. Modern sanitation, urbanization, and industrialization have altered the conditions of life in the Valley, but even in 1875, when these factors had not appreciably affected Indian society, the Valley was maintaining a population of more than half a million.[14] In other words, the colonial population, while it fell and rose sharply, always did so within the limits of the environment's declining potential, our tests for which are the higher populations of the periods preceding and following.

Many changes followed upon the decline in population. Those who survived confronted a physical environment on which a smaller Indian population was making fewer demands. Thus despite the deterioration of the land and the social disruption brought about by conquest, a certain easing of environmental tensions distinguishes the colonial from the late Aztec period. The Valley's upper slopes were depopulated, people moved to lower altitudes, and the original higher locations were not later reoccupied. In the Lake Xaltocan area, as the water level fell in the sixteenth and seventeenth centuries, agricultural land became alkaline and infertile. Indians moved to depopulated sections of the lake shore where fresh-water streams kept the soil free from salt and where chinampa agriculture could be maintained. Such movements would have been impossible under the crowded conditions of pre-conquest times.[15]

An adjustment of special interest relates to the new status of *maguey* cactus, which thrived on dry, infertile soils and yielded *pulque,* an intoxicating beverage. Under the stress of Spanish occupation and with the lessening of Aztec restrictions, a reduced population depended increasingly on pulque to help allay the rigors of Spanish exploitation. Supported by two changed conditions, one cultural and the other geographical, maguey came to be grown in areas that had once been more fertile and had supported much larger populations.

Archaeologists identify change in the pre-conquest period by means of dissimilarities among categories of objects, and they look to natural changes as determinants when other causes are unknown. The investigator of the colonial period, on the other hand, uses written sources, applying them to a shorter time span. He is preoccupied with political and religious and military events and committed to problems of European morality. It is evident that conquest marks a discontinuity not only in the human and environmental history of the Valley, but also in the perspective with which these subjects are traditionally viewed.[16]

To understand the role of environment in the colonial period it is not enough simply to transfer the terms of pre-conquest studies to the later era. After 1519 an immense variety of new influences came to bear on Indian life. Hapsburg imperialism drew its incentive from peninsular traditions and neglected regional adaptations. The Valley was never an "environment" for Spaniards save in the most circumstantial way. Spaniards established their colonial capital in the Valley, but they resolutely connected it by road to Veracruz and then by sea to Seville. They rarely adopted Indian styles in dress or design or house construction. Instead, they exaggerated their own Spanish styles, as if to deny their provincial situation. The "culture" of Indian civilization had for them at best an exotic appeal. Spaniards consumed chinampa produce, but they ignored chinampa agricultural methods until the eighteenth century, and even then they examined them not as a model for their own food production but only with the scientific curiosity that marked the age of Charles III. The Valley's lake system, so ingeniously used by Indians, was to Spaniards an obstacle to be drained away after the pattern of the Spanish Netherlands. Spaniards filled the canals of Tenochtitlan, introduced vehicular traffic and mule trains, and left Indians to paddle the canoes.

For local studies such as this, the significant fact is that while Spanish colonial civilization drew its dominant ideas from abroad, it relied upon native resources for the means to implement them. The paradox of a developing Spanish colonialism within a deteriorating environment is explained by a relationship of absolute dependence. Only through the direct use of natural and human resources was the Spanish colony able to flourish.[17] No changes in the relation of natural environment to human population could match the changes wrought by Spanish exploitation. Indian farmers were affected more by appropriations of land than by erosion, more by Spanish control of the irrigation system than by absolute lack of water. In pre-colonial studies, as we have said, the reasons for cultural changes are often in doubt, and are sometimes ascribed to nature rather than to man. But in the colonial period there is less occasion for doubt. The controlling forces were human, and it is to the direct pressures of Hispanic domination on native society that our primary attention will be directed.

CHAPTER II

Tribes

Indian peoples of the sixteenth century understood their own early history through a series of tribal narratives. Their original divisions into groups and the movements of these groups along recorded routes were subjects of keen historical interest to them. Each tribe had its traditional starting point, each had encountered difficulties in migration, and each had taken up residence in the Valley only after strife and hardship.[1]

How is the modern historian to interpret the records of tribal migration? At first, these tales seem remarkable for the precision of their toponymic and chronological detail. But this precision may be in part the consequence of subsequent standardizations. In passing through oral and pictorial phases and translations from one language to another, the narratives were surely subjected to stylization and other distortions. There is evidence that a rivalry in legend-making had come into being by the early sixteenth century and that the relative antiquity of a migration, real or supposed, served as a source of local pride.[2] As historical documents in the usual sense, then, these materials are not wholly reliable. The truth is that modern students are far from reaching a full understanding of the names, routes, dates, and relationships of the migrating peoples. We begin not at a fixed point but in a flux of disoriented data.

So far as the materials permit us to judge, the most important migrant peoples pertinent to Valley history in the Post-Classic or late pre-colonial period were the Olmeca, Xicalanca, Tolteca, Chichimeca, Teochichimeca, Otomi, Culhuaque, Cuitlahuaca, Mixquica, Xochimilca, Chalca, Tepaneca, Acolhuaque, and Mexica.[3] The first five of these were historically extinct, absorbed, or expelled by the time of the arrival of Europeans. The remaining nine maintained separate and recognizable identities, and they constituted the basic ethnic divisions at the time of the Spanish conquest.

OTOMI. Once believed to have been the earliest inhabitants of the Valley, the Otomi have in modern times been correctly classified as relatively late arrivals.[4] Their simple or "primitive" way of life, evident in both Aztec and Spanish times, undoubtedly contributed to a belief in their great antiquity.[5] In the sixteenth century they were the only major Indian group in the Valley possessing a separate, or non-Nahuatl, language, and Nahuatl-speaking peoples generally looked down on them. We may note that three grades of pulque were recognized in colonial times: fine, ordinary, and Otomi.[6]

The Otomi probably arrived in the Valley of Mexico from the west following the fall of Tula, and the apogee of Otomi power occurred in the thirteenth century. Xaltocan, in the northern part of the Valley, was the capital of a large Otomi empire when the Mexica passed through it in the mid-thirteenth century on their way to Tenochtitlan. In the fourteenth century Otomi hegemony rapidly declined, and the peoples ruled from Xaltocan were subjected to a century of devastating war, waged partly by the Mexica and partly by Cuauhtitlan.[7] In one of the foremost native chronicles, the Anales de Cuauhtitlan, we may read selected details of Otomi imperial decay in the fourteenth century. The Anales record the successively diminishing boundaries of Xaltocan at critical periods and the final collapse in 1395. The inhabitants are reported to have fled to Tecama on the eastern shore of Lake Xaltocan and to Meztitlan and Tlaxcala, outside the Valley.[8] Colonial texts state that refugees from Xaltocan were befriended by the Acolhuaque and that they were given lands in Otumba (Otompan, place of the Otomi).[9] Xaltocan itself was subsequently occupied by a Nahuatl-speaking tribe, and the Otomi underwent a dispersal so complete that throughout the colonial period they remained a diffused and subordinated people, more densely distributed in the north than in the south, but always lacking a fixed or integral territory.[10] In conquest times, Cortés described them as "mountain people" and as slaves of Tenochtitlan.[11]

CULHUAQUE. With respect to the Culhuaque (or Colhuaque) a problem of terminology must first be confronted. The Culhuaque (sing. Culhua) were the inhabitants of Culhuacan, near the tip of the peninsula separating Lake Mexico from Lake Xochimilco, and this is the sense in which we now refer to them. Several colonial sources, however, speak of the area governed by Texcoco as the empire of Culhuacan; and Cortés identified the Culhuaque as the subject people of Tenochtitlan or simply as all those within the authority of the Aztec empire. Of these usages the second may be dismissed as a variant of Acolhuaque.[12] Cortés's usage and many similar references, on the other hand, reflect the ideological dependence of the Mexica upon the earlier authority of Culhuacan.[13]

The migrant Culhuaque who settled in Culhuacan, possibly in the twelfth century, are most celebrated as the masters of the Mexica prior to the establishment of Tenochtitlan. For a period of some twenty years in the early fourteenth century, Mexica peoples remained subject to the Culhuaque.[14] Culhua expulsion of the Mexica, and Mexica emancipation, brought a renewal of enmity, but Culhuacan fell in the mid-fourteenth century, mainly as a consequence of Tepaneca expansion from Azcapotzalco. The Culhuaque, though less drastically than the Otomi, were dispersed. Some fled to the Tepaneca communities of Cuauhtitlan and Azcapotzalco, others to the Acolhua communities of Coatlichan and Huexotla.[15] Culhuacan itself was secondarily conquered by Tenochtitlan about 1428, but it remained an important Valley town in late Aztec times, rendering services and warriors to the rulers of Tenochtitlan. Its last act of resistance occurred in the 1470's, when the Culhuaque supported Tlatelolco in an unsuccessful effort to escape Tenochtitlan domination.[16]

Special conditions of Culhua history make it difficult to reconstruct the tribal territory of Culhuacan. Care must be taken lest the later and more general sense of "Culhua," pertaining to the empire under the Mexica, interfere with an understanding of conditions before that empire arose. The chronological point of separation may be taken as the reign of Acamapichtli, the son of a Culhua noble and the founder of the dynasty of the Mexica in the fourteenth century. Acamapichtli's successors in Tenochtitlan preserved the title Culhua Tecuhtli (Culhua Lord), and within a few decades they were dominating the territories of Culhuacan.[17] These territories surely included Tizapan, which was the small lake-shore site assigned by Culhuacan to the Mexica when the Mexica first arrived in the southern part of the Valley.[18] Huixachtecatl, the Cerro de la Estrella, may also safely be attributed to the original territory of Culhuacan. It became a location of significance to the Mexica as the scene of their New Fire ceremony, which they celebrated every fifty-two years, even during the late period of the domination of Tenochtitlan.[19] Apart from the town of Culhuacan itself, Ixtapalapa, Mexicalzingo, and Huitzilopochco (Churubusco) were the principal Culhua communities in the present sense. In the sixteenth century the Franciscan ethnologist Sahagún spoke collectively of the Nauhtecuhtli, or "Four Lords" of Culhuacan, Ixtapalapa, Mexicalzingo, and Huitzilopochco.[20] And the affiliation of the latter three to Culhuacan is confirmed by Diego Durán, who, following the Indian Crónica X, states that Culhuacan, Ixtapalapa, Mexicalzingo, and Huitzilopochco comprised the four *señorías* of Culhuacan.[21]

→ CUITLAHUACA. The Cuitlahuaca occupied an insular community called Cuitlahuac (or Tlahuac), which was located between Lakes Chalco and Xochimilco and connected with the mainland by causeways to the north and to the south. Surrounded by the Xochimilca, Mixquica, and Chalca to the south and by the Culhuaque, Mexica, and Acolhuaque to the north, Cuitlahuac never, so far as is known, extended its authority over any major community. It waged war with the Xochimilca, the Tepaneca, the Mexica, and the Acolhuaque. But the main conquest of Cuitlahuac was accomplished by the Mexica. The four subdivisions of Cuitlahuac—Tizic, Teopancalcan, Atenchicalcan, and Tecpan (Tecpancalco)—were among the earliest tribute prizes received by the Mexica.[22] There seems no reason to suppose that Cuitlahuaca territory at the time of the Mexica conquest was any more extensive than in the sixteenth century, when the boundaries and subjects of Cuitlahuac were recorded. The sixteenth-century record indicates an area of very limited dimensions, extending to Zapotitlan and Cuauhtli-Itlacuayan (Santa Catarina) in the north and to Tulyahualco in the south.[23] Thus the known territories of Cuitlahuac barely reached the mainland beyond the small insular location of Cuitlahuac itself.

→ MIXQUICA. The Mixquica were another people of limited authority, frequently associated with the Cuitlahuaca in a condition of subordination. The migration texts give them scant treatment, and their territory was a tiny strip between the lands of the Xochimilca and the Chalca, with both of whom the Mixquica found themselves at war. In the period prior to the rise of Tenochtitlan, the Mixquica fell under the sway of both Xochimilca and Chalca.[24] Acamapichtli, the first Mexica ruler, conquered Mixquic in the late fourteeth century, undoubtedly in a campaign directed by the Tepaneca. Chalca texts record a Mexica thrust directed against both Cuitlahuac and Mixquic in 1403. The definitive Mexica conquest of Mixquic occurred about thirty years later under Itzcoatl, and through most of the fifteenth century and into the sixteenth century the Mixquica remained directly subordinate to Tenochtitlan.[25]

→ XOCHIMILCA. The Xochimilca migration terminated in the southern part of the Valley, where the chinampa town of Xochimilco became the capital of an extensive territory. This territory is described as having once been larger than Chalca territory and half as large as Acolhua territory—conditions that no longer applied in 1519. There exist few exact data on the early expansion, but the Xochimilca are recorded as genealogically or politically related to the inhabitants of Ocuituco, Tlayacapa, Totolapa, and other towns in modern Morelos, as well as to the people of Chimalhuacan, Ecatzingo, and Tepetlixpa in the southern part of the Chalca area. To the east, even in the later period of the Mexica conquests, the Xochimilca area was described as extending as far as Tuchimilco (Ocopetlayuca), or to a point just south of the summit of Popocatepetl. The three peoples considered immediately above—those of Culhuacan, Cuitlahuac, and Mixquic—were likewise claimed as subordinate to or derivative from the Xochimilca.[26] Sixteenth-century writers in Tetela del Volcán and Hueyapan, both south of the Chalca area, considered themselves descendants or subjects of Xochimilco, where their ancestors had paid tribute and rendered service.[27] There can be small doubt that the Xochimilca were once an influential and formidable people. Even so unobservant a Spanish chronicler as Francisco de Aguilar recorded that the Xochimilca province of the sixteenth century was much smaller than it had been in the past.[28]

In its early stages, the Xochimilca decline appears to have been not so much the result of Mexica attack as of attack from outside the Valley. The Xochimilca towns of Totolapa and Tlayacapa warred with Huejotzingo, Tlaxcala, and Cholula to the east. The Xochimilca were "destroyed" by "Chichimeca" and Cuauhtinchan peoples in the late twelfth century. With the growing power of towns north of Xochimilco the center of opposition then shifted to the Valley itself. The Xochimilca were at war with the Culhuaque in the thirteenth century. Mexica and Tepaneca attacks on Xochimilco are recorded in the late fourteenth century.[29] Nezahualcoyotl and the Acolhuaque, aided by Itzcoatl and the Mexica, subdued Xochimilco in the fifteenth century at the time of the reduction of Tepaneca Azcapotzalco.[30] Under Aztec authority the real area of influence of Xochimilco was reduced to the lake shore between the Pedregal and the border of Cuitlahuac, and to the adjacent upland communities to the south.

→ CHALCA. The "province" of the Chalca was located in the southeastern corner of the Valley, between the Xochimilca on the west and the high

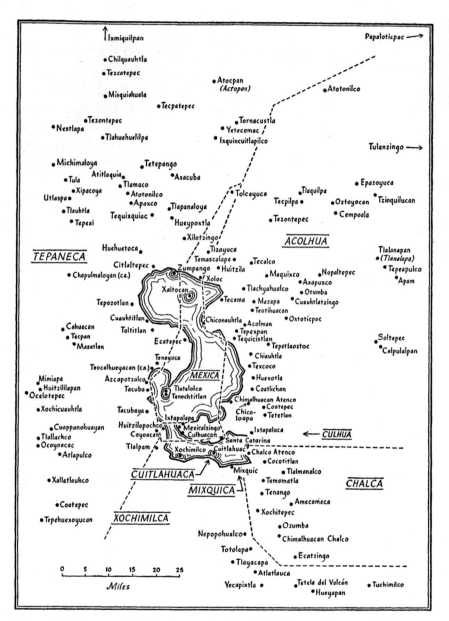

Map. 2. Tribal areas of the late pre-conquest period. Xaltocan, shown as Mexica, was originally Otomi, was captured by the Tepaneca, and became an Acolhua *calpixqui* location under Nezahualcoyotl. Mexica extension into Chalco province is not shown. The Culhua area is the narrow rectangle with Culhuacan in the center.

volcanoes on the east. Chalca records, extremely detailed in the *Relaciones* of Chimalpahin, indicate a less extensive influence than that of Xochimilco. Tlalmanalco and the other governing towns of Chalco province in the colonial period—Chimalhuacan Chalco, Tenango, Amecameca—were also leading communities in the pre-colonial period. The southern part of Chalco province, including Chimalhuacan, Tepetlixpa, and Ecatzingo, was additionally claimed, as we have said, by Xochimilco, and it appears possible therefore that a substantial area south of Ozumba had been won by the Chalca from the Xochimilca at an unknown time before the period at which our more detailed record begins. The Chalca area extended at one time to Coatepec and Chimalhuacan Atenco in the north and to Mixquic in the northwest. And in the late fourteenth century, according to Chimalpahin, the Chalca subordinated the Matlatzinca peoples in the Valle de Toluca to the west.[31]

Military losses, some of which can be precisely documented, account for the reduction of Chalca territory to the region between Tlalmanalco and the Ecatzingo area to the south. The Chalca were very frequently at war. Their enemies to the east, beyond the Valley, included the peoples of Tlaxcala, Huejotzingo, Tepeaca, and Cuauhtinchan. To the south hostilities occurred with Atlatlauca, Totolapa, and Tlayacapa.[32] Within the Valley, prolonged efforts were made by the Tepaneca, the Acolhuaque, and the Mexica to defeat the Chalca. The Tepaneca attacked the Chalca in the fourteenth century but failed to bring them under their domination. In the late fourteenth and early fifteenth centuries a state of war, which Chalca records describe as a *xochiyaotl* or formal war, existed between the Chalca and the Mexica.[33] Chalco was brought within the Aztec imperial system in the middle fifteenth century during the rule of Montezuma I, but it revolted several times after this and the history of its tributes to the Mexica suggests that it was not held firmly until the time of Montezuma II.[34] Chimalhuacan Atenco and Coatepec were probably separated from the northern part of Chalca territory in the fifteenth century. Records of the separated communities indicate that this was a local movement, but there is reason to suppose that it was accomplished under Acolhua auspices, for the Coatepec area became a part of the land under Acolhua jurisdiction.[35] Thus Cortés could describe Tlalmanalco as the Chalca "frontier" against the Culhuaque. At the time of the Spanish conquest, then, Chalco province, like other parts of the Valley, had fallen under the domination of Tenochtitlan, but its traditions of resistance were still alive and it retained enmities with Huejotzingo and Huacachula in the south and with the Culhuaque (at Ixtapalapa) in the north.[36]

TEPANECA. The Tepaneca, in their early history, appear to have been closely associated with the Otomi and to have received strong Otomi cultural influences. Probably they moved into the southwestern part of the Valley as a branch of the same migration that brought the Otomi in the thirteenth century. They occupied the territory along the western edge of the lakes, between the Otomi to the north and the Xochimilca to the south. Little precise record remains of early Tepaneca relations with the Otomi. But it is interesting that Crónica X, recorded in the sixteenth century by Durán, gives the early Tepaneca settlements as Tacuba, Azcapotzalco, Tacubaya, Tlalnepantla, and Tenayuca, for this suggests that the Tepaneca originally settled in the southern part of what was later to be their territory and then expanded northward as Otomi power declined.[37]

Tepaneca authority in the Valley of Mexico is associated first with the military conquests of Azcapotzalco, which for a time in the fourteenth and fifteenth centuries dominated Valley affairs. The site of Tenochtitlan was probably a possession of Azcapotzalco when the Mexica first arrived there.[38] The conquest of Culhuacan by Azcapotzalco, about 1347, initiated a century of extraordinary Tepaneca strength. Many of the military victories traditionally listed for the Mexica in the fourteenth century were probably Tepaneca victories to which the Mexica contributed, for throughout this period and until about 1428 Tenochtitlan was subordinate to Azcapotzalco.[39] The Tepaneca of Azcapotzalco, assisted by Tenochtitlan, waged war against the Chalca, against Cuitlahuac, and against the Otomi peoples of Xaltocan, Cuauhtitlan, and Tepozotlan in the late fourteenth century. To the northeast the Tepaneca extended their conquests to Tulanzingo, and an Acolhua chronicle states that Tezozomoc controlled the entire area from this town to the "limits of Chalco province." Thus, for a brief period in the fifteenth century Tepaneca power extended over the whole of the Valley.[40]

The death of Tezozomoc, probably in 1426 or 1427, marked a sharp turning point in Tepaneca affairs. It provided an opportunity for the usurpation of a new ruler, Maxtla, and this in turn initiated the decisive Tepaneca War of the late 1420's and early 1430's, which brought about a rapid diminution of Tepaneca strength. The Tepaneca were defeated by their two foremost subject tribes, the Mexica and the Acolhuaque, operating in alliance. The chief Tepaneca communities—Azcapotzalco, Tenayuca, Tlacopan (Tacuba), Toltitlan, Cuauhtitlan, Xaltocan, Tacubaya—were all vigorously attacked by these allies. The death of Maxtla and the conclusion of the Tepaneca War about 1433 permitted the rapid development of Acolhua power under Nezahualcoyotl as well as the semi-independent expansion of Tenochtitlan under Itzcoatl.[41] Azcapotzalco was reduced in importance, and by agreement with the Mexica and the Acolhuaque the town of Tacuba became the capital of the Tepaneca region. The post-war agreement produced the Triple Alliance—of Tenochtitlan, Texcoco, and Tacuba —and the Tepaneca territory was again limited to the western part of the Valley and adjacent areas to the west and south. Its extent is recorded in two colonial documents, the Memorial de los Pueblos, and Códice Osuna. Within the Valley its eastern boundary extended in an oblique line from the communities southwest of Coyoacan in the south to Ixcuincuitlapilco and its region in the north.[42]

ACOLHUAQUE. The term Acolhuaque (sing. Acolhua) signifies generally the inhabitants of the eastern part of the Valley, as the term Tepaneca signifies the inhabitants of the west.[43] Acolhua history is abundantly documented, primarily by a magnificent pictorial text, Códice Xolotl, and the running commentary on this text written by a colonial descendant of the Texcoco lords, Fernando de Alva Ixtlilxochitl. The Acolhuaque probably arrived in the Valley of Mexico in the thirteenth century in the same large movement that brought the Otomi and the Tepaneca.[44] Through the fourteenth century Acolhua history was one of gradual expansion. The center and capital of this expansion appears to have been Coatlichan, identified by Ixtlilxochitl and other writers as practically synonymous with Acolhuacan (place of the Acolhuaque). Texcoco, though it may have been a capital city under the earlier Tolteca and Chichimeca regimes, appears to have taken the leadership in Acolhua affairs only in the middle fifteenth century, and it probably remained a dependency of Coatlichan in the intermediate period.[45]

Acolhua expansion was halted in the early fifteenth century by the aggressions of the Tepaneca led by Tezozomoc. With his Mexica allies, Tezozomoc won over many subordinate Acolhua communities, subdued

Acolhuacan, and divided its territories with Tenochtitlan and Tlatelolco. When Maxtla succeeded Tezozomoc in Azcapotzalco, Nezahualcoyotl and the subordinate Acolhua rulers were forced to flee. But in the Tepaneca War, Nezahualcoyotl regained control of the Acolhuaque, and under his leadership the Tepaneca were subdued. The Acolhuaque then joined the Mexica in the Triple Alliance.[46]

Nezahualcoyotl, who ruled to the 1470's, and his son and successor Nezahualpilli, who died in 1515, governed Acolhuacan with a cultural and imperial luxury described as surpassing even that of Tenochtitlan.[47] Nezahualcoyotl restored the rulers of some towns and assumed personal jurisdiction over others.[48] He seems to have subdivided the area of Teotihuacan —which until his time ruled Otumba, Tepeapulco, and Tlaquilpa as a single "province"—and he instituted or reinforced Acolhua control over Acolman, Teotihuacan, Tequicistlan, and Tepexpan.[49] As a powerful member state in the Triple Alliance, Acolhuacan joined with Tenochtitlan and Tacuba and waged expansionist warfare on numerous fronts remote from the Valley. The Ixtlilxochitl text, and a documentary fragment entitled Pintura de México, indicate the far-ranging scope of these movements, which extended throughout central Mexico, to Michoacan on the west, to Tuxpan on the northeast coast, and as far as Soconusco in the south. Thus the "Aztec empire" was to some degree the achievement of the Acolhuaque under Nezahualcoyotl and Nezahualpilli. In the region of Texcoco direct Acolhua control was established over the northeastern sector of the Valley and its extension as far as Papaloticpac.[50]

Immediately preceding the Spanish conquest a dynastic crisis occurred in Acolhuacan. Upon the death of Nezahualpilli the succession was disputed by his sons, especially Ixtlilxochitl and Coanacochtzin.[51] The controversy was settled through the intervention of Montezuma, who installed another brother, Cacama, as Nezahualpilli's successor.[52] Of the two pretenders, Coanacochtzin supported Cacama, while Ixtlilxochitl undertook to lead a rebellion against him. Ixtlilxochitl secured the support of a number of towns in the northern Acolhua area, including Tulanzingo and Tepeapulco, and won over Otumba by force, making himself its ruler and centering his resistance there.

This internal Acolhua dispute had serious implications for the Triple Alliance. A revolt against Cacama was tantamount to a revolt against the authority of Montezuma, a point that Ixtlilxochitl is said to have made an explicit part of his appeal for support. Against the combined forces of Montezuma and Cacama, Ixtlilxochitl fortified his garrisons along a curving east-west line (Huehuetoca, Zumpango, Tecama, Chiconauhtla, Acolman, and Papalotla), undertook unsuccessfully to lay siege to Tenochtitlan, and secured the support of eastern peoples from Tlaxcala and Cholula against Montezuma. With Cacama himself Ixtlilxochitl reached a temporary agreement, whereby Cacama was to retain the rule and Ixtlilxochitl was to receive a share of the tribute. But the anti-Mexica aspect of Ixtlilxochitl's position was to figure significantly again two years later, for he and the areas he controlled sided with Cortés against Montezuma and Tenochtitlan.[53]

MEXICA. The entry of Mexica peoples into the Valley from the north, their settlement at Chapultepec, their subordination to Culhuacan, the establishment of their dynasty, and the foundation of their double city, Tenochtitlan-Tlatelolco, are among the familiar events of Aztec history. Here, as elsewhere, dating is irregularly recorded, but the total process of settlement undoubtedly took place in the thirteenth and fourteenth centuries. The Mexica people's early enemies, the Tepaneca, the Culhuaque, and the Otomi of Xaltocan, expelled them from Chapultepec. During the captivity of the Mexica under Culhuacan they warred against the Xochimilca and the Culhuaque. Settling in Tenochtitlan (the traditional date is 1325), they became subject to Azcapotzalco, the Tepaneca capital.[54]

Mexica annals tend to gloss over the subordination of Tenochtitlan to Azcapotzalco during the first century of its existence and to suppose a greater degree of local independence than actually existed. The first Mexica rulers—Acamapichtli (ca. 1370–96), Huitzilihuitl (ca. 1396–1417), and Chimalpopoca (ca. 1417–27)—paid tribute to Azcapotzalco. Acamapichtli is reported to have conquered Mixquic, Xochimilco, Cuitlahuac, and Chimalhuacan, and to have assisted Azcapotzalco in the defeat of the Otomi at Xaltocan. In the Huitzilihuitl period Mexica warfare took place at Acolman, Otumba, Chalco, Texcoco, and other communities, in conjunction with the Tepaneca expansion. Chimalpopoca's participation in wars initiated by Azcapotzalco resulted in his death. Under his successor, Itzcoatl (ca. 1427–40), Tepaneca hegemony was overthrown, Azcapotzalco was subdued, and the Triple Alliance furnished an opportunity much more favorable to Mexica expansion than any that had existed in the past. The sources record a sweeping Mexica-Acolhua imperialism. The rule of Itzcoatl brought victories over Tepaneca towns (Toltitlan, Azcapotzalco, Coyoacan, Xaltocan, Tacubaya, Teocalhueyacan, Cuauhtitlan) at the time of the overthrow of Azcapotzalco. Montezuma I (ca. 1440–69), the successor of Itzcoatl, was the ruler under whom Mexica imperialism for the first time broke out of the Valley on a large scale. The conquests of Montezuma I, some achieved independently and some with the help of allies, spread over most of central Mexico. Axayacatl (ca. 1469–81) brought Toluca and its adjacent regions under Mexica control, and within the Valley he subordinated Tlatelolco to Tenochtitlan. The victories of the three last Mexica rulers prior to the Spanish conquest—Tizoc (ca. 1481–86), Ahuitzotl (ca. 1486–1502), and Montezuma II (ca. 1502–20)—were almost entirely in remote regions to the east and to the south.[55]

Despite the enormous power represented by these conquests, Mexica territory within the Valley remained small. The reasons are evident. As late arrivals, the Mexica found the lands of the Valley already appropriated by other tribes. The site of Tenochtitlan itself fell originally within the Tepaneca territories.[56] To be sure, the Mexica might have usurped lands from neighboring tribes and made them their own, after the manner of other expanding states. But they generally avoided this course. Instead, through systems of alliance and the sharing of tribute, they looked to their neighbors for military aid, acquired tributary communities in distant localities, took over scattered properties throughout the Valley, and limited their own integral territory to the narrow borderland between the Tepaneca and the Acolhuaque. Mexica holdings extended from Tepopula, in the central part of Chalco province, northward along the western shores of Lake Texcoco to Ecatepec, and thence to the northern limits of the Valley at Tizayuca and Tolcayuca.[57] In their relations with neighboring tribes, the Mexica exerted powerful pressures and more than compensated for the small size of their own area. Some Acolhua towns, such as Cempoala and Tlaquilpa,[58] transferred their tribute payments to Tenochtitlan, as did the Chalca and the Xochimilca. Over the Mixquica, the Cuitlahuaca, and the Culhuaque the Mexica exerted even more direct forms of authority, virtually including them, by the time of Montezuma II, within the Mexica area itself.[59]

The tribal arrangements of 1519 were the end product of a complex history. For centuries, the rise and fall of tribes in the Valley of Mexico had been governed by military victory and defeat, and the expansion and reduction of controlled areas had been reciprocal, complementary processes. Unstable relations between one people and another mark the Otomi decline, the Tepaneca usurpation, and the compromise of the Triple Alliance. Códice Xolotl is eloquent on this point; in a series of pictorial maps it indicates by the size of the glyphs and the scale of the drawings the relative importance of each community in each new balance of power.[60]

We may now ask what connections existed between the tribal histories and the composition of Valley peoples as of 1519. It should be clearly stated at the outset that our summary of these histories is far from being an exhaustive commentary on tribal interrelations. More towns than we have discussed preserved migration legends, either as derivatives of the main migrations or as independent movements. The nine peoples we have mentioned are the ones described in the more comprehensive annals and codices, and we may assume that the form in which the narratives survived developed both from the migrations per se and from the competitions for domination during the centuries between first settlement and Spanish conquest. But it is precisely these competitions that concern us, for the outcome of the "crude wars over mine and thine," as one conquistador called them,[61] had appreciable consequences for colonial history.

The tribal movements have customarily been understood as successive ethnic influxes, distributed chronologically from the Otomi to the Mexica. For a historical reconstruction this may be regarded as appropriate and right, but the same tribes may also be examined—and in roughly reverse order—in their status and power relationships of 1519. In this perspective, we find at one extreme the Mexica, the principal rulers of the Valley and of the entire empire. At the opposite extreme are the Otomi—reduced, dispersed, lacking a capital community, and either omitted from the conventional migration texts or assigned a separate and minor role in them. Between these then fall the remaining groups: Culhuaque, Cuitlahuaca, and Mixquica all in low status, as inhabitants of towns without surrounding provinces; Xochimilca and Chalca in intermediate status, as provincial peoples of moderate size within the empire; and Tepaneca and Acolhuaque in superior status, with large territories but in unequal equilibrium vis-à-vis the Mexica. The hierarchy of power and status in 1519, in an approximate descending order, would be: Mexica, Acolhuaque, Tepaneca, Chalca, Xochimilca, Cuitlahuaca, Mixquica, Culhuaque, Otomi.

The enduring influence of these tribal entities in late Aztec times has often been overshadowed by the spectacular imperial achievements that marked the century before the Spanish conquest. But the Triple Alliance must itself be regarded in some sense as an affirmation of tribal self-preservation, of the failure of the Mexica to dominate Valley affairs absolutely or to exterminate the tribal concept. Moreover, the institutions of the late Aztec empire show not only that the tribal units were preserved, but also that they occupied the approximate order of importance listed above. Thus in Aztec military organization, the Crónica X describes an army composed in part of tribal cadres, of which the five Valley contingents were the Mexica, Acolhuaque, Tepaneca, Chalca, and Xochimilca, with a sixth cadre drawn from Culhuacan, Ixtapalpa, Mexicalzingo, and Huitzilopochco.[62] Here the first five tribes appear as distinct army units. Culhuacan appears with the other communities of the Nauhtecuhtli. Cuitlahuac, Mixquic, and the Otomi are not mentioned. In religious sacrifice, the captives taken by the Acolhuaque were assigned to one location, those of the Tepaneca to another, those of the Xochimilca to another, and those of the Chalca to yet another.[63] With respect to labor organization, the work on the construction of the Acuecuexco aqueduct, carried forward under Ahuitzotl, was divided among tribal groups: the Acolhuaque contributed light and heavy stone; the Tepaneca brought heavy stone; the Chalca, stakes and other materials; the Xochimilca, digging tools and canoes loaded with earth.[64] Evidence of this sort, which could be expanded upon, suggests that in the administration of Aztec imperialism each of the chief tribal entities—Mexica, Acolhua, Tepaneca, Chalca, Xochimilca—performed continuing and specific functions. Culhua, Cuitlahuaca, and Mixquica peoples are mentioned less frequently as separate entities. And there is no documentation whatever on the Otomi.

Is it possible that these peoples maintained real and separate identities through Aztec times? In all the expansion and contraction of territories, all the commercial and political interchanges, all the dense mingling of peoples in the Valley, did not biological and cultural mixture intervene to blur the tribal distinctions? Undoubtedly it did. Yet the evidence suggests that miscegenation was a factor of limited importance in pre-conquest history and that determined efforts were made to preserve tribal affiliations. Numerous internal migrations occurred, as well as numerous refugee movements and some systematic administrative insertion of peoples of one tribe in the area of another. But the result was the formation of enclaves, not mixtures, of populations. Separate wards or subdivisions of Mexica, Culhua, and Tepaneca peoples are recorded in the Acolhua capital, Texcoco. Chimalhuacan, in the southern part of Acolhua territory, included a subdivision called Culhuacan, presumably populated by Culhua peoples. Mexicapan (area of the Mexica) was a section in the Acolhua community of Tezayuca. Peoples from outside the Valley, such as the Chimalpaneca and the Tlaillotlaque from the south, were represented in similar enclaves in Texcoco.[65]

The precision of boundary delineation in Aztec times provides further evidence in support of tribal continuity. The subject is frequently dismissed with the assertion that boundaries shifted and were characteristically ill-defined. It is true that some pre-conquest peoples reserved frontier areas between competing jurisdictions as buffer territories and battlegrounds for conflict,[66] and it is likely that no exact limits were fixed where no human need required them or where unwanted or unusable lands separated two jurisdictions. But in the crowded, competitive conditions of the Valley interior, this was not the case. The statement of Xaltocan's boundaries in the Anales de Cuauhtitlan shows how carefully the deterioration of one tribal entity, the Otomi, was defined during the fourteenth-century war.[67] Equally exact boundaries are reported for the Acolhua area under the direction of Nezahualcoyotl. Here the border with the Mexica and the Tepaneca on the western side of Acolhua territory extended from near Cuitlahuac across the water to Tequicistlan and to the outlet between Lakes Xaltocan and Texcoco, thence north to Xoloc, and northeast outside of the Valley to Tototepec. Nezahualcoyotl placed walls and frontier markers, "morillos muy gruesos," along the line, the key points of which are specifically recorded.[68] On the eastern side, Nezahualcoyotl placed similar markers to divide Acolhua territory from Tlaxcala, along a line to the east of Soltepec and Calpulalpan.[69] We have records of precise limits for other tribal groups in Aztec times, and, although in many cases the details are still insufficient for modern cartographic reconstruction, the clear intent of demarcation remains.[70]

Hundreds of colonial documents, furthermore, record the limits of individual communities, and repeatedly such limits were defended as derivative from pre-conquest jurisdictional precedents. When adjoining communities fell in distinct tribal territories, community boundaries and tribal boundaries necessarily coincided. This was the case in the border litigation of 1561 between Azcapotzalco and Tlatelolco. The dispute concerned the rights to a spring, certain water ditches, and swampland that had been used for fishing and the collection of rushes. Azcapotzalco stated that it had included the area within its claimed limits, free from Tlatelolco intrusion, since the time of Tezozomoc, the fourteenth-century ruler of Tepaneca Azcapotzalco. Witnesses affirmed that the demarcation had been fixed by Tezozomoc himself when he sent his son Quaquapitzahuac to govern Tlatelolco. The boundary sites thus established were (Santiago) Tlatepantla, Coquiscaloco, Tilcoatitlan, Chalchiuhtatacoyan, and Mazatzintamalco, and these, it was argued, had ever since determined the border between Tepaneca Azcapotzalco and the Mexica of Tlatelolco.[71] The contested area was itself minuscule, but the principle of fixed and long-standing demarcation was never called into question. Such cases are too frequent and their use of historical evidence too detailed to allow us to dismiss them as colonial rationalizations.

The colonial cases, it should be noted, always applied to the jurisdictions of towns, and only when these were towns of different tribes did the disputes extend to tribal areas. There is no known colonial record of corporate litigation between one entire tribe and another—nor, indeed, of any kind of colonial legal action by a tribe acting as a unit. Does this mean that the tribes were of no importance in the colonial period, or that the Spanish state, intent on the pursuit of other ends, completely suppressed the Indian tribal jurisdictions? We may answer first by examining the effect of Spanish imperialism on the tribal areas in relation to five subjects: conquest, the church, *encomienda*, political jurisdiction, and draft labor. Each of the five required new subdivisions of Valley territory, and the areas all criss-crossed in complex patterns. Did any of these areas follow pre-Spanish boundaries? If so, what criteria of selection determined Spanish retention of aboriginal tribal limits in some instances and not in others?

The conquest furnished an opportunity for the Chalca to join the Spaniards and to reassert their long-standing resistance to the Mexica. It is an impressive fact that Cortés—who seems to have been unaware of the existence of the Triple Alliance—referred in his report of 1520 to the "province" of the Chalca in terms that indicate almost no difference in status or authority between it and the "province" of the Acolhuaque. Cortés, to be sure, did not comprehend immediately the distinction between a subject and an allied people in Aztec imperial organization. Cortés was looking for, and hence made reference to, the disaffected peoples in either category with whom he could make alliances against Tenochtitlan. He described in some detail the readiness with which the Chalca made alliance with the Spaniards and the effectiveness with which they fought during the remainder of the conquest.[72] In different degrees, this same course of Spanish alliance was adopted by the Xochimilca, the Cuitlahuaca, the Mixquica, and the Culhuaque.[73] In no case, however, was the action unanimous or unequivocal, and even in Chalco there occurred some defections to Tenochtitlan.[74] Acolhua leadership and territory were cleanly split by the crisis of the conquest. The internal Acolhua schism, as we have seen, antedated the conquest, but the arrival of the Spanish army added a new and complicating factor to this division and in effect determined the outcome. Our sources are not in agreement concerning events in Texcoco during the years 1519 to 1522, but it is probable that Ixtlilxochitl supported Cortés as part of a campaign against Coanacochtzin, Cacama, and Montezuma, and that the internal disorder of the Acolhua area was intensified accordingly. Ixtlilxochitl brought Otumba, Huexotla, and some other communities over to the Spanish side, while Xaltocan supported Coanacochtzin and the Mexica.[75] In terms of power relationships, one could say that conquest served to weaken the position of the strongest tribal units, notably the Mexica and the Acolhuaque, while it recognized and even reinforced (to be sure within the terms and limits of the Spanish victory) the positions of intermediate peoples such as the Chalca and the Xochimilca.

The Spanish ecclesiastical jurisdictions were in general not suited to any kind of dependence upon pre-conquest tribal divisions. The Valley as a whole was too small an area to comprise a bishopric, and its tribal provinces were for the most part too large for individual parishes. Cuitlahuac and Mixquic, it is true, became parishes, but they did so as communities, not as tribal entities with surrounding provinces. Colonial ecclesiastical organization required parish churches so distributed that effective communication could be maintained with a surrounding Indian population, and this meant the foundation of a large number of ecclesiastical establishments. But the sites were selected for the size or status of their communities or the density of their population, and without regard for tribal boundaries. It would have been possible, certainly, to assign the Acolhua area to the Franciscans or the Tepaneca area to the Dominicans and thus preserve a sense of the tribal jurisdictions in ecclesiastical government. But the course of Mendicant history ran counter to any such scheme, for the Franciscans came first and were already settled in key locations when the Dominicans and Augustinians arrived.

3   Encomienda, a system of private labor and tribute jurisdiction (see Chapter IV), was rather more flexible in its requirements and proved suitable both for individual communities and for provinces of moderate size. Tenochtitlan was too populous and its tribute yield too great to allow its assignment as an encomienda to any Spanish holder. Moreover, as the city of Mexico (or Mexico-Tenochtitlan) it became the colonial capital, in direct relationship to the crown. The plan to adapt Tenochtitlan and the Mexica area to the encomienda system therefore came to naught. In the same way the Acolhua and Tepaneca provinces, the largest zones of the central Aztec territory, would have made immense encomienda prizes and were therefore subdivided into a number of grants rather than assigned intact. Their towns came to be allocated without reference to the tribes. The towns of the Culhua area were all first granted to the capital city but were soon subdivided and reassigned.[76] This left Cuitlahuac, Mixquic, Xochimilco, and Chalco to become colonial encomienda jurisdictions. The encomienda status of Chalco and Xochimilco was brief, however, and the reasons surely relate in part to their size. These areas strained the accepted limits of encomienda, and they were rich tribute regions of interest to the crown. The smaller Cuitlahuac and Mixquic jurisdictions had also been assigned to the city,[77] but they soon became private encomiendas instead and survived in this form well into the seventeenth century. They were no different in status, however, from other encomiendas that survived, and one would be hard pressed to argue that their persistence as encomiendas was in any way related to their original tribal composition.

4   With regard to the political jurisdictions (called *corregimientos* or *alcaldías mayores*), considerations of tribute wealth were less relevant, the relationship of a capital town to a surrounding province was wholly appropriate, and greater opportunities were afforded for utilizing the existing tribal domains. The Acolhua and Tepaneca territories were still too large to be converted into single corregimientos or alcaldías mayores. They were accordingly subdivided: the Acolhua into four parts (Coatepec, Texcoco, Otumba, Teotihuacan), and the Tepaneca into three (Cuauhtitlan, Tacuba, Coyoacan). The totality in each case preserved, with some modifications,

the Acolhua and Tepaneca tribal regions of the Valley. Chalco and Xochimilco, on the other hand, being of suitable size for political jurisdictions, became corregimiento areas in their own right, with borders directly derivative from those of pre-conquest times. The four Culhua towns were incorporated in a single jurisdiction. Cuitlahuac and Mixquic, at the northern limits of Chalco, were attached to the Chalco corregimiento. One could conclude that the political areas, with some discrepancies, preserved a degree of tribal continuity.[78]

The Spanish institution that did most to maintain the pre-conquest tribal precedents was the labor draft, called *repartimiento*. Some years elapsed before full use of Indian labor was possible within the viceregal system. One opportunity appeared in 1555, after the free use of Indian labor had been denied to encomienda holders, and on the occasion of the first major colonial flood in Mexico City.[79] The organization of labor for this emergency derived directly from late Aztec tribal units. The Indian workers were assigned to the labor from four "provinces"—called Mexico, Texcoco, Tacuba, and Tlalmanalco—which corresponded to the four pre-Spanish tribal areas of the Mexica, the Acolhuaque, the Tepaneca, and the Chalca.[80] Later drafts for agricultural labor modified this arrangement, but they did so only gradually, and as late as the early seventeenth century traces of the Aztec tribal structure were still visible in the labor organization of the Valley.

This return to pre-conquest tribal boundaries in the colonial labor drafts is the more impressive because the continuity had been broken during the first generation following the conquest. One may assume that the tribal territories were remembered by Indians throughout this period and that they were overlooked by Spaniards in the fragmentations of encomienda. But they were then reinvoked deliberately and made explicit in viceregal orders. Viceroy Velasco "asked the (Indian) governors of the three main towns of Mexico, Tacuba, and Texcoco for the ancient paintings showing the foundation of the city and the methods they and their ancestors had used for protecting it from flood." Having studied various proposals the viceroy "decided that it could be done most quickly and effectively in accordance with the painting and as the Indians used to do it."[81] In the viceregal order Xochimilca labor was included with that of the Mexica. Except for this, the labor organization in 1555 bears a striking similarity to Ahuitzotl's organization of labor for the Acuecuexco aqueduct in the pre-Spanish period. That the two were related historically, and that the similarities were not merely coincidental, cannot be doubted.

The inclination toward tribal separation, which we have noted as a characteristic of pre-conquest Indian life, to some extent continued. Spanish administrative and ecclesiastical policies favored programs of Indian resettlement (*congregación*), and these occasionally resulted in new associations of peoples derivative from separate "tribes." A conspicuous instance is Tlalnepantla, an ecclesiastical foundation of the sixteenth century established to accommodate two pre-existing peoples, the Tepaneca of Tenayuca and the Otomi of Teocalhueyacan. But even in the single community of Tlalnepantla, Tepaneca and Otomi peoples remained separate, with distinct internal governments.[82] At other times tribal groups successfully resisted plans for common congregación, in part by citing their long-standing hostility to each other.[83] The subdivisions of Mexicapan and Culhuacan, and other communities whose names suggest tribal origins, persisted, and in many instances they are retained today.[84] The main center for migrant tribal groups in the colonial period was the city of Mexico, which by the seventeenth century was accommodating an influx of people from many areas. In some cases the alien groups grew to sufficient size to comprise whole political subdivisions in the city; among these sectors were San Juan Chichimecos (Otomi), San Juan Tlaxcaltecapan, and a unit of Tarascans from Michoacan, who were governed by their own *capitán* and four Indian *alguaciles*. The metropolitan agglomeration included, obviously, tribal entities from areas far beyond the Valley. But it illustrates, in an exaggerated degree, the reluctance of one Indian group to merge indiscriminately with another even in the congested conditions of the colony's capital city.[85]

Considerations of geographical size played an obvious role in the colonial adjustments noted above. The selective criterion—the suitability of an area of given size for the particular institutional function concerned—operated in such a way that the tribal areas of moderate size displayed more viability in the colony than did the larger ones. Thus the Xochimilca area, too small to comprise a labor unit, was of convenient size for corregimiento, and it remained a well-defined political entity throughout the colonial period. Chalco province, also of moderate size, is the most striking example. It was too large, of course, to constitute an ecclesiastical parish; it was large, though not impossibly so, for encomienda. But it was of the proper size for corregimiento and for the labor draft. Chalco did become an early en-

comienda jurisdiction in the 1520's. It was an integral, undivided corregimiento from the 1530's on. It was a labor draft area continuously from the
1550's to 1633, when such drafts were abolished, and it never in this time
suffered the alterations that affected the larger Acolhua and Tepaneca
labor provinces. In the political reforms of the late eighteenth century this
same Chalca area became the jurisdiction of a *subdelegado*. Even the prefecture organization of the nineteenth century and the modern subdivision
of the Distrito Federal have retained in some measure the pre-conquest
Chalca territory in an uninterrupted tradition.

Another consideration relates to timing. In many ways the mid-sixteenth century was the period of greatest harmony in Indian-Spanish relations. The immediate stresses of the post-conquest period had ended, and
a new generation of Indian leaders, schooled by friars and not yet disillu-
sioned by Spanish exploitation, had come into being. Spaniards of the middle sixteenth century showed more respect for Indian civilization, and
Indian leaders more respect for Spanish civilization, that at any other time.
In a sense, it is to be expected that Spanish dependence upon native jurisdictions—as in corregimiento, and especially in the labor draft of 1555—
was of this period rather than earlier or later. Attitudes of militarism could
not be abandoned immediately in 1521, and some time had to pass before
peace could be assured. Furthermore, the main Spanish institutions of the
early post-conquest years—encomienda and the mission church—were in
competition with each other, and neither encomienda holders nor friars
had much opportunity to inquire into tribal jurisdictions. All the tribes,
except the lowly Otomí, spoke the same Nahuatl language, and all appeared
equally accessible for exploitation or conversion. It mattered less that they
were Acolhuaque or Tepaneca than that they became tribute-payers or
Christians. But with the advent of non-encomienda labor and the critical
flood of 1555, the Spanish state for the first time required and brought into
being an organization based on Indian tribal groups. The gradual abandonment of aboriginal systems of labor organization in the later sixteenth and
seventeenth centuries, then, signifies the temporary character of this mid-
century accord and the re-establishment of Spanish methods of control.

Beyond geographical convenience and fortunate timing, another factor
was pertinent here. Students have frequently noted that it was the most
obvious or flagrantly incompatible features of Indian society that yielded
to Spanish influence. Spanish Christianity eliminated human sacrifice and

conspicuous pagan rituals, but it permitted lesser pagan practices to maintain a covert existence. Spanish political policies operated to depose the
imperial leaders of the Aztec state, but they preserved local structures and
their personnel. For the tribes, this principle meant that the main groups
suffered a loss of identity under Spanish rule whereas subordinate groups
survived.

In this connection we may note not only the destruction of the Triple
Alliance and the continuance of Xochimilco and Chalco but also the remarkable persistence of the Otomi. As a dispersed people, the Otomi were
unfit for any of the types of jurisdictional survival we have mentioned. So
thorough was their pre-Spanish collapse that no major community in the
entire Valley was ruled by the Otomi in the sixteenth century. Instead, the
Otomi occupied subordinate or outlying parts of communities that were
dominated by Nahuatl-speaking peoples. A seventeenth-century observer,
commenting on the condition of the Otomi in the community of San Jerónimo, in the hills west of Azcapotzalco, found them to be eating grasses,
with little agriculture, scanty clothing, and a rude material culture.[86] The
same description would fit the Otomi of many peripheral Valley locations
at the time of the conquest—and, with few modifications, in the twentieth
century as well. As a subordinate population, with a distinct culture and
language, the Otomi escaped the full destructive effect of Spanish influence.
Like other inconspicuous elements of Indian civilization, they did not
attract Spanish attention and were thus preserved by default.

Could one say that the concept of tribal units was itself a covert survival
in colonial Indian culture? Did the Indian mind retain the idea of tribal
organization in the seventeenth and eighteenth centuries, while Spaniards
moved progressively farther from an administration based on tribal divisions? Our answer would be that Indians retained such memories only
during the first few generations after the conquest. In the 1550's Indians
still possessed a detailed knowledge of the tribal form and were able to
translate this form, on demand, into action. But a hundred years later
this would not have been possible, for new colonial modes of organization
displaced the tribal concepts and prevented them from being put into
practical operation.

By the late sixteenth century, knowledge of tribal divisions was drawn
mainly from Indian legend and historical records. Those Indian writers who
took up this subject, and the Spanish historians who used their material,

depended on documentary sources from the early post-conquest period: Durán and Alvarado Tezozomoc relied on Crónica X; Fernando de Alva Ixtlilxochitl used Mapa Quinatzin and Códice Xolotl. The written migration legends, such as Códice Azcatitlan and Códice Boturini, also contributed a little to the lingering memory.[87] Indian poetry and oral tales occasionally touched upon the military glories of Chalco or Acolhuacan. But these were weak reminders of the tribal structure, and they were deliberately nostalgic. Insofar as this lore occupied itself with the historical past at all, it tended to single out particular towns, to fix its attention on celebrated individuals like Nezahualcoyotl, or to speak vaguely of a composite Indian (in contrast to the dominant Spanish) culture. Ultimately, even Indian folklore allowed knowledge of the tribal entities to fade into obscurity.

CHAPTER III

Towns

To Spaniards, Indian towns were more impressive and meaningful than Indian tribes. Differences between one tribe and another were not of a sort to attract Spanish attention, for the full significance of the tribes could not be immediately grasped and no consistent tribal adaptation to new colonial conditions evolved. Far more obviously, the Aztec empire appeared to be a "mosiac of towns,"[1] towns that were self-evident, exotic, and exploitable clusters of people. "One does not require witnesses from heaven," Las Casas wrote, "to demonstrate that these were political peoples, with towns, inhabited places of large size, villas, cities, and communities."[2]

Spaniards, including Las Casas, brought a developed body of urban concepts to bear upon the communities they found, and the outcome was an orderly differentiation based partly on Castilian and partly on Indian understanding. A superior urban rank was created when Spaniards designated four Valley sites as cities (*ciudades*). The four were Tenochtitlan, Texcoco in 1543, Xochimilco in 1559, and Tacuba in 1564.[3] Two others, Coyoacan and Tacubaya, which fell within Cortés's *Marquesado* area of 1529, were ranked as *villas*. All remaining population centers of moderate or large size were held to be *pueblos* in a uniform categorization. The ciudad-villa-pueblo classification was derived from Castile, where it was still observed in the sixteenth century: ciudades, such as Guadalajara or Toledo, occupied a rank above villas, such as Madrid or Alcalá, and both outranked the more numerous pueblos; all were superior to lesser entities called *aldeas* and *lugares*.[4] In Mexico, as in Spain, this kind of status depended partly on size (no small town could be a ciudad) and partly on local campaigns for privilege. It is a striking fact in the history of native learning processes that within a generation after the conquest Indians were addressing letters to the king requesting that pueblos be recognized as ciudades or that communities receive coats of arms or other honors.[5]

In practice, these designations and the coats of arms, which were duly granted, had little meaning either for Spaniards or for Indians.[6] Of far greater importance was the Spanish institution called *cabeza* or *cabecera*, which became fundamental to colonial political and economic organization, and which requires particular attention for its bearing on Indian history. In Castile a cabeza was the secular or ecclesiastical capital of a district.[7] A ciudad might be the cabeza of a district that included one or more villas, and a villa might be the cabeza of a district embracing a number of pueblos, aldeas, or lugares.[8] In the colony, the variant form cabecera was preferred to the common Castilian term cabeza, and *sujeto* was adopted in preference to aldea and lugar. Subdivisions of Indian towns were called *barrios* (wards) if they were connected parts of their cabeceras, and *estancias* if they were located some distance away.[9] Barrio, like cabecera, was a recognized but not a widely used term in sixteenth-century Spain, where the equivalent *colación* (or *collación*) was much more common.[10] Colación did receive occasional notice in the early history of the Valley of Mexico,[11] but it soon dropped almost completely out of usage.[12] The word estancia appears to have been introduced into Mexico by way of the West Indies, where it was applied to any cluster of Indian dwellings.[13] Under Mexican conditions estancia was an appropriate term for the separated, as opposed to the connected, portions of native towns. The colonial rejection of the Castilian term aldea—within a decade of the conquest a colonist could state that there was no such word in Mexico[14]—is presumably to be explained by the adoption of the more functional term sujeto. Although in certain cases colonists were unable to decide whether a given sujeto should be a barrio or an estancia,[15] and although the whole distinction tended to break down in time, Mexican terminology for the most part was remarkably uniform. This terminology also included, as might be expected, diminutive variants—*pueblecito, barriesito, barriesillo*[16]—and a number of related words of toponymic reference: *sitio, loma, pago,* or the characteristic phrases *donde llaman* and *donde dicen*.[17]

The key step was the selection of cabeceras, and in this several courses of action were open to the first Spaniards. They might have made the choice on the basis of size, designating as cabeceras only the larger communities and assigning to each a group of nearby sujetos. They might have chosen the capital cities of the tribal areas or divided the Valley into Tepaneca, Acolhua, and Mexica districts, reducing all communities except Tacuba, Texcoco, and Tenochtitlan to sujeto rank.[18] They might have selected the locations of the imperial tribute collectors (*calpixque,* sing. *calpixqui*) of Montezuma, locations which Indians continued to remember and which they recorded for one of the great native documents of Mexico, the Matrícula de Tributos. Or Spaniards might have established new settlements and subordinated all Indian areas to cabeceras inhabited by whites.

In fact, Spaniards chose none of these possible courses of action. Instead they found a basis for the classification of cabeceras and sujetos at what may be termed a sub-imperial or pre-imperial level within Indian society. Here the leading communities were traditionally governed by native rulers called *tlatoque* (sing. *tlatoani*) and were already subdivided in the Indian system, the unit part being the *calpulli* or *tlaxilacalli,* which was a group of families living in a single locality. In general the Indian calpulli became the Spanish sujeto, whether barrio or estancia, and it was made subordinate to the cabecera where the tlatoani resided. A cabecera, therefore, was identified as the capital town of a local Indian ruler who bore the title tlatoani. More specifically, the term cabecera meant the collection of barrios that comprised this capital,[19] each calpulli within the jurisdiction of the tlatoani being a sujeto (barrio or estancia) of that cabecera.

Before the conquest, a tlatoani had ordinarily inherited his position as his predecessor's son, or as some other close relative, at the time of the predecessor's death. He held the position for life and bequeathed it to his heir, and in most instances one may properly speak of dynastic succession in tlatoani rule.[20] In the late Aztec period there were some fifty tlatoque in the Valley of Mexico, supported in all cases by the tributes and labors of the persons subordinate to them. They were distributed unevenly among the tribal bodies, from the single ruler of the Mixquica to the twenty-five who at one time governed in the communities of Chalco province. In preconquest struggles for power, a tlatoani might usurp the position of another tlatoani and himself occupy both positions; he might permit a conquered tlatoani to retain his office under specified terms of obligation; or he might destroy a neighboring tlatoani's office entirely, reducing the town from the status of tlatoani capital to the status of non-tlatoani dependent. In the period prior to the Spanish conquest all peoples in the Valley had been subordinated by way of tribute and military service to the tlatoque of Tenoch-

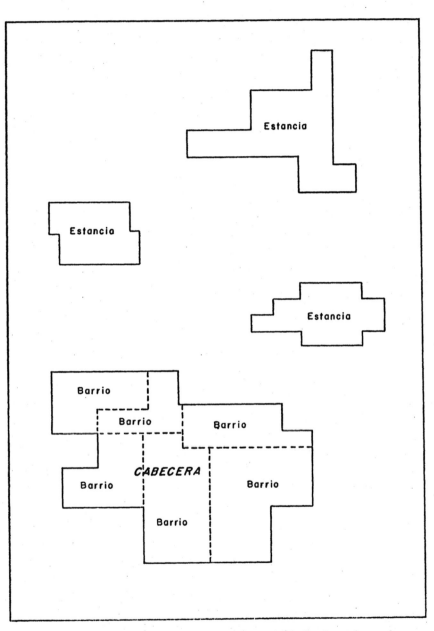

Figure 1. Schematic representation of a cabecera with its barrios and estancias.

titlan, Texcoco, or Tacuba. But because Aztec leaders did permit local officers to retain their positions and titles, the tlatoani principle remained to serve as the basis for the colonial cabecera organization.[21] It should be emphasized that in establishing this colonial cabecera system, Spaniards passed over both Montezuma's imperial tribute organization and the organization by tribal groups. Spaniards frequently referred to the cabeceras as *pueblos por sí*,[22] a phrase that by implication disregarded or deliberately denied tribal or imperial connections.[23]

Two circumstances, however, interfered with an absolute equation of tlatoani communities with the colonial cabeceras. One was closely related to the new Spanish terminology, for Spaniards also spoke of the tlatoani regimes as *señoríos*, and of the tlatoque as *señores, señores principales, señores naturales*, or *caciques*. These terms were consistent with other Spanish usages, but their application here meant that Spaniards everywhere neglected the proper Nahuatl term, tlatoani. Señor, of course, was a Spanish word.[24] Cacique was an Arawakian word, one that Spaniards had adopted in the West Indies and carried, naturally and easily, to Mexico.[25] Their failure to employ the local Nahuatl title in Mexico had important implications, for it meant that Indians might claim to be caciques, and that communities might claim to be cabeceras, without fulfilling the original criteria. The colonial terminology therefore provided an opportunity for exceptions to the rule, particularly since, with the passage of time, the original standards no longer pertained.

A more basic and immediate difficulty arose from the circumstance that not all tlatoani towns could be identified in the early post-conquest period. In most areas of the Valley in the 1520's, to be sure, the traditions of local tlatoani rule or of subjugation to another tlatoani rule remained clear and unequivocal. But in a few areas such traditions were ambivalent, and arguments could be made to support or oppose colonial cabecera rank. We may recall the reorganization effected by Nezahualcoyotl in the Acolhua zone, where, after the elimination of the Tepaneca overlordship, some tlatoque were restored to their positions while some were suppressed, their areas reverting to Nezahualcoyotl's personal control. These communities betrayed a broken or interrupted tlatoani history and an alternation of tlatoani and non-tlatoani status.[26] An impressive illustration is afforded by Chalco province, where at one time the government was in the hands of the twenty-five tlatoque mentioned above, but where less than half this number were ruling by the time of the conquest. In such cases, cabecera status depended not only upon events antedating the Spanish arrival but also upon variant interpretations of these events set forth in self-interested Indian testimony. The Spanish criterion for cabeceras, accordingly, was not always an absolute or applicable one. We may examine the problem most satisfactorily by reviewing the tlatoani traditions in each of the Valley's tribal areas.[27]

MEXICA. The tlatoani or *hueytlatoani* (great tlatoani) of Tenochtitlan was the dominant figure of Aztec imperialism, but as tlatoani in the present sense his jurisdiction was Tenochtitlan and its immediate sujetos. Tenochtitlan was divided into four barrios—Cuepopan or Tlaquechiuhcan, Atzacualco, Teopan or Zoquipan, and Moyotlan. It was unique among colonial Indian communities of the Valley in that a large section of its center was marked off to house the Spanish colonists. Moreover, it was the only Valley location to maintain a *cabildo*, or municipal council, of Spaniards.[28] But its four barrios—under their colonial names Santa María, San Sebastián, San Pablo, and San Juan—remained as sites of Indian habitation, its estancias were for the most part preserved, and its status as a colonial cabecera was never called into question.[29]

Tlatelolco, a separate community on the same island site as Tenochtitlan, traced its tlatoani history back to Quaquapitzahuac in the late thirteenth century.[30] The outstanding incident of its dynastic history was the rebellion of the early 1470's, when it rose against Tenochtitlan. Tenochtitlan suppressed the uprising and the local Tlatelolco rule was "destroyed."[31] The government of Tlatelolco persisted, however, under a military ruler, or *cuauhtlatoani*, appointed from Tenochtitlan.[32] Tlatelolco records such as the Carta of 1537 speak of an unbroken series of rulers and a continuous señorío separate from Tenochtitlan.[33] Spaniards admitted this cuauhtlatoani principle within the terms of their criteria, and Tlatelolco became a cabecera. Its close relationship with Tenochtitlan prompted some use of the terms *parte* and *parcialidad*,[34] as if Tenochtitlan and Tlatelolco were subordinate parts of the same city, but these terms did not in this instance imply any denial of cabecera status. In the 1570's, after Tlatelolco had entered upon its prolonged decline, Spanish ecclesiastics disputed in their own interest over the question of its independence from Tenochtitlan.[35] But in the early post-conquest years no doubt was raised.

Tenochtitlan and Tlatelolco were the original and principal tlatoani sites of the Mexica area. But in the fifteenth century, with the expansion of Mexica power, two other Mexica lineages had been established, in the communities of Ecatepec and Azcapotzalco. Both were recognized as cabeceras in the early colonial period. The first known historical tlatoani of Ecatepec was Chimalpilli, a member of the dynastic family of Tenochtitlan, who was installed in infancy in 1428, probably by the Mexica themselves on the occasion of the Tepaneca War.[36] Subsequent tlatoque in Ecatepec were all closely related to the dynasty of Tenochtitlan: Tezozomoc was the son of Chimalpopoca; Matlaccohuatl, the father-in-law of Montezuma II; Chimalpilli II, the son of Ahuitzotl; and Huanitzin, the son of Tezozomoc, Montezuma's brother.[37] Spaniards recognized the special Mexica affiliation of Ecatepec in several ways, notably by granting it in encomienda to Montezuma's daughter, and this presumably reinforced its cabecera status.[38] In any case, it was acknowledged by all to be a cabecera.

In the second community, Azcapotzalco, a former Tepaneca capital, the Mexica introduced a new dynastic lineage while permitting the existing Tepaneca lineage to continue. As a result, after about 1428 Azcapotzalco consisted of two subdivisions, Tepanecapan and Mexicapan, each with a tlatoani.[39] Spaniards, seeing a single community, tended to speak of Azcapotzalco as one cabecera with two partes or parcialidades. But the division was retained, and the dual principle was universally accepted.[40]

The progressive strengthening of the Mexica in late Aztec times resulted in a number of interventions in the tlatoani tenures of non-Mexica tribes. When Montezuma first received news of the arrival of Spanish ships, he undertook to establish his own nephews or sons as tlatoque, not only in Ecatepec and in Mexicapan of Azcapotzalco, which were Mexica communities, but also in Tenayuca, which was Tepaneca, and in Xochimilco.[41] At other times, members of the dynastic family of Tenochtitlan gained local tlatoani positions in non-Mexica areas through marriage. These interventions might eventually have obliterated the non-Mexica tribal jurisdictions entirely, but they were still far short of this result at the time of the Spanish conquest.

CULHUA. The dynastic history of the Culhua area is concerned with the four señoríos mentioned above: Culhuacan, Huitzilopochco, Mexicalzingo, and Ixtapalapa.[42] Culhuacan itself possessed one of the longest recorded tlatoani histories of the Valley. Although one Mexica annal states that the Culhua dynasty came to an end in the fourteenth century, other sources demonstrate clearly that it survived the period of Aztec imperialism and remained separate from the Mexica dynasty to which it gave origin. Thus Crónica X reports various activities of the "señor" of Culhuacan in the Aztec period and we know that a tlatoani named Tezozomoc was the Culhuacan ruler in 1519.[43] The tlatoque of Huitzilopochco, Mexicalzingo, and Ixtapalapa in 1519 were respectively Huitzilatzin II, Tochihuitzin, and the famous Cuitlahuatzin (Cuitlahuac) who became Montezuma's successor during the Spanish conquest.[44] The tlatoani history of the Culhua region is well documented. It includes a celebrated narrative concerning Huitzilatzin I, who was executed in the late fifteenth century by order of Ahuitzotl of Tenochtitlan for exposing the city to flood.[45] All four dynasties were closely related to the ruling family of Tenochtitlan through consanguinity and marriage. Spaniards recognized the four tlatoani locations (and no others in the Culhua area) as cabeceras in the sixteenth century.

—▷ MIXQUICA. In the tiny Mixquic area the Spaniards found one tlatoani, Chalcayaotzin, in 1519.[46] In accordance with the practice elsewhere, Mixquic itself, the tlatoani's residence, became the single cabecera.

—▷ TEPANECA. In the Tepaneca zone the cabecera situation was less simple. Azcapotzalco contained the two partes or parcialidades mentioned above, one of which preserved its Tepaneca affiliation. The many towns with indisputable Tepaneca tlatoani lineages—Tacuba, Coyoacan, Cuauhtitlan, Toltitlan, Tenayuca, Tepozotlan, Hueypoxtla, Tequixquiac, and Xilotzingo—were promptly granted cabecera rank. Zumpango, Citlaltepec, and Huehuetoca (as well as Utlaspa, which fell outside the Valley to the northwest) were sites of long-standing native dynastic regimes, but all appear to have been governed in 1519 by Aztatzontzin of Cuauhtitlan, in a remarkable instance of local tlatoani encroachment within one tribal jurisdiction.[47] The Spanish solution here was to accept Zumpango and Citlaltepec as cabeceras, leaving Huehuetoca's status in dispute.[48] In Tacubaya, pre-conquest evidence indicates at least an occasional local ruler but no real dynasty and no known tlatoani as of 1519.[49] Cortés, in his own interest, solicited the monarch to list Tacubaya separately in the grant of towns in the Marquesado del Valle, and the question of its rank was disputed between Cortés and the *audiencia*. Although the audiencia at first declared Tacubaya to be a sujeto of Coyoacan, Cortés's views prevailed and Tacubaya was admitted to cabecera status.[50]

Thus all tlatoani towns in the Tepaneca zone were accorded cabecera rank in the early colony. None was demoted to the position of sujeto. The

Tepaneca situation is summarized in Table 1, where the Memorial de los Pueblos commentary is taken as implying the existence of a tlatoani tradition.[51] The Memorial omits Huehuetoca, which was governed from Cuauhtitlan in 1519. It also omits Tenayuca, possibly because of the dynastic development of Tlalnepantla. But we know from numerous sources of Tenayuca's long dynastic tradition, and the Tacuba cacique of 1561 explicitly remarked upon Tenayuca as falling within the former Tepaneca jurisdiction.[52] Apart from these locations, Spaniards established two additional cabeceras in the Tepaneca zone, Tlalnepantla and Teocalhueyacan, the special circumstances of which will be separately discussed.[53]

⟶ ACOLHUA. As shown in Table 2, twelve towns of the Acolhua area had unquestioned tlatoani histories and were accorded cabecera status in the early colony. These were Texcoco, Chimalhuacan Atenco, Coatlichan, Huexotla, Chiauhtla, Tepetlaoztoc, Tezayuca, Tepexpan, Chiconauhtla, Acolman, Otumba, and Teotihuacan. The Anales de Cuauhtitlan records the names of seven of the tlatoque of 1519,[54] and from a variety of sources the pre-conquest dynasties of Chimalhuacan Atenco, Coatlichan, Huexotla, and Texcoco may be reconstructed in some detail.[55] Of the towns mentioned, however, Chiauhtla, Coatlichan, Tezayuca, and especially Huexotla had difficulty in maintaining their cabecera status in the sixteenth century as a consequence of the ambitions of Texcoco.[56]

A special feature of Acolhua history in the fifteenth century, as we have observed, was Nezahualcoyotl's demotion of a number of tlatoque, whom he replaced with calpixque under his rule. Our sources indicate that Nezahualcoyotl established such calpixque in Ixtapaluca, Coatepec, Xaltocan, Papalotla, Tizayuca, Aztaquemecan, Ahuatepec, Axapusco, Oxtoticpac, and Cuauhtlatzingo, at least some of which had the status, in 1519, of former tlatoani capitals.[57] Of the calpixqui locations that became early cabeceras, only Tizayuca gives no evidence of having been a tlatoani capital.[58] An apparent peculiarity of Coatepec was that a single tlatoani lineage governed four lesser "cabeceras"—Acuauhtla, Tetitlan, Quitlapanca, and Tepetlapa.[59] Finally, Tequicistlan and Tezontepec are recorded with "señores" in the late fifteenth century, and though the dynastic history appears to have been a broken one, both were granted cabecera status under the Spaniards.[60] In addition, early colonial cabeceras were established at Tecama and Chicoloapa. Chicoloapa traditions recorded a cacique-founder named Apaztli Chichimecatl, and possibly a later cacique named Apaztli

TABLE I

Tepaneca Area

Community	*Tlatoani in Memorial de los Pueblos*[a]	*Tlatoani in 1519*[b]	*Early Colonial Status*
Azcapotzalco[c]	*yes*	[Tlaltecatlçin]	Cabecera
Citlaltepec	*yes*	Aztatzontzin	Cabecera
Coyoacan[d]	*yes*	Cuappopocatzin	Cabecera
Cuauhtitlan[d]	*yes*	Aztatzontzin	Cabecera
Huehuetoca	*no*	Aztatzontzin	Cabecera (disputed)
Hueypoxtla	*yes*	*unknown*	Cabecera
Tacuba	*yes*	Totoquihuatzin	Cabecera
Tacubaya	*yes*	*unknown*	Cabecera (disputed)
Tenayuca	*no*	Moteucçomatzin	Cabecera
Teocalhueyacan	*no*		Cabecera
Tepozotlan	*yes*	Quinatzin	Cabecera
Tequixquiac	*yes*	*unknown*	Cabecera
Tlalnepantla	*no*		Cabecera
Toltitlan[d]	*yes*	Citlalcohuatl	Cabecera
Xilotzingo	*yes*	*unknown*	Cabecera
Zumpango	*yes*	Aztatzontzin	Cabecera

[a] ENE, XIV, 118–19. [b] *Códice Chimalpopoca*, p. 63.

[c] The Anales de Cuauhtitlan (*Códice Chimalpopoca*, p. 63) lists only the Mexica tlatoani, Teuhtlehuacatzin. For the Tepaneca tlatoani see Torquemada, *Monarchia indiana*, I, 254, and Barlow, "Los tecpaneca," p. 286.

[d] Dynasties of these towns are tabulated in García Granados, *Diccionario*, III, 410, 412, 437.

who governed for forty-five years, but in 1519 Chicoloapa was subordinate to Coatlichan. For Tecama there is no evidence of either calpixqui or tlatoani rule. Our information concerning its pre-conquest status is surprisingly slight, and it may have been a former dependency of Tlatelolco and not an Acolhua town at all.[61]

xochimilca. By native standards, Xochimilco consisted of three dynastic governments with three tlatoque. The subdivisions were Olac, Tepetenchi, and Tecpan, each the jurisdiction of one tlatoani. Each maintained a separate dynasty through the conquest and after,[62] and Spaniards were therefore confronted with a problem of cabecera designation similar to that posed by Azcapotzalco. Xochimilco appeared to be a single community. But a strict application of the tlatoani principle would require it to be three cabeceras, a condition remote from Castilian concepts of the cabeza, and one that Spaniards were not always willing to admit. For these reasons,

Spanish documents of the sixteenth century sometimes refer to Xochimilco as one cabecera and to Olac, Tepetenchi, and Tecpan as barrios, for to a casual Spanish observation this is what they appeared to be. At other times Spanish references to Xochimilco conformed to the tlatoani principle and indicated the three subdivisions as cabeceras. Occasionally, after the example of Azcapotzalco and Tenochtitlan-Tlatelolco, the three subdivisions were called partes.[63] No other tlatoani governments existed in the rest of the Xochimilco area, and in accordance with the criterion Spaniards assigned no other early cabeceras there.

CUITLAHUACA. Cuitlahuac, although smaller than Xochimilco, nevertheless maintained four tlatoani dynasties in the pre-conquest period, at Tizic, Teopancalcan, Atenchicalcan, and Tecpan. The four tlatoque of 1519 were, respectively, Atlpopocatzin, Ixtotomahuatzin, Mayehuatzin, and Acxochitzin.[64] Thus in Cuitlahuac Spaniards again confronted a problem of multiple tlatoani rule, this time in an especially acute form and compressed within an extremely small population and area. Our information on early colonial Cuitlahuac is not sufficient to permit an adequate explanation of what occurred. In any case, Spaniards never completely accepted the notion of four cabeceras in Cuitlahuac, and the status of the subdivisions was glossed over in such phrases as "pueblo de Cuitlahuac de Atenchicalcan." By the late sixteenth century the four Cuitlahuac areas were understood to be barrios, with Cuitlahuac itself the only cabecera.[65] The solution here resembled the solution in Xochimilco, but with a stronger insistence on one cabecera and its barrios.

CHALCA. Spanish preconceptions as to what constituted a cabecera met their most severe test in Chalco province, where the situation was even more complex and variable than in Xochimilco and Cuitlahuac. The twenty-five tlatoque of Chalco province had ruled prior to the Mexica-Chalca wars of the fourteenth and fifteenth centuries, and under a subsequent Mexica domination many changes had occurred in the Chalca towns. About a dozen tlatoani lineages still existed in Chalca territory in the fifteenth century when the Chalca revolted against Tenochtitlan. All these terminated with the suppression of the revolt, and the Mexica conquerors thereupon established military rulers (cuauhtlatoque) in four communities: Amecameca, Tlalmanalco, Tenango (Tenango Tepopula), and Chimalhuacan (Xochimilco Chimalhuacan).[66] In the 1480's the Mexica rulers Tizoc and Ahuitzotl restored ten tlatoani regimes, of which five—Iztlacocauhcan, Tlaillotlacan,

TABLE 2

Acolhua Area

Community	Ruler under Nezahualcoyotl[a]	Tlatoani in 1519[b]	Early Colonial Status
Acolman	Señor (tlatoani)	Coyoctzin	Cabecera
Ahuatepec	Calpixqui		Sujeto
Axapusco	Calpixqui		Sujeto (disputed)
Aztaquemecan	Calpixqui		Sujeto
Chiauhtla	Señor (tlatoani)	*unknown*	Cabecera (disputed)
Chicoloapa			Cabecera
Chiconauhtla	Señor (tlatoani)	Tlaltecatl	Cabecera
Chimalhuacan Atenco	Señor (tlatoani)	Acxoyatlatoatzin[c]	Cabecera
Coatepec	Calpixqui	*unknown*	Cabecera
Coatlichan	Señor (tlatoani)	Xaquinteuctli	Cabecera (disputed)
Cuauhtlatzingo	Calpixqui		Sujeto
Huexotla	Señor (tlatoani)	Tzontemoctzin	Cabecera (disputed)
Ixtapaluca	Calpixqui	*unknown*	Cabecera
Otumba	Señor (tlatoani)	Cuechimaltzin	Cabecera
Oxtoticpac	Calpixqui		Sujeto (disputed)
Papalotla	Calpixqui		Sujeto
Tecama			Cabecera
Teotihuacan	Señor (tlatoani)	Mamallitzin	Cabecera
Tepetlaoztoc	Señor (tlatoani)	Tlilpotonqui[d]	Cabecera
Tepexpan	Señor (tlatoani)	Teyaoyaualouatzin[e]	Cabecera
Tequicistlan	*unknown*	*unknown*	Cabecera
Texcoco	Nezahualcoyotl	Cacamatzin	Cabecera
Tezayuca	Señor (tlatoani)	*unknown*	Cabecera (disputed)
Tezontepec	*unknown*	*unknown*	Cabecera
Tizayuca	Calpixqui	*unknown*	Cabecera
Xaltocan	Calpixqui	*unknown*	Cabecera

[a]Ixtlilxochitl, *Relaciones*, p. 234. Ixtlilxochitl, *Historia chichimeca*, pp. 167–69. Motolinía, *Memoriales*, pp. 353–54.

[b]*Códice Chimalpopoca*, p. 63, unless otherwise noted. Cacamatzin is not included in the list but is mentioned in *Códice Chimalpopoca*, p. 61.

[c]PNE, VI, 72.　　　　　　　　　　　　　[d]*Códice Kingsborough*, fols. 210r ff.

[e]See "Mappe de Tepechpan," note 23.

Tzacualtitlan Tenango, Tecuanipan, and Panohuayan—were located in subdivisions of Amecameca. Three others—Opochhuacan, Itzcahuacan, Acxotlan Cihuateopan—were located in subdivisions of Tlalmanalco. The final two were at Tenango (Tenango Tepopula) and Chimalhuacan (Tepetlixpa Chimalhuacan). At least nine of these ten tlatoani governments were in

existence at the time of the conquest, and all nine survived beyond it. Only
Acxotlan Cihuateopan in Tlalmanalco disappeared as a tlatoani seat before
or during the conquest.[67]

The Spanish solution to the multiple tlatoani rule in Chalco province was
to consider Amecameca and Tlalmanalco as single cabeceras and their tlatoani subdivisions as barrios. The barrio status of Panohuayan, of Tecuanipan, of Tzacualtitlan Tenango, of Tlaillotlacan, and of Iztlacocauhcan is
frequently documented in the sixteenth century.[68] Spaniards considered
Chalco to be a province of four cabeceras—Tlalmanalco, Chimalhuacan,
Tenango, and Amecameca—after the precedent of the cuauhtlatoque sites
of the fifteenth century and in spite of the restorations by Tizoc and Ahuitzotl. Nevertheless, some sixteenth-century Spanish records speak of the
five parts of Amecameca as cabeceras, all within the major cabecera of
Amecameca, and unquestionably in reference to tlatoani rule.[69]

In sum, in all jurisdictions the towns with firm, unitary tlatoani traditions
became cabeceras. Towns with interrupted or divided tlatoani traditions, or
with records of some degree of subordination, became cabeceras in certain
cases and sujetos in others. Towns with multiple tlatoani lineages such as
Xochimilco or Amecameca occupied an intermediate or unresolved status,
the tlatoani locations being classified sometimes as cabeceras, sometimes as
sujetos. In the typical instances, the tlatoani lineages were maintained and
at least an approximation of the rules of Indian succession continued in the
early colonial period.

If the towns indicated above were the early cabeceras, it follows that all
others were sujetos. A sujeto may be defined as a community owing tribute,
service, and other obligation to the officers of the cabecera. A sujeto was
commonly a single calpulli, whose members were governed through local
calpulli officers under the authority of the cabecera tlatoani. Occasionally,
sujetos were themselves broken into barrios, a condition that suggests calpulli combinations or sub-calpulli divisions, although the truth is that we
know very little of such processes.[70] In the colony, tributes and services continued to be paid by sujetos to their cabeceras. In the sixteenth century the
liability of a community to a cacique's tribute and service requirements,
and a history of obedience to his demands for other labor, were consistently
cited in evidence of sujeto status.[71] Also, within a sujeto a cacique or other
privileged person might hold private lands with retainers or tenants.[72]

We are not yet able to identify all Valley sujetos or to clarify certain distinctions between a calpulli subject to a cabecera and the private property of a cacique or other Indian landholder. It is possible, however, to locate a large number of the sujetos and to examine details of the geographical and of some of the institutional relations between them and their cabeceras in the early colonial period. Estancias were for the most part situated within a few miles of their cabeceras, the total area of each cabecera and its estancias being fixed by the *términos,* or boundaries, of each tlatoani jurisdiction. In a small cabecera jurisdiction, such as Mixquic, all sujetos were situated within a radius of approximately one mile.[73] But in other cases, as Map 3 shows, sujetos might be located at much greater distances.

The cabeceras were concentrated in the lake area, with estancias fanning out toward the Valley rim. Only in the north and in the spurs of the main Valley—as in Chalco province or the "sub-valley" of Teotihuacan—did cabeceras occupy non-lacustrine locations. This fact recalls the controlling influence of the lakes, which determined not only the distribution and density of populations, but the administrative networks and local economies of capital and subordinate towns. As cabeceras tended to cluster near the main bodies of water, sujetos tended to occupy higher land, often in relation to small streams. The sujetos of Xochimilco, Coyoacan, and Tacuba extended up the Valley slopes away from the shores. The sujetos of the non-lacustrine cabeceras, on the other hand, might be distributed in more symmetrical patterns, as may be seen in Otumba, a central cabecera with its estancias grouped about it on all sides.

These "normal" distributions, however, were sharply broken in the northern lakes, where Cuauhtitlan, blocked to the south and west, asserted a jurisdiction extending into and across the waters. Similar extensions under the Tepaneca cabeceras farther south were prevented by the proximity of Tenochtitlan-Tlatelolco. On the eastern side of the Valley north of Texcoco, a situation of such complexity occurred that a regional mapping of controlled territories becomes nearly impossible. The Tepexpan and Acolman cabeceras did not govern integral territories; the lines of their jurisdiction crossed each other in a northerly direction, and the area was pocketed by scattered estancias of both. Hueypoxtla in the north was the cabecera of nearby Tianquistonco, but it was also the cabecera of Tezcatepec and Tlacuitlapilco, which were many miles distant and well outside the Valley.[74] Tacuba's authority likewise extended for an enormous distance: two six-

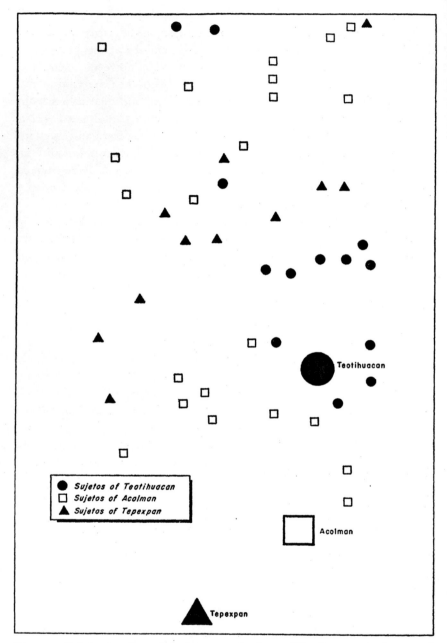

Figure 2. Relative locations of the interspersed sujetos of Teotihuacan, Acolman, and Tepexpan, from the map of ca. 1580 published in PNE, VI.

teenth-century subjects of Tacuba—Cepayautla and Ciuhtepec —were located near Tenango del Valle in the Valley of Toluca, some fifty miles to the southwest.[75]

The cabeceras with the most irregularly patterned estancias of all were Tenochtitlan and Tlatelolco. Tlatelolco estancias in the sixteenth century included Santa Ana Zacatlan, San Bartolomé Cuauhtlalpa (Tlalpam), and San Lucas Xoloc far to the north, as well as San Andrés Tecalco, San Pablo de las Salinas, and Santa María Ozumbilla north of Ecatepec.[76] In the Lake Texcoco area, Tlatelolco had estancias at Tolpetlac, Xaloztoc, and numerous other locations. And in the Chalco area far to the south, Tepostlan and part of Santiago Tepopula were likewise Tlatelolco sujetos.[77] Tenochtitlan estancias in the north included San Francisco Cuaquiquitla, San Pablo Tecalco, and San Pedro Ozumba (Ozumbilla).[78] South of the city Ixtahuacan (Aztahuacan), Los Reyes, and Santa Marta were Tenochtitlan subjects, and far to the south in Chalco province the list includes Santos Reyes Acatlixcoatlan, San Juan Coxtocan, and another part of Santiago Tepopula.[79] We know that some of the estancias of Tenochtitlan—Tecalco, Tepopula, Ixtacalco, Popotla, Coatlayuca—were calpixqui locations under the Aztec rulers, and that some—notably Coxtocan, Tepopula, Tecalco, Caxhuacan—included lands owned by Indians in the city.[80]

The general distribution of cabeceras and estancias in the sixteenth century appears in Map 3, where cabeceras are related to their estancias by connecting lines. Barrios are not shown, nor are those estancias that were situated at short distances from their cabeceras. The map therefore emphasizes the longer distances and the irregularities of the cabecera-sujeto relations. With few exceptions, these irregularities were of Indian, not of Spanish origin, and they represented derivations from the tlatoani jurisdictions of the pre-conquest period. As we have mentioned, the early colonial cabeceras can be demonstrated to have been locations of pre-conquest tlatoque in all cases save five: Tlalnepantla, Teocalhueyacan, Tizayuca, Tecama, and Chicoloapa.

The five instances of Spanish promotion from non-tlatoani to cabecera status, occurring at the time of the conquest or shortly after, were the first such instances of the colonial period in the Valley of Mexico. Four of them —Teocalhueyacan, Tizayuca, Tecama, and Chicoloapa—are to be explained as consequences of encomienda creation (see Table 4), while the fifth—Tlalnepantla—is to be explained as a consequence of religious congregation.

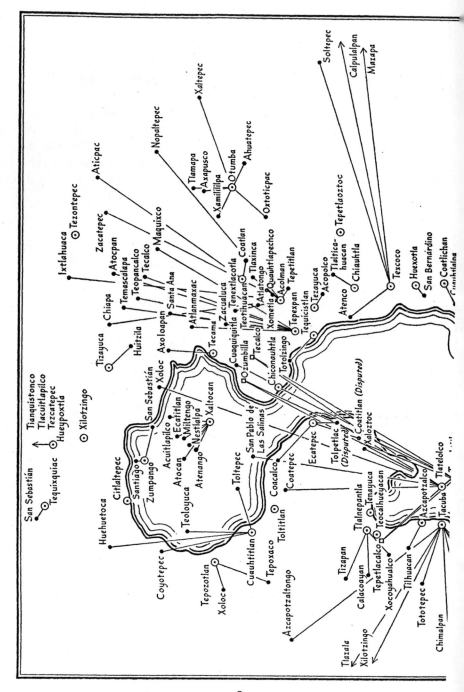

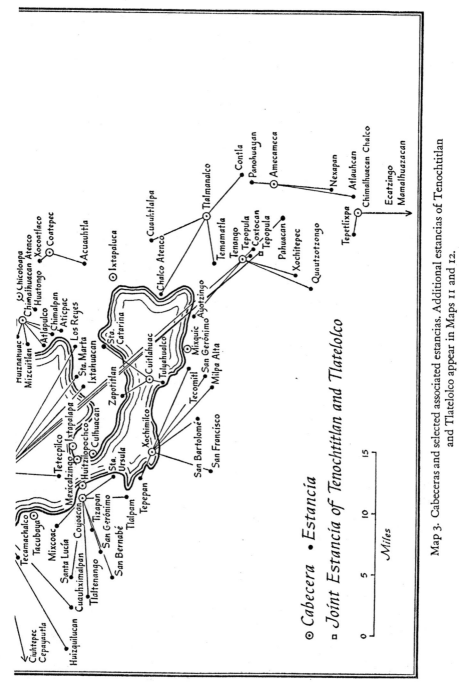

Map 3. Cabeceras and selected associated estancias. Additional estancias of Tenochtitlan and Tlatelolco appear in Maps 11 and 12.

⊙ *Cabecera* • *Estancia*

□ *Joint Estancia of Tenochtitlan and Tlatelolco*

Miles

0 5 10 15

Thus the first colonial departures from the Indian tlatoani-cabecera system are explicable in terms of two of the most fundamental Spanish institutions of the early period. The relations of the church and of encomienda to the cabecera-sujeto patterns are topics to which we will devote special attention in later chapters. For the moment, our purpose will be to enumerate other influences of the sixteenth century, and after, that brought about changed circumstances for cabeceras and sujetos.

The principal motivation for change in the existing cabecera-sujeto situations was not Spanish but Indian. For the most part, it took two forms: one in which interested Indian caciques sought to re-establish some of the patterns of the Triple Alliance, with Tenochtitlan, Texcoco, and Tacuba exercising controls over other cabeceras; and a second in which local Indian leaders in sujetos sought to escape the domination of their cabeceras and to promote their communities to cabecera rank. The first represents a reactionary Indian tendency pointing toward a restoration of pre-conquest status. The second represents opportunism and change depending on new circumstances.

In the sixteenth century, the three caciques of Tenochtitlan, Texcoco, and Tacuba, both separately and jointly, formally protested the loss of authority that their communities had suffered on the coming of the Spaniards. Their contention was that these three cabeceras, and no others, had existed before the Spaniards came.[81] The assertion ran counter, of course, to the Spanish policy of government through local tlatoque, and it implied a redefinition, in Triple Alliance terms, of the whole cabecera concept. In the separate campaigns, the Tenochtitlan cacique was now the weakest of the three. The Indian leaders of post-conquest Tenochtitlan and Tlatelolco had to accept the alienation of Ecatepec, which had been granted in encomienda to Montezuma's daughter Leonor, but they argued for the retention of some of the supposed Ecatepec sujetos, even to the point of carrying their suit to the Consejo de Indias in Spain.[82] The case was conducted more actively by Tlatelolco than by Tenochtitlan, chiefly because the former sujetos of Tlatelolco were the ones principally involved. The Spanish policy of recompensing Montezuma's heirs with encomiendas (Ecatepec to his daughter Leonor, Tacuba to his daughter Isabel, and Tula, outside the Valley of Mexico, to his son Pedro) operated to reduce any Indian inclination to combine the Tenochtitlan campaign with an argument based on legitimate Indian inheritance. Tenochtitlan, moreover, was the Indian capital that had been most conspicuously defeated in the conquest, and Spaniards were particularly alert to any reactivation of its pretensions.

The campaigns conducted by Tacuba and Texcoco were less inhibited by such factors. The Tacuba claim related partly to a group of alienated dependencies lying outside the Valley to the west, between the cabecera and its remote estancias of Ciuhtepec and Cepayautla. The Indian officers of Tacuba enumerated Tlallachco, Xochicuauhtla, Huitzililapan, and a number of other towns in this area, and in 1561 petitioned for the return of all or some of them. The towns had been granted in Spanish encomienda, and their tributes removed from Tacuba control. Antonio Cortés, the cacique, and other Indians of Tacuba stated in 1561 that the communities whose return was requested represented less than a hundredth part of the total deprivation.[83]

Our more immediate concern is with Tacuba claims within the Valley. As with Tenochtitlan and Ecatepec, Tacuba could not successfully protest against the alienation of Teocalhueyacan, a non-tlatoani sujeto of Tacuba granted in separate encomienda and elevated to cabecera status.[84] But Tacuba could, and did, protest against the disposition of other former sujetos as dependencies of Teocalhueyacan. The dispute related especially to Tlazala and Xilotzingo, Otomi estancias on the western edge of the Valley, and it took the form of a suit at law, Tacuba vs. Teocalhueyacan, which also proceeded on appeal from the audiencia in Mexico to the Council of the Indies in Spain. Indian witnesses for Tacuba stated that Tlazala and Xilotzingo had always been estancias of Tacuba in the pre-conquest period, that they had obeyed Tacuba and delivered tributes and rendered services there. Indian witnesses for Teocalhueyacan argued against this that Tlazala and Xilotzingo fell within the términos of Teocalhueyacan, and they asserted, probably falsely, that Teocalhueyacan had been a cacique residence before the Spaniards came and that it had been a cabecera for "as long as the memory of man." An interesting sidelight of the issue is that in the 1560's witnesses for Teocalhueyacan were shown to be professional perjurers who had received money and gifts from Indian authorities in Teocalhueyacan for making false depositions.[85]

The Texcoco claim was so similar in wording to the Tacuba claim that one may assume collaboration or modeling of the one upon the other.[86] Indian officials in Texcoco asserted that all Acolhua towns had been sujetos of the lord of Texcoco in the pre-conquest period—as, in a sense, they had—

and they made repeated reference to the loss of these under Spanish rule.[87] Texcoco entered its claim for "a large part of the pueblos of New Spain" in a petition to the audiencia in 1551–52.[88] The more practical campaign, however, was limited to the nearby Acolhua communities of Huexotla, Chiauhtla, Coatlichan, and Tezayuca, all of which had had pre-conquest tlatoque and all of which were colonial cabeceras and pueblos por sí, separate from the Indian government of Texoco. All of them had however been briefly granted together in encomienda with Texcoco, and all were, at one time or another in the sixteenth century, considered to be Texcoco sujetos.[89]

The Texcoco campaign for true cabecera-sujeto relations was directed most particularly against Huexotla. Huexotla continued to maintain an Indian cacique and to support the type of Indian government appropriate to a cabecera during the 1530's and 1540's, and yet Texcoco interests continued to hold it as a sujeto.[90] Texcoco entered into legal conflict with Huexotla in the early 1550's. Huexotla secured a *cédula* (royal order) favoring its side in 1551 and its Indian representatives asserted in court that it was a "true cabecera and pueblo por sí," that it had been independent "from time immemorial," that it had always had "rulers . . . by direct descent," and that its obligation to Texcoco related only to labor on public works. Huexotla asserted that Texcoco was seeking to subject it in unprecedented ways and that if the Texcoco claims were admitted Huexotla would lose its traditional "liberties." The dispute resolved itself into a discussion of the kinds of control that Nezahualcoyotl and Nezahualpilli had exerted over tlatoani communities in the Acolhua area, and the Huexotla Indian witnesses insisted, quite properly, that these controls were different from those of a cabecera over a sujeto. Texcoco's counter-assertion declared these statements to be false or irrelevant and characterized Huexotla as a true estancia, a community that from time immemorial had been a sujeto of Texcoco. Viceroy Velasco, rather unexpectedly, favored the Texcoco side in 1555, and by a compromise viceregal order some of Huexotla's Indian officials were chosen by its putative cabecera, Texcoco, while others were chosen from within Huexotla itself.[91] The interesting feature of the case is that although Huexotla in no way differed from other tlatoani locations of the Acolhua area, it nevertheless fell victim to Texcoco to this degree. It later successfully escaped from Texcoco control,[92] but the sixteenth-century dispute clearly demonstrates Texcoco's pretensions and its effort to gain advantage from a Triple Alliance precedent. Essentially, the Indians of Texcoco were denying the colonial equation of tlatoani site with cabecera.

The campaign of Temascalapa, a distant estancia of Tepexpan, exemplifies the second type of Indian motivation in effecting changes in cabecera-sujeto relations. Temascalapa's effort to secure independent status was reinforced by its geographical location, for it was one of Tepexpan's northernmost sujetos, and it was situated in the complex jurisdictional region mentioned above. Tepexpan itself qualified as an undisputed cabecera, with a tradition of pre-conquest tlatoani government, and Temascalapa was included with it in a single Spanish encomienda grant of the 1520's. During the next two decades Temascalapa was understood to be a sujeto of Tepexpan,[93] but in the mid-sixteenth century four Indian leaders, not natives of Temascalapa, succeeded in winning the support of its Indian population and in instituting a movement for separation. In the Spanish courts in the early 1550's Indian witnesses favoring Temascalapa testified that it had always been a "pueblo por sí" and that its enforced subjugation to Tepexpan was of recent date. Tepexpan witnesses, on the other hand, asserted that Temascalapa had been a sujeto of Tepexpan "for as long as men could remember," that its tributes and services had been paid there, and that it was situated within the Tepexpan limits.[94] In all these ways the terms of the dispute strikingly resemble those of the dispute between Texcoco and Huexotla.

In 1552 the audiencia decided in favor of Tepexpan, but in the early 1560's a new faction in Temascalapa was able to appeal this decision. Following a legal authorization of transfer, duly signed by Philip II, the case was transmitted in 1562 to the Council of the Indies. The Council likewise decided in favor of Tepexpan, but on renewed appeal the case was taken up again in the later 1560's, and the whole history was reviewed once more. Temascalapa meanwhile organized its own municipal government and assumed authority over certain local "sujetos," alleging that this authority entitled it to cabecera rank. Both sides continually sought out new arguments in the hope that Spanish courts might regard them as relevant. Temascalapa cited its pre-conquest market place and pagan temple (*casa de diablo*) as proof of its cabecera qualifications. Indian witnesses for Tepexpan argued the town's great antiquity, claiming that it was founded even before Texcoco, and its numerous pre-conquest sujetos. Tepexpan witnesses testified that Temascalapa had been founded by settlers from Tepexpan. The fact that Temascalapa was situated four leagues away was dismissed in the Tepexpan argument with the assertion that Santa María Chiapa, an estancia of Acolman, lay even farther from its cabecera.[95] In 1590 and as late as 1656 Temascalapa was still seeking to evade its sujeto responsibilities.[96]

A number of other sujetos in the Valley made similar efforts to escape their obligations and to establish themselves as cabeceras in their own right. Cabeceras in turn sought to retain their estancias in order to collect tributes from them and use their labor.[97] Factions in estancias, aided by ecclesiastics, royal officials, or other Spaniards with particular interests, advocated independence from cabeceras in campaigns for local power. A class of Spanish lawyers made its living by encouraging or provoking Indian litigation. Estancias situated in political or ecclesiastical jurisdictions different from those of their cabeceras argued that they were already at least partly separate and that they were therefore entitled to full independence in Indian terms.[98] Pre-conquest relationships were repeatedly cited as precedents for post-conquest status, and "the memory of man" was appealed to. Traditions of local señorío were evoked in demonstration of cabecera rank, but Indian testimonies on the one side and the other took opposite positions on what the pre-conquest status had been. Fraud and perjury in Indian testimonies were common occurrences. Moreover, the disputes elicited new criteria for cabecera status—markets, churches, geographical location, date of foundation, population size, and others—until finally the original tlatoani criterion became obscured or totally lost from view.[99] Not all the campaigns were successful, but there was a notable tendency in the later sixteenth and the seventeenth centuries toward the progressive transformation of sujetos into cabeceras.

Among the other forces modifying cabecera-sujeto relations was population loss, which in some cases extinguished sujetos completely. Town maps after the sixteenth century carried inscriptions such as "barrio now uninhabited," and the early baptismal books, as a curate noted in the eighteenth century, listed "many barrios that no longer exist."[100] In the official and unofficial redistributions (congregaciones) that followed population loss, opportunities were again offered for upsetting cabecera-sujeto systems. Thus when some sujetos of Tlalnepantla were congregated at Azcapotzaltongo, a sujeto of Tacuba, in the 1590's, the Indian leaders of Tacuba sought to take advantage of the change in location to control their tributes and services.[101] In the early seventeenth century Santa María Xochitepec, a sujeto of Tepexpan, requested and received permission to be congregated at San Felipe Zacatepec, a sujeto of Acolman. In Huitzilopochco in the early eighteenth century, where one barrio had been reduced to four families, another to two, and a third to none at all, the local curate, acting on his own authority, moved families from one barrio to another and combined the depopulated communities to make a single unit.[102]

In the middle and late colonial period, tribute and service came to be paid in far greater amounts to Spanish than to Indian authority, and Spaniards organized their exactions with progressively less attention to the cabecera-sujeto structures. Caciques everywhere lost authority, new systems of Indian government appeared, and increasing numbers of former sujetos separated as pueblos por sí, without caciques and in some instances without sujetos. As Spanish haciendas and ranchos came into being, there appeared new clusters of Indian population that were wholly distinct from the former cabeceras and sujetos.[103] In the programs of civic reform in the eighteenth century, communities were subdivided in new ways, frequently in four or more barrios or *cuarteles,* after the model of Mexico City and Madrid.[104] By the late eighteenth century, population lists commonly ignored cabecera-sujeto relations entirely, classifying communities simply as haciendas, ranchos, or pueblos.[105]

The distant estancias also came, in time, to be attached to new jurisdictions for reasons of convenience and practicality. By the eighteenth century Ciuhtepec and Cepayautla, the remote western sujetos of Tacuba, had been removed from Tacuba and attached to the closer cabecera of Tenango del Valle.[106] Other distant estancias were similarly attached to adjacent jurisdictions, the allegiance to the original cabeceras being pared away by degrees or destroyed in a single act. Tlatelolco and Tenochtitlan, like the others, lost their hold over the remote estancias.[107] Tlatelolco still had jurisdiction over part of Tepopula in Chalco province in 1788, when it successfully defied the efforts of Tenango to exercise new controls; and Tenochtitlan still preserved its status as the cabecera of San Pablo Tecalco and Ozumbilla to the north and of Coxtocan, Acatlixcoatlan, and the rest of Tepopula to the south. But in 1790 even these ancient Mexica estancias fell victim to the political rationalism of the late Spanish empire. Indians of Tepopula went up to Tenango to drink and engage in brawls, and when the local authorities put them in jail the question of jurisdiction came to the attention of Spanish authorities. One of the foremost Mexican legalists, Eusebio Bentura Beleña, explained what was happening in a letter to the viceroy. Tepopula, Acatlixcoatlan, and Coxtocan, he said, were traditionally subject to Tenochtitlan and Tlatelolco; but since the long-standing relationship brought no benefit to either side, the viceroy would be well advised to declare them attached to the nearest Chalco cabecera. The viceroy sought to discover the origins of the subjugation of these towns in the archives of the General Indian Court (Juzgado General de Indios), but failing in his search, he did as advised.[108]

The deterioration of the cabecera-sujeto concept may be seen more concretely in the case of Tlalnepantla, the early ecclesiastical site founded in the intermediate territory between Nahuatl Tenayuca and Otomi Teocalhueyacan. In the sixteenth century Tlalnepantla was regarded as the cabecera, but the two communities of which it was composed did not lose their identities.[109] Tenayuca, the more important of the two in pre-conquest history and the residence of a tlatoani in 1519, continued to be regarded as a cabecera in the sixteenth century.[110] Teocalhueyacan, formerly only an Otomi sujeto of Tacuba,[111] was variously classified as an estancia, a barrio, a cabecera, a parte, and a pueblo.[112] The two subdivisions were distinct early encomiendas. Teocalhueyacan remained an encomienda far into the colonial period, but Tenayuca was taken from its holder in 1544 as a result of the New Laws.[113] In the sixteenth century no other cabeceras and no other encomiendas were recognized between Azcapotzalco to the south and Toltitlan to the north. Both subdivisions maintained Indian governments,[114] though their separate sujetos were frequently confused by Spaniards, who tended to regard all subject towns as subordinate to Tlalnepantla or to think of Tenayuca and Tlalnepantla as a single town.[115] The cabecera-sujeto situation under Tlalnepantla was by no means a simple one. It was further complicated by the close proximity of several sujetos of Tlatelolco, including Santa María Coatepec, San Jerónimo Tepetlacalco, San Pablo de las Salinas, and San Jerónimo Cagualtitlan.[116]

The seventeenth-century history of the Tlalnepantla region was one of deterioration for Tenayuca and Teocalhueyacan and of expansion for Tlalnepantla. Tlalnepantla became the acknowledged cabecera, and Tenayuca and Teocalhueyacan were much more uniformly regarded as its barrios. Nevertheless, each continued to maintain an Indian government. Teocalhueyacan gradually dropped from notice, save as an Otomi barrio called San Lorenzo.[117] The viceregal congregación of the early seventeenth century assumed that Tenayuca had been incorporated within Tlalnepantla and ordered the concentration of the populations of the entire area into five locations: Tlalnepantla, Santa María Nativitas, Tecpan, Cagualtitlan, and Azcapotzaltongo. The congregación order defied the existing cabecera-sujeto relationships, for Santa María Nativitas and Tecpan were sujetos of Tlalnepantla, Cagualtitlan was a sujeto of Tlatelolco, and Azcapotzaltongo was a sujeto of Tacuba. This congregación, like many others, met Indian objection and appeal; its form was revised, and it was never completely put into effect.[118] A number of the larger sujetos, whose removal had been ordered in 1603, survived through the seventeenth century.[119] Meanwhile, haciendas continued to develop in the area in the seventeenth century and their *mayordomos* disturbed the community organization further by coercing labor and exacting payments in kind.[120]

In the eighteenth century these same processes continued. Tlalnepantla, still sometimes indicated as a cabecera, was now about five times the size of Tenayuca.[121] Teocalhueyacan had been nearly forgotten, and the surviving encomienda was understood as applying to a portion of Tlalnepantla, and not to Teocalhueyacan.[122] Santa María Coatepec and other former sujetos of Tlatelolco lost their connection with their original cabecera. The magnificent hacienda of Santa Mónica, just west of Tlalnepantla, dominated the area. Other haciendas and ranchos pressed upon the territories formerly belonging to cabeceras and sujetos. By the 1790's the concept of undifferentiated pueblos had gone far toward displacing the concept of cabecera-sujeto organization. More than twenty communities that antedated the congregación of 1603 survived to achieve pueblo status in the late colonial period.[123]

Similar changes took place throughout the Valley. In the sixteenth century the cabecera had been the seat of Indian government, the residence of the highest Indian nobility, the center of tribute collection, and the concentration point for the recruitment of labor. The abandonment of a system basic to Indian history, occurring gradually through individual changes in status, through depopulation, through congregación, and through many administrative modifications, was a part of the progressive yielding of Indian to Spanish institutions. After the early period, as we shall see, the Indian nobility lost its authority, and Spaniards reorganized the procedures for tribute collection and labor recruitment. In the late eighteenth century, there occurred repeated specific rejections of Indian systems of organization and a new emphasis on pueblos. The hacienda became the supreme community. The cabecera concept was not universally given up, but the terminology of the eighteenth century—hacienda, rancho, pueblo, barrio—reflected the real condition of the Valley.[124]

CHAPTER IV

Encomienda and Corregimiento

The Spanish institutions of greatest consequence for Indian civilization during the first fifty years of colonial Mexican history may be classified as private, political, or religious. Of these the private jurisdiction, or encomienda, was the first to establish itself in a position of power. Immediately, encomienda became the most openly exploitative of all modes of contact with Indians and the most aggressively competitive in relation to other Spanish institutions. Though it was also the first to lose out in competition, it served briefly as an instrument of authority for Spanish colonists and a source of terror for native peoples.

In legal principle, encomienda was a benign agency for Indian Hispanization. Its essential feature was the official consignment of groups of Indians to privileged Spanish colonists. The grantees, called *encomenderos,* were entitled to receive tribute and labor from the Indians delegated to them. The Indians, though liable to the demands for tribute and labor during the effective period of the grant, were regarded as free for the reason that they were not owned as property by their encomenderos. Their freedom established a legal distinction between encomienda and slavery, and between encomienda and more refined types of feudal tenure. A grant of encomienda conferred no landed property, judicial jurisdiction, dominium, or señorío. It entrusted to each encomendero the Christian welfare of a designated number of Indians. Encomienda was a possession, not a property, and it was per se inalienable and non-inheritable, save insofar as the terms of particular grants might allow. A vacant (unpossessed) encomienda reverted to the monarch, who might retain its Indians under royal administration or reissue them to a new encomendero.[1]

Encomienda had arisen from prototypes in Spain and during the early years of the sixteenth century it had become the chief means of private Spanish control over Indian peoples in the West Indies. It was already an institution of terror there. But the transfer to Mexico brought new opportunities for the abuse of regulations, and the regulations were in any case imperfectly defined until the middle sixteenth century. The wealth and size of Aztec population intensified Spanish cupidity, enlarged the possibilities of exploitation, and gave rise to an encomendero class bent on making of itself a hereditary colonial aristocracy.

But the encomenderos faced a monarch who was determined to reduce their pretensions. Through the sixteenth century, as encomiendas reverted to the crown, a progressively greater share of Indian tribute was directed to the royal treasury, and encomienda was weakened and brought under royal law. In a longer view, the monarch's victory served as a preliminary to the emergence of a third powerful group, a new land-owning *hacendado* class, which developed more gradually, assumed private working forces, and escaped royal direction. The encomendero class, by appearing suddenly in the aftermath of conquest and by establishing so conspicuous a domination over Indian tribute and labor, made itself vulnerable to royal attack. The later hacendados, profiting from the experience of their predecessors, scrupulously avoided this. But the hacendados had the advantage of living in another age, when a less active monarchy could more easily condone colonial excesses.

Cortés assigned encomiendas in the Valley of Mexico immediately upon the conclusion of the conquest, and encomienda was already an established institution in 1523, when Cortés received the royal order prohibiting it. His refusal to obey the order may be regarded as the first act of defiance by Mexican encomienda interests against the king.[2] He defended his position by citing his soldiers' demands, the strategic need that Indians be placed under regulation, and his belief that encomienda would liberate Indian peoples from their own native rulers.[3] Whatever the justification for Cortés's whole argument, it is certain that there was a compelling reason for his insistence on encomienda—as well as for the qualified approval that the monarchy soon granted—in the continued strength of the conquistadores. Though many Valley encomiendas were subsequently to be issued to non-conquistadores, and though the classification "conquistador" was to become blurred by redefinition, the early encomienda class did consist largely of soldiers recently released from war. In the Valley the first encomendero generation included some of the foremost soldiers of Cortés's army. The city of Mexico was from the first the residence of other encomenderos whose possessions fell outside the Valley, and many Spaniards simultaneously held encomiendas within the Valley and elsewhere. Thus the Valley emerged at the beginning of the colonial period as a focus of encomendero strength.[4]

Cortés's defense of encomienda was the consequence not only of his soldiers' demands but also of his own ambition. There is strong evidence that he hoped to secure Tenochtitlan as his private holding in the early 1520's and that he made vigorous efforts to prevent it from falling to the crown in 1526.[5] Outside the city he assigned to himself the encomiendas of Texcoco, Chalco, Otumba, and Coyoacan.[6] The latter two were large cabeceras with numerous sujetos. Texcoco was a "provincia" that included Huexotla, Chiauhtla, Tezayuca, and Coatlichan.[7] By Chalco, Cortés understood all the cabeceras and sujetos of Chalco province. The size and distribution of these areas suggest that he clearly comprehended the role that the Valley was to play in colonial affairs, and that he was seeking to assume direction over Indian tribute and labor in the capital and in its densely populated environs.

In practice, Cortés was able to maintain his early encomiendas only while he was present in person to enforce his claims. He nearly lost Texcoco to the assertive royal officials during his expedition to the south between 1524 and 1526, and after he left for Spain to plead his case before the court in 1528 his enemies proceeded rapidly to usurp his holdings. Nuño de Guzmán, members of the audiencia, and other royal officers seized Texcoco, Chalco, Otumba, and Coyoacan, taking tributes and using the Indian laborers of these towns.[8] The municipal council of Mexico City, following suit, urged that all of Cortés's Indians be reassigned to deserving conquistadores.[9] In Spain in 1529 Cortés received title to a large number of Mexican towns with 23,000 Indian "vassals," while other royal orders made him a marqués and granted him civil, criminal, and ecclesiastical (patronato) jurisdiction in his Marquesado.[10] These favors, far exceeding the customary privileges of encomienda, were to make Cortés the wealthiest man in America, and perhaps in the whole Spanish world.[11] The actual number of his tribute-paying "vassals" was far in excess of the 23,000 specified.[12] But of the towns only two, Coyoacan and Tacubaya, were located within the Valley, and it is possible that the monarchy acted deliberately to restrain his ambitions here and to direct his attention to other areas.[13] After Cortés returned to the colony in 1530 he successfully established his authority in the new Marquesado, but he was never able to resurrect his earlier encomiendas. Within a few years Otumba, Chalco, and Texcoco were all declared to be crown provinces. Though Cortés was permitted for a time to receive tributes from them, the use of their labor was denied him and the tributes of Texcoco and Otumba soon reverted to the monarch.[14] Chalco tributes continued to be assigned, in part, to the Cortés estate through the whole middle and late colonial period; the formal justification for this rested, however, not upon his original claim but upon the release of Tehuantepec to the crown.[15]

With the failure of Cortés's larger ambitions, the number of encomiendas in the Valley as of the mid-1530's stood at thirty, with an estimated 180,000 Indian tributaries. The average encomienda thus contained some 6,000 tributaries. The largest was Xochimilco, with some 20,000. The smallest was Tequicistlan, with about 450. The crown, incidentally, was on record in 1528 with a rule prohibiting encomiendas of more than 300 Indians.[16]

Of the thirty encomiendas of the 1530's, twenty-six could be described as normal in the sense that they were assigned to individual Spanish holders for their lifetimes, with an implicit assumption, at least for the encomenderos, that subsequent inheritance would be approved. The remaining four, though repeatedly classified as encomiendas, represent exceptions to this norm. Tacuba and Ecatepec, held respectively by the two daughters of Montezuma, qualified as "perpetual" holdings, inheritable from generation to generation without restriction. It is true that their status in this respect remained unresolved in the 1530's and was later to be the subject of dispute. But their possession by Indians and the special circumstances of their foundation already set them apart. A third, enjoying similar perpetuity and carrying additional privileges as well, was Cortés's Marquesado, which consisted of Coyoacan and Tacubaya and their sujetos. Finally, Ixtapalapa in the 1530's was a temporary encomienda of the corporate city of Mexico, the result of an earlier grant of jurisdiction by Cortés.[17] Brief histories of these and the other encomiendas of the Valley will be found in Appendix I.

In general, the encomendero class remained a powerful influence upon both the Spanish and the Indian societies through the 1530's. Encomenderos began to suffer restrictions as the mid-century period approached, not so much as a consequence of Indian resistance as of an intensified application of royal law. The encomienda of Xochimilco reverted to the crown in 1541, on the death of Pedro de Alvarado and his wife, and royal officials later refused a request for its reassignment.[18] The reform legislation of 1542–43, which forbade the holding of encomiendas by colonial officials, brought about the escheatment of another of the Valley's encomiendas, Tenayuca-Coatepec, held by the Treasurer Juan Alonso de Sosa.[19] The New Laws further urged the audiencia to reduce the largest holdings, precisely indicating the Valley encomenderos Vásquez de Tapia, González de Benavides, and González de Avila as possessors of too great a number of Indians.[20] The most stringent article of the New Laws required each encomienda to revert to the crown upon the death of its holder, and thus in effect forbade inheritance. Its repeal in 1545 amounted to a temporary victory for the encomenderos; but an earlier law (1536), restricting inheritance to one heir (a span of two "lives"), was still in force, and at least some of the Valley encomiendas were already in their second "life" in the 1540's.[21] Moreover, in 1545 the Indian population was stricken by its first serious epidemic and reduced by one-third or more, and this eliminated a substantial portion of all encomienda income. Finally in 1549, after the epidemic had passed, the crown ruled that encomenderos might continue to receive the tribute, but might no longer govern the labor, of the Indians assigned to them.[22] When this rule took effect, a crucial element in all encomendero relationships with Indians was formally terminated.

Immediately following these events, royal limitations upon encomendero tribute practices became effective for the first time. At the outset encomiendas had been granted without specification of the amounts that might be exacted, and encomenderos had exploited their opportunities accordingly. In the 1530's and 1540's royal officers undertook to fix limits in encomienda tribute and to specify in written regulations (*tasaciones*) the amounts that encomenderos might demand. Such specifications were ignored at first, and even in 1550 certain Valley towns had received no tasaciones.[23] But Francisco de Montejo, the encomendero of Azcapotzalco, was required in 1547–48 to pay back to the Indians of his encomienda the excess tribute that he had received, and Juan Ponce de León, the encomendero of Tecama, was arrested in the early 1550's for mistreatment of his Indians.[24] These cases served as a warning to the entire encomendero class. The most forceful restrictions upon the exaction of tribute during the mid-century period were those imposed by the royal *visitador* Diego Ramírez, who examined more than a dozen Valley encomiendas between 1551 and 1553, drew up new regulations, reduced tributes, and brought charges against the holders for their misconduct.[25] In brief, the Ramírez regulations and others similar to them in the 1550's and 1560's brought to an end the encomenderos' period of license. After the early 1550's tribute quotas were consistently specified by royal officers and recorded in contracts between encomenderos and Indians.[26] A viceregal court and the audiencia were available to hear Indian complaints, and colonial lawyers were always ready to accept, and profit from, Indian cases.[27] Under these circumstances, the famous encomendero conspiracy of the 1560's may be interpreted as evidence not of the power but of the desperation of the encomienda interests. The suppression of the conspiracy was a further warning and a display of royal strength. Cortés's son and heir was exiled, and other Valley encomenderos were arrested. Two brothers, Alonso de Avila and Gil González de Benavides, were executed, and the encomienda of Cuauhtitlan and its affiliates, the richest surviving possession in the Valley, was immediately taken over by the crown.[28]

In Table 3 the thirty-six documented encomiendas of the Valley of Mexico—the thirty previously mentioned plus the six that came to an end before 1535—are enumerated approximately in the order of their Indian population and tribute values. The population figures are derived from records of about 1560, and although by this time a number of the tributes were being paid to the crown rather than to individual encomenderos, the relative values may be taken as applying roughly to any period of the sixteenth century. In general, the largest and most lucrative grants were the first to come to an end: the eleven encomiendas shown as reverting to the crown before 1570, including all of the first eight, represent about three-quarters of all encomienda tribute income. The evidence suggests that by 1570 the victory of the crown over the encomenderos had been won, and we may suppose that the remaining encomiendas were permitted to survive because nothing more was to be feared from the encomendero class.[29]

Relations between encomienda and the cabecera-sujeto structure of Indian society are shown in the second column of Table 3, where differences among the several encomienda types are indicated. An encomienda might be a single cabecera, with sujetos, possessing a unitary tlatoani lineage; it might be a multiple cabecera or several cabeceras, with sujetos, possessing

TABLE 3
Encomiendas

Encomienda	Status	Tributaries ca. 1560[a]	Escheatment[b]
Texcoco, etc.	Five cabeceras of which four were disputed	16,015	1531
Chalco province	Four cabeceras	14,842	Ca. 1533
Tenochtitlan	Cabecera	12,971	Ca. 1525
Xochimilco	Three cabeceras considered as one	10,583	1541
Tlatelolco	Cabecera	8,665	Ca. 1525
Otumba	Cabecera	5,550	1531
Cuauhtitlan, etc.	Three cabeceras and one disputed cabecera	5,020	1566
Tepozotlan	Cabecera	2,971	Ca. 1546
Tacuba	Cabecera	2,700	Perpetual
Coyoacan	One cabecera and one new or disputed cabecera	2,130	Perpetual
Tenayuca-Coatepec	One cabecera and one multiple cabecera considered as a unit	1,890	1544
Hueypoxtla	Cabecera	1,800	After 1658 (?)
Teocalhueyacan	New cabecera	1,750	Before 1653
Tequixquiac	Cabecera	1,600	After 1666
Azcapotzalco	Two cabeceras considered as one	1,500	Ca. 1702
Toltitlan	Cabecera	1,500	Ca. 1702
Teotihuacan	Cabecera	1,400	Before 1658
Ecatepec	Cabecera	1,390	Perpetual
Tizayuca	New cabecera	1,191[c]	1531
Tepetlaoztoc	Cabecera	1,100	Before 1628
Xilotzingo	Cabecera	1,100	Ca. 1600
Acolman	Cabecera	1,000	After 1678
Axapusco	Sujeto	940[d]	Before 1603
Tepexpan	Cabecera	850	Before 1678
Chimalhuacan Atenco ..	Cabecera	800	1670
Cuitlahuac	Four cabeceras considered as one	800	After 1658
Ixtapalapa	Cabecera	700[e]	1582
Oxtoticpac	Sujeto	600	Before 1675
Tecama	New cabecera	600	1554
Culhuacan	Cabecera	560	Ca. 1659
Mixquic	Cabecera	550	Ca. 1702
Tezontepec	Cabecera	530	Before 1658
Huitzilopochco	Cabecera	420[f]	After 1640
Ixtapaluca	Cabecera	370	After 1597
Chicoloapa	New cabecera	300	Before 1597
Tequicistlan	Cabecera	220[g]	Ca. 1600

several tlatoani lineages; or it might be a new cabecera, with sujetos, or a sujeto alone, possessing a broken tlatoani tradition or none at all. It is clear that Cortés and other authorities did not feel obliged to confine a particular grant to a single cabecera with its sujetos. Moreover, when the demand for encomiendas exceeded the supply and additional encomiendas had to be issued, the solution was not necessarily to divide the compound encomiendas into their respective cabecera units. The customary solution was rather to form the last kind of variant—to separate out one or more sujetos from an existing encomienda and to assign these as a new grant.

Despite exceptions, a one-to-one relation between tlatoani community and encomienda was surely regarded as a norm. Following the practice of the West Indies, encomienda grants in Mexico were originally expressed as assignments of Indian señores with their followers rather than of designated towns with their inhabitants.[30] So pervasive was this early identification that even encomienda grants of sujetos, as of Chicoloapa to Pedro López, were understood as assignments of the "señor and his Indians."[31] The variants upon the normal grant of a single cacique and a single cabecera to each encomendero are then attributable to special circumstances: conquistador rivalry, personal influence, monarchical demand, the strength of certain communities and tlatoani dynasties in comparison with others, the confusion and temporary character of the encomiendas issued during

---

NOTES TO TABLE 3

[a]The tributary figures given are approximations of varying degrees of precision. Most derive from the two Ibarra lists published in ENE, IX, 2 ff., and BAGN, XI, 195 ff. The lists refer to pesos of tribute income after the deduction of the tithe. They are inaccurate guides to tributary population, especially in the cases of Texcoco, Xochimilco, Chalco province, Otumba, and Tepozotlan. For these as well as for Tenochtitlan and Tlatelolco the table records other tributary data from the 1560's, from *El libro de las tasaciones*; ENE, X, 23, 25; PNE, III, 82–83; and *Sobre el modo de tributar*, p. 77.

[b]The dates given for escheatment follow the second assignments (e.g., of Azcapotzalco, Toltitlan, and others to Luis de Velasco) but in general precede the grants of pure annuities. For some encomiendas one cannot speak of an absolute date of escheatment.

[c]The Ibarra list combines Tizayuca with Tolcayuca. It had 1,191 tributaries in 1565. See *El libro de las tasaciones*, p. 473.

[d]This includes Caguala.

[e]Ixtapalapa is not on the Ibarra lists for it was neither a crown town nor under a private encomendero. López de Velasco, *Geografía y descripción*, p. 194, assigns it 700 tributaries.

[f]The Ibarra list combines Huitzilopochco and Huamuxtitlan. The former had over 400 tributaries in 1569. See García Pimentel, *Descripción*, p. 225; López de Velasco, *Geografía y descripción*, p. 194.

[g]This represents the encomendero's share, approximately one-half the full amount. The crown received 200 pesos.

the 1520's, and presumably in some instances failure to recognize the tlatoani traditions for what they were. The various resolutions differed in degree
and character from community to community, and repeatedly they left
legacies of conflict to be settled in the future, sometimes by prolonged inter-
community dispute, sometimes by arbitrary decision on the part of the
encomendero.

We may direct our attention first to the composite encomiendas, those
that included more than one tlatoani lineage. This type occurred as a multiple-tlatoani community (Xochimilco, Cuitlahuac, Azcapotzalco); or as
a "province" (Chalco, Texcoco); or as a pair or group (Tenayuca-Coatepec, Coyoacan-Tacubaya, Cuauhtitlan and its associated towns). Encomiendas of this composite type were customarily of brief duration: Xochimilco, Azcapotzalco (though it was later reassigned), Tenayuca-Coatepec,
Texcoco, and Chalco had all reverted to the crown by 1545.

The case is different with Cuauhtitlan, which continued as an encomienda until 1566, and which offers in any event the most revealing history
of the group. Concerning the tlatoani history of Cuauhtitlan itself there
could be no question; its dynastic lineage may be traced from the seventh
century.[32] The four nearby communities of Zumpango, Huehuetoca, Citlaltepec, and Utlaspa (only the first three of which fell in the Valley and only
the first two of which were assigned to this encomienda) were associated
in the Indian system as Nauhtecuhtli, or four related offices of rule, similar
to Ixtapalapa, Mexicalzingo, Culhuacan, and Huitzilopochco in the south.
In the case of Cuauhtitlan, as we have said, all four were governed in
1519 by Aztatzontzin, the tlatoani of Cuauhtitlan.[33] In other nearby communities the pre-conquest separation from Cuauhtitlan may be dated with
some precision. Tepozotlan began its tlatoani dynasty in 1460 (7 Tecpatl
by the Indian calendar) under the stimulus of Montezuma I. Toltitlan
became separated from Cuauhtitlan in the time of Tezozomoc.[34] Finally,
Xaltocan, farther to the east, with a broken tlatoani history, differed from
these in its affiliation to the Acolhuaque rather than the Tepaneca.[35]

Out of this complex situation there emerged the huge encomienda of
Cuauhtitlan, consisting of Cuauhtitlan itself, Zumpango, Huehuetoca, and
Xaltocan. From the point of view of Indian Cuauhtitlan, the encomienda
appeared as an unwarranted interference and recomposition. "When the
Marqués del Valle came," wrote the Indian commentator of the Anales de
Cuauhtitlan (1570), "then the city of Cuauhtitlan decayed, for Tepozotlan,

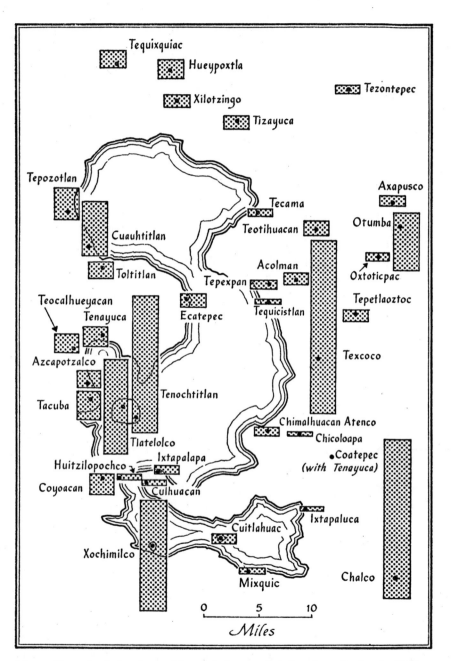

Map 4. Encomienda locations with population graphs taken from the data in Table 3.

Utlaspa, Citlaltepec, Zumpango, and Toltitlan were separated from it."[36] Tepozotlan and Toltitlan were of course already dynastically separate by 1519, and to this extent the Cuauhtitlan complaint has an artificial ring. But all five had been accorded the status of colonial cabeceras by 1570, and it is doubtless to this that the Indian annal more specifically refers. Tepozotlan, Toltitlan, Utlaspa, and Citlaltepec were separated also in the sense that none was included with the Cuauhtitlan encomienda. The point of interest is that the Indian annalist regarded Zumpango, which had its own Indian government[37] but which fell within the encomienda, as also separated.

Zumpango thus emerged in Spanish understanding as a cabecera. And since the cabecera status of Cuauhtitlan and Xaltocan was never in doubt, this made an encomienda of three cabeceras, each with its local Indian government. In Spanish references all the towns could be regarded as sujetos of Cuauhtitlan, the "cabecera" of the encomienda. To put the matter this way, of course, was to do violence to the Indian relationships and to apply the cabecera concept in a special sense. Spaniards could refer also to the encomienda towns as subject to Cuauhtitlan and Xaltocan together, presumably regarding Zumpango still as a sujeto of Cuauhtitlan, and recognizing only the two essential Tepaneca and Acolhua cabeceras of the encomienda.[38] Perhaps the most interesting consequence was the dispute between Cuauhtitlan and Huehuetoca, in which Cuauhtitlan claimed Huehuetoca as an estancia and Huehuetoca claimed independence as a pueblo por sí. On the side of Huehuetoca was the argument that its pre-conquest status had been no different from that of Zumpango and Citlaltepec and Utlaspa, all of which had become "separate" from Cuauhtitlan, and that its post-conquest status should be no different from Zumpango, which was a cabecera within the encomienda. On the side of Cuauhtitlan was the argument that prior to the conquest Huehuetoca had been ruled by the tlatoani of Cuauhtitlan. Significantly, the Indian annalist did not include Huehuetoca among the "separated" towns of 1570, for Huehuetoca, which had sought independence since at least 1551, was still being claimed as a sujeto by Cuauhtitlan.[39]

The multiple-tlatoani cases contrast with the assignments of non-tlatoani communities in individual encomiendas. The Valley affords six instances of this phenomenon[40]—Chicoloapa, Teocalhueyacan, Tecama, Tizayuca, Axapusco, and Oxtoticpac—and it will be remembered that the first four

TABLE 4

Non-Tlatoani Sites in Encomienda

Encomienda	Original Status	Original Cabecera	Colonial Status
Axapusco	Sujeto	Otumba	Sujeto (disputed)
Chicoloapa	Sujeto	Coatlichan	Cabecera (undisputed)
Oxtoticpac	Sujeto	Otumba	Sujeto (disputed)
Tecama	Sujeto	Tlatelolco (?)	Cabecera (undisputed)
Teocalhueyacan	Sujeto	Tacuba	Cabecera (undisputed)[a]
Tizayuca	Sujeto	Ecatepec	Cabecera (undisputed)

[a]Tacuba did make an ineffective protest against the loss of Teocalhueyacan. Moreover, the cabecera status of Teocalhueyacan was affected by the development of Tlalnepantla.

of these figure as the four instances of early cabecera creation resulting from encomienda. The other two continued in a disputed sujeto status, even though they were separate encomiendas. The sujeto-cabecera conditions of these six are summarized in Table 4. Of them, only Chicoloapa and Oxtoticpac give evidence of partial or broken tlatoani traditions in their pre-conquest histories. That four became cabeceras immediately, and that the remaining two made strong, though not immediately successful, bids for cabecera status, strikingly suggests the role of encomienda in the creation of new cabeceras. In the case of Tecama, the elevation to cabecera status occurred very rapidly, and we cannot be certain of its pre-conquest affiliation; it is possible that Tlatelolco was its original cabecera.[41]

For four of the communities—Tizayuca, Chicoloapa, Oxtoticpac, and Teocalhueyacan—we possess quite detailed records of the early encomienda assignments, and accordingly of the change from dependent to undisputed cabecera or disputed sujeto status. Tizayuca, at first included with Cortés's grant of Ecatepec to Leonor Montezuma, appears to have been removed from the encomienda and taken by Cortés himself; omitted from the Marquesado grant of 1529, it was royalized in 1531.[42] Chicoloapa, with the failure of its pre-conquest dynasty, became subordinated to Coatlichan, and it was still under Coatlichan at the time of the Spanish conquest; Cortés then removed it from Coatlichan in order to make the encomienda grant to Pedro López.[43] With respect to Oxtoticpac, we know that it served Cortés as part of the Otumba encomienda, and that after he was compelled to give up Otumba it was separated and transferred to his agent, Diego de

Ocampo, as encomendero.[44] Teocalhueyacan, as a sujeto of Tacuba, had been part of Cortés's grant to Isabel Montezuma. About 1527, after the grant of Tacuba, Alonso de Estrada and his wife "begged and pleaded with Hernando Cortés to give them certain estancias with Teocalhueyacan." (The quotation is from a witness's deposition in a lawsuit of the early 1560's.) Cortés complied, knowing that Isabel and her husband would not welcome the loss, as indeed they did not.[45]

Following the assignment of these non-tlatoani communities in encomienda, the tasks of organization facing the encomenderos were less difficult than might be supposed. In practice, if an encomienda contained no tlatoani, a simple internal adjustment could make it operate as if it did. Though lacking resident tlatoque, estancias were always organized to provide tribute and service to some native authority. In encomienda it was a matter only of designating one of the estancias as a capital, elevating one of the leading Indian personages to cacique status or its equivalent, and channeling the tributes and services of other estancias through this new center. So far as can be ascertained, encomenderos in every one of the six cases accomplished these adjustments without difficulty.

But to isolate an estancia or a group of estancias in this way invariably entailed disruption of the Indian services and tributes on which the former cabecera had depended. The cabecera suffered a loss in consequence. If it were to insist on its claim, Indians in the encomienda would owe obligation to two masters: their own encomendero, and the Indian rulers of their former cabecera outside the encomienda jurisdiction. It was to the encomendero's advantage, accordingly, to claim cabecera status for his encomienda capital and to assert the subordination of his sujetos to it, despite the absence of any historic tlatoani.[46] He could rely in this matter on the support of his encomienda Indians, who could expect emancipation from traditional obligations. Indeed, in such cases the Indian community was often the most avid supporter of cabecera status, and its opponents were the Indians of its earlier native jurisdiction.

The six instances of cabecera creation differed markedly in timing and degree. Tecama, Tizayuca, and Chicoloapa were immediately accepted as cabeceras, despite the weakness, or total absence, of tlatoani traditions. Their encomenderos were strong enough to prevail, or the former cabeceras failed to protest, or the precedent was established in such a way as to disarm or forestall opposition.[47] The Indian authorities of Tacuba, the original cabecera of Teocalhueyacan, protested Teocalhueyacan's change of status, but they accepted the loss, and in the 1560's, as we have seen, they engaged in a lawsuit with Teocalhueyacan concerning the affiliation of other sujetos, thus in effect recognizing it as a rival cabecera.[48] Oxtoticpac, which could boast a partial pre-conquest tlatoani dynasty, offered the most convincing case in terms of the normal cabecera criteria.[49] But despite this fact, and though the legalities of its situation in no way distinguished it from the others, it continued to be held as an estancia by its cabecera, Otumba, into the late sixteenth century.[50] Axapusco was incidentally described as a cabecera in a viceregal order of 1565, but Otumba continued to claim it, too, and far into the sixteenth century the Indian government of Otumba was still seeking to compel Axapusco to perform the traditional labor obligations of a sujeto. Against these demands, Axapusco Indians insisted in the seventeenth century that Axapusco was a cabecera, and they asserted, quite falsely, that it had never been a sujeto of Otumba.[51] In summary, the original Indian relations were not maintained in Chicoloapa, Teocalhueyacan, Tecama, and Tizayuca, and the effort to maintain them in Axapusco and Oxtoticpac brought prolonged controversy and trouble.[52]

In encomienda, sujetos were also occasionally disengaged from their cabeceras in order to attach them to other cabeceras. An encomendero possessed strong motives for usurping a sujeto, for if he could acquire a neighboring sujeto and join it to his own encomienda, his tribute income and reservoir of manpower would be increased by that amount. But the opportunities for aggrandizement of this kind were always limited. It may be remembered that the common conception of the encomendero as a ruthless extortioner relates to his dealings with Indians already within the encomienda, not to his aggressions outside. Any extension of his authority implied a corresponding loss to a neighboring and competing encomienda or crown community. Royal officials and rival encomenderos, as well as Indian communities, were always alert to such incursions. The legal facilities made available to Indians for protesting against excesses within the encomienda were available likewise for protest against attack from without. Moreover, the crown sent additional agents to control the abuses of encomienda. That encomenderos were able in any instances to circumvent this formidable array of obstacles and to acquire communities outside their first grants appears more remarkable than that they did not do so more often.

Encomenderos were, of course, vitally concerned with defining the precise areas that fell within their jurisdictions, and self-interest impelled them to place as generous an interpretation as possible upon the intention of the granting agency. In the profusion of native place names, no written assignment of encomienda ever enumerated all the barrios, estancias, and fields that would identify with precision the tribute-paying localities to be included. Though the documents referred to the "señor and his Indian peoples," encomiendas were customarily identified by their cabeceras, and in all cases the sujetos of the cabeceras were assumed—by the encomendero, by rival encomenderos, and by the courts—to be contained within the grant. In uncomplicated cases this sufficed. In encomiendas made up of several cabeceras, reference might be made to all, especially if the cabeceras were geographically separated and otherwise unrelated, as with Tenayuca and Coatepec; or one particular cabecera might be regarded as the "cabecera" of the encomienda, as was occasionally the case in reference to Cuauhtitlan. A grant might, on the other hand, specify the cabecera and one or more sujetos as well, presumably to ensure their inclusion, and official listings of the encomienda at a later date might preserve this terminology.[53] Hueypoxtla was commonly cited with its remote estancias Tianquistonco, Tlacuitlapilco, and Tezcatepec; Tepexpan was spoken of in conjunction with its remote sujeto Temascalapa; and references to the encomienda of Tequicistlan commonly included its estancia Totolzingo.[54] In such instances there could be no doubt that the listed communities fell within the encomienda. But an opponent of the encomendero might argue that sujetos not enumerated fell outside it, or rival interests might use the specification as a pretext for cabecera status, taking the position that if the community were a genuine sujeto it would not have required specification.[55]

The most common type of dispute concerning sujetos was the conflict over boundaries between two Indian communities. If a contested area were inhabited, and if it could be represented as falling within an encomienda jurisdiction, the encomendero's interest was immediately affected. The result might be conflict between one encomendero and another, or between an encomendero and a neighboring Indian population. In this respect, Coyoacan, backed by the encomienda power of Cortés, was a particularly aggressive community in the early period. Coyoacan acquired three estancias of Huitzilopochco and engaged in a protracted border conflict with Xochimilco from the 1520's on. The estancia of San Agustín Tlalpam was taken from Xochimilco in the 1520's, returned by court order, and reacquired by Coyoacan in the 1540's. In an altercation over conflicting border claims between the two towns in 1531, five Indians were killed and others wounded, and there is evidence that the violence was ordered by Cortés.[56] But in all these cases the matter was of greatest importance to the Indian communities, and the encomenderos appear as persons taking advantage of cleavages that were Indian in origin.[57] It is worth noting that all the cited instances involved Indians of diverse ethnic or tribal affiliation—Tepaneca, Culhua, and Xochimilca.[58]

In a more complex series of cases, claims arising from encomienda itself threatened certain cabeceras with the loss of estancias. The issue arose with particular force in the north, where the estancias of Tenochtitlan and Tlatelolco were situated close to undisputed cabeceras held by encomenderos. To the encomenderos, the estancias were alien enclaves within the encomienda territories, unwarranted intrusions upon encomienda jurisdiction. In the 1530's Gil González de Benavides, the encomendero of Cuauhtitlan, brought suit against the Indian leaders of Tenochtitlan and Tlatelolco concerning the estancias of Xoloc, Ozumbilla, and Tecalco. He was accompanied in his suit by the Indian governor of Xaltocan, who claimed that the estancias were sujetos of Xaltocan. If this could be demonstrated, the estancias could presumably be included within the encomienda, for Xaltocan was specified as one of the communities of the Cuauhtitlan encomienda. Indian witnesses testified in the familiar way that the disputed communities had been Xaltocan sujetos "since the memory of man," and that the Tenochtitlan-Tlatelolco claim represented an innovation of recent date, a usurpation by violence. The Tenochtitlan-Tlatelolco argument rested not simply on a denial of these assertions but on an authorization by Nuño de Guzmán and others, who were said to have granted (*encomendado*) half of Xaltocan with additional communities to the Indian ruler of Tlatelolco.[59] The essence of the dispute related to the distinction between sujetos and landed properties. Lands in all three disputed communities had been held by the Mexica rulers Huitzilihuitl, Itzcoatl, Montezuma I, and Axayacatl, and lands in Xaltocan had been held by relatives of these rulers.[60] The encomendero and the Xaltocan Indians won their case before the audiencia in 1531 and 1536, but the Indian leaders of Tlatelolco appealed to the Council of the Indies in Spain and the decision was reversed.[61] In 1537, when the Council's decision was made, Gil González de Benavides was in possession of Xoloc and Ozumbilla, and presumably of Tecalco as well.[62] But the decision was adhered to, and the disputed estancias were assigned to Tlatelolco and Tenochtitlan. Both Tecalco and Ozumbilla were divided sujetos, Tenochtitlan being the cabecera of one part and Tlatelolco of the other.[63]

The encomienda of Ecatepec, like Cuauhtitlan, was situated to the north of the city and some of the estancias of Tenochtitlan and Tlatelolco appeared to fall within its jurisdiction. To Leonor Montezuma, who married the conquistador Juan Paz, Cortés granted Ecatepec and its estancias as a dowry in 1527. In his statement of that date Cortés specified Acalhuacan, Coatitlan, and Tizayuca (Tecoyuca), as estancias of Ecatepec included in the grant, and he justified the whole as Leonor's legitimate patrimony. Because Ecatepec had "belonged" to Montezuma, it appeared proper to Cortés that it should be assigned to Montezuma's daughter.[64] The Indian officers of Tenochtitlan and Tlatelolco countered with the assertion that the estancias of Ecatepec should revert to Montezuma's successors in office, that they should be "sujetos" of the señores and upper-class Indians (*principales*) of Tenochtitlan and Tlatelolco.[65] In this connection it will be remembered that a close tie had previously existed between the ruling family of Tenochtitlan and the successive tlatoque of Ecatepec. The issue came before the audiencia and the Council of the Indies in a series of suits between 1531 and the 1560's. Tizayuca, royalized in 1531, was eliminated from the case. In 1553 the audiencia accorded Acalhuacan the status of a "true sujeto" of Ecatepec. Protesting that Acalhuacan had formerly paid its tributes to Tlatelolco, the Indians of Tlatelolco appealed the decision to the Council of the Indies, but were denied in 1561.[66] The other estancias— Coatitlan, Tolpetlac, Coatepec, and even Ozumbilla and Tecalco again— became the subjects of further dispute. Some had been included in Cortés's grant to Leonor, but Cortés himself testified afterward that he did not know exactly what he had granted. An interesting secondary position taken by the Indians of Tlatelolco was that Cortés had no legal right to make the Ecatepec grant, since Luis Ponce de León, the royal visitador sent to take Cortés's *residencia,* had already arrived in New Spain at the time when it was issued.[67]

The audiencia in 1536 had asserted that Ecatepec and its estancias were of the patrimony of Montezuma, that the estancias contained slaves and subordinates of Montezuma, that they had paid tribute to him as the lord of Ecatepec, and hence that they were rightfully assigned to Leonor. The audiencia added that they would properly be tributaries of Leonor even if Cortés had not made the grant. The Council of the Indies, however, took exception to this reasoning. The estancias, in the view of the Council, did not constitute a property and hence were not inheritable in the way the audiencia assumed. Thus the Council in 1538 took a legal position favorable to the Tlatelolco claims, namely, that Ecatepec and its estancias had been sujetos of the Indians of the city, that Cortés lacked the king's authority to issue the encomienda, and that even if he had had the authority it expired with the *visita* of Ponce de León.[68] The practical outcome was that the matter was left to the discretion of the viceroy, and in the aftermath most of the disputed estancias were successfully held by Tlatelolco. Coatitlan continued to pay tributes in the Ecatepec encomienda and to be regarded as falling within its jurisdiction.[69] But Tlatelolco was able to demand labor services from Acalhuacan, Tolpetlac, Coatepec, and others.[70]

An interesting feature of these cases is that they bring into close relationship three institutions that at first glance would seem to be quite different: Spanish encomienda, Indian sujeto, and private Indian land tenure with tenants and dependents. Spanish law was clear on the nature of encomienda. But Spanish law had not yet determined the precise status of the sujeto. If a sujeto owed its allegiance not to the corporate cabecera but to the incumbent tlatoani personally, then it consisted of a group of Indians paying tribute and labor to a specified individual and fitted the essential requirements of encomienda. Likewise, retainers who inhabited the "private" lands of other Indians and paid labor and tribute to them occupied a status not easily distinguishable from the status of Indians in encomienda. When such obligations were confirmed by Spanish authorities, the acts came close to being grants of encomiendas to Indian encomenderos, and every indication suggests that the two processes—one of patrimonial confirmation and the other of encomienda grant—were indeed confused. The Indian leaders of Tlatelolco could argue that the first audiencia had placed in encomienda half of Xaltocan and Tepeaquilla and other communities in Indian possession, whereas the audiencia's decision of 1536 classified these grants not as encomienda but as confirmations of private inheritance in the estancias of Xoloc, Ozumbilla, and Tecalco.[71] The Suma de Visitas (ca. 1548) listed Tecalco, the divided estancia of Tenochtitlan and Tlatelolco, in an enumeration of encomienda and crown towns, with the notice "they serve the caciques of Mexico."[72] When the crown in the early colonial period granted specified locations to noble Indians as "patrimony," no one could tell whether the outcome would be private Indian landholding or encomiendas held by Indians.[73] It is entirely possible that Cortés's original grants of Ecatepec to Leonor Montezuma and of Tacuba to Isabel Montezuma were intended to be confirmations of inheritance, not acts of encomienda creation. The supposition is reinforced by the fact that both grants enumerated the subordinate Indian households (*casas de renteros*) to be included, and that in Tacuba itself Cortés assigned only 120 casas to Isabel, far fewer than she would have received in a full encomienda grant.[74] The remarkable feature is that these Indian inheritances later came to be classified as permanent encomiendas in the Spanish sense. Though not all the details are at hand, it would appear that this outcome was due in no small part to the deft legal maneuvering of the Indian women's Spanish husbands.

The legalities of the cases of Isabel and Leonor Montezuma, for all their intricate meshing of Indian and Spanish thinking, have nevertheless an abstract quality remote from the ordinary Indian life of the Valley of Mexico. Fascinating to the legal minds of the Consejo de Indias as the technical arguments appeared, the problems were in fact solved by royal officers on the scene, who determined by summary compromise and arbitration which of the disputed estancias were to be assigned to which claimant. To a modern observer the individual decisions appear quite arbitrary. Cases were variously resolved, as private Indian holdings, as Indian encomiendas, or as sujetos of communities in encomienda or in the crown. Of the Indian encomiendas, however, Valley history offers only the two examples of Tacuba and Ecatepec, and these passed, in the second generation, from the category of encomiendas held by Indians to the category of encomiendas held by *mestizos*. In the history of the relations between encomenderos and Indians these encomiendas differ from others only with respect to their unusual origin in the early period and their status as perpetual holdings later.

Encomienda is much better known for its direct subjugation of Indian peoples than for its consequences in cabecera-sujeto relations. The basis for its reputation as an instrument of evil, first forcefully enunciated by Las Casas in the sixteenth century, was the severe means used by the encomenderos to compel Indian labor and tribute payment. In modern times Silvio Zavala, L. B. Simpson, and José Miranda have refined and extended our knowledge of these aspects of encomienda in colonial Mexico. Miranda has called special attention to the constructive role of the encomenderos in the economic development of the colony.[75] The new interpretations are altogether acceptable and applicable to the Valley of Mexico.

The severity of the early encomenderos may be explained in part as an extension of conquest militarism into the post-conquest years. Overt warfare in the Valley terminated in 1521, but the areas peripheral to the Aztec empire remained to be won, and the leaders of secondary expeditions found in encomienda a convenient reservoir of military manpower. Several thousand Indians were taken by Pedro de Alvarado from his Xochimilco encomienda for military expeditions to Guatemala and Honduras and Panuco, and according to the statement of the Indians of Xochimilco all of these were killed. The incidents imply a drastic, presumably coercive, impressment. But the need for such impressment was relatively brief. It ceased with the effective conclusion of the peripheral conquests and was confined almost entirely to the 1520's.[76]

Again, the early encomenderos made heavy demands upon Indian workers for city labor. Because most encomenderos became residents of the capital,[77] Indians of the Valley encomiendas became especially liable for construction labor on the encomenderos' residences. Cortés's palace, the outstanding private dwelling in the capital, was built by workers from Coyoacan and from his other possessions.[78] The homes of Francisco de Montejo, Alonso de Avila, and other Valley encomenderos were capital showplaces of the mid-sixteenth century.[79] But, as in the matter of the peripheral conquests, the greatest needs were the early ones; after the private palaces had been built the labor demands diminished.

Finally, the formal distinction between encomienda and slavery failed to gain acceptance in the early period. The reasons are obvious. The whole anterior history of encomienda in the Antilles had been closely related to enslavement. The careful differentiation set forth in royal law had a distant and impractical aspect.[80] Indians captured in war might be legitimately enslaved even in the monarch's view, and there was a sense in which all the native inhabitants of the Valley had been captured in war. This interpretation of conquest lent itself readily to the conquistadores' sense of personal achievement and power. The encomendero of Tecama administered physical abuse, addressed his Indians in the foul language of the period, and presented himself before them in an oppressive and despotic role.[81] Similarly, encomienda was regarded as property, not simply for inheritance but for negotiation or sale. Pedro de Alvarado and Francisco de Montejo privately contracted for the transfer of Xochimilco with its inhabitants, and Juan Ponce de León rented out his Indians' services and tributes to second parties.[82] Cortés branded Indians in Texcoco and then sold them as slaves.[83] Encomenderos justified such illegal and exploitative measures in the assertion that white rule was in danger, that the conquest had not been conclusive, and that Indians might rebel to reassert native domination.[84]

The record of the first encomienda generation, in the Valley as elsewhere, is one of generalized abuse and particular atrocities. Encomenderos used their Indians in all forms of manual labor, in building, farming, and mining, and for the supply of whatever the country yielded. They overtaxed and overworked them. They jailed them, killed them, beat them, and set dogs on them. They seized their goods, destroyed their agriculture, and took their women. They used them as beasts of burden. They took tribute from them and sold it back under compulsion at exorbitant profits. Coercion and ill-treatment were the daily practices of their overseers, calpixque, and labor bosses. The first encomenderos, without known exception, understood Spanish authority as provision for unlimited personal opportunism.[85]

We have abundant evidence from the testimonies given to Diego Ramírez and from other sources concerning the demands that the early encomenderos made upon the Indians of their towns. The provisions of daily food, fodder, and fuel were common to all tasaciones, and through these the encomenderos and their families were assured of regular sustenance at no cost. Tributes included precious metals, grains, textiles, and a multitude of additional materials by which encomenderos could directly increase their wealth. The provision of Indian servants was a common feature of encomienda tribute. Goods were commonly deposited at the encomendero's residence in Mexico City, and Indians worked their encomenderos' fields, wherever they might be.[86]

The most fully documented record of encomienda abuses in the Valley pertains to Tepetlaoztoc, a cabecera located in the Acolhua foothills northeast of Texcoco.[87] In its early encomienda period it reflected the characteristic domination over Indians as well as the struggle for power among Spanish colonists. Cortés first took Tepetlaoztoc for himself, as he took Texcoco, Otumba, Chalco, and Coyoacan. It passed quickly to two of Cortés's supporters, Diego de Ocampo and Miguel Díaz de Aux, and then to one of Cortés's most formidable enemies, Gonzalo de Salazar.[88] In the early 1520's Cortés reduced the number of tributaries who paid to the cacique and other Indian leaders of Tepetlaoztoc and took for himself large supplies of mantles, maize, and gold objects. The levies continued under Ocampo and Díaz de Aux. Under Salazar the native upper class lost more of its own tribute income to the encomendero. Cloth, foodstuffs, gold, fuel, Indian servants, and laborers were pre-empted, and the Indian community constructed houses and mills in and near Mexico City for Salazar and his wife, and for his mayordomos. Heavier tributes were demanded for Salazar's journey to Spain in 1530, and over two hundred Tepetlaoztoc Indians died carrying his goods to Veracruz for embarkation. During Salazar's absence his mayordomos continued to collect tribute and to mistreat the native officers of the town. On his return, Salazar himself beat the Indian rulers and demanded more tributes. Though no less a royal officer than Sosa, who had to give up Tenayuca and Coatepec following the New Laws, Salazar successfully held Tepetlaoztoc through the period of crisis and bequeathed it to his son.[89]

In his economic enterprises Salazar usurped communal Indian lands within Tepetlaoztoc and herded sheep, pigs, goats, and horses on lands taken from Indians. He seized the *casas de comunidad* (the native assembly quarters for community affairs) and transformed them into a textile mill. In the process he deposed and expelled the cacique, forcing him to become a shepherd on another property near Mexico City. The fulling mill and canals for water to operate the textile enterprises were built by community labor, under force and without compensation. The mill utilized the water supply of the town, originally a pre-conquest construction for drinking water and irrigation, to which improvements had been made under the early Dominican friar Domingo de Betanzos. Salazar now forbade the town the use of this water. From the late 1540's on the town suffered from water shortages and Indian petitions for relief were consistently refused. Not until the 1550's did the audiencia grant some water to the town, and then only between noon on Sunday and eight o'clock on Monday morning of each week. The audiencia further required that the encomendero return the casas de comunidad to the town, but this was not done. Some community lands were returned briefly, but they were reacquired by the encomendero's son, Juan Velázquez de Salazar, under a system of rental, and in the 1550's he continued to operate the textile mill as the encomendero of the second "life."[90]

The Indian inhabitants of Tepetlaoztoc were aware of opportunities for legal action, but, as they later stated, they were reluctant to protest because Gonzalo de Salazar was a fearsome person, a man of "rigorous and harsh character," for whom abuse was a constant habit. The Indian community finally achieved legal redress in the 1550's, at the time of the Ramírez visitas. The Tepetlaoztoc case came before the audiencia in 1552 and before the Council of the Indies, in Valladolid, in 1555. Other suits followed. The Indian record was presented in a series of court depositions, and in a native pictorial history (Códice Kingsborough), both graphic testimonies of encomienda exploitation. The legal campaign was wholly successful. In the 1550's tribute was reduced to a "normal" 1,100 pesos, and labor was removed from the encomendero's control and placed within the viceregal system of labor draft.[91] Juan Velázquez de Salazar then proceeded to devote himself to the representation of the Mexico City interests in Spain and to the composition of a theoretical defense, in Latin, of royal authority over the Spanish American empire.[92]

Characteristic features of the Tepetlaoztoc history are the extreme early domination and the rapid changes occurring in the 1550's. The transition from outright usurpation of lands and houses to the more refined technique of rental emerges with clarity and is typical both within and without encomienda. The community's delay in seeking justice is expressly indicated as a function of terror inspired by the encomendero and his agents. The 1550's appear as a period when the encomenderos' powers were waning and when the Indian communities successfully took action in Spanish law.

For all its early abuses, encomienda did not destroy Indian society. As usurpers of land, collectors of tribute, exploiters of labor, or intruders upon native systems of political rule, encomenderos strained but never obliterated the Indian community. Encomienda resulted, in Tepetlaoztoc and elsewhere, in a compression of Indian social classes, a reduction of the authority of caciques, loss of life, and a severe economic drain; but after the 1550's it would be difficult to find in all the Valley of Mexico any new instances of Indian exploitation attributable to it.[93] In the latter half of the sixteenth century, encomenderos had no more authority than other colonists in the allocation of Indian labor. They continued to receive tribute payments from their Indians, but it does not appear that they did so in excess of the tributary rates assigned by the crown.

In the continuing struggle between the encomenderos and the king in the later sixteenth century, the primary issue was encomienda inheritance.

In the 1590's, though a number of Valley encomiendas had terminated under the haphazard application of the New Laws, others were already in their third "life." [94] The surviving encomenderos continued to press for perpetuity, reiterating familiar arguments: that encomienda would ensure the Christianity of the Indians, abolish idolatry, and pacify the land.[95] Cedulas of the seventeenth century permitted the third life and even allowed subsequent inheritance.[96] But meanwhile, with new epidemics and progressive Indian depopulation, tribute income steadily declined. Numerous new grants, called encomiendas but of a wholly different character from the earlier grants, were issued in the later sixteenth and seventeenth centuries. For the most part, these were annuities of fixed amount, drawn from the tributes of designated areas, from expired older encomiendas, or from one or another branch of the royal treasury. They were assigned to noble families in Spain or in the colony, and all the processes of tribute collection and disbursement of funds remained in royal hands.[97] The typical encomendero of the late colonial period never saw the tribute-paying Indians whose funds he received. The Marqués de Salinas, the Marqués de San Román, the Conde de Cifuentes, and the other beneficiaries of Valley tribute funds in the eighteenth century were royal pensioners, utterly unlike their encomendero predecessors of the earlier period. Except for the three original grants in perpetuity—Tacuba, Ecatepec, and Coyoacan-Tacubaya—all surviving encomiendas in the Valley in late colonial times were of this type. And except for these three the crown never acceded to the demands for permanent encomienda. By 1600, with Indian labor denied, with tribute determined by population, and with Indian population reduced by eighty per cent or more from conquest times, the encomenderos' authority had all but disappeared.

The progressive decline of encomienda was accompanied by the progressive expansion of civil government under the king. The principal representatives of royal government, in descending order of rank, were the viceroy, the *oidores* or members of the audiencia, and the local magistrates called *corregidores*. The hierarchy was established in the late 1520's and the 1530's. It was the agency through which royal orders and nearly all official political acts were expressed, and, unlike encomienda, it remained an effective governing instrument to the end. Our chief attention will be devoted to the corregidores, for it was at the lowest level that Spanish government most intimately affected Indian life. These Spanish officials were variously entitled *jueces, justicias, alcaldes mayores, corregidores,* and in the late eighteenth century, *subdelegados.* For present purposes, these titles reflect no significant differences, and we shall refer to the office and jurisdiction as corregimiento and to the officials as corregidores, without regard to the terms particularly and locally employed.[98] In the Valley, the term corregidor was most common in the sixteenth century; the term alcalde mayor gained currency in the seventeenth century and was everywhere employed in the early eighteenth century; and the term subdelegado was introduced after 1786.[99]

In the instructions to the second audiencia, issued in 1530, corregimiento appeared as an alternative to encomienda, a system of government and tribute collection for Indians under the crown. That it did briefly fulfill this role helps to account for the early hostility between encomenderos and corregidores.[100] A few corregidores were appointed immediately in the early 1530's, but the first appointees were confined to Mexico City and allowed to visit their jurisdictions only on permission. The restriction suggests that the audiencia feared that corregidores might come into conflict with encomenderos or that they might use their positions for exploitation, after the manner of encomenderos.[101] Even in the 1540's, when corregidores were at least part-time residents of their areas, it was still customary to think of Indians as falling within the jurisdiction either of an encomendero or of a corregidor.[102] But the authority of corregimiento was soon extended to include Indians in encomienda, and in the 1550's corregidores were granted civil and criminal jurisdiction in cases involving Indians and Spaniards as well as in cases involving Indians alone. Thus within the same twenty-year period that witnessed the climax and turning point of the encomenderos' powers, corregimiento became an institution of full royal justice.[103] After the mid-century, as encomienda became progressively weaker, corregimiento came to embrace local civil government in its entirety.

In the beginning, encomienda and corregimiento were intimately related. All communities that were not in encomienda in the normal sense could be regarded as being in encomienda to the king, and corregidores accordingly could be regarded as the calpixque or mayordomos of royal encomiendas. We can scarcely doubt that the first corregidores thought of themselves as short-term, substitute encomenderos. Indeed, it was the crown's original position that the office of corregidor might be assigned to dispossessed encomenderos, as compensation for their losses.[104] The corregidores, of course, were salaried officers, as the encomenderos were not; but in the early period their salaries depended exclusively upon tribute. In Huitzilopochco and Mixquic the corregidor of the 1530's was to receive tributes to the amount of 260 pesos and his salary of 250 pesos was to be taken from this, so that only the tiny sum of ten pesos remained for the royal treasury. In Chiconauhtla in the 1530's tribute and the corregidor's salary alike came to 140 pesos, and nothing at all remained for the treasury. In other instances, depending upon encomienda status and population and salary, more substantial amounts accrued to the crown.[105] But corregidores and encomenderos, whatever the difference in gross amount of income—and it should be noted that the smallest encomiendas yielded incomes larger than the best-paid corregimientos—at first derived their pay from the same source. It is especially interesting to see, in the last quarter of the sixteenth century, the names of encomenderos appearing on the list of corregimiento appointees: Juan Velázquez de Salazar, the encomendero of Tepetlaoztoc, as corregidor of Texcoco and Cuauhtitlan;[106] Francisco Verdugo Bazán, the encomendero of Teotihuacan, as corregidor of Cuauhtitlan and Otumba;[107] Bernardino Vásquez de Tapia, the encomendero of Huitzilopochco, as corregidor of Ecatepec.[108] The duplications suggest one way in which the early antipathy between encomenderos and corregidores became reconciled, as encomenderos sought additional sources of income.

The early corregidores received their daily food, fodder, fuel, and Indian service as an additional portion of their salaries, just as encomenderos received theirs in the form of extra tribute. In Chalco during the 1540's, the corregidor and his assistant legally received from the Indians of the jurisdiction daily goods and services that included three chickens, one and one-half fanegas of maize, 200 chiles, a loaf of salt, twelve loads (*cargas*) of fodder, torch pine (*ocotl*), a load of charcoal, twelve loads of wood for fuel, and the work of eight Indian servants. Two-thirds of this was for the corregidor and one-third for his assistant.[109] The corregimiento Indians were further required to maintain and repair the corregidor's house and to provide other services.[110] It seems probable that Indian tribute-payers saw little difference between this kind of payment to corregidores and the tributes and services they owed to encomenderos and to their own Indian officers. In the case of Chalco, the food and other supplies were converted in 1552 to an annual payment of 500 pesos.[111] Nevertheless, in Chalco and elsewhere the demands by corregidores for Indian servants, supplies of fodder, and other goods continued through the colonial period. After the first few decades, corregidores were expected to pay for the goods and to recompense the servants, but the requirement that goods and services be provided was not changed.[112]

In each developed corregimiento, a corregidor's full staff consisted of a *teniente* (deputy), an *alguacil* (constable), an *escribano* (secretary), and an interpreter. But corregidores did not consistently operate with full staffs, and of the various aides the teniente and alguacil were always the most important.[113] In principle, the appointments were made by viceregal authority, but in reality some corregidores were appointed from Spain, and some assumed the power to appoint their own subordinates.[114] Appointment was usually by the year, but tenures were often extended for longer periods. When corregidores died, tenientes were sometimes appointed to succeed them, and when they were incapacitated, tenientes took charge.[115] The corregidor and his staff normally resided and held court in one of the cabeceras that lay within the corregimiento jurisdiction; at other times the officers alternated among cabeceras, or divided the duties in such a way that the corregidor maintained a principal headquarters in one cabecera while the teniente maintained a subordinate headquarters in another.[116] The capitals or places of residence were sometimes also known as cabeceras of the jurisdictions,[117] and we need note simply that this usage refers to the Spanish organization of corregimiento and should not be confused with other meanings of the term cabecera.

No comprehensive jurisdictional change affecting corregimiento occurred between 1550 and the introduction of the French-derived intendancy in 1786.[118] Corregimientos were legally abolished by the intendancy laws, the corregidores' positions being taken by subdelegados under the supervision of intendants. Salaries of the earlier type were now abandoned; instead, subdelegados received five per cent of the tribute income of their areas as salary.[119] The change was intended as a reform measure, to eliminate the corruption of corregimiento, but in this, as in many other respects, it failed.[120] The entire Valley, and a large surrounding region as well, fell within the single intendancy of Mexico. The territorial jurisdictions of subdelegados in the 1790's did not differ from those of the earlier corregidores. Viceroy Revillagigedo spoke of corregidores continuing in their offices "under the name of subdelegados," and the new officers' titles sometimes emerged in the form "corregidores subdelegados." The term corregidor was still being used in the early nineteenth century.[121] In its effect on Indian society, the late colonial transition to the intendancy system was hardly noticeable.

Corregimiento, like encomienda, required a delineation of areas and a new Spanish mapping of the Valley, and for this the cabecera-sujeto units again provided the essential basis. The new mapping could not be fixed in any permanent form until the 1550's, when corregimiento achieved full political authority over the encomienda areas. The first corregidores took charge of miscellaneous towns and regions as they were released from encomienda, a process that gave an unsystematic character to the corregimiento distribution of the 1530's and 1540's. By the 1550's nine corregimientos had come into existence in the Valley, but our documentation remains insufficient to demonstrate their boundaries precisely.[122] Since corregidores were frequently called upon to perform tasks outside their areas —usually in adjacent corregimientos—the evidence regarding geographical limits must be applied with caution. In the later sixteenth century, viceregal orders still occasionally required a corregidor to cross the border of his jurisdiction for the verification of a land grant or the performance of some other task. But from about 1575 on, we may speak with more certainty of the established jurisdictions of corregimiento.

The Valley of Mexico corregimientos in the 1570's numbered fifteen. Twelve of these lay completely within the Valley. The corregimiento of Texcoco extended across the mountains to the east beyond Calpulalpan to the Tlaxcala border. The corregimiento of Pachuca included Tizayuca and Tezontepec and a large area to the north toward the Pachuca mines. The corregimiento of Hueypoxtla extended beyond the northern part of the Valley to include Tornacustla. To the northwest the corregimiento of Tula, and to the northeast that of Epazoyuca, approached but did not touch the Valley.[123] The boundaries established by the 1570's were to remain generally stable through the seventeenth and eighteenth centuries; the principal later changes affected jurisdictions over Toltitlan, Tepoxaco, Acolman, and Xaltocan.[124] Further details on these boundaries may be found in Appendix III.

It was of the nature of corregimiento, as it was of the centralized Spanish monarchical system out of which corregimiento arose, that its jurisdictions were compact territorial units. An encomendero might hold widely separated communities simultaneously, but a corregidor was expected to render competent justicia within a region any part of which might require his immediate presence. In theory, corregimientos were limited in size, carefully demarcated, and contiguous with one another. But in practice, the Spaniards, like the Indians before them, made more exact boundary distinctions in the densely settled Valley lowland than in the remote and sparsely settled mountains. Convenience and policy dictated that Indian boundaries be preserved in the corregimiento jurisdictions—convenience because the boundaries were already in existence, policy because the alternative would have been a further disruption of Indian society. To designate a cabecera or several adjacent cabeceras was in effect to designate a demarcated and integral territory, for in corregimiento, even more than in encomienda, sujetos accompanied their cabeceras. Thus in the case of Xochimilco, the Spanish state needed simply to install a corregidor in the multiple cabecera of Xochimilco itself, whereupon a complete and well-defined corregimiento was immediately at hand. And in most other instances, it was a matter only of selecting the requisite number of cabeceras to yield a region of the approximate size desired.

Less powerful motives appeared in corregimiento than in encomienda for the creation of new cabeceras or for the separation of cabeceras from their sujetos. To this extent, corregimiento may be regarded as a stabilizing force, for an Indian area fixed in corregimiento possessed a durability acceptable to both societies. There was little inclination among corregidores to exploit the territorial disputes of Indians with a view to enlarging their jurisdictions. If we recall the losses suffered by the Xochimilco area prior to the Spanish conquest, and the loss of Tlalpam to Coyoacan in the early colonial period, then the later territorial history of Xochimilco, under corregimiento, offers a contrasting and impressive continuity.

The remote estancias, however, those that were separated from their cabeceras by intervening jurisdictions, did not always fit the pattern of corregimiento as an integral territorial unit. For this problem several solutions were possible. One was to make the corregimiento boundaries ample enough, or so otherwise to rearrange them, to include the remote estancias. Thus Tepexpan and its distant estancia of Temascalapa both fell within the corregimiento of Teotihuacan, though a corridor to the lakes had to be established to accommodate Tepexpan. Another was to assign an estancia to a nearby corregidor for purposes of political government, but to leave it

TABLE 5
Political Jurisdictions

Jurisdiction[a]	Sixteenth-Century Title[b]	Source and Date	Eighteenth-Century Title[c]
Chalco	Alcalde mayor	AGN, Mercedes, vol. 10, fol. 74r (1575).	Alcalde mayor
Citlaltepec	Corregidor	AGN, Mercedes, vol. 9, fols. 272v–273r (1568).	Alcalde mayor
Coatepec	Corregidor	AGN, General de parte, vol. 2, fol. 233r–233v (1580).	Alcalde mayor
Coyoacan	Corregidor	AGN, Mercedes, vol. 12, fol. 149r (1585).[d]	Alcalde mayor
Cuauhtitlan	Corregidor[e]	AGN, Mercedes, vol. 10, fol. 106r–106v (1576).	Alcalde mayor
Ecatepec	Corregidor	AGN, General de parte, vol. 1, fol. 203r (1576).	Alcalde mayor
Hueypoxtla	Alcalde mayor	FHT, II, 363 (1580).	Alcalde mayor
Mexicalzingo	Corregidor	AGN, General de parte, vol. 1, fols. 36v–37r (1575).	Alcalde mayor
Mexico	Corregidor	ENE, XI, 233 (1574).	Corregidor
Otumba	Corregidor	AGN, Mercedes, vol. 10, fol. 67r (1575).	Alcalde mayor
Pachuca	Alcalde mayor	AGN, Mercedes, vol. 11, fols. 109v–110r (1582).	Alcalde mayor
Tacuba	Corregidor[f]	AGN, Mercedes, vol. 7, fol. 70v (1563).	Alcalde mayor
Teotihuacan	Corregidor	AGN, Mercedes, vol. 11, fols. 117r–118r (1582).	Alcalde mayor
Texcoco	Alcalde mayor	AGN, Mercedes, vol. 8, fol. 197v (1565).	Alcalde mayor
Xochimilco	Alcalde mayor[g]	AGN, General de parte, vol. 1, fol. 196r–196v (1576).	Alcalde mayor

[a]For the geographical areas see Appendix III.
[b]Note that the text refers to all such officers uniformly as corregidores.
[c]AGI, Contaduría, leg. 816, et passim.
[d]Indicated elsewhere as alcalde mayor (e.g., AGN, Mercedes, vol. 11, fols. 49r–49v, 88r–88v).
[e]Indicated at other times as alcalde mayor (e.g., AGN, Mercedes, vol. 10, fol. 254r–254v) or by both titles simultaneously (e.g., AGN, General de parte, vol. 1, fol. 98r).
[f]Indicated at other times as alcalde mayor (e.g., AGN, Mercedes, vol. 10, fols. 96v–97v, 98r–98v, 109r–109v).
[g]The corregidor title was also used in Xochimilco in the sixteenth century. See AGN, Mercedes, vol. 7, fols. 207v–208r; vol. 9, fols. 135v–136r; vol. 11, fol. 232r–232v.

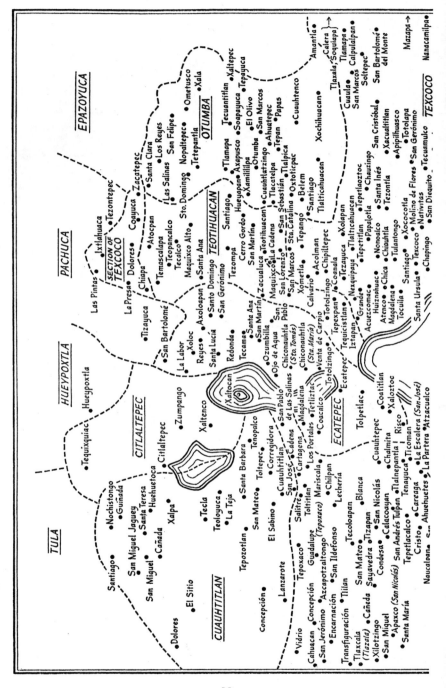

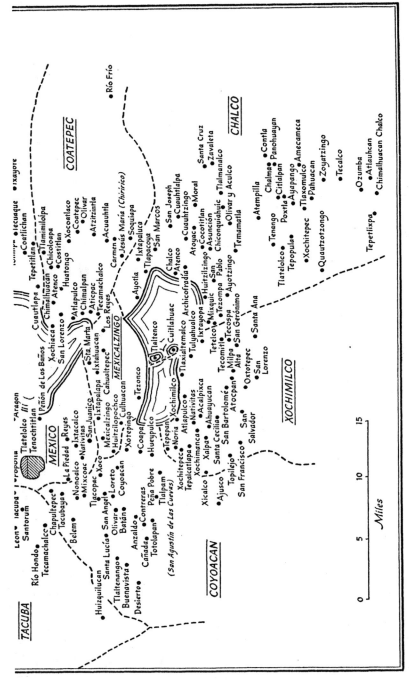

Map 5. Political jurisdictions of the late colonial period. For sources and changes from an earlier period see Appendix III.

connected with its distant cabecera in another corregimiento for purposes of tribute payments and other obligations. This was the case with Santa Marta and Los Reyes, both estancias of Tenochtitlan falling in the corregimiento of Mexicalzingo, and with various Tlatelolco estancias to the north.[125] A third solution was to have a corregidor rule over a distant enclave, as in Texcoco, where the corregidor governed the cluster of communities lying to the north of the corregimiento of Teotihuacan. These various solutions became less urgent as former estancias became cabeceras in their own right. But the solutions, once established, had a certain durability, too, and the three corregimientos mentioned all continued into the eighteenth century.[126]

The organization of corregimiento jurisdictions (Map 5) displays the familiar sector pattern, with the several areas fanning out from the central lakes. Characteristic corregimientos such as Chalco, Coyoacan, Texcoco, and Xochimilco possessed frontages of lake shore and widened as they extended outward to the edges of the Valley. The pattern was derived, as is obvious, from the original Indian cabecera and estancia locations. It did not hold for the two centrally located corregimientos of Mexicalzingo and Ecatepec, but these in turn reflect other conditions of the Culhuaque and the Mexica in the pre-conquest period. An evident geographic basis underlies the corregimiento boundaries of the peninsula of Mexicalzingo, but the attachment of Huitzilopochco to it again demonstrates the viability of the Culhua Nauhtecuhtli.

The influences of corregimiento, like those of encomienda, upon Indian society are measurable not simply in geographical allocations; they are to be seen far more directly in overt behavior and in the relations between corregidores and native peoples. Instructions to corregidores in the sixteenth century—addressed anonymously and requiring only the filling in of name and jurisdiction—stressed the Christian mission, spoke of the obligation to deal justly with Indians, urged the appointee to ensure that elective Indian offices in the towns be filled by good Christians, enjoined him to prevent injury to Indian agriculture by Spanish cattle, and referred to some other standard themes in Spanish-Indian relations.[127] Instructions drafted in the seventeenth century were similar but longer and more detailed. In these, the Christian doctrine again received first attention, and the remainder of the instruction was an extended list of specifications: that tributes be exacted only in the amounts designated; that no Indians be compelled to sell their produce at subnormal prices; that no goods be taken from the Indian community without payment; that Indian officeholders in the communities be removed from their offices only with cause; that the corregidor engage in no cattle ranching or commercial activity. The corregidores' instructions at all times constituted a precise enumeration of requirements and prohibitions designed to protect Indian society against interference, including interference by the corregidor himself.[128] Furthermore, corregidores were always liable to special viceregal orders for the performance of administrative tasks relating to crime, markets, roads, land grants, local agriculture, and an almost endless list of other affairs.[129]

But although corregidores occupied the Spanish civil office closest to Indian life, the truth is that ordinary Indians came into personal contact with them only infrequently. The religious life of the Indian community functioned in the absence of supervision by the corregidor. His direction of community political life was confined chiefly to attendance at local elections, in the company of a small and select portion of the Indian community. Tribute exaction and the administration of labor fell, in part, within the corregidor's jurisdiction, but the house-to-house contact required by these functions was delegated to Indian officials.[130] Especially in the distant estancias and in the cabeceras remote from the corregimiento seat, communication between Indian and corregidor was rare. In the late sixteenth century, even in a large and frequented community such as Tizayuca, Indians saw the corregidor only a few times each year, when his presence was particularly required or when he traveled to or from Mexico City.[131]

Corregidores personally confronted Indians mainly in court, where Indians appeared as criminals or civil litigants. Accusations and arrests were made by the teniente and alguacil, and the affected parties—Indians, Negroes, mestizos, mulattoes, or Spaniards—were brought before the corregidor as judge. The records of these courts are registers of the minor crimes and punishments of colonial society. Petty squabbles over lands, debts, thefts, and women were routine features of community life. A seventeenth-century corregimiento blotter might read as follows: Ana, Indian, for selling pulque illegally, fined six reales; Francisco and Mariana, Indians, for concubinage, fined sixteen pesos; Gaspar, Indian, for carrying a knife illegally, fined twelve reales; Diego de Saavedra, Spaniard, for selling wine with incorrect measures, fined ten pesos; María, Indian, for concubinage, fined six reales; Francisco, mestizo, for theft, fined fifty pesos; Martín

Vásquez, Spaniard, for selling wine illegally, fined nine pesos; Fernando, Indian, and Luisa, Indian, for concubinage, fined eighteen reales apiece; Tomás, mulatto, for wounding a man, fined six pesos; Francisco, Indian, for concubinage, fined four and one-half pesos; and so on for page after page.[132]

Unofficially, corregidores used their offices to gain personal advantage over Indian communities, in open disregard of their instructions. At the outset, the corregidores' opportunities for authority and private gain had been limited by encomienda, but corregimiento came quickly to supplant encomienda as an instrument of power over Indians. A Spanish colonist of the 1530's (not, however, an impartial one) reported that corregidores.were already treating Indians more severely than were encomenderos.[133] Two examples, taken from the 1560's, suggest the nature of corregimiento rule in the later sixteenth century. In Chalco, the corregidor Jorge Cerón y Carbajal employed Indian labor without pay to build his houses and tend his horses, used Indian materials in his house construction, forced Indian servants to carry his water and prepare his food without pay, and demanded mats, beds, firewood, and other materials, all gratis.[134] In Tenayuca, the corregidor Francisco Magariño committed Indians to the stocks, sequestered Indian lands and other property, abetted land seizures by non-Indians (including Isabel Montezuma's mestizo son, Gonzalo Cano, who had become the encomendero of Tacuba), and exacted money, cattle, and food valued at more than 10,000 pesos.[135] The examples suggest a certain uniformity of technique, and in Magariño's case reveal collusion between encomendero and corregidor.

As legal prohibitions developed, all such irregular conduct was in principle to be exposed in the hearing (residencia) held on the conclusion of a corregidor's term of office.[136] Indians as well as Spaniards gave testimony in residencias. But only rarely were corregidores punished for their illegal acts, which were not sufficiently distinguishable from acts of other Spaniards to justify an exclusive punishment.[137] In extreme cases, family connections and friends helped to protect them. Fraud was a commonplace in the residencia hearings, and the punishments, if legally imposed, were light or not enforced. Thus Francisco Magariño had dealings with the oidor Villanueva and was aided by numerous acquaintances in high positions. He bribed the Indian leaders to remain silent at the testimonies, and though sentenced to imprisonment and to a fine of 1,000 pesos, he was quickly set free and did not pay the fine.[138] It is clear that corregidores, however subordinate their position in the total administrative bureaucracy, nevertheless held a royal office of esteem. In the late sixteenth century the corregimiento in Ecatepec went to a descendant of one of the first settlers; in Citlaltepec it went to a grandson of a conquistador; in Chalco it went to a participant in the conquest of Nueva Viscaya.[139] These were not simply fortuitous attributes of the appointees, but justifications for the appointments, and the appointments themselves were rewards and opportunities for enrichment. In the seventeenth century many corregidores left office without residencia, or "composed" the hearings for a fee of 800 or 1,000 pesos. For the most part, the surviving records of residencias reveal only perfunctory investigations.[140]

In the seventeenth and eighteenth centuries, with the further development of colonial economic life, the emphasis in corregimiento came to lie still more in its perquisites and opportunities for gain. Corregimientos were in demand among would-be officeholders to the extent that they offered favorable circumstances for business and finance. Like the encomenderos before them, the corregidores performed economic functions of far-reaching implications, and, as in encomienda, a substantial portion of the burden fell upon the Indian community. In this respect three features of late corregimiento deserve mention: tribute collection, *derramas*, and commerce.

Colonial law made corregidores responsible for the delivery of tribute to the treasury officers, but it forbade their making collections directly from Indian tributaries.[141] The reasons have to do with the corregidores' known propensity to divert tribute funds into their own pockets. Corregidores did receive food and goods from Indians, however, and from the start their practice was to sell these materials for profit. According to a viceregal statement, embezzlement of tribute funds had become a common corregidor's procedure by the seventeenth century.[142]

The term derrama, in its colonial usage, refers to extra or unauthorized tributes. Exaction of derramas was not an exclusive device of the corregidores—clergymen and local Indian officials were also adept in this—but it consistently served corregidores as a means of raising money.[143] Fees for the performance of official duties and fines for transgressions of the law were closely associated with derramas, particularly if they were larger than customary. The organization of tribute collection furnished all the mechanisms needed for the levying of derramas. A corregidor's visita of his jurisdiction—a tour of its communities and a form of inspection easily represented as a proof of responsible government—provided abundant opportunities. Colonial law restricted visitas in the seventeenth century to one per term of office.[144] But more than law was required to limit visitas and prevent derramas. In Tacuba, in the eighteenth century, corregidores regularly made several visitas of their jurisdiction, traveling with retinues, requiring communities to supply food and lodging and to care for the horses, and exacting payment. Each Indian *gobernador* furnished food and gifts to the visiting entourage and contributed thirty pesos for each of his years in office. Each town gave a separate payment, depending on its size and the number of its inhabitants, exactly as in regular tribute.[145]

The corregidores' interest in commerce appears in part as an outgrowth of the concern with tribute and with derramas. As recipients of Indian payments and with access to a variety of commodities, the early corregidores enjoyed some particular commercial advantages.[146] With the systematization of Indian tribute in the mid-sixteenth century, corregidores could no longer count on a supply of commodities other than maize, and they expanded their activities into new areas of procurement and sale. In the late sixteenth and seventeenth centuries colonial law belatedly listed and ineffectively forbade the enterprises into which corregidores were known to be expanding: the marketing of wheat and maize, the marketing of chickens and other fowl, the raising of pigs and cattle, farming, and the ownership of land.[147] In the developing hacienda economy of the seventeenth century, local officials with influence to dispense were in a favorable position to speculate in commodities and control markets. The corregidor's common procedure was to buy cheaply, often from Indians themselves (a method not greatly different from levying a derrama), and then to make a forced distribution (repartimiento), again to Indians, at inflated prices. Thus in the seventeenth century cows and mules were sold in Indian communities at profits of several hundred per cent, intoxicants were illegally sold, and luxury goods, including silk stockings, were disposed of to native buyers under the corregidores' direction.[148]

In the Valley of Mexico such practices reached their most developed form in the jurisdiction of Chalco. Here the hacienda economy and the large Indian population created conditions particularly favorable to coercive sale and commercial exploitation. The administration of Phelipe Díez de Palacios in the 1720's is typical of the late colonial period. In

TABLE 6

Corregimiento Salaries, Seventeenth Century[a]

Jurisdiction	Salary in pesos	Jurisdiction	Salary in pesos
Mexico	550	Ecatepec	200
Chalco	525	Mexicalzingo	200
Pachuca	500	Tacuba	200
Otumba	450	Citlaltepec	150
Xochimilco	450	Teotihuacan	150
Texcoco	250	Coyoacan	?
Coatepec	200	Hueypoxtla	?
Cuauhtitlan	200		

[a]AGI, México, leg. 326; leg. 327; Contaduría, leg. 768.

Tlalmanalco, the seat of his corregimiento, the town furnished him an Indian woman to prepare his food without pay, and various barrios provided him with fuel and fodder in weekly donations. His principal economic activity was the forced distribution of animals. He maintained a ranch for cattle and horses, demanded the unrecompensed service of three Indians per week in caring for the herd and equipment, and disposed of the animals by compulsory sale to Indians at prices imposed by himself. His procedure of sale was to issue an order to each pueblo in the jurisdiction whereby individuals and groups were required to accept cattle, mules, and colts. Following the distribution, he sent Indian subordinates to collect the money, often approving in advance their use of extortionist methods, which included the imprisonment and kidnapping of Indian women. Díez de Palacios conducted a regular business on these lines, keeping books, recording the names of Indians in debt from previous transactions, and accepting surplus animals from the neighboring haciendas for disposition in the same way. Animals costing five pesos were sold at twelve. Mules costing from six to twelve pesos were sold at twenty-eight and thirty pesos.[149]

In the eighteenth century it was universally admitted that a corregidor's legal salary comprised only a small fraction of his real income. Emoluments were precedented, customary, and wholly expected. Approximately half the corregidores of the colony were living in Mexico City, neglecting their offices, engaging in commerce, and in other ways disobeying the law.[150]

A guide book for political aspirants in the colony, written in 1777, suggests how systematic the benefits of corregimiento had become. The guide book lists and classifies the jurisdictions, ranking them in terms of material gain. In the Valley of Mexico, Chalco qualified as of the first class in the opinion of the writer. Its many large haciendas offered ample opportunities, the repartimiento of wax candles to the Indians for All Souls' Day being one of the Chalco corregidor's choicest prerogatives. If "well administered," the report stated, Chalco was worth 16,000 pesos per year, or some thirty times the corregidor's official salary. The other corregimientos of the Valley ran the gamut of categories in opportunism: Texcoco, Coyoacan, and Tacuba in the second class; Cuauhtitlan in the second or third class; Otumba (with a modest repartimiento in maize, wheat, barley, and pigs) in the third class; Xochimilco, Teotihuacan, and Coatepec (with "some slight repartimiento") in the fourth class; Zumpango (Citlaltepec) in the fifth; Ecatepec in the sixth; and Mexicalzingo ("of little profit") at the end.[161]

The development of custom is one of the most important themes of corregimiento history. Corregimiento was absolutely defined in law and circumscribed by legal prohibition. But in its effective history this was insignificant. What mattered was the growth of precedent, which was wholly uniform with respect to an exploitative tendency and differed only in detail from one corregimiento to the next. No compelling historical cause assigned the repartimiento of wax candles to the corregidor of Chalco; under other circumstances, this repartimiento might have fallen to the clergy or to some other imperial agent. In practice, it fell to the corregidor, who in the eighteenth century had inherited it from his predecessors and would have been outraged if another had sought to divest him of it. Only in a few instances may such traditions be traced to their historical origins, which, when they appear, have always an unintended or fortuitous quality. The traditions stemmed from unique early concessions or acts of aggrandizement, not from any conscious creation of precedent. The deliberate royal and viceregal attempts to create precedent, in law, were evidently sincere and usually of no avail. But the law repeatedly cautioned against innovation; and innovation, once established, became custom, hence inaccessible to law.

These interrelations of conduct, custom, and law applied not only to corregimiento, but also to a whole range of official and unofficial influences upon Indian society. The remarkable feature of encomienda is that royal law prevailed. That the royal victory over encomienda was of only limited consequence for Indian society becomes clear in the history of corregimiento. The encomenderos' methods were refined to meet new conditions and passed to other hands, including those of the corregidores. A huge accumulation of royal and viceregal law came into being, but it proved ineffective in controlling the crown's own administrative officers.

CHAPTER V

Religion

Spanish imperialism sought to justify its acts by its Christian mission. The conquest was a Christian enterprise because it destroyed a pagan civilization, and encomienda and corregimiento were Christian institutions because they ensured a Christian society. With the papal consignment of the New World to Spain, all aspects of Hispanic colonization became subject to a Christian interpretation and subordinated to a Christian function.[1]

But this is not to say that a united colonial church consistently adapted itself to imperial ends. Within the church, the regular Mendicant friars and the secular clergy comprised two powerful opposing groups. The former were the Franciscans, Dominicans, and Augustinians, to whom parochial and sacramental powers had been entrusted for the realization of missionary goals. The latter were the clerics of the episcopal hierarchy, the traditional possessors of these powers, who saw parochial control by the regular clergy as an unwarranted intrusion. In this usage, of course, "regular" means living by rule (*regula*), and "secular" means living within the world or within the age (*saeculum*) instead of in monastic retreat. Although hundreds of monasteries (*conventos*) were constructed in Mexico under Mendicant direction, the friars did not live in retirement or seclusion. On the contrary, and especially during the first fifty years, they were the active agents of a flourishing conversion program.

The earliest Mendicants were itinerant missionaries lacking ecclesiastical headquarters and dedicated to the task of baptizing as many converts as possible. The natural limits of mass baptism, however, together with doctrinal criticisms of its superficiality,[2] soon brought demands for more meaningful conversions and for fixed ecclesiastical locations. The foremost Indian towns—Tenochtitlan, Tlatelolco, Texcoco, Tlalmanalco, Xochimilco

—were occupied by Franciscans. The Dominicans settled in the scattered communities of Chalco province and in the two villas of the Marquesado, Coyoacan and Tacubaya. The Augustinians, with fewer sites than either of the others, established churches and monasteries in Acolman, Culhuacan, and Mixquic. Controversies among the orders over the occupation of towns, and movements from one site to another, are reminiscent of the early disorders of encomienda.[3] But one must look to the Franciscans for the primary impetus and motivation and for the character that the whole movement came to express. Most long-term ecclesiastical assignments rested upon Franciscan priority or concession. The principal Dominican and Augustinian centers, including Acolman, Amecameca, Coatepec, Coyoacan, and Cuitlahuac, as well as the sites of the secular clergy in the northern part of the Valley, had been early Franciscan locations. In general, it may be said that Franciscan leadership and Franciscan precedents dominated the missionary enterprise.[4]

The "apostolic twelve" Franciscans who came to Mexico in 1524 were products of a Mendicant reform movement in Spain led by Cardinal Jiménez de Cisneros. Their episcopal head after 1527, the Franciscan Bishop Juan de Zumárraga, undertook to apply the precepts of Erasmian humanism to the American mission. Everywhere the first Franciscan friars founded schools and sought to inculcate literacy and Hispanic values as well as Christian doctrine. To this end, they conceived a broad program within which cultural education and social reform were second only to the propagation of the faith. The educational institutions of the early colonial period were not seminaries; all, or almost all, proposals for the creation of an Indian clergy were rejected in the sixteenth century.[5] They were rather institutions for the Christian training of young upper-class Indians who would subsequently occupy high places in their own society.[6] The school founded by Pedro de Gante in Tenochtitlan served as a model for those that later came to be associated with the conventual establishments in the towns.[7] The outstanding center of humanistic education was the Franciscan Colegio de Santa Cruz in Tlatelolco, where selected native students studied Latin and were exposed to the traditions of European learning.[8]

The foremost expression of humanistic social reform lay outside the capital in the model community or "hospital" called Santa Fe, on the western edge of the Valley. Founded in the early 1530's, it was patterned directly after Thomas More's Utopia. Its regulations provided for a literate Indian population engaged in an economy of agriculture and skilled crafts, holding common property, and rotating in political office.[9] The site was chosen in an area removed from the centers of Spanish lay influence, and Christianized Indians were drawn to it from other pueblos. The objective of its founder, Vasco de Quiroga, was to cultivate the natural morality of Indian peoples and to recreate the conditions of primitive Christianity in a single exemplary community. Although its effective history was brief and its population small, Santa Fe stands as the purest of the efforts to remold Indian life in Christian humanist terms and as a practical expression of the intellectual and moral conviction of the first missionaries in Mexico.[10]

The efforts of the friars did bring about a virtually immediate elimination of a number of non-Christian elements in Indian society, notably pagan temples, the Aztec class of priests, and the acts of human sacrifice.[11] The overt aspects of the Christian religion were the ones that Indians embraced most readily—the great churches and monastery buildings, the ceremonies, the processions, and the images of the saints. The Aztec religion had included practices analogous to some of the practices of Christianity, notably marriage, penance, baptism, fasting, and offerings.[12] But in no case were the similarities so exact as to permit a simple or unqualified transfer, and the differing contexts within which similar practices functioned invalidated any synthetic reconstructions on Christianity's behalf.

The dilemma of Christianity in the colony was not simply that it failed to indoctrinate the mass of its communicants with its fullest meaning, but that Indian acceptances were strongly colored by residual and antithetic values. In general, the Indians did not abandon their polytheistic view. The standards of Christian behavior—whether communicated by teaching, encouraged by precept, or enforced by compulsion—failed to make understandable the basic Christian abstractions of virtue and sin.[13] The community of saints was received by Indians not as an intermediary between God and man but as a pantheon of anthropomorphic deities. The symbol of the crucifixion was accepted, but with an exaggerated concern for the details of an act of sacrifice. The Christian God was admitted, but not as an exclusive or omnipotent deity. Heaven and hell were recognized, but with emphasis on concrete properties and with obtrusive pagan attributes. Christian worship was acknowledged without a distinction among the degrees of worship, and Indians continued to act as if the object of worship relied upon the worshiper for its sustenance and upkeep. Indians confessed, but the Aztec preference for confession in time of crisis competed with the Christian requirement that confession be performed at least once a year. Indians accepted the concept of the soul, but they extended it to animals and inanimate objects.[14]

Idolatry and pagan superstition persisted. They were most fully described in the seventeenth century by Hernando Ruiz de Alarcón in the *Tratado de las supersticiones* (1629) and by Jacinto de la Serna in the *Manual de ministros* (1656).[15] Idolatry was discovered in the eighteenth century in Mexicalzingo, Huitzilopochco, Xaltocan, and Citlaltepec. In 1803 one entire town in the Valley was found to be worshiping idols in secret caves. Even where idolatry itself was not practiced, idols were surreptitiously cherished, springs and hills continued to be places of superstition, and pagan deities were remembered.[16] The Franciscan friar Toribio de Benavente, usually called Motolinía, asserted in the late 1530's that idolatry had been wiped out as completely as if it had disappeared a century before and that Indian witchcraft and diabolical illusions had been wholly eradicated. This was indeed what the early missionaries believed, but it differs sharply from what modern students have discovered. Later in the same century the Franciscan ethnologist Bernardino de Sahagún took issue with Motolinía's point of view ("a darkness has been spread to preserve the early fame of both the baptizers and the baptized"). But few ecclesiastics were so perceptive, or so outspoken, as Sahagún.[17]

The first friars confronted administrative problems akin to those of encomienda and corregimiento. Fixed sites required first of all geographical jurisdictions and new delineations of boundaries. The colonial parochial jurisdiction was variously entitled *doctrina, curato, partido,* and *parroquia,* the term doctrina (which we shall use) being generally preferred in the early period, and the term curato in the later.[18] A doctrina consisted of a principal town called a cabecera (or cabeza) de doctrina, where the church and clerical residence were located, and a cluster of surrounding towns called *visitas*.[19] Each town was given a Christian prefix to its native name. This new pattern and terminology appeared early and uniformly in the Valley, both in the establishments of the three Mendicant orders and in the areas ministered by secular clergy.

As in encomienda and corregimiento, Indian society itself furnished jurisdictions that were internally structured and of appropriate size for ecclesiastical purposes. Integral cabecera-sujeto units were easily transformed into parishes, with the Indian cabeceras becoming cabeceras de doctrina and the sujetos becoming visitas. The adaptation of the cabecera-sujeto system held many advantages for the friars, who could rely upon it for labor, church attendance, and orderly payments. Moreover, it fitted one of their most successful techniques of Christianization, namely to convert the caciques first, in the expectation that the people as a whole would follow the examples of their leaders.

In normal or uncomplicated cases the church complied absolutely with the existing cabecera-sujeto jurisdictions. The modifications that were made principally affected sujetos situated farther from their cabeceras than was consistent with effective ministration. Since doctrinas had to be of manageable size, distant estancias were in some instances assigned to the doctrinas of alien cabeceras. If cabeceras were not conveniently located to serve as cabeceras de doctrina, sujetos were sometimes selected for the purpose. This was the case prior to 1570 in Milpa Alta, Calpulalpan, and Chalco Atenco, each of which was located at a distance from its cabecera, and none of which could appropriately be assigned to another doctrina. In Santa Fe and Tlalnepantla new communities were established to serve as cabeceras de doctrina.[20]

Although ecclesiastics in encomienda towns received their support from the encomenderos, the church did not maintain or recognize the readjustments in cabecera-sujeto distributions that had been made under encomienda. In the great multiple encomiendas such as Cuauhtitlan and Chalco, the ecclesiastical decision was to separate the communities again, and to equate the doctrinas more evenly with the Indian cabecera jurisdictions. Of the six non-tlatoani communities that became distinct encomiendas, only one, Tizayuca, became a cabecera de doctrina during the first fifty years. A second, Tecama, was granted doctrina status in the early seventeenth century. The other four—including Chicoloapa, which like Tizayuca and Tecama was granted early cabecera rank in political and other non-religious affairs—were retained as visitas in the ecclesiastical organization.[21]

In this process, also, the church refrained from interfering with Indian cabecera-sujeto connections, permitting sujetos to remain subordinate to their traditional cabeceras in Indian society even when they became cabeceras de doctrina, or visitas in other doctrinas, in the ecclesiastical structure.

TABLE 7

Doctrinas, 1570

Doctrina	Tributaries	Clerics	Doctrina	Tributaries	Clerics
FRANCISCAN			DOMINICAN (cont.)		
Texcoco	8,000	5	Cuitlahuac	1,500	3
Otumba	6,500	4	Chimalhuacan Atenco	800	3
Xochimilco	5,800	3	Tacubaya	800	2
Tacuba	4,700	4	TOTAL	20,200	30
Tlalmanalco	4,000	5	AUGUSTINIAN		
Cuauhtitlan	3,400	4			
Tlalnepantla	3,400	3	Acolman	4,100	2
Milpa Alta	2,800	2	Culhuacan	1,300	2
Ecatepec	2,600	2	Mixquic	1,200	3
Huexotla	2,500	2	Tezontepec	800	2
Calpulalpan	1,300	2	TOTAL	7,400	9
Chalco Atenco	550	2	SECULAR CLERGY		
TOTAL	45,550	38			
			Huehuetoca	4,800	1
			Tizayuca	4,400	1
DOMINICAN			Tequixquiac	3,700	1
Coyoacan	4,400	5	Zumpango	2,900	1
Tepetlaoztoc	3,500	2	Hueypoxtla	2,700	1
Tenango	2,500	4	Tepozotlan	2,400	1
Azcapotzalco	1,800	2	Ixtapalapa	700	1
Chimalhuacan Chalco.	1,800	4	Huitzilopochco	420	1
Coatepec	1,600	3	Santa Fe	130	1
Amecameca	1,500	2	TOTAL	22,150	9

SOURCE: López de Velasco, *Geografía y descripción*, pp. 193 ff. The number of doctrinas appears to be complete for 1570, with the possible exceptions of Teotihuacan and Toltitlan. The former is listed with 2,000 "vecinos" (plus 500 in Chiconauhtla) in 1569. The latter was under construction, with 3,000 "vecinos" (plus others in the visitas) in the same year. See NCDHM (1941), II, 13 ff. The tributaries in this table total 95,300. The difference between this and the 117,270 tributaries listed for 1570 in Table 10 results from the omission of Mexico City here and the omission of Hueypoxtla, Tizayuca, Tezontepec, and Santa Fe in Table 10.

A few native cabeceras were kept as visitas into the eighteenth century— the conspicuous examples are Tezayuca, Tepexpan, and Chiconauhtla— and in no case is it possible to detect any effort at subordination with respect to established Indian status.[22] Similarly, where the organization of the church separated sujetos as cabeceras de doctrina, there was no corresponding inclination to elevate these to Indian cabecera rank. Thus the departures from the native system undertaken by the church had less effect upon the classification of cabeceras and sujetos than did encomienda departures. On occasion, cabeceras de doctrina were reduced to the role of visitas, but this was a rare and temporary expedient resulting from momentary shortages of religious personnel or occurring in intervals of transfer from one order to another.[23]

In two regions of the Valley, however, ecclesiastical departures from the cabecera-sujeto affiliations appeared in a particularly pronounced form. One was the region of the estancias of Teotihuacan, Acolman, and Tepexpan in the northeast; the other was the region of the estancias of Tenochtitlan and Tlatelolco to the north and south of the capital. In both areas changes were accomplished over a long period, so that at any given moment a single jurisdiction might include the remote estancias of an original cabecera-sujeto unit in addition to nearby estancias of alien cabeceras. In 1570, for example, Acolman was an Augustinian cabecera de doctrina ministering to a variety of cabeceras and sujetos of Indian government. Its visitas included the cabecera of Tequicistlan with its estancias, the cabecera of Tecama but not the northern Tecama estancias, the cabecera of Tepexpan and one of its estancias but not the other estancias farther to the north, and a miscellany of estancias of Texcoco, Tenochtitlan, and Tlatelolco. Meanwhile, the doctrina retained the distant Acolman estancias of Chiapa and Zacatepec, requiring the friars to travel a distance of twenty miles, beyond the ordinary limits of the Acolman doctrina and past communities ministered in other doctrinas.[24] Likewise, the estancias of Tenochtitlan and Tlatelolco in the second area had been assigned by 1570 as visitas to a number of doctrinas, including Zumpango, Guadalupe, Ecatepec, Tenango, Acolman, and, of course, Tenochtitlan and Tlatelolco themselves.[25] The two areas represent local situations of unusual complexity. They illustrate, nevertheless, a basic fact: that cabecera-sujeto units, encomiendas, corregimientos, and ecclesiastical jurisdictions might all have different boundaries.[26]

Such boundaries, moreover, were in constant process of change. The original church jurisdictions underwent progressive transformation as new doctrinas were formed and as new adjustments were made in the disposition of visitas and cabeceras de doctrina. In the ecclesiastical procedures no original grants assigned the patterns in so fixed a form as in encomienda, and there occurred continuous opportunities for shifting sujetos about and reassigning the parochial affiliations.[27]

Factional rivalries within the church brought about further departures from the cabecera-sujeto patterns. Mendicants protested that the seculars habitually intruded into sujetos, encouraging separation from cabeceras and fostering Indian dispute. They contended that Indians preferred the regular to the secular clergy and that support for the seculars was confined to opportunistic Indian leaders anxious to remove sujetos from traditional cabecera control.[28] The complaint that seculars were intruding into sujetos was not unfounded. In the Valley, as of 1570, it was applicable to the secular clergy's doctrina of Guadalupe.[29] With less justification, because of their tlatoani status, it was applicable to Huehuetoca and even to Zumpango. An additional point might have been made regarding the visitas of these and other doctrinas of secular clergy, for many of the local churches had originally been built under Franciscan direction.[30] Despite its tlatoani tradition, Huehuetoca was still claimed by Cuauhtitlan as a sujeto in 1570 and thus offered the most appropriate example with which to support the Mendicant charge. It is an interesting commentary on Mendicant justification that Huehuetoca was cited in this connection in a Franciscan protest of about 1569. The Franciscans asserted that Huehuetoca was a sujeto of Cuauhtitlan and that it was being ministered by a secular cleric against the will of its Indian inhabitants.[31] The protest is further connected with reports made by the secular clergy in 1569, which stated unequivocally that Huehuetoca was a cabecera and that its visitas, Teoloyuca and Coyotepec, were pueblos por sí.[32]

The friars were also generally correct in observing that intrusion into the sujetos was more common among seculars than among themselves. But the Mendicant orders were liable to countercharges on the same score. Thus Tlacuitlapilco and Tezcatepec, the distant northern estancias of Hueypoxtla, came under the doctrinal jurisdiction of the Augustinians of Ixmiquilpan, while Hueypoxtla itself was ministered by secular clergy.[33] And in the continuing rivalry between one Mendicant order and another, intrusion into sujetos was a recognized competitive technique. An aspect of the bitter and complex dispute between Franciscans and Dominicans in Chalco province was that the visita of Ayapango was connected to Franciscan Tlalmanalco but was simultaneously retained as a sujeto by Tenango, a Dominican cabecera de doctrina. This connection, like others, defied contrary claims argued on the basis of proximity, for Ayapango was farther from Tlalmanalco than from Tenango.[34]

The situation of cabeceras de doctrina and their visitas at approximately

TABLE 8
Parochial Foundations and Secularizations

Parish and Period of Foundation[a]	Date of Secularization[b]	Parish and Period of Foundation[a]	Date of Secularization[b]
FRANCISCAN		DOMINICAN (cont.)	
Atlapulco*	After 1764	Coatepec*	1752
Atocpan	After 1764	Coyoacan*	1752–53
Calpulalpan*	After 1764	Cuitlahuac*	1754
Chalco Atenco*	1761	Ecatzingo	1751
Chapultepec	1770	Ixtapaluca	1761
Chiauhtla*	By 1768	Mixcoac*	1754
Coatlichan*	1768	San Agustín de las Cuevas	1754
Cuauhtitlan*	1754–56	San Angel (San Jacinto)*	1756
Ecatepec*	1761	Tacubaya*	1765
Huexotla*	1771	Tenango*	1772
Ixtacalco	1770	Tepetlaoztoc*	1777
Mexicalzingo	1770	Xochitepec	1751
Milpa Alta*	1772–74		
Naucalpan	By 1768	AUGUSTINIAN	
Otumba*	1756	Acolman*	1754
Ozumba	1765–69	Ayotzingo*	By 1768
Popotla	By 1768	Culhuacan*	1756
San Antonio de las Huertas	1770	Mixquic*	By 1768
Santa Marta	After 1764	Tecama	1768–68?
Tacuba*	1754–55	Tenochtitlan*	
Tecomitl*	After 1764	San Pablo	1772
Temamatla	1765–69	Santa Cruz Coltzinco	1772
Tenochtitlan*		Tezontepec*	By 1768
San José de los Naturales	1772		
Santa María la Redonda	1772	SECULAR	
Teotihuacan*	1771–72	Guadalupe*	
Tepepan	After 1764	Huehuetoca*	
Tepetlatzinco (Nativitas)	After 1764	Hueypoxtla*	
Texcoco*	After 1800	Huitzilopochco*	
Tlalmanalco*	1768	Huizquilucan	
Tlalnepantla*	1754	Ixtapalapa*	
Tlatelolco*	1772	Nestlalpa	
Toltitlan*	1754	Santa Fe*	
Tulantongo	After 1764	Teoloyuca[o]	
Xochimilco*	1786	Tequixquiac*	
		Tizayuca*	
DOMINICAN		Xaltocan-Xaltenco	
Amecameca*	1774	Zumpango*	
Azcapotzalco*	After 1800		
Chimalhuacan Atenco*	1770	JESUIT	
Chimalhuacan Chalco*	1789	Tepozotlan*	1767

the mid-point in colonial history is illustrated in Map 6. The representation is generalized in time, in the sense that it depicts these connections as of no one moment but is drawn instead from numerous seventeenth-century sources. The map disregards the large number of visitas that were situated at short distances from their cabeceras de doctrina, and it should be viewed therefore in the knowledge that many communities in addition to those shown were incorporated in the ecclesiastical jurisdictions. It represents an over-all transition. In the seventeenth century more doctrinas were in existence than in 1570, but still more were to come into being in the eighteenth century. Absolute dependence upon the cabecera-sujeto relations is indicated in the seventeenth century in such doctrinas as Otumba, where all the visitas were sujetos of the cabecera. In the Xochimilco area, on the other hand, the original cabecera-sujeto pattern was substantially revised, with the foundation of new cabeceras de doctrina at Tepepan, Atlapulco, Tecomitl, and Milpa Alta. Atocpan, shown on the map as a visita of Milpa Alta, was to become another distinct cabecera de doctrina in the late seventeenth century.[35]

It will be observed that all acts of separation in the Xochimilco area occurred under Franciscan direction. They qualify as modifications made for effective ministration in a densely populated area, rather than as solutions to the problems of Mendicant rivalry. The case is different in the Chalco area, where competition existed among all three orders (although chiefly between Franciscans and Dominicans) and where the visita affiliations represent sequential acts of settlement. In the Texcoco region the native

---

NOTES TO TABLE 8

[a]Asterisks indicate parishes founded in the sixteenth century; parishes without asterisks were founded between 1600 and 1750. The list includes known parochial communities outside the city except some late anexos and asistencias. Four parishes of Tenochtitlan are included; the histories of others are not easily reduced to a tabular form.

[b]Precise dates for secularization are not always clear. We rely in general on the notices in Vera, *Erecciones parroquiales*, pp. 3 ff., and Ocaranza, *Capítulos*, pp. 499–501, and on the anonymous eighteenth-century map in the Museo Nacional de Historia in Chapultepec, reproduced in Apenas, *Mapas antiguos*, lám. 22. This map we date at 1765–68, for it shows Tacubaya (secularized in 1765) under secular clergy, and Tlalmanalco and Coatlichan (secularized in 1768) under Franciscans. It thus allows for a provisional dating of some secularizations by 1768 or after 1764. See in addition for Ozumba and Temamatla, *Compendio histórico del concilio III*, III, 247–48; for Tlatelolco, Sedano, *Noticias de México*, II, 156; for Xochimilco, AGN, Clero regular y secular, vol. 215, exp. 1, fols. 3r ff.; and for Coyoacan, Castro Santa-Anna, *Diario*, I, 120.

[c]The doctrina was in existence in 1603 (AGN, Congregaciones, vol. 1, fols. 65v–66r) and may have been a sixteenth-century establishment.

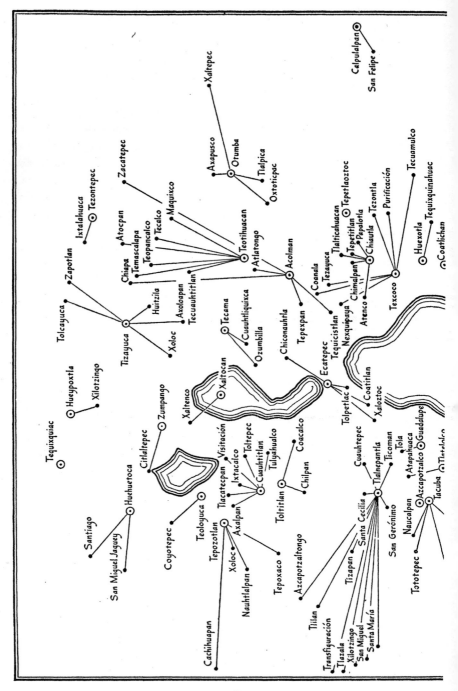

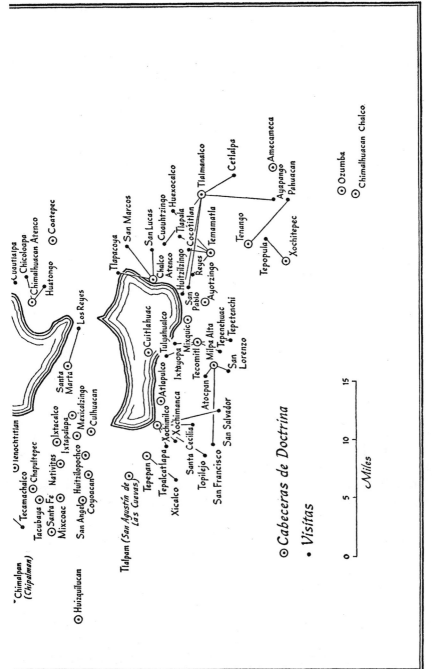

Map 6. Ecclesiastical cabeceras de doctrina and their selected visitas in the seventeenth century.

cabeceras had been separated to a greater extent than in encomienda (thus Chiauhtla and Huexotla were cabeceras de doctrina), but Tezayuca, Tepexpan, and Chiconauhtla, which were cabeceras, remained as visitas. On the eastern edge of the Valley, Calpulalpan was both a cabecera de doctrina and a sujeto of Texcoco. In the complex area north of Acolman, the vestiges of the interspersed sujetos persisted. Zacatepec, the most distant sujeto of Acolman, was ordered to change its visita affiliation only in 1603, and Map 6 shows conditions of the first years of the seventeenth century.[36] Finally, the secular clergy's doctrina of Tizayuca, which had formerly included the visitas of the Temascalapa-Maquixco region, was being intruded upon by Franciscan Teotihuacan.[37]

Further changes and a continuation of the regular-secular rivalry marked the late seventeenth and eighteenth centuries. Ecclesiastical doctrinas to the middle eighteenth century, together with dates of monastic secularization, are shown in Table 8. The tabular form distorts the evidence somewhat, for sites continued to be transferred from one order to another, and intermediate categories (anexos and asistencias, not all of which are shown in the table) came into being. The final process of secularization, like the intendant-subdelegado innovation which was its political counterpart, occurred in the latter half of the eighteenth century and followed upon royal orders requiring the cessation of each Mendicant administration on the death of its clerical personnel.[38] By the first years of the nineteenth century only Texcoco (Franciscan) and Azcapotzalco (Dominican) remained in Mendicant hands,[39] and the long dispute between the secular and the regular clergy for parochial control was at an end.

Ecclesiastical disputes in the early period had engendered a more vigorous partisanship among Indians than had the disputes of encomenderos. As we have seen, Indian loyalty to the encomendero was a secondary feature of encomienda rivalry, for encomenderos in effect strategically exploited Indian claims. In ecclesiastical controversies Indian loyalty was an immediate and central issue. In Amecameca during the 1530's and 1540's the competition between Franciscans and Dominicans was intensified when one cacique faction supported one order and a second cacique faction the other.[40] In Tenochtitlan in 1569 the viceroy sent secular clergy to say Mass where Franciscans had previously officiated, and the entire Indian congregation rose up against them. Indians stoned the secular clergy, Spaniards were obliged to defend themselves with swords, Indians stoned a Spanish judge sent by the viceroy, and in the furor the Franciscans were restored.[41]

In Teotihuacan, where the Augustinians planned a monastery in 1557, and where the Indian community, originally indoctrinated by Franciscans, feared a long period of construction labor like that imposed on neighboring Acolman, a prolonged and successful Indian campaign for the Franciscan return followed. The crisis in Teotihuacan was marked by extreme Indian partisanship, chiefly for the Franciscans but on occasion for the Augustinians on the other side. The alcalde mayor of Texcoco, other judges, the friars, an Indian judge appointed by the viceroy, and an oidor all came to Teotihuacan to restore order, and all failed. Imprisonment, exile, whippings, threats of hanging (a gallows was constructed), and other measures were applied, but to no avail. The Indian community maintained its resistance with extraordinary perseverance, assisting prisoners to escape, defacing the image of San Agustín, sacking the church to prevent the Augustinian entry, and vacating the town for an entire year until the Franciscans were permitted to return.[42]

These incidents of the sixteenth century contrast with conditions of the later period, when relations between friars and Indians came everywhere to be marked by estrangement. The Indians' early love for the friars, in the words of a Franciscan writer of the late seventeenth century, "has been changed to hatred by their descendants."[43] In the eighteenth century even the disputes between regulars and seculars no longer served to enlist Indian support. Native peoples offered no objections to the secularization of the parishes, because, as the viceroy stated in 1755, they hated the friars.[44] The dispute between the regular and the secular clergy was conducted, through the whole latter part of its long history, in an atmosphere of Indian hostility or indifference.

The beginnings of this estrangement from the church occurred earlier than might be supposed. At the end of the first fifteen years of Mendicant labors, Motolinía described Indian society in terms that suggested a thorough conversion to Christianity, as we have seen. But church attendance was already declining in the 1550's.[45] In 1556, Indian men were reported to be less concerned with church attendance than women. In 1562 it was stated that only a third of the native population of the city of Mexico were receiving sacraments. In 1569 the Franciscan Provincial reported that even in the most Christianized areas only about one-fifth of the population attended church.[46] We may suppose that Motolinía's description exaggerated the positive response to Christianity and understated the resistance. But even if one accepts his version of the history of early evangelism, a very brief duration for the success of the proselytizing program must be postulated. By the middle of the sixteenth century Indian communities were not responding with full enthusiasm to ecclesiastical persuasions.

The failure of the church to complete a conversion program so earnestly begun may be ascribed to a number of interrelated causes. Among the clergy the early optimism waned and a reconciliation took place with other Spanish classes. Encomienda had at first served the Mendicant orders as a foil and a focus of hostile attention; but after the middle sixteenth century churchmen accepted encomienda and could no longer convincingly maintain their position as defenders of the life of the spirit in opposition to the encomenderos' oppression. Ecclesiastical strictures against forced labor and tribute exaction appeared incompatible with the church's own dependence upon Indian tribute and labor. As caciques lost authority over their communities, the church could no longer rely on a native hierarchy to unify the response to Christianity. In the early period church attendance had taken place in a regulated order, in unison, and by barrios. But with the progressive disruption of the native social order, attendance became a matter of personal decision, lacking communal sanction and incapable of enforcement by the clergy.[47]

The alienation of Indians from the church was not the result of any quantitative decline in ecclesiastical personnel, for it proceeded while the number of ecclesiastics increased and while the number of Indians decreased. Numbers of clergy in the various doctrinas as recorded about 1570 (Table 7) indicate sharp variations in the ratios to native population from one area to another. The maximum ratio, one cleric to 130 families, was achieved in Santa Fe (as a result, however, of Santa Fe's small Indian population); the minimum ratio, one cleric to 4,800 families, occurred in Huehuetoca.[48] The average number of families per cleric outside the capital in 1570 was about 1,125, but this fell to about 280 in the middle seventeenth century with the further population decline. In 1570 clergy outnumbered encomenderos by about three to one and corregidores by about six to one. The crown in the late sixteenth and seventeenth centuries sought to reduce the number of clergy,[49] but with no real success until the expulsion of the Jesuits in 1767, and the Jesuit expulsion had little effect on the ratio of Indians to clergy in the towns. In the doctrinas a maximum of five clerics and a minimum of one were normal for all periods. The total number of clergy ministering to Indians in the Valley increased from about 85 in 1570 (Table 7) to about 120 at the end of the colonial period. Meanwhile, the

TABLE 9
Number of Parochial Clergymen, ca. 1800

Parish	Clergymen	Parish	Clergymen
Acolman	2	Mexico City (*Cont.*)	
Amecameca	3	Santa Ana	3
Axapusco	3	Santa Catarina Mártir	3
Ayapango	2	Santa Cruz Acatlan	1
Ayotzingo	2	Santa Cruz y Soledad	4
Azcapotzalco (Dominican)	?	Santa María la Redonda	2
Chalco	2	Santa Veracruz	4
Chiauhtla	2	Santo Tomás de la Palma	2
Chimalhuacan Atenco	2	Milpa Alta	3
Chimalhuacan Chalco	4	Mixcoac	4
Coatepec	1	Mixquic	2
Coatlichan	1	Naucalpan	2
Coyoacan	3	Otumba	3
Cuauhtitlan	4	Ozumba	2
Cuauhtzingo	1	San Agustín de las Cuevas	3
Cuitlahuac	2	San Angel (San Jacinto)	2
Culhuacan	2	Santa Fe	1
Ecatepec	3	Tacuba	4
Ecatzingo	1	Tacubaya	2
Guadalupe	?	Tecama	2
Huehuetoca	2	Tenango Tepopula	4
Huexotla	2	Teoloyuca	2
Hueypoxtla	2	Teotihuacan	3
Huitzilopochco	1	Tepetlaoztoc	2
Huizquilucan	2	Tepexpan	2
Ixtacalco	3	Tepozotlan	3
Ixtapalapa	3	Tequixquiac	2
Ixtapaluca	2	Texcoco (Franciscan)	?
Mexicalzingo	4	Tezontepec	2
Mexico City		Tizayuca	2
Sagrario de la Catedral	8	Tlalmanalco	2
Salto del Agua	1	Tlalnepantla	5
San Antonio de las Huertas	2	Toltitlan	3
San José	2	Xaltocan (with Xaltenco)	2
San Miguel	6	Xochimilco	7
San Pablo	4	Xochitepec	2
San Sebastián	4	Zumpango	2

SOURCE: "Noticias de Nueva-España en 1804," pp. 9–16. The list for the Valley correlates with the list given in Navarro y Noriega, *Catálogo de los curatos*, pp. 13–19, save that the latter gives Xaltenco instead of Xaltocan. The parroquia center was moved from Xaltocan to Xaltenco ca. 1740, but the two names clearly refer to the same parish. See Villa-señor y Sánchez, *Theatro americano*, I, 84–85. Several changes from the seventeenth century (see Map 6) will be noted. The list excludes the several thousand non-parochial clergymen, located chiefly in Mexico City. For the statistics on these see Humboldt, *Political Essay*, II, 62–63.

number of clergy in the capital city increased to something over 8,000. This means that only about one cleric in seventy had anything to do with Indians in the late colonial Valley of Mexico.[50]

The Archbishop of Mexico in 1556 argued a direct connection between the small numbers of clergy and the inadequacy of the conversion program. Visitas, he said, were located up to twenty leagues from their cabeceras de doctrina. The more remote communities received clerical attention only twice a year, and they did so under conditions in which only Mass and perfunctory ceremonies of marriage and baptism could be performed. Some writers of the second half of the sixteenth century, on the other hand, took the position that a single ecclesiastic sufficed, even for doctrinas of large population.[51] The differences of opinion resulted from differing criteria concerning an acceptable Christianization program, as well as from factors of rivalry among the several classes of missionaries. Partisan statements, of course, are not reliable sources for relations between clergy and Indians. A more accurate understanding of this subject may be gained from the official instructions issued to ecclesiastics in the latter part of the sixteenth century, and still more from the direct reports by ecclesiastics concerning the performance of their tasks.

The official instructions issued in 1576 to Bernabé López, curate of the doctrina of Tequixquiac in the northern part of the Valley, are a precise listing of ecclesiastical obligations. He was required to learn the Indian language, or languages—in Tequixquiac this meant not only Nahuatl but Otomí—within six months, and to become capable of preaching and hearing confession directly. The instructions further required of him: to preach in each cabecera and church every two weeks; to make a census of the confessors in each sujeto, enumerating the houses, husbands, wives, and children old enough to confess (generally boys of fourteen and over, and girls of twelve and over); to hear confession by sujetos in sequence, with all the confessors in a given sujeto assembling periodically for instruction; to sign a statement on each occasion confirming the confessions; to compile a list of all Indians capable of receiving the Eucharist, to observe their conduct, and to instruct them in this sacrament with care; to examine those about to marry, again with care; to declare and preach the obligations of penance and extreme unction; to record the place names, the baptismal names, and the names of parents and patrons in baptism; to teach the sacrament of confirmation; to adapt the Mass and other ceremonies to the Tridentine missal and the breviary, and to ensure the observance of all proper ceremonies. No ornament or other religious object was to be removed from the church or the sacristy. The curate was not to charge fees (*derechos*) for confession or baptism. His charges for burial and marriage were not to exceed customary usage. Alms (*limosnas*) for Masses and for other purposes were to be recorded, with dates and the names of donors. The curate was himself to make confession each week. No women, and no men outside the immediate family, were to reside in his house. He was to have no more than two horses or mules, and was forbidden to raise colts or dogs, to hunt, or to engage in business, "because of the scandal and bad example to the Indians." Indian fiscales were to be examined in the doctrine. López was not to issue unauthorized orders for Indian labor on the church building or the clerical residence. In the convocation of children for daily lessons, an Indian alguacil was to compel attendance, to keep a record of the pupils, and to report any resistance by the fathers of the pupils. A report was to be made to the curate's superiors regularly every three months.[52]

Statements of 1569 from Tizayuca, Tequixquiac, Tepozotlan, Hueypoxtla, Zumpango, Huitzilopochco, and Huehuetoca record the clergy's own attitudes and actual conduct in this period of evangelism. Each community supported one curate and together the seven ministered to some 21,000 Indian families. They stated that they celebrated Mass in their cabeceras de doctrina on Sundays and festival days, while on week days they traveled to the visitas, providing Mass and sacraments where necessary. In some visitas Mass was said once a year on the titular day. The curate of Tizayuca indicated that he needed another minister in these tasks, for one alone could not accomplish what was required, and the curate of Tepozotlan stated that the houses were too far away for proper visitation of the sick. The seven curates preached in Nahuatl on the main festival days, heard confessions on special days, and recorded the names of confessors so that delinquents might be identified. Confession was required once or twice each year, and Indians who failed to confess were punished. The curates gave instruction to betrothed couples and inquired in each case if the marriage were being undertaken voluntarily or under compulsion. They kept marriage and baptismal books, confessed the sick, and administered the Eucharist. They pronounced the Christian doctrine according to the text of Alonso de Molina or its equivalent, and they did this through Indian spokesmen in the courtyards of the churches, with responses by the congregation. By these means the Pater Noster, Ave Maria, Creed,

Salve Regina, Articles of Faith, Commandments, Seven Mortal Sins, General Confession, and other elements of doctrine were taught. In Zumpango and Huehuetoca, instruction in Christian doctrine was given in three languages—Nahuatl, Otomi, and Latin. Indians offered alms, the curates said, for candles and for church ornaments. Certain Indians were deputized to ensure attendance at Mass, and persons who failed to attend were punished. The Otomi were reported to be less perfectly instructed than the Nahuatl-speaking Indians, partly because their dwellings were scattered through the hills and partly because they resisted Christian teaching. In the words of the curate of Huehuetoca, they were "excessively brutish," and he recommended that they be compelled with all necessary force to adopt Christianity. With respect to social conduct, the ministers spoke feelingly of their difficulties in controlling drunkenness, concubinage, and truancy. They commented on the evil example of the Indian leaders of the towns, who inflicted heavy punishments and levied derramas. They complained that town moneys were spent in drink and in festivals, and that no funds remained for the church. The curate of Tequixquiac explained that he had not dared to speak out against native witchcraft and sorcery because if he were to do so the Indians would refuse to provide him with food. He could not live, he stated, on his salary alone. The curate of Huitzilopochco felt that he was unable to prevent the Indian ceremonies and amusements and debaucheries, "because these are very ancient practices among them."[53]

The reports, as would be expected, express differences in personality among the writers and varying degrees of satisfaction with the Christianization program. They give special stress to sacramental performance and make it clear that the ministers were not uniformly able to perform all the obligations outlined in their instructions. As would likewise be expected, they are silent on the subject of clerical immorality (although other sixteenth-century documents speak candidly on this subject)[54] and on the business operations so precisely forbidden them. All the writers found themselves compelled to overlook immorality on the part of the Indians, and the remarks on witchcraft in Tequixquiac are suggestive of an implicit agreement between the curate and his parishioners: that they would continue to provide him with rations, while he would overlook their lapses into superstition. Notable throughout is the concentration upon the Nahuatl-speaking population and the sense of frustration in dealing with the Otomi.

Finally, the reports take for granted the necessity of punishing delinquents and the use of compulsion.

Punishment and force played a larger role in Mexican conversion than is customarily recognized. As early as the 1530's the church executed an Indian idolator from Texcoco, condemned another to lifetime imprisonment in Spain, and tortured a third with water and the garrote. The church sentenced an Indian bigamist to local imprisonment, and sent Indians guilty of concubinage into exile and service in the monasteries.[55] More common than these cases, which are reported in the records of the early Inquisition, were the routine beatings and imprisonments in the doctrinas. The Franciscans in Tlatelolco in the sixteenth century heard the civil and criminal cases of Indians, punished culprits, and sentenced them to a local Franciscan jail.[56] In the procedures of convocation in the doctrinas, Indians were assembled and counted and the absentees were later whipped.[57]

Clerical punishment of Indians soon came under attack, not because punishment was thought to be unnecessary but because the clergy were thought to be intruding upon the prerogatives of royal authority.[58] Franciscans justified their conduct in the assertion that Indians "want to be disciplined," that native mentality was equivalent to that of children of ten or twelve years, and that the punishments were administered, in most cases, not by the friars themselves but by Indian alguaciles.[59] Church jails, forbidden by royal order in the sixteenth century, were still in evidence in some doctrinas in the late seventeenth century.[60] Indians were still being counted at the churches and given *papeles* or confirmations of attendance in the eighteenth century. Ecclesiastical courts in the eighteenth century continued to celebrate *autos de fe,* in punishment of Indian sorcerers and bigamists.[61] But the infliction of punishment by parochial clerics gradually fell into abeyance. The curate of Cuauhtitlan in 1780 boasted that in his entire thirty years of professional life he had never ordered the beating of a single Indian.[62] And when a curate in Ixtapalapa in 1780 demanded the public whipping of an Indian who had failed to produce his "papel," the result was a legal accusation. Indian witnesses testified on this occasion that the curate habitually lived in Mexico City during the week, that he appeared in Ixtapalapa only on Saturday nights, and that he departed again following Mass on Sunday. The accused Indian testified to having attended Mass in another town, explaining that the curate had not appeared in Ixtapalapa before noon on Sunday. The archepiscopal fiscal charged

the curate both with maintaining his residence in the city and with requiring the whipping.[63] The case reveals something about clerical "laxity"
in the eighteenth century, but it also suggests that clerics were no longer
so free to inflict physical punishment on Indians as they had been in the
first fifty years.

One might imagine that the partial abandonment of corporal punishment would have promoted a reconciliation between the Indians and the
friars. This was not the case, however, and other factors must be cited in
explanation. The heart of the matter may in fact lie in the Franciscan
assertion of 1569 that Indians "want to be disciplined," for there is abundant evidence from the early period that native peoples adopted toward
the clergy the same attitudes of respect and fear that they adopted toward
encomenderos and caciques. The clerics everywhere made alliance with
the caciques and depended on the existing authority of Indian leaders,
while opposing the encomenderos. But caciques, encomenderos, and clergymen all lost power after the first generation.[64] In the early 1560's the Franciscan Gerónimo de Mendieta personally inquired of Indians about their
response to Christianity and recorded their answer in this way: "Before
Christianity no one acted according to his own will. Instead everyone did
what was ordered. Now we have great freedom and it is bad for us because
we are not forced to hold anyone in fear or respect."[65] There was, in other
words, an Indian point of view according to which the church of the
1560's was exerting not too much but rather too little force. In terms of
their own traditions, Indians under Christianity were living a life deficient
in controls.

This attitude pertained also to labor. Given the nature of Indian society,
the essential administration of any labor enterprise was in the cacique's
hands, and in the early campaigns of church-building, the crucial step for
the missionaries was to enlist the cooperation of the caciques. When the
caciques' powers failed, there appeared that "great freedom" to which Indians were unaccustomed. As the native sanction for labor declined, then,
Spaniards created their own organization of compulsory work to take its
place, and Spaniards quite naturally saw the process as a change from free
to forced labor. Indians simultaneously saw a transition from an ordered
to a disorderly or free state. The last major "donation" of a cacique's
laborers—a grant of 3,000 workers over a period of three months by Antonio
Cortés, cacique of Tacuba, for the Jesuit church in the city—occurred in

the 1570's.[66] But for a long time before this the church had been receiving workers in the system of forced labor imposed by Spaniards.

Forced labor for religious purposes developed in the 1530's and 1540's through various devices that bear a close relation to encomienda and to the early labor organizations in Mexico City. When an encomienda became vacant its tributes and labor services reverted to the crown, as we have seen, and royal authority was then free to transfer these to other recipients. The crown might do this by a second formal encomienda grant, or by a short-term assignment for specific purposes. The evidence of the 1530's and 1540's is not wholly clear, but it would appear that workers from Texcoco were temporarily assigned in this way to the Augustinians after the removal of Texcoco from Cortés's holdings, and that tribute, probably including or implying labor, was similarly required for the Dominicans from Chalco province.[67] We know of no actual encomienda grant of Valley Indians to any ecclesiastic or to any church institution, and in any case such grants were forbidden by the New Laws of 1542. In the labor repartimiento drafts of the sixteenth century and after, however, Indians were required to work at tasks outside of encomienda and the employers were required to pay them a wage. In this procedure not only were Indians assigned to ecclesiastical construction work but the church was issued funds with which to make the wage payments. By the 1560's Indians from various towns of the Valley were being required to work on the Cathedral and on the churches of the Augustinians and Dominicans in Mexico City. Dominicans and Augustinians each received from the royal treasury 12,000 pesos per year in the late 1560's, and the Franciscans, who stated that they were receiving nothing, found themselves at a competitive disadvantage. But the record demonstrates conclusively that the Franciscans were in fact receiving labor drafts for the monastery of San Francisco in Mexico City by 1564.[68] In the 1570's the organization for compulsory labor service in the city was providing workers for a large number of ecclesiastical institutions, including the Cathedral, the Inquisition buildings, La Concepción, Santa Clara, La Veracruz, Nuestra Señora de Guadalupe, San Antón, Santa Catalina, and the three Mendicant monasteries of San Francisco, San Agustín, and Santo Domingo.[69] Since Tacuba was already giving 300 workers per week in the 1560's for ecclesiastical service in the city, the "donation" by the Tacuba cacique in the early 1570's may have involved only the transfer of these workers to a new task.[70]

In summary, Indian labor for the construction of church buildings and
clerical residences depended on the asserted power of caciques ("voluntary") or on organized labor drafts ("forced"), and the latter were, in some
degree, a consequence of the weakening of the caciques' control. On the
other hand, the loss of authority by caciques might signify, in its initial
stages, only the failure of a cabecera to control effectively the labor of its
sujetos. The integral communality of cabeceras and sujetos declined somewhat, but in the sujetos a sense of native loyalty might linger. While the system of labor drafts developed as a means of recruiting workers for ecclesiastical construction in the cabeceras de doctrina and for the building of monasteries and churches in Mexico City, no such Spanish controls were required for construction in other towns or in the barrios and estancias. All
sujetos were liable to the Spanish labor draft, but within them local
churches continued to be built by traditional native labor organizations.

Such local churches were called *hermitas* or *iglesias de visita*. They were
small and unpretentious in comparison with the churches of the cabeceras
de doctrina, but they reflected rather more—most notably after the development of Spanish systems of forced labor—the sense of communal identity
to which we have referred. Deficiencies and delays in the provision of royal
funds might slow the campaigns for building monasteries, but church
construction in the sujetos was independent of royal funds and could proceed at times when work in the cabeceras de doctrina came to a halt. The
iglesias de visita, like all the early ecclesiastical constructions, were dependent upon Indian provision of materials and donation of labor.[71] After the
early years the iglesia de visita, rather more than the monastery and church
of a cabecera de doctrina, fitted the Indian conception of labor, for the iglesia
de visita was an Indian-directed enterprise, it never involved excessive
exertion or time, and it contributed to the honor of a community and of
its saint at the most local level.

The fullest construction record for an iglesia de visita in the Valley
occurs in documents of San Juan Ixhuatepec, north of Guadalupe. Here
the first building was erected in 1539. Indians assembled to plan the construction voluntarily, according to the native report, and "with enthusiasm."
All agreed upon San Juan Bautista as patron. The small, straw-covered
building (*jacal*) was built rapidly, and the community offered a donation to the curate for its benediction. The curate urged all Indians to attend
church and declined the donation, accepting only "some bread and fowls."

About sixty years later, at the end of the century, a new masonry church was designed. Although the records are not completely clear, the first lime for mortar was apparently purchased by the community about 1598 and some six or seven cartloads of lime were collected before construction began. The first several cartloads were paid for by the Indian government in assessments on the inhabitants; the wife of one of the leading Indians of the town provided another; and three others were donated by civilian Spaniards. Building began in 1603, four or five years after the initial lime purchases. Lime was the most costly item in the budget of this second construction, its price varying over the years from 23 to 35 pesos per cartload, and its total cost, 201 pesos, exceeding the total cost of stone and labor combined. Professional masons, almost certainly Indians, were hired by the community, but it is probable that the unskilled labor was provided free by the inhabitants. The church was completed in 1616, at a cost of 347 pesos. Both campaigns of building were Indian enterprises, planned and executed by officers of the community. The Spanish donors, in the second instance, were presumably local residents performing acts of charity. The two campaigns differ in the degree to which a small Indian town became involved in the developing colonial economy of wages and prices. But the sense of communality pervades both accounts, and we reckon here with Indian labor undertaken for Christian purposes and not subject to Spanish rules. It is clear that this communal aspect of Christianity, to which Indians were already accustomed, remained active long after the personal estrangement of Indians and the clergy.[72]

Differences among the types of labor performed for the church are thus explained not only by differing requirements but also by Indian attitudes toward work. Labor demands by caciques were familiar to the native society, but they could not continue long under colonial conditions. Labor on the iglesias de visita might still be accommodated within the institutions of service to communities in the late sixteenth and early seventeenth centuries. Through the whole colonial period, moreover, Indians served the ecclesiastical institutions as gardeners, janitors, cooks, sacristans, carriers, acolytes, and musicians.[73] Their willingness to do so may in part have been the result of the sixteenth-century rule that service in the churches exempted individuals from tribute liabilities.[74] An additional explanation lies in the local prestige and perquisites that such service entailed. (Even the sweeping of the temples had been an honorific assignment in pre-conquest society, reserved for sons of the upper class.)[75] But unprecedented or extreme demands[76] could elicit no such response, with the result that the church received both forced and voluntary labor.

Questions of voluntary and coerced donation also arise in the history of Indian payments to the church. Here, in the early period, supplies were provided in the form of gratuities upon which the church in no sense depended. Later changes added new revenues and required that the ecclesiastical institutions be supported by the communities. The over-all transition was toward compulsion. The matter may be traced in the history of clerical salaries, tithes, fees, lands, and *cofradías*.

As crown officials under monarchical patronage, members of the clergy received their salaries either from the royal treasury or from funds that would otherwise have been paid to the royal treasury. In encomienda towns clerical salaries were supplied by the encomenderos. In crown towns they were supplied from royal funds. Where a doctrina included both crown Indians and encomienda Indians the solution was an exact or approximate pro rata division.[77] Encomenderos were additionally liable for oil and wine, and sometimes for a portion of the costs of church construction. In the sixteenth century the crown undertook to establish an annual encomendero's responsibility at one hundred pesos and fifty *fanegas* of maize (or its equivalent in money) for each cleric, and though some clerics received more than this and some less, these represented an approximate average.[78] With the progressive escheatment of encomiendas, payments by the crown in the seventeenth and eighteenth centuries were generally to the exact amount, one hundred pesos and fifty fanegas of maize, but with the maize now commuted to money at the standard rate of nine reales per fanega.[79] With all this it could plausibly be argued that because Indians paid tributes to encomenderos or to the crown, and because these in turn paid clerical salaries, the real costs devolved from the first upon the native peoples. As population declined tribute amounts likewise declined, and the ratio between the clergy's share and the crown's or encomenderos' share changed markedly. In the seventeenth century Indian tribute in Cuitlahuac fell to the point at which the one hundred pesos and fifty fanegas of maize received by the friar exceeded the amount that remained for the encomendero.[80] In Hueypoxtla in the early seventeenth century the encomendero reported that he had to operate under a deficit, for tribute income from the Indians of the encomienda was not sufficient to allow him to support the clergy.[81]

From the beginning proposals had been made for more direct kinds of Indian payment to the church. From the 1530's through the 1550's, the issue concerned liability to the *diezmo* or tithe, a tax of ten per cent on income or commodity increase, which would have supported the clergy and paid the costs of church-building and other expenses. Much discussion centered on the propriety, justice, and feasibility of Indian tithing, with the regular clergy in general opposing it and the secular clergy supporting it. One argument against it was that Indians were already building and repairing churches, providing ornaments, supplying the clergy with sustenance, and doing everything else that would justify a tithe.[82] Indians repeatedly insisted that they should not be tithed, and a legal hearing on the matter took place in 1558 with the archbishop on one side and Indian witnesses on the other.[83] The decision reached at that time was that Indians were not to pay tithes on native goods and native properties, but that they were liable in transactions involving either Spanish goods, such as cattle, wheat, and silk, or lands that had formerly belonged to Spaniards.[84]

In the 1530's and 1540's, however, the crown had decreed a substitute procedure that in effect accomplished the objective of a full Indian tithe. By this rule native peoples were to pay no tithe as such, but their normal tributes to encomenderos or to the crown were to be raised by the amount necessary to provide the clergy with food and other necessities, and to pay for the oil, candles, and similar goods that might be required. The king cautioned specifically that Indians were not to be informed of the true intent of this rule.[85] It was not immediately acted upon, but the procedures outlined did come to be established and they involved expenditures over and above any other tithe liabilities to which Indians might be subject. Additional Indian support of the clergy during ecclesiastical tours was sanctioned both by the religious council and by secular tribute rules from the 1550's on.[86] Regulations of the 1560's raised the tribute payments further and set aside a portion of community funds as tribute residues (*sobras de tributos*) in the local treasuries, from which community and ecclesiastical expenses, though not clerical salaries, were to be met.[87] Occasionally, segments of particular tributes were granted to the church for the payment of building costs.[88]

Clerical abuse of these financial privileges received immediate and unfavorable notice.[89] Payments to the church through community treasuries allowed a far more systematic financial relationship between Indians and the clergy than had previously been possible. The archbishop of Mexico stated in 1556 that the *cajas de comunidad* were already being exploited and that friars were taking funds from them with impunity.[90] Records of town finance demonstrate that community treasuries were in fact used principally for fiestas and other religious purposes from this time on.[91]

But the clergy did not depend upon these sources alone. If community funds were insufficient, it was possible for unscrupulous friars to exact derramas after the manner of the corregidores, to demand extra amounts for sustenance during visitations, or to charge the communities inflated costs for small tasks. Tithes could be levied not only on sheep, pigs, wheat, and other Spanish commodities but also on Indian goods.[92] Tithes already paid, or commuted and included in other payments, were often demanded again, so that the Indians paid twice the legal amount. As in corregimiento, local prerogatives became customary. An Indian official might be required to collect money from the parishioners to pay for maintaining the curate's horses or for other purposes "in accordance with long-standing custom among the Indians."[93] Cases were reported in which ecclesiastics collected tithes in kind from Indians and sold the goods back to them.[94] It was the custom everywhere that the Indian communities supplied food to the clergy quite apart from the cajas de comunidad or the tithe or any other payment.[95] Though less openly than corregidores, ecclesiastics conducted business operations, raised horses, mules, and pigs, and engaged in commercial dealings involving wine, native mantles, chickens, wheat, and maize. An oidor reported in 1584 that he knew of Indians with fifteen or twenty pairs of shoes, bought from clergymen under compulsion and never worn. Some clerics are known to have made fortunes by these means and to have returned to Spain, after the manner of civilian opportunists.[96]

Direct payments to the church occurred also in the form of the alms or charitable contributions called limosnas, and wealthy Indians are known to have given huge amounts in the early period. Private donations of three, four, six, and seven thousand pesos are recorded. Contributions from native society paid for the great Capilla de San José, attached to the Franciscan monastery in Tenochtitlan. Isabel Montezuma, the Indian encomendero of Tacuba, gave so prodigally in the post-conquest period that the Augustinian beneficiaries felt obliged to ask her to desist. The Franciscans announced that they had not received the regular payment of one hundred pesos and fifty fanegas of maize from the crown and the encomenderos as had the other orders, and that the abundance of Indian contributions made these unnecessary.[97]

Some of this donation to the church undoubtedly represented a continuation of pagan practices transferred to the Christian organization. The large bequests by Isabel Montezuma and others appear to have been wholly voluntary. But the church came increasingly to enforce payments from its native parishioners and to budget its finances upon a predictable income from this source. Many such payments, though still frequently classified as alms, were understood to be in recompense for specific clerical services. The ecclesiastical council of 1555 had ruled that clergy were not to charge fees for performing sacraments, and that all payments were to be "voluntary." But at this time curates were already charging more than the amounts specified for their support.[98] It will be recalled that the instructions for secular clergy in the 1570's forbade fees for confession and baptism but allowed fees at a customary rate for burial and marriage.[99] The curate of San Pablo in Tenochtitlan in 1570 received in lieu of any formal salary a donation of one peso in limosna per week from his Indian parishioners and another peso from his Spanish parishioners, to make a total of 104 pesos per year. His income was supplemented by fees received for Masses and by some 30 pesos per year for burials.[100] Though orders continued to be issued in the late sixteenth century forbidding the charging of money or goods for sacraments, the demands for such fees did not diminish.[101] The compulsory aspect of limosna payment was fully established by the early seventeenth century.

Payments for services performed by the clergy came in the seventeenth and eighteenth centuries to be specified in what were called *aranceles,* published statements designating fixed or maximum prices to be charged. The payments themselves, in a terminology that abandoned any pretense of volition on the part of the donor, were called obventions (*obvenciones*) or "derechos parroquiales."[102] Price lists and local customs varied. Native peoples under Jesuit jurisdiction in Tepozotlan in the seventeenth century stated that they were being charged nothing at all for baptisms, marriages, burials, or fiestas.[103] Elsewhere regulations specified six reales for a marriage, with additional payments for separable parts of the ceremony such as banns and veiling, in amounts up to twenty-four reales. Charges for burials varied with the status of the dead person (*persona grande* or *persona pequeña*), the costs ranging from three to twelve reales. Prices generally increased in the eighteenth century. Aranceles of late colonial times allowed forty reales plus an offering (*ofrenda*) and up to sixty-four reales for marriage and veiling, and from five to fifty-six reales for a burial. Baptisms were commonly priced at four reales. Sung Masses ranged from sixteen to eighty reales, and sermons might cost thirty-two reales.[104] The Franciscans in Tlatelolco in 1749 asserted that no native parishioner there had ever been required to pay for confession, clearly implying that the same could not be said elsewhere, or, within Tlatelolco itself, for other sacraments.

Moreover, churchmen did not feel obliged to abide by the amounts specified in the aranceles. The rules were expressed in terms that allowed for some individual interpretation, and established customs were allowed to stand in spite of the aranceles.[105] Though particular Masses were paid for by community cajas, in the eighteenth century it came to be the practice in all towns for the Indian gobernador or some other official to call the roll following the weekly service, at which time each Indian parishioner gave his contribution of one or one-half real. These payments, as well as other payments for Masses on Christmas, Easter, and Holy Thursday might still be called limosnas. The terms tlapalole, tlapalolistli, and tlapohualli (presumably the original word, with the meaning of a thing that is counted), were also used.[106] And the "papeles" that were issued to Indians who attended Mass were, in effect, not simply proofs of attendance but also receipts for payment.

Some Indians were property owners in the Spanish sense, but most owned no land outright and could not legally grant or bequeath their usufruct titles to the church. Native wills typically mention only small tracts of land or specify the rental or liquidation of some minor property so that money might be bequeathed for Masses.[107] Yet the total accumulation, as is well known, made the church the largest corporate landowner in the colony. All church-held land had originally belonged to Indians, but it is by no means true that all was received in the form of Indian bequests. Clergymen, like others, did sometimes seize Indian lands.[108] But far more often civilian colonists were the intermediaries, acquiring native land in various ways, and later, often generations later, leaving or selling it to the church. It should be noted that the church as a single unit did not own the land; instead, separate properties were held by individual orders or religious institutions. Thus in the seventeenth century the Dominican colegio in Mexico City derived an income from its own haciendas near Azcapotzalco. The sanctuary of Nuestra Señora de Guadalupe was the owner of the Hacienda de Las Salinas and various ranchos near Teotihuacan and Otumba in the later colonial period, and its clergy disputed with the neighboring Indian communities over property ownership just as did the non-clerical hacendados.[109] The institutions of the Jesuit order, by various means, became the principal ecclesiastical landholders. It is not true, as has sometimes been stated, that the Franciscans owned no land.[110] The accusation often made against the clergy that Indians were forced to bequeath lands to the church remains unverified in the known instances of bequest in the Valley of Mexico.[111]

The church of the late colonial period was a complex and wealthy institution. Its individual doctrinas received incomes from land rents, mortgages, sodalities, charitable organizations, and other funds and investments, in addition to the regular contributions by parishioners.[112] For the most part, such income falls outside the limits of this study. Of the several financial institutions mentioned, only one, the sodality or parishioners' association (cofradía), was to an appreciable extent a part of Indian life.

The cofradía represents, for the most part, a delayed Indian response to Christianity. It was not a product of the early period of missionary activity. Although some Indian cofradías were founded in the sixteenth century,[113] the years of greatest vigor were those after 1600. By the late seventeenth century several hundred were in existence in the Valley, and the evidence suggests that at least in some towns all or nearly all the community inhabitants were members.[114] In general, the larger towns developed the greater number—the Capilla de San José in Mexico City maintained eight in the late seventeenth century—while small towns might have only one or two. But there was no necessary relation between population size and the number of cofradías. San Gregorio Atlapulco supported six in the late seventeenth century, but Teotihuacan, three times its size, had only two, one of them restricted to white colonists.[115]

Cofradías offered their members a spiritual security and a sense of collective identity otherwise lacking in seventeenth-century native life. Though they were of enormous material benefit to the church and to the clergy, compulsion alone is insufficient to explain their growth.[116] The cofradía was an enduring institution outliving its members, and this fact may have instilled a sense of stability in a population seriously reduced in numbers and undergoing hardship of many kinds. Racism and distrust of the Spanish population were also attitudes relevant to the Indian cofradías, which were normally, though not always, separate institutions from cofradías for whites, with distinct organization and ceremonies.[117] In some cofradías members were guaranteed an "Indian" burial. As the patent of the Cofradía de la Purísima Concepción de Nuestra Señora in Cuauhtitlan stated, "it is agreed that this burial will be with Indians only and not with Spaniards, Negroes, mestizos, mulattoes, or chinos."[118]

The cofradías were of various sizes and degrees of complexity. An example of the relatively simple organization is the Cofradía de la Veracruz in Xochimilco, which, during the seventeenth century, confined itself to the support of one sung Mass per month, at a cost of three pesos. This was its sole function. Its record is a week-by-week notation of receipts and expenses surrounding the monthly Mass. Expenses for Masses varied hardly at all. Income was received in *cacao* beans, reales, and half-reales provided by the members. In 1610, in an average month, the cofradía received 680 cacao beans and eight and one-half reales in money. This income was paid to the Franciscans of Xochimilco, who accepted cacao beans at a ratio of approximately 400 per peso, with slightly changing rates of exchange from time to time. The Franciscan guardian or his delegated agent in the monastery sometimes issued receipts for payments and sometimes failed to do so. Ecclesiastical visitadores from Mexico City occasionally audited the cofradía's books, criticizing its Nahuatl keeping of records and its confused listing of income and expense. The criticism had no appreciable effect during the seventeenth century. For long periods the cofradía recorded no surpluses, but only a regular income of approximately three pesos per month and a regular expense of the same amount. Payments for Masses sometimes fell into arrears but were always made up again. The cofradía in the late seventeenth century had lost the documentary title of its own foundation. It served by custom as a collecting agency to finance the twelve sung Masses per year, and one may suppose that this was characteristic of Xochimilco, for its financial books are parallel in every significant way to those of its sister organization, the Cofradía de la Soledad, during the same period.[119]

The records of the Cofradía del Santísimo Cristo de Burgos in Culhuacan during the 1770's illustrate the operation of a later and more complex cofradía. Here members paid to the mayordomo or his subordinates two reales on admission, one real per month, six reales on the Feast of the Ascension (the *fiesta titular* or titular holy day of the town), and one real in November for All Souls' Day—a total of nineteen reales per year, slightly higher than the average amount paid in royal tribute. The largest item of cofradía expense was the payment made for about forty-five Masses per year, for the souls of dead members, at three and a half pesos per Mass. The regular monthly Masses supported by this cofradía were less expensive, costing only one peso apiece. Celebrations for holy days cost about twenty-seven pesos per year. The fiesta titular required a contribution of about fifteen pesos. Over a two-year period in 1770–72 the cofradía was obligated by the terms of its patent to spend 412 pesos. In addition, it made irregular payments to the curate of approximately 130 pesos per year, an amount that fell far short of the obligation agreed upon at the time of the cofradía's establishment. At the conclusion of one such period in the 1770's, the cofradía remained in debt to the curate in the amount of some 350 pesos, and in this desperate condition the cofradía's Indian officials ordered the printing of new patents requiring each member to pay two reales instead of the customary one real a month. The intention was denounced as fraudulent by Spanish authorities, for most members were unable to read the patents.[120]

The costs of membership in the Culhuacan cofradía were much higher than in Xochimilco, but the compensating rewards were superior. These included monthly Masses at the cofradía altar for the members, living and dead; several special Masses throughout the year to the same effect; payments for shrouds, coffins, Masses, vigils, and burials in the cofradía chapel on the death of members; and extra payments in case of death outside the town. It was well known to the members, furthermore, that by the terms of their association and by concession of Pope Innocent XI (1676–89) plenary indulgence was granted on the day of a communicant's entrance into this cofradía and again on the day of his death. Members in good standing were therefore spared expiation in purgatory. The cofradía, in other words, was an elaborate organization of ecclesiastical insurance, maintained by regular premiums, covering Masses and remissions of punishment resulting from sin, and contributing twelve and one-half pesos to the largest single expense that many Indians ever incurred, that of a Christian funeral. The organization was economically severe; if payments were not maintained the benefits did not accrue. The regulations specified that indebtedness to the cofradía at the time of death disqualified a member from the funeral privileges.[121]

Of equal interest are the unofficial cofradías, which derived their income not from the contributions of Indian members but from agricultural lands. Five institutions of Chimalhuacan Atenco in the eighteenth century were of this type. Their names, each referring to one of the images of the church, were La Asumpción, Santa María Magdalena, Nuestra Señora de Guadalupe, San Gregorio, and Santo Ecce Homo. Each cultivated about ten acres of land. Each was administered by an Indian mayordomo who directed the cultivation and the finances. The lands were "saints' lands" and they were understood to belong to the images of the saints. The images in this conception were not inanimate representations but the actual possessors. An Indian could refer, without sensing any peculiarity in the idea, to "the lands held by the holy images that are within the church."[122]

All five institutions in Chimalhuacan Atenco operated on a small scale. None spent more than 100 pesos annually, the customary limit being sixty or seventy pesos. The mayordomos raised maize and maguey, sold the produce, and spent the proceeds on celebrations for the saints. Expenses, fixed by custom and agreement, varied hardly at all from year to year. Income depended on the agricultural year and the market price of the produce. Losses always had to be made up from the private funds of the mayordomos, whose records are repeatedly annotated, in years of poor harvest, with the statement "paid by me from my own pocket." Expenses were for seed, plowing, hired labor, fiestas, Spanish candle wax, flowers, fireworks, gunpowder (for fiestas), and soap (for cleaning the church ornaments). Income was from the sale of maize, pulque, and hay, and occasionally from the rental of a portion of the saints' lands. In good years the cofradías earned profits of ten to twenty pesos. In exceptionally poor years a mayordomo might spend thirty or forty pesos to meet the fixed expenses.[123] The precise origin of the cofradías or saints' lands in Chimalhuacan Atenco is obscure, but evidence from other towns indicates that such lands might have been former private Indian properties bequeathed to the saints in testamentary donations, or common lands granted by the Indian government or by the community as a whole.[124] The mayordomos of saints' lands were not salaried officials of the towns. It is probable that they were rewarded only by their dedication to an honorable task and by the prestige that this dedication earned them in the community.

The five cofradías of Chimalhuacan Atenco did not require a formal membership or an official association of communicants. Hence, although they were known in Chimalhuacan as cofradías and brotherhoods (hermandades), these terms are not in a strict sense to be applied to them. Despite the absence of salaries, their operation lies as close to municipal finance as to normal cofradía business, a fact made clear by the techniques employed in other eighteenth-century towns to finance Masses and to maintain the faith.

In eighteenth-century Huitzilopochco, for instance, the income from particular lands was devoted directly to ecclesiastical purposes. An area of about thirty acres supported the fiesta titular; another poorer tract of four or five acres supported six lesser fiestas throughout the year; and a small pasture supported a weekly Mass in a capilla outside the town. Seven other segments of about twenty-five acres in all supported Masses for various saints on the appropriate days. The lands devoted to fiesta expenses were common or community land, "possessed" however by the Indian governor of the town with the obligation of financing the designated ceremonies. The pasture and some of the other lands for Masses were regarded as possessions of the resident curate, and it is worth noting that the Masses that these were intended to support were no longer provided in the later eighteenth century. Most of the tracts dedicated to saints were understood to be the possessions of particular Indians who, for the privilege of working and profiting from them, were obliged to contribute the specified amounts for the Masses. In some cases the Indian possessors were called mayordomos; in others the lands were "inherited from ancestors" as were other sections of common land that Indians cultivated.[125]

It has occasionally been suggested that in their origin or essential meaning cofradías may have been guilds designed to protect and unify groups of native craftsmen. The conception is supported by the religious and economic calpulli institutions of the Aztec pre-conquest period and by certain craft guilds that had patron saints, religious insignia, and even full cofradías in Spanish society. Cofradías supported by groups of Indian craftsmen did appear in Mexico City in the later colonial period,[126] and a quasi-cofradía institution developed among the thousands of tobacco workers, mostly Indians and mestizos, in the city in the late eighteenth century. One-half real per week was deducted from each tobacco worker's pay to provide a fund used for burials, hospital expenses, clothing, and charitable gifts for widows in the organization.[127] But these late urban institutions had little if any connection with pre-conquest practices, and records of the earlier Indian cofradías in the towns fail to indicate any craft functions of this type.

Much more plausible is an explanation of the cofradía that takes into account its communal function, its utility for nonspecialized Indian populations and for the church, and its development in the late sixteenth and seven-

teenth centuries. To Indians, the cofradía appeared as an institution acceptable to whites, but non-white and in some measure anti-white.[128] To the
clergy, the Indian cofradía was a means of ensuring a steady church income
from a reduced population. Especially interesting is the close connection
between the finances of Indian governments in the towns, with their cajas
de comunidad based on tribute, and the finances of the cofradías, with their
funds based on the monthly payments by members. The expenses of town
treasuries and the expenses of cofradías have many points of similarity in
the seventeenth and eighteenth centuries, for both included payments to
the clergy, support of particular ecclesiastical functions, and provision for
church ceremonies. The cajas de comunidad and the cofradías thus divided
between them the Indian obligation to underwrite the church. It is probable
that cofradías developed when they did at least partly because the secular
town treasuries had then become unable to provide, without assistance, the
funds that the church required. To a Christianized or partially Christianized Indian population, the cofradía offered a communal organization at
a time when the traditional communities, the pueblos, were suffering huge
population losses and were under attack from Spaniards. Hence the rise of
the cofradías may be regarded in some measure as a response or alternative
to the decline of the towns.

This interpretation of the cofradía may be supported by a consideration
of other institutions of Indian Christianity possessing some or all of these
same traits. One was the fiesta, financed by both the community and the cofradía, in which each community celebrated the day of its titular saint and
other holy days of the Christian calendar. Fiestas were occasions for public
ceremony, with church services, processions, food and drink, dances, floral
decorations, fireworks, costumes, and music. They combined elements of
Christian observance with traditional forms of Indian ritual, and in numerous ways they reconciled the Spanish Christian and the Indian pagan
worlds. On the side of Christianity were the specific calendar holidays and
the Christian worship that attended them. On the Indian side were the
costumes and dances and masks, the public displays, and the sense of special
participation in collective functions. The sixteenth-century missionary
Pedro de Gante described the way in which he had deliberately fostered
this fusion in the early period. Having observed the singing and dancing of
Indians in pagan worship, he composed a Christian song and drew new

patterns for the mantles to be used in a Christian dance. "In this way," he said, "the Indians first came to show obedience to the church."[129]

The clergy naturally opposed the drunkenness and the license occasioned by fiestas and were especially outspoken against the Indian town officers whose conduct set a "wrong example" for the community. But it is likely that the clergy never truly understood the custom that had for so long sanctioned periodic collective Indian orgies.[130] Nor did colonial Spaniards understand the interpretation of the fiesta that commends itself to the social thinking of the twentieth century: that it was a communal release and act of self-protection, a propitiation of supernatural forces, and a demonstration of the community's being. The festival community, as it were, expressed itself in excess by breaking its normal rules of behavior.[131]

A second institution similar to the cofradía was the local cult that surrounded a community's patron saint or the relics of one of its early missionaries. In the Valley of Mexico one might compile a lengthy catalogue of saints possessing mysterious powers and of images known to have bled, moved, perspired, or wept.[132] The principal cults relating to remains of early missionaries were those honoring Martín de Valencia at Tlalmanalco and Amecameca,[133] and Domingo de Betanzos at Tepetlaoztoc.[134] The foremost of all colonial cults, as is well known, was that of the Virgin of Guadalupe at Tepeyacac, which had been a pre-conquest sanctuary and pilgrimage center.[135] The legendary date of the Virgin's first apparition, 1531, remains a matter of dispute.[136] But unquestionably by the 1550's an incipient Indian ceremonial had come into existence surrounding the Virgin's miraculous powers and cures.[137] Clerical efforts to arrest the growth of the cult, on the grounds that an image painted by an Indian was being represented as miraculous,[138] were uniformly unsuccessful, and Spanish society came to be reconciled to it. But the Guadalupe cult was essentially an Indian phenomenon, in some ways rivaling the Spanish patronage of the Virgin of Los Remedios.[139] Its fiesta in the seventeenth and eighteenth centuries, as in modern times, was the greatest Indian religious event in all Mexico.[140]

Saints' images, religious paintings, and objects of devotion played an important role in Indian lives. One has only to read the wills of upper-class Indian of all periods to appreciate the enormous number of such objects that they owned and valued.[141] But it is important to distinguish a private from a public devotion. The image that each community venerated was an embodiment of the inner meaning of the town. The Spanish conception of the patron saint was enthusiastically adopted by the Indian communities, and in town records a contrived antiquity for the local church may sometimes be found, as if reputation and status depended upon an early date for a church and Christianization.[142] In Santiago Tlatelolco the image of Santiago mounted on a horse and carrying a sword was borne in procession as "conquistador and auxiliary" of the town; and when the town suffered a calamity, as in the plague of 1737, Santiago was dressed as a penitent with a crown of thorns and a penitential whip (*disciplina*) in place of his sword.[143] In this way the image was made to respond in Christian fashion to the town's misfortunes. But the pagan attitude might survive intact. When the curate of Huitzilopochco in the eighteenth century took stone from a ruined temple platform to the north of the town in order to make repairs on the church, the Indian community protested the act as a desecration. The community boldly informed the curate that "in that spot lies all the strength (*fuerza*) of the town."[144] Again, when the curate of Cuauhtitlan undertook to make repairs on the image of the Virgin in an Indian chapel in 1785, the result was revolution. Indians charged that the alterations were destructive and that the repaired image differed from the original. The ecclesiastics were threatened with death. The curate fled, and a company of dragoons from the regiment in the capital had to be sent to restore order.[145]

What, finally, did the church accomplish? On the surface it achieved a radical transition from pagan to Christian life. Beneath the surface, in the private lives and covert attitudes and inner convictions of Indians, it touched but did not remold native habits. Our fullest evidence for pre-conquest survivals derives from modern Indian practices rather than from colonial records, for the latter, however informative in individual incidents, are unsystematic for the whole. Modern Indian society, on the other hand, abundantly and consistently demonstrates a pervasive supernaturalism of pagan origin, often in syncretic compromise with Christian doctrine.[146] Although it cannot really be demonstrated, it may be assumed that the pagan components of modern Indian religions have survived in an unbroken tradition to the present day.

But whatever the depth of individual responses to Christianity, it is clear that the Church, in pursuing its own ends, nurtured and preserved communal forms of life among Indians. At point after point, interests of the Indian community were made to coincide with Christianity and were expressed in Christian terms—in finance, in fiestas and cults, in church buildings, in labor, in local histories, in images, in the new names of the towns, in cofradías, and in numerous other ways. Thus viewed, Christianity appears as a cohesive force, not always displacing but repeatedly implementing and abetting Indian preferences for communal organization. It seems probable that the aspects of Christianity contributing to these ends were the more acceptable to Indians for the reason that in so many other ways Spanish colonialism operated to destroy native communality.

CHAPTER VI

The People

Population figures for colonial Mexico suffer from a multitude of statistical defects. We know that the ecclesiastical and tribute counts, from which most of our data are derived, were not always made with the utmost care.[1] Exaggerated losses were sometimes reported so that relief benefits might be increased, or for other purposes. Indians, clergymen, hacendados, and other interested persons were all accused of complicity in preventing accurate enumerations.[2] Accidentally or deliberately, many persons escaped the census lists.[3] Particularly in times of crisis, there was open or surreptitious movement from place to place, and the population changes resulting from such migration become indistinguishable from changes caused by fluctuating birth and death rates.[4] As a whole, the magnitude of the unrecorded population seems unrecoverable, nor is there any sure method for determining whether the later counts were more accurate or less accurate than the earlier ones.[5]

Spaniards offered many explanations for the Indian population losses. Excessive labor requirements, excessive tributes, mistreatment, drunkenness, the Indians' "flaca complexión," starvation, flood, drought, disease, and divine providence were all mentioned in the colonial period as causes.[6] In more recent times the rigors of Spanish treatment and the visitations of disease have seemed to provide the most probable explanations. But the view that Spanish mistreatment of the Indians was primarily responsible for large-scale population decline has now lost much of its earlier acceptance; among all causes, epidemic disease is now recognized as paramount.

A large number of major and minor epidemics afflicted the Valley of Mexico in the colonial period (Appendix IV). The most severe and widespread occurred in the years 1545–48, 1576–81, and 1736–39. But the lesser epidemics were often intensely destructive for limited areas, and in the sixteenth and early seventeenth centuries depopulation continued between epidemics.[7] Infection often spread at the beginning of the dry season, in the late summer and autumn, and abated in the spring.[8] None of the three most serious epidemics has been clinically identified (varieties of smallpox, typhus, typhoid, or measles appear to be the most likely possibilities), and it is probable that none had any pre-conquest analogue.[9] Spanish methods of treatment, consisting in large part of bleeding, added anemia to the other debilitating consequences of disease.[10]

Most population statistics of the sixteenth century are informative for particular communities but incomplete for the Valley as a whole. The Suma de Visitas of the 1540's, an immensely valuable document in other respects, fails to include some important towns. The several Mendicant surveys relate only to the regions ministered by individual orders. The two complementary Ortuño de Ibarra lists, one of crown towns and the other of encomienda towns, are expressed in pesos of tribute income rather than in population units, and while a one-to-one equation between tribute payers and pesos is acceptable for many towns it is by no means so for all of them.[11]

Only López de Velasco, about 1570, undertook to record the tributary population of the whole Valley. Although he rounded the figures to the closest hundred, the correspondence between his and known ecclesiastical records is at times so close as to leave no doubt concerning the sources he used (thus 4,092 and 4,100 for Acolman, 6,472 and 6,500 for Otumba, 3,398 and 3,400 for Cuauhtitlan).[12] No one, of course, could argue that the López de Velasco figures are truly accurate, even as rounded approximations, for the discrepancies between his data and those of still other known ecclesiastical reports are sometimes considerable.[13] Moreover, truancy, migration, and the additional disturbing factors apply as much to his statistics as to others.[14] The 125,000 tributaries that he reported as of about 1570 may be somewhat high (he probably overestimated the Indian population of Mexico City by 10,000 or more), but they compare fairly closely with the results of more complex calculations deriving from different sources, and they imply a total population of about 325,000 or 350,000, counting women and children and all non-tributary classes.[15]

Since López de Velasco's is the first reasonably reliable figure that we have for the entire Valley, the problem becomes one of extrapolating backward to arrive at the figure for 1519. The decline between the conquest and 1570 was estimated by contemporaries at well over one-half. Alonso de Zorita, writing about 1555, stated that the decline had been in excess of two-thirds. Mendieta in 1565 reported a decline of two-thirds or five-sixths. The Indians of Xochimilco in 1563 asserted that population had declined in their province from 30,000 to 6,000 or 7,000.[16] Many further indications of the extent of the first half-century of decline are available, but none is more precise or more plausible than these. If we estimate the population of the Valley at the time of the conquest to have been four or five times that of 1570 we arrive at about 1,500,000, and with present evidence this is as nearly true a figure as we are likely to discover.[17]

The process of decline continued after 1570. The epidemic of 1576–81 accounted for a further loss, probably of over one-quarter.[18] In the late sixteenth and early seventeenth centuries it was common to speak of a total decrease since the conquest of 90 per cent or more.[19] Reports for individual communities indicate local declines, for the whole period, from 8,000 to 300, from 6,000 to 200, and from 4,000 to 150.[20] Many community counts of this time are accessible, the profusion of statistics stemming in large part from revisions of the labor drafts. The revisions were made necessary by, and they amply demonstrate, continuous depopulation. But such sources are incomplete, and they become less frequent as one approaches the mid-seventeenth century. The labor drafts no longer served so consistently as a vehicle for population figures after the early 1620's, and the main drafts were abolished in 1633. The tribute record, which includes payments in a form that may be readily translated into data on tributary population,[21] was so severely damaged in the archival fire in Seville in 1924 that until the surviving papers, scorched and faded, are systematically restored, the collection must be regarded as virtually inaccessible.[22]

Preliminary samplings of the tribute record, together with such additional data as may be brought to bear on the problem, demonstrate a gradual modification in the rate of decline, with the low point occurring in the middle years of the seventeenth century.[23] It should be noted, however, that a figure for a given date may apply to a count made some years previously. In Milpa Alta the low point is recorded for 1670, but the same figure continued to be given in 1682, evidently in the absence of any new count. The sample communities shown in Figure 3—Milpa Alta, Otumba, and the several towns of the Coyoacan jurisdiction[24]—differ not only in

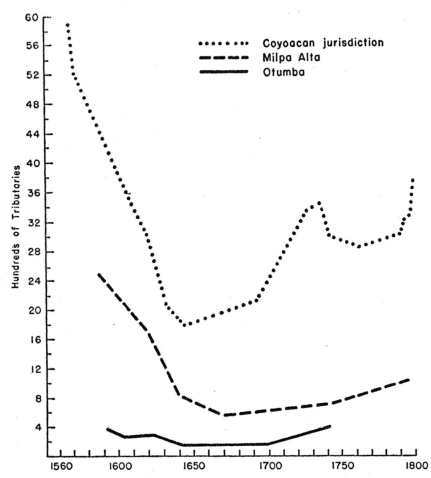

Figure 3. Selected population trends. Population of the Coyoacan jurisdiction, Milpa Alta, and Otumba. Sources: see Appendix VI.

their rates of decline and in their points of lowest population but also in their rates of recovery. Milpa Alta and Otumba show regular increases after the late seventeenth century. The Coyoacan towns show a second decline of shorter duration in the eighteenth century, seemingly the consequence of the epidemic of 1736–41. But the essential feature—decrease in the sixteenth and early seventeenth centuries followed by rise in the late seventeenth and eighteenth centuries—is common to all.

Because of the nature of our evidence, the increasing population of the late colonial period is most satisfactorily examined not by ecclesiastical areas or by separate towns but by political jurisdictions. For the corregimientos a fairly regular series of statistics may be compiled. It is true, as we have seen, that the boundaries of the corregimientos underwent some changes, and these changes render any accurate comparisons impossible. Moreover, figures are lacking altogether at several points in the series, and we do not know whether the absence of data represents an absolute omission or whether these populations were included within those of neighboring jurisdictions. In Table 10 we have regrouped the López de Velasco figures in order to make the ecclesiastical jurisdictions roughly equivalent to the political jurisdictions and thus to provide as continuous a sequence as possible from 1570 to 1800. The procedure cannot be defended as a precise one, but it is probably sufficient to allow for some further calculations of population change by area. Transposing several groups of figures in the form of a graph (Figure 4), we conclude that four southern jurisdictions and three northern ones underwent an equivalent decline until the middle seventeenth century but that the rate of subsequent recovery was substantially more rapid in the south than in the north, especially in the eighteenth century. The difference is probably to be attributed to the decreasing moisture of the northern part of the Valley and to the preservation of the southern lakes, and changes in birth rate and migration may both be involved.

Our figures show an Indian tributary population in 1800 of approximately 60,000, or half the number of 1570. However, the difference between the total Indian populations of these dates was less extreme than the figures would suggest, for the ratio of tributaries to total population was not the same under the conditions of decrease as it was during the population expansion of the late eighteenth century. For the period of population decline in the sixteenth century one may compute a total population between 2.8 and 3.3 times the tributary population, depending on the date of the enumeration and the types of persons classified as tributaries.[25] The late eighteenth-century statistics for the Valley jurisdictions (outside of Mexico City) indicate that total population was from 4.06 (Chalco) to 5.79 (Teotihuacan) times the tributary population.[26] Although many more, and many more intricate, computations might be undertaken, we may hazard the following conclusions about Indian population in the Valley of Mexico:

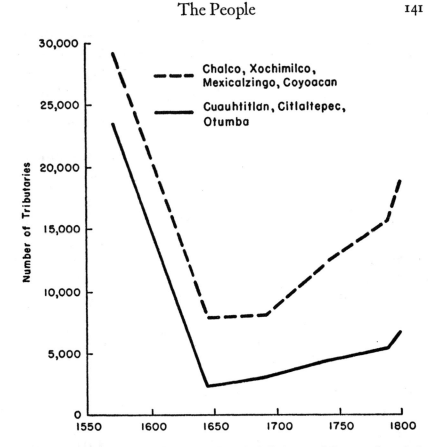

Figure 4. Population changes in four southern jurisdictions and three northern jurisdictions. Sources: see Table 10.

an initial population at the time of the conquest of about 1,500,000; a decline to about 325,000 by 1570; a further decline to about 70,000 in the mid-seventeenth century; an increase to about 120,000 in 1742; and a further increase to about 275,000 by 1800.[27]

Indian population figures of the colonial period commonly show more women than men for all recorded ages.[28] Many local ecclesiastical archives contain birth and death records in abundance, but these still await systematic analysis. We have no satisfactory colonial statistics on infant mortality, but nineteenth- and twentieth-century records suggest that half or more of the Indian children born alive in the colonial period died in their first

TABLE 10

Indian Tributaries by Political Jurisdiction

Jurisdiction[a]	1570	1644	1692	1742	1763–1765	1782	1787–1794	1797–1804 (old)	1797–1804 (new)
Chalco	13,050	2,910	2,689	5,071	5,180	6,372	7,182	8,623[b]	9,830[b]
Citlaltepec	6,600	661	720	1,206	1,021	902	745	1,362	1,596
Coatepec	2,400			827	845	842	1,118	1,319	1,543
Coyoacan	5,200	1,781	2,168	2,988	2,887		3,011	3,722	4,401
Cuauhtitlan	10,600	1,182	1,861	2,513	2,725	3,094	3,479	3,978	4,495
Ecatepec	2,600	362	260	1,024	1,631	1,834	1,762[c]	2,573	3,024
Mexicalzingo	2,420	462	318	882	825	1,585	1,761	2,222	2,518
Mexico	30,000[d]	7,631	7,631	8,400			8,893	9,672	12,061
Otumba	6,500	480	509	709	853	1,246	1,088	1,361	1,634
Tacuba	9,900	2,430	2,916	3,965	3,571	5,210	5,951	6,561	7,383
Teotihuacan				860	1,273	1,674	1,577	1,813	2,168
Texcoco	19,400	2,074	2,711	5,969	4,793	7,540	6,847	7,546	9,011
Xochimilco	8,600	2,686	2,783	3,440	4,314	4,730	3,666[e]	4,281	4,821
Total, Valley of Mexico	117,270	22,659+	24,566+	37,854			47,080	55,033	64,485
Total, New Spain[f]				316,099+ (1729)	397,900+ (ca.1770)	458,251 (1784)	483,282 (1794)	676,683 (1807)	763,813 (1807)

SOURCE: Except where noted this table depends on the following sources: for 1570, López de Velasco, *Geografía y descripción*; for 1644 and 1692, Miranda, "La población indígena"; for 1742, Villa-señor y Sánchez, *Theatro americano*, I; for 1763–65, AGN, Tributos, vol. 2, exp. 1 (the figures are repeated in AGN, Tributos, vol. 2, exp. 2, with some slight changes); for 1782, BNM, ms. no. 455, fols. 205v ff., and BNP, no. 258, fols. 3r ff. (population is computed from the one-half real tribute; there are slight differences between the two versions); for 1787–94, AGN, Tributos, vol. 37, exp. 6; for 1797–1804, AGN, Tributos, vol. 43, final exp., fol. 4r–4v.

a We omit the jurisdictions of Hueypoxtla and Pachuca, a relatively small part of which fell within the area we treat as the Valley of Mexico. This means subtracting the doctrinas of Hueypoxtla, Tizayuca, and Tezontepec from the 1570 record. Santa Fe is also subtracted, as a community exempt from tribute.

b The figures given in AGN, 12,318 and 14,043 for the old and the new respectively, include Tlayacapa. These are reduced by 30 per cent in accordance with the Chalco-Tlayacapa ratio of 1770 recorded in AGN, Tierras, vol. 1518, exp. 1, fols. 28r ff.

c The figure is for 1787. But a new count in 1789 recorded 2,205 tributaries. See BNM, ms. no. 451, fol. 295r.

d The figure is probably too high by 10,000 or more. See Figure 17.

e AGN, Padrones, vol. 29, fol. 3r, gives 5,396 (5,394) Indian men and 5,970 (5,960) Indian women in Xochimilco about 1790.

f Figures for the whole of New Spain are arbitrary and incomplete in various degrees. Negro and mulatto tributaries are included in some of the statistics. Sources: for 1729, the Gazeta of that year, published in León, "Bibliografía," no. 4, pp. 89–90 (the figure omits Mexico City, the Marquesado, and some other jurisdictions); for ca. 1770, Gálvez, *Informe general*, p. 87; for 1784, BNM, ms. no. 455, fol. 217r; for 1794, AGN, Tributos, vol. 37, exp. 6; for 1807, Zamora y Coronado, *Biblioteca de legislación*, VI, 96.

143

year and that three-quarters or more died in early infancy.[29] Despite isolated instances of remarkable longevity, persons over the age of fifty were always rare.[30] Figures for Mexico City in the year 1790 (Figure 5) show an over-all parallel between Spanish and Indian age groups, but a higher percentage of Spaniards over the age of forty (19.5 per cent as compared with 15.2 per cent). Figures of the late eighteenth century indicate that the age of fifty was passed by 8 per cent of the creole white population and by 6.8 per cent of the Indian population.[31]

Data on the history of racial mixture are notoriously unreliable, and despite a huge amount of miscellaneous information for the early period the problems can hardly be confronted statistically before the eighteenth century. Even then, one would be exceedingly rash to accept the figures at their given values. The late colonial statistics for each jurisdiction (Table 11, Figure 6) suggest that areas with the largest number of Indians had also the largest populations of non-Indians, while the highest percentages of non-Indian populations occurred in Mexico City, Coyoacan, and the sparsely populated northern jurisdictions of Otumba and Citlaltepec. The southern areas of Xochimilco and Coatepec display disproportionately small non-Indian intrusions. All available information indicates that ethnic mixture was greater in Mexico City and in the larger towns and haciendas than in small towns and the countryside.[32]

Because formal marriages between Indians and non-Indians were rare, it is safe to say that the great majority of first-generation mestizos were the bastard offspring of Spanish men and Indian women.[33] Although the late Spanish colonial language contained a number of esoteric terms for the various refinements of ethnic mixture, the only ones in common usage were mestizo (mixed Indian and white), mulatto (mixed Negro and white), and to some extent *pardo* and *coyote* (mixed Indian and Negro).[34] We do not know the criteria used for defining and identifying these in colonial records, and it is unlikely that the problems that they raise can ever be solved satisfactorily. On the one hand, it is possible that the rise in "Indian" population in the late seventeenth century and after may have reflected the emergence of a mestizo class. On the other hand, no such significant mestizo increase is recorded or appears to have been identified at the time. External or visual criteria for Indians were physical features, native dress, and the *balcarrotas* or Indian hair style, any or all of which might equally have applied to mestizos.[35] One may suspect that the Spaniards

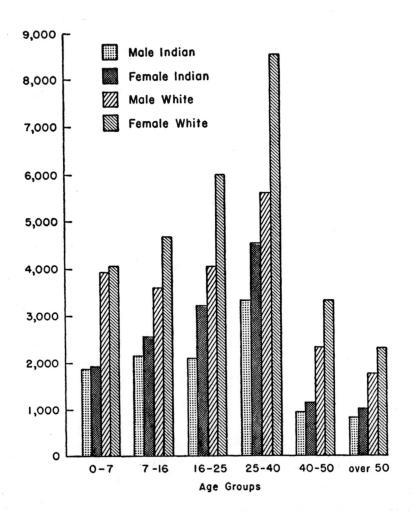

Figure 5. Indian and white age groups in Mexico City, 1790. Whites of European birth, ecclesiastics, military troops, and mixed classes are not shown. Indians number 25,603 (11,232 males and 14,371 females). Whites number 50,371 (21,338 males and 29,033 females). Whites of European birth were counted at 2,335 (2,118 males and 217 females); ecclesiastics at 8,166; pardos or mulattoes at 7,094 (2,958 males and 4,136 females); and other castas at 19,357 (7,832 males and 11,525 females). Thus the total for the city exclusive of military troops was 112,926. Sources: *Gazetas de México, compendio de noticias,* V, fac. 224. Humboldt, *Political Essay,* I, 254. "Noticias de Nueva-España en 1805," p. 8.

TABLE II
Population Figures, 1790–1804

Jurisdiction	Indians, ca. 1800[a]		Non-Indians, ca. 1790[b]					Ratio: Indian tributaries to Indian total	Non-Indian percentage of total population
	Tributaries	Total	Spaniards	Mestizos	Castas	Pardos	Total Non-Indians		
Chalco	8,623	35,029[c]						1:4.06	
Citlaltepec	1,362	6,534	500	988	304	38	1,830	1:4.79	22
Coatepec	1,319	5,767	300	61	91	9	461	1:4.37	7
Coyoacan	3,722	15,590	2,198	840	371	522	3,931	1:4.19	20
Cuauhtitlan	3,978	18,701	1,014	1,506	731	219	3,470	1:4.70	16
Ecatepec	2,573	12,769	809	513	239	204	1,765	1:4.97	12
Mexicalzingo	2,222	10,090						1:4.54	
Mexico[d]	25,603	25,603	52,706				79,157	1:3.55[e]	76
Otumba	1,361	6,841	1,118	563	372	130	2,183	1:5.03	24
Tacuba	6,561	33,516	1,826	2,436	1,087	308	5,657	1:5.11	14
Teotihuacan	1,813	10,507	895	166	222	266	1,549	1:5.79	13
Texcoco	7,546	32,601	3,459	1,282	910	69	5,720	1:4.32	15
Xochimilco	4,281	18,577	1,145	557[f]	161	204	2,067	1:4.34	10

[a]Tributary and total Indian population are derived from AGN, Tributos, vol. 43 final exp., fol. 4r–4v. The dates range from 1797 to 1804.

[b]Most of the material concerning non-Indian population is derived from AGN, Padrones, vols. 3 through 29. Data for the Citlaltepec jurisdiction are from AGN, Historia, vol. 72, fol. 48r. Data for Mexico City are from Humboldt, *Political Essay*, I, 254. Some of these same figures are recorded in Aguirre Beltrán, *La población negra*, pp. 228–29, although my count differs from his at several points.

[c]These are derived figures. The original gives 12,318 tributaries and a total of 50,041 for Chalco and Tlayacapa together. I have reduced these by 30 per cent for the approximate equivalents of Chalco alone. See Table 10, note b.

[d]Mexico City had 9,672 tributaries and a total Indian population of 34,289 according to counts made in 1800–1801. We use the figure 25,603 (ca. 1790) because it occurs in the same record as the figures for non-Indians and is thus directly comparable.

[e]This ratio is computed from the figures mentioned in note d: 9,672 and 34,289.

[f]This figure includes 75 persons classified as mulattoes.

usually classified mestizos as Indians in order to render them liable in tribute payment and other kinds of obligation; a document of 1790 refers to
"mestizos and half-castes who are also called Indians."[36] In any event, the
Spanish state never confronted the facts of miscegenation in a forthright
way. The earliest racial problems pertained to Spaniards and Indians, and
the tendency was to continue to think in these terms long after the mixed
classes developed.

Negroes, mulattoes, and mestizos received attention in the early years
mainly as intruders upon Indian society. In 1544 persons classified as Negroes and mestizos were accused of forcing their way into Indian homes
in the community of Coyoacan and compelling the occupants to load
wagons with lumber and fuel. Mulattoes were implicated in similar activities at least by the 1550's.[37] Court records of the middle years of the sixteenth century and after contain a large number of related cases involving
forced entry, the seizure of market goods, and the impressment of native
peoples for temporary labor. The early incidents took place chiefly in the
city and its environs,[38] but Negro overseers in encomiendas and rural
properties engaged in similar activities throughout the Valley.[39]

The Spanish state sought to eliminate or control such assaults upon Indian
society by three official methods. One was to punish offenders under the
Spanish law. A second was to grant permission to Indian communities to
arrest intruders and deliver them to Spanish authorities.[40] A third and
more drastic technique was to prohibit the residence of non-Indians in
native communities. In 1543 a viceregal order required all Spaniards to
move from Texcoco within six days.[41] In a cedula of 1578 the king prohibited mestizos, mulattoes, and Negroes from "being in the company of"
Indians in the pueblos.[42] The policy of separation was also urged in the
sixteenth century by the three caciques of Mexico, Texcoco, and Tacuba,
who deplored the "many bastard offspring" resulting from contact between
the two societies.[43] But all efforts at separation failed. Legal exceptions
were made in the Texcoco dismissal, and no effective measures for isolat-
ing the communities from Spanish pressures were ever devised.[44]

The cultural Hispanization of Indian peoples proceeded meanwhile in
ways both planned and unpremeditated, and most of the deliberate attempts
to induce it fell short of their objectives. Hispanization in language, which
received a primary and official attention from the Spanish state, was
achieved only in a limited degree. At first Spanish language training was

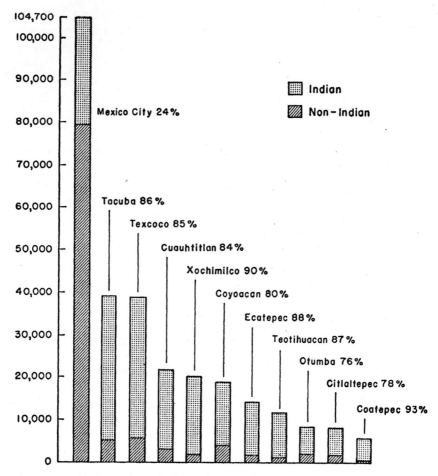

Figure 6. Population at the end of the colonial period. Percentages refer to the number of Indians in the total population. Data are transposed from Table 11. Except for Mexico City, the figures for Indian population are from about 1800, while those for non-Indian population are from about 1790. This has the effect of slightly increasing the percentages.

regarded as an adjunct of Christian education, and schools were maintained
in the ecclesiastical doctrinas. Royal law in the seventeenth century required
curates to teach Spanish directly to their parishioners.[45] Later the ecclesiastical schools were superseded by civil schools, and the financial burden
of their support was shifted from the church to the towns.[46] In its extreme
form the program of linguistic Hispanization was devoted to nothing less
than the eradication of all indigenous languages.[47] But though a number
of Indians learned Spanish, very few gave up their native speech. All
through the colonial period Indian wills, public notices, cofradía ledgers,
and other kinds of record continued to be written in Nahuatl by professional native scribes. Spanish courts always required the services of interpreters as did directors of labor, civil and ecclesiastical visitadores, congregación officials, and all other authorities in contact with native society.[48]
In the sixteenth and early seventeenth centuries, Indian court witnesses commonly denied knowledge of Spanish and testified through interpreters. In
the late seventeenth and eighteenth centuries Indian witnesses sometimes
admitted a knowledge of Spanish but still chose to speak through interpreters.[49] Only occasionally in late colonial times did Indian witnesses
depose wholly in Spanish.[50] Colonial peoples often used the terms *ladino*
and *españolado* in reference to Spanish-speaking Indians, and the usages
undoubtedly carried some wider connotations. As a Spaniard stated in
1692, native people were "more humble" when speaking their own language.[51]

The history of Indian literacy had a somewhat similar development, but
with more emphasis on instruction and social rank. In documents of all
times there appear fluent and practiced Indian signatures,[52] but at all times
also there appear records of Indians unable to sign their names. In the
eighteenth century most of the highest officials in the towns could and did
sign their names, but in the year 1802 not a single Indian officer in Xilotzingo was able to sign.[53] Evidence of this type relates only to signatures, not
to complete literacy, and it applies only to selected upper-class Indians, who
were always preferred as signatories in official capacities.[54] It is quite clear
that the majority of the native population remained illiterate.

In social behavior, Hispanic colonialism provided significant but unpremeditated stimuli to vagabondage and intoxication. From the first years
of the colony Indians were inclined to change their residences, to abandon
their homes and families, and to wander from place to place. A drought,

a tribute collection, or any other crisis in the precarious economy of their lives became an occasion for large-scale truancy.[55] The details of the tribute registers relating to absentees suggest that young men and bachelors were more prone to vagabondage than were heads of families.[56] But the practice was universal. Viceroy Mendoza, unaware of the scope of the problem, at first granted permission for full freedom of movement. But he was soon obliged to rescind this rule, and efforts were later made to forestall Indian wandering and to compel migrants to return to their original locations. Despite many notices of absence, this subject also is one that cannot be statistically analyzed with confidence. Indians were normally permitted to change their residences if their full tributes were paid for the year in which the move was made, and new arrivals quickly became registered tribute payers in a second location.[57]

As for intoxication, it should be noted first that the use of pulque had ordinarily been confined to the sick and the aged in pre-conquest times, though a *licencia general* had been granted for public ceremonies and religious celebrations. Consistent popular drunkenness had been unknown. But following the conquest the native population rapidly took to drink. Motolinía observed that women as well as men were drinking when he arrived in 1524.[58] Consumption increased despite the population decline. Indian practice was to drink to saturation, to induce vomiting, and to begin again.[59] Clerics preached against drink.[60] Efforts were made to halt the manufacture of intoxicant pulque. Laws were enacted forbidding the sale of liquor to Indians and severely punishing Indian drunkards. Taverns and *pulquerías* were prohibited in the towns.[61] In 1664 a determined corregidor confiscated and destroyed all the pulque in all the pulquerías of Mexico City.[62]

The failure of the efforts to control drunkenness may be attributed to the deep-seated distress of native society, from which intoxication offered a relief, and to the eagerness of liquor sellers to capitalize on this distress.[63] Pulque production became a major industry of the Spanish haciendas. On a smaller scale, Indian and non-Indian vendors established prosperous retail trades against which prohibitions were totally ineffective.[64] Legislation, abrupt confiscation, and punishment never had more than the most temporary effects.

Intermittently Spaniards forbade other customs that were loosely identified as uncivilized or non-Christian. The native ball game came under criticism and was eliminated in the sixteenth century, for it was said to involve witchcraft and satanic pacts.[65] The *volador* ceremony, wherein skilled native performers swung from great upright poles, was repeatedly denounced for similar reasons, but it nevertheless persisted and was even occasionally favored by Spaniards as a form of entertainment appropriate to viceregal celebrations.[66] The *ahorcado* ceremony and the dances called *huehuenches,* which continued in Ixtacalco, Mexicalzingo, and Ixtapalapa until the eighteenth century, were sharply forbidden in 1780 as residual pre-Christian rites.[67] The popular Indian dances with costumes and masks, and the licentiousness that attended fiestas, were accepted in practice while they were condemned by religious and civil authorities.[68]

Spanish influences affected native family life in a variety of ways. The church sought everywhere to introduce the institution of Christian marriage, and weddings accordingly fell under the control of Spanish clerics from the mid-sixteenth century on. The custom whereby Indians married only with the permission of their own native leaders was forbidden.[69] Concepts of incest had to be revised in accordance with Christian rules, for pre-conquest taboos had applied only to marriages between brothers and sisters, and between parents and children. The Indian ruling class, which had practiced a type of polygamy, was now obliged to comply with monogamous Christian standards.[70] Earlier traditions, continuing after the conquest, may well explain the many cases of bigamy and concubinage among the leaders of native society.[71] Among the masses, monogamous unions and single family groups were always assumed in Spanish ecclesiastical records and in the regulations governing tribute and labor. There is some evidence—although it is not conclusive—that Indians tended to marry at earlier ages than Spaniards.[72] But an Indian might choose a lifetime partner at an early age and live the remainder of his life without the formality of marriage, such an act being interpreted as ideological resistance to Christianity, as a way of avoiding clerical marriage fees, or simply as negligence.[73]

We have only very limited evidence concerning relations within families, for no Christian sacrament was involved in these and no Spanish civil institution required an examination of the details. Several descriptions of the rearing of children in pre-conquest times are available,[74] but there are no satisfactory post-conquest data until the ethnographic descriptions of the twentieth century. The *calmecac* and other Aztec institutions for the instruction of children appear to have come to an end almost immediately with the conquest and supplanted by the missionary schools. Women performed certain tasks that struck Spaniards as inappropriate or bizarre, such as the making of adobes, and Spaniards sometimes commented on these as peculiar features of Indian life.[75] Plague probably accounted for the most drastic modifications in relations between parents and children, for it left poverty and abandoned homes, as well as a large number of orphans. In Coatepec in 1580 most of the four hundred children of the town were reported to be orphaned.[76] The increase in the number of orphans may help to explain the widespread Indian adoption of the Spanish institution of *compadrazgo,* or dependence on godparents in place of the natural parents. Baptismal records from the sixteenth century uniformly include the names of male and female godparents,[77] and we may suppose that Indians valued their *padrinos* and *madrinas* the more highly because of the danger that a family unit might be broken up through death.

The calpulli (also called chinancalli and tlaxilacalli), the group unit in which a number of Indian families were associated, persisted in most areas through colonial times. The term was applied both to small groups of families and to much larger entities, including Tepetenchi, the cabecera of Xochimilco.[78] Baptismal and other documents consistently recorded the calpultin in identifying the origins and affiliations of the members of the community. In some instances the terms calpulli and tlaxilacalli were interchangeable and synonymous with the Spanish terms barrio or estancia. In other instances they referred to lesser subdivisions. Where the calpulli was of substantial size and where it was recognized as a barrio by Spaniards, it filled obvious administrative needs as a unit for tribute and labor and as a functioning political division in its town. It might further endure through its subordination to an Indian leader, its maintenance of an iglesia de visita, its control over the assignment of lands, or the craft specialty of its inhabitants.[79] With population decline, on the other hand, the surviving members of diminished barrios often moved to other barrios, and in some instances groups of migrants established completely new barrios in alien locations. When Indians from Tula founded a new barrio in Xochimilco during the 1570's, the act may have resembled an original pre-conquest calpulli foundation in a new territory.[80] Mestizos, mulattoes, and other non-Indians were frequently spoken of as originating in certain barrios, and these may also have induced some colonial modification of the original calpulli form.[81] If any calpultin were patrilinear exogamous "clans," as the first students of this subject in the nineteenth century supposed, these seem to have disappeared at an early date. The oidor Zorita remarked in the mid-sixteenth century that the calpultin were in disorder and could never be set to order again,[82] and it remains quite possible that more substantial modifications than those now known may have attended the earliest colonial history of the calpulli.

The effect of Spanish colonialism on the class stratifications of Indian society was to equalize and compress, to move all classes toward a single level and condition. Ordinary Indians, comprising the majority of the native population, were called *maceguales* (Nahuatl *macehualtin*, sing. *macehualli*). The subordinate peoples, who owed private tribute and service to members of the upper class, were called *esclavos, renteros, terrazgueros,* or, in a derivative and Hispanized Nahuatl, *tlalmaites* and *mayeques.*[83] The terms denote at least two degrees of sub-macegual status, roughly equivalent to the European conditions of serfdom and slavery. Motolinía, a strong opponent of slavery, described a slave in Aztec society as one who might occupy the land of his master, work in part for the master and in part for himself, possess a home and family, and own property, including other slaves. The children of slaves, he said, were born free.[84] Other early Spanish writers stated that possession of slaves in Indian society might imply only a lien on labor without control over their liberty or property.[85] An obvious difficulty of these and similar accounts lies in distinguishing a slave group from other peoples of the lower or even of the intermediate class in Aztec society. The audiencia referred in 1531 to the difficulty of discovering the true facts about an Indian slave class,[86] and the difficulties remain today.

Distinctions were made, however, and sixteenth-century commentaries indicate that a slave group is properly distinguishable as the lowest of the original Indian classes. The Nahuatl *tlacotli* was translated as esclavo. The conquistadores witnessed numbers of "esclavos" being bought and sold in Indian markets. Individuals had sold themselves into slavery because of inability to pay Aztec tributes or for other reasons, and in times of famine the number of slaves was said to have sharply increased. Enslavement was at times a penalty for crime. Male, female, and child slaves might be sacrificed, and in some instances slaves were bought to be fattened, sacrificed, and eaten.[87]

All these aspects of Indian slavery came quickly to an end following the conquest. Whatever the true differences between slaves and other peoples in the Aztec state, and however much the matter may have been distorted in Spanish understanding, there can be no doubt that slaveholding by Indians was a short-lived colonial institution. Quite expectably, it was forbidden by royal law.[88] Indian masters were reported to be voluntarily freeing their slaves in the 1540's,[89] and Motolinía reported that by 1540 almost no slaves were being bought or sold by Indians. A document of 1553 stated that the remaining Indian slaves were few and old, and commentaries of the later sixteenth century speak of Indian slavery as totally or practically extinct.[90]

Less rapidly and less obviously the non-slave subordinate classes were likewise eliminated. The essential point is that persons called tlalmaites and mayeques had paid tributes only to local recipients and not to the Aztec state. When Spaniards took control of tribute collection such persons retained their exemption and were excused from making payments to Spaniards.[91] But Spanish society was able to afford this condition only during a period of transition and only so long as a large additional tributary population remained. With a population decline and with the need to exact the full limit of Indian tribute and labor, Spaniards declared all such subordinate peoples liable in the same manner as macegual tribute payers. It is true that mayeques and tlalmaites as well as maceguales sometimes became the slaves of Spanish masters. But this kind of slavery was also unable to withstand official prohibitions,[92] and Spaniards developed labor institutions that did not depend on enslavement, as we shall see. Records of the 1550's indicate that a substantial fraction of the Indian population was still occupying a sub-macegual status at this time: 160 in a population of 826 in Culhuacan, 46 in a population of 278 in Huitzilopochco, 1,667 in a population of 6,361 in Tepetlaoztoc.[93] As late as 1587 there remained 600 members of this class in Texcoco.[94] But when these were transferred to the category of tribute payers—as they all were in the latter half of the sixteenth century—they became indistinguishable from maceguales in the Indian social system.

Change in status for the upper classes occurred more gradually than for the lower classes, partly because Spaniards maintained a certain respect for aristocratic values and hereditary Indian rule, and partly because the recognition of the Indian upper classes was a practical expedient in early colonial administration. Two essential upper-class ranks were involved: the tlatoque or caciques, and the *pipiltin* (sing. *pilli*) or principales. Tlatoque were everywhere understood to be the "natural lords" (señores naturales) of Indian society, and in principle the colonial cacique of any cabecera was the heir of its pre-conquest tlatoani. Principales were the relatives of the caciques or the heirs of the pre-conquest pipiltin.[95] In the original Indian society both tlatoque and pipiltin were classified according to a system of titular designations that recalled to Spaniards the noble orders of Europe. The ranks ranged from the position of *cihuacoatl*, close to Montezuma at the top of the hierarchy, through many subordinate positions in the towns. Indians holding such titles were generically called *tetecuhtin* or *teteuctin* (sing. *tecuhtli* or *teuctli*) in Nahuatl, and Spaniards sometimes used these words in adapted forms such as *tecuhtlis, tecles,* or *teules*.[96]

The conquest and the disorders of the 1520's disrupted the position of the Indian ruling class, although not to the point of eliminating the class itself as an intermediary authority. Spaniards made many new demands upon the tlatoque and the pipiltin. Cortés and other encomenderos interfered with succession rules, approved or disallowed particular cacique inheritances, and at times assumed full powers of cacique appointment. Spaniards seized lands, goods, and retainers by force. In 1525 the three incumbent tlatoque of the Triple Alliance cabeceras—Cuauhtemoc of Tenochtitlan, Coanacochtzin of Texcoco, and Tetepanquetzatzin of Tacuba—were executed by Spaniards.[97] Thus through coercion and punishment Spaniards of the 1520's made it clear that resistance by the Indian ruling class would not be tolerated.

Through privileges and honors, on the other hand, Spaniards favored those Indian rulers who cooperated, assuring them of their positions, confirming their titles, and approving their possession of lands and vassals. Caciques and principales for their part were quick to appreciate the policy of favoritism and to request benefits. In the early period they were sometimes permitted to accompany official missions to Spain and to present their requests directly to the royal court.[98] The favors granted by kings and viceroys allowed caciques and principales to carry swords or firearms, to wear Spanish clothing, to ride horses or mules with saddles and bridles, or in other ways to demonstrate their status within Indian society.[99] Cortés undertook to preserve or recreate the office of cihuacoatl and other Indian ranks. Viceroy Mendoza sought to maintain the native orders of nobility in a colonial form through the appointment of several "tecles" in the name of the king.[100]

In time, caciques and principales became thoroughly Hispanic in their material culture while they retained their status as privileged Indians. Unlike maceguales, they built their houses in Spanish colonial styles and adopted beds, mattresses, pillows, tables, chairs, chests, and other Spanish furnishings.[101] Following the example of the economic promoters of the colony, they established sheep ranches and other enterprises.[102] Wills and inventories of their possessions show a progressive adoption of the articles of Spanish civilization, sometimes even including Negro slaves.[103] Caciques and principales continued to marry within their own upper class, thus preserving the purity of native rank. Though the project for gaining royal sanction for native orders of nobility proved abortive, Indians in their own communities preserved the tecuhtli titles in the sixteenth century and in some instances into the seventeenth century.[104] Nahuatl texts such as the Crónica Mexicayotl betray an obsession with Indian genealogy and pedigree rivaling that of the Spanish *hidalgo* class itself.[105]

It is not surprising that maceguales in some instances made efforts to escape their condition and to pass as principales. Vacancies left by the loss of local leaders in the conquest period were sometimes surreptitiously occupied by ambitious maceguales, and time and custom reinforced these usurpations until their colonial origin was forgotten, or, if remembered, ignored.[106] The maceguales' techniques reveal an adept exploitation of the conditions of the Spanish colony. A macegual might engage in commerce, gain a measure of wealth and local influence, and become accepted as a principal. Or he might serve in a monastery, make himself a favorite with the friars, escape the tribute and labor rolls of his community, and come to be regarded as a principal. Again, he might win the favor of his encomendero and be elevated to a position of gubernatorial power in defiance of the electoral principle and the claims of caciques and principales. Spanish critics commented that such illegal principales constituted over half the total number and that they amounted to a quarter or a third of the entire Indian population.[107] But like a number of other Spanish commentaries on Indian society, such reports were much exaggerated. Community records indicate that the principales varied in number from place to place but that they were normally confined within a range of 2 to 10 per cent of the total population.[108]

It is possible that some cacique and principal families preserved lands and retainers continuously to the seventeenth century and thus effected the transition to the hacienda era.[109] Most, however, did not, probably for reasons relating more to the loss of retainers than to the loss of land. When Antonio Cortés, the cacique of Tacuba, requested permission to use Tacuba Indians to work his lands in 1565, the viceregal government granted his request under conditions quite different from those of pre-conquest Aztec society: the laborers were not to be private tlalmaites but hired workers, and the cacique was to provide them with food and a wage of twenty cacaos per day.[110] In other cases in which retainers were removed from Indian control, temporary recompense was sometimes provided by the community. Thus a principal who had received tribute from his barrio might for a time receive a stipulated payment instead from the town treasury or caja, together with the services of one or two Indians. Excess caja funds, if any, might be distributed among the principales, and caciques might receive regular salaries from town funds.[111] All these, however, were temporary expedients attending the loss of private services, and almost all such cases occur in the second half of the sixteenth century, when the remaining sub-macegual classes were being extinguished under the Spanish program for full tribute payment. In any event, the abolition of the lowest or dependent classes necessarily entailed a loss of income, power, and prestige for caciques and principales.

Surviving *cacicazgos*, if they were efficiently managed, maintained archives with records of family transactions, records that today provide detailed information on the colonial life of the Indian upper class. In the seventeenth century the cacique family of Tepetenchi in Xochimilco still traced its ancestry back to Acamapichtli, the first Mexica tlatoani. The surviving papers of the cacicazgo include the series of caciques' testaments, listing their possessions and heirs, together with the titles to their properties, documents of purchase and sale, payments by the community, receipts for such payments, maps and plans of properties and houses, and many similar materials. The property titles were neat Nahuatl documents, duly signed by the caciques and other authorities.[112] The truth is, however, that few cacicazgos were able to keep their records intact in this way, and a lawsuit in which all cacicazgo papers were in order was a rarity.[113]

For the Tepaneca area the community of Coyoacan offers a well-documented example of the institution of cacicazgo. Its tlatoani at the time of the Spaniards' arrival was Cuappopocatzin. He "married" the daughter of Huitzilatzin, tlatoani of Huitzilopochco, and granddaughter of Huehuezacatzin, the brother of Montezuma I.[114] Their eldest son, Cetochtzin, baptized as Hernando, inherited his father's position as tlatoani of Coyoacan after the father died in the conquest, and he then accompanied Cortés to Guatemala, where he died in 1525.[115] His younger brother, Juan de Guzmán Itztollinqui, was installed as tlatoani in Coyoacan by Cortés in 1526 and held this position until his death in 1569.[116] He spoke some Spanish, served the Spaniards in suppressing the Mixton uprising in the west, and as the viceroy stated was "always treated as a Spaniard."[117] He figured in the Coyoacan lawsuit against Cortés for land usurpation and excesses in labor and tribute demands. He wrote to the king calling attention to his father's and his brother's services to the crown, complaining that Spaniards treated his Indians as if they were slaves, and objecting to the excessive tributes.[118] Royal cedulas were issued to him in 1534, 1545, and 1551, granting him a coat of arms and confirming his private properties "by just and legitimate right and title." Viceroy Mendoza authorized him to carry a sword after the Spanish manner.[119] He married a *cacica* from Texcoco, and their combined properties included an enormous number of lands and houses in the vicinity of Coyoacan, as well as properties in Xochimilco and elsewhere.[120] He was an affluent native aristocrat, continuously provided for by his community. His retainers are duly recorded by place name and number: 13 in one location, 2 in another, 68 in another, 51 in another—totaling about 400. By a regulation of 1560 Juan de Guzmán received from Coyoacan each year some 600 bushels of maize and 300 bushels of wheat; each week he received the labor of four Indian servants, provided and paid for by the town. Each day he received 10 chiles, 100 tomatoes, one-half loaf of salt, two fowls, three loads of wood, two loads of fodder, and two bunches of pine knots for light. The community was to cultivate four plots of land for his use, of which two were to be sown in maize and wheat each season and two to lie fallow. By another assessment he received each day three fowls, two baskets of maize, 400 cacaos, 200 chiles, one loaf of salt, six loads of wood, five loads of fodder, and the labor of ten male and eight female servants. The natives of Coyoacan were required to build his house and to hold ten masons and ten stonecutters in readiness for its repair, and they had to pay him fees for the privilege of selling their goods in the market of Coyoacan.[121]

In Nahuatl notices Juan de Guzmán was designated as tlatoani. In Spanish documentation he was indicated as señor of Coyoacan in the 1520's, as señor natural in the 1530's, and as cacique and gobernador in the 1540's.[122] But in Coyoacan, as elsewhere, the hereditary cacicazgo and the elective position of gobernador were not continuously held by the same individual. The earliest documented accession of a second party to the governorship in Coyoacan is dated 1554, and although Juan de Guzmán regained the office after this he did not hold it continuously. He made a special appeal to the viceroy in 1561 urging that the cacique's powers not be lost through the creation of a separate governorship in Coyoacan, as was occurring in other cabeceras.[123]

After Juan de Guzmán's death in 1569 his oldest son Juan de Guzmán the younger inherited the cacicazgo, with its houses, lands, and properties. But the son felt that he was never permitted to enjoy the cacicazgo privileges in the way that he had a right to expect. His only salary from the town was as gobernador. Moreover, in the 1560's the Marqués del Valle seized and redistributed a number of lands belonging to the principales of Coyoacan and to the cacicazgo, an act that Juan de Guzmán the younger never forgot. In his will he urged his heirs to try to recover this lost patrimony. He sold some additional lands and engaged in a number of business transactions, borrowing money at various times from the Coyoacan hospital, the cofradía, the mayordomo (130 pesos to buy a horse), and the community treasury itself. Debts to all these were still outstanding at the time of his death in 1573. Like other caciques of his period he had to pay wages to maceguales for labor on his fields and service in his house.[124]

At his death, Juan de Guzmán the younger left four children. The oldest, Felipe, a child of six, was designated by his father to inherit the cacicazgo and was declared the cacique successor by the viceroy, but he was too young to assume full charge. In accordance with standard Indian principles of succession, then, his uncles, Lorenzo de Guzmán and Hernando de Guzmán, brothers of Juan de Guzmán the younger, successively became caciques in his stead. When both uncles died in the epidemic of 1576 the cacicazgo suffered decline.[125] The retainers that Felipe inherited were far fewer than those of his grandfather's estate. A listing of 1575, shortly after his father's death, contains only fifty-one names. Most gave four reales, to make an annual income of only twenty-three pesos. Moreover, the list was shrinking. In the record that survives, several names are crossed out with the notification *"murio"* (died) and one is marked *"huyose a mex(i)co"* (fled to Mexico[City]). In 1581 Felipe de Guzmán received 300 pesos from the community's excess tributes, but he was still too young to serve as governor. At a later time the viceroy granted him permission to serve as governor, but he was removed from the office again by viceregal order in 1594. Felipe fell under the influence of Spanish land buyers who persuaded him to sell some of the cacicazgo lands at a low price.[126]

In the seventeenth century several of the Coyoacan cacicas married Spaniards, and all the heirs became mestizos.[127] A crisis in the inheritance occurred following the death of the incumbent cacique Juan Estolinc (Itztollinqui) y Guzmán. The succession of Juan Hidalgo Cortés Moctezuma y Guzmán Carbajal was confirmed first in 1683, but his full possession was hindered by the claims of the son-in-law of the preceding cacique, Alonso de Guzmán. The suit was actively prosecuted in the middle 1680's, the audiencia reaching its decision in 1687 in favor of the daughter of Alonso de Guzmán. She thereupon took possession of all that had been granted to Juan Hidalgo, but she died without succession and the inheritance was promptly disputed by Ignacio de Tapia and Carlos Patiño. While these intra-family controversies were taking place in the late seventeenth century, Spaniards and mestizos were steadily appropriating the lands and houses of the cacicazgo. In the middle years of the eighteenth century, the long-standing litigation resolved itself into a conflict between Theresa de Guzmán and the heirs of Carlos Patiño. By the end of the eighteenth century the extensive landed properties officially confirmed to the cacicazgo in the sixteenth century had in large part been lost. The prodigious efforts of the late colonial cacique to recover them proved unavailing. He carried on a thirty-year lawsuit, worked his passage to Spain as a sailor, worked as a carpenter in Madrid, engaged in protracted conflict with Godoy and other royal ministers, and finally died in prison.[128]

A more complex form of cacicazgo is exemplified in the multiple cabecera of Amecameca. It will be recalled that here the suppression and restoration of tlatoani offices in the late fifteenth century had resulted in five dynastic divisions at the time of the Spaniards' arrival: Tecuanipan, Tzacualtitlan Tenango, Tlaillotlacan, Iztlacocauhcan, and Panohuayan. All five survived through the sixteenth century, together with the tecuhtli ranks with which each was associated. Several tlatoque shifted from one tecuhtli title to another. Several held two tlatoani offices, first in one of the five cabeceras, then in another. Interruptions, restorations, and impositions occurred. A governorship was created in 1560, the first gobernador being Juan de Sandoval Tecmauxayacatzin, tlatoani of Tlaillotlacan, who was at this time the oldest of the five caciques. His authority over all five cabeceras was recognized by 1563. Gobernadores of the later sixteenth century included some of the five tlatoque. One, Juan Maldonado, served as gobernador before 1591, the date at which he succeeded as tlatoani at Iztlacocauhcan. Rivalries took place among the cacique heirs when the competing caciques allied themselves with the competing Franciscan and Dominican orders in Amecameca, to create a situation of mingled Spanish-Indian antagonisms resembling that of the period of military conquests.[129]

The five cacique dynasties of Amecameca underwent many stresses and crises after the sixteenth century, all of immediate concern to the individuals involved but sufficiently uniform to suggest the limits within which legitimate cacicazgo could survive and function. Joseph de Santa María, cacique of Panohuayan in the middle sixteenth century, had received weekly tributes of 300 cacaos, one Spanish chicken, the work of one male and one female servant, 20 Indians to work his fields, and 300 pesos per year from the town treasury. But his son and heir, Felipe Páez de Mendoza, received none of this. As in Coyoacan, mestizos were introduced in the cacique families in the seventeenth century. An order issued to place the caciques in the possession of their cacicazgos was disputed by the gobernador and other officials of the Indian government. When Domingo Páez, cacique of Panohuayan, died in the eighteenth century, his son Luis was a minor and too young to assume the position. This provided an opportunity for Francisco Páez, a cousin of Luis, to intrude in the succession and seize the cacicazgo with its properties, privileges, and documentary titles. Succession by sons and succession by brothers or nephews occasioned intricate suits at law, contested for long periods, and the trials brought to light conflicting testimonies and much evidence of the abuse of cacique authority. Testaments, baptismal records, and land grants were repeatedly cited to establish legitimacy.[130]

Such controversies, characteristic of cacicazgo life everywhere in the seventeenth and eighteenth centuries, were further complicated by some imprecision and local variation in the popular as opposed to the legal concept of the term cacique. Technically, a cacique was the single possessor of the cacicazgo and the heir of the pre-conquest tlatoani. But this technical sense was not universally recognized among Indians. In later colonial times the sons and daughters of a cacique might all successfully adopt the cacique title, to the confusion of viceregal investigators. Audiencia regulations of the eighteenth century brought to light instances of multiplication, as in Tacubaya, where the seven sons and daughters of a cacique had all been "reputed to be caciques."[131] A criterion sometimes advanced for cacique status was the holding of office in Indian government, particularly the office of gobernador. But while it is true that caciques did sometimes hold the gubernatorial office in the seventeenth and eighteenth centuries, as well as in the sixteenth, and while it is probable that their candidacies to this position were strengthened by their status as caciques, still neither the cacique's position nor the governorship was a legal prerequisite to the other.[132] Outright cacicazgo inheritance by females was accepted from an early date, and very clear instances of mestizo succession and the assumption of cacique titles by mestizos in violation of the law are recorded. In Xochimilco in the late eighteenth century a Negro or mulatto became gobernador and was addressed as cacique.[133] On the other hand, pretenders to a cacicazgo might seek to disqualify their opponents by accusing them of being mestizos or bastards and hence ineligible for the succession. Colonial courts of the early period did not take either *mestizaje* or illegitimacy very seriously, and in any case a cacique on his deathbed might marry his lifelong "wife," thus legitimizing the heir.[134]

In the confusion of inheritance, with the establishment of new cabeceras, and with the movement of cacique relatives from place to place, a number of efforts were made in later colonial times to create new cacicazgos, or to secure official recognition of local cacique pretensions. A branch of a legitimate cacique family, resident in another town, could acquire copies of cacicazgo documents, establish the relationship, and have a chance of legal authorization as members of a cacique lineage. In this way cacicazgos increased in number, and caciques appeared in the seventeenth and eighteenth centuries in communities that had never had tlatoque.[135] Their campaigns for legitimacy sometimes included the manufacture and presentation of false or misdated documents. In the seventeenth century a branch of the Tello Cortés cacique family of Xochimilco, resident in Mexico City, presented papers allegedly signed by Cortés in 1519 and testifying to the original declaration of the cacicazgo.[136] In the eighteenth century a cacique pretender in Axapusco presented false documents supposed to have been signed by Cortés in 1526 and containing romantic allusions to ancient prophecies and the vision of Acamapichtli.[137] Such forgeries are often clearly recognizable now through their linguistic and factual anachronisms (one document dated 1490 speaks of the conquest and the early baptisms) and to informed Spaniards in the seventeenth and eighteenth centuries they were equally recognizable.[138] Official Spanish confirmation of cacique status sometimes required detailed genealogical proof of descent, but at other times viceroys confirmed cacique status after only the most perfunctory inquiries.[139]

Some cacique families remained vigorous, but their vigor depended only indirectly upon their position as caciques. By late colonial times cacique status could in some degree buttress a family's prestige, but it could no longer in itself be regarded as a rank of major authority.[140] Inheritance failed or the cacicazgo properties were alienated to such an extent that disputes over inheritance were not worth while. Where caciques were still powerful, their power rested upon forms of economic and social domination common to all ruling families regardless of origin. Whereas in the sixteenth century caciques had imitated Spaniards, in the eighteenth century "caciques" and "Spaniards" might both be mestizos, and if they remained successful they managed their lands, rents, agricultural production, and mode of life after the manner of all hacendados and rancheros. Their properties were enlarged by methods that cannot be meaningfully distinguished from the methods of the propertied class in general. The Panohuayan cacique in Amecameca outstripped his cacique colleagues decisively in this matter of late-colonial adjustment. He was a wealthy mestizo, owner of the hacienda of San Antonio Tlaxomulco and other properties producing wheat and maguey and yielding an income of thousands of pesos per year. Like any Spanish hacendado, the cacique received payments from Indians who cut wood and grazed animals on his property. His great house was equipped with Spanish furniture, silver dining service, and rich tapestries. He possessed a private arsenal of guns, pistols, and steel and silver swords. His stables and storehouses and other possessions compared favorably with those of wealthy Spaniards.[141] But Panohuayan was an exceptional case, and it is worth noting that no known circumstance in the sixteenth-century history of this cacicazgo can be demonstrably related to its later affluence.

One further example may be selected to suggest the limitations of late colonial cacicazgo, that of the Cortés lineage in the former imperial capital of Tacuba. In the sixteenth century Tacuba supported a cacique family in pride and ostentation. The family was the possessor of a coat of arms granted to Antonio Cortés by Philip II in 1564. The entire cacicazgo family was descended from Totoquihuatzin, the tlatoani of Tacuba at the time of the arrival of the Spaniards.[142] The cacique of the sixteenth century wrote letters to the king and, as we have seen, received citation for his commitment of 3,000 Indians in Tacuba for the construction of the first Jesuit church in Mexico City.[143] His son, Juan Cortés, was descended on his mother's side from Diego Huanitzin, tlatoani of Tenochtitlan. It was this son who directed the construction of the first Franciscan church in Tacuba and who was further celebrated as a witness of the apparition of the Virgin of Los Remedios.[144] The seventeenth- and early eighteenth-century caciques enjoyed their privileges and displayed their arms on the church tower beside the royal arms. But in the last quarter of the eighteenth century, with an intrusion in the succession, the traditional privileges were lost, the family came to be "treated as maceguales and *plebeyos*," and the cacique heir, José Jorge Cortés Chimalpopoca, was placed on the tribute lists. He had been baptized as a bastard at the time of his birth in 1738, but his parents married in 1769, two months before his father's death. After this the Tacuba native family of Alvarado—a name that the Cortés family insisted was a false one —supported by the curate and other Spaniards, denied the Cortés genealogy and testified that the descendants of Antonio Cortés had been tribute payers, as indeed they had. José Jorge Cortés Chimalpopoca appealed to the viceroy for the restitution of his privileges as the cacique of Tacuba and in 1810 was confirmed in a long list of specific favors, of which the following are examples:

1. Representatives of the jurisdiction of Tacuba should attend the Cortés family funerals.

2. In community functions the cacique should be separately seated, in a chair bearing his name.

3. The cacique may be excused from serving in any minor capacity in the town government.

4. The cacique is excused from tributes, repartimientos, and other exactions.

5. The cacique is excused from Sunday worship and from the contributions of one or one-half real.

6. The cacique's servants are not liable for road repair or other public or private services.

7. The cacique might never be imprisoned for debt, nor might his house, arms, horses, oxen, clothing, or furniture be sequestered.

8. The cacique's imprisonment, in the event of serious crime, should be in the community house, and not in the public jail.

9. In visiting the Spanish subdelegado, the cacique should be given a chair and not be kept standing.

10. The caciques' names may be included in the registers of nobility of all the cities of the kingdom.

11. All these privileges are to apply equally to the caciques' wives and widows.[145]

Even to an ear unaccustomed to the tonalities of Mexican history, this list has a hollow ring. Legitimate cacicazgo had little meaning beyond family pride in the conditions of the late colony. Alexander von Humboldt, one of the most perceptive observers of the Mexican scene of any period, noted in the first years of the nineteenth century that caciques were by that time hardly distinguishable from the mass of the Indian population in their economic circumstances and mode of daily life.[146] Neither the urban economy of Mexico City nor the hacienda economy of the countryside favored the preservation of cacique status, in the earlier sense, on the eve of independence. The desperate Spanish monarchy had nothing further to offer to the heirs of the fifteenth-century tlatoque. The long series of royal laws favoring caciques was about to come to an end, and nothing in the subsequent ideologies of political independence, liberal egalitarianism, or creole supremacy was to restore the decayed prestige of the Indian nobility. The conditions of Mexican independence were only superficially seen as opportunities for the re-creation of Indianist values. A descendant of Montezuma who sought to take personal advantage of independence was invested as Mexican emperor in a Paris hotel room—such at least was the report—but in Mexico itself his pretensions were ridiculed.[147] The term principal lost its colonial meaning in the nineteenth century. The term cacique had already been internationalized, and figured as one of the hereditary, noble, landowning ranks in John Locke's Fundamental Constitutions of Carolina. But in nineteenth-century Mexico, by a process already under way in colonial times, the term cacique lost its hereditary significance and acquired the meaning of political boss or local tyrant. It is symptomatic of these later transformations that Emiliano Zapata's Plan de Ayala (1911) could classify caciques with hacendados and *científicos* as the greatest enemies of reform.

CHAPTER VII

The Political Town

When the Spanish administration took possession of the collapsed Aztec empire after 1521, Indian control over a central government was permanently lost. Montezuma's descendants received encomiendas or were absorbed into the lower levels of the peninsular nobility. In the Acolhua zone the heirs of Nezahualcoyotl and Nezahualpilli became Texcocan caciques, powerful for a time in the immediate area but with a dwindling influence. Indian overlordship similarly declined in the Tepaneca zone, where the native Cortés family was reduced to its local cacicazgo. Thus the Triple Alliance organization, although not absolutely destroyed, was fragmented and its powers severely limited. As we have seen, members of the three imperial families protested against their reduced status in the mid-sixteenth century.[1] Their letters to the monarch spoke with deliberate pathos of vast domains shrunk to the confines of single cabeceras. Their ramified affiliations of family power had deteriorated or collapsed altogether, and no Indian lineages could compare with those of the period prior to 1519.

Reducing Indian jurisdiction to individual cabeceras was an initial step in political Hispanization. For a number of practical reasons, the Spanish state could not permit native government to survive above the cabecera level. Within the cabecera-sujeto units, the Spaniards created administrative links with a mass Indian society by allowing the caciques to retain their authority. But the caciques themselves were only temporarily useful in this respect. The reduction of their powers after the mid-sixteenth century was consistent with a second phase of political Hispanization, a phase in which elected Indian officers filled town offices patterned on those in Spanish municipal government.

The chief political institution in Spanish towns was the cabildo or municipal council. Cabildos in the Spanish world contained two principal offices, that of *alcalde* and that of *regidor*. Two alcaldes and four or more regidores were common in each municipal government. Both alcaldes and regidores, as councilors, were concerned with the political administration of the community, but alcaldes also served as civil and criminal judges in local courts, and they had greater authority and prestige than regidores. The establishment of a cabildo was frequently the first official act in the foundation of a new colonial town, and the cabildo staffed by Spanish colonial alcaldes and regidores was a customary feature of the Spanish towns everywhere in America. The Valley of Mexico had one such cabildo, in Mexico City; nowhere else in the Valley was there a concentration of white population large enough to justify a second cabildo of white councilors. But cabildos staffed by Indian alcaldes and regidores came into being in all cabeceras of the sixteenth century, and the political Hispanization attendant upon this was one of the most dramatic achievements of the Spanish state.

The history of municipal offices held by Indians begins, however, not with cabildos but with the creation of what Indians called *gobernadoryotl*. In this, the presiding native figure in each cabecera was to be entitled gobernador or *juez gobernador*,[2] and his office was to signify the separate, nonsujeto status of the cabecera under his rule. It is quite impossible to say when gobernadoryotl began. Spaniards spoke loosely of Indian gobernadores as early as the 1520's,[3] and they anticipated Indians in the use of the term. Confronted with the necessity of establishing gobernadoryotl, native communities rendered the change less abrupt by putting forth the existing tlatoani as gobernador and continuing to refer to him by his Nahuatl title. Spaniards recognized the temporary duality of such cases in the phrase "cacique y gobernador," which was frequently used in the sixteenth century. The combined tlatoani and gobernador office is to be found in Texcoco in the Pimentel family, in Tacuba in the Cortés family, in Coyoacan under Juan de Guzmán, in Ixtapalapa in the person of Alonso Axayaca, and in the native dynasties of many other towns.[4]

But the significant fact for Indian government was that the office of gobernador came to be differentiated from that of tlatoani, with the two offices held by different persons. Even where cacicazgo remained strong, elected or appointed non-tlatoani gobernadores were introduced in the middle sixteenth century and after, serving terms of one or more years. The occasion for the insertion of an elected or appointed non-tlatoani gobernador was customarily some crisis in the tlatoani inheritance, as when succession was in dispute or when a tlatoani heir was too young to rule. Such a crisis occurred in Chimalhuacan Atenco on the death of the conquest tlatoani, Pedro Pacheco (Acxoyatlatoatzin). His son and heir, Thomas Pacheco, was not of age to inherit the succession, and the circumstance provided an opportunity for a gubernatorial tenure in adult, non-tlatoani hands.[5] Similarly, in Azcapotzalco, when Diego de León, "gobernador y señor" of the Tepaneca portion, died in 1555, his son Diego Ossorio was too young to inherit. The viceroy appointed a principal as interim gobernador and the non-tlatoani gobernadoryotl was established.[6] It was a deliberate viceregal policy in the sixteenth century to take advantage of such opportunities to introduce the desired Hispanic institution and simultaneously to reduce the powers of hereditary caciques.[7] Sometimes, as in Coyoacan, tlatoque reappeared as gobernadores in later years, but they did so in competition with others, with reduced prerogatives and for short terms. One cannot overgeneralize about the implementation of Spanish policy, for it was different in each cabecera, but with local modifications the pattern we have described applies to Texcoco, Tacuba, Tenochtitlan, Tlatelolco, and other major and minor cabeceras of the Valley of Mexico.

Both the progressive restriction of Indian imperial authority and the transition from tlatoani government to gobernadoryotl are represented in the succession in Tenochtitlan following the rule of Montezuma.[8] Montezuma himself was killed in 1520 under circumstances that are variously reported.[9] His brother, Cuitlahuac, tlatoani of Ixtapalapa, was appointed immediately by Indian electors as tlatoani of Tenochtitlan; he ruled for only a few months before he died in the epidemic of 1520.[10] Cuauhtemoc, who was probably Montezuma's nephew and son-in-law, became Cuitlahuac's successor, capitulated to Cortés at the conclusion of the conquest, and was killed by Cortés on the Guatemala expedition in 1525.[11]

The careers of the three rulers of Tenochtitlan during the decade and a half following Cuauhtemoc's death reveal the rapid rate of the dynasty's decline. Juan Velázquez Tlacotzin, the first to succeed Cuauhtemoc, died in the south before the return of the Guatemala expedition.[12] His successor, Andrés de Tapia Motelchiuhtzin, who served as cuauhtlatoani of Tenochtitlan for five years, was *amo pilli* (not a noble) or *zan cuauhpilli* (only a noble warrior), and he was incidentally referred to by Spaniards as a former slave.[13] After his death on the Nuño de Guzmán expedition, Pablo Xochiquentzin, who was *zan calpixcapilli* (only a noble calpixqui) served as cuauhtlatoani of Tenochtitlan for five years, dying in 1536.[14]

The "legitimate" dynasty in Tenochtitlan was restored in the late 1530's with the elevation of Diego Huanitzin (Panitzin), grandson of Axayacatl, son of Tezozomoc, and Montezuma's brother. At the time of his selection Diego Huanitzin was serving as tlatoani of Ecatepec, and he received the full tlatoani title in Tenochtitlan. Although his predecessors had been called gobernadores in a loose Spanish usage, he was the first to be given the official title under the new viceregal government.[15] His successor, Diego Tehuetzqui, was the grandson of Tizoc, Montezuma's uncle, and served as the second gobernador in the 1540's and early 1550's.[16] In 1554, following Diego Tehuetzqui's death, a new rule was ordered by the viceroy under Esteban de Guzmán, who was then gobernador of Xochimilco. As Indian *juez de residencia* in Tenochtitlan, Esteban de Guzmán held office from 1554 to 1557, after which he performed similar duties at viceregal direction in a number of other communities, including Tlatelolco.[17] The successor in Tenochtitlan, from early 1557 until his death in 1562, was Cristóbal de Guzmán Cecepatic, son of the first gobernador, Diego Huanitzin, and known both as tlatoani and as gobernador.[18] The last of the gobernadores descended from the imperial ruling family was Luis de Santa María Cipac, grandson of Ahuitzotl. He assumed the gubernatorial position in 1563 after the lapse of a year and died in late 1565.[19]

With the death of Luis de Santa María Cipac the dynastic office came to an end in Tenochtitlan. From the beginning of the Aztec dynasty to 1565 the rule had been confined to the members of a single family, save for the period of cuauhtlatoque following the execution of Cuauhtemoc and for the interlude of Esteban de Guzmán's residencia from June 1554 to January 1557.[20] "The government of the revered rulers of Mexico Tenochtitlan came to an end," lamented an Indian chronicler. "No more were the natives of Mexico to be gobernadores or to rule the *altepetl* of Mexico Tenochtitlan. No more were there to be descendants of the great tlatoque or the *tlaçotlatocapipiltin*. There were to be only people from other places, some pipiltin, some not pipiltin, and others mestizos, whose Spanish ancestry is not known, nor do we know if they were pipiltin or maceguales."[21]

In 1568, after another interval and the failure of efforts to find an acceptable candidate within Tenochtitlan, Francisco Jiménez, a principal from Tecamachalco, was appointed gobernador.[22] His successor in 1573 was Antonio Valeriano, the Indian Latinist and informant of the Spanish chroniclers Bernardino de Sahagún and Juan de Torquemada.[23] By native standards Antonio Valeriano was also amo pilli, not noble, but he reflected fully the new Hispanized Indian culture, and he married into the dynastic family, his wife being the daughter of Diego Huanitzin.[24] He served as gobernador for more than twenty years, from the 1570's into the early 1590's, and after several intermediate incumbents his grandson, Antonio Valeriano the younger, came to hold the same office in the 1620's.[25] For the remainder of the seventeenth century and throughout the eighteenth century, Indian gobernadores of Tenochtitlan were elected, served terms of various lengths, and governed as did other gobernadores in other cabeceras, in the absence of any genealogical or dynastic connection with the family of Montezuma.

With respect to Texcoco, the second cabecera of the Triple Alliance, it will be remembered that after the death of Nezahualpilli in 1515, Montezuma settled the conflicting claims in favor of Cacama. Cacama was Nezahualpilli's son by Montezuma's elder sister, and the succession thus fell to the heir by a *cihuapilli* of Mexico.[26] Cacama, as tlatoani of Texcoco, greeted Cortés in 1519 but turned against both Montezuma and the Spaniards. After his duplicity was discovered he was jailed and killed in 1520.[27] Cortés's own candidate as his successor was Cacama's brother, Cuicuizcatl, who was chosen on the advice of Montezuma and who became the victim of a fratricidal plot sponsored by the resistance movement in Tenochtitlan under Coanacochtzin and Cuauhtemoc.[28] The tlatoani who surrendered to Cortés in 1521 was Coanacochtzin, son of Nezahualpilli, who had fought to the end in Tlatelolco, and who was baptized by the Spaniards as Pedro de Alvarado.[29] But Cortés's particular protégé was still another of Nezahualpilli's sons, Hernando Ixtlilxochitl. He assisted the Spaniards in the rebuilding of Tenochtitlan and accompanied Cortés on the Honduras expedition. In 1525 Cortés killed Coanacochtzin.[30]

After brief rules by other brothers, Hernando Ixtlilxochitl was installed as tlatoani in Texcoco.[31] At least two other sons of Nezahualpilli—Jorge Yoyontzin and Pedro Tetlahuehuetzquintzin—ruled after Ixtlilxochitl's death in 1531.[32] When the second of these died in 1539, his brother Carlos proclaimed himself successor. Carlos was the Indian idolator who was executed under the inquisitorial authority of Juan de Zumárraga in 1539, at which time the gobernador of Texcoco was Lorenzo de Luna.[33]

The tlatoani succession in Texcoco became more orderly after the execu-

tion of Carlos, under Antonio Pimentel (1540-45), another son of Nezahualpilli, and under Hernando Pimentel (1545-64), son of Coanacochtzin.[34]
Antonio Pimentel was identified as gobernador both before and after he
succeeded to the tlatoani rule.[35] His successor was repeatedly designated
gobernador after 1545. Following the death of Hernando Pimentel other
gobernadores served for one or more years as elected officers, as in Tenochtitlan, and were disassociated from the continuing tlatoani succession.[36]

In Tacuba the tlatoani of 1519, Totoquihuatzin, was killed in the conquest, and his successor, Tetepanquetzatzin, was executed by Cortés, together with the tlatoque of Tenochtitlan and Texcoco, on the Guatemala
expedition.[37] From 1525 to 1550 a number of persons held office, and they
were variously designated by the titles señor, cacique, and gobernador.[38]
In 1550 the succession devolved upon Antonio Cortés Totoquihuatzin, son
of Totoquihuatzin, and thus a legitimate tlatoani. His election as gobernador was confirmed by the viceroy in April 1550, and he was addressed
as gobernador and cacique continuously after this.[39] In 1565 a principal of
Acolman received viceregal confirmation, to interrupt the rule.[40] With the
death of Antonio Cortés in 1574, and after a short term under a rival candidate, his son Juan Cortés continued to be regarded as cacique but alternated with others as elected gobernador.[41] In the 1590's the alien cacique
from Tlaxcala, Leonardo Xicotencatl, became gobernador,[42] and though
the cacicazgo family continued to the end of colonial times, it never regained the exclusive privilege of gobernadoryotl.

A number of problems remain to be solved in the reconstruction of the
post-conquest dynasties of the Triple Alliance cabeceras; discrepant sources
still require resolution, and statements contradicting those made above may
be found in the literature. But it is quite clear that in all three of the cabeceras the office of gobernador was accorded to the tlatoque during a transitional period, and that in all three the office was taken from them. The
new non-tlatoani gobernadores were for the most part from the class of
principales, but they lacked hereditary claims upon the tlatoani's office, and
in some cases they were outsiders appointed by viceroys to assume control
at critical periods. The appearance of new rulers from Xochimilco, Tecamachalco, and Tlaxcala in the Triple Alliance cabeceras indicates a continuous
viceregal imposition and assignment working side by side with the electoral
and hereditary systems. Certain principales of the late sixteenth and seventeenth centuries shifted from one cabecera to another as professional gober-

nadores. In the early seventeenth century, for example, the historian Fernando de Alva Ixtlilxochitl served as gobernador both of Tlalmanalco and of Texcoco.[43] And at various times in the late sixteenth and early seventeenth centuries, Jerónimo López served as gobernador of Tenochtitlan, Tlatelolco, Texcoco, Xaltocan, and Tecama.[44]

The process of transition from rule by tlatoque to rule by gobernadores may be clearly traced in these and other cases, and one might imagine that similar processes attended the change from the other offices of pre-conquest government to the alcaldes and regidores of the colonial Indian cabildos. The tlatoque, of course, had never ruled unaided. Various texts indicate the existence of pre-conquest "councils," ruling together with or subordinate to the tlatoque in Tenochtitlan and other communities, and colonial writers referred to these in the Spanish terms familiar to them. Thus as Montezuma was called "rey," certain of his subordinates were termed "oidor" or "gobernador" or "capitán general" in Spanish commentaries.[45] A sixteenth-century notice identifies the calpulli officials as alcaldes and regidores.[46] Modern students, alert to the limitations of Spanish understanding and nomenclature, have nevertheless been prone to assume derivations from such pre-conquest offices to the post-conquest cabildos, below the level of the tlatoani.[47] But it seems certain that no such derivations took place. The class of principales remained the officeholding class, but too long a time intervened before cabildos were established, and in all known cases the continuity was interrupted. With present knowledge no Indian alcaldes are recorded for the Valley until the late 1530's, and even in 1550 the full cabildo system was not yet operating in all cabeceras.[48] Only after 1550 can one speak of uniformly distributed cabildo systems, generally with two Indian alcaldes and three or four Indian regidores in each cabildo and one cabildo in each cabecera.

In Tenochtitlan the last known appearance of the Aztec "council" occurred with the selection of four assistants to Cuitlahuac in 1520 before the completion of the conquest. In late 1523 or early 1524 Cortés officially recognized one of the "council" offices, that of the cihuacoatl, in the early colonial government of Tenochtitlan, and this same cihuacoatl, Tlacotzin, became Cuauhtemoc's successor, as we have seen.[49] But the Aztec "council" as a corporate body yielded wholly to the personal rule of Motelchiuhtzin and his successors. Some twenty-five years then elapsed before the creation of a full cabildo system with alcaldes and regidores in Tenochtitlan. Two alcaldes for Tenochtitlan and Tlatelolco are mentioned in 1543.[50] The Indian annal Códice Aubin remarks on the establishment of alcaldes in 1549 as if a completely new body and institution were being created in the absence of any memory of the Aztec imperial "council."[51] The names of at least ten alcaldes of Tenochtitlan are known from the period 1549–54 and the suggestive observation of the 1560's that "order and system" in their election began in 1555 argues further in favor of innovation.[52] The offices, and the persons serving in them, so far as we can see, had no relation to any known institution in pre-Spanish political life. The cabildo thus appears as a colonial institution deliberately introduced by Spaniards.

The phrase "order and system" referred to the distribution and rotation of the cabildo offices among the four barrios of Tenochtitlan. It will be remembered that these four subdivisions, derived from pre-conquest jurisdictions, were Santa María Cuepopan (Tlaquechiuhcan), San Sebastián Atzacualco, San Pablo Teopan (Zoquipan), and San Juan Moyotlan. Beginning in 1555 each was represented in the Indian cabildo of Tenochtitlan by one alcalde every other year, and the four barrios thus rotated in pairs. In its mid-century intricacy and precision, the system has no known antecedents in any pre-conquest political government. It evokes instead the precedent of municipal organization in medieval Spain.[53] The perfection of the pattern during its period of most sustained operation (1555–68) is demonstrated in Table 12.

Similarly, there appear no pre-Spanish prototypes for the cabildo office of regidor. Indian regidores were first proposed by the monarch in 1530 in a cedula urging their appointment and their combined service with Spaniards in a joint body.[54] The experiment of an interracial cabildo was actually attempted in Puebla, but in Mexico City, although the Spanish cabildo seriously contemplated such a system, it never admitted Indians to its ranks. In practice, in the Valley, Indian regidores, like Indian alcaldes, came to be members of exclusively Indian bodies in the cabildos of the cabeceras.[55]

The number of regidores varied from cabecera to cabecera, ordinarily with the largest numbers in the largest towns. Tenochtitlan with twelve and Texcoco with ten had the most sizable regimientos in the sixteenth century. Regidores normally served one-year terms in representational and rotational tenures, but occasionally the terms were prolonged beyond the usual one year, and other variations were made upon the standard form.

TABLE 12
Indian Alcaldes in Tenochtitlan, 1555–68

Date	Alcalde	Barrio
1555	Alonso de San Miguel	San Pablo
	Miguel Díaz	San Juan
1556	Miguel Sánchez Yscatl	San Sebastián
	Cristóbal de Guzmán	Santa María
1557	Tomás de Aquino Yspopulac	San Pablo
	Luis de Santa María	San Juan
1558	Martín Cano	San Sebastián
	Pedro de la Cruz (Tlapaltecatl)	Santa María
1559	Pedro García Tenylotl	San Pablo
	Lucas Cortés Tenamaz	San Juan
1560	Miguel Sánchez Yscatl	San Sebastián
	Melchior Díaz Suchipepena	Santa María
1561	Luis de Paz (Huehuezaca)	San Pablo
	Toribio Vásquez (Tlacuscalcal)	San Juan
1562	Martín Cano	San Sebastián
	Pedro (de la Cruz) Tlapaltecatl	Santa María
1563	Tomás de Aquino Yspopulac	San Pablo
	Lucas Cortés Tenamaz	San Juan
1564	Martín de San Juan (Ezmalin)	San Sebastián
	Antonio de Santa María (Mexicaytoa)	Santa María
1565	Pedro Dionisio	San Pablo
	Toribio Vásquez (Tlacuscalcal)	San Juan
1566	Miguel Sánchez (Yscatl)	San Sebastián
	Francisco Xuárez	Santa María
1567	Luis de Paz (Huehuezaca)	San Pablo
	Martín Hernández Acatecatl	San Juan
1568	Juan García Totoco	San Sebastián
	Diego de Tovar	Santa María

SOURCES: The fullest notices of these alcaldes' names, offices, dates, and barrio affiliations are to be found in AGN, Civil, vol. 644, exp. 1 (published as "Transcripción del texto inédito" in *Códice Osuna*, pp. 11 ff.) and in the Códice de Juan Bautista in MNM, Colección Gómez de Orozco, no. 14. Numerous other texts refer to these same alcaldes. For a more detailed discussion of the problems involved in this reconstruction, see Gibson, "Rotation of Alcaldes."

In Tenochtitlan in the 1560's the barrio of San Juan regularly furnished four regidores to the cabildo while the other three barrios together sent only two or three, and occasionally four, in various combinations.[56]

The election of tlatoque had been traditional in Indian practice, and Spaniards were repeatedly astonished, in the early period, at the regulated electoral procedures of the native communities. When Ramírez de Fuenleal responded to the royal proposal for interracial cabildos in 1533 he opposed the combined form, asserting that Indian elections were already more orderly than those of Spanish cabildos, and that to introduce Indians as regidores into cabildos of Spaniards would be to acquaint them with all "the evil that is to be found among Spaniards."[57] Vasco de Quiroga, taking a similar view, described an Indian tlatoani election in Otumba in 1535, after the incumbent cacique had died. The election was accomplished and notification made, he said, "with such good efficiency and deliberation that one could hardly believe it."[58] Such traditional Indian elections in the towns, of course, had occurred not annually but only on the death of a cacique. To Indian eyes, then, a principal innovation in the new cabildo governments was not the election itself but its periodicity and frequency. In most cabeceras an entire new cabildo was to be chosen each year. The fact that native custom favored life tenure surely explains, in part, the colonial Indian tendencies to retain tlatoque as gobernadores, to prolong the terms of gobernadores, and to resist Spanish directives requiring annual elections and rotation in office.

Spanish regulations, including instructions to corregidores, repeatedly made reference to these tendencies, insisting on annual elections and forbidding or limiting re-election of the same individuals.[59] One difficulty was that with population decline and the continued confinement of officeholding to the class of principales, sheer lack of personnel might militate against such rules. Thus in Tequixquiac in 1569, one gobernador, two alcaldes, and four regidores were to be selected annually from among thirteen principales. In Xilotzingo, where a full cabildo had similarly to be chosen, only five principales remained as candidates in 1569.[60] In these and other instances it is evident that the demands upon the privileged class strained and even exceeded its ability to fill the positions with new officials each year. The prohibitions against immediate re-election were repeatedly flouted and came to be evoked mainly when ulterior goals might be served. Re-election, contrary to law, occurred in both small and large cabeceras. In Tenochtitlan, Antonio Valeriano held the position of gobernador for over twenty years. In the seventeenth century in Cuauhtitlan a native of Tlatelolco remained in the gubernatorial office for over thirty years.[61] These are extreme examples, but the practice that they illustrate was universal in the cabeceras of the Valley.

Like the officeholders, the electors—called *vocales* in Spanish accounts— were normally the principales of the community. In the Nahuatl voting records of the seventeenth and eighteenth centuries, the criteria for tlatoque and pipiltin continued to apply as criteria for eligibility to vote.[62] At times of dispute or at other critical periods, a viceroy might make appointments in the absence of local elections.[63] But election by the principales was customary.

We have an enormous number of colonial notices on the varieties of electoral procedure. It was a procedure that differed substantially from cabecera to cabecera, but one that was strictly maintained in each by custom and precedent, for any innovation was liable to denunciation and disqualification as a local irregularity. These varieties may be illustrated by a series of brief descriptions, extracted from election records of the seventeenth century. In Otumba in 1639 the *principales y común* elected a gobernador, but the Franciscan guardian brought together the *cantores* and other Indian officers of the church and presented one of this group as gobernador, disallowing the election. In 1669 in Tenochtitlan, 129 voters assembled in the *tecpan,* or community house. It was announced that only legitimate votes were to be cast because in the preceding election some false balloting had resulted in the election of a mestizo. Three nominations were made, the result of the vote being the election of Felipe de Aguilar, "a legitimate Indian and cacique." He received 79 votes. His two opponents received 49 votes and one vote. In 1676 in Cuauhtitlan, 34 electors chose a gobernador, but the election was disputed on the grounds that a cabecera faction had excluded certain sujetos from the vote and that some of the voters had been maceguales. In Tacubaya in 1677 a group of electors met in the casas de cabildo and elected the existing gobernador, Gabriel de San Juan. Another group of electors chose a second and rival gobernador, Juan Domingo, who had held the office in 1675. Faced with a schism, the Spanish teniente approved the election of Juan Domingo because Gabriel de San Juan could not legally be re-elected. A witness signed for Juan Domingo, who was illiterate.[64]

Eighteenth-century records indicate similar varieties in procedure. In

1724, in Tenochtitlan, 400 electors chose Felipe de Jesús as gobernador by a vote of 394 to 6. In Coyoacan in 1726 a "large number" of Indians, "who were said to be legitimate electores and vocales," congregated in the tecpan and re-elected by acclamation the gobernador of the previous year. In San Agustín de las Cuevas (Tlalpam) in 1736 a gobernador was unanimously elected by the voters, but the corregidor refused to confirm the election, alleging that the candidate was "seditious, contrary, and faultfinding." In Chicoloapa in 1740 the electors were the principales, past gobernadores, past alcaldes, past regidores, past alguaciles mayores and "the entire community," but the effective votes numbered only 29. In Tacubaya in 1783 three nominees were proposed for gobernador. One received 17 votes, another 11, the third none; the winning candidate then appointed the alcaldes. In Santa Fe, the vocales comprised all married males in 1790. They gathered in the church in the presence of the curate and each voted for one of three candidates. The curate counted the ballots and announced the winner, who then traveled to Mexico City to receive the confirmation of the viceroy.[65]

Viceroys always retained the power to disallow election results, and corregidores and their tenientes were instructed to employ their influence to prevent the election of unsuitable candidates: drunkards, rebellious or uncooperative men, persons of "bad character," persons who had served during the previous year, or any but pure Indians.[66] To the other qualifications was added, in one of the seventeenth-century efforts to induce Indians to Hispanize their speech, the requirement that a candidate possess a knowledge of the Spanish language.[67] But no such legislation could take effect, and the requirement proved unenforceable.[68] The legislated restriction of officeholding to pure Indians also proved unsuccessful in the progressively mixed population. Mestizos appeared as alcaldes and regidores in the Indian cabildos of the seventeenth century. Mestizo gobernadores appeared in the major towns, including Texcoco, Xochimilco, Cuauhtitlan, and Azcapotzalco.[69] A Negro or mulatto and his son by an Indian woman became gobernadores in Xochimilco.[70] In 1635 a Spaniard was elected to the governorship in Texcoco and received the reluctant authorization of the viceroy.[71] In the early seventeenth century a Spaniard, Juan Pérez de Monterey, became gobernador of Tenochtitlan.[72] A campaign by another Spaniard to secure the governorship in Tenochtitlan later in the seventeenth century included entertainments, banquets, gifts, and extravagant election promises.[73]

Elections might be held in the tecpan, the cabildo quarters, the house of the incumbent gobernador, the church, or some other location.[74] Voting occurred most often in January or February, but sometimes in December of the preceding year or as late as March of the year for which the election was to take effect.[75] Preliminary nominations might or might not be made. Factions in local political struggles might introduce new election procedures to influence the results. Election might be withheld in order to maintain incumbents in their positions. Elections might be disputed on the grounds that an elected official had not filled other offices, or that he had served in the same capacity in a previous year, or that he owed arrears in tributes, or that he was illiterate, or that he was a *pulquero*, or that he was too young or too old.[76] Elections might also be disputed if they were not held at the customary times, with the "legitimate" electors, with the customary nominations, or before a notary.[77]

Surviving documents point to a high incidence of electoral controversy, but this is partly because the disputed and litigated cases were the ones that came under Spanish scrutiny and thus entered the record. Spaniards continued, in general, to describe native election procedures as peaceful, and to regard the disputes, if any, as the result of partiality by mestizos, corregidores, clergymen, or other non-Indians. If left alone, Bishop Palafox stated in the seventeenth century, Indians chose the most deserving candidates, those distinguished by rank, literacy, "commanding presence," physical size, or "ostentación."[78] Many of the known electoral disputes seem to have had a personal character, with active contention by factions based on the loyalty of intimates and family rather than on political policies or ideological principles.[79] A gobernador might introduce his sons into strategic community offices below the cabildo rank, and cultivate their assumption of the succession. Or he might yield the governorship in such a way that a member of his family would be his successor.[80] The election controversies provide fragmentary evidence of feuds between influential Indian families and occasionally of long-term hostilities engendered by local regimes. Against the tendency to resist annual changes in government, electoral rules could be evoked legalistically and made effective at critical times in the pursuit of private or factional objectives. For Indians the electoral system came to be a flexible instrument, useful alike for prolonging or for overthrowing an existing administration.

Spanish interference in elections was common. Lawsuits and accusations,

1. The church at Acolman

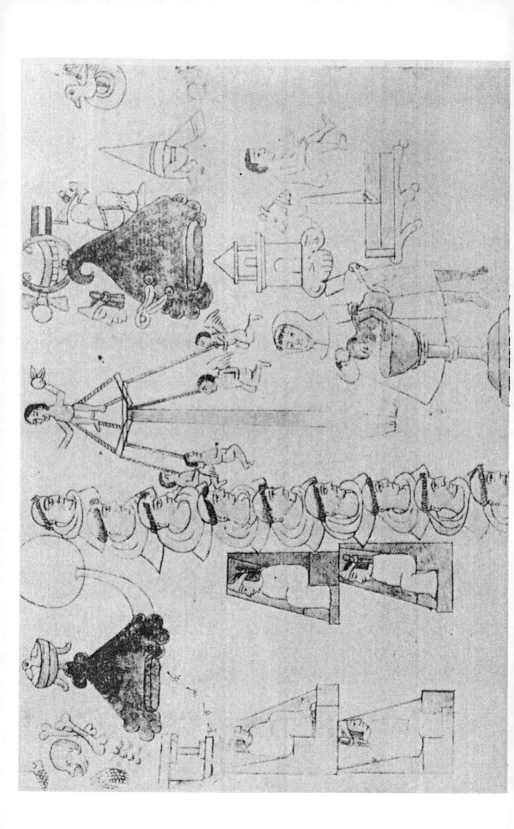

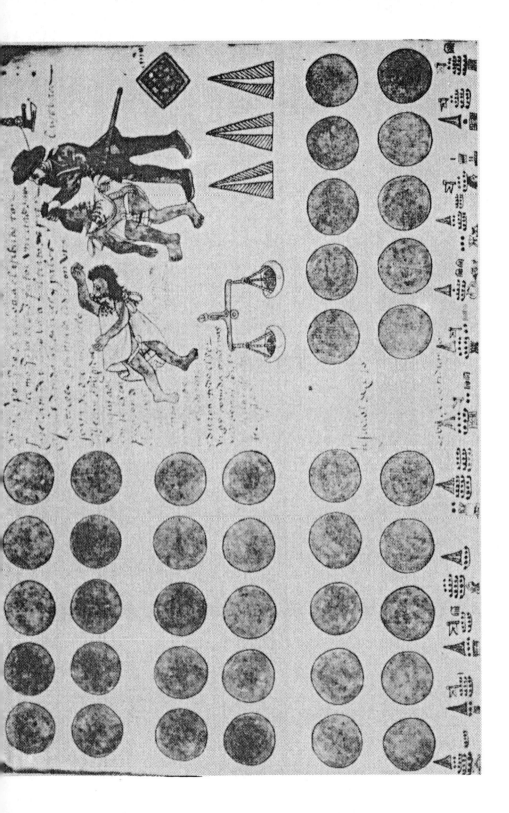

iv. Standing Indian figure (*Códice del Museo de América*)

lian types: farmer, tailor, and carpenters (Sahagún)

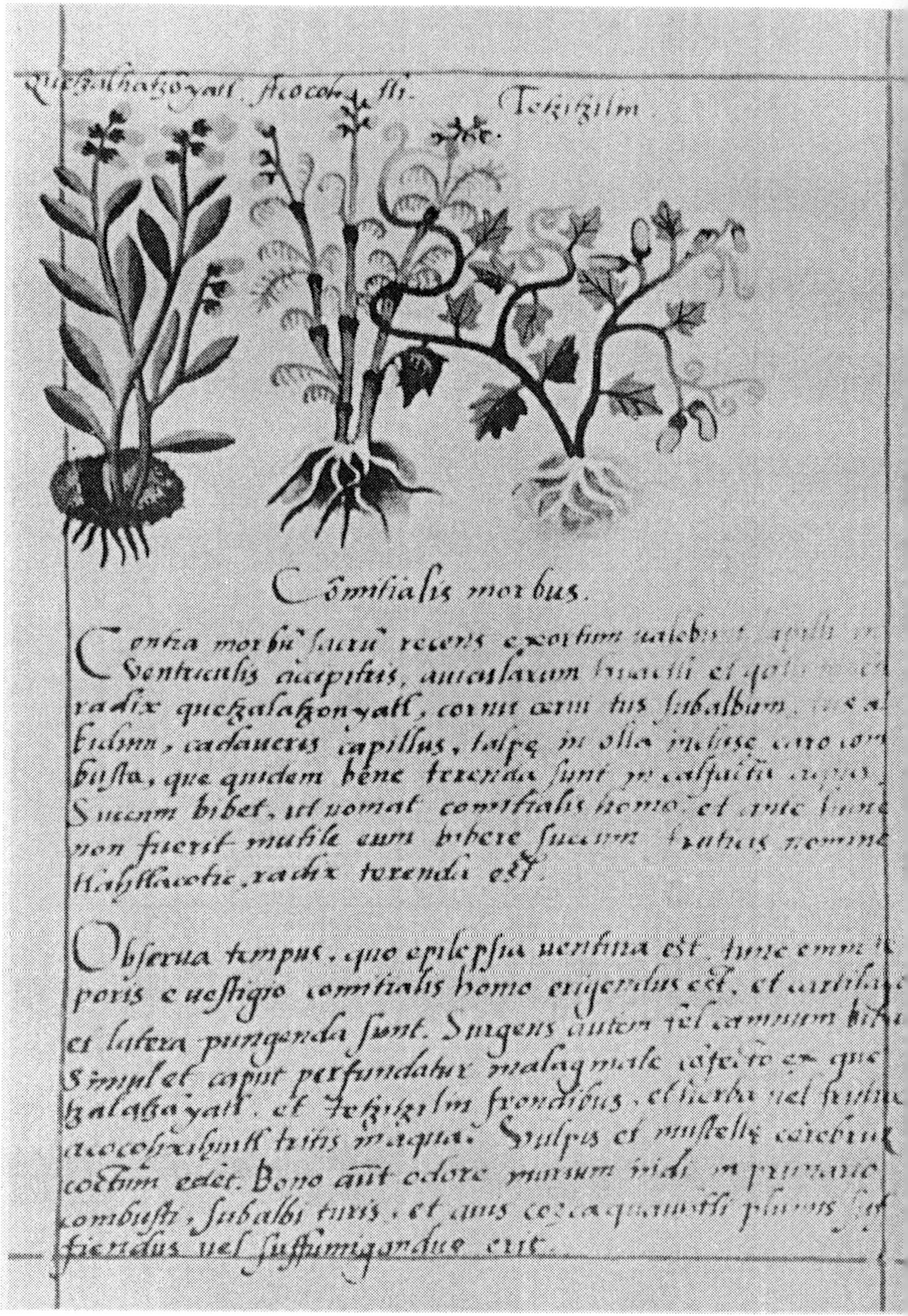

vi. A page from the Badianus Herbal

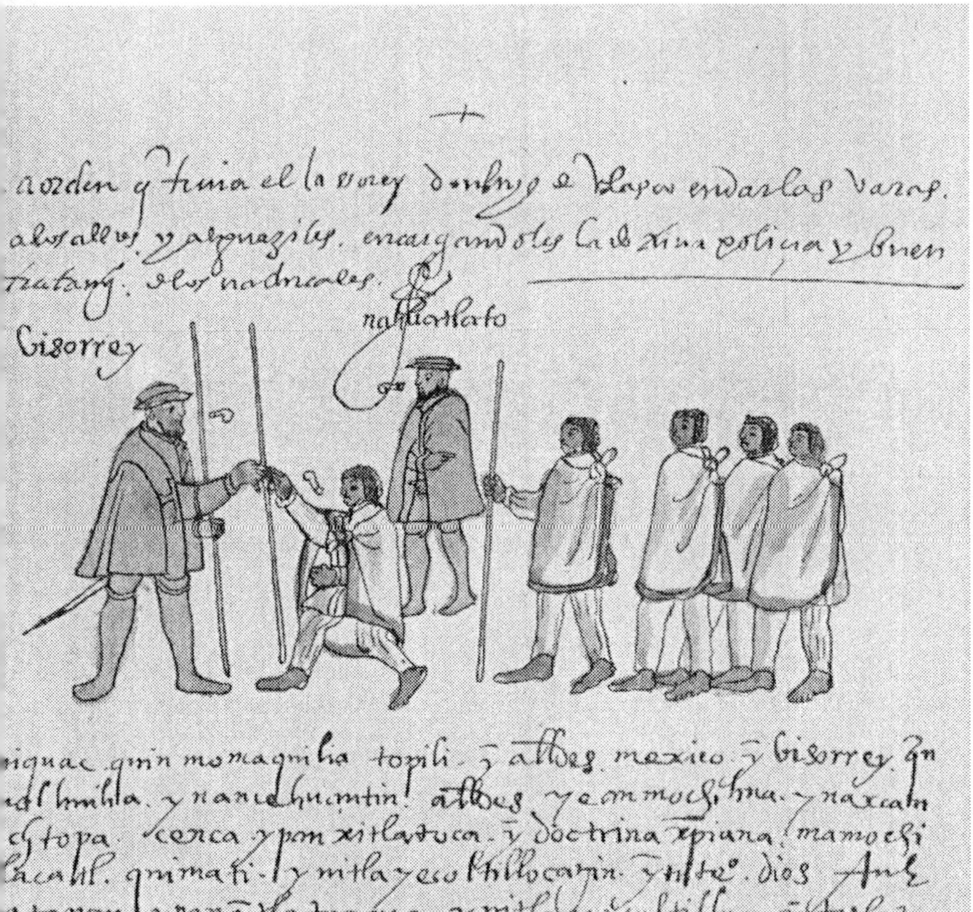

a orden q̄ tenia el la virey don luys de Velasco en darlas varas.
alcalldes. y alguaziles. encargandoles la policia y buen
tratamy̅. delos naturales.

Visorrey   nahuatlato

Investment of Indian political officers by the viceroy (*Códice Osuna*)

VIII. Tribute records: Top, Antonio Valeriano testifies to the death of a tribute payer (*Códice Valeriai* Bottom, Indians serve as tamemes and providers of food in encomienda (*Códice Kingsborough*) real or supposed, constituted the justification or pretext.[81] From the six-teenth century to the end of colonial times, Spanish oidores, corregidores, and clergymen supervised elections, either in person or through Indian agents and protégés. Encomenderos deposed and exiled recalcitrant native officers in the early period.[82] Clerics manipulated elections to place their own candidates in office or removed elected officials from their posts, and the fre-quency with which elections were held in church buildings in late colonial times suggests a pervading ecclesiastical interest. Conflict between a curate and a corregidor might be reflected in two Indian factions, and in two op-posing Indian candidates for the office of gobernador, each supported by his Spanish patron.[83] Sometimes in the eighteenth century curates and corregi-dores chose community officials outright in the absence of any pretense of election.[84]

In the sixteenth century, and frequently in the seventeenth and eighteenth centuries as well, newly elected Indian officers traveled to Mexico City to receive viceregal confirmation of their positions, as pre-conquest tlatoque had traveled to Tenochtitlan to receive confirmation from Montezuma. In the eighteenth century such confirmation was often given on the rec-ommendation of the curate.[85] With this, the officers received their *varas* (staffs) of office, and were charged with their obligations. Standard state-ments—written or printed forms with blanks for name of the official and town were sometimes used—required them to govern honorably and well, to ensure "good treatment" of the maceguales, to deliver tributes and com-ply with labor drafts, to control drunkenness, to refrain from derramas, to promote the Christian doctrine, to control crime, and to eliminate idolatry.[86]

As with clergymen and corregidores, the duties of Indian officials were only partially expressed in their instructions. A cabildo's functions related to all routine political processes in the life of the cabecera and its sujetos. Cabildos held regular and irregular meetings throughout the year. In most cabeceras and at most times, cabildo officers were responsible for tribute collection and delivery. The provision of labor quotas for Spanish em-ployers, as well as the regulation of the internal local labor for community affairs, fell within the cabildo's jurisdiction. Cabildos enacted rules con-cerning local markets, public buildings, water supplies, roads, and all local projects. The officers regarded themselves as representatives of the com-munity as a whole, bound to defend their town against land usurpation or other intrusions—"por sy y en nonbre de los maceguales concejo, y vniversidad" in the full formal phrase.[87] Lodging protests against excessive tribute exaction and handling community lawsuits with neighboring towns or haciendas were always regarded as cabildo functions. Such suits might be costly in time and funds. In extreme cases, as we have seen, they involved a full appeal to the Council of the Indies, and while this normally required only the submission of written depositions and the payment of lawyers' fees, it might also include the sending of Indians to Spain.[88] Municipal pageants and ceremonials, for viceregal receptions or religious fiestas, likewise fell within the cabildo's jurisdiction. In all this, much depended upon local precedent and circumstance. An inclination appears at times to transact business outside the established institutions; the Tenochtitlan cabildo, for instance, was designed to meet twice a week, on Mondays and Fridays, but it was already failing to do so by 1560.[89]

Indian gobernadores and alcaldes (not, so far as we know, regidores) held court for minor local offenses, and the cabildos maintained local cabecera jails for the imprisonment of drunkards and other persons sentenced for crime. Criminal and civil cases involving Indians were heard and settled before native alcaldes in regular sessions.[90] The cases decided by Indian judges, like those decided by corregidores, provide a revealing record of the petty squabbles of Indian life—over property, debts, horses, women, market goods, and other matters without end. Spaniards occasionally complained that Indian alcaldes possessed only a limited understanding of their judicial obligations and that they jailed maceguales unjustly.[91] On the other hand, records of Indian judicial procedure indicate at times a remarkable sense of legalism, in absolute imitation of Spanish procedures. A number of records of Nahuatl court minutes have survived, with accusations, charges, interrogations, depositions, sworn testimonies, sentences, and the full corpus of Hispanic legal form. Official Indian land sales conducted before native alcaldes often adhered rigidly to Spanish legal precedents. The Nahuatl land records include statements of possession, testimonies of witnesses, contracts of sale, records of measurement and survey, records of payment, and maps of the affected properties.

The Spanish residencia, the court trial for officeholders, was introduced into the new Indian governments almost as soon as they were created. The record suggests that this was established as an emergency measure, one not employed for every change in political office but applicable when circumstances required, as in instances of malfeasance or dispute. Residencia judges in Indian government might be Spaniards or other Indians.[92] At least three residencias by Indians in the Valley are recorded as early as 1544: in Tecama by a native of Xochimilco;[93] in Chalco Atenco by a native of Xaltocan; and in Cuitlahuac by a native of Cuauhtitlan.[94] Some residencias occurred long after the incidents that they were established to investigate,[95] and communities sometimes spent large sums in the attendant litigation. Or the viceroy might make a residencia-like appointment of a gobernador, in the absence of a local election, in order to conduct an inquiry into the political practices of preceding officers without disturbing the continuity of local rule. Records of the sixteenth century especially are filled with assignments of principales to serve as gobernadores in alien communities, to conduct general or limited residencias, and to perform special tasks, such as the revision of labor drafts or the settlement of disputes in cacique succession.[96] Such appointments might accomplish their purpose, or they might provide opportunities for new demands, derramas, or campaigns of terror on the part of the newly appointed officials.[97]

At levels below the gobernador and the members of the cabildo, the Hispanized community governments further required that functionaries keep records, guard properties, and maintain an administrative order. Escribanos, literate Indians associated with the alcaldes' courts or with the cabildos, were to copy documents for the court archives, to act as court stenographers, or to keep cabildo minutes. Regular Indian escribanos were functioning in most community governments by the late sixteenth century. Small communities had one or two, larger communities three or four or more. The office required special training and skills, and some remarkable examples of the calligraphy of Indian scribes survive.[98] The colonial scribe's function was in part a Hispanization of the role of the pre-conquest *tlacuilo* or pictorial draftsman, and in the post-conquest period Indian records normally had a larger pictorial content than comparable Spanish records—in notices of genealogies, census lists for tribute, maps of land properties, or accusations against gobernadores and corregidores. After about 1590 the pictorial forms were abandoned in Indian records, and for much community business the services of the Indian escribanos were dispensed with altogether.

The Indian mayordomos were officers responsible for community properties: common lands, the town's sheep herd, the jail, or any other possession that required direction or maintenance or yielded an income. Many towns supported *mayordomos de la comunidad* in the sixteenth century, often with subordinates for special tasks. It will be recalled that each of the five cofradías of Chimalhuacan Atenco in the eighteenth century was under the charge of a mayordomo, and that these were not organizations of cofrade membership but rather institutions of community landholding for particular saints. Mayordomos sometimes held their positions for long periods and at other times were regularly appointed by gobernadores or cabildos. Tenure might be by rotation, with one mayordomo for a cabecera and another for the sujetos, the latter being chosen from a number of sujetos periodically and by turns.[99]

At the lowest levels of community government a less deliberate Hispanization occurred, and aboriginal forms of rule persisted for a longer time. Despite loss through attrition and merger, the calpultin, as we have seen, survived as barrios or estancias or subdivisions of these. In the pre-Spanish political system calpultin had been presided over by pipiltin with tecuhtli or other titles. They occurred most often as *tlayacanque, tepixque, tequitlatoque, topileque, achcacauhtin, calpixque,* or *calpulleque.*[100] The members of a calpulli recognized as their head a person who was one of their group, who served a life tenure, and whose son might inherit the office after his death. The tequitlatoque, or *tequitlatos* as they were known in the colony, kept records of changes in macegual landholding, verified tribute receipts from macegual members of the calpulli, and collected tributes. Topileque (or *topiles*) and achcacauhtin had a police function, and the latter served also as judges in minor crimes.[101] Calpixque were collectors of tribute or guardians of property.[102] Within the calpultin, families appear to have been grouped in vigesimal units, each with its officer. Many notices comment especially on the *centecpanpixqui* (20-*pixqui*) with jurisdiction over twenty families, and the *macuiltecpanpixqui* (100-*pixqui*) or centurion, with jurisdiction over 100 families.[103]

This calpulli structure survived virtually intact to the mid-sixteenth century, although at least in some areas the organization by twenties and hundreds had fallen into decay by that time.[104] The offices of tequitlato, topil, calpixqui, and tepixqui were retained almost everywhere.[105] In the colonial period the barrio and estancia officers adopted in some instances equivalent Spanish titles—*mandón, capitán, alguacil, merino,* or *mayoral*—but the offices continued to be hereditary, at least in part, and in some barrios the merinos of the late sixteenth century still held their positions by family descent from the period prior to the conquest.[106] Spaniards indicated an equivalence between the achcacauhtin and the capitanes, between the topiles and the alguaciles, and between the (te)pixque and the mandones.[107] But such correspondences may be accepted only in the most general sense. The terminology of office varied from community to community within a uniformly operating hierarchy, and it is probable that local differences were not innovations but reflections of pre-conquest nomenclature and function. In any town a colonial collector of barrio or estancia tribute might be variously entitled tequitlato or topil or mandón. Tlalmanalco in the late sixteenth century had nine alguaciles and five tequitlatos, while Tizayuca, reversing the emphasis, had two alguaciles and forty tequitlatos. In Huehuetoca the hierarchy included thirty-two principales of whom eight were mayores and twenty-four were capitanes in lower rank.[108] In Xochimilco in 1561 the organization consisted of fifty-two centurions and twenty-four 80-pixque.[109] In Coyoacan, where a profusion of tequitlatos, alguaciles, and mandones held office, and where the holding of office became a means of avoiding labor obligations, the viceroy in 1580 introduced a reform that reduced the number of officers for each group of one hundred families to one tequitlato mayor, three tequitlatos menores, and one alguacil.[110] In Tenochtitlan in the late sixteenth century, in addition to the usual officers, four *alguaciles chichimecas* and four *alguaciles tarascos* held office.[111]

The lower levels of Indian officialdom were also used by the church to enforce religious attendance. Indian alguaciles were charged with summoning and gathering congregations, with inflicting the beatings and other punishments prescribed for absence, and with searching out and eliminating pagan survivals. In the early period, centecpanpixque circulated through the barrios notifying the Indian population of their fiesta obligations, and the congregations attended in files or groups, by barrios, each with its banner honoring its barrio saint. Often systems of rotation were established, such that a person serving non-religious functions in one year as alguacil, would be assigned to the gathering of congregations in the next year as ecclesiastical tepixqui.[112] But many towns of the sixteenth century maintained separate religious alguaciles, called alguaciles de la iglesia or alguaciles de la doctrina, for these purposes, a common ratio being one for each barrio. An equivalent Indian officer might be called fiscal, or topil de la

TABLE 13

Numbers of Indian Officers in Selected Towns, Late Sixteenth Century

Town	Date	Gober-nador	Alcalde	Regi-dor	Fiscal	Mayor-domo	Escri-bano	Cantor	Mayoral	Algua-cil	Tequi-tlato (or equivalent)
Acolman	1580	1	2	8		2	1	12			
Amecameca	1578	1	2	5		1	1	8		2	34
Azcapotzalco	1580	1	1	3		1	1	8		1	26
Chimalhuacan	1580	1	2	6		1	1	10		3	26
Coyoacan	1581	1	2	6	1	2	2	16			24
Otumba	1578	1	2	4	1	1	3	12	7	4	8
San Juan Temamatla (sujeto of Tlalmanalco)	1581		1	2		1	1	15		1	7
San Martín (sujeto of Tlalmanalco)	1581		1	3		1	1.	5		1	5
Tacuba	1574	1	2	7		1	1	20			
Tacubaya	1580	1	2	4		2	1	4		2	11
Tepetlaoztoc	1580	1	2	6	1	2	2	12		4	19
Tequixquiac	1581	1	2	4		2	1	8		1	
Tizayuca (sujeto of Otumba)	1578	1	1	2	1	1	3	8		2	40
Tlalmanalco	1581	1	2	9	1	1	4	20		9	30

SOURCE: AGN, General de parte, vol. 2, fol. 153r–153v, and AGN, Indios, vol. 1, *passim*. All communities except San Juan Temamatla, San Martín, and Tizayuca were cabeceras. Occasional officers under other titles are not shown.

iglesia.[113] Tlalnepantla (Teocalhueyacan) had a fiscal de la iglesia, an alguacil de doctrina, a maestro for the cantores, and a maestro for the instrumental musicians. In Tepozotlan in 1568 the barrio officials for church congregation were mandones or capitanes, and the barrios were called capitanías. In Hueypoxtla the same function was performed by tequitlatos and tepixque under the direction of an alguacil. In many towns the Indian cantores de la iglesia were municipal officials charged with the teaching of Christian doctrine on Sundays and holidays. The office of cantor was an honorable one, and the high regard in which cantores were held appears to have been continuous from pre-conquest times, when the tlatoque maintained groups of noble singers.[114] In the later colonial period, ecclesiastical fiscales, alguaciles, and their equivalents might be elected by the vocales following nomination by the curate, and in the performance of his duties such an officer might carry a large staff, five feet or more in length, capped with a silver cross.[115]

The political officers, related as they were to existing social organizations, continued at first to depend for their recompense upon Indian perquisites and methods of payment. As we have seen, caciques and principales lost their private incomes of tributes and services drawn from lands and retainers. By way of substitution for traditional forms of income, and also in the interests of Hispanization, salaries were established for the political officers in the towns. Here the transitional period was the sixteenth century, when tlatoque were losing their private tribute payers and simultaneously being removed from positions of community control. Salaries further served as inducements to seek and to hold office. By the 1580's salary scales had been established everywhere in the cabecera governments of the Valley and fully separated from the remaining private tributes and perquisites of caciques and principales. The funds were drawn from community treasuries (cajas de comunidad) and fixed in amount by viceregal order. In certain towns the transitions from private to public income may be documented with great precision. In the early 1550's in Otumba, for example, three principales—Martín Vásquez of Tizayuca, Martín García of Ahuatepec, and Martín Dircio of Aztaquemecan—were supported by tributes from their respective sujetos. Beginning in 1555, by order of a Spanish visitador, these principales became salaried officials in the Otumba government: Martín García received eighty pesos, Martín Vásquez received sixty pesos, and Martín Dircio received forty pesos, payable as annual salary in money or in kind. Each was given the services of two male and two female Indian servants, provided by the community in weekly alternation.[116]

Food, fuel, and services, in addition to money, were the miscellaneous components of the political salaries of the sixteenth century. Only in the later sixteenth and early seventeenth centuries did these come officially to be distinguished from salaries, and in reality it may be doubted that they were ever given up. A comparison of the financial salaries of gobernadores of various towns in the late sixteenth century indicates an extremely wide range, related directly to the population size of the communities. Community funds were provided by tribute, and in the absence of disturbing conditions, the larger tributary populations generally provided the larger town treasuries. In the period shown in Table 14, gobernadores continued to receive, in addition to their money salaries, an authorized but now limited service from the communities: four male and four female servants in Xochimilco (1561), two male and two female servants in Zumpango (1579), and one male servant and one female servant in Chimalhuacan Atenco (1579).[117]

Changes in gubernatorial salaries with the passage of time reflect shifting municipal circumstances and serve as a rough index of a town's prestige. Texcoco was still a highly reputable community in the sixteenth century and its gobernador continued to receive a large salary, 300 pesos per year. But by 1628 Texcoco had fallen sharply in size and importance, and its gubernatorial salary had been reduced to 150 pesos.[118] Xochimilco illustrates the reverse process. The gubernatorial salary there was increased from

TABLE 14

Salaries of Gobernadores in Selected Towns, Late Sixteenth Century

Town	Salary in pesos	Date	Town	Salary in pesos	Date
Tenochtitlan	400	1564	Chimalhuacan	40	1576
Xochimilco	350	1598	Tecama	40	1575
Texcoco	300	1593	Tequicistlan	40	1577
Tlatelolco	300	1590	Zumpango	40	1577
Acolman	100	1583	Mixquic	30	1578
Coyoacan	100	1581	Chiconauhtla	20	1577
Tequixquiac	50	1581	Coatlichan	20	1577
Tlalmanalco	50	1576	Huitzilopochco	20	1581

SOURCES: Data for the first four towns are from UT, G-42; AGN, Indios, vol. 4, fol. 219v; vol. 6(1), fol. 171v; vol. 6(2), fol. 240r. Data on other towns are from AGN, Indios, vol. 1, *passim*.

TABLE 15

Salaries of Principal Indian Officers in Selected Towns,
Late Sixteenth Century

Town	Date	Annual Salaries in Pesos				
		Alcaldes	Regi-dores	Mayor-domos	Escri-banos	Can-tores
Acolman	1580	8	4	6	10	2
Chiconauhtla	1577	8	5	6	6	
Chimalhuacan	1576	15	6	6	6	
Citlaltepec	1563	7	5	6		
Coatlichan	1577	6	3	6	4	
Coyoacan	1581	12	6	10	6	2
Mixquic	1578	10	6	6	6	2
Otumba	1579	10	3	5	3–5	2
Tacuba	1574	12	8	12	8	2
Tecama	1575	8	4	4	4	2
Tenochtitlan	1564	50	20	20		
Tequicistlan	1577	8	6	8	6	
Tequixquiac	1581	10	4	4	4	2
Zumpango	1577	10	6	8		2

SOURCES: These data are taken from AGN, Indios, vol. 1, *passim.*, except for Tenochtitlan (UT, G-42) and Citlaltepec (AGN, Mercedes, vol. 7, fol. 55r). Occasional additional payments (e.g., to a fiscal or a regidor mayor) are omitted.

100 to 200 to 350 pesos between the mid-sixteenth century and 1598.[119] The Indian gobernador of Xochimilco in the seventeenth century received a higher payment than many Spanish corregidores. The salaries of gobernadores, to be sure, were the highest in the Indian scale. Many lesser officers never appear in the salary schedules, and we must suppose that their rewards were in power and prestige and in the informal payments that were characteristic both of Spanish and of Indian political life.

Beyond this, Indian gobernadores and other officials used public funds for personal and community affairs, and in general they did so to the extent that such funds were available. Spaniards repeatedly noted that Indian community treasuries were squandered by the principales, an observation determined in part by the differences between Spanish and Indian concepts of "public" property. By custom, as Zorita remarked in the sixteenth century, the fiesta was a necessity in the Indian communities, for if rulers failed to provide fiestas, their people "neither hold them in esteem nor obey them."[120] The records of town finances in the colonial period indicate a fairly loose system of gubernatorial and other salary payments, with disbursements made at irregular times and with additional allotments in years of surplus.[121] At other times coercion and extortion are recorded on the part of Indian town officers, with the levying of derramas, the confiscation of tribute receipts, the alteration of records, the taking of bribes, and other illegal procedures.[122] In the late eighteenth century, with the introduction of the intendancy, the close functional connection between tribute collection and community salaries was legalized for gobernadores. Salaries in the former sense were abolished, and by the same order that abolished them for the corregidores-subdelegados, the gobernador, alcalde, or other Indian tribute collector in each community was authorized to receive one per cent of the tribute amount as salary.[123]

As would be expected, Indian governments were always intimately related to the problems of cabeceras and their sujetos. The office of gobernador and the existence of a local cabildo came to be the single most important criterion for the cabecera status of any community. The transition from tlatoani rule to gobernador-cabildo rule is of the greatest significance in this respect, for it denotes the full substitution of a Spanish formula in the determination of cabecera rank. After the middle sixteenth century communities could no longer justify cabecera rank exclusively in terms of a cacique lineage. Connections between cabecera status and the cabildos were now universally recognized by Indians and Spaniards alike. For the most part the multiple cabeceras ceased to be regarded as such, evidence for unity being found in the unit cabildo. Repeatedly, the several elements of the multiple cabeceras found expression not in separate Indian governments but in the various subordinate offices within cabildos, particularly at the ranks of alcalde and regidor.

Some examples will illustrate these processes as they operated in the Indian governments of the Valley. In the three putative cabeceras of Tenango —Tepostlan, Tenango, and Tepopula Amilco—the governorship was a single office in the middle years of the sixteenth century while the three subdivisions were represented in the alcaldía and regimiento. Here one alcalde represented Tepostlan, the other alcalde represented Tenango and Tepopula Amilco in annual alternation, and two regidores represented each of the three.[124] Xochimilco, originally a triple cabecera, maintained three tlatoque, called gobernadores, for its three divisions in the 1540's. In the early 1550's the governorship in Xochimilco rotated from one cabecera to another. But in 1555 Agustín Osorio, a principal of Huejotzingo, was appointed as single gobernador and charged with settling the disputes among the three tlatoque. Later in the sixteenth century the Xochimilco governorship again became multiple, but in the seventeenth century, when the three cabeceras were generally regarded as barrios of a single community, each was represented in the Indian government by a single alcalde.[125] The five cabeceras of Amecameca, as we have noted, recognized a single gobernador in 1563.[126] On the other hand, the two cabeceras of Tlalnepantla—Tenayuca and Teocalhueyacan—retained separate gobernadores and separate alcaldes even in the seventeenth and eighteenth centuries.[127] Cuitlahuac shifted back and forth between a unitary and a multiple governorship, and for a time a cacique of Tlaxcala simultaneously held the governorship in Cuitlahuac and Mixquic.[128] In Azcapotzalco the two subdivisions of Tepaneca and Mexica preserved their Indian gobernadores and their separate cabildos to the end. At times each of the Azcapotzalco alcaldes possessed a distinct jurisdiction in his area, while at other times they shared a joint jurisdiction. Occasionally the two parts came into conflict, each seeking to influence the election in the other.[129] Once in the mid-seventeenth century, after a series of elections that were nullified by the viceroy, the Tepaneca and Mexica factions agreed on a single gobernador for both.[130]

These various arrangements became more complex when the status of cabeceras and sujetos was disputed and when sujetos campaigned for recognition as cabeceras. Two cases to which we have referred above—one concerning Texcoco and Huexotla, the other concerning Tepexpan and Temascalapa—are especially revealing in this respect. It will be recalled that in 1551 the Indians of Huexotla used as an argument for cabecera status their tradition of "rulers . . . by direct descent."[131] The argument was wholly appropriate in 1551, when tlatoani traditions still served to justify cabecera status. The terms of the conflict between Huexotla and Texcoco, however, were quickly adjusted to the new cabildo governments. A decision of 1555 recognized the authority of a Huexotla alcaldía, but the single alcalde was to serve in the cabildo government of Texcoco and his appointment was also to be made in Texcoco. Later Huexotla was able to increase its participation to two alcaldes chosen within Huexotla, but the choice became subject to the confirmation of the Texcoco cabildo.[132]

In the dispute between Tepexpan and Temascalapa, Tepexpan was the acknowledged cabecera, and Temascalapa strove for separation from it.

To the standard arguments justifying their position the Indian officers of Tepexpan added the new political criteria in 1552: that the alguaciles of Temascalapa were being appointed by the gobernador of Tepexpan; that the alcaldes of Tepexpan journeyed to Temascalapa to render justice in local suits; that Temascalapa had never had a cabildo of its own, with gobernador, alcaldes, and regidores; that the only Indian officials in Temascalapa were alguaciles, tequitlatos, mandones, and "mandoncillos"; that these collected tributes for Tepexpan and sent workers from Temascalapa for labor in Tepexpan. Against these claims the Temascalapa principales presented counterarguments, and once in the middle sixteenth century even elected a pseudo-gobernador. In 1552 the viceroy granted Temascalapa one alcalde who was to be a native of Temascalapa, to reside there for two weeks, and then to reside in Tepexpan one week.[133]

In the course of time all Indian governments changed. The progressive promotion of sujetos to cabecera status meant that many new governments under separate gobernadores appeared. The conflicts of status between cabeceras and sujetos repeatedly took the form of disputes over political organization. Sujetos sought to establish their tequitlatos as regidores, their regidores as alcaldes, and their alcaldes as gobernadores. Sujetos with one alcalde sought to elect two.[134] The increased number of cabeceras in the seventeenth and eighteenth centuries offered many opportunities for refinement and elaboration in officeholding. Existing cabeceras created internal grades and new positions. Community officials came to be designated by rank and number. Alcaldes became alcalde de primer voto, alcalde presidente, alcalde juez, alcalde ordinario, or alcalde menor.[135] Of four regidores one might be mayor and the other three ordinarios or menores.[136] *Contadores mayores* and *contadores ordinarios* appeared.[137] Xochimilco enlarged its cabildo to include thirteen distinct alcaldes.[138] San Agustín de las Cuevas (Tlalpam), which had been only a sujeto of Coyoacan in the sixteenth century, became a separate pueblo with a gobernador and ten alcaldes, each from a different barrio. In the Ecatepec jurisdiction, nine pueblos had independent governments under gobernadores by the late eighteenth century. In the Texcoco jurisdiction the number was twenty-three.[139]

But in general, and despite this progressive elaboration, the 1550's and 1560's rather than the late colonial years appear as the period of greatest prestige, confidence, and affirmation on the part of the Indian governments.

In the middle decades of the sixteenth century a newly indoctrinated generation had come to power, and the pressures of the later period were not yet fully in evidence. The mid-century spirit is reflected in the rotational systems and the operating cabildo forms, and in the campaigns for new public buildings to house the Indian governments and express their functions. The tecpan of Tenochtitlan and the tecpan of Tenango were both products of construction campaigns begun in the 1550's.[140] In Tlatelolco in the 1550's the community jail and the house of the gobernador adjoined the great plaza, which contained a fountain and gallows in its center, in imitation of municipalities of Spaniards. Tlatelolco built its new tecpan between 1576 and 1581 with funds provided by a gobernador in the 1550's and 1560's. The construction was a huge municipal enterprise, directed by the gobernador and cabildo, with numerous salons and offices, a prison and garden, a reception hall, and rooms for lodging.[141] The cabildo of Xochimilco was organized according to an elaborate set of rules drafted in 1553: that meetings would be held every two weeks in the *casas reales*; that absentees from the cabildo meetings would pay fines of five pesos; that proper minutes would be kept; that the gobernador and his family must reside in the casas reales. The cabildo decided in 1561 that the status of the community as the cabecera of a "provincia" and as an official ciudad required a new campaign of official building and public works. The cabildo determined to construct new casas reales, with a courtroom and jail, a wall enclosing the monastery on four sides, and a fountain in the plaza.[142] Other town governments likewise took pride in their constructions in the sixteenth century, as well as in their cabildos, their lawsuits, their archives, their water supplies, their ceremonies, and their consultations with the viceroy.

All this changed in the seventeenth and eighteenth centuries. Ceremony lost some of its Indian character and became mandatory under Spanish direction, as in 1721 when the gobernadores of Tenochtitlan and Tlatelolco were requested to participate in the bicentennial of the "felicitous conquest" and to celebrate the "singular benefits" that Indians had received under church and state.[143] Late colonial Indian governments functioned principally to collect tribute and to dispense minor punishments. The gobernadores of Tenochtitlan and Tlatelolco spent a large part of their time in a routine daily accounting of prisoners. By the end of the colonial period the word tecpan had come to be virtually synonymous with jail.[144]

Town buildings fell into disrepair. The community of Coyoacan in the late seventeenth and early eighteenth centuries had no casa de comunidad at all, and only a ramshackle adobe jail, from which prisoners regularly escaped. Its elaborate water conduit was in ruins, and only vestiges remained of its plaza fountain.[145] In eighteenth-century Cuauhtitlan, the casas reales were in serious disrepair and prisoners were breaking through the adobe walls of the town's prison. The casas reales of Texcoco were in ruins and near the point of collapse. The community house of Amecameca was "very dilapidated" and that of Tlalmanalco was "almost completely ruined."[146]

In the immediate aftermath of the conquest Spaniards had been in a position to govern the Indian communities through the tlatoque, the existing Indian leaders. To some degree they succeeded in this during the first thirty or forty years. But the need to Hispanize Indian rule, to reject the authority of the tlatoque, and to introduce municipal cabildos in Hispanic form was urgent. The urgency arose both from the total program of Hispanization and from the Spaniards' desire to control Indian municipal finance. In the atmosphere of the first viceregal administrations, municipal Hispanization provoked some of the optimism and enthusiasm that attended the early missionary effort, of which it may be regarded as a secular counterpart. Indian governments responded affirmatively to it, as the records of many communities attest. It is possible that the rotational and representational features of the sixteenth-century municipal governments appealed to an Indian aesthetic sense, for they were patterned institutional systems depending upon essential community relationships. The alcaldía of Tenochtitlan in the mid-sixteenth century had some of the cyclical intricacy and symmetry of the ancient Aztec calendar.

But such appreciation could hardly endure. Spanish pressures upon Indian governments, with demands for tribute and for the provision of laborers from a declining population, created new and more rigorous political conditions. Under the influence of the clergy and the corregidores, Indian governments became exploitative after the Spanish example. One could say, of course, that Indian community governments had always been exploitative and that their yielding to Spanish conceptions of exploitation hardly represented a significant change. But change was expressed in the native attitude toward political office and in the decay of the mid-century feelings of community pride. In the 1590's the corregidor of Texcoco had to compel the elected Indian alcaldes and regidores to accept the positions for which they had been chosen.[147] Officeholding came to be understood not as a spontaneous affirmation of rule, but as an obligation required by Spaniards. The rewards had become too limited, the demands and responsibilities too great, to permit an enthusiastic political activity in the earlier sense. "The Indian population in general is free from the vice of ambition," Bishop Palafox observed in the seventeenth century; "few Indians now aspire to be gobernador or alcalde."[148]

Occasional references in the historical literature to informal bodies of elders (*viejos* and *ancianos*) suggest a residual community power that survived all colonial pressures. This influence appears not in the cabildo tasks of tribute collection or labor regulation but in those areas of life where a covert Indian symbolism was called into question or where community traditions were at stake. We have mentioned above an incident in Huitzilopochco in the eighteenth century, when the community denounced its curate for tampering with a sacred hill and hence with the source of the pueblo's "strength." Here the curate criticized the gobernador for his pagan superstition. The gobernador responded that he himself "would not have intervened, but the viejos and viejas demanded it." On another occasion the same curate selected as his fiscal an Indian twenty-six years old, married and with children. The gobernador protested the choice, asserting that "it would be said in other pueblos that a boy was governing us."[149] Election disputes might center on the dominant position of the older generations, particularly at those periods of transition when power was passing to younger hands. A gobernador defeated after many years in office was likely to interpret his defeat as a rejection of tradition. As a losing candidate stated in 1734, "I am an old man," and the new gobernador and alcaldes are "young men of small experience" who have brought "pressure against their elders."[150] Such crises of transition are common to all governments. But in Indian society a special authority resided in the venerable aged, who were the guardians of the community's heritage and were at times willing to defy all external authority in its defense.

CHAPTER VIII

Tribute and Town Finance

While Montezuma was still alive, Spaniards were able to profit directly from Aztec imperial tribute procedures. During the early stages of the conquest, Spanish and Indian collectors circulated together under Cortés's and Montezuma's direction to secure a Spanish booty.[1] But by the conclusion of the conquest this was no longer possible. The Aztec tribute system rapidly fell into a state of disintegration.[2] The deaths of Montezuma and Cuitlahuac, the many independent decisions of Indian leaders to support or resist the Spaniards, the military campaigns in the Valley of Mexico, the dislocations of peoples, all contributed to the failure of native tribute organization in the years 1520–21.

Even after the disruptions, this Aztec tribute structure might have been re-established under certain circumstances. A centralized exaction under Cortés's control might have apportioned tributes among conquistadores, assigned appropriate amounts for the crown, and preserved an orderly continuity. What made such re-establishment impossible in practice was encomienda, the institution most clearly expressing post-conquest decentralization in Spanish tribute exaction. For the most part encomienda was based upon the tlatoani communities and their sujetos, as we have seen. When the conquistadores demanded encomiendas of Cortés, when the tlatoque of the cabeceras visited Cortés with gifts in Coyoacan,[3] Spanish assessment and collection of tribute became inseparably linked with the cabecera-sujeto structures.

The locations of Montezuma's tribute collectors (calpixque) were thus overlooked or rejected by the Spaniards. If we read the evidence of the Matrícula de Tributos and Codex Mendoza correctly, there had been over fifty of these locations in the Valley,[4] and fewer than half of them were tlatoani communities. The fact that only two of the non-tlatoani calpixqui locations mentioned in these documents—Tizayuca and Chicoloapa—became separate encomiendas illustrates again the thoroughness and effectiveness of the decentralization based on the tlatoani communities. Other non-tlatoani communities were of course granted in encomienda, and several of these were calpixqui locations under Nezahualcoyotl. But traditional encomienda required that a native cacique and his people, not simply an imperial tribute collector and the persons whose tributes he collected, comprise the essential material of the grant. In any case, there is little connection between the celebrated texts of Aztec tribute—the Matrícula de Tributos and Codex Mendoza—and the tribute jurisdictions that were established by the Spaniards.

In a very broad sense one could say that each encomienda contained two classes of Indian taxpayers: those who had formerly paid to local recipients, and those who had formerly paid to the imperial calpixque or to the agents of non-resident Indian recipients. It was the Spanish reduction of Aztec imperial tribute to an encomienda form that inspired the mid-century tlatoque of Texcoco and Tacuba to make protest, to specify the original tribute-paying communities, and to cite the various alienations resulting from encomienda.[5] We may note again that the successors, heirs, and relatives of Montezuma in Mexico City engaged in legal dispute with encomenderos over Acalhuacan, Coatitlan, and Tecalco, all of which were non-tlatoani calpixqui locations listed in the Matrícula de Tributos. The Indian leaders, making an appeal to Hispanic legalism, argued that these locations, as a part of Montezuma's "patrimony," could not legally be assigned in the Spanish encomienda system.[6]

If the first Spaniards rejected the Aztec tribute structure, one might suppose that they would have concentrated instead on the techniques of assessment and collection in their immediate cabeceras and sujetos. A direct encomendero concern with tribute at these levels would have been consistent both with decentralization and with the greed of encomenderos. To suppose this, however, would be to attribute to the encomenderos a greater interest in the details of Indian tribute methods than they in fact displayed. In practice they were far more concerned with gross tribute receipt than with a precise understanding of its sources, and they were quite willing to leave problems of assessment and collection to the tlatoque and principales. Upon the assignment of encomienda, in the words of Motolinía and Olarte, each encomendero "negotiated with the cacique, señor, and principales of the town of his encomienda concerning how much they were to give him."[7] During the entire first generation of encomienda, encomenderos received tributes from the caciques, and paid small attention to the distribution of assessments through the ranks of Indian society. Tributes were first received, and continued to be received, "from the hand of the señor."[8] The result was a critical relationship between encomendero and cacique, one that prolonged the rule of caciques who cooperated with encomenderos and cut short the rule of those who did not.

It is clear that the early demands made by Cortés and the encomendero class, as well as by royal officers and members of the first audiencia, strained to the full the native capacity to pay. "Their word was the only measure, for all that they could take," wrote Motolinía and Olarte,[9] and all evidence confirms the observation. A large part of the commentary on tribute during the first post-conquest generation relates to excesses in Spanish exactions. Occasionally, as in Chalco province, Cortés made some effort to base the new tribute requirements upon pre-conquest precedents.[10] But Spanish demands rapidly transcended such scruples. Documentation for Cortés's own levies is to be found in his residencia record of 1529 as well as in texts concerning his relations with Texcoco, Xaltocan, Coyoacan, Tlalmanalco, and other communities.[11] Extreme tributes by Matienzo, Delgadillo, Salazar, and many other leaders of the early colony are amply documented.[12]

Our most concrete account of tribute collection in the early encomiendas, based on data obtained from conquistadores and other "creditable persons," is provided by Fernández de Oviedo. Each tequitlato, he stated, had charge of the collection from some forty houses. At harvest times the tequitlato examined the land cultivated by each tributary, counted the ears of maize harvested, and counted the women and children in each house. Computing then the number of ears that all individuals in the household would require until the next harvest, the tequitlato left this amount and delivered the remainder to the Indian señor (cacique). The tequitlato made a similar division of beans, chiles, and other produce, in each case leaving for the tributary family only "as much as each needed for sustenance during the year." In addition he collected the tributary's payment in mantles, gold, silver, chickens, cacao, honey, or other produce. This was done periodically, at sixty- to ninety-day intervals, according to custom or prior arrangement. All materials were taken to the cacique, and from the total the amount due was paid to the Spanish encomendero or corregidor.[13]

The retention of an operating control in the hands of caciques and principales meant that the upper native classes were themselves able to make extreme demands upon tequitlatos and tributaries and then deliver only a portion of the yield to the Spanish recipient. Within native society, payments in excess of Spanish assessments by several hundred per cent and more were reported,[14] and Spaniards spoke frequently of the derramas, "robberies," and extreme impositions by the Indian rulers.[15] A reduced assessment imposed by the viceroy or audiencia for any community might result in a smaller amount for the encomendero, but it might have no effect at all upon the amounts paid by maceguales.[16] Thus in the sixteenth century a corollary to the limitations upon encomenderos' tributes was the formal Spanish demand for restrictions on the tributes taken by Indian leaders. The monarchy itself favored a reduction of caciques' tributes in the belief that the royal treasury would benefit.[17]

Tributes paid to local tlatoque in the pre-conquest period had consisted of most of the familiar materials paid in Aztec imperial tribute: mantles of various kinds, loincloths, feathers, torch pine, mats, baskets, vessels, and similar goods. Daily provisions included maize, turkeys, cacao, tomatoes, chiles, and salt. The authorized tributes for caciques in the middle sixteenth century included these same goods, with an occasional addition of new colonial products such as money, wheat, and fodder for horses.[18] But in accordance with Spanish regulations, the authorized amounts received by caciques after 1550 were progressively reduced. By 1560 very few caciques were receiving the equivalent of one thousand pesos, and the income of many amounted to only a small fraction of this figure.[19] The elimination of caciques from the governing position within the Indian towns implied a further reduction of their income, and at the same time a continuous depopulation took place within the sub-macegual classes on whom caciques had previously depended for large parts of their support.[20]

In an average community of about 1550, the Indian criteria for liability in payment continued to prevail. This meant the exemption, in various degrees, of caciques and principales, of those who paid to private Indian recipients, of the aged and infirm, of children and youths still living with their families, and in some instances of merchants and craftsmen.[21] Just as maceguales who supported the Aztec temples had paid no tribute in the preconquest period, so those serving in Christian monasteries and churches—including singers and players of musical instruments—were commonly exempted from early colonial tribute.[22] In the middle sixteenth century each tributary in a community might be required to pay a quantity of maize, a turkey, firewood, or some other product, in addition to a certain number of reales. The tax might still be graded among maceguales, with those cultivating large allotments of land paying one peso or one-half peso and those with small amounts paying only one real or a fraction of a real or a number of cacao beans.[23] Craftsmen (*oficiales*) might be required to pay in the products of their manufacture, or in what they could make in one week's work.[24] The women of the community might pay specified amounts of cotton cloth, from which the principales and tequitlatos would receive an allotment of mantles. Lands were still worked in common for the community. The town's gobernador and the cabildo officials would receive payment in commodity tributes as well as in money and required service. Dishes, bowls, grinding stones, and similar goods might be paid so that they could be redistributed to the community as a whole for use on festival occasions.[25] Extra and exorbitant demands of money and goods might still be made by principales, under any of a number of pretexts.[26] Collection might still follow a common aboriginal pattern of eighty-day tributes.[27] Special requirements would be made for fiestas. The encomendero or the crown would receive a stated amount, but this would still be only a fraction—to be sure, a steadily larger fraction—of the total amount exacted by the Indian officers of the town.[28]

Tribute records after 1550 reveal many partial and compromise solutions to the demands for reform. The official Spanish objective, however imperfectly achieved, remains clear. It included first the further legal escheatment of encomienda towns to the crown. For both encomienda towns and crown towns the viceregal government now sought a precise, quantitatively fixed differentation between tributes destined for Indian authority and tributes destined for Spanish authority. The viceregal government proposed in addition to eliminate the multiple commodity tributes, reducing all payments to money and maize. The equalization of tribute was a similar objective, with each family head a tribute payer and each paying an equal sum. Lands worked in common were regarded as inappropriate to a system of equalized tribute payments. Spaniards looked to the total abolition of sub-macegual classes, and to an established scale of salaries for Indian municipal officials. Finally, the Spanish government now proposed that there be local treasuries or cajas de comunidad and annual records of all town finances. For no known community was this program ever achieved in its entirety. Yet every tribute regulation of the period represents a step in the direction of its realization. No two towns were exactly alike. But the regulations for all clearly express the effort to introduce the new uniformity in tribute procedure. New specifications were made as opportunity afforded, as Indians complained of irregularities or excesses, as encomienda heirs or cacique heirs died, or as other special circumstances warranted.[29]

The elimination of tributes from lands worked in common was a necessary initial step in the establishment of the uniform head tax. Originally a large number of these lands had been "lands of Nezahualcoyotl" or "lands of Montezuma," and their produce had been paid to their "owners."[30] In the early colonial period lands worked in common—undoubtedly in some instances the identical lands—were used to supply tributes both to encomenderos and to the crown.[31] The amounts to be harvested and delivered were set forth in the tribute regulations. Common plantings might be subdivided by barrios, and occasionally two sujetos might combine to make a joint "planting for His Majesty."[32] That extensive fields and labor and a large agricultural operation were involved in the common plantings is suggested by the case of Xochimilco, which was still required in 1563 to supply the crown with five thousand fanegas (about seventy-five hundred bushels) of maize from fields cultivated "in common."[33] The main practical difficulty with common labor in the raising of tribute goods, of course, was the variation in annual yield. Everything depended on the season and the harvest. Occasionally the new Spanish assessments compensated for the variation in annual yield by requiring additional and personal taxes in poor harvest years, or by delivering the excess in good harvest years to the community. At other times Indians had to make up deficits through derramas on their own authority.[34] But the most common solution of the 1550's and 1560's, and the solution consistent with the program of a uniform head tax, was to abandon the common plantations altogether and to assess each tributary directly. Towns were still held liable for bulk amounts in a form of assessment that would continue to the end of the colonial period, but the amounts were now determined by population counts and each tributary was expected to contribute an equal payment.[35]

Reduction of the multiple commodity payments to stated amounts of money and maize was for the most part accomplished during the same period.[36] The process can be traced in the tribute history of every community for which a record is available. In encomienda towns it meant the elimination of the food, fodder, firewood, textiles, and other materials delivered to encomenderos. In crown towns it meant chiefly the conversion of the corregidores' food to a money equivalent. The change began in some instances before 1550, and it was at times delayed by the resistance of corregidores and encomenderos.[37] Moreover, it was never fully accomplished; even a hundred years later multiple commodity goods were still being paid in certain towns.[38] To the extent that it was accomplished, it received criticism in the later sixteenth century as a cause for reductions of supply and increases in prices.[39] Multiple tribute goods had been marketed to consumers through sale or auction, and the shift to maize and money, while it helped to regularize Indian tribute, operated as a deterrent to the production and exchange of goods.[40]

Many of the exemptions derivative from pre-conquest rules likewise became inoperative in the 1560's. In any given community the addition of previously exempt classes to the tributary lists might occur as a gradual process involving progressive stages of liability to the new assessments.[41] Or change might result from viceregal ruling, as in 1563, when two hundred Indians reserved as laborers for the gobernador and principales in Teotihuacan were declared to be tribute payers. The change received a special impetus following the Valderrama visita, the express purpose of which was to increase the tribute yield.[42] Whereas Diego Ramírez in the 1550's and other royal agents had tended to abide by the original Indian criteria of exemption, Valderrama uniformly rejected these criteria. In the far-reaching changes of the 1560's the sub-macegual classes were almost without exception classified as tributaries, and even caciques were sometimes placed on the tribute rolls.[43]

The new regulations commonly required full tributaries to pay nine and one-half reales of silver and one-half fanega of maize apiece per year. Half-tributaries—widows, widowers, bachelors, and unmarried women living apart from their parents—were to pay half this amount.[44] The Indian schedule of eighty-day payments now yielded almost everywhere to the Spanish schedule of payments every four months or by the *tercios* of the year, a system with existing precedent in the payment of private debts.[45] Full exemptions were now limited to the aged, children, the blind, the crippled, the sick, and bachelors and spinsters (*solteros*) living with their parents. The phrase "even though they have lands" (*aunque tengan tierras*), frequently attached to the exemption regarding bachelors and spinsters, sought to separate the new system completely from Indian landholding.[46]

Much discussion among Spanish administrators attended this last point. Philip II in Spain and the viceroy and audiencia in the colony debated the issue of a uniform head tax (*tributo personal*) as opposed to a graduated tax based on landholdings or on property (*tributo por haciendas*). The king favored the latter, in the belief that Indian properties (including maize, wheat, and cattle) were sufficiently extensive to warrant such taxation.[47] At times graduated taxes were imposed by viceregal authority, as in Xochimilco, where principales were assigned varying amounts ranging from four reales to eight pesos, and where widows were assigned two or four reales, depending on their holdings of land and other property.[48] But for the most part, the viceroy and audiencia favored the uniform head tax,[49] and in the second half of the sixteenth century regulations providing for unequal payments by full tributaries became rare. Even after Spanish authority specified uniformity for full tributaries within each town, however, Indian governments sometimes continued to apportion the amounts by landholdings or by social rank, so that those with several land parcels paid more than those with only one, and principales paid more than maceguales.[50] Thus the new Spanish requirements were interpreted by native society according to its own terms, and not always in literal obedience to Spanish rules. And long after the change, individual Spaniards continued to argue ineffectively for a full reversion to the Indian system.[51]

Spanish rules regarding the age limits of tributaries were likewise subject to Indian interpretation. The rules themselves were by no means precise or consistent, and practice varied from town to town. Ecclesiastical records, on which tribute records were frequently based, sometimes included children of ten years and over as confessors, while at other times the lower limit was fixed at twelve or fourteen years.[52] Indian taxation prior to the 1560's sometimes included children under fourteen. The tribute record for Tepetlaoztoc in the 1550's included not only a category for bachelors and spinsters but also one for youths (*mozos* and *mozas*), excluding as tributaries only the small children. In other cases even unweaned infants were included in the lists and counted as tributaries.[53] But in general the age of fourteen was regarded as the initial year of liability in Spanish assessments.[54] The distinction between those living with their parents and those living separately undoubtedly served to reduce the number of recorded tributaries, but Indian governments are known to have disregarded this distinction and to have required youths of both classifications to pay equally.[55] And a royal order of

1578 ruled that Indians were to pay tribute at age twenty-five even if living with their parents.[56]

The new regulations, finally, made a precise distinction between the portion of the tribute that would be paid to the crown or the encomendero and the portion that would be retained by the community for its expenses. The purpose here was twofold: to prevent Indian governments from collecting excess tributes, and to limit the degree to which clergy or others might exploit community funds. Insofar as this matter had been specified at all prior to 1560, a ratio of three to one had been established, with the crown or encomendero taking three-quarters of the total tribute income, and the community keeping one-quarter. Thus in certain towns two reales of every peso paid in tribute had been designated for the community government.[57] The new rules reduced this amount, generally to one and one-half reales, and made it additional to the peso paid in Spanish tribute. From the income of one and one-half reales per tributary the town governments were to pay the salaries of their Indian officers, meet other common expenses, and in some cases provide for the support of the clergy.[58]

Thus by 1570, in a short span of years, substantial tribute changes had been brought about and a far greater regularity had been achieved than during the preceding decades. The largest encomiendas had reverted to the crown. The Spanish head tax had at least legally displaced the Indian common plantings and tributes based on land. Tributaries were defined by law in accordance with new Spanish requirements, and exempt classes had been brought within the tributary classifications. Regulation penetrated to the lowest levels of Indian society. The amount to be paid by each tributary was specified, and the Indian collectors were forbidden to collect in excess of this amount. Both the tributes designated for Spanish recipients and the tributes designated for town governments were fixed. The tribute system was intricately and permanently associated with Indian municipal finance.

Students of colonial tribute have often asserted that a uniform payment had been achieved by 1570, but the truth is that individual payments still varied and would continue to vary from town to town. The assertion that each tributary paid one peso and one-half fanega of maize is not wholly correct as regards payments to Spaniards, and it overlooks the additional payments made to the community. In Toltitlan each full tributary was required to pay six reales and one fanega of maize. In Tlalmanalco the payment was seven and one-half reales and one fanega. In Azcapotzalco it was eight reales and one-half fanega. In Xochimilco it was nine and one-half reales and one-half fanega. In Hueypoxtla it was ten reales and one-half fanega.[59]

Despite such variety, certain Indian documents of the later sixteenth century reveal a scrupulous effort to conform to the new Spanish tribute regulations. The most striking example is Códice Valeriano (1574), a native record of tribute receipt in San Pablo Teocaltitlan, a portion of Mexico City. The manuscript lists the tributaries as heads, five to a page. In three pictorial columns of red, orange, and blue, it enters the payments made by the tributaries at each of the three times of the year. When a tributary died, the drawing of his head was blackened, the certificate of his death was inserted in Nahuatl, and the notice was signed by the gobernador or by an alcalde. Separate sections denote married persons, half-tributaries, and persons who had moved to the jurisdiction during the tributary year, with explanatory notes by the Indian collectors. The document is evidence of a remarkable willingness to adjust to the Spanish tribute rules.[60]

On the whole, the procedures of tribute exaction from the 1550's to 1575 may be understood as Spanish responses to Indian depopulation, notably to the plague of 1545–48. The effect of the plague of 1576, after this, was a new insistence upon maize plantings. A rule of 1577, designed to prevent the abandonment of native agriculture in the crisis of further depopulation, required that contributions to the community were to consist not of money but of the produce of maize or wheat plots to be sown by the tributaries. Each full tributary was to cultivate a plot of ten *varas* (about nine yards). Each male half-tributary was to cultivate a plot five by five varas. Widows and spinsters were to pay one real apiece for the community instead of serving in the new agricultural labor force. The work was to be communal and enforced by the Indian officers, and only the gobernadores and alcaldes were to be exempted. After selling the produce, communities were to retain the income for their expenditures, and Indians were to contribute to the town treasuries in no other way than this.[61]

The rule regarding ten-vara plantings was less than explicit on a number of points, and some of its ambiguities were never completely resolved. The liability of the non-agricultural Indian craftsmen, notably in the larger communities such as Texcoco and Mexico City, remained in doubt.[62] The ten-vara measurement was not defined. The rule specified only ten varas, and this might be interpreted as ten varas in both directions (one hundred square varas) or as ten varas marked along a strip of arbitrary width. In any case the measurement for half-tributaries, five by five varas, could not be understood as half of a measurement of ten by ten varas.[63] Moreover, later notices indicated ten *brazas* rather than ten varas.[64] Later also the ten-vara distribution was sometimes confused with the distribution of community agricultural land, as if the rule of 1577 had been designed to fix a maximum amount for each Indian's own cultivation rather than an additional amount for community funds or a substitute for the contribution of one and one-half reales.[65]

Despite such uncertainties, it is clear that the new rule represented a determined Spanish effort to maintain maize supplies in a period of agricultural decline. The change was already in effect in a large number of towns in time for the spring planting of 1578. It meant that in good harvest years after this date Indian communities received substantially more than they would have received if the system of money payments had remained in effect—supposing, at least, the absence of derramas or covert exactions. Thus in 1579, a year of abundant harvests, Coatlichan, with 1,015 tributaries, would have had a community income of 190 pesos with payments of one and one-half reales from the tributaries. One real continued to be collected, in 1579, from each widow and spinster, the result being a cash income of 63 pesos. From the five-vara and ten-vara plantings of the remaining tributaries 200 fanegas of maize were collected in 1579. With the income from widows and spinsters, and at the current price of two pesos per fanega, only 64 fanegas had to be sold to reach the equivalent of 190 pesos. This left 136 fanegas of maize by which the town profited as a result of the change from money to maize payments.[66]

Four additional tributes remain to complete an accounting of exactions during the first century following the conquest. The first was the Medio Real de Fábrica, instituted in 1552 as each tributary's share of the costs of the metropolitan Cathedral construction. Proceeds from this tax were gathered by local corregidores and alcaldes mayores and by them delivered to a Cathedral treasurer. The tax continued in force during the period of the Cathedral construction and into the eighteenth century, with the rate remaining at one-half real per tributary per year.[67] The second exaction, instituted by Viceroy Velasco in 1592, required the substitution of one chicken for one real of existing tribute per tributary. Its purpose was to ensure the production of chickens during a period of shortage. But instead of increasing their production and reducing prices as expected, Indians now bought chickens at the tribute sales and maintained existing prices at from one and one-half to three reales. The chicken tribute was therefore regarded as a failure and was abolished in 1600–1601.[68] The third additional tribute was the Servicio Real, a tax of four reales per tributary for monarchical expenses, instituted in 1592 and ostensibly to be continued as long as the king maintained a fleet in defense of the Indies. Though deliberately entitled "Servicio," it was in effect a tribute, and it remained in force to the end of colonial times.[69] Finally the Medio Real de Ministros, inaugurated in 1605, was a tax upon each tributary to defray costs of Indian litigation and judicial protection. Its proceeds paid the salaries of Spanish court scribes, attorneys, ministers of justice, and other officials with jurisdiction over Indian cases, and it was intended to take the place of the fees (derechos) that would otherwise have been charged against Indian litigants. It also continued to the end of the colonial period.[70]

Thus in the early seventeenth century an average Indian tributary in the Valley of Mexico was required to pay eight reales and one-half fanega of maize to encomendero or crown, one real for Fábrica and Ministros, and four reales for Servicio Real. He also contributed to the treasury of his community on the basis of ten varas of agricultural land. To this list of his obligations might be added the compulsory, but remunerated, "servicios" still levied upon certain towns, the sales tax (alcabala) that Indians were expected to pay in transactions involving Spanish goods, legal or illegal fees and special local taxes, and the various labor provisions for Indian gobernadores and others.[71] It may be noted also that free Negroes and mulattoes became formal tributaries in 1580, following a series of regulations of the preceding decade, at a rate of one or two pesos per year depending upon marital or professional status.[72] Mestizos remained exempt from tribute payment.

The standard tribute procedure of the seventeenth and eighteenth centuries required a careful listing of cabeceras and sujetos and a detailed record of tribute collectors. In all jurisdictions except Mexico City, corregidores and alcaldes mayores were nominally responsible in final tribute deliveries, for which, in late colonial times, they customarily provided security through bondsmen (fiadores) at the time of taking office.[73] Tribute payments to Spanish authority continued at a normal rate of one peso and one-half fanega of maize per tributary, but still with numerous variations from place to place.[74] Maize in royal tribute was commutable, for most of the seventeenth and eighteenth centuries, at nine reales per fanega.[75] Half payments by widows, widowers, bachelors, and spinsters persisted. The ten-vara plantings, or a money substitute, remained in force in the seventeenth and eighteenth centuries, with occasional personal exemption in cases of age or illness or necessary absence, but without reservation for principales, alcaldes, mandones, or other Indian officials.[76] Half-tributaries might still pay one real per year in lieu of service in the ten-vara plots. Communities were permitted to spend up to twenty pesos per year with the approval of the corregidor, and more than that at viceregal discretion.[77] Temporary relief from all or a part of the taxation continued to be granted in local crises, or during periods of community construction or repair of a church, provided, as a seventeenth-century viceroy stated, that there was no fraud by the local ecclesiastics.[78]

Spaniards continued to the end of colonial times to assess the cabecera-sujeto units in bulk amounts, to compute such amounts as multiples of the tributary population, and to entrust actual collection to the Indian authorities. Each municipal government continued to be held responsible for the annual tax. Tribute officials based their counts at least partially on ecclesiastical records of baptism, marriage, and death.[79] The tax was usually paid by tercios, with payments in April, August, and December. Payment was made to the Spanish "collector," who might be the corregidor or alcalde mayor of the jurisdiction, the owner of a hacienda or a workshop (obraje), or a civilian licensee.[80] Communities of the jurisdictions of Xochimilco and Chalco continued to pay part of their tributes to the Marquesado del Valle.[81] The administrative structure of tax collection by Spaniards above the level of Indian municipal government varied widely in place and time, but it never greatly affected the procedures of tribute collection in the towns, nor was it a matter of special concern to Indians. Royal tribute maize continued to be auctioned—sometimes before the harvest, with the highest bidder becoming in effect a licensed collector of tribute. Preferential sales were still made to oidores or other influential Spanish authorities.[82] Beginning in the late sixteenth century, royal tribute maize from the whole Valley was periodically purchased by the Spanish cabildo of Mexico City, which thereupon assumed some of the responsibility for its collection.[83]

More important for Indian history is the late colonial procedure for collection within the towns. Here the actual collectors—those who went from house to house receiving payments from the tributaries—continued to be the lesser Indian officials: tequitlatos, mandones, merinos, tepixque, alguaciles, regidores, or simply *cobradores de tributos*. The collectors kept records of payers and amounts.[84] They delivered what they received to higher Indian authorities in the cabecera-sujeto systems: to alcaldes for certain barrios and estancias; to alcaldes or gobernadores for other sujetos; to gobernadores for hacienda workers still regarded as residents of the towns. These authorities in turn delivered the tributes to Spanish officials: to corregidores, alcaldes mayores, or subdelegados, or sometimes directly to the treasury officials.[85] Printed or manuscript receipt forms were sometimes issued with the payer's name, the date, and the signature of the gobernador.[86] In some eighteenth-century communities payments were still not equalized among tributary maceguales but continued to depend upon land allotments, as in the ancient Indian system. In Coyoacan gobernadores granted usufruct land privileges to maceguales. From their lands the maceguales supported themselves and paid their tributes, some paying one tax (*tequitl*) and others one-half or other amounts, the distinction being governed not by the Spanish definition of a half-tributary but rather by the size of the land allotment.[87]

Criteria for tribute liability varied markedly even in the late colonial period. As a rule, in the eighteenth century a tributary consisted of a man and his wife, or two half-tributaries—widows, widowers, bachelors, spinsters—all between the ages of eighteen and fifty.[88] Tribute lists distinguished in separate columns the married persons, the widows and widowers, the single persons of age, the youths, and the total tributaries. Persons approaching tributary age (*próximos a tributar*) were normally of twelve to seventeen years and were included in anticipation of the next tributary count. Those listed as "boys and girls" were under twelve.[89] But much depended on local custom. Some counts and categorizations were far more elaborate than others.[90] Caciques and their eldest sons were uniformly exempted, but other members of a cacique's family might or might not be required to pay.[91] Special local exemptions sometimes prevailed, as in Ticoman, where ex-alcaldes paid no tribute.[92] Indian spinsters were exempted by a rule of the 1720's which required that married women and widows be the only female classes liable. But the rule for spinsters was still in dispute in 1755, and in 1758 both spinsters and widows were formally exempted.[93] Elaborate guides for verifying exemptions were drafted in 1739, and new forms were introduced to distinguish Indian from other tributaries and to specify names, ages, residences, occupations, and marital status.[94]

The ordinances for intendants, which began to be applied in part in 1786, identified as full tributaries all Indian males from eighteen to fifty years and exempted men under eighteen (even though married), all women, legitimate caciques and their eldest sons, and gobernadores and alcaldes during their terms of office.[95] The new tribute forms of the late eighteenth century were in some instances elaborate documents of eleven or twelve categories: caciques; gobernadores and alcaldes; exempt persons of both sexes; absentees; widows and spinsters; boys and girls; married Indians of age; married Indians not of age; Indian men married to mulatto or absent women; Indian widowers and bachelors; Indian women married to mulattoes; and Indian youths about to become tributaries.[96] The definition of a tributary as a male aged eighteen to fifty proved extremely difficult to enforce, and viceroys reported in the late 1780's and 1790's that it was not yet in effect. Tributary counts continued to be made according to the old form.[97] In test areas where the new form was introduced as an experiment (to determine the increase in the number of tributaries under the new definition) the results were inconclusive, because Indians who were adversely affected moved to areas where the former system was still operating.[98] But a stricter application of the new rules in the early nineteenth century resulted in a statistical increase in the number of tributaries by about seventeen per cent (Table 16).

TABLE 16

Tributaries by Old and New Counts (1797–1804)

Jurisdiction	Indian Tributaries		Percentage Difference
	Old System	New System	
Chalco-Tlayacapa (1800–1803)	12,318	14,043	14
Coatepec (1799)	1,319	1,543	17
Coyoacan (1799)	3,722	4,401	18
Cuauhtitlan (1797)	3,978	4,495	13
Ecatepec (1803)	2,573	3,024	17
Mexicalzingo (ca. 1800)	2,222	2,518	13
Otumba (1800)	1,361	1,634	20
Tacuba (1799)	6,561	7,383	13
Teotihuacan (1804)	1,813	2,168	20
Texcoco (1802)	7,546	9,011	19
Xochimilco (1801)	4,281	4,821	13
Zumpango (1801)	1,362	1,596	17
Mexico (1800–1801)	9,672	12,061	25

SOURCE: AGN, Tributos, vol. 43, final exp., fol. 4r–4v.

Several changes in tribute amount occurred in the eighteenth century. The Medio Real de Fábrica was abolished by a series of royal orders beginning in 1739.[99] A new tribute, the Medio Real del Hospital, originating in the 1720's, was a similar tax, but it was dedicated to the support of the Hospital Real de los Indios in Mexico City. The new tribute took the place of an earlier arrangement, nominally in force since the late sixteenth century, whereby one fanega of maize out of every hundred received by each community had been contributed for the support of the hospital.[100]

Thus a normal payment per tributary in the mid-eighteenth century consisted of one peso, one-half fanega of maize convertible at four and one-half reales, four reales of Servicio Real, one-half real for Spanish judicial salaries, and one-half real for the Indian hospital, a total of seventeen and one-half reales per year. The ordinances for intendants undertook to reduce this to seventeen reales per Indian tributary,[101] but a uniform seventeen-real payment was never achieved. Jurisdictions varied in their enforcement of the rules, and local custom remained the principal factor in determining tribute liability and payment. Of 102 cabeceras in the late eighteenth century, 57 were paying 17½ reales per tributary, three were paying more than this, and 42 were paying less. The entire range of payment extended from 13 reales to 22½ reales.[102] The highest recorded amounts "legitimately" demanded in colonial Spanish tribute occur in records of the Marquesado towns of Coyoacan and Tacubaya, where 28 and 29 reales per tributary were taken in the seventeenth century.[103] At the opposite extreme a total tribute exemption remained in force in Santa Fe.[104]

The difficulties of tribute assessment in the seventeenth and eighteenth centuries were aggravated by the complex and shifting relations of cabeceras, barrios, and estancias. By a custom originating before the conquest, sujetos deposited their tributes in the cabeceras, in effect "paying" each cabecera tlatoani. Indeed, the tribute relation had been one of the main criteria used in identifying cabeceras and sujetos.[105] Spanish rules of the sixteenth century, however, had introduced a further refinement. They required barrios to deposit all, and estancias to deposit half, of their "sobras de tributos" in the cabeceras, thus engendering Indian disputes over what constituted a barrio and what constituted an estancia. The distinction intruded upon Indian financial relations between cabeceras and their sujetos, and encouraged barrios to seek to become estancias, and estancias to seek to become cabeceras.[106]

Collection in the multiple cabeceras was complicated by changes in cabecera status as well as by the progressive separation of former sujetos. In Tlalnepantla the subject towns of each of the two cabeceras had to be distinguished for tribute purposes.[107] At times newly created cabeceras were able to pay their tributes as separate transactions, wholly distinct from the payments made by their former cabeceras. At other times the traditions of past payment persisted, and separated towns continued to pay through their former cabeceras without change.[108] Special problems arose in the regions of confused or interspersed estancias and where two sujetos had merged into one. In 1739 Colhuacapilpan, nominally a barrio of Tepexpan, possessed twenty tributaries, but nine and one-half of these were tributaries of Tepexpan and ten and one-half were tributaries of Teotihuacan.[109]

Additional difficulties arose from the deficiencies in tribute assessment. Even when records were revised every five years, deaths and absences could take a heavy toll during the interval. By a rule continuously enforced from the sixteenth century, towns were liable for the full amount assessed at the most recent count.[110] Since it was easier to formulate a new listing by reference to the old one, names of truants and deceased persons tended to be retained from one assessment to the next. Those who moved from one barrio to another might be listed twice.[111] Moreover, by universally observed custom, any determined effort to collect tribute was accompanied by an exodus from the community. Indians sought many means to escape; they went into hiding, took false names, changed residence, and feigned bachelor, mestizo, or even cacique status.[112]

Actual fraud in tribute collection is as difficult to measure in the seventeenth and eighteenth centuries as in the sixteenth. But there is no doubt that it took place. There occurred embezzlement and extra collection by corregidores and Indian gobernadores. Corregidores charged "derechos" and additional payments in food, money, and other goods—for assessments, tribute counts, election confirmations, investments in office, and other services—and they frequently continued to charge for the Medio Real de Fábrica after its abolition.[113] Similarly, Spanish judges continued to charge separate fees for litigation after the establishment of the Medio Real de Ministros, and Indians continued to offer fruit or chickens or money to the court, in a custom whose origins antedated the arrival of the Spaniards.[114] Gobernadores still demanded payments for fiesta decorations, unofficial "salaries," new population counts, and other community and private expenses.[115] The maize tribute was illegally commuted by interested recipients at high market prices or even at several times the market prices, although the official commutation rate remained at nine reales. Licensees deliberately postponed collection of tribute maize, permitting it to spoil so that money might be collected instead, at a high rate of exchange.[116] Moreover, special local tributes—tributes lacking all sanction save that of custom and similar to the corregidores' local privileges of repartimiento sale—continued to be collected. Thus a tax called Real de los Aves was exacted of all tributaries in Amecameca by "ancient custom" in the eighteenth century, ostensibly as a tithe substitute for chickens, pigs, and magueyes raised.[117]

In all towns, the intimate relation between tribute and Indian government was retained. The basic fact was that the officers of Indian government were the ones truly responsible for tribute delivery. Their own salaries and the community funds depended on the amounts collected, and problems of finance came to be their principal preoccupation. Following the ten-vara enactment towns received their highest incomes in good harvest years. When floods in the southern lake waters destroyed crops in Cuitlahuac, Mixquic, Culhuacan, and other communities, the governments of these towns could exact nothing from the ten-vara plots. They accordingly sought viceregal permission to abandon the system of ten-vara plantings and to revert to the direct assessments levied upon tributaries. Cuitlahuac and Culhuacan were authorized to charge two reales per tributary in lieu of the ten-vara income as early as 1580. Chalco Atenco and Mixquic were authorized to charge one and one-half reales in 1583.[118] Other towns made similar transitions in later years, with or without viceregal permission. In the mid-seventeenth century most of the income of Xochimilco came from money payments by the tributaries. The system of ten-vara plantings and the system of money assessments existed side by side in the seventeenth and eighteenth centuries as alternative, complementary, or combined measures for supporting the community governments.[119]

Some towns supplemented their incomes by herding animals on community lands. The animals were town properties, and herding became a communal enterprise under the direction of the town government. The practice developed rapidly in the sixteenth century, and the first viceroys granted or confirmed many common lands for this purpose. Chalco Atenco maintained a herd of between two and three thousand sheep, with ranch houses and corrals, in the 1570's.[120] Sheep were preferred, for wool and meat, but towns also herded cattle and horses, and they continued to do so into the eighteenth century.[121]

But in the late colonial period the most common types of town financial enterprise were those involving sales or rentals of community property. Rentals by town governments, rare in the sixteenth century, became customary in the seventeenth and eighteenth centuries. The lessees or tenants were usually Spaniards or mestizos, and the transactions were often initiated under their pressure at times of known financial need in the community.[122] Rentals might be forced upon communities by persons who had become creditors precisely in order to obtain such rentals at reduced rates. A Spaniard might contract for the usufruct of community lands in exchange for assuming the costs of the Servicio Real, or some other part of the tribute obligation, and might then deliver this payment directly to the royal treasury officials.[128]

In some communities the transfer to the system of income by rental came to be absolute. By 1731 in Coyoacan, for example, the only remaining community land not worked by maceguales in the traditional agricultural assignments was rented to a neighboring hacienda for one hundred pesos per year.[124] Other towns adopted the common labor and the rental systems concurrently. In Otumba the community harvested some sixty fanegas of maize in the good agricultural years of the late colonial period and sold this as income for its treasury, while at the same time it rented out lands for about five times what it received for the maize. Communities also tended to shift from maize to maguey in late colonial plantings. Otumba, in a rich maguey area, had some six thousand community-owned maguey plants in the 1790's, and its treasury regularly received 150 pesos per year from their produce. Since labor both in the maize and in the maguey plantations was contributed as a service by the Indian inhabitants, the expense to a town's treasury for such plantations was very slight.[125] Even so, the preponderance of rented land in comparison with land still worked by communities indicates that late colonial Indian governments found rental to be the more secure source of income. It came to be accepted by Indians and Spaniards alike.[126]

In all such operations, gobernadores, as the persons most responsible for tribute payments, necessarily assumed control over community funds and properties. In repeated financial emergencies gobernadores sold community lands and community animals. Rentals were ordinarily paid to the gobernadores, and as rentals came to be the chief source of community income it became possible for gobernadores in effect to govern with private treasuries, the income and expense of which merged with their own personal finances.[127] Land could be "rented" in accordance with a "title of perpetual sale," and, once rented, a tract of land might be forever alienated from the community. Gobernadores found frequent opportunities for borrowing town funds and for delaying in repayment. Instances of collusion between gobernadores and Spanish authorities—corregidores, tenientes, hacendados, curates, subdelegados—for the alienation of property are numerous and unmistakable.[128]

The provision for community finance required the establishment of cajas de comunidad in all cabeceras, after the manner of Spanish towns. The caja was a box for the safekeeping of town moneys, and it was equipped with three locks so that it could be opened only by three separate keys. Here again, however, gobernadores found means to exert a late colonial influence. In 1554, when the crown ordered the establishment of cajas de comunidad, one key was to be held by the cacique and the others by two principales.[129] In the transitional period during the establishment of Indian government, the three holders of keys were the cacique, an Indian alcalde, and the corregidor.[130] But after the mid-eighteenth century the three keys, by audiencia order, were to be held by the curate, the corregidor, and the gobernador.[131]

A large number of community financial records for the towns of the Valley have survived.[132] Ordinarily the statements show income and expenses in separate accounts, arranged chronologically, item by item, through the year. New accountings were made necessary each year—by the annual elections of Indian officers, by the seasonal agricultural income, by the annual tribute in tercios, by the festival calendar that governed most community expenses, and by the rental system that normally required a yearly payment. Spanish law, on the other hand, came to forbid annual audits of community finance by corregidores, for the reason that corregidores took advantage of such audits for their own financial profit. By a rule of 1611, corregidores were forbidden to examine the cajas more than once during their terms in office and were forbidden to take money from the cajas "even though it be loaned."[133]

In summary, town financial accounts indicate that the chief sources of community income were the following:

1. Community lands worked in common or as ten-vara plots by the Indians of the town without recompense.

2. Payments of one and one-half or two reales in lieu of the ten-vara plantations.

3. Rental of community lands to Spaniards, mestizos, or Indians.

4. Sales of community lands to Spaniards, mestizos, or Indians.

5. Regular or irregular derramas imposed by the Indian governments.

6. Community business or commerce, especially agriculture and herding.

7. Rental or fees in the plaza market.

8. Sale or rental of water rights.

9. Investments, mortgages, and interest.

The first six of these were the most common and substantial sources of income in the Indian towns. Market fees and sales or rentals of water yielded limited or occasional incomes for some towns.[134] Mortgages and interest on loans occurred with increasing frequency in the records of town income of the late eighteenth century, when communities sometimes found themselves in a position to loan money to Spaniards for special purposes, such as the purchase of haciendas or city houses.[135] Within certain limits, gobernadores could manipulate these various funds to ensure a fairly predictable budget and to offset poor seasons or land alienations or other factors outside their control.

Viceregal rules of the sixteenth century, which specified the amounts that community treasuries would handle, assumed that the funds would be devoted not simply to civil community expenses but also to the support of the clergy, and, in the standard colonial phrase, the *ornato del culto*.[136] As early as the 1550's the archbishop of Mexico could assert that "most of what is spent from the cajas de comunidad is spent at the will of the clergy."[137] The statement occurs in a partisan context, but it is wholly true. A small town such as Mixquic might spend as much as a thousand pesos on church supplies in a single year in the late sixteenth century.[138] As population dropped and town income became less secure, surviving community properties provided the funds for ecclesiastical expenses as well as for community expenses as a whole. This might be by a particular provision in an emergency, as in 1727, when the community of Xochitepec paid for convento repairs by renting out previously unrented lands. Or it might involve a designation of particular herds, the income from which would serve ecclesiastical needs. Finally, it might involve a designation of lands for specified fiestas or other financial burdens, as in Huitzilopochco.[139] In the seventeenth and eighteenth centuries, Indian governments were regularly spending three-quarters or more of their income on church and fiesta supplies: wine, flowers, gifts to the clergy, food, fireworks, feathers, costumes, and masks. Secular expenses included agricultural labor, lawsuits, guards, and transportation charges, in addition to the salaries of Indian officials.[140] The reception of a new viceroy required lavish outlays. The introduction of the secular teachers (*maestros de escuela*), following a royal cedula of 1770, involved heavy new expenses, for the teachers' salaries were to be paid from community funds, or, if these were insufficient, by special levies on the families of the children who were to be taught.[141] Moreover, by the intendancy ordinances of 1786 two per cent of the gross annual income in each community caja was to be deposited in the intendancy treasury, to be used for the intendant's salary and expenses, and insofar as this rule was obeyed it constituted another drain on community funds.[142]

Royal law forbade the spending of community funds on feasts and celebrations. The prohibition presumably derived from early accusations that towns were spending too large a portion of their incomes on the frivolities that attended fiestas, and especially on intoxicating drink.[143] Viceregal rules in the tribute reforms of the 1560's had sometimes restricted and specified the occasions when officials of the town might hold their festivals.[144] But in the seventeenth and eighteenth centuries fiestas were always regarded as Christian ceremonies entirely appropriate to the Indian communities, and those that were not supported by cofradías were supported by the towns.[145]

The margin between income and expenditures in the financial arrangements of any town was customarily small, for communities, like individuals, spent freely when funds were available and underwent privation when they were not. In Tlalmanalco, in the sample years of the late seventeenth and early eighteenth centuries shown in Figure 7, the town government regularly spent more than it received. After excesses in the 1690's the gubernatorial administrations in Tlalmanalco were able to control expenses to an almost fixed amount and to reduce the annual deficit. Annual expenses ranged from about 300 pesos in the 1670's to over 1,000 pesos in 1696. In Axapusco the community government made substantial profits, including a net gain of 170 pesos in 1699, but it incurred losses in 1707, 1712, and 1713. Towns differed, too, in the amounts of liquid capital maintained in their local cajas. As with property held in land, liquid funds were a sign of community strength, but they were also a precarious possession liable to sudden and radical depletion. The totals by jurisdictions in 1785 (Table 17) ranged from nothing at all in Ecatepec and Otumba to more than 2,000 pesos in Tacuba.

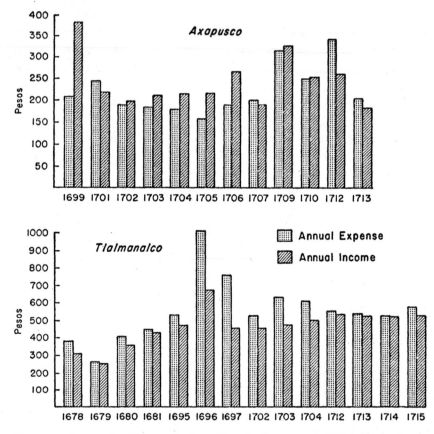

Figure 7. Community finance. Profit and loss in Axapusco and Tlalmanalco in the late seventeenth and early eighteenth centuries. Sources: AGN, Tierras, vol. 1923, exp. 6; vol. 1466.

TABLE 17

Caja Funds by Subdelegación, 1785

Subdelegación	Fund in pesos	Subdelegación	Fund in pesos
Tacuba	2,058	Xochimilco	533
Cuauhtitlan	1,538	Coatepec	265
Chalco	1,192	Citlaltepec	121
Texcoco	1,029	Otumba	0
Teotihuacan	702	Ecatepec	0

SOURCE: AGN, Intendentes, vol. 33, fols. 189r ff. Other jurisdictions are not recorded.

The largest single expenditure of the Indian communities, however, was the Spanish tribute described above. This was a burden that no community was able to bear consistently over a long period, and it was the one that brought the greatest stress to community finance. The 1560's, the period of major changes from Indian to Spanish systems of tribute exaction, mark the beginnings of large-scale tribute deficit in the towns.[146] Arrears developed gradually, through delays in payment and modest accumulations of debts, to become a standard condition of community financial life. In the 1570's and 1580's many towns fell seriously into debt for back tributes. Even in 1570 Tenochtitlan and Tlatelolco owed ten thousand pesos and Texcoco owed nine thousand pesos.[147]

The Spanish government adopted various measures to resolve the problems of tribute arrears. Indian officials were told to use force in tribute collection, and new gobernadores were sometimes appointed to ensure the payments.[148] Wherever maize supplies were low, it was common to facilitate collection by the conversion of maize deficits into money, at first at varying rates and later at the standard rate of nine reales per fanega.[149] Methods were outlined for prorating the payment of back tributes in annual installments, or for converting the indebtedness to labor obligations or to the supply of materials.[150] New land rentals imposed expressly for the payment of deficits might be arranged. Loans might be contracted with Spanish creditors. And the system of bonds and bondsmen operated with a fair degree of efficiency in the several jurisdictions in late colonial times to transfer, though not to cancel, the community indebtedness.[151]

But the principal Spanish method for ensuring as high a return as possible within the tribute assessments was punishment. In this, Spanish governments ignored the individual Indian tribute payers as well as the Spanish "collectors" and held the Indian government of each town responsible. After the late sixteenth century, community tribute debts were treated as the personal debts of the gobernadores and of members of the cabildo. Indian officials unable to pay were jailed as criminals.[152] Their houses, lands, and other properties were seized and sold, and the proceeds were taken as full or partial payment of tribute debts. The debts were held to be inheritable by the descendants and executors of deceased gobernadores. Cases are on record in which the daughters of deceased gobernadores were made responsible for tribute arrears.[153] Long delays and sudden peremptory Spanish demands attended the arrears.[154] Incumbent administrations might be made to pay a tribute debt incurred in earlier periods, and Indian officers were sometimes jailed even after collecting thousands of pesos in arrears.[155] When the intendancy ordinances fixed gubernatorial salaries at one per cent of the tribute in an effort to induce reform, the effect was to link communal and gubernatorial finance even more closely.[156]

The establishment of a percentage ratio between tribute and gubernatorial salaries accelerated a process already in effect—the abandonment of cajas de comunidad and reliance on the personal responsibility of the gobernador.[157] It was a common practice of Indian political officials in the late period to complete the final, and even the second, tercio payment from their own pockets. Gobernadores might enter upon their offices in solvent circumstances and leave them impoverished. "Appointing an Indian as gobernador here is simply condemning him to destruction," wrote an eighteenth-century curate of Tacubaya, a town where gobernadores had been compelled to liquidate their private possessions and where one gobernador had incurred tribute debts exceeding nine thousand pesos.[158] Especially in periods of agricultural crisis the arrears multiplied, and although the deficits might be partially made up in subsequent years they were rarely made up completely. In times of flood and limited harvests in the seventeenth century, maize payment fell disastrously behind.[159] Universal inability to meet the quotas occurred again in the famine years of 1785 and 1786. But by the eighteenth century arrears in tribute obtained in all jurisdictions and in all towns of the Valley, and the total tribute indebtedness in the colony amounted to some one and one-half million pesos.[160]

This desperate situation was brought to a legal end only by independence. The tribute yield of the late eighteenth century came to four or five times the yield of the mid-seventeenth century, but for the Spanish government it was far surpassed by the income from other financial departments such as Tobacco and Alcabala.[161] Liberal Spaniards began to campaign for the abolition of Indian tribute in the 1790's,[162] but gobernadores were still being jailed for arrears as late as 1809.[163] Finally, in 1810, as a consequence of the independence movement, exemption from tribute was decreed for all Indians by the Consejo de Regencia, and the decree was ordered executed by a viceregal *bando* in Spanish and Nahuatl in the same year.[164]

In sum, the tribute obligation was a continuing annual burden for the Indian communities. Tribute represented a direct exaction, a device through which in its initial stage a privileged Spanish class, and subsequently the Spanish political state, obtained a calculated revenue from the Indian population. Two major developments of the sixteenth century were the decay of encomienda tribute and the intensification, or Hispanization, of the rules relating to liability and payment. These were consistent with the sixteenth-century changes in Indian class structure, as well as with the imperial government's increasing financial needs. Spaniards rarely collected tributes directly from the local Indian taxpayers. Instead, Indian officers were the intermediaries and the ones held answerable in instances of default. The procedure allowed Spanish government to remain aloof from the petty tasks of collection and to concentrate on a relatively small number of Indian leaders who could easily be held accountable. It allowed also for some perpetuation of ancient Indian practices, including the graduated liabilities based on rank or land, which ran counter to Spanish head-tax assessments. Moreover, it reinforced the authority of Indian town governments, which were able to collect in excess of the assessments and to exploit the payers. But when this authority proved insufficient, the result was an accumulation of community debt, punishable through jail sentences. Finally, there was an intimate connection between tribute and community finance. Because a fraction of the tribute was assigned to the town governments for local expenses and support of the clergy, both Spanish and Indian revenues became linked with the Indian community organization.

CHAPTER IX

Labor

In Aztec society, labor had been prescribed and carefully regulated. Agricultural labor was a primary responsibility of maceguales in the system of common landholding.[1] Labor in the towns or in the town subdivisions, as for the construction or repair of community buildings, was required of the able-bodied inhabitants of all cabeceras and sujetos. Local Indian rulers depended upon groups of workers to perform communal tasks, with minimal individual assignments. What impressed the Spanish oidor Alonso de Zorita concerning Indian labor in the early sixteenth century was the sense of contribution, the "merriment" and "great rejoicing" that attended it.[2] Beyond this, and in some measure exploiting it, had been the imperial labors of Aztec society, including the military services demanded by Montezuma.

It is evident that native peoples of the conquest period were vulnerable to the Spaniards' demands for labor. Accustomed to providing their own sustenance and to both local and distant service without pay, Indians appeared to be ready to perform, and even to derive satisfaction from, occupations that were monotonous or degrading in European eyes. In Europe, unskilled mass labor carried implications of coercion or enslavement. In the Indian tradition the same mass labor, if not too onerous, might be considered rewarding as a shared and pleasurable experience.

Spaniards quickly took advantage of the Indian attitude toward directed labor. By controlling the tlatoque, Cortés and other Spaniards easily manipulated masses of workers. A major change under Spanish rule, however, was that Indian peoples lost the sense of joyous participation and adopted an attitude of resignation. From the mid-sixteenth century until the end of the colonial period they acceded to Spanish demands for employment without the ceremonial communality that had attended the pre-conquest and the first post-conquest labor enterprises. Labor tended thus to move from the social, moral, and spiritual categories, in which Indians had placed it, into the economic or physical categories of Europe. The memory of earlier Indian values was retained, however unsympathetically, in Spanish society. As a colonist stated in the seventeenth century, "It is well known that Montezuma gave tasks to Indians with no other purpose than to entertain them."[3]

Spaniards did not need any mass enslavement of Indians in the Valley of Mexico. Slavery was not unknown in the early colonial period, but it derived mainly from Spanish experience with societies of other types. In individual cases it operated under a guise of legitimacy whenever Indians could be shown to be occupying a "slave" status already in Indian society—for this could be understood as a change of masters rather than as an initial enslavement. When Spaniards asked for slaves from upper-class Indians, non-slaves might be delivered instead, for, in the words of Ramírez de Fuenleal, if an Indian ruler called a macegual a slave, "lo era."[4] Moreover, Spanish raiding expeditions introduced Indian captives from outside the Valley, and these also were sold as slaves in the capital in the early years.[5]

But the native institutions of mass labor were more appropriately controlled by encomienda than by slavery, and encomienda proved to be the more important institution. In practice, both slavery and encomienda had a considerable flexibility, for workers under either system could be sold or hired to other employers and utilized in illegal ways. Furthermore, the early relations between Spaniards and Indians brought into being a variety of lesser labor institutions. In the corregimientos of the 1530's and after, labor provisions were specified in tribute regulations. The early church, by persuading and influencing the caciques, employed Indian workers in the construction of ecclesiastical buildings and in other *servicios personales*. In Tenochtitlan and Tlatelolco the first Spanish tribute exactions consisted almost wholly of demands for labor, with service to the viceroy, the construction of civic buildings, the repair and filling of canals, and other tasks contributing to the maintenance of the colonial capital.[6] Only in mining, because the Valley itself possessed no precious metals, did difficulties arise in the employment of the Valley's laborers.[7]

In labor as in tribute, one effect of encomienda and of other types of early Spanish control was to decentralize the imperial Aztec organization and to place emphasis on the separate town units of cabeceras and sujetos. For a generation after the first labor drafts for the rebuilding of the city, no other

single large-scale endeavor required the mobilization of more than local segments of the laboring population.[8] Service to encomenderos and corregidores and the construction of ecclesiastical buildings were town enterprises.
The Spanish recipients of Indian labor depended upon town organizations,
profiting from the authority of each community's tlatoani, from the many
calpulli subdivisions, from the tequitlatos, and from the macegual classes
accustomed to orderly direction. In Indian society the labor obligation of a
sujeto to its cabecera constituted a fundamental relationship recognized by
all, and it was universally turned to Spanish uses.

Spaniards used the term *llamamiento* to signify the act of summons
whereby a tlatoani convoked the laborers of the sujetos for the construction
of community houses, common agricultural labor, personal service, or other
work. The Nahuatl term, *coatequitl,* implied in practice a division of tasks
among the calpulli subdivisions, in a labor structure wherein each calpulli
might be responsible for a different specialty and a given portion of the
work. In the service continuously provided by sujetos to their cabeceras,
these Indian arrangements still applied. Thus in Xochimilco in the late
sixteenth century barrios still recognized their special tasks in coatequitl
service.[9] Even in the eighteenth century, when a cabecera's community
houses required repair or when local road work was to be done, the provision of materials and the work itself were parceled among the sujetos.[10] But
from the beginning the sujeto obligations were extended to include service
to Spaniards. For the early Spanish construction labors in Mexico City, the
drafts were subdivided by barrios and were governed, in part, by barrio
specializations. When the Marqués del Valle ordered Indians of Coyoacan
to build the house of the oidor Quesada in 1548, the workers supplied the
materials, the labor was organized by sujetos, and each sujeto worked on a
designated task. In Quesada's construction 340 Indians were directed to
bring seventeen wooden beams, an indication not only of the continuing
use of a vigesimal organization, but also of the high ratio of laborers to
labor units, with twenty Indians for each beam.[11]

Encomenderos, ecclesiastics, and employers of all sorts relied on *tamemes*
(Nahuatl, sing. *tlamama*), or Indian carriers, for the provision of goods
and for transport. Human carrying had pre-conquest antecedents—since
native society lacked vehicles and beasts of burden—but the early colony
greatly expanded its role and its dimensions. Royal orders forbidding human carriers on humanitarian grounds met strenuous opposition and were

accordingly modified or revoked.[12] Many types of tameme regulation were attempted—voluntary carrying, licensing, confinement to fixed routes, reduction of the distances to be traversed, limitations on the size or weight of loads—but for the most part in vain.[13] Ultimately certain supply routes, notably those connecting Mexico City with the coasts, were served by animal pack trains in numbers sufficient to absorb the commodity traffic, and the problem was in some degree resolved.[14] But as late as the early seventeenth century royal orders were still being issued forbidding tamemes, and colonists were still arguing their necessity.[15]

The royal orders are indicative of a more general monarchical attitude with regard to Indian labor. By many means in the sixteenth century the crown sought to create a working force that would be free to choose its own tasks and adequately recompensed in wages. Such a working force never came into being in the colonial period, but royal efforts to implement it contributed to major changes in the relations between employers and workers during the middle years of the sixteenth century and after. As a first step, the crown resolved to eliminate unrecompensed labor from the tribute schedules. The basic order of 1549 and subsequent orders in ensuing years announced this prohibition and proposed as a substitute a rotational system of hire, with moderate labor, short hours, limited distances of travel, and wages. The rules were to apply in both encomienda and corregimiento. They implied that coercion was unnecessary and that Indians would work voluntarily if a sufficient wage were provided.[16]

Officials in New Spain took the royal orders seriously, and tribute regulations in encomienda and corregimiento after the mid-century sharply reduced, although they never fully eradicated, unrecompensed labor. The cabildo of the city denounced the rules and attributed to them the labor shortages of subsequent years.[17] Long afterward Suárez de Peralta recorded his childhood recollections of the consternation that the mid-century restrictions had created among the affluent white class. "Previously everyone's house was filled with whatever the land provided," he asserted, "but the moment that these rules took effect everything had to be bought, properties began to deteriorate, and people found themselves in need."[18]

It is not surprising that the recipients of the cheap mass labor of the first colonial generation attributed the decline of the working force to royal legislation against encomienda services. But other causes were simultaneously at work to bring about modifications in the conditions of Indian employment during the mid-century years. Whether by accident or design, the labor legislation of 1549 appeared at one of the critical moments in the shifting population ratio of whites and Indians—the period following the plague of 1545–48. Although encomenderos tended to blame the king, it became increasingly evident to the growing class of non-encomenderos that encomienda could not meet the needs of the whole white population. The uneconomical labor institutions of the first colonial years would no longer suffice. After the mid-century there were not enough workers to support such institutions, and many new non-encomendero landowners[19] were making claims upon Indian manpower.

The resolution of these problems was repartimiento. The word means distribution or apportionment, and it was applied to a series of diverse colonial procedures, including encomienda grants, land allotment, tribute apportionment, forced sale, and draft labor. For the moment, we adopt the most common usage of the sixteenth and seventeenth centuries, identifying as repartimiento the institution that dominated the recruitment of Indian workers for a period of about seventy-five years after the mid-century.[20] It was a system of rationed, rotational labor, purportedly in the public interest or for the public utility, affecting both encomienda and non-encomienda Indians, and benefiting a much larger employer class than had been possible under encomienda.[21] In fact, it did not fulfill the royal demands for short hours, moderate tasks, or voluntary labor for wages. But it subjected the labor procedures of the colony to administrative scrutiny for the first time, and it satisfied, at least temporarily, the needs of the new colonial employers.

The origins of repartimiento, as would be expected, antedate 1549. The principles of compulsion and rotation, which were essential to it, had precedents in both pre-conquest and early colonial labor. Communities had alternated in service for Nezahualcoyotl in the fifteenth century, and they alternated in service for the viceroy in the early sixteenth century.[22] It is a remarkable fact that Cortés's earliest encomienda regulations relate closely to procedures later established for repartimiento. In the 1520's Cortés ordered a rotational system for encomienda whereby Indians would work for their encomenderos in shifts of twenty days, with thirty-day intervals between working periods for each laborer. Cortés's rules provided for means of inspection, forbade the involvement of women and children, allowed for overtime pay and sustenance, and limited the daily labor to the period between sunrise and one hour before sunset.[23] Such regulations were never seriously enforced in encomienda. But Cortés's principle of rotation and some of the details of his humanitarian regulation were reactivated in repartimiento, when repartimiento labor became separated from encomienda.

Given these antecedents, it appears entirely natural that the Mexico City flood crisis of 1555 should have been met by a repartimiento organization. This was the first of a long series of inundations and threatened inundations in the colonial history of the city. Exceptionally heavy rains, beginning in mid-September, raised the level of the surrounding lake and damaged the city's streets and causeways.[24] In early November the viceroy summoned a huge labor force of about six thousand Indians.[25] Unofficially, the labor force was estimated at over two million.[26] The work began in early December and continued for about four months. Remedial measures included the closing of the sluice openings of certain causeways, the shifting of the courses of several streams, and especially the construction of the new Albarradón de San Lázaro, a protective dike lying closer to the city than its pre-conquest counterpart and extending from the Guadalupe causeway along the entire eastern edge of the urban zone.[27] The dike was approximately twenty feet wide and over four miles long.[28] Vast supplies of lumber and other materials were required.[29] Labor was organized by enforced rotation, with the Indian workers returning to their homes at the end of a week's work to be replaced by a new shift. The work was of unusual severity, much of it was performed in and under the water, and many workers died.[30]

This repartimiento of 1555–56, created as it was by viceregal order in response to emergency conditions, occupies a significant, but short-lived, role in repartimiento history. The more important, because longer lasting, repartimientos of the middle sixteenth century were those dedicated to urban construction (see Chapter XIII) and to agricultural labor on the wheat farms of the area surrounding the city.[31] The new emphasis upon non-encomienda employment in agriculture is readily explained. The capital had become a major Spanish metropolis and market, with a white population of some fifteen hundred or two thousand families[32] and a correspondingly greater demand for foodstuffs. With escheatment and population loss, encomienda had deteriorated as an instrument of agricultural supply. Land grants had been issued to private colonists in many areas, and wheat and cattle farms had become numerous. The privately owned farm was already rivalling encomienda as a supplier of food when suddenly, in 1549, the royal prohibition of labor services in encomienda further limited encomienda's role in agricultural provision. For all these reasons a new agricultural repartimiento was called for and came into being.

Our earliest record of the new agricultural repartimiento is dated July 1550.[33] The date follows so closely the prohibition of labor services in encomienda that an immediate causal relation may be supposed. As one of his last acts in office, and at a time of acute shortages of wheat and maize in the city, Viceroy Mendoza ordered the "caciques y gobernadores, alcaldes y principales" of the area surrounding Mexico City to send workers in specified numbers for the cultivation of wheat plantations.[34] During some five years the repartimiento served officially as a combined draft for the wheat farms and for the Spanish citizens of the city, in house construction and other tasks. When in August 1555, a month before the flood, the urban labor was forbidden (except by Indian residents of Tenochtitlan and Tlatelolco) the fact signified a full viceregal commitment to the agricultural draft.[35] At the same time the official in charge of repartimiento, entitled *repartidor,* was given power to use force, to make arrests, and to sentence culprits to prison.[36] By the early 1560's the repartimiento was officially engaging the labor of approximately 2,400 Indian workers per week, distributed among 114 Spanish agriculturists at an average of about twenty workers per employer.[37]

Throughout the rest of the sixteenth century, agricultural repartimiento was a systematically functioning institution. There was installed in each of three subdivisions of the Valley a *juez repartidor,* who was responsible for the administration of the Indian workers and their distribution to Spanish agriculturists. The jueces repartidores were assisted by tenientes, by Indian alguaciles, and by interpreters. Indians were furnished from the towns of the repartimiento jurisdictions in weekly shifts at fixed quotas and were delivered to those Spanish agricultural employers whose properties were located in the same jurisdictions. The detailed procedure, altered only slightly in the last decades of the sixteenth century,[38] was as follows.

Population records were first collected for every contributing community, and from these a percentage quota, at first approximating two per cent of the tributaries, was computed. Each community was then expected to furnish its assigned number of workers each week. The Indian governments of the towns were provided with written or pictorial records listing the names, sujeto affiliations, and tequitlatos of all Indian laborers. As in tribute, temporary reductions might be permitted in periods of epidemic or of labor on local churches.[39]

Every Monday morning the Indians from the towns of each repartimiento area assembled at a given distribution point. They were dispatched, in time for the Monday arrival, by the Indian officials of their communities and conducted to the repartimiento center by local Indian alguaciles. On Monday morning, inside a corral, the juez repartidor issued to the Spanish farmers (*labradores*) or to their agents the Indians assigned to them, in accordance with the amount of wheat each had under cultivation and the requirements of the fields, a matter that depended upon the judgment of the juez repartidor. At the same time the juez repartidor received from the Spanish employers one cuartillo (one-fourth real) for each Indian granted, and from this sum he paid the local alguaciles one real for each eight Indians delivered. Once each year the juez repartidor collected from the labradores one-half real for each fanega they had sown. The income received from the cuartillos and half reales formed a fund from which he paid a salary of twelve pesos per year to the several alguaciles who assisted him. The remainder he kept to supplement his own salary of 250 pesos.[40] All transactions were duly recorded in the account books of the repartimiento.

On Monday morning each labrador or his agent returned to his farm with the Indians assigned to him. There the Indians worked the fields, commonly under a Negro or some other overseer,[41] for a period of one week, from Tuesday to the following Monday, Sunday being a day of rest.[42] On the afternoon of the second Monday, the Indians received their pay and were released to return to their communities. Their places were immediately taken by a new group, which had been collected, assigned, and delivered in the same manner.[43] Thus the qualified Spanish agriculturists were assured of a steady working force in weekly rotation, the drain upon any contributing community was minimized by the quota system, and no single individual was held liable to the draft more often than three or four times per year. An Indian laborer's guaranty against excessive summons was a receipt issued to him by the juez repartidor, indicating the number of terms he had served since the beginning of the year.

The local operation of repartimiento, with which Spaniards were rarely concerned, continued to follow the procedures of the indigenous coatequitl. In the sixteenth and early seventeenth centuries Spanish repartimiento and Indian coatequitl existed side by side, influencing each other.[44] In repartimiento as in tribute, Indian governments sought to maintain existing Indian organizations and existing exemptions applying to sub-macegual classes, who remained in the service of local Indian rulers.[45] Occasionally

Indians arranged a labor differentiation among barrios by assigning coatequitl to certain sujetos while making others liable to repartimiento.[46] Since the Spanish state did not normally regulate the procedures for the selection of workers, but instead made Indian governments responsible for the delivery of a stated number, repartimiento could, at first, be adapted to the Indian organization of cabeceras, sujetos, and calpultin, wholly or almost wholly under Indian control.

In one other fundamental way labor repartimiento depended upon Indian precedents.[47] We revert here to the pre-conquest imperial labor organization and to the jurisdictions of the aboriginal tribes. The repartimiento subdivisions of the 1550's—the areas of Mexico, Texcoco, Tacuba, Chalco— were original Indian tribal areas, and, as we have observed, the viceroy of 1555 deliberately sought out information on the organization of imperial Aztec labor to provide a model for repartimiento.[48] This reliance on the imperial Indian system pertained to labor but not to tribute, since labor, unlike tribute, had been separated from encomienda in 1549 and centralized under the repartimiento system. Changes affecting the points of distribution were made after 1555, but as late as the 1570's the main Indian jurisdictions of the Acolhuaque, the Tepaneca, and the Chalca were still clearly distinguishable in repartimiento administration.[49]

Later, however, repartimiento jurisdictions underwent continuous modification, and the structural relationship with Indian precedents became obscured. The derivative Acolhua jurisdiction shifted its capital to Tacuba, thence to Azcapotzalco, and finally back to Tacuba. The derivative Tepaneca jurisdiction came to be divided, with capitals at Tacubaya and Tepozotlan, and the Tepozotlan jurisdiction for a time maintained its capital at Cuauhtitlan.[50] In the early seventeenth century the agricultural repartimientos of the Valley were variously centered at Chapultepec, Chalco, Chiconauhtla, Cuauhtitlan, Mexico City, Ecatepec, and Tepozotlan. The Indian tribal jurisdictions, on which they had originally been based, were virtually forgotten. Only Chalco, in this as in other matters, preserved a continuity with the Indian past.[51]

As the native population declined in the late sixteenth century, and as new stresses were imposed upon the methods of recruitment, other elements of continuity from Indian labor traditions were likewise progressively abandoned. Indian governments compelled women, disabled persons, and skilled workers (oficiales) to pay a charge for exemption, or to hire substi-

Map 7. Labor repartimiento jurisdictions of the late sixteenth century. Towns south of the city at this time provided urban labor and services and were not involved in the agricultural drafts.

tutes in labor obligation.[52] Alcaldes sometimes sought to make principales liable, and the officers of town governments themselves were not always excused. With the decline of sub-macegual classes, principales tended to divert workers from coatequitl and repartimiento to private labor on the principales' own fields.[53] When quotas could no longer be met, the sub-macegual exemptions failed, and the remaining sub-macegual peoples were required to contribute to the drafts. Even tequitlatos, alguaciles, and man-dones—the very Indian officials responsible for the delivery of workers— were in some instances declared liable in repartimiento labor.[54]

Spaniards, of course, demanded additional workers, both in farming and in other forms of employment. The non-agricultural repartimientos did not cease with the establishment of the agricultural assignments, but re-mained as simultaneous competing labor drafts. The viceregal government adopted a lenient policy with regard to Spanish petitions for extraneous Indian laborers, and the systematic labor pools provided by repartimiento were a tempting source from which to derive workers for other purposes. In the northern part of the Valley some towns became subject to the repartimientos for the Pachuca mines.[55] Drafts outside the Valley were permitted to draw workers from the Valley's repartimientos in times of critical need.[56] The demand for workers on various construction jobs in the city could not be met from within the city itself, and repartimiento Indians from Xochimilco, Chalco, Texcoco, Tacuba, and other jurisdictions were used for public works, monasteries, the casas reales, the Cathedral, the streets, or the city's water supply, all in addition to agricultural reparti-miento.[57] At times the recipients of agricultural laborers leased them infor-mally to private employers in the city, so that Indians nominally designated for the farms found themselves engaged instead in illegal urban labor for individual Spaniards.[58] A count made by the protesting Spanish employers of Chalco in 1599 enumerated eighty-three repartimiento Indians who were being occupied each week in extra tasks, an annual total of about 4,300 laborers, all from the Chalco repartimiento jurisdiction. In a single year, according to the same report, 5,470 Indians from Chalco had labored on the hospital at Oaxtepec. The customary viceregal response to such protests was to suppress some of the additional drafts, but the problem always re-curred, and no over-all policy was ever achieved to resolve the conflicting claims of agricultural and non-agricultural employers.[59]

Further drains upon the manpower of the Valley appeared in the form of the *servicio de zacate*, the *servicio de piedra*, and other "servicios" demanded by the viceregal government. These exactions were intermediate between labor and tribute. They required the provision of material goods, but Spaniards in general did not classify them as tribute because the goods were paid for. The requirement that the goods be provided nevertheless constituted a labor demand, and Spaniards referred to the operation as repartimiento. From the earliest days of the colony designated towns had to bring to the city daily canoe loads of fodder, fuel, fish, eggs, chickens, stone, lumber, and other materials for the royal officials and other citizens. The payments for these were lower than the market prices of the goods, and it often happened that gobernadores and principales took all the payment, leaving nothing for the suppliers. The communities known to have been particularly affected by these demands for servicios were Coyoacan, Huitzilopochco, Tacuba, Cuauhtitlan, Tenayuca, Culhuacan, Toltitlan, Tepozotlan, Coyotepec, Teoloyuca, Huehuetoca, Zumpango, Ecatepec, Chiconauhtla, Chimalhuacan, and Tacubaya. The specifications as to quantity and frequency of delivery underwent continuous change.[60] But throughout the sixteenth and early seventeenth centuries a royal official in the capital could expect a regular, preferential, and inexpensive supply of necessary goods—a canoe-load of fodder each day, two loads of firewood per week, and food and service to supply his needs.[61] In time the servicios became less demanding, but they continued through the whole period of agricultural repartimiento.[62]

As would be expected, the decreasing population and the various drains on manpower had consequences for the quotas and the number of workers actually provided. During the first thirty years of agricultural repartimiento, quotas for the growing season continued to approximate two per cent of tributaries. Quotas for other periods of the year approximated one per cent, and the year was equally divided between the *sencilla* (November through April) and the *dobla* (May through October).[63] Actual percentages varied. The largest cabeceras, including Xochimilco, Tlalmanalco, and Tacuba, were required to give one hundred workers per week. For all towns giving over fifteen workers the early quotas were expressed in multiples of ten. Until the plague of 1576 the Indian population was sufficiently large and the number of Spanish employers still sufficiently limited to permit low quotas and rounded numbers in agricultural drafts.[64] But with the depopulation of the late 1570's and after, jueces repartidores, on their own authority, resorted to quotas in excess of two per cent. Viceregal rules of the late sixteenth century authorized quotas of four and five per cent in the sencilla and ten per cent in the dobla, at times varying these percentages depending upon liabilities to other drafts or other special circumstances.[65] Occasionally in the early seventeenth century the viceroy offered options to Indian towns: two per cent in the sencilla and ten per cent in the dobla, or four per cent in the sencilla and eight per cent in the dobla, or five per cent over the year.[66] But whatever the quota for any individual town, the trend was toward an increase in the required percentages from the 1550's to the early seventeenth century.[67]

In addition the dobla periods changed. Doblas of the 1580's were commonly granted in periods of four, six, eight, or ten weeks, depending on the season and the urgency of the Spaniards' petitions. Two annual dobla periods were granted in the 1590's, one for weeding in July or August, and one for harvest in November or December. In the 1590's grants for eight-week and ten-week doblas became more frequent, and a total annual dobla of sixteen to twenty weeks came to be regarded as normal during the years when the dobla of ten per cent was adopted.[68] In the 1590's, too, this schedule was progressively disrupted by the demands of those labradores who had adopted irrigated wheat, the harvesting of which usually occurred in May or June. At first irrigation was slight, and the extra demand could be accommodated by temporary doblas in selected towns. But by the late 1590's all agricultural repartimiento jurisdictions had to make adjustments for irrigated wheat. This was done principally by anticipating the dobla for designated communities, discounting the regular dobla proportionately, and providing the irrigated fields with sencilla quotas during the regular dobla. In times of special need all workers might be utilized for the irrigated crop.[69] Scheduling difficulties became more serious with the development of partially irrigated wheat fields, which required weeding when the fully irrigated wheat fields were ready for harvest.[70] During the overlapping doblas of the early seventeenth century Indians from the public works (*obras publicas*) in the city were sometimes diverted to farm labor.[71] Meanwhile dobla periods were increased to twenty-four or thirty weeks per year, thus approximating and even exceeding the original six-month periods.[72] And the doblas of ten per cent in the seventeenth century, of course, imposed a far heavier burden upon the contributing communities than the doblas of two per cent in the early years.

The conditions of repartimiento accordingly became more burdensome. Indian communities found themselves progressively harder pressed to supply the workers demanded. As in tribute, the increased pressures brought about an abandonment of traditions, an adoption of new and more coercive measures, and a steady accumulation of arrears. As in tribute, Indian governments were held responsible, and gobernadores who were unable to supply their quotas were threatened with arrest and jail sentences.[73] At the same time the competition among Spaniards for Indian workers became more intense, and the frequency and sophistication of malfeasance increased. Spaniards sequestered laborers, beat them, refused to pay them, seized their food and clothing to prevent their escape, and undertook to acquire private native workers outside the drafts.[74] Jueces repartidores repeatedly sought to procure more Indians than the quotas permitted.[75] The repartimiento system of the late sixteenth century was everywhere one of compulsion and abuse, and it received continuous criticism from the clergy.[76]

The meaning of these developments for the actual delivery of workers is suggested by records of the Chalco repartimiento in the years 1619–20 (Figure 8). Surviving documents give the sencilla and dobla quota for each community of the Chalco repartimiento in these years and the numbers in fact delivered week by week. The records demonstrate that the Chalca towns at this time were making no exact differentiation between the sencilla and the dobla, and that they failed to meet their quotas, rarely sent the same number twice in succession, and at times defaulted entirely. The total numbers delivered during successive weeks in these years present a most irregular pattern. The dobla periods for weeding and harvesting were periods of increased provision of workers, but the increases were not uniform and at no time was the full dobla, 647 workers, ever delivered to the Spanish employers.[77]

In the seventeenth century the evident deficiencies of repartimiento resulted in attempts to reform the entire structure of colonial labor. The initial royal reform order in 1601 forbade compulsion in the recruitment of laborers and ruled that repartimiento was to be terminated in agriculture, building, and all other occupations except mining. Indians were to choose their Spanish employers voluntarily, the office of juez repartidor was to be abolished, and corregidores were to require only that Indians offer themselves in appointed places for hire.[78] It is clear that the royal intention in 1601 was

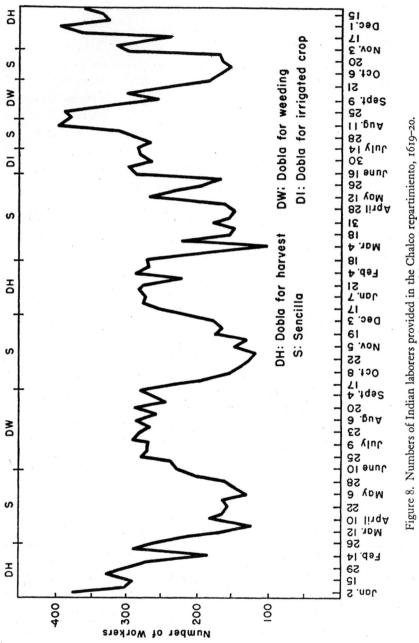

Figure 8. Numbers of Indian laborers provided in the Chalco repartimiento, 1619–20.

Source: AGN, Indios, vol. 8, fols. 111 ff.

to bring to an end the evils of repartimiento. Yet the orders granted discretion to the viceroy with respect to the jueces repartidores, and the provision that Indian workers were to convene in appointed places under the charge of corregidores could be interpreted as entailing no radical departure. The former jueces repartidores did assume new titles—notably, the title *juez comisario de alquileres*.[79] The repartimientos for public works in Tenochtitlan and Tlatelolco were formally abolished, and the viceroy personally visited the plazas of both communities to ensure that Indians would hire themselves "freely and voluntarily."[80] But all attempts to halt repartimiento permanently by means of such legislation uniformly failed. In the metropolitan plazas, where the viceroy demonstrated a desire for genuine reform, "voluntary" labor became farcical. The financial transactions of repartimiento persisted without appreciable change. Labradores paid the jueces comisarios as they had paid the jueces repartidores for Indian laborers, in consideration of the amount of wheat sown, and the jueces comisarios in turn paid the Indian officers who recruited the workers.[81] Private payments, bribery, and fraud frustrated efforts to reform the system. In agricultural repartimiento even the nominal recognition of jueces comisarios de alquileres was soon abandoned. By 1607 the former title, juez repartidor, was again making its appearance, and in subsequent years the old and new titles were indiscriminately employed.[82] The provision that jueces might compel attendance by force, still in accordance with the system of quotas, rendered the new institution essentially unchanged from the old.

The crown sought again in 1609 to bring repartimiento to an end, this time more gradually, through the exercise of viceregal controls. By degrees after this date new viceregal and audiencia rules did bring about formal abolition. In the 1620's the audiencia forbade certain features of urban repartimiento, and of the remaining servicios. Finally, a viceregal order of 1632 issued the definitive repartimiento prohibition. The termination of all repartimientos, except those in mines, was to take effect January 1, 1633.[83]

In Mexican history significant changes have rarely occurred as a consequence of law. Law provides an approximation of historical happening, or a commentary upon it. In the case of the abolition of 1632 it would be an error to suppose either that repartimiento labor came to an end[84] or that law alone was responsible for the transition to other forms of labor organization. It is true that repartimiento played a negligible role in agricultural labor thereafter. But it is also true that it played a negligible role in the period just prior to the abolition. The deficiencies of the Chalco repartimiento at the beginning of the 1620's were wholly characteristic, and a steady deterioration occurred during the next decade. From 1630 to 1632 the labradores of Tacuba received no Indians in repartimiento. The 130 farms of the Tepozotlan repartimiento received an average of one Indian per month.[85] The labor failure, as is obvious, had little relation to the royal and viceregal prohibitions. Instead, two other factors, originally independent but progressively interrelated in the early seventeenth century, brought about the decline of the agricultural repartimiento. One of these was Desagüe labor. The other was hacienda labor, which was dependent upon private working forces and peonage.

In the history of the Valley of Mexico, the term Desagüe refers to the process by which the lake areas of the conquest period were converted into the salt-dust flats of today. During colonial times labor on the Desagüe was organized manual labor, differing from agricultural labor in the erratic character of its employment and provision. The size of the Desagüe working forces was determined by irregular floods and by the successive states of anxiety experienced by viceregal administrations. In times of emergency available resources were strained to the limit. At other times, and for long periods, the Desagüe was permitted to languish.

Whenever prolonged rains occurred, lake levels rose, flood conditions prevailed, and the low-lying areas became inundated. But Spanish authorities rarely paid attention to floods elsewhere than in the city.[86] Flood danger and Desagüe operations were almost invariably measured in terms of potential damage in the capital. In the early city the streets and plazas were situated at higher levels than the houses, which suffered first from increases in the water level.[87] The chief measure of earlier control had been the pre-conquest dike (*albarradón*), constructed in the late 1440's under Montezuma I and Nezahualcoyotl, and enlarged at the end of the fifteenth century under Ahuitzotl.[88] The most critical sixteenth-century emergency, the inundation of 1555–56, resulted in the construction of the new dike, the Albarradón de San Lázaro.[89]

Spaniards in the sixteenth century, like Indians in the pre-conquest period, favored a system of flood protection by dike. But Spaniards proposed, without ever executing, large-scale remedial measures of other kinds. Initial plans were made in 1555–56 to divert the Río de Cuauhtitlan, and to construct a lengthy drainage canal from Lake Texcoco north to the Río de Tula, a distance of more than twenty miles.[90] Subsequent proposals for the drainage of the waters surrounding the city were advocated in the belief that the urban site would become more healthful and that lands might be reclaimed for use.[91] On the occasion of a minor flood in 1579–80, surveys were made for a drainage operation from Ecatepec to Huehuetoca. Humanitarian criticism of these plans took the position that the heavy labor involved would destroy the Indian workers. The humanitarian opposition did not prevail, but other factors—notably the natural decline of flood waters and the failure to appreciate the magnitude of the problem—operated to forestall any effective action.[92] As a whole, and apart from the years 1555–56, the sixteenth century may be regarded as a period of complacency with regard to water levels.

More serious flooding, accompanied by heavy damage in the city, occurred in 1604 and 1607. It is probable that the city's vulnerability to flood waters had been steadily increasing during the late sixteenth century as a result of the cutting of the surrounding forest and the progressive silting of the lake. City life had also changed in ways that made flood waters far more injurious: canals had been filled, boat traffic had declined, new houses had been built in an assumption of safety, and city ways had become increasingly farther removed from the amphibious living of the late Aztec and early colonial period. With the floods of the early seventeenth century, small causeways and wooden bridges reappeared and canoe traffic revived in the city.[93] The flood of 1607 was more severe than that of 1604, but together they stimulated a program of relief and repair far more ambitious than any undertaken in the sixteenth century. The Albarradón de San Lázaro was now rebuilt;[94] the causeways of Guadalupe, San Cristóbal, and San Antonio Abad were repaired; and work was begun on a dam, the Presa de Acolman, to contain the waters of the Río de Teotihuacan (Nexquipaya).[95] Most important, a new and far larger program of Desagüe General was now inaugurated under the direction of the master engineer Enrico Martínez. The plan was to construct a tunnel through the mountains at the northwestern corner of the Valley, near Huehuetoca, and to direct the excess water into it by a series of canals. The main canal was designed to drain Lake Zumpango as well as to carry water from the Río de Cuauhtitlan, the largest river of the Valley.[96]

After prodigious labor by thousands of Indians during eleven months in 1607 and 1608, the subterranean channel and its approaches were completed. The mouth of the tunnel was about thirteen feet across and thirteen feet in height, and the whole tunnel was about four miles long. It was excavated in sections, with underground cuts made from a series of perpendicular shafts along its route.[97] At its deepest part it fell approximately 175 feet beneath ground level.[98] The cutting of shafts and the processes of earth removal closely resembled the operations of mine construction. On its far side the tunnel opened at the Boca de San Gregorio, from which waters were conducted by an open trench for a distance of about five miles to empty into the Río de Tula.[99]

In late 1608 the new Desagüe seemed to be complete and successful, requiring only modest improvements and ordinary maintenance. But circumstances quickly rendered it ineffective. The drainage trench from Lake Zumpango became blocked, and the tunnel received water only from the diverted Río de Cuauhtitlan. Martínez's project received criticism as a "negative" Desagüe, one that limited the increase of water levels but did nothing directly to reduce them. In any case, the tunnel was deep enough to drain only Lakes Zumpango and Xaltocan. It could not drain Lake Texcoco, the surface of which was lower than the tunnel's mouth.[100] The tunnel was also criticized for being too small, with an opening too narrow to carry the volume of water that an emergency would require. Even those who criticized it on this score were sometimes unaware that it narrowed deceptively in the interior and that at its narrowest point it measured only about a yard in width and a yard in height.[101] In addition it was imperfectly constructed. Much of its wall consisted of loose earth. Intermittent arches of wood or masonry were insufficient to support its walls and roof, and undermining, crumbling, and blockage occurred. Many new plans were proposed after 1607, including proposals to strengthen the tunnel, to enlarge it, to clear it of obstructions, and to remove its earth cover entirely and convert it to a large open ditch.[102]

When the Spanish court sent the Dutch engineer Adrian Boot to review the Desagüe operations in 1613–14, still another plan was proposed: to abandon the drainage principle entirely and revert to the Indian and sixteenth-century principle of protection by dike. Boot's proposal was for a strong dike, after the manner of Dutch dikes, to separate Lake Texcoco from the waters surrounding the city.[103] The two experts, Enrico Martínez and Adrian Boot, came into conflict over fundamental procedure. New flood waters entered the city in the summer of 1620. Boot asserted in 1622 that everything accomplished so far had been ineffective and that the whole operation had been a waste of money.[104] Viceregal authority, after some vacillation, decided against the tunnel, and work on it was ordered to cease.[105] In 1623, after a brief period of drought, the viceroy ordered the Cuauhtitlan and Tepozotlan rivers redirected into Lake Zumpango in order to test the effectiveness of the tunnel, and the result was a progressive increase in the water level. In 1627 the city's streets were again inundated and large-scale repairs had to be undertaken on these and on the dike. Work on the tunnel began again in 1628, but it was already too late. As the rainy season of 1628 approached, the danger of still more serious flooding in the future was evident to all.[106]

The consequence, in 1629, was the most devastating flood in colonial history. Its immediate cause was the exceptionally heavy rainfall at the opening of the rainy season. Martínez, who had closed the Zumpango channel in order to save the tunnel from the destructive currents, was held responsible for it and placed in jail. The city's canals, which received most of the waste and refuse from the houses, had not been cleaned in the preceding dry season and, with their overflow, the city remained flooded for four years. Streets, plazas, and causeways stood under several feet of water and were again heavily damaged. Canoes and canoeists were brought from surrounding towns for transportation.[107] As the food shortages became acute, three-quarters or more of the city's population fled in a mass evacuation. Houses collapsed. Trade was halted. The king, when informed of the crisis, again proposed the transfer of the city to the mainland.[108]

Reduced rainfall in subsequent years finally brought the great flood to an end.[109] In 1637, with the viceregal transfer of Desagüe control to the Franciscan commissary, Luis Flores, the plan for uncovering the tunnel and converting it into an open trench was implemented. After 1637 most Desagüe labor was applied to the conversion from tunnel to open cut. The tunnel had been constructed, under critical conditions, within a period of eleven months. The transfer to the open cut occupied more than a century. Labor slowed or came completely to a halt during dry periods, only to be vigorously renewed under threat of flood. The transfer to the open cut was finished in the late eighteenth century, but work continued with the object of reducing the pitch of its sides and preventing the sliding of earth into the channel. Thus, with some interruptions and variations in intensity, Desagüe labor was continuous from the early seventeenth century to the end of colonial times.[110]

At all stages of these operations Desagüe labor was regarded as exceptionally arduous. That involving excavation resembled mine labor not only in its character but also in its severity. The repair of causeways required the carrying of stone and earth in large quantities, often in accelerated campaigns of great urgency. Indians were tied to beams at the water's edge and obliged to perform dredging operations while suspended in the current. Darkness, dampness, and cold made the tunnel labor extremely disagreeable. Disease took a heavy toll. Even in the very late colonial period the Indian population was reported to be living in dread of the Desagüe.[111]

We lack precise figures on the numbers of Indians employed in these labors except for short periods. The recorded expense account of the operations, however, gives some indication of the relative size of the labor force at successive times. Desagüe expenses suggest that the decade 1628–37 was the time of heaviest labor, that an irregular decline occurred during the subsequent hundred years, and that an expanding activity characterized the middle and late eighteenth century as the open cut came to be a reality (Figure 9). Figures on the Desagüe laborers do not always distinguish between numbers working at a given time and cumulative numbers working successively. But between 1,500 and 2,000 men were reported to be working daily on the Guadalupe causeway in 1604–5. Records of 1616 show that over 10,000 Indians worked on the Desagüe in that year, each for a two-week period, with some repetition. In the heavy labors of 1628, approximately 3,000 persons worked simultaneously. In 1637, at the end of the decade of extreme labor, between 600 and 900 Indians were working each day.[112]

The decade of most intense Desagüe activity was also the decade within which agricultural repartimiento was finally abolished. The connection is an obvious one. Desagüe labor cut sharply into the agricultural labor supply. In times of need viceroys always ordered jueces repartidores to divert Indian workers from agriculture to Desagüe employment, and irregular withdrawals had thus been made upon the system of agricultural recruitment for this as for other non-agricultural tasks. No fundamental change in the labor recruitment occurred with the inception of Desagüe General. The earliest detailed labor records of Desagüe General date from 1609, and they clearly show the reliance of Enrico Martínez and his subordinates upon the existing counts, quotas, and delivery systems of the agricultural repartimiento. Workers came in groups from individual towns; they were conducted by principales and alguaciles and mandones; their arrival and their periods of labor were recorded by number and by town just as in the drafts for the farms.[113] At first the heaviest demands were made upon the agricul-

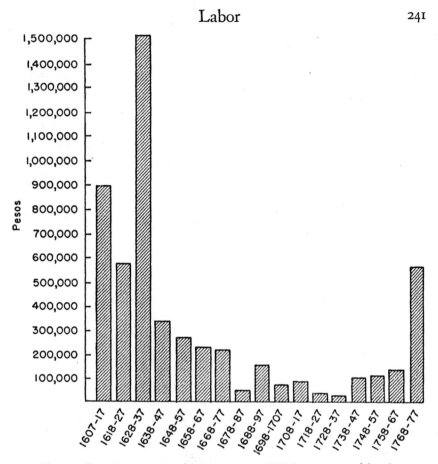

Figure 9. Desagüe expenses, 1607–1777. Source: BNM, ms. no. 450, fol. 358r.

tural repartimiento jurisdictions of Tepozotlan and Tacubaya. Many fewer workers were drawn from the jurisdiction of Tacuba in the early years, and even in 1616 Chalco was giving no regular workers.[114] But with the crisis of 1627–28, the demands upon the repartimiento system became exceptionally severe. The repartimiento of Tacuba now became liable for biweekly shifts of 233 men. The Tacubaya repartimiento became liable for 315. Chalco, which had experienced such difficulties in raising its quota for farm labor a decade before, was now required to furnish biweekly shifts of 250 for the Desagüe.[115] Orders for the provision of Desagüe workers were still being issued to the regular jueces repartidores in the early 1630's, on the eve of abolition. The last known orders to be so directed occurred in May 1633, after the abolition of agricultural repartimiento had been announced but before it had taken full effect.[116]

The Desagüe was thus manned to 1633 by means of the existing institutions for the coercion of labor.[117] Although the repartimiento for farm labor came to an end in 1633, the Desagüe repartimiento did not. It did not matter that the viceregal order of abolition applied to all repartimientos except those for mines. The Desagüe could not function through voluntary workers alone. Its labor records do occasionally mention voluntary workers, but they occur in ones and twos while the repartimiento workers number in the thousands.[118] From 1633 and continuously in the eighteenth century, orders for the delivery of Desagüe workers were issued in the familiar form, addressed now to the corregidores and alcaldes mayores rather than to jueces repartidores. At the end of colonial times the Desagüe repartimiento still persisted, an anachronistic corvée, as Humboldt observed, in a country where even mine labor had become "voluntary."[119]

Gradually the Desagüe drafts cast a wider and wider net. At the outset of Desagüe General in the early seventeenth century, only a few towns outside the Valley contributed labor. By 1616 additional towns, notably from the repartimiento of Zimapan, were being drawn upon.[120] With the crisis of 1627 new specifications were drafted and Indians were brought from much greater distances. The mining repartimiento of Pachuca and the Ixtlahuaca and Toluca areas now contributed.[121] Thousands of laborers from Cholula came to work in 1627. A decade later and toward the middle years of the century still more distant towns were added: Ixmiquilpan and Calpa in the north; Cuernavaca, Totolapa, and Tlayacapa in the south; and Tlaxcala, Huejotzingo, and Puebla in the east.[122]

The introduction of workers from outside the Valley followed upon the failure of nearer sources of supply. The city's Spanish cabildo, which had an interest in maintaining labor in the environs of the capital, proposed in 1630 that Desagüe workers be drawn exclusively from other districts of the viceroyalty. The cabildo asserted that the towns of the Valley ought to be excused from the Desagüe labors to which they were still sending hundreds of workers, for they were exhausted by the preceding three years and much weakened by disease. They were further needed for the repair of the city and for service to the Valley's Spanish agriculturists, who had "suffered so long from the lack of workers."[123] The agriculturists, of course, were soon to experience the complete cessation of the government-directed supply of agricultural labor. But the truth is that they had no real need for the cabildo's concern, for insofar as possible in the declining population, the Spanish agriculturists had already solved their problem by restoring the arrangements for private employment.

The sequestration of Indians for private labor outside encomienda and repartimiento began not on the Spanish farms but in workshops for the production of woolen cloth, known to colonial peoples as obrajes. Although the weaving of cotton was a familiar Indian technique, nothing like the obrajes had been known before the conquest. They were a purely Spanish innovation, a natural corollary of the colonial sheepherding industry, which had established itself very rapidly in central Mexico in the post-conquest years. Woolen looms worked by Indians under Spanish direction were first established in Texcoco in the 1530's or before. During the mid-century period, sheepherding and woolen manufacture enjoyed promotion under the highest auspices. The entrepreneurs included the oidor Lorenzo de Tejada and Antonio de Mendoza, the first viceroy.[124] The obraje thus emerged as a form of labor utilization open to influential non-encomenderos, a fact that may go far to explain its role as a forerunner and prototype in the development of systems of private employment.

The usual obraje was a single enterprise housing its own employees. The technology of manufacture was subdivided and specialized, the chief operations being washing, carding, spinning, and weaving.[125] Most employees were Indians. Negroes and mulattoes were often used as guards.[126] In the early seventeenth century Mexico City had twenty-five obrajes manufacturing cloth and ten manufacturing hats. Texcoco had eight obrajes, Xochimilco four, Azcapotzalco two. They averaged approximately forty-five employees; the smallest required a labor staff of about thirty, while the largest on record in the early seventeenth century had 120 workers.[127]

From the beginning, obraje labor had a sordid reputation. The work was hard, food and living conditions were unsatisfactory, and physical abuse was a commonplace.[128] The mayordomos of obrajes, who were themselves paid in accordance with the obrajes' output, coerced workers with severity and in overtime periods.[129] A captured English sailor, Job Hortop, who was sent to one of the Texcoco obrajes about 1570, spent his time carding wool, as he later reported, "among the Indian slaves." Hortop's companion, Miles Philips, who was similarly sentenced, described his experiences as follows: "We were appointed by the Vice Roy to be carried unto the town of Texcuco . . . in which towne there are certaine houses of correction and punishment for ill people called Obraches, like to Bridewell here in London:

into which place divers Indians are sold for slaves, some for ten yeers, and some for twelve."[130] These statements do not represent any English misunderstanding of the status of the obraje workers. Spaniards described the workers in much the same terms, and viceregal laws and other Spanish statements identified them as slaves. Some were Chichimec Indians enslaved during frontier hostilities.[131] More common, however, and historically more interesting for their role in the history of labor procurement, were the Indians condemned for crime, whom Spaniards also regarded as slaves.

In the sentencing of culprits, judges specified terms of service, and obraje operators utilized the convicted workers as private employees. If the sentence took the form of a fine, this might be paid by the employer, who thus "bought" the convict in the same transaction that reimbursed the court. The employer would in turn be reimbursed in labor. The sentences were regarded as differing only in degree from sentences to service in the Philippines or to galley labor in Spain. They were imposed for less serious crimes, and they met an obvious local need.[132] Technically, only members of the audiencia and certain other judges were entitled to issue such sentences.[133] But this technicality was repeatedly disregarded. It came to be the custom that corregidores and their assistants, and other judges, even including Indian gobernadores and the clergy, condemned Indians in the same manner. Viceregal legislation on court jurisdiction makes it clear that judges regularly exceeded their authority in this matter and that they continued to do so to the eighteenth century, often in complicity with the obraje owners.[134]

For the employers, advantages of economy and security lay in possessing a working force of condemned criminals, and judicial sentence provided them with a means of labor procurement far cheaper than Negro slavery. A Negro slave sold for about 400 pesos in the early seventeenth century, and an obraje of average size at this time would thus have required an outlay of some 15,000 to 20,000 pesos for the labor force alone.[135] The obraje employers' self-interest is made emphatic in the protests of the early seventeenth century against royal legislation requiring Negro workers.[136] Convict labor guaranteed to the employer a supply of workers at reduced expense and it allowed time for specialized training. But even in the sixteenth century the obrajes were unable to rely upon criminals alone. Even the widespread abuses in the system of judiciary sentencing were insufficient to satisfy their needs. Moreover, unlike the labradores, the obraje owners could not depend upon repartimiento. Not only were the obraje tasks unsuited to the rotational labor of repartimiento, but repartimiento was commonly held to be inapplicable to obraje conditions on grounds of public good. When obrajes did occasionally receive Indians in repartimiento, this was for peripheral and unskilled tasks, such as the cutting of firewood.[137] In addition, Indian laborers in the obrajes were sometimes regarded as liable to repartimiento drafts in other enterprises, precisely as were the Indians in the towns.[138] It is not surprising, therefore, that the obraje entrepreneurs became the first class of employers to develop supplementary techniques of employment, distinct from encomienda, repartimiento, judicial sentence, and Negro slavery.

They began by negotiating privately with individual Indians. It was not difficult to locate native peoples in need of money, and the many stresses of the sixteenth and seventeenth centuries made Indians the more willing to accept offers of employment.[139] The terms of labor were recorded in written contracts, partly because this seemed to fit the royal ideal of voluntary labor. In a contractual agreement the employer and the Indian laborer appeared as free agents, the legal formalities were complied with before royal judges, and the wages, hours, and perquisites of the workers were explicitly set forth. In a colony of corruptible judges, however, contracts were susceptible to many varieties of abuse, all favoring the employers. Judges permitted exploitative contracts and agreed to conditions that would apply in jurisdictions other than their own. Most important, no procedure was ever devised to ensure that the contracts would be fulfilled.[140]

A related technique of the early period was the incarceration of the contracted workers behind locked doors, to make of the obraje, in effect, a prison workshop. Incarceration was already an established procedure by the 1560's, and it may have represented at first only an employer's precaution with respect to a working staff of convicts. But it quickly affected non-convict laborers as well. Viceroy Velasco asserted in his own defense in the 1560's that he had ensured the opening of the obrajes and the removal of guards for the non-criminal employees.[141] We do not know exactly what Velasco accomplished, but it was at best no more than a temporary reform. When the Indian draftsman of Códice Osuna pictured an obraje in Mexico City in the 1560's he carefully delineated its stone façade and massive closed doors.[142] Incarceration continued despite criticism by the church and repeated viceregal denunciation in the late sixteenth century.[143] It was par-

ticularly difficult to control because convicts and other laborers worked
side by side. Royal law shifted its position and the viceregal administrations
legislated rules with distinctions too subtle to be enforced—that escaped convict workers, for example, might be compelled "con prisiones" to return to
their labors, while the obrajes themselves had to be kept open.[144] The law
called for a degree of responsibility that obraje employers refused to assume,
and judges continued to support the employers in defiance of the law. The
obrajes of the seventeenth century contained Indians who had been lured
inside as children under the guise of apprenticeship or committed to obrajes
by the judges as orphans. Once inside, they spent the remainder of their
lives behind locked or guarded doors.[145] The sentencing of Indians to labor
in this manner was still being forbidden in the eighteenth century. But the
closed obraje persisted until the end of colonial times.[146]

The sequestration of Indians for private labor in agriculture has a somewhat different history, much more closely related to repartimiento. Slave
labor and criminal labor were negligible in agriculture, and force and incarceration less prevalent. In agriculture, with the decline of encomienda,
repartimiento operated temporarily to fill the need for labor. Agricultural
work was well adapted to repartimiento; it was relatively unskilled and
was always regarded as falling within the public interest; it could be adjusted to seasonal demands; and excess laborers could be channeled into
other employment. It required, however, an Indian population sufficiently
large to accommodate its uneconomical features. Probably the epidemic of
1576–81 provided the chief sixteenth-century impetus to private employment in agriculture, just as the epidemic of 1545–48 had provided the chief
impetus to repartimiento. Thus the sequence of agricultural labor institutions—encomienda, repartimiento, private employment—may be understood as a progressive adjustment to a shrinking labor supply. As towns
failed to supply their repartimiento quotas, labradores undertook to secure
laborers by independent means. Like obraje owners, labradores made individual contracts that bound Indian workers to private service. The process
was delayed by the perpetuation of repartimiento, and it could not succeed
completely until repartimiento had been demonstrated to be a failure. The
fifty-year period 1580–1630, the period of competition between the systems
of private and repartimiento labor, was the critical one in the transformation
of agricultural employment. With every failure of repartimiento, private
labor in agriculture gained an additional advantage. And it was abetted by

the circumstance that private labor in the obrajes had gone before it and established its precedents.

In the wheat farms of the Valley, private Indian workers (called *gañanes*) were already being employed by the 1580's. In 1583 the owner of an hacienda near Tepozotlan testified that he had employed gañanes from Teoloyuca, Tepozotlan, Huehuetoca, and Coyotepec for "many years," and he protested against the principales of the town who were sending his gañanes to Mexico City as carriers.[147] His complaint was a typical one, for as labor supplies were reduced the first impulse of labradores was to circumvent the gañanes' obligations in Indian society. In this they received some viceregal support. The viceroy in 1586 ruled that gañanes were not liable to extra community tasks. Their sole obligation was to the repartimiento, and the Indian town held no other labor claim upon them. With this rule a labrador might hold his gañanes at all times of the year except when they were called to the repartimiento, and the Spanish institution gained an advantage over the Indian institution. In test cases—as in 1599 when the gobernador and alcaldes of Toltitlan sought to use the gañanes of a labrador in working the fields of Indian principales—the viceroy took the Spaniard's side and ordered the town authorities to desist. On occasion Spanish agriculturists influenced the viceroy to rule that towns could not elect gañanes to local offices. The rule was made explicit with regard to the Indian government of Tlalnepantla in 1604, on the appeal of a local Spaniard.[148]

By the late sixteenth and early seventeenth centuries, then, the agricultural employers were making large strides in the direction of full gañán labor. The principal obstacle at this time was repartimiento itself. Employers continued to receive Indians in repartimiento, but their own gañanes were likewise liable to repartimiento drafts and had to serve other employers when their turns came. Occasionally in the late sixteenth and early seventeenth centuries labradores were permitted to receive their own gañanes in repartimiento drafts, although Indian towns made efforts to prevent this and to use gañanes in other service obligations.[149] Spaniards were likewise sometimes able to receive Indians in repartimiento directly, without attendance at the repartimiento center.[150] Moreover, as repartimiento began to fail conspicuously in the early seventeenth century, those Spaniards possessing gañanes actively encouraged its decline. Their interests now sharply diverged from the interests of those who still had to depend on repartimiento. The employers of gañanes opposed the efforts of jueces repartidores to enlarge or maintain the quotas because—as an interested employer group declared in 1617—any extension of repartimiento would result in the depopulation of the haciendas.[151]

A major period of trial immediately preceded the repartimiento abolition of 1632–33. In the Valley this was a time of epidemic, severe flooding, and the collapse of agricultural repartimiento, virtually all the resources of which were being diverted to the repair of flood damage and to the Desagüe. The Spaniards with gañanes were able to survive, while those who still depended on repartimiento abandoned their farms or shifted, if they could, entirely to gañán labor. Gañanes who had been acquired without legal formality came to occupy positions equivalent to those under legitimate contract. The crises of the 1620's and early 1630's were radically selective forces in the transformation of agricultural employment. In repartimiento jurisdictions such as Tacuba-Azcapotzalco, where the number of operating wheat farms fell from two hundred to sixty,[152] the abolition order of 1632-33 could appear only as a coup-de-grâce. In 1601, when the monarchy had sought to abolish repartimiento, the labradores had not been ready for abolition and had successfully opposed it. But by 1633 it could not affect them; repartimiento was an institution they had already rejected and passed beyond.[153]

Within Indian society, the 1620's brought about another kind of selectivity. Here the division lay between those Indians responsible for the maintenance of community obligations and those who found a personal solution in becoming gañanes. The crises of these years served as inducements to Indians to seek employment in haciendas, and in some instances to move completely from town to hacienda residence. To Indian refugees from the towns the hacienda offered an escape, and the interests of the hacendados and the gañanes converged in opposition to traditional community obligation. The situation contributed to a conflict between Indian communities and Spanish haciendas, a conflict that continued into the twentieth century. But in the early seventeenth century the lines of division were still far from clear. Many gañanes were residents of towns. In Texcoco, where the normal tendencies favoring gañán labor operated side by side with a developed obraje economy in 1630, three-quarters of the Indian population were in direct non-repartimiento service to Spaniards. In Tequixquiac, where the surviving encomendero was an influential hacendado, the Indian gobernador took the hacendado's side and compelled Indians to labor in the hacienda. Caciques and other Indians who themselves became hacendados opposed the Indian town officers who sought to divert the hacienda workers to community tasks.[154]

The hacienda was the culminating institution in the long history of Indian agricultural labor, but it was less overtly coercive in its policies of labor recruitment than any of the antecedent institutions. Enslavement, encomienda, repartimiento, and the obrajes all required compulsion. The hacienda did not, at least to the same degree. The hacienda was not a simple institution. Its internal operation and its relation to the economic environment were intricate and shifting. Its role was one of progressive domination over land (Chapter X), over agriculture (Chapter XI), and over other forms of supply (Chapter XII), and as it dominated these it necessarily extended its control over Indian labor. The hacienda could afford to reject outright coercion in the procurement of workers because the accumulation of other pressures upon Indian society had rendered such coercion unnecessary. Haciendas had no need of the prison atmosphere of the obrajes. The economic environment had developed, or deteriorated, to the point at which the hacienda, for all its rigors, offered positive advantages to Indian workers.

These observations would appear to conflict with the common assumption that the hacienda acquired and retained its workers through debt servitude. It has been argued, quite plausibly, that hacendados, like other employers of Indian labor, did use coercion, that they contrived to become the creditors of individual Indians and thereafter compelled debtors to labor in discharge of the amount owed. An examination of this thesis in relation to labor in the Valley will require first a survey of the history of wages and other remunerations in the types of labor thus far discussed.

Most early labor—in encomienda, in urban construction, or in other duties—was either unrecompensed or recompensed only with respect to the Indian officers responsible for the delivery of workers.[155] Labor hired for wages, however, is recorded occasionally for both skilled and unskilled workmen in the 1530's and after. As of 1549, before the separation of the agricultural repartimiento from labor in the city, the normal wage for a day's hire in unskilled labor was one cuartillo (one-fourth real, or 8½ maravedís) per day.[156] This was officially rejected as inadequate recompense, and under Viceroy Velasco's rule in the early 1560's wages were set at $\frac{6}{17}$ real (12 maravedís) per day for unskilled workers (*peones*) in the labor drafts on the farms and $1\frac{2}{17}$ real (24 maravedís) for carpenters, masons, and other skilled workers (oficiales) laboring principally at urban tasks.[157] In the repartimiento for farms all workers were regarded as unskilled. Wages were increased to one-half and one real per day respectively in 1553,[158] and hence Indian laborers were receiving one-half real per day in 1555, when the agricultural repartimiento was formally separated as a distinct institution.[159] The wage was increased to two-thirds and then to three-fourths real for peones in the 1560's and 1570's,[160] and to one real for unskilled and two reales for skilled workers in several enactments around 1590.[161] Wages for peones in repartimiento were raised to 1½ reales per day in the period 1603–10 and to two reales per day by 1629.[162]

Wages for unskilled hired labor outside repartimiento approximated the repartimiento figures but were more variable. In the 1560's wages for unskilled hired labor varied from one-fourth real per day in Xochimilco to 1½ reales per day in Mexico City.[163] Skilled craftsmen working outside repartimiento were earning at this time one-half real per day in Xochimilco and 3 to 4 reales in Mexico City.[164] Skilled workers practicing their own trades in Mexico City in the late sixteenth and early seventeenth centuries received up to 8 reales (one peso) per day.[165] Hired agricultural labor by peones was recompensed at a normal rate of 1½ reales per day in the early seventeenth century.[166] Labor services for corregidores were to be paid for at a rate of one real per day in the 1590's.[167] In obrajes a wage of 3 to 4 pesos per month, amounting to one real per day or less, was common in the early seventeenth century.[168] The cost of hiring substitutes in repartimiento labor ranged up to double the repartimiento pay, rising from 8 reales per week in 1570 to 10 or 12 reales in the 1590's, and to 18 reales per week in the 1620's.[169] In the late sixteenth century a skilled Indian worker might avoid his week's repartimiento obligation through a payment to the employer of 3 or 4 pesos (4 to 5 reales per day). In obligatory service to Indian gobernadores and caciques, peones of the sixteenth century received much more modest sums, generally 20 or 25 cacaos and daily food.[170]

Desagüe labor was paid for by the state—unlike agricultural labor which was paid for by the private employers—and it accordingly received a lower wage. Few if any of the albarradón workers of 1555–56 received compensation.[171] The Desagüe plans of 1604–5 called for a wage of one peso per week, but the first workers of the seventeenth century received nothing. Later the Desagüe wage rose from 5 to 7 reales per week in 1620, to 9 reales by 1628, and to 12 reales per week or two reales per day by the 1640's.[172]

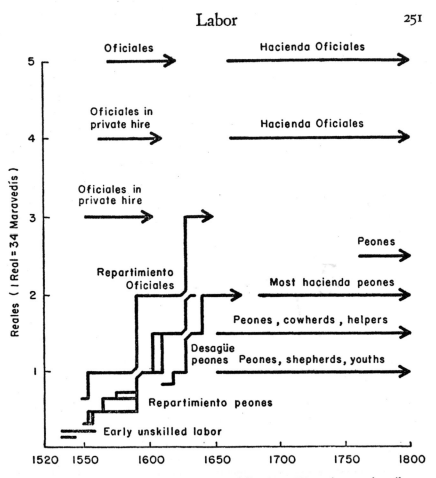

Figure 10. The Indian laborer's average daily wage. Wages increased until the mid-seventeenth century and then remained steady.

Wages for Indian labor in each category thus increased during the period of population decline. From the 1630's to the end of the colonial period, on the other hand, wages were much more stable. Rates in the late eighteenth century were in some cases identical with those of a hundred and fifty years before. "Free" workers in late colonial obrajes still received only 3 pesos per month.[173] The common daily wage for peones at the time of the abolition of agricultural repartimiento—1½ or 2 reales per day—remained standard until the last quarter of the eighteenth century. The hacienda wage was commonly 2 reales per working day for peones,[174] with equivalent rates for other employees: 2 reales per day for mule keepers and field workers; 1½ or 2 reales per day for cowherds and their helpers; one real per day for shepherds, youths, and miscellaneous assistants; and 3 or 4 reales per day for skilled masons.[175] At the end of the eighteenth century wages for peones varied between 1½ and 2½,[176] and oficiales were commanding wages of 3 to 5, reales per day.[177] The highest recorded peones' wage is 3 reales per day in the early nineteenth century.[178]

To these wage scales were added, under certain circumstances, provision of daily food and extra pay for travel to or from work. In repartimiento and Desagüe labor, five or six leagues (approximately fifteen miles) of travel were regarded as the equivalent of one day of labor, and, with a variety of exceptions, were paid for accordingly.[179] Travel did not normally figure in the wages paid by haciendas. The provision of food to workers was common in obrajes and in the late repartimientos, including the Desagüe.[180] Food provision in haciendas was standard and universal, but the provisions were not always in addition to the wage. If the wage were two reales per day, one might be issued in money and the other as a maize ration; alternatively, the full monetary payment might be made and a part received back by the hacienda in maize sales.[181] Even haciendas that did not produce maize for sale customarily raised a supply for their own workers.[182] Haciendas commonly issued monetary wages on Sunday—this ensured that workers would have the means to meet their ecclesiastical obligations—and deferred the maize payments to Tuesday or Wednesday, after the weekly labor had begun. As the manager of the hacienda of Molino de Flores, near Texcoco, stated in 1785, this schedule was deliberately established and had "a thousand advantages," for it meant that the workers would be induced to stay on the premises.[183]

Debt labor, like much else in labor history, received its earliest impetus in the obrajes and spread from them to other employment institutions.[184] Debt could be incurred in many ways. An advance in wages to a "free" obraje laborer placed him immediately in debt. An Indian laborer might be forced to accept money payable in work, or he might be required to purchase, with borrowed funds, the equipment he was to use in obraje labor. Deductions might be made against a worker's account if his finished cloth weighed less than the raw wool with which he started.[185] Forced sales, with price markups and the prohibition of purchases elsewhere, might prolong or increase his debt.[186]

Royal legislation on debt labor in the sixteenth century sometimes forbade loans by employers to their workers and the discharge of debt by labor.[187] But other rules tended to compromise in favor of the employers. As in so many other matters, laws shifted between prohibition and regulation. Loans were to be transacted before judges, but other loans, for tribute or for food or for "necessities," could be transacted privately.[188] Restrictions were placed upon the amount of loans and on the periods for which debts could be effective.[189] Viceregal legislation in 1595 supported the employers even to the point of forbidding payments of debt in money and specifying payments in labor. But labor debts were entirely forbidden again by royal and viceregal legislation in the early seventeenth century.[190] When communities had to perform special Desagüe labor in commutation of tribute arrears, a supervised public debt servitude was established.[191] Limitations on the duration of the debts were attempted, as well as limitations on the amounts, expressed as salary for a given number of months. The law also recognized those employers who paid tributes for their Indian employees, tribute payment sometimes being regarded as a separate transaction, not to be included in computing the maximum legal debt.[192]

No one could argue that the Valley's hacendados absolutely refrained from using the devices of debt employment, for countless records indicate that they did use them. But many other employers used them as well, and one must be cautious in evaluating the special role of debt employment in haciendas. A comparison between the hacienda and the obraje is revealing here, for while both were institutions of debt labor, the obraje was in addition a closed and guarded workshop. Obraje history indicates that debt labor alone was incapable of holding obraje workers, and it may be concluded that it was likewise incapable of holding hacienda workers. In any case, indebtedness was a legal technicality. An Indian worker bent on leaving his hacienda could find occasion to do so despite his indebtedness—just as any Indian could default and escape his tribute debt to a town or his private debt to any creditor. From the viceregal point of view, even the legal technicality could be regarded as inapplicable in the late eighteenth century, for the viceroy was on record in 1784 with the assertion that Indians might freely leave the haciendas regardless of the amount they owed.[193]

An examination of hacienda records is further revealing. During any agricultural year the working force of a large Valley hacienda might vary from fifty to three hundred or more persons, depending on the seasonal de-

TABLE 18

Tributary Classifications

Jurisdiction	Indios de pueblo	Laborios and vagos	Jurisdiction	Indios de pueblo	Laborios and vagos
Chalco (and Tlaya- capa) (1800–1803)	11,800	517	Mexico (1800–1801).	9,672	
Coatepec (1799)	1,306	12	Otumba (1800)	1,342	19
Coyoacan (1799)....	3,548	174	Tacuba (1799)......	6,561	
Cuauhtitlan (1797)..	3,897	80	Teotihuacan (1804) .	1,813	
Ecatepec (1803).....	2,573		Texcoco (1802).....	7,546	
Mexicalzingo (ca. 1800)	2,222		Xochimilco (1801) ..	4,278	3
			Zumpango (1801)...	1,310	52

SOURCE: AGN, Tributos, vol. 43, exp. último, fol. 4r–4v. Numbers refer to tributaries. The jurisdictions of Hueypoxtla and Pachuca, which lay mainly outside the Valley, are not included.

mand for agricultural labor.[194] The nucleus of this labor force consisted of resident workers, the "gañanes radicados" of the hacienda, who might be expected to work regularly six days a week. For the remainder of their workers haciendas relied on a fluid supply from nearby communities. The seasonal operations entailed a continuous influx and departure of workers, under conditions quite different from those of the closed obraje.[195] Records of the late eighteenth and early nineteenth centuries (Table 18) show that by far the larger number of Indians were "de pueblo," only a small percentage being included in the double category of hacienda residents (laborios) and homeless persons or vagrants (vagos). The finances of the hacienda of Santa Ana Aragón in 1771–72, shown in Figure 16, indicate weekly expenses for wages ranging from under five to over sixty pesos throughout the year.[196] Santa Ana Aragón had at this time forty-two gañanes radicados, of whom fewer than half were in debt to the hacienda, and indeed the largest debts amounted to only a few weeks' wages. All but four of the debtors owed less than a peso apiece.[197] In a great hacienda such as Los Portales, approximately 100 persons owed a total of 367 pesos in 1778, with individual debts ranging from a few reales to 28 pesos. But Los Portales was at this time hiring weekly shifts of more than twice the number of debtors.[198]

The total indebtedness in these instances appears slight in comparison with the reputation of debt peonage as a controlling and universal hacienda technique. The matter would require documentation through the study of a large number of hacienda records, both in the Valley and elsewhere, and in the nineteenth and twentieth centuries as well as in the colonial era. A document of special interest in this connection is a survey of the economic condition of New Spain written from the point of view of the Spanish employers in 1788. The report speaks of the great shortage of hacienda workers, a shortage that operated to increase the amount of indebtedness in labor peonage. It was impossible, the writer stated, to find Indians who would work with a debt of only five pesos, at this time a legal limit. By "ancient custom" Indians were demanding advances of forty to eighty pesos, and if an employer were to refuse to raise his offer over five pesos, the Indian would desert and move to another hacienda where conditions were more attractive.[199] Here the emphasis is reversed from the conventional interpretation of debt labor, for it assumes relative freedom among the workers, whose objective was not to escape but to enlarge the indebtedness. The writer recognized that regional customs varied in New Spain with respect to the amounts owed, and we may suppose that his comments applied far more to other areas than to the Valley of Mexico, where conditions were less extreme than those described. In any case, the amount of the debt may be considered in some degree as a measure of the bargaining power of the worker. The relatively dense population of the Valley may have reduced this bargaining power, and accordingly reduced the amount of indebtedness and the role of peonage.

Present evidence for the Valley suggests that in late colonial times debt peonage affected fewer than half the workers on haciendas, and that the large majority of these owed debts equal to three weeks' labor or less. But a full explanation for the hold of the hacienda over its workers cannot stop with debt servitude. To Indian workers the hacienda offered solutions to economic conditions not to be found elsewhere. As monetary values came to occupy a large role in Indian society—in tribute, in ecclesiastical charges, in economic exchange—the hacienda offered a regular or irregular income. To Indians who had lost their lands (largely, of course, to haciendas) the hacienda provided a dwelling and a means of livelihood. Under conditions permitting only tiny margins between income and sustenance, the hacienda was an institution of credit, allowing Indians freely to fall behind in their financial obligations without losing their jobs or incurring punishment.

If these conclusions are accurate, we confront the further problem of explaining the evil reputation of the hacienda in Mexican labor history. In part, this reputation may represent an extension, with respect to labor, of a reputation gained in acts of land usurpation. In part, it may relate to areas remote from the Valley or to areas where haciendas were larger and workers less numerous. It may also reflect conditions of the nineteenth century and attitudes of justification relating to the Revolution of 1910, for in the national period Indian enslavement and repartimiento were obsolescent, and industrialization depended upon a mestizo urban population. In rural areas, where Indian civilization persisted, only the hacienda exploited labor, and an Indianist ideology consequently focused its attention here. But in the Valley in colonial times the hacienda offered an acceptable livelihood to Indians who had lost their lands. The alternatives—starvation, vagabondage, abandonment of town and family—were less attractive for most workers than hacienda labor itself. Moreover, the same hacienda labor might appear moderate in comparison with other circumstances of the colonial period, and harsh only in comparison with a twentieth-century liberal ideal. To say this is to suggest that in areas such as the Valley of Mexico Indian labor for Spanish employers became progressively less severe, and that it became least severe under the hacienda.

CHAPTER X

Land

Despite some discrepancies, colonial sources agree upon five essential or major classes of Aztec land: (1) *teotlalli,* or land of the temples and gods; (2)
tecpantlalli, or land of the community houses; (3) *tlatocatlalli* (*tlatocamilli*)
or land of the tlatoque; (4) *pillalli* and *tecuhtlalli,* or land of the nobles
(pipiltin and tetecuhtin); (5) *calpullalli,* or land of the calpultin.[1] All five
came to be substantially modified under the impact of Spanish colonization.
The teotlalli ceased to exist; the tecpantlalli and tlatocatlalli were first
sharply limited and then almost wholly extinguished; the pillalli, tecuhtlalli, and calpullalli were preserved in reduced amount. Much land shifted
from one category to another, several new categories came into being, and
ultimately the greater part of the land passed from Indian possession and
control altogether.

The subject of colonial land transformation is technical and complex.
With present knowledge it may most satisfactorily be treated under five
somewhat different headings, representing a rearrangement and adaptation
of the five categories of original Aztec land. We shall consider in sequence:
teotlalli; other lands worked in common; new land grants to Indian communities; private Indian properties; and calpullalli. We shall proceed then
to examine the history of land acquisition by Spaniards.

For comment on the sizes of Indian land tracts we must depend upon the
basic linear units employed in the colonial period, the vara and the braza.
The vara can usually be identified as the vara de Castilla, also called the
vara of Burgos, of Toledo, and of textile measurement (*de medir paños y
sedas*). It was the approximate equivalent of .84 meters or 33 inches and
was divided into three "feet" (*pies*), each of about .28 meters.[2] The braza,
which was less precise, appears most often as the equivalent of two varas or
1.68 meters.[3] But other brazas, and even other varas, are recorded in dif-

ferent contexts, and the measurement intended is at times obscure. Especially in dealing with native lands Spaniards were likely to adopt local Indian variants of the braza in such a way that the computation of equivalent modern measurements becomes difficult or impossible. We have records of "brazas" of three pies in Tequicistlan, of six pies in Teotihuacan, of nine pies in Tepexpan, of ten pies in San Angel, and of twelve pies in Coyoacan.[4]

TEOTLALLI. Land called teotlalli consisted originally of tracts located in each community or calpulli and worked in common by inhabitants who delivered the proceeds exclusively to the temples.[5] For present purposes the major fact concerning these lands is that they were not systematically converted into colonial church properties. Christian churches were sometimes constructed on the sites of destroyed pre-conquest temples, but there is no evidence of any transfer of the supporting lands. The earliest churches were supported not by lands but by tributes, bequests, and labor. It is true that a royal cedula of 1534 urged the audiencia to determine to what extent aboriginal temple lands might be secured for the support of Christian churches.[6] But every item of information suggests that this action came too late. Temple lands had been taken either by Spaniards or by other Indians and diverted to secular functions.[7] When the church eventually acquired land it was from sources other than the teotlalli.[8]

OTHER LANDS WORKED IN COMMON. Other lands worked in common for secular tribute in the Aztec state demonstrate a more direct continuity into the colonial period.[9] Much of the "land of Montezuma" and similar land was also seized by acquisitive Spaniards and Indians.[10] But Spaniards frequently insisted on common plantings for tribute purposes, and occasional evidence suggests that identical lands were used for Aztec tribute before the conquest and for Spanish tribute later.[11] In 1552 maize fields in common plantings for Spanish tribute appear on the order of 1,000 by 160 brazas in Acolman (the braza in this instance being from the foot to the extended hand); 400 by 100 brazas in Culhuacan; and 200 by 100 brazas in Huitzilopochco.[12] Wheat fields in common plantings occur as 415 by 102 brazas in Chicoloapa and 150 by 100 brazas and 250 by 60 brazas in Ixtapaluca.[13] Successive tribute notices of the middle sixteenth century record varying dimensions and shifts from maize to wheat; in Ixtapaluca the fields in 1543 measured 800 by 160 brazas for maize and 200 by 100 brazas for wheat; in 1552, when both were for wheat, they measured 150 by 100 and 250 by 60 brazas.[14] Dimensions are lacking in cases where lands of this type were specified not by linear measurement but by yield in maize or wheat, a stated amount of grain being designated as due to the encomendero or the crown. This practice is mentioned for Texcoco as early as 1531.[15]

Lands worked in common for the benefit of local caciques and principales are described as adjoining the towns and worked by "all the people together" for periods of two or three hours per day.[16] Such lands were not the personal possessions of the caciques and principales concerned; they were "common" lands for the support of the offices of rule. But it is not completely clear to what extent the colonial lands of this type are to be identified as continuations of the earlier tecpantlalli and tlatocatlalli. Pre-conquest tecpantlalli is described in colonial notices as having been dedicated to the "households and palaces of the kings and señores" and inhabited and worked by persons called *tecpanpouhque* or *tecpantlaca* (tecpan people), who paid no tribute but served in the repair of the house or tecpan. Tecpantlalli appears in at least one account as land not worked in common at all but divided into individual plots, with succession from father to son, and with reassignment in case of removal or failure of succession.[17] By tlatocatlalli (tlatocamilli) was seemingly meant land divided into plots of 400 by 400 measures (*medidas*) in each town and rented to maceguales for the maintenance of the tlatoani. The plots were attached to the offices of rule (señoríos), and the incumbent tlatoque were not permitted to dispose of them in any way save by rental.[18]

The terms tlatocatlalli and tecpantlalli do occur in reference to colonial land types, though not in a form that permits close comparison with the pre-conquest tenure described.[19] However, lands attached to the office or to the rule of the Indian leaders and distinct from personally owned land are found with sufficient frequency to suggest widespread early survival. Thus Ramírez de Fuenleal, writing in 1532, described the lands of certain communities "attached to the rule" (*anexas al señorío*) and worked by the maceguales. The Altamirano report of 1553 distinguished private land of Indian rulers from land attached to their "government" (*gobernación*). Records of Cuauhtitlan in 1554 and of Huitzilopochco in 1564 make an unmistakable differentiation between the personal landed property of a cacique and the land of his office.[20] In Tepetlaoztoc in 1559 the encomendero usurped some land specifically referred to as tecpantlalli, and witnesses in his behalf sought to prove that this land was the cacique's personal property. Against these assertions Indians of Tepetlaoztoc affirmed that the land was properly tecpantlalli (*tequepantale*), that it was "common land," that it comprised "land of the community," and that it was worked for "common purposes" (*cosas tocantes al común*).[21] The case is suggestive concerning the technique of Spanish justification (private lands, by Indian canons, could be alienated, whereas community land, in general, could not) and it also reveals an Indian tendency to identify community interests with the interests of caciques and principales.

In certain communities, lands under common cultivation were adapted to the new offices of colonial Indian governments. The most detailed instances occur in two communities bordering the Valley of Mexico—Utlaspa to the northwest and Totolapa to the south. In Utlaspa, in addition to other forms of tribute received by the Indian officers, the gobernador of 1549 received the produce of a plot measuring 400 by 400 brazas worked by the community as a whole; for each alcalde a plot of 200 by 200 brazas was maintained; and the community cultivated plots of 160 by 160 brazas for each regidor and 200 by 200 brazas for the mayordomo.[22] In Totolapa in 1559 the produce of 240 by 200 brazas went to the gobernador; 40 by 20 brazas supported the escribano; each of six principales in charge of public works received the produce of 40 by 20 brazas; each of certain other principales received produce from 120 by 60 brazas; and tracts of 20 by 10 brazas were cultivated for the tequitlatos. Any Indian principal elected to the governorship in Totolapa was required to contribute his personal income to the community treasury and to receive, during the period of his tenure, only the yield of the gubernatorial land.[23] These two cases demonstrate that a type of "office land" was maintained for the support of the officers of Indian government in the middle years of the sixteenth century; and the evidence, although not conclusive, suggests that such land was worked in common and not inhabited by tecpanpouhque or rented to maceguales.

Distinct "office lands" were not retained consistently, however, and several instances suggest what took place. A cacique-gobernador, in office for a long period, might establish the position that office lands were part of his cacicazgo. A gobernador who was not a cacique might take over the same lands and argue personal possession based upon years of receipt of their produce.[24] In Teotihuacan, principales brought suit before the audiencia against the cacique heir over possession of tlatocatlalli and tecpantlalli, which were then judged to be part of the cacicazgo.[25] In Tepetlaoztoc, following a ruling by Cortés, the cacique's retainers (renteros) were reduced in number to 265, and it was stated that these retainers "have been attached and continue to be attached to the governmental office" (*an andado y andan con la gobernación*). When the Tepetlaoztoc cacique died, the rule was inherited by his nephew, who already had twenty-eight families (casas) of retainers "as part of his patrimony inherited from his father." The two groups were then joined under the successor.[26] In this case, tecpantlalli or tlatocatlalli and private or personally inheritable land, each with retainers, were seemingly combined under a single holder. In any event, after the middle sixteenth century, notices of "office land" virtually disappear from the record, and this leads us to believe that the tecpanpouhque became absorbed in the entire body of maceguales and that tecpantlalli and tlatocatlalli were converted into other kinds of property—pillalli, calpullalli, or Spanish-held land.[27]

It is possible that in some instances lands classified as tlatocatlalli were converted into the "common cultivated lands" (*sementeras de la comunidad*) that figure in the tribute assignments of the 1540's and 1550's prior to the tribute reforms of the 1560's. These were lands whose produce was to accrue to the communities, and viceregal insistence on their cultivation reflected Spanish alarm at the decline of Indian agriculture. In its most forceful expression of concern, the viceregal government stipulated in 1554 that all unworked lands in all towns of the capital environs were to be cultivated for the communities, with the threat that such lands would otherwise be forfeited and sold, either to Spaniards or to other Indians.[28] These common cultivated lands measured 1,600 by 800 brazas and 800 by 800 brazas in Utlaspa, and 400 by 400 brazas in Citlaltepec, measurements that would seem consistent with the dimensions of the tlatocatlalli (400 by 400 measures).[29] Tribute regulations of the 1560's replaced the common cultivated lands by direct money payments, but community taxation was again directly connected with land in the ten-vara legislation of 1577. When the original ten-vara rule was interpreted as implying ten brazas (presumably twenty varas), towns did in fact assign lands in this amount.[30] But it is not certain whether these were worked individually or in common. Moreover, we have no secure sources of information on the earlier classification of the lands so used. They may have been lands formerly worked in common for the community or other lands rendered vacant by depopulation.

NEW LAND GRANTS TO INDIAN COMMUNITIES. The most important of the various new types of common land followed upon viceregal grants (*mercedes*) to corporate Indian towns. That communities requested and received official land grants indicates, obviously, a developed Hispanization and an Indian cognizance of Spanish legalism. There is some evidence, on the other hand, that Indian towns made their requests less for the procuring of formal title to land (the Indian community already understood itself to be the owner) than for the procuring of viceregal authorization for common flocks of sheep. Viceregal titles for Indian sheep pastures required the herding of two thousand head in an area of about three square miles and forbade the sale of the property assigned, thus seeking to ensure that communities would indeed use the estancias for herding and not for speculation or other purposes.[31]

Grants for agriculture were sometimes made separately and sometimes combined with grants for herding—always with provision that the lands be used by the Indian community for these purposes. Therefore the receipt of a viceregal grant placed some responsibility on the community, in default of which the land was, at least legally, assignable to another owner. Indian towns did engage in community sheepherding in the sixteenth century and later, both as a means of contributing to town treasuries and as a means of securing funds for tribute.[32] Had they done so on a larger scale, and had they in all cases secured formal viceregal land grants, their later legal position as corporate owners of land would have been much strengthened. So far as we know, lands assigned to towns by viceregal grant were in all cases lands already within the limits (términos) of the recipient Indian communities and still unclaimed by any other party. But Spanish occupation was much facilitated by the circumstance that only a limited amount of original Indian land was ever so confirmed.[33]

A viceregal land grant to a native community was issued only on formal petition from the native inhabitants and only after specified requirements had been fulfilled. After a gobernador and his officers had entered a petition, the viceroy ordered the corregidor to make a survey. The Indians of the town were notified of the pending survey on a Sunday or fiesta day following religious services. Announcements were duly read, recorded, and witnessed. The corregidor, the Indian officers, an interpreter, and a number of other Indians traversed the area in question and made a record of its measurements and topographical features. The corregidor was required to summon ten Spanish and Indian witnesses to testify concerning the land: that it fell within the known Indian limits of the town; that it was suited to sheep pasturage; that any maize plantings found within its boundaries were common property and not privately owned; and that these could be abandoned without hardship. If all seemed in order the corregidor then recommended to the viceroy that the merced be issued, and that the land be held by the town in an inalienable condition. The merced itself was a formal document enumerating the boundary points and designating the Indian community as the possessor.[34]

PRIVATE INDIAN PROPERTIES. In the colony, private Indian lands derived from many sources. But their pre-conquest prototypes probably fall in the two main classifications of pillalli and tecuhtlalli. Land called pillalli is described in terms that suggest an alodial holding, for it could be bequeathed or sold and was not attached to an office-holding position. Land classified as tecuhtlalli is more difficult to identify. The name obviously implies a connection with the members of the tecuhtli class. But the tecuhtlalli seems to have been used particularly for the settlement of foreign refugees, from whom the tecuhtli class received tribute or rent.[35]

In any case, we have many notices of private land assignments of the late Aztec period. When Xochimilco was conquered in the time of Itzcoatl, he distributed some of its lands to Mexican conquerors. When Nezahualcoyotl's Acolhua forces conquered Tequicistlan, he assigned lands there among his sons. When Chalco was conquered under Montezuma I, lands there were distributed among the ranking personages of the Triple Alliance in such numbers that every "person of significance" in the three ruling families received land, the three tlatoque taking as much as they wanted for themselves.[36] Lands might be bestowed as a marriage dowry. Calpullalli plots might be acquired by private individuals in purchase from principales. Some merchants had "private lands" (*tierras propias*).[37] Unquestionably, lands owned in this way were bequeathed to heirs, both male and female, in Aztec custom, and the services of their sub-macegual occupants were similarly inherited.[38] Thus at the time of the conquest individual Indians owned scattered lands and were supported by the tributes of the persons attached to them.

A striking feature of Aztec landholding is the geographical extent and wide separation of the holdings of single individuals. We have the evidence of Montezuma's son-in-law that Montezuma possessed—as patrimonial inheritance from his father, before inheriting the rule, and apart from lands attached to the office—properties in or near Tacuba, Tacubaya, Azcapotzalco, Chalco, Xochimilco, and Cuitlahuac. In the same way Montezuma's wife held lands in Tlalmanalco, Mixquic, and Cuitlahuac.[39] A single principal might own lands in Otumba and Cuernavaca.[40] Principales of Teotihuacan had lands and vassals in Texcoco, Tenochtitlan, Tlatelolco, Ecatepec, and other places. Principales of Tepexpan had lands in Toltitlan, Azcapotzalco, and Xochimilco.[41] Records of Texcoco indicate private possession of lands in Chalco, Cuernavaca, Azcapotzalco, Xochimilco, and Cuauhtitlan. This meant also that in single communities lands were owned by numerous distant owners. Within the términos of Cuauhtitlan, there were properties held by Indians of Culhuacan, Ixtapalapa, Mexicalzingo, and Azcapotzalco.[42]

In principle, the Spanish state respected the legitimacy of private Indian properties.[43] But the intricacy of their distribution, the disruption caused by the conquest, and Spanish greed all operated to reduce native ownership. Because the subordinate inhabitants of such lands were immune from early encomienda tribute, it lay within the interests of the early encomenderos to reject the claims of private Indian possession in the encomienda areas. Under certain conditions Spaniards were able to deny native ownership outright and to assume property for themselves. It is not surprising that Spaniards in practice refused to recognize or to sanction all the complex interrelationships of Indian land tenure. The Spanish tendency was to simplify by placing an entire subject community under a single cabecera, to slough off alien tribute obligations, and gradually to eliminate or modify the properties occupied by retainers in the sub-macegual class. In many communities the lands that Montezuma had given to his officers reverted to the towns during the first decade following the conquest. Cortés's procedure was to reduce the amount of land and the number of retainers held by upper-class Indians, to confiscate distant possessions, and to reassign nearby possessions in progressive acts of consolidation.[44] In Tepetlaoztoc he removed the distant possessions of twenty principales and confirmed only the closer holdings. In Cuauhtitlan he denied the cacique heir his inherited properties in Chalco and other remote regions and gave him instead local lands that had belonged to Montezuma and to owners in Culhuacan, Ixtapalapa, Mexicalzingo, and Azcapotzalco.[45]

Such actions inevitably brought protests from upper-class Indians. Isabel Montezuma, the daughter of Montezuma, complained that the greater part of her inheritance had been dissipated by such Spanish acts.[46] Other de-

scendants of the Aztec rulers made formal appeal for the return of sequestered lands, and principales of Mexico petitioned for the restoration of their
usurped properties in Chalco, Texcoco, Tacuba, and Xochimilco.[47] Many
Indian claims referred to properties not simply as lands (tierras) but as
estancias, and it sometimes happened that a complaint was made by the
cacique and principales of a town in unison, so that the list of deprivations
included both estancias lost to the cabecera and lands lost to private persons.[48] These facts suggest again the close connection between land "owned"
by a cacique or principal, and an estancia subject to a cabecera. The first
Spaniards saw little difference between the two, for the land and its occupants would appear similar at first glance and in both cases tribute would
be paid to cabecera recipients. In effect, the purpose of private property holding in the Aztec system was the receipt of tribute, and it could be understood—as in the cases of the two daughters of Montezuma—that such ownership resembled encomienda more than any other Spanish institution.

The properties of principales and caciques were thus progressively alienated—in sequestration by Spaniards, in conversion to encomienda, and in
seizure by other Indians.[49] But principales also took advantage of the tur-
bulence of the early colony to acquire new properties in compensation. They
exploited weaknesses in cacicazgo tenure to seize land from caciques, and
disputed with them over land possession. Principales took teotlalli and calpullalli and land of Montezuma, retaining the inhabitants for their own use
or reducing macegual inhabitants to sub-macegual status.[50] As late as 1619
terrazgueros in the distant Tenochtitlan sujetos of San Juan (Coxtocan),
Santiago (Tepopula), and Los Reyes (Acatlixcoatlan) were still paying half
the produce of the lands they occupied and worked to Indian principales in
the city.[51]

In the sixteenth century Indian private properties were considered to be
legally held if they could be demonstrated to be inheritances in private Indian possession from pre-conquest times. In disputes over cacicazgo, audiencia decisions normally granted to the victor not only the cacique title but
also the lands and houses attached to the cacicazgo, such a decision amounting to a legal Spanish confirmation of properties. In the absence of confirmation following litigation, prudent caciques and principales fortified their
possessions by requesting viceregal mercedes, after the manner of towns.
Individual land grants to caciques and principales in the sixteenth century
compare in size, but not in number, with those issued for Spaniards. As in

the land grants to corporate communities, mercedes were issued either for agriculture or for herding, but the viceregal government did not enforce these specifications, and a document of merced was commonly regarded as proof of possession, both for the grantee and for his heirs, regardless of how the land might be used.[52]

The lands of a characteristic seventeenth-century cacicazgo combined inherited and acquired properties, some guaranteed by viceregal mercedes of possessions, others based solely upon Indian inheritance. A number of cacicazgos still consisted of scattered properties, which might be located in the cabecera, in various estancias, or, despite the sixteenth-century Spanish consolidations, outside the cabecera-sujeto limits entirely. Cacicazgos were often made up partly of lands that were in dispute—with principales, with Spaniards, or with Indian community governments. Caciques in the seventeenth century, unlike their ancestors in the sixteenth century, did not normally refer to lands in Indian terms, such as tlatocatlalli or pillalli; instead, they identified their properties after the Spanish manner, as plots (*suertes*) of 400 or 800 or 1,400 varas or brazas, located in particular sujetos and known to the principales of the localities. Measurements were vigesimal and often vague ("400 braças o mas y sea de 800 braças"), and varas and brazas were confused. Caciques distinguished lands that had been purchased from those that had been inherited from pre-conquest ancestors. Cacicazgo archives contained Indian paintings or maps to identify the possessions. Caciques were on guard against usurpation by communities, and to defend their properties they might insist that disputed lands "had never been part of the community," that the facts were well known to the people of the town, and that the lands had supported the cacique's ancestors before the Spaniards came.[53]

By the eighteenth century viceregal mercedes and legal disputes over possession had determined the ownership of most private Indian properties. A cacique or principal possessing formal viceregal title or the text of an audiencia decision in his favor was in a legal position similar to that of any white property owner. Thus the Indian origin of cacicazgo lands ceased to be pertinent, and questions of property came to be settled wholly, or almost wholly, in terms of Spanish law. In the late colonial period "caciques" and "Spanish" property owners might both be mestizos, and their interests with respect to Indian communities might be much the same. The Alva Cortés cacicazgo in Teotihuacan and the Páez de Mendoza cacicazgo in Amecameca became estates differing from Spanish haciendas only in their Indian origin and in the cacicazgo rules that governed their inheritance.[54] Propertied caciques in the eighteenth century were known as hacendados.[55] Like other hacendados they bought and sold land, rented land to outsiders, bequeathed their properties to their heirs, and disputed with Indian communities over possession.[56]

CALPULLALLI. For the mass macegual population the most important type of Indian land was the calpullalli, or land controlled by the corporate calpulli. The term *altepetlalli*, used synonymously or almost so with calpullalli,[57] seems to have implied land of a corporate town (*altepetl*) and presumably represented not a distinct area but rather the sum total of the calpullalli. Whatever the distinction, calpullalli was the more commonly used term. It signified both the house sites and the agricultural plots of calpulli members, no matter how distributed.[58] Although the calpullalli might be identified as "common" land, it was not worked in common but was subdivided into individual plots. Spaniards referred to calpullalli as "repartimiento lands" (tierras de repartimiento) or "lands apportioned to the natives" (tierras repartidas a los naturales), and to the individual plots as *milpas*.[59] The more precise Nahuatl word for a plot or segment in the calpullalli—*tlalmilli*—was rarely used by Spaniards.[60]

In the Aztec system a macegual family head did not "own" his tlalmilli in the calpullalli, nor could he legitimately sell it, but he possessed usufruct privileges so long as he cultivated it and paid his tribute from it. He had the traditional privilege of bequeathing his tlalmilli and his house to his descendants, but he forfeited his tenure if he failed to work the plot or moved elsewhere.[61] If escheatment to the community took place, a tlalmilli might be reissued to a new user. Plots not worked for two years might be worked temporarily by the community, so that the tribute due on them might be paid, and this circumstance may have underlain, at least in part, the common plantings for caciques and principales. Unassigned plots were retained for those about to marry or for others who had no lands.[62] Calpulli land in some cases also supported the non-agricultural population: craftsmen, hunters, fishermen, masters of singing and dancing, and others.[63] Control over the allocation of plots appears to have been exercised in Aztec times by tlatoque, tequitlatos, elders (viejos), or other calpulli officers.[64]

Spanish government accepted the Indian principle that maceguales exercised no dominium over calpullalli, which was understood to be held only for "labor and cultivation" (*labrar y beneficiar*). Accordingly, the official Spanish position during the plague of 1545–48 was that the tlalmilli of an Indian who died without heirs was to revert to the native community.[65] But the procedures concerning reversion to the community were severely weakened by the radical diminution of the macegual population, for depopulation created unprecedented quantities of vacant lands which both Spanish and Indian land interests were always ready to exploit.

Calpulli properties were at times adapted to the movements of Indians, as in 1579–81, when Otomi and other native migrants from Tula, Apaxco, Texcoco, Axacuba, and Tequixquiac received land in Xochimilco.[66] Some vacated calpulli properties were seized by principales as recompense for the loss of retainers and income, and the principales involved here may well have been calpulli officers whose positions provided them with an initial authority over calpullalli.[67] Or viceroys might appoint alien Indian judges to redistribute vacant lands among surviving macegual populations, as in Xaltocan in 1558, when the viceroy named an Indian repartidor, Antón de Santa María, to visit the town, distribute all unused lands among the maceguales, record the result in a painting for viceregal approval, and at the same time assign a plot for the community.[68] But so rapid was the depopulation of the latter half of the sixteenth century that lands were left unoccupied faster than any such redistributions, or even Spanish seizures, could absorb them. By 1600 much land formerly cultivated by the Indians of Xaltocan in the higher ground toward Ozumbilla had been abandoned, and the town's agriculture had come to be concentrated in the lower chinampa area. The population was too small to cultivate the vacant lands in common, according to the original Indian custom.[69] But above all, with the development of the new Indian municipal governments, the community representatives in this matter became the gobernadores, who operated everywhere as agents in the alienation of common lands. With progressive depopulation, and with continuous Spanish demands for tribute payment, it was a natural step for gobernadores not to reissue calpullalli to surviving maceguales but rather to sell or rent it to Spaniards.[70]

All texts indicate a wide variation, both within single communities and between one community and another, in the form and size of tlalmilli plots. Certain colonial commentaries do refer to plots of equal sizes, but they indicate that some individuals held one, others two, and others three or more.[71] Cortés observed that the plots ranged from a one or two hundred magni-

Land

269

TABLE 19

Sample Tlalmilli Dimensions, Chalco Province, 1603

Community	Tributaries	Land worked by each Tributary (in brazas)
Acapan	17	100–300 x 40–50
Amanalco	11	200–300 x 100
Atlauhtla	5	80–100 x 80–100
Cencalco	6	300–400 x 20–30
Cihuatzingo	15	80–100 x 80–100
Ococalco	8	400–600 x 20–30
Pahuacan	20	100 x 40
Quautzotzongo	80	100–200 x 30–40
Tecalco	14	100 x 100
Tenango	5	160–200 x 100
Tepopula	20	200 x 20–30
Tepopula Tenango	160	200–300 x 100–120
Tepostlan	10	200–400 x 160
Tlacotetelco	12	200–300 x 20–30
Tlacotlan	8	300–400 x 20–30
Tlacuitlapilco	11	150–200 x 30–40
Xochitepec	60	600–700 x 20–30

SOURCE: AGI, México, leg. 665, cuad. 2, fols. 97r ff. Material of this nature derives from the congregación records. For similar data on Amecameca in 1599 see BAGN, ser. 2, II, 22 ff.

tude to a one or two thousand magnitude.[72] In Utlaspa in 1547 the plots were uniformly forty brazas in width but they ranged in length from twenty to as much as 1,600 brazas.[73] Códice Vergara and Códice de Santa María Asunción, which provide our most detailed illustrations of Indian families, houses, and lands in the early colonial period, demonstrate that plots were of rectangular or irregular shape and that they differed radically in size.[74] Tlalmilli plots were often elongated strips, as in Utlaspa. In Ococalco in the early seventeenth century the measurements were 400 to 600 brazas in length and only 20 to 30 brazas in width (Table 19). In Huitzilopochco in the eighteenth century new allocations were made of plots measuring 113 by 15, 170 by 15, and 195 by 13½ varas.[75] The two codices and the documents of survey in Xaltocan in 1599 are among those that record both family size and tlalmilli dimensions, and they show that land apportionments tended to vary in accordance with the number of persons per family. Thus in Tenamitlan, a sujeto of Xaltocan, a man and wife alone might have 40 brazas of community land; a couple with one child might have 50 to 60 brazas; a bachelor or widow would be likely to have only 10 brazas. Such adjustments were by no means universal, however, and in many other cases families with children had less land than families without children.[76] In the tlalmilli dimensions of Utlaspa in the sixteenth century a range from 800 square brazas to 64,000 square brazas is recorded: a ratio of 1 to 80. In those of Chalco province in the seventeenth century the total range was from 3,200 to 64,000 square brazas, a ratio between smallest and largest of 1 to 20. If the braza in the Chalco example be equated with 1.68 meters, a distribution from slightly over one to about 26 acres per family may be supposed.

In summary, the situation of all Indian lands underwent progressive modification during the colonial period. At the outset everything within the Indian términos of a community had been the possession of individuals or of the town, and an intricate scale of payments had governed relations between those who cultivated land and those who received tribute. The territorial limits, enclosing land of all types, had separated the area pertaining to one community from the area pertaining to its neighbors. Some lands within the términos had "belonged" to Montezuma or to his military leaders or to other owners elsewhere, and depending on circumstances these were worked either by special classes of occupants or by the community as a whole. Communities ranged from densely populated urban settlements, such as Tenochtitlan, to combinations of scattered house sites and agricultural lands, such as Hueypoxtla.[77] A community's lands within its términos might include not only the calpullalli in which each macegual worked his tlalmilli, but also a forest (*monte*) used for stone or firewood or pasturage or protection against a neighbor. So precise was the Indian concept of términos that viceregal grants of land to Spaniards in the sixteenth century customarily identified the tracts as falling within the areas of one or another Indian town.[78]

In the late sixteenth century a town's productive land might still consist of its calpullalli and its properties in private Indian ownership. One Spaniard in the middle sixteenth century asserted that these were then the only surviving types of Indian land.[79] The statement must be qualified, but its sense may be accepted, for it means that the aboriginal variations in landholding were much simplified during the first two colonial generations. Many communities still had their non-agricultural montes in the late sixteenth century, and some had pasture areas that had been confirmed by viceregal grant. But by the late eighteenth century cacicazgo lands and calpullalli and montes and términos, though still to be found, were everywhere interspersed with the properties of ecclesiastical institutions and of private whites or mestizos. All original types had been reduced with the pre-emption of Indian land. One could still speak of the términos of an Indian community, but the términos now separated the community from Spanish haciendas and ranchos as well as from Indian properties.

Throughout the colonial period the native community prized and guarded its lands in full awareness of the dangers of alienation. In the first postconquest years, as in the late Aztec period, land disputes between one town and another were a standard feature of Indian life.[80] But in the developed colony, though controversy within Indian society continued, the more characteristic disputes occurred between Indians and Spaniards. The communities' ideology of land protection was expressed most forcibly in their "títulos," documents of uncertain origin, of indisputable native composition, of considerable persuasive power, but of limited legal validity. In a combination of exhortation, history, and religion, the títulos expressed protection and foreboding with regard to property. A typical example reads:

"This is what our grandfathers and fathers left. . . . My sons, you must guard it as the town of God. . . . Never abandon what is God's. . . . Our grandfathers and fathers won it against attack. . . . The enemy was pushed back. . . . This occurred because God ordained it. . . . They erected a Virgin and Señora and put a royal staff in her hand. . . . You must preserve this divine protection. . . . Thus we leave you knowledge of the way to live. . . . All must not be lost when we die. . . . Spaniards come to seize what we have justly won. . . . We urge our sons to know, guard, and keep the water, monte, streets, and houses of the town. . . . Sons of the town, guard the lands. . . . Here are its limits and its boundaries. . . . Do not forget. . . . Guard this paper."[81]

But the eloquence of the títulos could not combat intrusion by Spaniards. The process was one of cumulative usurpation. Very few properties, once alienated, ever reverted to Indian ownership. The broad outlines of Spanish land acquisition and its outcome are well known. But a special interest attaches to its tempo and periodization, and to the techniques, legalities, and secondary effects of land transfer.

For several related reasons, no large-scale usurpation of the Valley's land by Spanish colonists took place in the earliest post-conquest years. So long as a large Indian population existed, tribute and labor were the preferred modes of economic control, and power was expressed at first in encomienda. Wealth could be derived from landholding—in agriculture and herding—only after the development of a Spanish colonial market, and such a market did not develop immediately. Even when a sizable market did come into being, the first tendency was to supply it through encomienda and the regulation of Indian labor rather than through productive Spanish land ownership. Indian occupation of the land operated as an inhibiting factor, and all responsible authorities agreed that legitimate Indian possession ought not to be jeopardized. When infringement first began, Spaniards took pains to declare that the Indian possession had not been legitimate, or that the Spaniards were within the law, or that the injury was in some way beyond their control. Self-justification, of course, attended the history of land acquisition through the entire colonial period; but the terms of self-justification and the concepts of legitimate Indian possession changed markedly in the course of three hundred years.

Spanish authority for the granting of land was disunified in the early years. The monarchy, as would be expected, only rarely exercised its prerogative in direct mercedes in the Valley of Mexico.[82] Cortés, in the first flush of his power, granted plots in Mexico City, and assumed authority to issue and revoke land titles.[83] The Spanish cabildo of the city, relying upon royal permission, made land grants as far afield as Michoacan before its pretensions were effectively limited. The early audiencia likewise regarded itself as a royal agent for land entitlement.[84] Only after 1535 did the viceroy, or the viceroy and audiencia together, bring an effective centralization to the process of land disposal.[85]

From the conquest to 1535, Spanish land interests in the Valley concentrated on one major area, the mainland lying west and southwest of Tenochtitlan. Here the communities of Tacuba, Coyoacan, and Tacubaya attracted the immediate attention of Cortés.[86] The city's cabildo took the position that Cortés had no right to the two Marquesado communities, Coyoacan and Tacubaya, either as encomienda or as property, and the region became a focal point for the struggle between Cortés and his enemies. The cabildo granted properties to its own regidores and to other Spaniards along the Tacuba causeway and on the mainland, countered Cortés's effort to direct urban interest to the south, and revoked earlier grants to Cortés in the area.[87] Moreover, the cabildo did not always act in accordance with the view that Indian possession was to be respected. In the process of securing city lands, it removed Indian families and destroyed their homes, and in its private sessions there appeared the assertion that any injured Indians could be bought off.[88] In Tacubaya the president of the first audiencia, Nuño de Guzmán, took land and water for mills. In Tacuba the oidores Matienzo and Delgadillo made similar appropriations. The oidor Tejada built flour mills, transacted for land, and made other kinds of territorial intrusion.[89]

The several arguments advanced in justification of these acts reflect the struggles among Spaniards as well as the various interpretations of pre-conquest Indian status. The Spanish cabildo asserted that the territories in question had belonged to the native rulers of Mexico, that they had been seized after the conquest by the Indians of Coyoacan, and that they should hence revert to the control of the now Spanish city.[90] Cortés based his claim on the contrary view, that the lands had been independent of Tenochtitlan in their pre-conquest condition. Some had belonged to the "natural rulers" (señores naturales) of Coyoacan and Tacubaya. Others had been given by Montezuma and his predecessors to Indian military captains who had died in the conquest and who thus forfeited their properties to Cortés.[91] Others had been temple lands and had escheated legitimately to Cortés's control, for as the destroyer of the idols he became the proper possessor of the lands thus "freed." Still other properties he had acquired in legal purchase from Indians.[92] Against such Spanish views the Indian communities arrayed opposite and self-interested arguments. Indians of Coyoacan and Tacubaya demanded the restoration of properties that had been taken by Cortés, including lands that had "belonged" to the maceguales. The Coyoacan statement that lands had belonged to the maceguales of Coyoacan conflicted with the Tacubaya statement that they had belonged to the maceguales of Tacubaya.[93]

The essential appropriation in this region had been accomplished and its impetus had already become irreversible by the time that the viceroy assumed control of land disbursement policies.[94] The same amount of land distributed throughout the Valley as a whole would not have amounted to incursion on a large scale. Its concentration in a single zone had been dictated in part by geographical proximity—the area was the closest mainland to the city and one of the most fertile agricultural regions of the entire Valley—and it gave an insight into the future.[95] A viceregal ruling of 1555 required presentations of titles by all Spanish landholders in the Tacuba-Coyoacan region, and another of 1563 forbade all further land grants in Tacuba.[96] But the attempts to bring legal order to land occupation or to halt it altogether came too late and failed. By the early 1560's Spanish intrusions in Tacuba had reached the point at which it could be said that Indians were barely able to settle around their church.[97] In the subsequent period Spanish land interests were to be dispersed over the larger, but initially less attractive, remainder of the Valley. This larger region, too, was to approach its point of saturation, but under economic and social conditions peculiar to the latter half of the sixteenth century.

Spanish colonists had three principal methods for acquiring land from Indians during the mid-century period and after. One, purchase from the Indian occupants or owners, was at first understood to be a legal preliminary to formal entitlement by colonial authorities, as outright usurpation in the absence of payment was not. The method was used even before the conquest was completed, and it continued for a long time thereafter. Official Spanish permission to purchase was sometimes granted, but purchase alone was ordinarily regarded as sufficient evidence of Spanish-Indian negotiation.[98] The procedure was readily liable to fraud. An Indian might sell property that was not his but communal and in Indian terms inalienable. A sale might be transacted under duress. It might involve deceit practiced by one Indian or group of Indians upon another or even upon a Spaniard.[99] More frequent frauds were those committed by Spanish purchasers, who might pay meager sums or trade poorer for more valuable land.[100] Both secular colonists and ecclesiastics forced unwanted land sales upon Indians. It became evident that purchase from Indians, however justifiable in principle, might involve only outright usurpation with a token payment, and on several occasions Spanish possessors, pressed to explain themselves, stated that their lands had been gifts from Indians.[101] In some cases it was possible to rent land from Indians and subsequently to take the position that the rental payment had been a payment in sale. Alternatively, lands might be seized and rented back to Indians, a device that ensured not only the possession itself but also a steady, often exorbitant, income from it. Moreover, purchase from Indians could result in the accumulation of extremely large holdings: it is recorded that 101 distinct properties were all acquired in this way by a single Spaniard in the years before 1583.[102]

y macamtu malco . y mimala Cerda . espanolti . ynoca cacate . ymintepã calav.
yyemochinti . ytepãpã tlaca . yna lte petlpãn tlaca . yqmilaca . arle ytequiuh
amochi gua . yashuateqnitl . y gua . arle y tlacalaquis. ymtechpohui
yraltepetl. õ tripoto . ymin mochinti. õ miculoto. qmopo huato. y juã gallego

espanol.

y ymin chon. espanolti. y hahua. y niqmiti. yyemochinti. ynaltepetli
pan. tlaca. ytepapã tlaca. camochinti. õ miculo. apo huato. y jua
gallevo. caalmonotle y tequius. amonoqchi gua. y co huateqnitl.
õmedaica teqnitl. y gtan. amonotle õ tlacalaquis. ymtechpo
hui . ynaltepetl. õ tripoto. ——

ndian labor in hacienda and obraje (*Códice Osuna*)

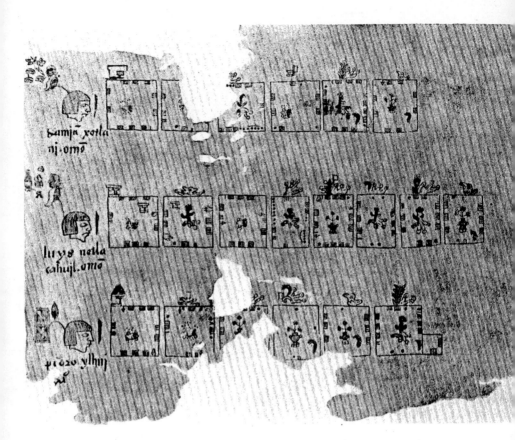

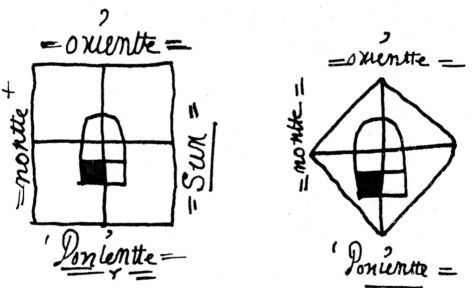

x. Indian land records: Top, lands and retainers (Humboldt Fragment VIII).
Bottom, varieties of the 600-vara measurement (Papeles de los Condes de Regla)

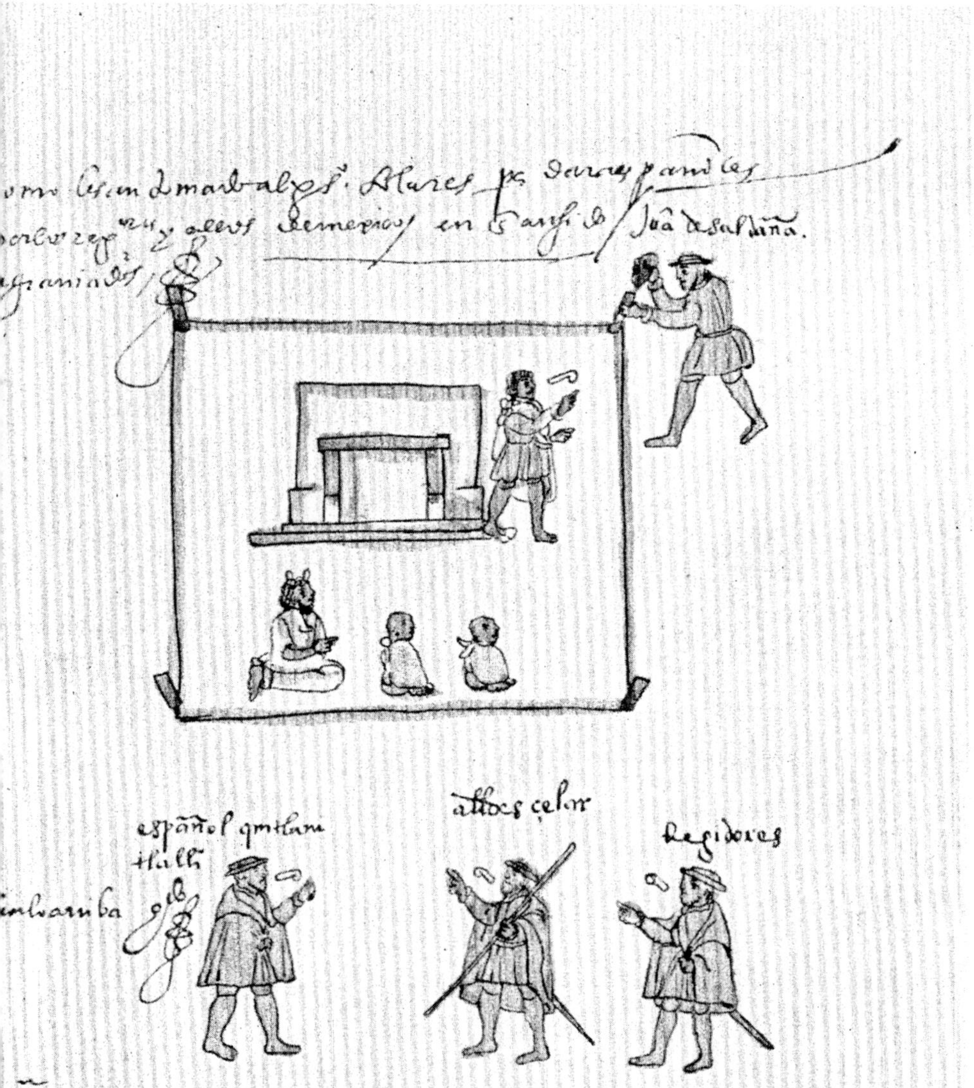

aniards usurp Indian lands (*Códice Osuna*)

xii. Land dispute in Ixtlahuaca (Papeles de los Condes de Regla)

A second method of acquiring land involved the use of encomienda privileges or of positions of political authority. It has been said that although encomienda did not itself allow for property ownership it facilitated property acquisition, and the statement is amply corroborated by Valley of Mexico evidence. The list of Valley encomenderos who held properties in or near the regions of their encomiendas includes the following persons: Cortés in Coyoacan and Tacubaya; Antón Bravo de Lagunas in Hueypoxtla; Alonso de Avila in Cuauhtitlan; Martín de Cuéllar in Ixtapaluca; Martín López in Tequixquiac; Juan Ponce de León in Tecama; Gerónimo de Baeza in Tepexpan; Alonso de Estrada in Teocalhueyacan; Gonzalo de Salazar in Tepetlaoztoc; and Francisco Verdugo Bazán in Teotihuacan.[103] Other encomenderos, among them Diego Arias de Sotelo in Xilotzingo, Blas de Bustamante in Tepozotlan, and Alonzo de Bazán in Teocalhueyacan,[104] acquired properties outside their encomiendas or in the encomiendas of others. The list of property-holding political officials is headed by Viceroy Mendoza, whose ranching interests and use of Indian labor received occasional unfavorable comment, and the oidor Luis de Villanueva Zapata, whose property near Coyotepec, containing large numbers of Negroes, Indians, and cattle, was sold for over 12,000 pesos before 1575.[105] Lesser examples are Constantino Bravo de Lagunas, corregidor of Cuauhtitlan, who held private property within his corregimiento area, and Francisco Magariño, the corregidor of Tacuba, who engaged in extensive land usurpation in the 1550's and 1560's.[106]

A third method, and the one that superseded and legalized the others, was the outright receipt of a merced. The usual procedure after 1535 was to petition the viceroy for a designated tract for agriculture or herding. The tract itself might be one on which the petitioner had already established his farm and his residence. Grants were issued as ranches for cattle (*estancias de ganado mayor*) or as ranches for lesser animals (*estancias de ganado menor*), usually sheep or goats, or as agricultural farm units (*caballerías*), for all of which Viceroy Mendoza had established the dimensions in 1536 (Table 20).[107] Grants for ganado menor commonly provided that 2,000 head were to be established within a year and that sale would not be permitted until the land had been held for four years. In agricultural grants it was stipulated that the larger part must be cultivated within one or two years and that the property could not be sold within the first six years.[108] For Indian welfare, the most pertinent requirement of the grants was that they

Land

TABLE 20

Land Grant Measurements

	Colonial Measures			Modern Equivalents		
Unit and Type	Varas de Castilla	23/8 vara	Pasos de Salomón	Square Leagues	Square Miles	Acres
Estancia						
Ganado mayor	5,000 × 5,000		3,000 × 3,000	1.00	6.78	4,338
Estancia						
Ganado menor ....3,333.3 ×	3,333.3		2,000 × 2,000	.440	3.01	1,928
Caballería						
Agriculture	1,104 × 552	384 × 192		.024	0.17	105

SOURCE: See Chapter X, note 107. Modern equivalents are approximate.

be "without injury," (*sin perjuicio*) and not in conflict with the legitimate claims of any other party. Examinations were made prior to the issuance of mercedes to ensure that the lands requested were unoccupied territories within the Indian términos. An elaborate formula of tracing boundaries, throwing stones, and giving possession was required. The process was sometimes protracted, with repeated examinations, delays, intrusions, objections, and countercharges. Indians, encomenderos, neighboring landholders, or others might protest against a proposed merced. The site might be examined a number of times before its title became secure. Alternative Indian proposals might be offered—for example, that part of the grant be authorized on the proposed site and the rest elsewhere. Landmarks might be altered and boundary posts moved by hostile neighbors, whether Indians or Spaniards. At other times the readiness with which Indian gobernadores and cabildos accepted the proposed land grants to Spaniards and formally affirmed that such grants would entail no injury to the Indian community strongly suggests collusion, coercion, or bribery.[109]

Despite the specifications of measurement and the extreme detail of the recorded surveys, considerable real differences in size distinguished one grant from another. Estancias were not necessarily regular rectangles of the dimensions specified. Rather, they were of irregular shape, and the areas enclosed by their boundaries were only approximations of the stated sizes. Official surveys of caballerías did not count the rocky areas (*riscos*), ravines (*barrancas*), or "unusable land" (*tierra inutil*), but only the cultivable land,

TABLE 21

Land Granted to Spaniards to 1620

Type	Documented	Estimated Total	Approximate Square Miles
Ganado mayor	7–8 estancias	10 estancias	70
Ganado menor	163 estancias	215 estancias	650
Agriculture	1,195 caballerías	1,600 caballerías	270

SOURCE: AGN, Mercedes, vols. 1–35.

with the result that several times the area of the official caballería might be granted. Linear measurements were sometimes understood to be approximations or were simply estimated by the amount of seed that might be sown.[110]

The records of land grants to Spaniards are incomplete. Surviving documents mention approximately 650 such grants in the Valley during the hundred years following the conquest,[111] and a correction for the missing periods might raise this figure to 850 or 900.[112] Most of the recorded grants were agricultural, but since the pastoral grants contained larger unit areas the total pastoral land amounted to between two and three times the total agricultural land. Individual agricultural grants were generally from one to four caballerías or from about 100 to 400 acres, and agricultural caballerías were sometimes attached to pastoral areas in combined grants. A rough computation for the period to 1620 suggests that between 700 and 750 square miles were assigned to Spanish colonists for herding as compared with 250 or 300 square miles for agriculture, the total amounting to approximately one-third of the area of the Valley. When it is recalled that about half the remainder consisted of lakes, swamps, and mountains, it becomes evident that an enormous part, considerably more than half, of the agricultural and pastoral area of the Valley was officially transferred from Indian to Spanish hands during the first century after the conquest. Furthermore, it was a universal tendency among Spaniards to encroach beyond the limits of the grants.[113]

The Tacuba-Coyoacan zone remained a favorite region for wheat growing. It was further filled in and extended westward during the period to 1560.[114] Meanwhile many Spanish pastoral holdings were established elsewhere. Grants of the mid-century were issued for herding ranches in the vicinities of Tlatelolco, Tepetlaoztoc, Tecama, Tacuba, Ixtlahuaca, Coyoa-

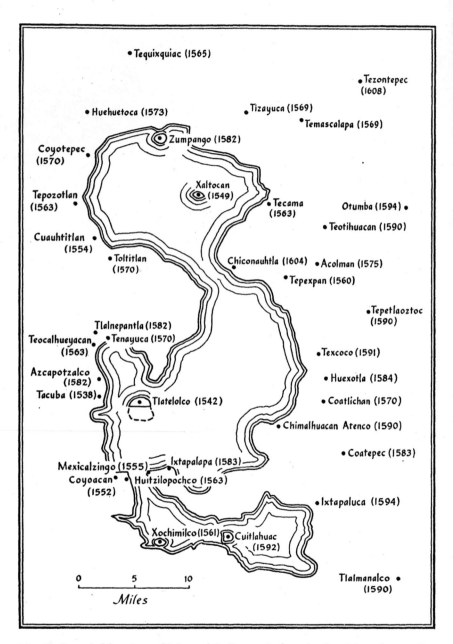

Map 8. Recorded locations of injury to Indian agriculture by Spanish cattle, to 1610.

The labels on the map:

- Tequixquiac (1565)
- Tezontepec (1608)
- Huehuetoca (1573)
- Tizayuca (1569)
- Temascalapa (1569)
- Zumpango (1582)
- Coyotepec (1570)
- Xaltocan (1549)
- Tepozotlan (1563)
- Tecama (1563)
- Otumba (1594)
- Teotihuacan (1590)
- Cuauhtitlan (1554)
- Chiconauhtla (1604)
- Acolman (1575)
- Toltitlan (1570)
- Tepexpan (1560)
- Tepetlaoztoc (1590)
- Tlalnepantla (1582)
- Teocalhueyacan (1563)
- Tenayuca (1570)
- Texcoco (1591)
- Azcapotzalco (1582)
- Huexotla (1584)
- Tacuba (1538)
- Tlatelolco (1542)
- Coatlichan (1570)
- Chimalhuacan Atenco (1590)
- Coatepec (1583)
- Mexicalzingo (1555)
- Ixtapalapa (1583)
- Coyoacan (1552)
- Huitzilopochco (1563)
- Ixtapaluca (1594)
- Xochimilco (1561)
- Cuitlahuac (1592)
- Tlalmanalco (1590)

0   5   10

Miles

can, Hueypoxtla, and other communities, on both sides of the Valley, on the slopes back from the populated lakeside towns, but still rarely in the drier, less productive regions of the north. The 1560's and 1570's brought heavier occupations to the northeastern and northwestern parts of the Valley, with many grants, both pastoral and agricultural, in the regions of Calpulalpan, Acolman, Tepozotlan, Huehuetoca, Teocalhueyacan, Azcapotzaltongo, Axapusco, Tequixquiac, Xaltocan, and Zumpango. This extended the penetration into areas only partially infiltrated previously, and, if our incomplete record may be trusted, it was accomplished by grants far more numerous than those of previous years. Meanwhile, Chalco province received its first heavy mercedes of lands. From 1580 to 1618 the record is one of an even more intense activity and of a continuously scattered distribution.[115] Grants of the 1580's include the north central area and the regions close to Mexico City as well as the other areas mentioned, and they surely reflect Spanish occupation of lands depopulated by the plague of the late 1570's. In the 1590's it was stated that Indians retained only small amounts of land throughout the Valley, and that their remnant possessions were either uncultivable or distant from Spanish centers of influence. Torquemada observed in the early seventeenth century that all the slopes of the environs of the city and of the Texcoco region were occupied by wheat farms and that there was left almost no segment of land without Spaniards.[116] By this time the towns of Tenayuca, Toltitlan, and Coyotepec had been surrounded by Spanish properties for fifty years. Their Indian inhabitants lacked land for crops and pastures, and emigration had been continuous.[117] The term hacienda had gained currency, and haciendas had begun to depend upon gañanes rather than upon repartimiento labor.[118] Gañanes in the early seventeenth century had already begun to make their homes within the hacienda confines.[119]

Apart from direct land alienation, certain secondary features of Spanish landholding seriously affected Indian welfare. The presence of a Spanish property near an Indian community commonly resulted in what were called "offenses" (*agravios*) by Negro servants, usually robbery and forced entry into Indian houses.[120] Permits and orders issued by the viceroy for the supply of lumber and stone from the montes of the Indian towns sometimes guaranteed that there would be no offense, the licenses nonetheless representing an exploitable incursion.[121] Spanish land use ordinarily required the use of water as well, for irrigation, cattle, or power for mills, and Spaniards were often able to pre-empt streams with the lands or to buy water rights from Indians at low prices.[122] Both the use of montes for fuel and the use of streams for irrigation or other purposes were incursions against which Indians repeatedly protested.[123]

But the most extensive of the secondary consequences, and the one that provoked the greatest Indian objection, was the pasturing of cattle on Indian agricultural lands. This first appeared in an acute form near Mexico City in the 1520's,[124] and it abated only in the seventeenth century after the cumulative transfer of Indian lands to Spaniards and the removal of the largest cattle herds to the northern ranges. Control in the sixteenth century was the more difficult because of traditional Spanish rights of common pasturage and because of the further Spanish custom, sanctioned by Mesta law in the colony, that animals might graze on agricultural stubble in alien properties after harvest and before planting.[125] Cattle were further permitted to graze freely in the *tierras baldías*, or unoccupied land, a rule signifying in effect that any lands not actually under cultivation were to be regarded as common pasture.[126] Cattle required water, and an additional consequence of the development of the herding industry was the pollution of drinking water and the desiccation of downstream irrigation.[127] Moreover, cattle and sheep multiplied prodigiously. The earliest grants proved insufficient to contain the expanding herds after only a few generations. Herds of sheep doubled in size in a year and a half or less.[128] Herds of 12,000 to 15,000 head are recorded as early as the mid-sixteenth century, and of 50,000 to 70,000 in the late sixteenth and early seventeenth centuries. The hacienda of Santa Lucía is said to have had 140,000 sheep and goats, 5,000 horses, and 10,000 cows and oxen in the late seventeenth century.[129] Spaniards grazed animals on the smaller properties granted for agriculture and cattle on the lands designated for sheep and goats.[130] Indian communities constructed corrals and fences and trenches to control wandering Spanish cattle and to surround and protect agricultural lands. Indians fought back with nets and traps and pits and dogs and fire.[131] But in general cattle were more successful in finding forage than were Indians in protecting their crops. Interested Spaniards accused Indians of purposely relocating their agricultural plots so that cattle would destroy them, thus furnishing a cause for complaint or establishing a perjuicio that could be argued against a merced.[132] The accusation may well have been justified. The entire community of Tepepan was said to have been constructed by Indians from Xochimilco in a period of twenty-four hours—complete with houses, agricultural plots, and even a church—in order to prevent the establishment of a Spanish cattle ranch.[133]

Genuine administrative efforts to curb excesses by Spaniards and to render a measure of justice to Indian inhabitants of the land occurred sporadically in the sixteenth century and after. Laws of the 1530's required that all Indian land sales be made voluntarily and be transacted before Spanish judges.[134] The viceregal government sought additionally to promote Indian agriculture and to ensure Indian use of vacated lands.[135] From 1571 Indian lands offered for sale were to be publicly auctioned each day for thirty days, in order to allow for higher bids and prevent prearranged sales coerced by Spanish purchasers.[136] Legislation prohibited the sale of non-inherited lands as well as the sale of communal property by Indian gobernadores and alcaldes, and it required Indian sellers to be the possessors of other lands in addition to the property sold. Occasionally local land sales were prohibited altogether.[137] But in land sale, as in other matters where Spanish law came into conflict with the private interests of Spaniards, the law proved impotent. Indian land sales in the Valley are repeatedly recorded without formal notaries, for extremely low prices, as punishment, and in unequal trades. In effect, Indians continued to sell land to Spaniards so long as there remained land to sell.[138]

Administrative incapacity applied likewise to cattle intrusion. At first even the capital city's Spanish cabildo took the matter seriously and ordered the revocation of grants and the abandonment of herding areas that interfered with Indian properties. The viceroy in the middle sixteenth century ordered offending Spaniards to pay for damages to Indians and undertook to reassign lands when it became apparent that injury to Indians was involved.[139] But dispossession proved extremely difficult to enforce, and as a regulating or punitive device it became increasingly rare. The viceroy instead sought to render the conduct of existing cattle owners less injurious and to protect Indian communities from their incursions. In 1567 each Indian town was officially allowed a surrounding area of five hundred varas (about one-quarter of a mile) in all directions, and a thousand varas were to separate each town from the nearest Spanish cattle ranches. In key areas of intrusion, viceregal rules extended these limits and forbade or restricted the pasturage privilege.[140] The viceregal order of 1558, that all usable vacant lands were to be distributed to the maceguales for cultivation, is noteworthy not because it was obeyed or enforced but because it indicates that Spaniards in the mid-century period still hoped to encourage Indian agriculture for the maintenance of Spanish society.[141]

No date can be fixed for the formal relinquishment of the policy of protection, for the policy was never formally relinquished. But events of the
late sixteenth and early seventeenth centuries resulted in a relaxation of the
efforts to control Spanish intrusion. The plagues, dislocations, and depopulations of the last quarter of the sixteenth century accelerated the progressive abandonment of Indian lands. Lands without Indian inhabitants could
be categorized by Spaniards as vacant, unowned, or unappropriated (baldías or *realengas*), and thus as lands available to Spanish intrusion "without injury."[142] Actual transfers were still accomplished in standard ways,
by sale transacted by Indian officials or maceguales, by forced sales coerced
by Spaniards, and by formal grant.[143]

Indian society contained within itself, as we have seen, traditional procedures for accommodating depopulated lands and preserving them under
the control of local communities. In essence these procedures involved the
retention of undistributed common lands under the authority of caciques
or calpulli officers. In a sense, therefore, the loss of more than half the Indian population in the last quarter of the sixteenth century need not have
resulted in loss of land. Indian society, however, found itself not simply reduced in size but debilitated and disunified by recurrent disease and death,
and it confronted an increasingly large white society. In any crisis, land represented to Indians an asset that could be sold and converted into money
for the purchase of food and the discharge of tribute obligations. Spaniards
might acquire properties from Indians through formal or informal sales of
private or community lands, by trading cattle or other goods, or in unauthorized sequestrations made as private punishment.[144] In areas severely
struck by epidemic, the Indian survivors regrouped, abandoned some barrios and attached themselves to others, neglecting the procedures of Indian
calpulli society, and exposing the vacated areas for new Spanish aggressions.[145]

How far such practices of regrouping might have extended in the normal
readjustment of Indian society to its crisis we cannot say. The fact is that
they were abetted, encouraged, and coerced in the late sixteenth and early
seventeenth centuries under the Spanish program called congregación. Congregación implied the resettlement of scattered Indian families or of entire
sujetos in compact communities. The program already had a tradition in
viceregal orders and in ecclesiastical removals, and it had been justified previously in terms of administrative efficiency and ease of religious conversion

rather than as a preliminary to land appropriations.[146] Yet Spaniards could hardly consider congregación without realizing that the proposed regroupings would make new tracts of land available for Spanish use.[147] On several occasions the Mexico City cabildo had proposed forms of congregación that would serve the immediate interests of Spanish landowners: that Indian lands in all the communities of the city's environs be taken for the white population, the Indian occupants being compensated with lands elsewhere, or that Indians be given the lands they needed for compact congregación while all other lands be reserved for Spanish use.[148] Such proposals suggest a degree of compromise, under duress, with the original recognition of the legitimacy of Indian occupation. And in the developing complexities of Spanish-Indian relations such compromises acquired a practical sanction, becoming progressively more urgent as attention was directed away from the ethical implications of a brazen grabbing of land. Thus congregación came to be supported as a program that would uphold rather than restrict Indian ownership, and the example of Tacuba, where Spanish inroads had been exceptionally severe, was cited as proof of the vulnerability of Indian lands in the absence of congregación.[149]

In the congregaciones of the 1590's and the first decade of the seventeenth century, the stated justifications were the teaching of Christianity, the elimination of drunkenness, the promotion of orderly Indian living, and the protection of Indians under Spanish law.[150] Surveys were first conducted under viceregal direction, and detailed plans were laid for each congregación movement. In each case it was decided which communities were to be abandoned and to which ones the affected Indians would be moved. In no known case in the Valley was an entire new community to be established. Instead outlying sujetos were to be vacated and their inhabitants moved to cabeceras or to other sujetos. Regulations were specific that Indian land possession was not to be disturbed. If the new settlement was to be located only a short distance from the old one, the original agricultural lands were to be retained. If greater distances were involved, new lands were to be assigned. Viceregal rules sought to prevent shortages in agricultural supply by forbidding maize purchase, hoarding, resale, and speculation by Spaniards during the period of change.[151] Congregación orders required that each Indian be provided with a site for his house and with lands for the sowing of his maize. New tlalmilli assignments were made under Spanish congregación authority, again with adjustments for family size.[152] In locations where available land was inadequate, congregación rules stated that land was to be taken from Spaniards (who would be recompensed for the loss) and given to the Indian community. Furthermore, agents were instructed to prevent Spaniards from purchasing the lands left vacant by Indian removals.[153]

The chief opposition to the program came from within Indian society and reflected the traditional attachment of native peoples to their lands. Indians argued that they were better provided for in the old locations, that Spanish cattle would more easily destroy their crops in the new locations, that the new lands were inferior to the old or too distant from their residences, that the new lands could not be protected against intruders, or that because of the differences of environment the whole economy and mode of life of the community would be changed.[154] In some instances they protested because the proposed congregaciones required persons of distinct tribal affiliations to mingle in single communities—as in the interspersed Mexica and Acolhua communities north of Acolman.[155] Occasionally Indian objections were successful, and congregación orders were modified in accordance with them.[156] But Indian resistance was never organized to prevent the accomplishment of the program as a whole. Opposition, however forceful, was always local and directed against particular manifestations of the congregación movement. Indian gobernadores sometimes favored congregación as a means of strengthening their own control over their communities. Once moved, Indians were forbidden to return to their former homes. Corregidores and other Spanish officers visited the new sites, examined the new houses to ensure that they were being occupied, and destroyed any houses of the old site that had not been abandoned.[157]

Known Valley documents make reference to about thirty distinct congregaciones—although since some documents relate only to the initial stages, we cannot yet assert that all of these were actually executed. Only in a limited number—Xaltocan, Otumba, Tlalnepantla, Amecameca, Tenango —have detailed records of activity survived.[158] The documentation, though far from complete, demonstrates that congregación did not achieve the anticipated results. The Spanish contention that congregación would bring about orderly government, eliminate drunkenness, or accomplish any of the other stated objectives proved false. The Indian contention that congregación would result in new Spanish intrusions and loss of land proved correct. Spanish colonists appeared in Indian communities even before congregaciones were under way to negotiate with Indians for the transfer of the lands that were to be vacated. Spaniards quickly moved in after congregaciones were completed, and viceroys issued many new mercedes in the depopulated areas.[159] When opportunities permitted, Indians returned to their original locations.[160] A land survey in a small area in Chalco province in 1668 recorded the sites of thirteen former towns, all abandoned in the congregación of 1603 and never reoccupied.[161] On the other hand, many communities that were originally scheduled for removal survived as occupied sites. Thus it is impossible to evaluate congregación in any precise way. But insofar as it did effect change, its tendency was to concentrate even further the surviving native population, to make this population more accessible to controls by hacendados and others, and to render lands formerly occupied by Indians available to Spaniards. In the early seventeenth century congregación represented one further Spanish response to Indian depopulation and one further preliminary to the full hacienda era.

Despite continued Spanish intrusion, imperial legislation of the period following congregación maintained the formal policy of protecting Indian communities. Royal laws of 1687–95 increased to a minimum of 600 varas the measurement that Indian towns were to hold in each direction and to 1,100 varas the measurement that was to separate Indian towns from Spanish estancias.[162] Additional legislation of 1713, implementing some earlier enactments, required that all Indian towns were to receive water, montes, and land for agriculture, and that each town should possess a common tract (*ejido*) of one square league for pasture.[163] Legally, then, a town of the late colonial period consisted of a square composed of the 600-vara measurement (known to nineteenth-century lawyers as the *fondo legal*), and an ejido of one league, in addition to whatever other lands the viceregal government might judge that it required. At the same time, however, royal legislation maintained the rules of the late sixteenth century relating to *composición,* which permitted the legalization of defective titles through the payment of fees, and colonial practice refined these procedures in the seventeenth and especially in the eighteenth centuries "in order that deficiencies and weak titles may be made good." A related late colonial device was the *denuncia,* wherein an individual might "denounce" a vacant or illegally occupied territory and "compose" the lands in question for himself.[164]

In the seventeenth and eighteenth centuries the procedures in all legal cases continued to be hedged in by formalities—declaration before Spanish judges, hearing of testimonies, sworn and witnessed measurements of the land, and public notifications in both Spanish and Nahuatl.[165] But late colonial courts often regarded all property outside the 600-vara measurement, and all property not duly issued to Indians in formal viceregal grants, as available for Spanish occupation. Under the conditions of the sixteenth century, as we have observed, Indian towns had frequently failed to secure such grants, for their properties lay within their términos and were already held, and no one could accurately foresee the altered circumstances of the later period.[166] In the seventeenth and eighteenth centuries the rules regard-

TABLE 22

Congregaciones

Location	Date	Citation
Acolman	1603, 1604	AGN, Congregaciones, vol. 1, fols. 25v–26r, 83r.
Amecameca	1599	BAGN, ser. 2, II, 17 ff. AGI, México, leg. 122 (1599).
Chiauhtla	1603	AGN, Congregaciones, vol. 1, fols. 25v–26r.
Chimalhuacan Chalco	1599	AGI, México, leg 122 (1599).
Citlaltepec	1592	AGN, Indios, vol. 6 (2), fols. 55r–55v, 182r.
Coatepec	1604 (ca.)	AGN, Vínculos, leg. 244, exp. 1, fols. 16r ff.
Coatlichan	1603	AGN, Congregaciones, vol. 1, fols. 25v–26r.
Cuauhtitlan	1604	AGN, Congregaciones, vol. 1, fols. 74r–74v, 104r.
Cuitlahuac	1599, 1603	AGI, México, leg. 122 (1599). AGN, Congregaciones, vol. 1, fols. 36v–37r.
Ecatepec	1603, 1604	AGN, Congregaciones, vol. 1, fols. 19r–19v, 101v, 114r–114v.
Huehuetoca	1594	AGN, Indios, vol. 6 (1), fol. 197r–197v.
Hueypoxtla	1592, 1603	AGN, Indios, vol. 6 (1), fols. 58v–59r; Congregaciones, vol. 1, fol. 57v.
Ixtapaluca	1603	AGN, Congregaciones, vol. 1, fol. 38r.
Mexicalzingo	1600	AGN, Civil, vol. 1271, exp. 1, no. 9, fols. 79r ff.
Mixquic	1599	AGI, México, leg. 122 (1599).
Otumba	1603	AGN, Congregaciones, vol. 1, fols. 30v ff.
Tacuba	1593	AGN, Indios, vol. 6 (1), fol. 178r–178v.
Tecama	1603, 1604	AGN, Congregaciones, vol. 1, fols. 19r–19v, 120v–121r.
Temascalapa	1604	AGN, Congregaciones, vol. 1, fols. 117v–118r.
Tenango	1599, 1603	AGI, México, leg. 122 (1599); leg. 665, cuad. 2, fols. 97r ff.
Tenayuca	1593	AGN, Indios, vol. 6 (1), fols. 127v–128r, 141v–142r.
Teotihuacan	1600, 1603	Gamio, La población del valle de Teotihuacan, I (2), 379–80. AGN, Congregaciones, vol. 1, fols. 5r, 8v–9r.

TABLE 22 (cont.)

Location	Date	Citation
Tepetlaoztoc	1603	AGN, Congregaciones, vol. 1, fols. 25v–26r.
Tepexpan	1604	AGN, Congregaciones, vol. 1, fol. 86v.
Tepozotlan	1593	AGN, Indios, vol. 6 (1), fol. 177v.
Tequixquiac	1592	AGN, Indios, vol. 6 (1), fols. 58v–59r.
Tezayuca	1603	AGN, Congregaciones, vol. 1, fols. 25v–26r.
Tlalmanalco	1599, 1603	AGI, México, leg. 122 (1599). AGN, Congregaciones, vol. 1, fol. 38r.
Tlalnepantla	1593, 1603	AGN, Indios, vol. 6 (1), fols. 127v–128r, 141v–142r; Congregaciones, vol. 1, fols. 46r–48r.
Toltitlan	1604	AGN, Congregaciones, vol. 1, fols. 112v, 121r.
Xaltocan	1593, 1599	AGN, Indios, vol. 6 (1), fols. 130v–131r; Tierras, vol. 1584, exp. 1, fols. 3r ff.
Xochimilco	1598, 1603	AGI, México, leg. 24, ramo 1 (April 25, 1598). AGN, Congregaciones, vol. 1, fol. 57r.
Xochitepec	1603	AGI, México, leg. 665, cuad. 2, fols. 97v, 106v ff. *Al severo tribunal,* pp. 28–30.
Zumpango	1593	AGN, Indios, vol. 6 (1), fols. 130v–131r, 196r.

NOTE: The list is confined to original cabeceras and to certain disputed or new cabeceras of the late sixteenth and early seventeenth centuries (e.g., Huehuetoca, Temascalapa, Xochitepec). A number of other records relate to sujetos of these. Some of these same congregaciones included sujetos of other cabeceras, notably the sujetos of Tenochtitlan and Tlatelolco. It is probable that other congregaciones, of which the record has not yet appeared, involved other Valley communities. Dates and citations in some instances refer to initial orders rather than to actual movements of people.

ing the 1,000 or 1,100-vara interval and the ejido of one league were in almost all cases ignored, and the 500- or 600-vara rules were reinterpreted as definitions of the maximum limits of an Indian town. Even this was disputed in its application, for it frequently happened that Spaniards already owned lands and houses within the 500- or 600-vara limits.[167] Adjustments were occasionally reached in particular cases, so that haciendas might be permitted to continue to hold land within the 600-vara limits while the community might be compensated with lands elsewhere.[168] But such compensations were never uniformly implemented. With the increased number of towns and haciendas in the later colonial period, it became physically impossible to abide by the 600-vara and 1,100-vara rules.

Communities without viceregal mercedes were able at times to produce their Indian "títulos" or some surviving pictorial codices purportedly showing original settlement by pre-conquest founders. Communities lacking these could argue only "ancient possession" or invoke old cedulas to the effect that Spaniards were not to live in the Indian towns or that Indians were not to live under conditions inferior to those of pre-Christian times.[169] Communities sometimes argued that they had once possessed but had subsequently lost not only their lands but their títulos as well. Documents had been sold or pawned, in order to obtain money for tributes or for liquor.[170] Forged documents of land assignment sometimes made their appearance, perhaps including the group of pictorial manuscripts that have since been entitled Techialoyan codices.[171]

Failing an adequate defense, Indian communities themselves resorted to denuncia and composición when their properties were threatened. They sometimes submitted, in a form of secondary exploitation, to private Spaniards who arranged composiciones for a price. But since composiciones were governed by bids for payment, Spaniards were normally in a position to pay more for them than Indian communities. When Azcapotzalco was compelled in the early eighteenth century to pay 200 pesos for a composición and for the repair of "defects in its título," it delivered the amount in simple reales. Affluent Spaniards, on the other hand, might bid thousands of pesos in composición settlements, which thereafter secured the titles against Indian or other claims.[172] Even an Indian victory in court, when it occurred, might be only temporary, since the properties might become liable at any later time to Spanish demand, and if they lay outside the 600-vara measurement they were subject to later denuncia. Time was always on the Spaniards' side. If a usurped property were held for a number of years its holder could point to his own peaceful possession for that number of years with Indian consent. Spaniards might begin by renting lands from Indian communities and end by asserting that the rental was really a sale, claiming possession through the intervening years as proof of ownership. Under pressure from the clergy, remnant Indian lands were progressively diverted to cofradías, or to the images of saints, or to clerics themselves. Furthermore, Indian society was not united against Spanish society. At times when individual Indians were pressed by Spaniards to sell their lands, a community adjustment might be made whereby the lands were sold instead to the Indian gobernador, who became the guardian and protector against the Spaniards. But gubernatorial ownership did not always ensure permanent Indian possession. Gobernadores, in control of the allotment of Indian common lands, continued to dispose of such lands to Spaniards in private negotiations, with or without the consent of the communities.[173] Under pressures of a markedly disruptive character, Indian society was rarely unanimous in its conception of self-interest.

The great haciendas of the Valley of Mexico came into being through legal grant, consolidation, expansion, purchase, composición, and denuncia. Their land titles include the original mercedes, subsequent documents of sale, composiciones, records of surveys, statements of boundaries, and related papers. The titles of the hacienda of Los Portales near Cuauhtitlan consist of three massive books of pertinent documentation extending from the mid-sixteenth century to the late eighteenth century. Some fifteen original mercedes issued to various recipients in the latter half of the sixteenth century formed the basic grants for Los Portales. The properties passed through a series of owners, were sold, became the subjects of legal suits, were augmented by other sales directly through Indian owners, and were gradually incorporated into a single property. The essential territory was entitled Hacienda de Los Portales by the early seventeenth century, but a continued accretion and consolidation occurred in the late seventeenth century, when several more haciendas were joined under the same title.[174] Other records of properties of haciendas, such as Santa Lucía near Xaltocan and Huatongo in the jurisdiction of Coatepec, demonstrate strikingly similar histories.[175] The hacienda of Xalpa can be traced from its original mercedes of estancias and caballerías through intermediate stages to its emergence as the celebrated Jesuit property of the eighteenth century.[176] All hacienda titles show that while viceroys made the original grants in relatively small sizes, individual Spaniards immediately bought land from the recipients and began the process of consolidation. An active Spanish land speculation was under way in the mid-sixteenth century, when properties were already being sold for sums as large as 40,000 pesos.[177]

In all, some 160 haciendas had come into existence in the Valley of Mexico by late colonial times.[178] The number is less significant than might at first appear, for the term hacienda had no precise definition and the difference between haciendas and other similar properties—ranchos, rancherías, estancias, "haciendidas"—was not always a matter of size. Moreover, some haciendas developed, reached their culmination, and declined, entirely within the colonial period. By the late eighteenth century the hacienda (rancho) called Tauregui, belonging to the Marqués de San Cristóbal, in the jurisdiction of Ecatepec, had fallen into ruins, and even the great hacienda of Santa Lucía had deteriorated markedly from its earlier splendor.[179] In the qualifications for hacienda status much depended on the condition of the buildings and the quality of the lands, as well as on other and quite arbitrary factors. Land prices varied sharply—from a few pesos per caballería for land of poor quality to a thousand pesos or more per caballería for good agricultural land.[180] In the evaluation of an hacienda, especially one located in the northern part of the Valley, a governing factor was the presence of water, a fact that accounts for the status of the hacienda Ojo de Agua, in the Ecatepec jurisdiction, as one of the most luxurious of its area.[181] Haciendas represented investments ranging from a few thousand pesos for unpretentious establishments to 100,000 pesos and more for a first-class estate.[182] Individual owners in the seventeenth and eighteenth centuries held three, four, and five haciendas apiece, in some instances combining them under one name, in other cases maintaining separate lands under different names.[183]

The largest transaction of the colonial period took place in the late eighteenth century, when the Conde de Regla purchased the former Jesuit properties—Santa Lucía, Xalpa, Los Portales, San Xavier, and a number of others—at a price of 1,020,000 pesos.[184] The four haciendas included a substantial fraction of all the land in the northern part of the Valley, and although owned by one person they were preserved as distinct estates. Even a single hacienda, however, was not necessarily a continuous or unit block of land. It might consist, as did San Xavier, of scattered lands extending over an extensive area, interrupted and broken by smaller possessions of other persons or Indian towns.[185] No map could now be drawn showing all the lands of all the Valley's haciendas at any one time, for the evidence is no longer available, and even in the colonial period not all hacendados knew the limits of their properties.[186] The map of the residential houses or headquarters of the haciendas (Map 9) shows, nevertheless, a distribution that contrasts, in significant ways, with the original Indian patterns of settlement. It is evident that haciendas tended to extend broadly around the Valley's slopes and that they did not concentrate in the lacustrine region. They were distributed fairly evenly in Chalco province and on the east and west sides of the Valley but were almost non-existent in the Xochimilco jurisdiction. The relatively small number north of Zumpango and Xaltocan was the consequence of the huge extent of Xalpa, Santa Lucía, and San Xavier. But even these assertions must be qualified, for the great haciendas were rented out as subdivided parcels, Santa Lucía alone being rented to over two

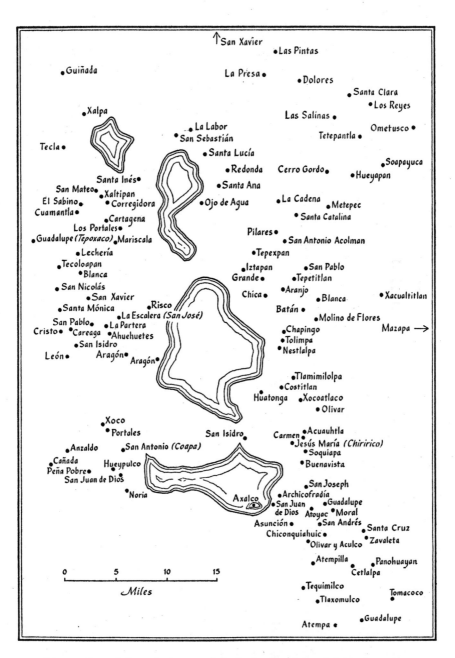

↑San Xavier

Las Pintas

Guiñada

La Presa

Dolores

Santa Clara

Los Reyes

Xalpa

La Labor
San Sebastián

Las Salinas

Tetepantla

Ometusco

Tecla

Santa Lucía

Soapayuca

Santa Inés

Redonda

Cerro Gordo

Hueyapan

San Mateo
El Sabino
Cuamantla

Xaltipan
Corregidora

Santa Ana

Ojo de Agua

La Cadena

Metepec

Cartagena

Santa Catalina

Los Portales

Pilares

Guadalupe (Tepoxaco)

Mariscala

Tepexpan

San Antonio Acolman

Lechería

Tecoloapan

Blanca

Iztapan
Grande

San Pablo

Tepetitlan

San Nicolás

Aranjo

San Xavier

Chica

Blanca

Xacualtitlan

Santa Mónica

Risco

Batán

San Pablo

La Escalera (San José)

Molino de Flores

Mazapa →

Cristo

Careaga

La Partera

Ahuehuetes

Chapingo

León

Aragón

San Isidro

Aragón

Tolimpa

Nestlalpa

Tlamimilolpa

Costitlan

Huatonga

Xocoatlaco

Olivar

Xoco

Portales

San Isidro

Carmen

Acuauhtla

Anzaldo

San Antonio (Coapa)

Jesús María (Chiririco)

Soquiapa

Cañada
Peña Pobre
San Juan de Dios

Hueypulco

Buenavista

Noria

San Joseph

Axalco

Archicofradía

San Juan
de Dios

Atoyac

Guadalupe

Moral

Asunción

San Andrés

Santa Cruz

Chiconquiahuic

Zavaleta

Olivar y Aculco

Atempilla

Panohuayan

Cetlalpa

0   5   10   15

Tequimilco

Miles

Tlaxomulco

Tomacoco

Atempa

Guadalupe

Map 9. Sites of the main houses of the haciendas of the eighteenth century.

hundred persons in the mid-eighteenth century.[187] In any case, the great hacendados were financial entrepreneurs, removed by wealth, taste, custom, preference, and culture from Indian society. Indian contact was not with the hacendado but with his mayordomo or with his tenants. For an Indian community there was little difference between intrusion by a great hacienda and intrusion by a minor rancho.

Some haciendas and ranchos, on the other hand, never emancipated themselves from the original Indian landholding but instead preserved a status comparable to that of an Indian barrio or estancia subject to a cabecera. Thus in the area immediately adjacent to the capital, the two haciendas of San Antonio Aragón and Santa Ana Aragón remained under the formal jurisdiction of the Indian governments of Tenochtitlan and Tlatelolco respectively. They were included as tributary subdivisions of the Indian communities and their Spanish proprietors rented the entire establishments from the Indian communities.[188] Such cases suggest that Spanish utilization of land in the Valley remained in some ways subordinate to the forms of Indian fiscal and territorial organization. But even here pressures on the Indian community might approach those exerted by the independent haciendas and ranchos. Thus the rancho of Tres Palos was the property of Quautzotzongo, one of the sujetos of eighteenth-century Xochitepec. The community, in debt to a Spaniard in the amount of some 650 pesos and unable to pay, arranged to rent the rancho to his heirs at 70 pesos per year for nine years. Each year the community received 40 pesos and the debt was discounted annually in the amount of 30 pesos.[189] The community retained formal ownership but the tenant held over the community a type of control comparable to that of debt service. He maintained his rancho not through the payment of a purchase price of some thousands of pesos but through an annual payment of 40 pesos per year. An equivalent property could hardly have been rented from a Spanish owner for so modest a sum. Quite apart from other kinds of exploitation that such a tenant might exert, his contractual relation with the Indian community represented a basic adjustment to his advantage. Such adjustments, like others, acquired the force of custom and precedent, their perpetuation justifying their acceptance and assuring their validity.

The history of relations between haciendas and Indian communities, then, was one of pressures and counterpressures with the long-term advantage on the side of the hacendados. Indians of the seventeenth century continued to construct temporary dwellings at the limits of their pueblos in order to revise, favorably for themselves, the starting point of the 500-vara measurements. The practice was encouraged following the 600-vara rule of 1687, for this rule stated expressly that the measurement was to begin at the outermost house of the pueblo. As might be expected, Spanish interests objected to this royal support of the Indians' tactics, with the result that the support was withdrawn in 1695. The measurement from then on was to be made from the center of the town.[190] Thus the 600-vara area of the eighteenth century was not an additional territory outside the town site itself. Under certain conditions it might be further reduced by half, for the law did not specify how the outer boundaries were to be drawn, and either of the situations illustrated (Plate X) was possible.[191]

Interested Spaniards undertook further to interpret the 600-vara legislation to their own advantage by limiting its application to certain classes of Indian community. The legislation itself spoke only of Indian "towns." It did not recognize the original distinctions of the sixteenth and seventeenth centuries regarding cabeceras and sujetos, and in the legalism of the eighteenth century this was to invoke again the question of the definition of an Indian town. Spanish proprietors of haciendas and ranchos argued that the 600-vara legislation ought to apply only to cabeceras, or to communities founded before the date of the Spanish mercedes, or to communities that fulfilled certain innovating criteria as pueblos, such as the presence of a church, the Holy Sacrament, a ministerial residence, an Indian gobernador, or even a Spanish corregidor.[192]

Three case histories will illustrate the conflict between haciendas and Indian communities: one involving Xochitepec in Chalco province; the second involving Ixtlahuaca, in the northern part of the Valley; and the third involving Tlilan, in the west.

In the congregación in 1603, the inhabitants of ten communities were moved and resettled at Xochitepec, in Chalco province.[193] In 1610, under threat of Spanish occupation, Xochitepec received a viceregal grant of one estancia de ganado menor and five caballerías, or about four square miles. Between 1610 and 1655, during a period of continued depopulation in Xochitepec, Spaniards, mestizos, and mulattoes, principally from Totolapa, infiltrated the area vacated by the congregación, cut the community's oak and cedar forest, and introduced cattle herds.[194] In 1667 a Spaniard petitioned the viceroy for a cattle ranch and six caballerías, about eight square miles in all, in the abandoned area. The Indian government of Xochitepec protested against this, arguing that lands depopulated in the congregación were not subject to Spanish alienation but remained Indian property. A survey of the area disclosed the ruins of the former houses, which in the late 1660's were held to be evidence of the original occupation, and the Spaniard's petition was therefore denied. But further infiltration occurred in the 1670's and 1680's. In 1694 Xochitepec protested the new incursions and the audiencia ruled that Xochitepec was to be protected in its use of the lands. The audiencia now referred to the area, however, as a monte, "on the assumption that it is unappropriated" (*suponiendo ques realengo*).[195]

The Indian government was able to rent some of the lands to tenants. But in 1744 the lands became the object of a denuncia by another Spaniard, who argued that as vacant territories they belonged to the crown and were being used by the community of Xochitepec without title. The area of the denuncia was surveyed and 155 caballerías, an area of about 26 square miles, were measured outside the 600-vara area and outside the limits of the merced of 1610. The Indian community, unable to produce the document of its merced, offered 100 pesos for a composición. The denuncia was further protested by the tenants and by the Dominican curate of Xochitepec, who now stated that the town had given some of the lands to the monastery. In 1745 an oidor declared the lands to be royal property and hence accessible to denuncia. A new survey indicated 252 caballerías, the difference of 97 caballerías between the earlier and the later surveys being attributed not to any error in measurement but to the different limits indicated on the two occasions. Some lands within the measured areas were shown to be the legal property of other persons. But after a payment of 1,000 pesos "by way of gratification or donation" the 97 caballerías were adjusted in favor of the denuncia and the remainder was composed in Spanish possession for the huge sum of 31,900 pesos.[196]

In an effort to prove Indian ownership, the gobernador of Xochitepec exhibited one hundred documents signed by the names of former viceroys, all but one of which were declared by viceregal examiners to be forgeries. The documents were consigned to the secret archive of the Juzgado de Tierras in order to prevent their further use. The summary argument by the Spanish lawyer supporting the denuncia asserted that the Indian community would benefit from Spanish ownership, for such ownership would bring to an end the Indian rental which had fostered laziness and been the source of money for drunkenness in the town.[197]

A feature of interest in the Xochitepec case is that Spaniards made two attempts to acquire lands abandoned in the congregación. One of these attempts, about sixty-five years after the congregación, failed for the reason that the memory of the congregación was still retained, and the ruins of the former houses were still in evidence. The other, about 140 years after the congregación, succeeded because congregación had been forgotten and was no longer regarded as relevant. The lawyer for the denuncia in the 1740's argued successfully that the lands had belonged to towns unrelated to Xochitepec, and that Xochitepec was falsely claiming the titles of these towns. The incident indicates again how the passage of time abetted the continuous process of Spanish land occupation, as successive generations modified the criteria.

The second illustration begins in 1559, when the viceroy granted to a Spaniard, Antonio Machado, an estancia de ganado menor within the términos of San Mateo Ixtlahuaca, the distant northern sujeto of Acolman. The Ixtlahuaca términos bounded an area of approximately fifteen square miles (shown as 30-31-32-33, or the entire area, of Plate XII), and Machado made an agreement with the Indians of Ixtlahuaca whereby he would return the land to the community and receive instead a region called Huacachula (A-B-C-D in Plate XII) for his animals. This was done and the community held the estancia granted to Machado. The community then brought suit against him, declaring that his possession of the estancia was not "sin perjuicio," and in 1570 Machado was ordered to remove his animals. Between 1580 and 1615 seven new land grants were issued to various Spanish recipients, including one of 1582 to Cristóbal Pérez duplicating the area granted to Machado in 1559. All seven fell wholly or partially within the Ixtlahuaca términos, where they comprised four estancias de ganado menor and fifteen caballerías and included several sites abandoned in the congregación of the first years of the seventeenth century. The Jesuit Order began to acquire the various titles in 1682 and by the late seventeenth century all seven were incorporated among the titles of the Jesuit hacienda of Santa Lucía.

In 1709 the community of Ixtlahuaca initiated a suit against the Jesuits, claiming that the four sitios and fifteen caballerías fell within its ancient términos. The community brought two principal arguments to bear upon its claim: that the original grant of 1559 had been revoked, and that by a viceregal ruling of 1603 towns were to retain lands held before the congregación. The Jesuit lawyers ridiculed both arguments. Haciendas everywhere, they said, included lands abandoned in the congregación. To agree with the Indian side, they added, one would have to declare all seven mercedes invalid, a proposition that appeared absurd. Even the community's claim to the 600-vara limits (the rectangle 16-17-18-19 in Plate XII), the Jesuit lawyers stated, should be denied, for the 600-vara rule applied only to "those that are truly towns" (*los que son verdaderamente pueblos*). Ixtlahuaca was not a pueblo, for it lacked a minister and Holy Sacrament, and was only a sujeto of Acolman. The Jesuits won the case. Ixtlahuaca could present no papers other than those mentioned. The Jesuit side was defended by skillful lawyers fortified with quantities of documentation, including the original mercedes in proper legal order. The Jesuits' side in this and similar cases depended on a detailed knowledge of late colonial land law, against which Indian communities were helpless.[198]

In the third case, with the continuous development of Spanish haciendas in the region back of Tlalnepantla, the community of San Miguel Tlilan (Hila) found itself surrounded and engulfed by the hacienda movement. The small community possessed fifteen tributaries at the beginning of the seventeenth century, and these were ordered to move to Azcapotzaltongo in the congregación. But the order proved ineffective. In the middle eighteenth century Tlilan had more than twice its earlier population, with 24 full tributaries, 19 half-tributaries, two reserved persons, five youths immediately under tributary age, and 38 children. Most of its workers were gañanes in the hacienda of San Ildefonso, one of several haciendas of the region.[199] The community's campaign for a 600-vara measurement centered upon the question of its status as a pueblo. The owner of the hacienda, Laureano González, argued the classification of Tlilan as a "pueblito" or "ranchería" included in and surrounded by the hacienda, and lacking independent status. Its inhabitants, in the hacendado's view, were wholly servile to the hacienda's control in agriculture and in pasturing. His permission was always required before the inhabitants could utilize any of the hacienda's pasture land, and in agriculture he "permitted them to plant only a few small *milpillas* around their huts (*chozas*)." The ranchería had never been a pueblo. It lacked curate, Sacrament, Spanish political officer, and everything else that a real pueblo required, and its tributes were paid to the Indian gobernador of Tlalnepantla by the hacendado himself. The last point was regarded as particularly convincing with respect to the status of the inhabitants as gañanes. Against these assertions Tlilan argued that no law required a pueblo to possess a minister or a corregidor. Only a church for Mass was required, and this Tlilan possessed. It was, in addition, a place of baptism—two of the hacendado's own sons had been baptized there—and of burial. Tlilan boasted an Indian alcalde, and, as a pueblo should, a sacristy. It had always been a pueblo.[200]

The Tlilan case is one of many that reveal the methods of late colonial hacendados in dealing with the Indian communities. Especially noteworthy in the eighteenth century are the ecclesiastical criteria evoked to establish or deny pueblo status. A community with a church, a baptismal font, ecclesiastical ornaments, church bells, and a tradition of Mass could, if all else failed, offer these as indications of its pueblo status. Hacendados could as easily deny the existence or relevance of these standards. A baptismal font of recent installation could be dismissed as an innovation. An "iglesia" could be deprecated as a "hermita," or a "visita." In the civil criteria, proximity to a cabecera could support the argument that the community was simply a barrio; its alcalde could be denounced as a mere topil, a false alcalde.[201] But increasingly in the eighteenth century the hacendados could claim for their side the massive argument of precedent, for the hacienda was no longer a new institution, the status of its laborers as gañanes had acquired legitimacy by long-standing custom, and no one could remember a period when haciendas did not exist. The hacendado's payment of tributes for his gañanes could be interpreted as an act of benevolence, the exercise of paternal care by an *amo* for his *sirvientes*.[202] A community had little to offer in response to an argument that its inhabitants were gañanes, for that is what they were; adversity had come to be sanctioned by custom and by law, and the existing status of the gañanes was cited as itself the sanction, the *costumbre*.

To the Indian towns the issue was an important one, for it threatened the communality of Indian life in an especially serious way. A community might lose a substantial part of its population and still survive as a corporate body, but the loss of lands threatened its very nature and existence. As town populations increased in the late seventeenth and eighteenth centuries, they included larger and larger numbers of landless Indians, those who remained after all the calpullalli, all the "tierras de repartimiento," had been distributed. In Chicoloapa in the middle eighteenth century, the total population had increased to over 187 families. Haciendas had taken most of the community's original land. Some 38 families and 28 single persons lacked community land for their own agriculture. Some, including two ex-gobernadores, rented land from the hacienda of Xocoatlaco. Others used lands of neighboring Santiago Cuauhtlalpa. The situation was becoming more serious in an expanding population, for no less than 44 youths, listed as "próximos a tributar," would soon become tributaries.[203] In Xochitepec the increased population amounted to some 350 families at the end of the colonial period, and several families were occupying each house. Some 45 others had fled to the unproductive monte, where they lived "sin ley ni rey." The town pastured its animals in the plaza and in the cemetery.[204] Whole communities in the late colonial period were completely landless save for the house sites themselves.[205]

Indian towns could no longer rely on their caciques to protect them. In the eighteenth century the notion of a cabecera identified by its cacicazgo was no longer valid, and towns were obliged to employ quite new criteria in demonstrations of "pueblo" status. Moreover the most powerful caciques, as we have observed, were virtually indistinguishable from hacendados, and they readily adopted hacienda arguments in their conflicts with Indian towns. It is interesting to see the consequences of the petition of the community of Santa Isabel Chalma, in Chalco province, for its 600 varas in the 1790's. The petition was protested not by a Spanish hacendado but by the cacique Luis Páez de Mendoza, some of whose properties were affected by the community's claim. The community argued that it was a pueblo. Páez de Mendoza, like any hacendado, argued that it was a barrio. The dispute occasioned much legal discussion concerning the monarch's real intention in the 600-vara rule, and Chalma presented a list of the ornaments of its church to demonstrate pueblo status.[206]

In brief, the haciendas had impinged upon the land of the pueblos. A variety of pressures had induced Indians to work on the haciendas, which incorporated them as gañanes. The benevolent monarchy sought to alleviate these conditions by granting 600 varas to the pueblos. And the owners of the haciendas asserted that this rule could not apply to them because the pueblos were no longer pueblos but "rancherías" or clusters of huts within the haciendas. Thus in certain instances Indians were prevented from arguing that they had been exploited beyond a certain point. Whereas a sixteenth-century protest could simply have cited damages in a straightforward way, an eighteenth-century legal claim required the assertion that Indians had maintained themselves "always in a pueblo form," that not all were really gañanes of the hacienda, and that they voluntarily worked in any of a number of haciendas as they chose.[207] The Indians' argument led, therefore, to the assertion not only that they should be free but that they were free. In this kind of discussion it lay in the hacendado's interest to assert that he or his forebears had restricted the freedom of the Indians, and hacendados did in fact point to their own strictness to demonstrate the non-existence of the pueblo. In practice, therefore, a legal advantage for the hacendado was gained by harsh treatment, and Indians were obliged to say that the treatment was not so extreme, that their pueblo had not been seriously affected by it, that they had always retained their freedom of labor choice, and that they did possess lands and other communal holdings. The legal advantage for Indians thus lay in a pretense of more communality in pueblo form than was in fact the case.

CHAPTER XI

Agriculture

The upper limits of agricultural cultivation in the Valley of Mexico were determined by the oak, cedar, and pine forests[1] of the elevated slopes, where soils were shallow and temperatures cold. Below the forest lines, and descending to the lakeshores, more moderate temperatures prevailed and the volcanic or alluvial soils gave way to deep chernozems and other rich soils. The transitional area was monte, a region of grass and brush, used chiefly for pasture and the collection of faggots, with soils inappropriate for agriculture save under the most extreme conditions.

Indians distinguished a number of soil types: *atoctli,* or fertile alluvial soil; *xalatoctli,* or sandy alluvial soil; *tetlalli,* or stony soil; *quauhtlalli,* or soil enriched by decayed trees; *tlazotlalli,* or soil enriched by decayed grasses; and *tlalauiac,* or soil enriched by dung.[2] They identified these varieties of soil in their pictorial records of land tenure; Códice Vergara, Códice de Santa María Asunción, and Humboldt Fragment VIII show stony, sandy, fertile, and other kinds of soil in hieroglyphs.[3] The Badianus Herbal, an Indian pictorial text of great beauty and distinction, distinguishes soil varieties not in relation to the agricultural plots of Indian families but in a scientific or botanical spirit, with reference to the suitability of plants to specific soils.[4] Spaniards did not adopt any of the Indian designations for soils of high fertility, but two Nahuatl terms for infertile soils became standard in Spanish usage. One was *tequisquitl,* used for soils impregnated with salts.[5] The other was *tepetate,* designating caliche or alluvial soils of yellowish brown color originally formed beneath the surface by lime deposits and later exposed at many locations.[6]

Although located in the Torrid Zone, south of the Tropic of Cancer, the Valley of Mexico has many characteristics of temperate climates. With regard to temperature, colonial notices often mention the coldness of the Valley in contrast to the *tierra caliente*.[7] Modern monthly averages of temperature indicate a moderate warmth, with an average variation of about nine degrees Fahrenheit from the coldest to the warmest seasons.[8] But it is important to remember that fluctuations within each month are always far greater than this, and that temperature, particularly as it affects agriculture, is properly understood not by monthly averages but by maximum and minimum limits. Maximum temperatures vary up to ten degrees between the coldest and the hottest months, while minimum temperatures vary slightly more than this and drop below the freezing point in winter. The annual growing season falls between March and October, and vegetation must adjust to an eight-month period without frost and a four-month period when freezing conditions may be expected, especially at night. Even in the coldest months, however, temperatures rise close to 86° Fahrenheit (30° Centigrade) during the daytime. The low latitude means that day and night do not markedly vary in duration, although they do in temperature, and that the sun's rays strike the earth less obliquely than in more northerly regions. Irradiation and evaporation are rapid in the Valley. The atmosphere tends to be clear and the sunlight intense. In general, these climatic features become modified as one ascends to the Valley rim, where special local conditions prevail on summits and in barrancas of different degrees of exposure and where agriculture is precarious or impossible. At upper elevations winds are stronger and temperatures much lower. The highest mountains are often hidden in clouds.[9]

The pattern of rainfall, with its characteristic sequence of dry and wet seasons, is of particular significance for agriculture in the Valley. The sequence results from low atmospheric pressures during the summer months alternating with high atmospheric pressures in the winter. Air circulating convectionally from the Atlantic or Pacific brings regular summer rainfall. In the winter this circulation is reduced, and rainfall is limited to the condensation precipitated by northern winds cooling in their passage over the mountains.[10] The rainy season normally begins in April or May, reaches its climax in July or August, and then declines. It ordinarily takes the form of a moderate or heavy shower falling in the afternoon or at night.[11] Within the Valley it operates with a consistent disparity between north and south. Figure 12 shows the marked decrease in rainfall as one proceeds from the Desierto de Leones northward toward Pachuca, a decrease that

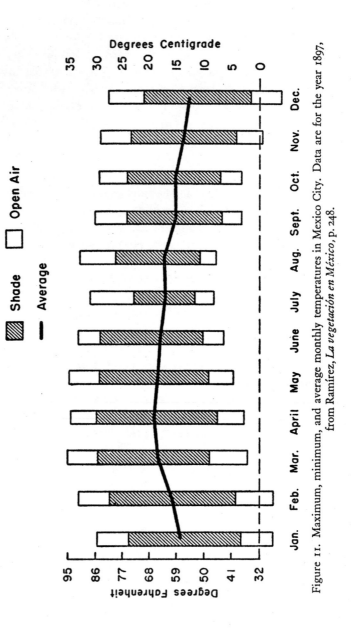

Figure 11. Maximum, minimum, and average monthly temperatures in Mexico City. Data are for the year 1897, from Ramírez, *La vegetación en México*, p. 248.

is reflected in the natural vegetation of the several regions and one that plays an important role in determining the character of agriculture. In Pachuca, to the north of the Valley, the wet season brings five times as much rain as the dry season. In the humid south, where the dry-season rainfall is approximately the same as in the north, the wet season has four times as much rain as in the north or twenty times as much as the dry season.[12]

The fluctuations of temperature, the sequences of wet and dry seasons, and the differences between north and south appear to have been stable Valley conditions since prehistoric times. The written record clearly indicates the influence of these conditions in the colonial period.[13] The record is less explicit, however, with reference to long-term climatic modifications, for until the 1760's, when Felipe de Zúñiga y Ontiveros and Antonio Alzate compiled the earliest tables, colonial peoples did not systematically measure temperature, and the records that remain of colonial rainfall occur as casual observations applying to abnormal periods.[14] Data on water supply in the towns of Chalco province in the seventeenth century demonstrate that colonial peoples recognized a connection between the cutting of forests and the disappearance of streams. A further decline in moisture was commented upon in the eighteenth century, and again it was related to removal of the forest cover.[15] The over-all evidence suggests a progressive colonial desiccation, related to deforestation, to increasingly rapid runoff, and to a declining rainfall.

Data on colonial changes in the distribution of land and water areas are more precise. Because the lakes were shallow, relatively slight changes in the volume of water created extensive changes in shore outline. Motolinía, who arrived in New Spain in 1524, asserted that the diminution of the lake area began in that year.[16] His reference was to the environs of Mexico City and explicitly not to its eastern side, which was still bounded by water long after his time. The original Indian dike, the new dike of 1555–56, and the northern and southern causeways of the city served as obstacles to the westward movement of the saline waters of Lake Texcoco, and the diminution mentioned by Motolinía probably applied only to the slightly more elevated area west of these barriers. A possible explanation for the decrease in water levels here appears in the cultivation and irrigation projects between Tenayuca and Coyoacan, the only agricultural zone to be vigorously exploited by Spaniards at the time of Motolinía's writing, and, given the efficacy of the dikes, the only one whose streams directly watered the area in question.

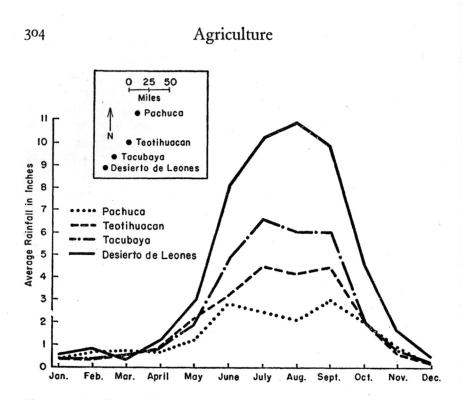

Figure 12. Monthly rainfall at selected sites. Averages for Pachuca, Teotihuacan, Tacubaya, and Desierto de Leones, 1921–34. Source: Ministerio de Agricultura y Fomento, Departamento de Meteorología, Tacubaya, D.F., published in Carlson, *Geography*, p. 406.

Diminution in the lake system elsewhere was also observed prior to the flood of 1555. A canal constructed between Zumpango and Xaltocan drained water from the northern lakes, with the result that by 1554 a part of the former lake bed from the Ecatepec-Chiconauhtla region north to Zumpango, as well as other areas in the territory north of Tepozotlan, had been dried. Water flowed from these sources into Lake Texcoco via the channel that colonial peoples called the Río de Ecatepec.[17]

After the flood crisis of 1555, the lake level and indeed the entire hydrographic system of the Valley are much more frequently mentioned in the literature, and except in times of heavy rains the notices point to a further and progressive shrinking. Visible desiccation continued to affect principally the northern lakes and the areas west of the city's north-south causeways. The former were much reduced and the latter wholly free from water during the dry season by the early seventeenth century, while the southern lakes remained full. Lake Texcoco, which had the lowest level of all the Valley waters, was conspicuously reduced in the early seventeenth century. Even so, the wet season temporarily restored high levels, so that the entire area surrounding the city, apart from the artificially elevated causeways, was periodically submerged.[18] The systematic Desagüe was attended by further slow and irregular decreases in the volume of lake water. But, if the maps of the period may be trusted, the average water levels in many areas in 1810 were still not greatly different from those of the seventeenth century.[19]

Changes in the lake levels are related to the history of erosion and the redistribution of soils. It is axiomatic that erosion did not begin with the coming of the Spaniards, but there can be no doubt that it was accelerated by Spanish plow agriculture and animal herding.[20] The first observer to comment with authority on this subject was Torquemada, who noted in the early seventeenth century the extensive cultivation of the Valley's lands up to the forest line and the downward movement of its soils. Extensive areas of cultivation were already lacking in topsoil, Torquemada stated, and their subsoil tepetate was exposed. Many planners and witnesses of the Desagüe, beginning with Torquemada's contemporary Enrico Martínez, made similar observations.[21] Their concern was not so much for the decreasing fertility of the upper regions as for the more pressing possibility that earth carried to the Valley bottom was elevating the bed of Lake Texcoco and thus increasing the danger of flood. The deterioration of the higher soils was also accelerated by deforestation, which was continuous and for the most part cumulative. The most accessible trees were cut for building material, for fuel, and for the setting of huge, deep pilings (*estacas*) as foundation material in Mexico City. In late colonial times 25,000 trees were cut down annually for estacas alone, and the process had been characteristic of urban building since the sixteenth century.[22] Wasteful practices were the rule in all uses of lumber. Forests on the upper slopes were still being burned away in the seventeenth century to clear land for the expansion of Spanish agriculture. Cedars, burned as fuel, were virtually exterminated by the late eighteenth century.[23] Many great stretches of tepetate, which appear as such striking features of the landscape of the modern Valley, were exposed well before the end of the colonial period.[24]

It was sometimes argued in favor of the program for a complete Desagüe that the dry lake beds might furnish new agricultural land. A counterargument asserted that the reclaimed lands would be unproductive and that their dust would blind the city.[25] In general this second position prevailed, and a complete drainage was never accomplished. But in dry seasons some of the predicted consequences of a complete drainage did come into being. The saline beds of Lakes Zumpango and Xaltocan were never agriculturally productive. Sub-surface alkaline waters continued to rise in drained areas and with their evaporation soils became impregnated with salts. As Alzate stated in the eighteenth century, wherever the waters receded, the alkali proportionately advanced.[26] Salinization was evident on the eastern shore of Lake Texcoco in the sixteenth century, where *lagunillas* had formed, where soils were alkalized, and where sterile years for crops were common. The first alkali dust storms occurred in the sixteenth century, and similar storms were regular features of the dry season during the rest of the colonial period.[27] Thus the draining of the lakes, far from creating new agricultural land, rendered existing agricultural land less serviceable. The process was not a rapid one, but it continued irresistibly. It accounts to a large degree for the decline of towns bordering Lake Texcoco and for the decline of Tlatelolco, which had once been surrounded by fresh water. The conjunction of desiccation and alkalization was nowhere so striking as in this once great Indian city, which had become barren and much reduced by the end of the colonial period. Its neighbor, Tenochtitlan-Mexico, was saved from a similar fate by the preservation of the canal route to the agricultural area of the south.[28]

For all this, the historical significance of desiccation and declining soil fertility in the Valley should not be exaggerated. The areas most affected were the salt lake beds and the upper slopes, neither of which ever comprised a major agricultural zone. Chinampas and bottom-land haciendas were only temporarily affected by flood.[29] For Indians the loss in productivity was more than matched by the decline in population, and the economic effects were therefore limited. Spring rains regularly brought relief from drought, and long-term changes were obscured by the annual alternations. From the Indian point of view, as we have noted, lands were lost far more obviously as a result of pre-emption by Spaniards than as a result of the impoverishment of the soil. And the most dramatic hazards to agricultural production were the unseasonable frosts and temporary droughts rather than the long-term desiccation or decline in soil nutrients. Moreover, the process of climatic change occurred so gradually that the adjustments to it merged with the adjustments to other and more immediate hardships, and it therefore passed virtually unnoticed except by the most perceptive observers.

For the Indian population, soils and climate were objects of concern chiefly for their effect upon maize, the major cereal plant of colonial Indian civilization and the one on which, in a variety of forms, the mass of the human population and much of the domesticated animal population depended.[30] Among all the world's cereals maize ranks highest in its combination of nutritional quality, abundant yield, and adaptability to a variety of environments.[31] The conditions of soil, temperature, and moisture in the Valley were, within certain limits, singularly appropriate for maize, which was a developed agricultural product in the colonial period, the outcome of centuries of selective Indian cultivation. The growth cycle of the maize plant had been a crucial element in pre-conquest native ceremonial, and it continued to govern Indian daily lives thereafter.[32] It was an annual plant with a maturation period of approximately six months, and it was thus accommodated within a probable margin of safety to the Valley's growing season. Plantings in March, April, or May could be expected to receive the warmest temperatures of the year in the absence of frost. Rainfall adequate to ensure germination in April became abundant at the time when the plant's rapid development required larger supplies of moisture. Cold temperatures and reduced rainfall late in the year, after maturation but before harvesting, hardened the grain and made it durable, so that it could be preserved as a food through the unproductive winter. Maize yielded harvests even where the soil was nearly pure sand or in very rocky ground. Its shallow root system required no great depth of soil preparation or soil fertility. It survived high temperatures and drought, its structure being such that it could absorb and retain moisture for considerable periods, but it was especially responsive to the conditions of rapid evaporation and recurrent replenishment of moisture, the periodic daily watering and intense sunlight of the summer rainy season. It was a hardy and resilient plant, capable of withstanding abuse but repaying devoted care. Nevertheless, its cultivation and growth were always attended by uncertainties, for it was by no means impervious to unusually adverse conditions of temperature and rainfall. Its poor years were years of depression for Indian society, and its good years were years of prosperity. It was a peculiarly Indian grain, intimately asso- ciated with the hand-to-mouth character of colonial Indian economy, and its rivalry with wheat reflects in a multitude of ways the stresses of Indian-Spanish relations.

Maize differed from location to location as a result of differing soils, differing climates, and differing seed varieties developed in special regions. Throughout colonial Mexico "white" maize was regarded as superior. The small, hard kernels of Epazoyuca and Toluca could be kept for years, while the maize of Tlaxcala had the reputation of deteriorating rapidly.[33] In the Valley the standard type was the maize of Chalco, which matured in approximately six months, could be kept for fairly long periods, and was preferred for human consumption while maize imported from Toluca was fed to animals.[34] The kernels of Cuernavaca maize, however, germinated in less than half the time that Chalco kernels required. Throughout colonial times, maize varieties that were ready for harvesting within a period of three months were available, and although these sometimes appeared in the city's markets as early as May and June, they were not cultivated by Valley agriculturists.[35]

It is true that with a greater awareness of possibilities and a greater interest in developing new methods colonial peoples might have accomplished more with maize varieties than they did. But in maize agriculture, which was the most vital single economic activity of Indians, the influence of costumbre was heavy and pervasive. With so much at stake, any innovation was precarious. With so much inevitable variation in temperature and moisture and condition of growth, any change deliberately introduced by human agency was suspect. The complex, highly developed, indigenous sense of time, which the colonial church adapted to the ecclesiastical fiesta calendar, persisted in agriculture in a more direct way. Maize ready for harvest was not harvested in Indian towns, even at the risk of loss of the crop, until the elders of the town announced that the time had come. As an Indian explained to an inquiring Spaniard in the late sixteenth century, "Everything has its count and its assigned day."[36] Additionally, the very abundance of the Valley operated to inhibit innovation, for years of poor harvest occurred only intermittently and no sustained periods of scarcity stimulated experimentation with new methods.[37]

Indians planted maize in the familiar way, in hills arranged in rows. An eighteenth-century source comments on the regularity of the rows and the even separation of the hills. Sahagún's illustration of Indian sowing appears to show five or six kernels per hill, though one must allow here for the possibility of a certain artistic license.[38] Clavigero speaks of one, two, or more kernels per hill, while other sources refer to three or four. We know of no colonial record that provides a measurement of the distance between hills. Modern Indian practice in the Valley is to sow hills at more or less regular intervals, slightly under or slightly over one meter apart. At four kernels per hill and approximately 4,000 hills per acre a normal colonial planting would require some 16,000 kernels per acre, not all of which, of course, could germinate or grow to maturity. The *fanega de sembradura* for maize was officially computed at 184 by 276 varas (8.8 acres), and if the fanega be computed at 1.5 bushels (78–84 pounds) a sowing of about nine pounds per acre, or between six and seven acres per bushel, may be estimated.[39] This compares with modern Indian practice ranging from five to ten pounds per acre and with modern United States practice at approximately eight pounds per acre (seven acres per bushel). In the United States corn belt, 10,000 to 12,000 stalks per acre make a moderate or normal stand, though 16,000 or more stalks per acre are quite possible in fertile fields with abundant subsoil moisture. In modern Mexico 12 kilograms per hectare (about 10 pounds per acre) are appropriate for poor to average soil and 22 kilograms per hectare (nearly 20 pounds per acre) for exceptionally well fertilized soil. Stands of 20,000 plants per acre (50,000 per hectare) are not unknown.[40] This relates, however, to commercial production with hybrid seed in the most favored areas, and amounts normally planted in colonial Mexico may have been considerably less than this. Moreover, colonial Indian maize plantings varied greatly from field to field, for much depended upon the soil, the slope, and the quantities of land and seed available.

Ordinary Indian cultivation continued to utilize the *coa* or digging stick (Nahuatl *huictli*) after the conquest,[41] although principales in some instances are known to have adopted plows and oxen in the sixteenth century,[42] and community plantings later employed a number of Spanish techniques. Eighteenth-century notices mention Indian burros, oxen, and plows as if these were fairly common Indian possessions. In the eighteenth century only the "indios pobres" were still making use of coas for planting. It was recognized even then, however, that hand planting with the coa was more economical with respect to seed and that it yielded larger harvests.[43] Indian irrigation was fairly widely practiced in the Valley at the time of the conquest, but as Spaniards appropriated the land irrigation came principally to be applied to wheat, with the result that native maize cultivation relied for the most part on natural rainfall.[44] With the exception of the chinampa areas, this was the case even in the hacienda maize plantation of the late colonial period.[45]

Data on maize yields, as one would expect, indicate harvests of great irregularity. Yield was often measured in Mexico as a relation between the amount planted and the amount harvested, ratios of 1 to 100 to 1 to 200 being regarded as normal to good. In extreme cases ratios of 1 to 300, 1 to 400, and even 1 to 800 were recorded.[46] Official evaluations of property in the late eighteenth century estimated from 70 to 125 fanegas as the yield of one fanega sown.[47] With a planting of 1.5 bushels per 8.8 acres, a "normal" ratio of 1 to 100 would yield slightly over 11 fanegas, or about 17 bushels, per acre. The maximum yield mentioned in the colonial period, 1 to 800, would be, by the same calculation, the equivalent of about 135 bushels per acre, an extraordinary harvest and one rarely exceeded even in the most favorable conditions of modern maize agriculture.[48] Recorded specific yields fall in the lower portion of the range indicated in the colonial Valley. Records of Axapusco in the early eighteenth century indicate annual plantings of one-half fanega with yields ranging up to 20 fanegas (ratios up to 1 to 40), probably on inferior land.[49] Tlalmanalco in 1757 planted about 1½ fanegas and harvested 200 fanegas,[50] a ratio of 1 to 133.

Maize was commonly eaten by Indians in the form of tortillas, prepared by women in the manner still familiar. Kernels were soaked in lime water (this greatly increased their calcium content), then ground on the metate, and cooked on the griddle, called the comal.[51] In times of shortage Indians of the lake area sometimes mixed insects in the dough, and occasionally tortillas were made with barley or with maguey.[52] Maize soaked and cooked in water was consumed as the beverage called atole.[53] The leaves and stalks of the maize plant were used as fodder—especially for pigs, horses, and mules[54]—or as human food, and stalks were used as fence material and as fuel.[55]

Following the harvest, maize was stored for the unproductive winter. Small amounts of the shelled kernels were kept in jars for domestic use. Larger quantities of cobs were stored in cribs (trojes) of a variety of designs and modes of construction, ranging from pure Indian models to the great hacienda storehouses of the eighteenth century.[56] Storehouses in Indian towns, like their pre-conquest prototypes, were adjuncts of the tribute system, but they might be opened by special dispensation and for relief in times of extreme need.[57] Maize in an immediately edible form could not conveniently be preserved for long. The tortilla becomes dry and almost inedible within a few hours and is accordingly made fresh for each meal. This explains why food carried by laborers in the early repartimiento was so subject to spoilage, and why women, serving as tortilla makers, accompanied the labor drafts of the Desagüe.[58]

To some degree, the Valley's maize economy may be understood in terms of average individual consumption and population numbers. Various enactments of the colonial period required food rations for laborers in specified amounts: one *cuartillo* (1/48 fanega) of maize per day in 1555–56; one *almud* (1/12 fanega) of maize per week in 1618; two almudes (1/6 fanega) of maize per week in 1769. The standard ration in Desagüe labor was one almud of maize per week. The standard ration in hacienda labor was two almudes (*celemines*) per week.[59] In modern Mexico a minimum daily ration is one-half liter for the poor and three-fourths to $1\frac{1}{2}$ liters for the average. The fanega of 12 almudes is probably the equivalent of about 54 or 55 liters. Hence a weekly ration of one almud would be the equivalent of about 4.5 liters, or .65 liters per day. The hacienda ration would be twice that, or 1.3 liters per day. In the colonial period one fanega may have sufficed to feed one person from 50 to 75 days, or up to 100 days for the very poor. Each person then required some 4 to 7 fanegas per year. One almud per week would amount to $4\frac{1}{2}$ fanegas per year. An average tributary's family may have required from 10 to 20 fanegas per year, and colonial maize production and consumption in the Valley may have approximated 15 fanegas per tributary.[60]

These averages and abstractions, however, are several steps removed from the realities of life in a maize economy. The truth is that Indians ate well when maize was plentiful and starved when maize was scarce. Abundance and scarcity are measurable, in part, in the price history of maize, for the maize price was always a key statistic in the colonial period, an index to the cost of a whole range of articles—meat, lard, wheat, beans, and other foodstuffs in both Indian and Spanish markets.[61] Maize progressively increased in price, most notably in the sixteenth and early seventeenth centuries when the Indian population was in sharp decline and cultivation was decreasing. The official money equivalent in the commutation of maize tribute rose from two to nine reales per fanega during this period, and the increase equates approximately with the over-all price increase in the maize market to 1627. After 1627 the commutation figure remained at nine reales.[62]

A more radical series of price changes, and one of more immediate concern to colonial Indian peoples than the over-all increase, involved short-term fluctuations from place to place, from year to year, and from month to month. Within Mexico as a whole, one location was frequently well provided while another suffered scarcity. Between the tierra caliente and the Valley of Mexico quite different rhythms of maize supply prevailed. Within the Valley less extreme but still considerable differences may be found. Thus in 1580 the maize price in Tlalmanalco was eight reales per fanega, while across the Valley at Tacubaya the price stood at twelve reales.[63] Such differences in part reflected transportation costs, which in turn related to the availability of draft animals, wagons, human carriers, and canoes. Maize could be moved from outside the Valley to Mexico City only at a price approaching that of the original maize itself.[64]

Within any one year the supply was customarily highest and the price lowest during the late winter, spring, and early summer, following the harvest and marketing of the crop.[65] The opposite extreme was reached in the late summer, fall, and early winter, when that season's supplies were reduced and the new crop not yet harvested. In certain circumstances the shift could be radical and sudden, as in June 1641, when the price doubled within a single month.[66] But the normal seasonal price fluctuation was repeatedly upset by the variable climatic factors—especially temperature and rainfall—that affected maize growth. Under conditions of relatively primitive agricultural production and limited transport there necessarily existed a direct and absolute relationship between weather and supply, and between supply and price.[67] When a poor harvest in one year was followed by a good harvest in the next, the changes in price from January to December were especially pronounced. Thus in 1780, the price per fanega stood at 16 reales in May, rose to 19 reales in October, and fell to 9½ reales in December.[68] Table 23 indicates a normal or standard variation during the year 1784, when the price in Mexico City remained almost entirely within a 10–11 real range to mid-September, rose in October, November, and December to 15 reales, and then started to fall.

TABLE 23

Maize Prices, Alhóndiga, Mexico City, 1784

Period	Reales per fanega	Period	Reales per fanega
Jan. 1–Jan. 11	10	Aug. 16–Aug. 19	11
Jan. 12–Mar. 20	11	Aug. 20–Sept. 14	10
Mar. 21–Apr. 24	10	Sept. 15–Sept. 16	11
Apr. 25–May 9	11	Sept. 17–Oct. 4	12
May 10–May 24	12	Oct. 5–Oct. 23	13
May 25–May 31	11	Oct. 24–Nov. 4	14
June 1–June 4	10	Nov. 5–Dec. 15	15
June 5–July 28	11	Dec. 16–Dec. 30	14
July 28–Aug. 15	10	Dec. 31	13

SOURCE: AA, Pósito y alhóndiga, vol. 2, no. 3695, exp. 86, fols. 1v ff.

Indians understood a good year to be one of ample harvests and low prices, a year of sufficient rain in the absence of unseasonable frost. Flood, although occasionally severe, was a less important factor than drought in determining the character of the agricultural year, and its effects on prices were felt mainly in the city of Mexico.[69] Drought and frost had comparably disastrous effects upon maize supplies, but they were calamities of different sorts and the colonial responses to them were quite dissimilar. A single day without rain was of little importance, but a single day of frost might be ruinous. Drought required a long series of dry days and a low cumulative rainfall. A rainy season late in beginning might be followed by heavy summer rains, and the effect only a relatively inconsequential retardation of the entire growing season. But a dry April was a fearsome phenomenon, and a drought continuing into May and June became progressively more alarming, for such conditions seemed to portend a serious interruption in the seasonal processes on which maize and life depended.

To counteract these variants and to ensure a satisfactory growing season, pre-conquest Indian peoples had elaborated a formal ritual of propitiation, sacrifice, and offerings to the rain deity Tlaloc, and this ritual persisted to some extent after the conquest. The Christian response to drought, on the other hand, was the appeal to the Virgin of Los Remedios, the bearing of whose image to the metropolitan Cathedral in 1597, 1616, 1641, 1642, 1653, 1663, 1667, 1668, and many later years was a demonstration of the colonial faith in the efficacy of divine intervention.[70] The decision to bring Los Re-

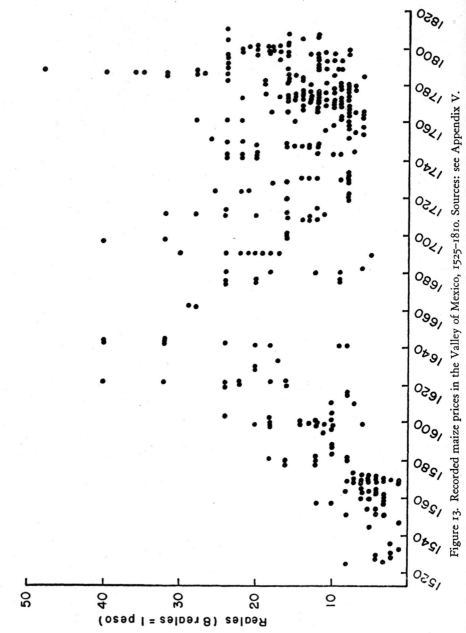

Figure 13. Recorded maize prices in the Valley of Mexico, 1525–1810. Sources: see Appendix V.

TABLE 24

Removals of Los Remedios to Mexico City, Seventeenth Century

Date	Cause	Date	Cause
1616, June 11	drought, famine, disease	1656, Nov. 12	flota peril
		1661, June 14–15	drought
1639, July 2	disease, famine, peril of flota	1663, June 17–29	drought, heat, disease
		1667, May 11	drought, disease
1641, June 13	drought, famine, disease	1668, June 13	drought, disease
		1678, May 30	drought, disease
1642, Aug. 31	drought, famine, disease, royal wars	1685 (1686?), June 2	drought, famine
1653, June 17	drought, heat, disease	1692, May 24	famine
1656, Sept. 16	English attacks in the Caribbean	1696, Aug. 28	peril of flota at Havana

SOURCES: The list follows the authority of Vetancurt, *Chronica*, pp. 130 ff., and Cabrera y Quintero, *Escudo de armas*, pp. 125 ff. There are some discrepancies between them; two dates are not listed in Vetancurt; two others are not listed in Cabrera y Quintero. Additional references are AC, XXI, 340, 344; XXXI, 343 ff.; XXXII, 225; XXXIII, 318, 358 ff.; AAMC, no. 14, pp. 672, 679; Guijo, *Diario*, I, 242, 459–60, 514–15; Robles, *Diario*, I, 36–40, 57, 239–41; II, 248; III, 13. There were also other ceremonies involving Los Remedios but without the removal of the image to the city, e.g., in 1618, 1621, 1623, and 1624 (AC, XXII, 136–37; XXIV, 78–79; XXV, 25, 145); all four of these were for drought.

medios was never lightly made. It was always preceded by serious consultation between secular and ecclesiastical authorities, and for the less important emergencies other images were appealed to. The image of Los Remedios customarily remained in the afflicted city until rains fell, a circumstance that undoubtedly reinforced confidence in the Virgin's powers.[71] She was brought, to be sure, to alleviate other crises as well as drought. But the connection between the appeal to Los Remedios and the delayed rainy season is suggested by the fact that of fifteen recorded appeals in the seventeenth century, ten occurred in the months of May and June (Table 24). In 1594 rain had still not fallen on July 25, and in many other years early rains were so sparse that drought conditions prevailed.[72] Nevertheless, because drought required time to achieve its full effects, it could in some measure be prepared for. Purchases could be made in advance or existing supplies could be husbanded. Moreover, drought was relative. It might damage the late sowings or the plants at high altitudes or those grown in tepetate or sandy soils, while the regular and most reliable stands were sufficiently mature to withstand the adverse conditions and to survive without injury.[73]

Frost, on the other hand, might destroy an entire crop in a single sudden catastrophe. Such frosts are known to have taken place in pre-conquest times, and in the colonial period they occurred with devastating effects in the years 1541, 1695, and 1785.[74] The gravest danger was not a spring frost, damaging as this might be, since new plantings might still be made in late spring with some chance of a successful harvest.[75] The great hazard was early autumn frost, striking at a time when all crops were planted and when no opportunity remained for new sowings. In this event there was little possibility of an adequate food supply until the next harvest, thirteen or fourteen months later. Thus the frost of September 13, 1695, created extreme shortages throughout the entire year of 1696.[76]

The most disastrous single event in the whole history of colonial maize agriculture was the exceptionally severe frost of August 27–28, 1785. To the one disaster of that night's temperature may be ascribed the great year of famine of 1786 and the highest maize prices of all time in the Valley. The rainy season ended early in 1785, and the frosts characteristic of November began instead in late August, before the crop had matured.[77] Shortages were already evident in September, when another frost occurred, and conditions of crisis appeared well before the time of normal harvest.[78] By October, in anticipation of the shortages to come, hacendados had closed their granaries and stopped selling. This artificially intensified the natural crisis, and consumers with money in hand were unable to buy.[79] The price rose to four pesos per fanega in September and October, to four and one-half and five pesos in November,[80] and to six pesos in the early weeks of 1786.[81] As shortages became acute, Indian trade declined and manufacture and labor deteriorated. The decline affected the supplies and raised the prices of meat, wheat, and beans. Tangential activities, such as pottery making and the collection and sale of zacate as fodder, also suffered. Indians ate roots and grass in 1786, and sold their animals and other possessions.[82] Disease attended the famine. With agriculture in collapse, native peoples wandered the countryside, died on the roads, and fled to Mexico City in search of livelihood and sustenance. Tribute collections were suspended.[83] Vast measures of relief were undertaken. A learned discussion took place on the merits of irrigation in maize agriculture, and efforts were made to encourage winter maize (planted between November and February, harvested in June) in the tierra caliente.[84] Pigs and other animals normally fed with maize were given other produce, and the government sought to reduce the number of coach animals in Mexico City in order to control the consumption of maize.[85]

It is interesting to observe that the image of Los Remedios had been brought to the city in 1785—not, however, to relieve the effects of the August frost, since all experience demonstrated that although its intervention might bring rain, it could not be expected to restore dead plants to life— but earlier, in May, and precisely to ensure the fall of spring rains.[86] The fact suggests a connection between drought and frost. A late rainy season always made early frost more dangerous, for the plants germinated late and were less developed when the season of frost began. Thus the growing season could be cut short at either end.[87] Rainfall and drought, high temperature and frost, could occur also in many other combinations. Hot weather could last into late October, as it did in the plague year of 1576.[88] The fall and winter months could be warm, as in 1769, when a "bad" year brought to an end a long series of "good" years.[89] To the multiple factors involved in successful maize agriculture, colonial peoples added others less relevant, such as solar eclipses and the phases of the moon.[90]

After maize, the most important cultivated product of colonial Indian agriculture was maguey (Nahuatl *metl*), a plant whose agricultural properties were quite different, but whose history is revealing in ways of its own.[91] Maguey is a perennial, requiring up to ten years to mature, and under proper treatment yielding juices for pulque (Nahuatl *octli*) during a period of a few months.[92] Its noteworthy feature is its capacity to remain alive with limited moisture. Indians planted maguey in rows and cultivated the plants in order to provide them with the most satisfactory conditions of growth.[93] But maguey depended much less than maize upon human cultivation. Its ability to withstand adverse conditions of soil, temperature, and rainfall in large part separated its history from the vagaries of climate and made it a permanent part of the agricultural scene regardless of weather. Maguey always survived the droughts and frosts that affected maize. Its reliability made it much less a factor in Indian augury, for what was never in doubt never aroused apprehensions. It grew, wild or cultivated, in nearly all soils. Even tepetate and tequisquitl supported maguey of mediocre quality, and artificial irrigation was quite unnecessary in the maguey fields. It served as an economical hedge against the loss of other crops, and ultimately as a major crop in its own right.[94]

In the preparation of pulque a hole was cut in the interior of the plant,

MAGUEY

from which the juice (*aguamiel*) was extracted. This aguamiel was cooked with roots or other adulterants to make the intoxicant liquor in various qualities and strength.[95] The aguamiel also yielded sweetening materials and was a common medicine or medicinal base in Indian society. Maguey leaves were used as fuel and as roofing material, and were the source of fibers used in sewing and in making cord, sandals, and cloth. The thorns were utilized as nails and as needles when extracted with the fiber attached.[96] A major obstacle in the program for exterminating Indian drunkenness was the circumstance that the maguey had so many uses and was so important a factor in Indian life.[97]

The area devoted to maguey underwent progressive expansion during the colonial period. In the sixteenth century maguey was reported principally in the northern communities: Tequixquiac, Acolman, Chiconauhtla, · Tecama, Ecatepec, Xaltocan, Teotihuacan, Tequicistlan, and Tepexpan.[98] The shifting emphasis from maize to maguey cultivation in the late sixteenth century may be documented in particular towns, such as Coatitlan, whose inhabitants were supplying taverns with pulque along the entire route to Mexico City by 1590. Men, women, and children in Coatitlan carried on a pulque commerce, and Indian maize plantings were abandoned for the more lucrative trade.[99] The new emphasis probably reflects both a declining moisture and an increased consumption. By late colonial times some of the most productive agricultural regions of the Valley were being devoted to maguey. The centers of pulque manufacture in the eighteenth century were still the dry northern areas, but large quantities were being produced also in the fertile zones around Cuauhtitlan and Otumba, and in the southern communities of Ixtapalapa, Chalco, Tlalmanalco, Amecameca, and Xochimilco.[100] Even in the north the area planted in maguey increased in the colonial period.[101]

Royal government, unable to prevent the manufacture of pulque, proceeded in the seventeenth century to license the shops (*pulquerías*) and to tax the producers. Native production for home use was not liable to such taxation, which was intended to apply to commercial sales and manufacture on a large scale.[102] But Indian producers habitually sought to supply the market while avoiding the tax, and a common feature of life in the pulque-producing communities of late colonial times was conflict between Indians and the Spanish tax collectors. An incident of 1770 in San Miguel Toltepec and adjacent towns of the Cuauhtitlan area illustrates the role of maguey and pulque at this period. Agriculturally, the Cuauhtitlan region was one of the most bountiful of the Valley: its soils were rich; its Río de Cuauhtitlan was, in the late eighteenth century, one of the few streams in the entire Valley that did not run dry in the winter. It was a region where the Indians' extensive plantings of maguey resulted not from aridity or impoverishment of soils but from the high profits to be derived from pulque sales. The markets of Cuauhtitlan were frequented by throngs of travelers, muleteers, merchants, and others on the route from Mexico City to the mining and ranching country of the north. The situation of Toltepec was one conducive to exploitation by Spanish officials, and the two most closely involved, the *asentista de pulques* and the alcalde mayor, conspired to exploit it. Together these two imposed an additional and illegal tax on pulque produced for family use. The asentista fixed a schedule of payments which were thereupon classified as tributes to be collected by an Indian deputy, and in 1769 the Spanish officials declared this tribute to be retroactive for a decade, holding a new Indian gobernador responsible for payments of arrears. The Indians could truthfully argue that they were being illegally taxed. The Spaniards, for their part, could assert that the Indians had been illegally making pulque under the pretense that it was for home use and covertly selling it in Toltepec and Cuauhtitlan. The native peoples resisted in a unified demonstration of community solidarity. A Spanish commission visited Toltepec to reach a settlement and found the town abandoned, with all its houses shut. The gobernador was imprisoned and then released by viceregal order. When the Spanish officials sought to return they were driven from the town by a determined band of Indian women, who brandished sticks, threw stones, and screamed abuse.[103]

Many other plants besides maize and maguey were raised in colonial Indian agriculture. Among the cultivated foodstuffs were American beans (*frijoles*); *chía* (a salvia, perhaps best translated as sage); *huauhtli* (an amaranth); *ají* (chile); squashes (*calabazas*); and tomatoes (Nahuatl *tomatl,* from which the English word derives).[104] Frijoles were in some instances retained as a tribute item in the sixteenth century. Chía and huauhtli, on the other hand, appear not to have appealed to Spaniards either as food or as articles of tribute or commerce. Judging simply by the number of references, we may infer that chía and huauhtli likewise came to be of less importance to Indians during the colonial period.[105] *Habas,* the traditional beans of Europe, were among the few Spanish horticultural introductions adopted by Indians for their own use. Others, in various degrees, were cabbages, artichokes, lettuce, and radishes.[106] *Tunas* (prickly pears) were cultivated in the Valley for fruit. In the barrio of San Agustín in Xochimilco Indians were caring for grape arbors by 1579.[107] In the eighteenth century a principal industry of Tulyahualco and Ixtayopa, near Xochimilco, was the production of olives.[108] Reed-like grasses (zacate) were grown in the shallow lakes as animal fodder.[109] In addition to these products grown for sustenance or market, a long list of native fruits and medicinal plants might be compiled.[110]

Indian horticulture and the cultivation of marketable foodstuffs reached their most intensive form on the fresh-water lakeshore, where chinampa agriculture was the common mode of production. Chinampas (or *camellones,* as they were generally known to Spaniards to the eighteenth century)[111] were segments of land artificially constructed in the lakes or canals and irrigated by the surrounding waters. The smallest were about five by fifty feet, the largest many times that size.[112] Whether they were ever literally "floating gardens" is an unresolved question. Despite numerous colonial references to movable gardens floating on the water, most modern students have rejected the possibility of the floating chinampa.[113] In any case, the non-floating chinampa was probably the normal type. Chinampas were originally established in all the lakes of the Valley, including the salt lakes of Zumpango and Xaltocan, and archaeological evidence appears to indicate their considerable antiquity in Lake Texcoco.[114] Chinampas could be effectively maintained in these lakes for the reason that the waters, though saline, were not saturated and could therefore be made to leach and purify a chinampa soil. But with the receding waters, this could no longer be done in a stationary chinampa. An initial corrective step in the event of water reduction was the lowering of the chinampa's top surface to achieve a moisture content sufficient to prevent impregnation by salts.[115] But when the water level fell radically the only recourse was abandonment of the chinampa. Occasional chinampas were still to be found in the salt-water lakes in colonial times—indeed chinampas have not been wholly unknown in the remains of Lake Texcoco in the twentieth century[116]—but the chinampa area came to be confined for the most part to the fresh southern waters. Most colonial references are to chinampas in the vicinity of Mexico City and the south, and it is probably true that even before the conquest the principal chinampa areas were confined to Lakes Xochimilco and Chalco.[117]

At the end of the colonial period the major chinampa region extended from Santa Ana, Ixtacalco, and San Juanico, south of the city, to Mexicalzingo and Xochimilco, and this is the same general area in which chinampas survived into the twentieth century.[118]

Chinampas yielded rich harvests because of highly intensive techniques of cultivation. These included fertilization with aquatic plants, regular irrigation, transplantation of the young plants from nursery beds (*almácigos*) (this allowed several crops per year), replenishment and replacement of soils, and mulching with cabbage or other leaves.[119] Alzate's eighteenth-century descriptions of this agriculture demonstrate the full repertory of chinampa techniques, and one may suppose, though the documentation is imperfect, that these same practices were uninterrupted from the period prior to the conquest. Colonial chinampa produce included turnips, onions, carrots, lettuce, cabbage, chiles, chia, squash, tomatoes, edible greens called *quilites,* and maize in large quantities.[120] The schedules were fixed and specialized in a series of activities continuing through the winter: chiles were planted in late September, tomatoes in October, squash in February. Chinampa maize, like many other plants, was propagated in the nurseries and later transplanted. We have no information on its yield, other than a statement of the sixteenth century that chinampas of 1 by 10 brazas produced one fanega of maize.[121]

More effectively than any agricultural methods that Spaniards could devise, the chinampa combined intensity of cultivation with Indian control over production and supply. Chinampas were among the most conservative and durable types of Indian agricultural holdings, and their persistence through the colonial period may be largely attributed to the urban market for vegetable foodstuffs. Colonial conditions favored the preservation of this agriculture in an unchanged state. Although the chinampa area was progressively reduced, Spaniards never succeeded in intruding into the zone of concentration south of the city. The low incidence of Spanish settlement, ethnic mixture, and hacienda foundation in the Xochimilco jurisdiction has been noted above, and the fact surely implies a Spanish willingness to retain chinampa agriculture as an Indian specialty.

In all non-chinampa areas, however, a continuous expansion of Spanish agricultural institutions and their progressive domination over Indian modes of production took place. Traditional Indian agriculture persisted insofar as communities were able to retain land, but no specific area preserved this agriculture as the southern lake area preserved the chinampas. In non-chinampa communities the lands that Indians regarded as most productive were precisely the lands that appealed to Spaniards, and Spanish occupation of such lands underlay the most important changes affecting Indian production. We have considered above the processes of Spanish land pre-emption with regard to techniques of acquisition and transfers of titles. In relation to agriculture the key stages of land acquisition and utilization were the development of Spanish wheat farms (*labores de pan*), commercial maize farming, and the multiple-product hacienda.

The Spanish farms of the sixteenth century, based on viceregal grants and repartimiento labor, provided Indians with their earliest experience in Spanish farming schedules and methods of cultivation. Almost exclusively, the early farms were producers of wheat. Our records indicate a variety of methods, including a type of planting resembling that used for maize, with several grains per hill.[122] The many references to weeding and cultivating in the wheat fields of the sixteenth century suggest a furrow or hill sowing rather than a broadcast sowing (although hand cultivation of wheat is not irreconcilable with broadcast sowing), and this may represent the influence of maize plantation methods, or a form of the furrow technique (*a chorrillo*) still practiced in Spain.[123] In the sixteenth century Spanish wheat farmers depended mainly on natural rainfall with planting in the spring and harvesting in November or December, a schedule approximating that of maize.[124] Irrigated wheat, which normally required planting in the fall and harvesting in May or June,[125] was not common in the sixteenth-century Valley. It was adopted sufficiently to affect repartimiento quotas only in the 1580's and after, a fact that may be related both to the decrease in moisture and to the transition to large-scale production.[126] In the early seventeenth century, with the advance of irrigation in wheat farming, Indian labor was required particularly at the two harvest times, May–June and November–December, and at periods of weeding and cultivation for the non-irrigated wheat, normally June or July.[127]

On their own land, Indians preferred maize and tended to resist Spanish efforts to promote native wheat cultivation independently of the Spanish farms.[128] Indian traditions, the reluctance to adopt new processes, the relatively smaller yield and higher price of wheat, and the fact that Indian wheat production was subject to tithe whereas maize production was not— all these may have operated to induce Indians to reject wheat as a staple grain for their own use. In some instances Indian communities were required to sow wheat for tribute, and at times caciques and principales, imitating Spaniards, required community service in wheat cultivation. Occasionally Indians also planted wheat for sale to Spaniards and established mills and ovens for the Spanish bread market.[129] But for most Indians wheat appears to have been associated directly with Spanish intrusion and domination. The native rejection of wheat provided some justification for the establishment of farms by Spaniards, and it surely accelerated their acquisition of land. Although each Indian laborer in repartimiento was required to serve only a few weeks each year in the sixteenth-century wheat farms, these farms marked the beginnings of a Spanish institution that was ultimately to control agricultural supply and to intrude seriously upon Indian production.

The transition to large-scale enterprise in wheat production occurred in the late sixteenth century, and a fairly exact measurement of it between the years 1563 and 1602 can be made. In 1563 the farms receiving repartimiento labor numbered 114 and 4,482 fanegas of wheat were planted. The records of the repartimiento of 1563 indicate that small farmers, those planting under 20 fanegas, numbered 26 and accounted for 23 per cent of the farms and 5 per cent of the grain. Farms of moderate size, sowing 20 to 87 fanegas, numbered 81 and accounted for 71 per cent of the farms and 73 per cent of the grain. Large farms, planting 100 to 215 fanegas, numbered 7 and accounted for 6 per cent of the farms and 22 per cent of the grain.[130] The official fanega de sembradura for wheat was ⅟₆₉ of a caballería, or the approximate equivalent of 1.5 acres. Thus the official estimate for wheat sowing was almost exactly one bushel per acre.[131] It would be a mistake, of course, to assume that this ratio was uniformly achieved in practice. But if we take it as an approximation of the cultivated land in the repartimiento farms of 1563, we may suppose the small farms to have planted less than 30 acres, the farms of medium size from 30 to 130 acres, and the large farms from 150 to about 325 acres.

These figures may be contrasted with figures relating to the Tepozotlan repartimiento jurisdiction in 1602. If we may regard this jurisdiction as typical, the data indicate a radical change in size and production during the late sixteenth century. The Tepozotlan repartimiento of 1602 contained 90 farms with plantings of 13,579 fanegas of wheat, or about three times the plantings of the 114 farms of 1563. Thus the total amount of wheat production vastly increased. But the increase was accounted for mainly by the large farms. In 1602 plantings over 100 fanegas accounted for more than 90 per cent of the grain, whereas in 1563 they had accounted for less than 25 per cent. The majority of the wheat farms of 1602 exceeded 150 acres, and the largest of the jurisdiction, planting 400 fanegas, may be estimated as a farm of some 600 acres.[132]

Wheat was the principal crop of the Tepozotlan repartimiento jurisdiction in 1602. Agricultural repartimientos had been established almost wholly for wheat, and they were officially known as repartimientos for wheat cultivation (*beneficio de las sementeras de trigo*) or for wheat bread (*pan de trigos*).[133] Viceregal orders sometimes required jueces repartidores to confine their allotments absolutely to the wheat farmers.[134] Only very occasionally were the repartimientos referred to as drafts "for wheat and maize."[135] We are able to specify the amounts of various grains planted in 94 farms of the Tepozotlan repartimiento of 1602, for the records indicate that 13,579 fanegas of wheat, 1,952 fanegas of barley, and only 138 fanegas of maize were sown. The average plantings per farm were 144 fanegas for wheat, 20 fanegas for barley, and 1.5 fanegas for maize. It is evident from these figures, and it is stated in the records explicitly, that all the maize and a part of the barley were grown for the use of the hacienda itself rather than as a commercial crop for sale.[136] We lack comparable figures for the various grains in the other agricultural repartimientos of the early seventeenth century, though it is known that the total number of fanegas sown in 1602 amounted to 11,124 in the Tacubaya repartimiento and 16,091 in the Chalco repartimiento.[137] It seems probable that the number of farms increased about four times and the amount of grain about twelve times between 1563 and 1602. In any case, there can be no doubt that the established Spanish agricultural institution in the early seventeenth century was the wheat-producing hacienda, raising maize in very small quantities, and barley in somewhat larger quantities, as fodder for its animals or food for its workers.

The next significant step was the development of a class of Spanish enterprises dedicated to the production of maize on a large scale, with extreme consequences for Indian maize cultivation. In the early colonial period maize had been produced entirely by traditional Indian methods, and it was the chief commodity of tribute. Between harvest and consumption, supplies fell under the control of encomenderos, corregidores, purchasers of royal tribute maize, and private dealers. Opportunities for private speculation in maize were thus present from an early date for certain classes of

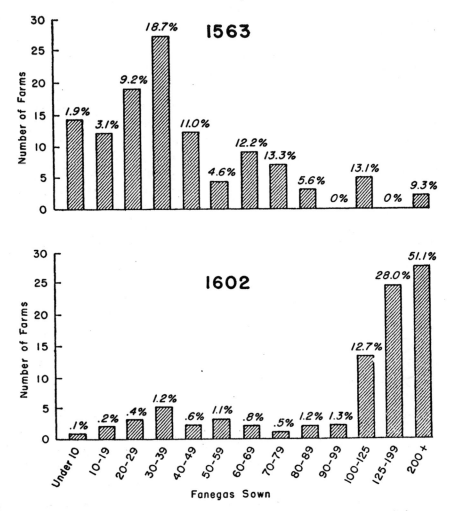

Figure 14. Sizes of wheat farms in 1563 and 1602. The shift from the small farm to the large hacienda in wheat production was accomplished during the forty years 1563–1602. Percentages indicate the portion of the total planting sown on the farms in each category. Sources: AGN, Mercedes, vol. 7, fols. 217v ff.; Tierras, vol. 70, exp. 8, fols. 17r–18r.

Spaniards. In the middle and late sixteenth century Indian maize lands came increasingly into Spanish hands, and Indian labor was diverted to a variety of new activities. Crisis in the traditional Indian maize economy was first noted during the epidemic of the 1540's, when the shortages caused by the epidemic were intensified and exploited by Spanish speculators. Viceregal action took two forms: prohibition of maize purchase for resale, and encouragement of additional Indian maize plantations in the towns. Viceregal orders for the expansion of Indian plantings were characteristic of the 1550's and after. Regulations became progressively more stringent. They included the commutations of multiple tributes to maize tributes; the promotion of maize cultivation on community lands and of the storage of maize in the Indian towns for future sale; and finally (1577) the requirement that each tributary cultivate ten varas of land.[188] The restrictions on private Spanish maize purchases from Indians were repeated. Spaniards were forbidden to buy in the Indians' houses or anywhere save in the markets, and purchases for resale had to be recorded before judges.[139] The viceregal efforts to make adjustments in the maize economy thus remained until the late 1570's within the limits of individual or communal Indian production. But with the failure of these efforts, maize joined wheat in the Spanish-owned commercial haciendas, now not simply as an adjunct of hacienda operation for fodder or local sustenance, but as a separate article of commerce.

The transition to commercial production of maize was accomplished in the fifty years between 1580 and 1630. In a revealing statement of 1630, one of the Spanish councilors of Mexico City observed that fifty years earlier the city had been supplied by Indians, either by direct sales or by tribute maize, whereas in 1630 Indian maize agriculture had been reduced to the status of local subsistence and the city was being supplied by "wealthy Spaniards."[140] By this date the hacienda as a maize producer had every advantage over the Indian community. It possessed lands for extensive production and facilities for storage and transportation already developed for wheat. The hacendados controlled Indian labor. They could profitably undersell small producers in bulk transactions or hoard supplies for a seller's market. They could offset the effects of variation in price by paying laborers in money when the price of maize was high or alternatively in maize when the price was low—a practice that transferred the burden of price fluctuation to the Indian workers.[141] Hacendados in the first half of the seventeenth

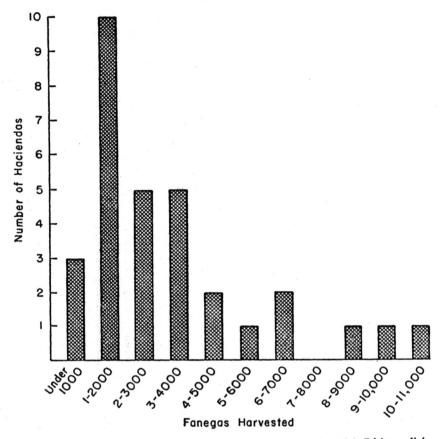

Figure 15. Maize production in 31 Chalco haciendas, 1773. Source: AA, Pósito y alhóndiga, vol. 2, no. 3695, exp. 65, fol. 13r–13v.

century were in a position to speculate heavily in the city's maize market, and they incurred the persistent wrath of civil authorities for their manipulations of price and supply.[142] They were continually active throughout the seventeenth and eighteenth centuries, particularly in periods of shortage. It is significant that following the acute shortages of 1692, which resulted in a popular uprising in the city, maize was immediately made available from the hacendados' stores.[148] It is also significant that before 1769, when harvests were abundant and prices low, hacendados were compelled to limit the areas under cultivation, and in some instances to abandon their operations altogether. They were saved by the droughts, frosts, shortages, and other troubles of 1769 and after.[144]

The commercial maize hacienda reached its most highly developed form in Chalco province, where conditions of soil and climate were particularly favorable.[145] Individual production figures for 31 Chalco haciendas, compiled in 1773, may serve as an index to the relative size of individual operations (Figure 15). The average yield per hacienda in 1773 was about 3,000 fanegas, or 4,500 bushels. The largest hacienda yielded 10,000 fanegas, or 15,000 bushels. Supposing a yield of between 15 and 30 bushels per acre, we may conjecture that the average Chalco hacienda planted 500 to 1,000 acres.[146]

Hacienda maize fields were sometimes prepared during the autumn and planted so that germination would start with the first spring rains. More often plowing took place in the spring and planting after the first two or three showers. A third planting, called *tardía,* might also be made when the ground was quite wet and when the danger of spring frosts was past. But apart from these variations, commercial maize was produced in a standard and fairly uniform schedule of operations: planting in March, April, or May; the first "labor" in May or June, with one Indian peón running the plow close to the plants while another heaped soil about the hills; the second "labor" in June or July, a repetition of the same process with higher mounds to support the plants; and a third cultivation with plow and a kind of moldboard called *cajón,* which raised a ridge of low earth along the row. Some haciendas employed a final plowing operation (*aporque*) with further mounding of the earth. Maize was harvested in December or January, by rows of basket-carrying peones who stripped the ears from the stalks.[147] This hacienda procedure was partially and gradually adopted by Indian communities in the plantings on community lands. Indian cofradías came to employ the same practices, with sowing, first and second "labores," the *cajonear,* mounding, harvest, and the gathering of stalks for fodder.[148]

Chalco hacienda maize was marketed almost entirely in Mexico City. Maize might be sold wholesale to a middleman or carrier (*trajinero*) who transported it to the city and disposed of it either in the city's storehouse and official grain market (*pósito* or *alhóndiga*) or to individual purchasers. Alternatively, an employed agent of the hacendado might perform the trajinero function, or a single trajinero might be the contractual agent for a number of haciendas. In each case the produce was transported first from the hacienda to one of the embarkation docks on the eastern or southern shores of Lake Chalco, where it was received by the embarkation administrator, and then moved by Indian canoe to the city markets. Most single canoes carried up to 65 or 70 fanegas of maize. The extent of the traffic always depended upon supply and price and the condition of the markets in the city.[149] Some 5,000 fanegas per week were sent in the harvest season in the late seventeenth century.[150] The figure for 1709 was 97,330 fanegas in 1,419 canoes. The figure for 1710 was 155,120 in 3,463 canoes.[151] In 1741, 113,701 fanegas were harvested from 57 Chalco haciendas. A harvest of 250,000 fanegas from 46 Chalco haciendas was reported as an average yield in the middle eighteenth century. In 1773, 91,200 fanegas from 36 Chalco haciendas, plus an additional amount by tenants to make 121,000 fanegas, were harvested.[152]

Even in the haciendas of Chalco some 60,000 fanegas of wheat were raised annually in the eighteenth century.[153] But outside Chalco province typical haciendas depended much less on maize and much more on diversified produce: wheat, barley, frijoles, straw, and other crops, as well as sheep, cattle, horses, and mules. The Cuauhtitlan, Coyoacan, and Otumba jurisdictions were major areas for wheat in the eighteenth century. Barley was raised principally in the jurisdictions of Coatepec, Cuauhtitlan, Tacuba, Teotihuacan, Otumba, and Citlaltepec. Pigs, cattle, and other animals came to be concentrated in the eastern part of the Valley, in Coatepec, Texcoco, and Otumba.[154] Hacendados in the central portions of the Valley characteristically depended on the production of wheat and adjusted lesser sowings of maize to the relative or expected prices.[155] Late colonial hacendados also capitalized heavily on the pulque market, competing directly and successfully with Indian private and community production. In the Zumpango area in the eighteenth century pulque production increased while sheepherding decreased.[156] In the late colonial period, a rancho such as San Nicolás Tlalticahuacan, in the rich maguey region near Otumba, regularly disposed of some fifty or sixty *cubos* of pulque per week, continuously through the year. The Jesuit hacienda of San Xavier, which overlapped the Valley of Mexico in the north, was primarily and essentially a hacienda for pulque. In the single year of 1770 San Xavier sold some 20,000 cargas (3,000 to 3,500 tons) of pulque, to earn over 40,000 pesos, one of the largest ha-

TABLE 25
Schedules in Hacienda Agriculture

Month	Regular Maize	Irrigated Maize	Regular Wheat	Irrigated Wheat	Regular Barley	Irrigated Barley	Beans (Frijoles)
January	harvesting, storing		harvesting, winnowing	irrigating	harvesting	irrigating	
February	harvesting, storing		winnowing	irrigating		harvesting	
March		plowing, sowing	plowing	irrigating		harvesting	
April	plowing, sowing	sowing	plowing, sowing	harvesting	plowing, sowing	harvesting	
May	sowing, first labor	weeding, irrigating	sowing	harvesting	sowing		
June	first labor, second labor	weeding, irrigating	sowing, weeding	winnowing	sowing, weeding		sowing
July	second labor		weeding	winnowing	weeding		sowing
August	other labores, mounding						
September	mounding			plowing		plowing	
October	guarding	harvesting	harvesting	sowing	harvesting	sowing, irrigating	harvesting
November	guarding, harvesting	harvesting	harvesting	sowing	harvesting	sowing, irrigating	harvesting
December	harvesting		harvesting	irrigating	harvesting	sowing, irrigating	

cienda incomes of all central Mexico. Haciendas were eminently suited for the commercial production of maguey, for they could afford extensive plantings, of which only a small fraction was productive at one time.[157]

A series of remarkable letters written between 1775 and 1785 by the administrator of the Hacienda de Molino de Flores near Texcoco to the hacienda owner in Mexico City describes more fully than any other known documents the daily life and economy of the late colonial hacienda. The letters effectively demonstrate that the hacienda was not maintained simply as a luxury estate for prestige in landholding, or in gentlemanly disregard of profit and loss. Molino de Flores concentrated on wheat, maize, and barley. The administrator recorded his daily preoccupation with weather, prices, Indian labor, and the detailed schedule of agricultural production. His constant concern was whether to sell his produce at existing prices or to hold it in expectation of higher profits in the future, and he and the hacendado sometimes argued over the decision to sell immediately or later. Maize and wheat supplies suffered weekly depletion in the payments of rations to workers, a drain necessarily calculated in the estimates of future supplies and the decisions for retention or sale. Grain sometimes had to be sold in order to pay the wages of the peones. The administrator kept close watch over neighboring haciendas, observing when and what they planted, how they were affected by frosts and droughts, and what their crop yields were, for all this determined his competitive success or failure. Favorable rains and temperatures he attributed to the *bondad de Dios*; all aberrations of weather were reported with alarm. Insofar as possible wheat and maize were irrigated in time of need. The administrator expressed apprehension in 1776 when the neighboring hacienda of Chapingo was sold, for the boundary between the two was indefinite and the property sale affected the use of the unsurveyed monte by Indian employees. The administrator lacked knowledge of titles to the monte, either by one party or by the other.[158]

Figure 16 illustrates in more concrete form the economy of a late colonial hacienda, that of Santa Ana Aragón in the irrigated lowland northeast of Tlatelolco. The lightly shaded area indicates expenses in addition to peón labor and the heavily shaded area shows financial losses of the hacienda as a whole. Throughout the whole period the correlation between total expenditures and peones' wages is uniformly evident. Wages accounted for considerably more than half the hacienda's weekly costs. In addition to the peones Santa Ana regularly hired a mulekeeper at 2 reales per day; a cattle

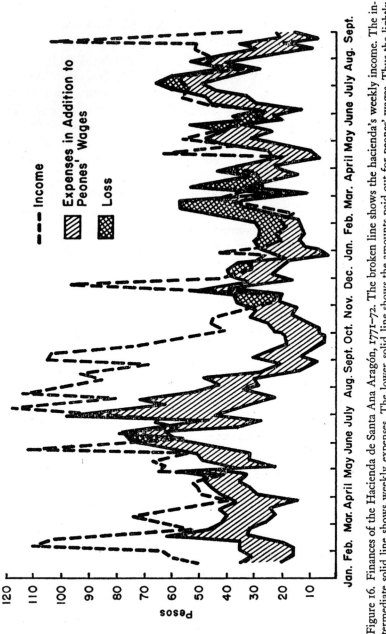

Jan. Feb. Mar. April May June July Aug. Sept. Oct. Nov. Dec. Jan. Feb. Mar. April May June July Aug. Sept.

– – Income

▨ Expenses in Addition to
   Peones' Wages

▩ Loss

Figure 16. Finances of the Hacienda de Santa Ana Aragón, *1771–72.* The broken line shows the hacienda's weekly income. The intermediate solid line shows weekly expenses. The lower solid line shows the amounts paid out for peones' wages. Thus the lightly shaded area shows expenses in addition to peón labor and the heavily shaded area indicates financial losses. Source: AGN, Tierras, vol. 991, exp. 4, fols. 1r ff.

guard (*vaquero*) at 1½ reales per day; a shepherd at one real per day; a watchman for the fields (*milpero*) at one peso and 6 reales per week; a mayordomo at 3 pesos per week; a first assistant at 3 pesos per week; and a herdsman for colts (*potrero*) at 3 pesos per week. The Indian workers earned 2 reales per day in irregular, seasonal labor. The hacienda hired workers in the largest numbers from April through August, but its hiring pattern was most irregular, being governed by special crops, the condition of its irrigation and drainage ditches, ecclesiastical festivals, and many other particulars. Employment sharply declined during the Easter and Christmas weeks. It rose to its highest points in May, June, and July of both years for plowing and the several labores, for the planting of maize, for the harvesting of barley, and for the cleaning of the ditches. In this hacienda the agricultural season for barley dominated the processes of hiring and discharge more than did the season for maize or beans or wheat, and the patterns were further complicated since both irrigated and non-irrigated barley was grown. Maize and bean plantings in May and June and the cultivation of these in July combined with the barley labors to make the summer months a season of intense activity. The sharp and irregular pattern of the hacienda's profits resulted mainly from the sale of its agricultural produce and the sale and rental of animals. In late June 1771, the hacienda had to purchase Toluca maize to feed its workers. In the first eight months of 1771 the hacienda recorded a net gain of 736 pesos. In the first eight months of 1772 it failed to make a profit, its net loss amounting to 43 pesos. The difference was due less to the seasonal variation in agricultural produce than to irregular transactions in animals.[159]

In summary, the haciendas occupied a special position among Spanish institutions affecting Indian agriculture and Indian life. Other exploitative Spanish institutions of the colony—encomienda, royal tribute, various "servicios," ecclesiastical payments—were expressed as direct exactions in agricultural goods or their money equivalents. The hacienda made no such exactions. In a more reliable and regular way than repartimiento it provided the Indian agricultural laborer with maize and money in exchange for work. The hacienda developed in a period of economic crisis, when Indian agriculture could no longer support the encomenderos or the urban markets or the "voluntary" ecclesiastical contributions. Whereas encomienda had continued to depend, while it could, on production by the Indian towns, the hacienda depended on the deterioration of native agriculture and supply. To an Indian society that had lost its surplus goods and lands and energies the hacienda offered food and agricultural jobs and wages. The "good" times of Indian agriculture might be times of hardship for the haciendas, for the well-filled hacienda granary was most effective under the prospect of rising prices. On the other hand, the critical years for Indian agriculture were periods of relative prosperity for the haciendas, which extended their controls from Spanish markets to Indian markets, notably in maize and pulque, displacing Indian supplies and continuously reducing Indian agriculture.

CHAPTER XII

Production and Exchange

It was not the intention of Spaniards to interfere in the more prosaic aspects of native commodity production. Indian housing, clothing, and food, the omnipresent Indian goods, the *metates* and *petates* for which Spaniards had small use, the exchange of simple materials in cheap markets, all were features of a native substratum beneath the notice of colonists. However disruptive Spanish demands may have been in other respects, they required no fundamental transformations in these areas of native economy. No secular Spanish body dedicated itself to the eradication of Indian crafts. No missionaries undertook to teach Indians new ways to fashion pottery. The point is obvious, but it explains why so much that was openly and conspicuously "Indian" was suffered to remain.

The basic materials of Indian house construction—stone, lime, adobes, straw, wooden poles, wooden slabs—continued unchanged through the colonial period. Only caciques and principales imitated Spanish styles in the building of houses.[1] The common macegual residence remained a one-room, rectangular hut with a small open doorway. Walls were of stone, or of adobe on low stone foundations. The roofs were usually low and flat, of slab shingles or straw laid on horizontal poles.[2]

Poles, wooden slabs, thatch, and soil for adobes were almost universally accessible in the Valley of Mexico. Towns lacking montes were always able to procure these materials from other communities.[3] Stone was less common but still widely distributed.[4] Lakeshore towns that lacked stone, such as Mexicalzingo, could bring it in canoes from outside or take it from abandoned pre-conquest buildings.[5] A full stone construction, however, required lime for mortar, and this was not so readily available. A limestone quarry was discovered in Xochimilco about 1550, but for the most part natural limestone was rare in the southern part of the Valley.[6] Communities such as Coatepec, Chimalhuacan, Chicoloapa, and Culhuacan lacked lime entirely, and either purchased it elsewhere or depended on adobe construction.[7] Lime was produced principally in the northern towns —Zumpango, Citlaltepec, Xaltocan, Hueypoxtla, and Tequixquiac—and its manufacture and sale offered a source of commercial profit to communities appropriately situated for it.[8] In Hueypoxtla the burning of limestone became a major industry. Spanish lime merchants carried on an active wagon commerce in the sixteenth century between Mexico City and the Indians of Hueypoxtla. Inhabitants of nearby towns such as Xilotzingo bought stone from Hueypoxtla, burned it, and sold the lime. The process required kilns and wood fuel, and some technical skills. The industry was brisk but not of long duration, especially as it applied to the major market in the Spanish capital, for most of the lime for Mexico City in the later colonial period was obtained from the Tula area farther north.[9]

The houses of maceguales were primarily places for eating and sleeping. Throughout the colonial period Indian peoples slept without beds or hammocks and ate without chairs or tables. They slept on petates or mats, the weaving of which was another important industry of Xaltocan, Zumpango, Citlaltepec, and many other lakeshore towns where the reeds (*tule*) were found.[10] Domestic food preparation required the metate (*metlatl*) or grinding-stone for maize, the comal (*comalli*) on which tortillas were cooked, the stone mortar (*molcajete*) for grinding, and earthen jars and pots for cooking and storage. These, with the petates, small Christian images, and a few other objects such as baskets and brooms, were the principal furnishings, often the only furnishings, of macegual homes.[11] Illumination at night was provided either by tallow candles, a European introduction of the sixteenth century, or by torches of pine knots (ocotl) in the traditional Indian manner.[12] Cooking fires were made with small sticks, leaves, maize stalks, zacate, or dry cactus. The houses did not provide for air circulation and were characteristically filled with smoke.[13]

The major Indian articles of dress introduced in the post-conquest period were shirts, trousers, and hats. The loincloth (*maxtlatl*), which with the cape or mantle (*ayatl, tilmatl, tilma*) formed the standard macegual male attire prior to the conquest, was generally abandoned in favor of trousers during the sixteenth century, probably under clerical persuasion and for reasons of decency. The cape was retained as an article of male dress.

Women's clothing continued to consist of the cape, the long skirt, and the outer shirt (*huipilli, huipil*) extending to the knee.[14] Some Indian men adopted hats in the sixteenth century, and some wore sandals.[15] Women commonly wore neither. Sandals (Nahuatl *cactli,* the modern term *huarache* being of uncertain origin) had been known before the conquest, but their use became more widespread.[16] Spanish styles (though not Spanish cloth) were legalized for Indians in the late sixteenth century but were never fully adopted.[17] Most of the changes in dress occurred in the sixteenth century, after which Indian clothing remained little altered to the end of colonial times.[18]

The basic textiles for Indian clothing were woven of maguey fiber, cotton, or wool. Of these wool was a colonial introduction, and cotton could not be raised in the climate of the Valley of Mexico. Maguey cloth, called *nequen* or *henequen* (a Taino word) by Spaniards, had been widely used in the Valley in the pre-conquest period. It was still in use during the sixteenth century and after,[19] but it was in large part displaced by cotton.[20] Cotton cloth also had been known and used in the Valley in the pre-conquest period, both as a tribute item received from afar and as a product locally woven from imported raw cotton. In the sixteenth century cotton from the tierra caliente to the east or south was brought to the Valley's markets and made into huipiles and mantles that could be worn, sold, or paid as tribute.[21] Mantles were of a variety of sizes, colors, and qualities.[22] To some extent the ceremonial mantles of aboriginal society were retained for use on formal occasions in the colony, as in the viceregal reception of 1640, when four hundred Indian participants performed native dances with *tilmas de gala* and feather decorations.[23] *Tochomitl,* a fabric of rabbit fur, also continued to have a decorative function in elaborate dress.[24] The making of cloth was primarily though not exclusively a woman's occupation, performed with the whorl spindle and belt loom.[25] Indians were introduced to the techniques of woolen manufacture in the obrajes, but they seem to have used wool mainly for mantles.[26] Mantles described in the sixteenth century as "large, gala, and of colored woolen cloth" may have been the forerunners of the later *serapes.*[27]

Indian foods were not confined to agricultural produce. Indeed, few areas of the whole of America were so richly supplied with non-agricultural food resources as the Valley of Mexico, and the native diet in the colonial period continued to be extremely varied. Salt extraction, fishing, hunting, and animal husbandry were activities through which agricultural diets were regularly supplemented, and each of these had its character and history.

The salt industry depended on the natural brines of the northern lakes and of Lake Texcoco, which contained mostly common salt (sodium chloride) and soda ash (sodium carbonate).[28] Supplied by streams and runoffs, without outlets, these lakes received a constant influx of minerals. So far as is known, colonial Indians did not obtain salt directly from the lake waters, but always from the surrounding soils where salts accumulated in higher concentrations than when in solution. Thus salt extraction was especially characteristic of dry seasons and periods of low water levels.[29] The process entailed the washing of soils to obtain concentrated solutions and the evaporation of these by artificial heat to obtain residue salts. Humboldt, who witnessed the extraction of salt on the shore of Lake Texcoco in the late colonial period, observed that technological change from pre-Spanish times had taken place only in the substitution of copper for earthenware containers.[30] Unsystematic commentaries on salt manufacture in the sixteenth century at least partially confirm this judgment, for they indicate the use of impregnated earth, washing in water, heating and distillation, and the final extraction of the salt.[31] So far as we know, the modern processes of solar evaporation were not employed in the colonial period. The end product was a block of various dry dark salts, shaped into a round loaf about the size of a large loaf of wheat bread. These loaves were trade objects over a fairly wide area in the sixteenth century and were the source of some substantial Indian fortunes.[32]

Salt manufacture is reported as an Indian industry in Mexicalzingo, Coyoacan, Mixcoac, Huitzilopochco, Guadalupe, Ixtapalapa, Ecatepec, and many other lake towns.[33] Towns on higher ground set back from the lakes obtained salt by trade from towns more advantageously situated.[34] All Indians, whatever their location, seem to have regarded salt as a necessity, and they consumed it in prodigious quantities. Food rations in Desagüe labor, reflecting native tastes, included three standard items, maize, chile, and salt, all others being described as "extraordinary rations."[35] Spaniards disdained this salt as an article for their own diet, holding it to be noxious and unhealthy, and preferred the produce of more salubrious deposits. They found the native material useful, however, for curing hams and for the salting of other meat, and Indians were therefore able to sell it in Spanish markets as well as in their own.[36]

Tequisquitl soils were also used by Indians for the making of soap, presumably for a Spanish market. Indians themselves did not use soap, at least in large quantities, for they preferred the native *temazcal* or sweat house for bathing, and *amoli* (*amol*) or other natural materials for the washing of clothing.[37] The tequisquitl soils of the Texcoco region were described in the sixteenth century, from a Spanish point of view, as fit only for the manufacture of soap, and in Xaltocan the extraction of tequisquitl for this purpose became an important Indian industry. Most of the communities subject to Xaltocan were described as profitably engaged in soap manufacture by 1599.[38] The use of tequisquitl as a dye is also recorded from the sixteenth century, again notably in the Xaltocan region. Santa María Tenamitlan, near Xaltocan, was an Indian weaving and cloth-making community where colored dyes were applied to fabrics.[39]

The only other recorded colonial use for these mineral earths was as an ingredient in gunpowder, but this was restricted by the adulterated and limited form in which saltpeter could be obtained from most tequisquitl soils. The Texcoco region yielded a saltpeter of inferior quality, and Spaniards used richer sources in the caves between Teotihuacan and Otumba.[40] Saltpeter is also recorded in Cuitlahuac, Mixquic, Cuauhtitlan, Mexicalzingo, and other communities, and it is mentioned precisely as an ingredient for gunpowder in Cuauhtitlan and Mixquic in the early seventeenth century. The probability is that saltpeter was used by Indians entirely in the manufacture of fireworks for fiestas.[41]

In sum, the colonial uses of the Valley's salt deposits were more varied than before the conquest, and Indian peoples diversified their activities in accordance with them. But the essential use of the Valley's salt in native diets persisted through the colonial period, and the process of extraction for this purpose appears to have remained an Indian monopoly.[42]

Fishing, like salt extraction, was restricted to the lacustrine regions of the Valley. The fresh-water lakes contained the fish called *xohuilin* (*juile*), and several species under the general designation *iztacmichin,* or *pescado blanco.* None was of large size, the pescado blanco being eight or nine inches in length, with the preferred *amilotl* being slightly larger.[43] The salt-water fish, notably white or yellow *charales,* were smaller.[44] The most successful fishing of the salt-water lakes was to be found where springs or the mouths of fresh-water streams reduced the salinity, as near Zumpango and Ecatepec, or in parts of Lake Citlaltepec. Pescado blanco were caught in the waters of Xaltocan, at Coyotepec on the shores of Lake Zumpango, and even in the artificially dammed laguna de Ozumbilla in the seventeenth century.[45] The taste of the fresh-water fish was described by a Spaniard as *sano* and *sabroso,* that of the salt-water fish as *malo* and *doliente.*[46]

Indians fished in the open water from boats, using hand nets, spears, and rods with lines.[47] The Uppsala map of about 1555 (Plate XV) suggests that many small canoes manned by one or two men were the rule, rather than cooperative enterprises with large nets and boats. Although Spaniards retained their taste for deep-sea fish, imported in dried form from the Gulf coast, the Indian population depended on the local supply, and no far-flung commerce developed. Salt fish were not unknown in native markets, but it is likely that the difficulties of preservation restricted the area of trade.[48] The known notices refer only to the sale of fish in Mexico City and neighboring towns. But the dimensions even of this commerce are suggested by an estimate of the early seventeenth century that over a million fish were being taken annually from Lake Chalco and Lake Xochimilco.[49]

Professional Indian fishermen are reported from Cuitlahuac, Huitzilopochco, Mixquic, Chalco, Mexicalzingo, Mexico City, and many other communities near the fresh-water lakes. A number of them are associated also with the salt-water communities, including Texcoco, Chimalhuacan, Tequicistlan, Chiconauhtla, Zumpango, Citlaltepec, and Xaltocan.[50] Spaniards interfered in native fishing far more than in native salt extraction, probably because the lakes were the only local sources of fish and because fishing was a familiar activity to Spaniards. The records indicate that fishing jurisdictions were as carefully demarcated and as jealously guarded as land jurisdictions in native society. Thus in Ecatepec the fishing waters formed an integral part of community property and the income was used for community expenses in the Indian tribute system, at least until Spanish judges and civilians sought to intrude and to appropriate the fish.[51] In Cuitlahuac, where the waters were likewise recognized properties of the native government, a series of bitter disputes centered on the lucrative fishing industry: the gobernador and alcaldes and principales of the sixteenth century extorted fish from maceguales; Indians confiscated the equipment of an intruding Spanish fisherman who set a large net in 1640; the town rented some waters to other Spanish fishermen and encountered difficulty in collecting the rent in 1651; Indian fishermen of the community had to submit to a survey and measurement assigning them one square league of lake water in 1662. The community suffered further losses and restrictions of jurisdiction before the end of the century when a Spanish intruder, exceeding the terms of his original privilege, claimed exclusive rights to half of the remaining fishing grounds. Here and elsewhere, lake waters were subject to measurement and the placement of boundary markers. Spaniards argued the availability of waters as realengos and compelled Indians to rent them. In the seventeenth century they were fishing freely in Lake Cuitlahuac, disregarding Indian jurisdictions and confining Indians to areas where the lake was filled with tule or excessively contaminated by salts. In the eighteenth century canoes carrying mulattoes armed with garrotes and knives drove the Indian fishermen out of the best Cuitlahuac waters.[52] The history of Indian water property has obvious similarities with the history of Indian land.

Many aquatic foods besides fish were traditional in the native economy and the diet of the Valley. The earliest founders of Tenochtitlan are reported to have gathered salamanders, dragonfly larvae, shrimps and crawfish, frogs, water snakes, water bugs, and various grubs.[53] These and a variety of other *animalitos* of the water continued to be elements of native diet through the colonial period and into modern times. Frogs, grubs, crustaceans, molluscs, polliwogs, crawfish, and other lake creatures receive frequent mention in pre-conquest and colonial records as food. The *axayacatl*, a water bug best known now as an exported bird feed, was eaten by Indians, as were its eggs (*ahuauhtli*), which were cultivated on reeds in the water and eaten in small cakes (*tortas*).[54] *Izcauitli* was consumed in the form of dense masses of worm-like grubs. The *axolotl*, white or black, a larval salamander about eight inches in length and resembling an eel in taste, was widely regarded as a fish in colonial times and widely eaten.[55] *Tecuitlatl*, a green or purplish lake scum, was gathered, dried, and eaten in tortas or as a material resembling green cheese and was an article of general commerce in the sixteenth century.[56] Most of these nutritious foodstuffs failed to appeal to Spanish palates, and even among Indians the use of some of them was a mark of inferior status. But an exception was ahuauhtli, which Spaniards ate on meatless days.[57]

Many types of waterfowl were also known to Aztec peoples. In the latter sixteenth century Sahagún was able to enumerate over forty varieties, with data on their appearance, traits, and habitat.[58] Ducks, geese, and other birds, wintering in the Valley in great flocks, had served the inhabitants as food from immemorial time. Their meat and eggs were a continuous and important source of protein in native diets.[59] Birds also had special meanings in ritual and augury and were prized for their white or colored feathers, which were used as ornaments or in the exacting feather arts.[60] The most plentiful of the birds used as food were the ducks, and the most important season was the dry period between October and March, when ducks were present in enormous numbers. Certain other birds were non-migratory, and fowling was therefore a year-round occupation, but one pursued with special intensity in the winter.[61]

The most popular native method for capturing ducks required the setting of large nets on poles at intervals in the water, then arousing the ducks at dusk with shouts and sticks, and retrieving those that became entangled. The *atlatl* or throwing stick was also used. Both methods were aboriginal and both continued into the twentieth century.[62] In the seventeenth century floating ducks were caught also by swimmers with their heads concealed in pumpkins.[63] Duck hunting took place in both the salt-water and fresh-water lakes, in Zumpango, Citlaltepec, Xaltocan, Chiconauhtla, Mexicalzingo, Coatepec, and a number of other towns.[64] Waters for duck hunting, as for fishing, were included in the jurisdictions of individual towns. Huitzilopochco received forty pesos per year in the eighteenth century for the rental of a backwater used for duck hunting, and towns south of the city—Ixtapalapa, Culhuacan, Mixiuhca, Ixtahuacan—all rented out local marshland.[65] Fowling was an economic specialty in communities such as Tepozotlan, which Spaniards called *pueblo de los patos*. The barrio of Mexico City called La Candelaria or Candelarita, came to be known as Candelarita de los Patos in the later colonial period, and its corporate body was a *común de tiradores*.[66]

Lay Spaniards expressed a minimal interest in the rituals that surrounded Indian duck hunting as well as in the feather art that depended, in part, on water birds. This art was still practiced in the late seventeenth century, though not with its earlier vigor. Indians continued for a time to make ceremonial mantles of feathers, and Spaniards found the feathers of certain ducks useful for writing quills.[67] But in the colonial period all these were ancillary to the utilization of ducks as food. Because the meat appealed to Spanish tastes, duck hunting became an activity in which Spaniards and mestizos competed with Indians. Spaniards and mestizos used guns rather than native methods, and at an undetermined time, possibly in the seventeenth century, Indians also adopted firearms. Firing mechanisms were constructed by placing guns at several angles, one for firing across the water's surface and startling the birds or killing those on the water, others for cannonading them in flight.[68] Despite the reduction in the supply caused by wholesale slaughter, duck hunting remained an important aspect of the Valley's economy. Even in the eighteenth century it was estimated that the annual consumption in the city averaged between 900,000 and 1,000,000 birds, and the effect of the opening of the winter duck season in October was immediately evident in the smaller number of animals in the city's slaughterhouses.[69]

Nevertheless, all the activities centering upon the lake waters declined somewhat in the colonial period. The progressive scarcity of both fish and birds was noted at least from the early seventeenth century.[70] Tecuitlatl, the lake algae that yielded a cheese-like food, was extinct for commercial purposes by that time.[71] The scarcity of the axolotl and its consequent increase in price were reported in the eighteenth century, although the adult salamander remained as a widely recognized land creature. The axolotl did not become adult in Lake Texcoco, and it was not recognized as the larval form of the salamander until the transformation was observed in a Paris aquarium in 1865.[72]

The extent and economic importance of hunting in the colonial Valley is problematical. Coyotes (Nahuatl coyotl, from which the English word is derived), wolves, and some other large animals inhabited the area, but their use as food remains imperfectly documented. The exception is deer, which were hunted by Indians camouflaged in skins, approaching on all fours, and shooting with bow and arrow at close range.[73] Smaller animals, especially the native hares and rabbits, were caught in nets.[74] Other quadrupeds that were shot or snared and marketed for Indian consumption were the armadillo, the pocket gopher (tozan, tuza), and the weasel (cuzatli). In addition, a whole small world of lesser mammals, rodents, reptiles, vermin, and insects—including snakes, moles, mice, worms, locusts, and ants—found their way into the Indian diet.[75] Wild animal skins played a role in colonial economy, for some clothing was made from the ocotochtli and the ocelot skins, and deerskin was used for shoes and jackets, presumably in the Spanish market. But colonial conditions in general afforded only limited scope for clothing of animal skins, for the elaborate war dress of Aztec times, made of the pelts of rabbits and other animals, was no longer used.[76] Indians sometimes hunted for bounties, notably in the case of the destructive pocket gophers, strings of which were sold to Spanish agriculturists in the eighteenth century.[77] Spaniards hunted also, but that they did so for food or skins in appreciable quantities seems doubtful. The great viceregal hunts of the sixteenth century were sporting ventures, after the manner of the aristocratic hunts of Europe, but they intimately affected Indian life, since they employed many thousands of Indian beaters and stalkers, armed with bows and arrows and *macanas*.[78] The Spaniards' interest lay in the leisurely slaughter of deer, bear, wild felines, and similar animals. It does not appear that they participated significantly in the hunting of rabbits and hares, at which Indians were so adept. One sixteenth-century Spaniard described Mexican rabbit meat as tasty and hare meat as edible, but in general Spaniards did not eat either until the late eighteenth century. That they did so then was not by way of adopting a habit from Indians but in deliberate imitation of the French fashion.[79]

Statements to the effect that Indians of the pre-Spanish period knew no domestic animals are incorrect. Domestication was limited, but it included, in the Valley of Mexico, the turkey (*huexolotl, cihuatotolin*) and the native dog (*chichi*), both of which were eaten.[80] After the coming of the Spaniards, domestication received a new impetus in Indian society, and European animals were widely raised. The most popular of the new animals was the chicken. One may speculate that its small size, dependable egg production, ease of rearing, and similarity to the turkey were all factors encouraging its use. Chickens multiplied rapidly in the early post-conquest years, suffered a loss in an epidemic in 1539–40, and then gradually regained their position of importance.[81] Among domestic animals they occupied a unique position, for they were, after money and maize, the most common item of tribute in the encomiendas of the middle sixteenth century. Even crown tribute for a time late in the century required a chicken payment, as we have seen. It may be suggested that Spaniards quickly exploited the Indians' readiness to raise chickens, came to rely upon the supply, and had no recourse except coercion when both the chickens and the Indians were struck by epidemic in the late 1530's and the 1540's. The mid-century shortages are reflected in the exchange ratio of chickens and turkeys. Turkeys, less frequently demanded in tribute, could be traded at one to three or four for Spanish fowl in the 1530's but characteristically only at one to two or three in the middle sixteenth century and after.[82] The complaints by Spaniards regarding shortages in produce have been mentioned above with respect to maize, and they apply also to chickens, which fed on maize.[83]

Although the raising of chickens and turkeys was described as the principal occupation of Teotihuacan in the late sixteenth century, it is likely that it was more often an accessory occupation of home life in the hands of Indian women than a distinct male profession. The domestic character of animal husbandry applied also, in different degrees, to other animals raised by native peoples: ducks and geese, pigs and goats, rabbits, native dogs, Spanish dogs, and even coyotes.[84] Indian possession of mules and burros is poorly documented before the eighteenth century, and with present knowledge the development of Indian possession of these animals cannot be traced in detail. Female mules were listed at a standard price of five and a half pesos, and males at twelve pesos in the early eighteenth century, and these prices do not appear prohibitive with respect to Indian purchasing power.[85] We know from an instance cited previously that the repartimientos of the corregidores in the late colonial period compelled Indians to purchase animals at much higher prices than these.

The pasturage of sheep, which in certain cases might also be a domestic side line, was elevated in others to the status of a moderate-sized Indian industry. In native society caciques and principales adopted sheepherding in imitation of wealthy Spaniards. A legal limit for Indian herds, in the absence of a special license or land grant, was fixed at 300 sheep and 250 goats in the late sixteenth century. The largest Indian herd recorded for the Valley belonged to a principal of Tecama, who had 8,000 head in 1714. The cacique Juan de Guzmán maintained a flock of 3,000 in the sixteenth century, and other private Indian owners had flocks ranging from several hundred to several thousand. Spanish sheep interests reacted with only mild alarm to the threat of Indian herding, presumably because the dimensions of the Indian activity, whether private or communal, were never sufficient to constitute a major competition. Sheep herds numbering in the thousands were rare in Indian society, and even these were small in comparison with the large Spanish herds.[86]

Indian, like Spanish, sheepherding served two main industries: the supply of meat and the manufacture of woolen cloth. For reasons not altogether clear, it has become a widely held belief in modern times that Indians were not meat eaters. Colonial evidence that they were is indisputable, both in the Valley and in other parts of New Spain. The colonial Indian consumption of chicken, pork, mutton, and beef may have been less an innovation in kind than an amplification of original native diets of duck, game, dog, or human flesh. The eating of human flesh, which had been a ritual

Aztec practice, came to an end immediately following the conquest. The eating of dog meat continued, but by the late sixteenth century it was confined mainly to festival occasions such as baptisms and weddings.[87] Spaniards were tolerant of Indian meat eating, raising objections only in times of shortage, and then principally with regard to beef. Of other forms of meat—fowl, pork, mutton, game, dogs—Indians were both producers and consumers. But with beef, Spaniards felt that Indians were consuming disproportionately, while failing to contribute to the maintenance of cattle herds. This was in fact an accurate evaluation of the role of the native peoples, whose taste for meat extended to beef but whose inclination toward animal husbandry did not. The care of cattle under Spanish auspices in the sixteenth century was a mulatto occupation, not an Indian one, a fact that may be related to Indian experience of damage to fields by cows and steers.[88]

A variety of causes, including slaughter to provide hides for the European market, and hides and tallow for the domestic market—activities conducted largely without Indian participation—resulted in depletion of the cattle herds in the 1560's and after. Spaniards immediately seized upon Indian meat eating as a contributing factor in the decline and made proposals to outlaw the slaughtering of cattle in Indian towns.[89] By this date slaughterhouses had been introduced into the larger Valley towns, including Texcoco, Coyoacan, Xochimilco, and Tlalmanalco. The order prohibiting such slaughterhouses was issued in the 1560's, but it is unlikely that it appreciably affected Indian meat eating, since it applied only to houses that did not receive viceregal confirmation, and such confirmation was immediately given to many existing establishments.[90] The extent of viceregal permissiveness in this matter is suggested by a new Xochimilco license of 1576, which permitted the slaughter of some 2,500 steers per year.[91] The slaughterhouses in Indian towns were licensed to bidders, and the evidence suggests that these were invariably Spaniards. "There is hardly an Indian city without its carnicería, to provide beef for the Indians, where an infinite number of cattle are killed," wrote the itinerant secretary of Father Ponce in 1584, "and for this there are Spanish contractors and everything is cheap."[92] Indian labor is documented for some of the slaughtering operations, but no evidence is known for Indian management. In any case, neither the numerous Indian beef markets nor the markets of the huge capital city populated with meat-eating Spaniards figured as a major incentive to Indians to raise cattle.

Increasingly, the city came to be supplied with its beef and mutton from the ranges of northern New Spain—the process was well advanced by the late sixteenth century—and with pork from Apam and Toluca.[93]

Supplies of potable water created no problem throughout large parts of the Valley, where springs and streams were abundant. Inhabitants of the shores of Lake Chalco were reported to be drinking lake water without ill effects in the eighteenth century.[94] There is no evidence that the saline northern lakes or Lake Texcoco (which received the refuse and sewage of the city) were ever so used. Although some northern towns had excellent water supplies, northern peoples in general suffered from lack of water. Where neither springs nor wells could furnish a supply, rain water was caught in pools.[95] Even in the southern community of Milpa Alta the inhabitants had to carry water from a source several miles away.[96] Spaniards, as we have noted, usurped or diverted some of the Indian streams.[97] At other times, however, Spaniards made prodigious efforts to improve community water supplies. The most celebrated construction was the aqueduct from Cempoala to Otumba, built in the mid-sixteenth century by Indians under the direction of Fray Francisco de Tembleque; it had more than a hundred arches and carried water over a distance of some fifty kilometers.[98] It should be added that later in the colonial period the tendency was toward poorer water supplies for the communities. Progressive desiccation meant the drying of springs, and Spanish usurpations became more serious. In the late colonial period, aqueducts were built more for haciendas than for Indian towns, and the existing community aqueducts were not maintained. In the eighteenth century the Texcoco water conduits were broken and not repaired, and the Coyoacan and Xochimilco aqueducts were in ruins. The huge arches of the Tembleque aqueduct remained intact but the water level had fallen and the great construction carried no water.[99]

Neither Spaniards nor Indians regarded milk as a beverage appropriate for adults. Coffee and tea, which achieved their European vogue in the late seventeenth and eighteenth centuries, were virtually unknown in the western world before that and were at no time used by Indians in the Valley. For a brief period in the early sixteenth century Spaniards hoped that Indians would drink beer, and a modest brewing industry was established, but the market proved to be an illusion.[100] Indian consumption of Spanish wine and brandy was limited by the efforts of Spanish authorities to prevent these beverages from falling into Indian hands. The efforts were motivated not so much by the fear that Indians would deplete the supply—as with cattle—as by a moral and social solicitude based on the universal Indian tendency to drunkenness.[101] But it is more likely that the failure of Indians to become wine drinkers on a large scale was the result of high prices. Indians drank pulque and exercised great resourcefulness in contriving other cheap intoxicants, the general literature on which, mainly under the category *bebidas prohibidas* (*chinguirito, mezcal, sangre de conejo,* and many others), forms an impressive record of ingenuity under duress.[102]

Among non-intoxicants, the remarkable fact is that Indian peoples preferred a beverage flavor that was not indigenous to the area and that came ultimately to be imported over a distance of several thousand miles. This was chocolate, made from cacao beans, and repeatedly identified in the colonial period as an Indian necessity.[103] The importation of cacao beans from Soconusco, Colima, and other areas of southern Mexico was well established in the pre-conquest period,[104] and the trade was continued during the first post-conquest decades. The southern plantations declined, however, in the 1540's, the chief cause apparently being native population loss in the plantation areas, and cacao came to be imported into the Valley and other highland areas of New Spain from Guatemala and from Sonsonate, in what is now El Salvador.[105] The main sources of cacao then remained Central American for about seventy years. In the early seventeenth century the export points fell still farther south, to Maracaibo, Caracas, Guayaquil, and Cartagena in northern South America.[106]

These changes were necessarily attended by corresponding adjustments in transportation techniques. The early transport of cacao from southern Mexico had been accomplished by Indian carriers, after the manner of the tribute transport under the Aztec rulers. Commercial travel by Indians from the central plateau to Soconusco and Guatemala is documented in 1556 as having existed for ten years, and this tallies with the decline of production and communication in southern Mexico after the plague of 1545. Evidence is still lacking that an overland trade by human carriers ever penetrated farther south than Guatemala. Sonsonate cacao was sent by sea as a cargo in Spanish holds to the southern Mexican ports of Huatulco and Acapulco, and the South American product of the seventeenth and eighteenth centuries also came by a maritime route. At the end of colonial times, ships from Campeche, Tabasco, Maracaibo, and other ports were carrying cacao to Veracruz, and mule trains from Acapulco were carrying Guayaquil cacao to Mexico City.[107]

Only a thoroughly conditioned taste can explain such extended supply lines for this exotic product. The extension of the supply line from Central America to South America evidently represented not a local intensification or expansion of this taste but rather a transfer to cheaper sources of supply. The price of cacao in the Valley of Mexico dropped by more than half between 1605 and 1625, as Central American sources were abandoned and South American sources introduced.[108] The taste was formed well before the early seventeenth century, and it becomes worth inquiring whether the acquisition of the cacao habit was a pre-conquest or a colonial phenomenon. The answer appears to be that cacao was used both as a medium of exchange and as a beverage in pre-conquest times but that its popularity as a beverage increased in the colonial period while its use as a currency declined.[109]

In any case, cacao continued to be looked upon as a necessity throughout the seventeenth and eighteenth centuries.[110] To prepare the drink the beans were pulverized and the powder then steeped in hot water or boiled with honey, maize, or other ingredients.[111] The price of the bean varied sharply as a result of unpredictable crops and the activities of middlemen, and an additional complicating factor lay in the precarious sea route.[112] Guayaquil and Caracas cacao beans were considered inferior and even injurious in the seventeenth century, and Maracaibo cacao, looked upon as preferable, then advanced sharply in price. The history of cacao in the Valley in other respects is remarkably like that of maize, with quick changes in supply and cost, interference by suppliers, government efforts to exercise controls (including price subsidies), an experiment with a cacao alhóndiga in Mexico City, and in 1716 the prohibition of cacao from Guayaquil.[113]

All these conditions of Indian housing, dress, and sustenance in the Valley required a commercial exchange and a specialized production of considerable variety. The relations of towns to their environments created regional specialties in salt, fish, wool, lime, petates, and other products, in addition to the agricultural foodstuffs. Local specialization beyond this had been a factor in the social structure of the Aztec period and one deliberately fostered by Aztec rulers. Thus the organization of Texcoco under Nezahualcoyotl had entailed a division of the community into thirty parts, each with its own economic function. Silversmiths, lapidaries, painters, feather workers, and others each occupied a barrio. In Aztec practice, sons normally adopted the trades or crafts of their fathers, and genealogy, location, and profession were thus identified in a single composite loyalty. Moreover, because the members of a barrio ordinarily worshipped their own local deity the integrity of the unit was further reinforced by religion.[114]

The colonial period modified but never essentially altered this aboriginal principle of community and barrio specialization. Modifications, when they occurred, resulted mostly from the decay of those cultural traditions that were unsuited to colonial life. The Indian arts of manuscript painting, feather design, and paper manufacture declined in the sixteenth century, for they were most closely connected with pre-conquest conditions. The production of native codices received a brief new stimulus in the sixteenth century, but by the late sixteenth and early seventeenth centuries this had become essentially a lost art. The same may be said for Indian silver work, which had been concentrated at Azcapotzalco. In the sixteenth century Spaniards continued to recognize Azcapotzalco as the "pueblo of silversmiths," the foremost center of silver, gold, and lapidary work in the Valley. Objects of wrought gold and silver continued to be demanded by Spaniards in tribute in the middle years of the sixteenth century, and the industry was to some degree prolonged under new conditions. But with progressive impoverishment Indians abandoned objects of precious metals. Sahagún reported that in his time gold bracelets were still being used in Indian dances, but gold ear pendants were no longer seen. The silver industry was still functioning in Azcapotzalco in the 1580's, and it still had the character of an intra-Indian trade. But silver workers had to pay the king's fifth (*quinto*) in taxes, and in any case Indians were at a disadvantage in working with a metal so valuable to the Spaniards.[115] Azcapotzalco shifted to bronze working, and in the eighteenth century lapidary work was practically unknown. Azcapotzalco produced bronze bells, nails, door hinges, and similar objects in an industry now adapted to colonial needs.[116]

Though clay soils suitable for pottery were found everywhere in the Valley lowland, and though pottery manufacture was an industry in a number of communities—including Huitzilopochco, Azcapotzalco, and Xochimilco—the major production center was northwest of Mexico City in Cuauhtitlan.[117] Indian ceramic wares from Cuauhtitlan were portrayed graphically in 1564, when four Indian potters, angered at the failure of an alcalde mayor to pay for their goods, registered their protest in a pictorial record of their pots, pitchers, bowls, human-head jars, and tripod vases. Notices of the seventeenth and eighteenth centuries refer to the Cuauhtitlan ware in such terms as common crockery (*loza ordinaria*); large earthen jars (*tinajas*);

clay vessels (*barros*) of various types, some very fine; pots (*ollas*); and special red jars of the Cuauhtitlan type (*jarros colorados llamados de Cuauhtitlan muy particulares*). Cuauhtitlan potters were still celebrated in the eighteenth century, and the industry continued into the twentieth century. At the end of the colonial period pottery manufacture was said to be bringing 100,000 pesos a year to Cuauhtitlan. We do not know to what extent this industry was intruded upon by non-Indians.[118]

Indian carpenters and masons worked in many towns of the Valley, and Spaniards relied on them as specialized laborers (oficiales as opposed to peones) for the urban repartimiento drafts. Towns such as Chimalhuacan, Coatepec, and Tepetlaoztoc maintained groups of professional carpenters and masons on whom Spaniards continuously drew.[119] The numbers of such oficiales varied greatly from community to community. When Ecatepec was required to give carpenters and masons in service to the city in 1591, the town had none to supply and the Indians were obliged to fill the order by hiring workmen from Texcoco. Tacubaya, on the other hand, supported huge numbers of masons for urban work, and the inhabitants of Coyoacan were famous and widely employed as masons and pavers of streets.[120]

In two communities outside the capital—Texcoco and Xochimilco—a full *oficio* tradition was preserved throughout the colonial period. Texcoco was the main obraje center of the Valley, but the great pre-conquest craft tradition of Texcoco was not wholly relegated to an obraje form. Indians of Texcoco in the late sixteenth century, seemingly independent of Spanish controls, served as carpenters, masons, smiths, lacquerers, tailors, lapidaries, and makers of spools, thimbles, rosaries, and lay and ecclesiastical hats. Texcoco Indians were also the principal stonecutters outside Tenochtitlan, and in the early Spanish campaigns of ecclesiastical building they traveled from site to site when new churches and monasteries were in progress.[121] In Xochimilco, which was a center of pre-conquest woodworking and mechanical arts, the larger part of the population in the middle sixteenth century held the rank of oficial as masons, woodworkers, smiths, canoe makers, and similar craftsmen.[122] Xochimilco, like Texcoco, was subdivided by barrio specialties, with carpenters and sculptors in Tepetenchi, carpenters, smiths, and potters in Tecpan, and presumably, though the evidence is not at hand, particular specialties within the lesser subdivisions. The occupational division in Xochimilco in some ways superseded the barrio division, for among the prominent Indian officers in the seventeenth century were the inspectors of the various crafts, and in public dances and fiestas the professions were represented by symbolic masks and instruments. Tribute payments were organized by groups of craftsmen rather than by barrios or other subdivision.[123] Xochimilco remained an industrial community specializing in woodworking and metallic arts, producing chairs, beds, cabinets, chests, doors, locks, nails, latches, and other furniture and hardware. The normal petate industry of a lakeside community likewise achieved the status of an oficio in Xochimilco, with the production of quantities of mats woven of tule.[124]

Economic interchange in the Valley was traditionally served by the *tianquiz,* or Indian market, which had been held at fixed locations within the Aztec towns, commonly at intervals of five, thirteen, or twenty days under the supervision of the community's tlatoani.[125] Certain pre-conquest markets emphasized their own specialties: dogs at Acolman; slaves at Azcapotzalco; and birds at Otumba.[126] The markets had operated partly by barter but with a few items—notably cacao beans, maize, and mantles—serving as common media of exchange.[127]

The foremost Aztec markets of the Valley of Mexico—indeed, the foremost of the entire American hemisphere—were those of the island city of Tenochtitlan-Tlatelolco. So profound an impression did the capital market exert upon the first Spaniards who witnessed it that it is now one of the most copiously documented features of late Aztec economy anywhere. Full accounts, with lists of the goods offered for sale, are furnished in the writings of Cortés, Bernal Díaz, and the Anonymous Conqueror. Among later arrivals and secondary authorities, Motolinía, López de Gómara, Las Casas, Sahagún, and Cervantes de Salazar all left detailed statements.[128] In most cases it is possible in the several descriptions to distinguish between purely aboriginal goods and goods derived from Spanish contact, with the result that a comprehensive listing of Indian trade objects and their progressive modification in the early colonial period can be reconstructed. The first observers were impressed not only by the variety and quantity of market goods but by the barrio specializations and the orderliness in display.[129] Their accounts describe an efficient administration by market judges, whom they compared with Spanish alguaciles or oidores, and whose function was to settle disputes and punish thieves.[130]

No immediate or drastic transformation occurred in native markets with the establishment of the Spanish colony. Even in the capital, which was the location of the most intimate contact between Indians and Spaniards, a large measure of continuity was preserved in native forms of exchange. Only when we compare the conquistadores' accounts of 1519–20 with those that derive from the later sixteenth century do changes become noticeable. The precious stones and precious metals, with which both Cortés and Bernal Díaz began their lists, received less attention in later reports. Cervantes de Salazar, about 1550, observed that Motolinía's list no longer applied with respect to the objects of gold, silver, feathers, and precious stones.[131] The slaves and animal skins of Bernal Díaz's list drop out or receive reduced emphasis in the subsequent accounts. Sahagún's list, in the later sixteenth century, was the first systematically to include items introduced by the Spaniards, and it is worth noting that these were principally foodstuffs: wheat and wheat flour, chickens (the *"gallinas"* mentioned by Cortés and Bernal Díaz were presumably turkeys), goats, sheep, pigs, and beef. Apart from these, in Sahagún's list, candles are the only items adopted by Indians from the Spaniards. The similarity of the lists is striking, and although in several instances this is purely a matter of documentary dependence it is by no means so in all. What the similarity suggests is the conservatism of Indian material culture. Also notable throughout is the absence of European tools, hardware, glass, and clothing, all of which lay beyond the ordinary Indian's needs or economic opportunities.[132]

Our most extensive record of an early colonial market outside the capital relates to Coyoacan in the time of the cacique Juan de Guzmán in the middle sixteenth century. Some fifty items are mentioned in several lists, with some duplication. They include building materials (stone, lime, lumber), clothing and textiles (shirts, wool, tochomitl), foods (*izquitl* or toasted maize kernels, tamales, chia, chile, fish, cacao), materials for food preparation or storage (firewood, pottery, baskets, comales, molcajetes), and house furnishings (petates, candles, torch pine). Other goods in the Coyoacan market were knives, metalware, spinning whorls (*malacates*), feathers, tumplines (*mecapales*), brooms, oak bark (used as a chewing gum), medicinal herbs, and various materials for smoking or incense.[133] Notices of individual sellers and their wares in other Indian exchanges reiterate the standard materials: wood, lime, stone, firewood, charcoal, and foodstuffs including fish. Indian women sold medicinal plants in the colonial markets and in the late eighteenth century still remained knowledgeable and skillful in their use. The small number of Spanish commodities mentioned among the wares of Indian traders in the sixteenth century—paper, knives, soap, indigo, blue and red thread, and generalized "merchandise of Castile"—may have been in part for Spanish consumption.[134]

In the case of a few products, the Spanish consumers' market operated to accelerate a purely Indian production. In general, when Spaniards needed goods that Indians could supply the result was the imposition of tributes or forced commodity "servicios," as we have seen. But when the Spanish demand could not be satisfied by these means, Indians seized the opportunity to sell directly to Spaniards. Apart from foodstuffs for human consumption, the outstanding example is fodder for Spanish horses. Here the servicios applied only to the equipages of high-ranking Spanish officers. Two kinds of fodder predominated: maize stalks and lake reeds (zacate).[135] Zacate grew the year round in the shallow lakes and was planted and harvested by Indians and sold as fodder. Its production was dependent on a canoe commerce, and it developed especially in the lake towns close to the capital, such as Mexicalzingo, Culhuacan, and Ixtapalapa.[136] Like fishing and fowling, it came to be an activity in which Spaniards and Negroes competed with Indians. Colonial ordinances restricting zacate production to Indians, like ordinances regarding other economic intrusions, were ineffective.[137]

One other material of Indian manufacture received a new stimulus in the colony as a result of Spanish demand. This was cochineal, a dye made from the dried bodies of insects cultivated on the tuna or nopal cactus. The greater part of the dye, transcending the colonial market altogether, was exported to Spain. Cochineal is of interest as the only item in the Indian economy that was so exported, but in fact its production in the Valley was minor in comparison with that in Tlaxcala or the Puebla region. Valley cochineal came principally from the northeast, between Otumba and Cempoala.[138] The industry declined steadily after the sixteenth century and its center shifted to Oaxaca. By late colonial times only a small amount was still being produced in Chalco province.[139]

The Spanish state became actively concerned in matters of native marketing after the plague of 1545–48, which created the first crisis in the city's supply. For the first time the Spanish government confronted the problem of priority assignment among Indian commodities. A typical viceregal reaction is illustrated by a case involving Tlalmanalco in the 1550's. Indians of this pueblo, situated on the slopes of the mountains in the southeast, brought wood from their monte to sell in the city. Although their trade clearly served to supply the city, the viceroy ruled emphatically that Indian maize production held first importance, and that no wood was to be cut in Tlalmanalco from March to May and from November to January, so that Indians would not neglect planting and harvesting.[140] The viceroy was here primarily interested in the supply of agricultural produce for Indian, rather than Spanish, consumption in the city.

In other acts relating to the city's supply after the plague, the audiencia ruled that all towns within a radius of twenty leagues were to bring to the city's markets every Saturday 100 turkeys, 400 chickens, 2,800 eggs, and all available firewood and fodder.[141] In the most stringent order, Viceroy Velasco in 1551 sharply restricted all Indian markets in the Valley except those in the city itself and in Texcoco. All save these were to be confined to sales of tortillas, maize meal (*mazamorra*), tamales, and native fruit. The viceroy's purpose was to ensure sufficient quantities of chickens, mantles, maize, and cacao in the city.[142] Alguaciles were instructed to enforce this order, but when Indians protested, the viceroy relented to the extent of permitting the sale of articles necessary for Indian sustenance in town markets. In two recorded cases—one applying to Ecatepec and the other applying to Xochimilco and Acolman—we have the lists of the Indian necessities that were allowed (Table 26).

Colonial changes further affected market regulation. In Tenochtitlan and Tlatelolco, an Indian market judge was still functioning in 1533, in the absence of any substitute Spanish officials. The duties of the judge extended to the settlement of commercial disputes, the punishment of offenders, and the collection of the fees that Indian sellers paid for the privilege of displaying wares.[143] But control of the two urban markets passed to Spanish authority shortly after, and it is probable that the Indian offices came to an end with the transfer. With the establishment of the new San Hipólito market in the city, no income was allocated to the native government, and the Spanish alguaciles of the Tenochtitlan and Tlatelolco markets extended their jurisdiction to San Hipólito. The viceregal government, the audiencia, and the Spanish cabildo of the city all introduced measures for market regulation, which progressively fell away from Indian control. The markets of Mexico City in the seventeenth and eighteenth centuries came to be totally subordinate to Spanish regulation.[144]

In the towns, Indian control lasted for longer periods. The pre-conquest

TABLE 26

Indian Market Goods Legally Sold, 1551

Ecatepec	Xochimilco and Acolman	
Chile	Firewood	Rabbit-fur textile
Tortillas	Griddles	Cotton
Tamales	Chile	Gourd containers
Salt	Salt	Needles
Native fruit	Digging Sticks	Tumplines
Pottery	Tomatoes	Ropes
Firewood	Torch pine	Tobacco
Mats	Lime	Grinding stones
Torch pine	Pottery	Native fruit
Atole	Mats	
Lime for tortillas	Melon seeds	
Rabbit-fur textile	Small canoes	
Cotton	Sandals	

SOURCE: AGN, Mercedes, vol. 3, fols. 293r–293v, 318v–319r, 320r.

practice whereby sellers paid the tlatoque for market privileges continued so long as caciques retained positions of authority over marketplaces. The schedule of payment to Juan de Guzmán, cacique of Coyoacan, recorded for the middle years of the sixteenth century, includes separate charges for the sellers of maize, chia, chile, fish, meat, herbs, petates, comales, baskets, and other goods, with a range from one-half real for the sellers of wool and sellers of tumplines to five reales for the sellers of firewood.[145] After the authority of caciques had been limited, the privileges of market collection were assumed by gobernadores and other community officials. In Texcoco in the eighteenth century collections were made by an Indian alguacil.[146] That Spaniards permitted Indian governments to retain a fiscal control of market duties outside Mexico City may be attributed to two conditions: the amounts paid for market locations were too small to attract Spanish attention; and the market places, customarily located near the center of Indian towns, were less vulnerable than outlying areas to Spanish pre-emption of land. It is interesting that the eighteenth-century cacica heir of Juan de Guzmán received seven to nine pesos per week from the Coyoacan market and sold the market plaza to the Marqués del Valle in 1746 for nine hundred pesos.[147]

Market schedules in the towns also shifted from the Indian periodization to the weekly intervals of the Christian calendar. In the Valley this change took place gradually in the early and middle sixteenth century. Some towns were holding weekly markets by the 1540's, while others did not do so until the 1550's and 1560's. The Monday market of Coyoacan was fixed in 1550. Huitzilopochco shifted from the twenty-day to the weekly schedule in 1563. Citlaltepec established its Wednesday market in 1565.[148] These are typical dates for the larger towns, but some smaller or more remote communities retained aboriginal market schedules for longer periods. Thus Mamalhuazacan, a sujeto of Chimalhuacan Chalco, received viceregal confirmation for its five-day market in 1580, and Tulanzingo, to the north, was still holding its market at twenty-day intervals in the seventeenth century.[149]

Indians also adopted certain Spanish units of measurement in commodity exchange. Tribute specifications commonly, though not in all instances, required maize payments in fanegas, and the Indian community therefore rapidly adopted this Spanish quantity and term. Sixteenth-century regulations undertook to enforce Spanish measures in Indian market transactions, notably the half-fanega, the almud (1/12 fanega), the half-almud, and cuartillo (¼ almud). Gobernadores, alcaldes, and other officers in Indian towns were required to maintain certified measures (half-fanega, almud, and cuartillo), which were to be approved by Spanish authorities in the city.[150] So far as is known Indian market goods were not measured by weight.[151] Fraud and false measurement receive some attention in the record of Indian markets, but not in a way that permits evaluation or comparison with Spanish practices.[152] Numerous vague measurements were used by Indians as well as by Spaniards, and the Indian vigesimal numbering continued to govern much measurement, as in the term *zontle* (400). Indians adopted commodity measurements of larger size than the fanega late in the colonial period. Cofradías and communities regularly reckoned their maize sales by the fanega through the seventeenth century, shifting to the carga (equal to two fanegas) only in the middle or late eighteenth century.[153]

The Spanish monetary system rapidly became an element in Indian life, and again the principal impetus was tribute. Caciques, merchants, wealthy Indians, and the officers responsible for community finance developed as sophisticated an appreciation of Spanish money as any colonist. The transition to a money economy involved at first only the addition of Spanish coins at standard rates with respect to the Indian cacao beans and other media of exchange. Indians are reported to have been skeptical of the value of copper coins and to have thrown them away in the lake, but at most this can have been only a momentary and aberrent response. Native economy emphasized the coins of small denomination. Even in transactions involving fifty pesos or more, payments were for the most part in reales.[154] False reales of Indian manufacture were observed as early as 1537—a modification of the Indian tradition of counterfeit cacao currency.[155] Barter, cacao, and metallic coins existed side by side in the markets throughout colonial times.[156] The ratios of cacao beans to reales declined from 200 to 1 and 180 to 1 in the middle sixteenth century to 150 to 1, 100 to 1, and 80 to 1 in the late sixteenth century. Rates of 140 to 1, 120 to 1, 80 to 1, 60 to 1, and 50 to 1 were reported in the seventeenth century and of 80 to 1 at the end of the colonial period.[157] Here, as in other aspects of lower-class Indian culture, the vigesimal numeration continued to prevail.[158]

Tlatelolco deteriorated more than any other of the Valley's marketplaces. Texcoco, which was a major market at the time of the conquest, and which was the only exception outside the capital to Viceroy Velasco's restrictive order of 1551, likewise declined as a trade center. In both towns the economic deterioration was attended by population loss and the decay of political power and prestige. The slave market in Azcapotzalco and, more gradually, the dog market of Acolman decayed as their specialties fell into disuse.[159] Communities offering goods for which there was continued demand maintained their specialized markets, the conspicuous example being the pottery market of Cuauhtitlan. Other communities increased in importance as market centers. By the late seventeenth and eighteenth centuries the Friday market of Chalco Atenco had come to be a major event, to which large numbers of persons came overland and by canoe. It was one of the most celebrated in all the colony, displaying fruits, grains, and other foodstuffs from the tierra caliente and as great a variety of merchandise as was displayed in the plaza of the city. Goods remaining from the Friday market at Chalco Atenco were transported to Mexico City for Saturday sale in the plaza. A spectacular change likewise occurred in Chicoloapa. Its sixteenth-century market appears to have been in no way outstanding, but by the eighteenth century it had become an important commercial town, where every Wednesday a large concourse of people gathered to exchange clothing, grains, fruits, animals, and many other articles.[160]

The environment of the colony was not conducive to the preservation of the Aztec merchants (*pochteca*) as a privileged group. As the pochteca lost their distinctive position, they were replaced by new Indian traders. The change was first observed after the plague of 1545-48, and the decline in agricultural productivity appears to have been due not only to the absolute loss in population but also to a shift from agriculture to trade among the survivors. Spaniards complained that new Indian traders were neglecting their other occupations and were motivated by laziness and greed.[161] Occasionally Indian merchants of the period following the plague could declare themselves to be merchants by hereditary Indian descent (*mercaderes de padres y abuelos*), but many others could make no such claim.[162] A macegual of the 1550's might already have acquired ample experience to fit him for the role of itinerant merchant. Foot travel and the carrying of loads over long distances might be familiar to him in his capacity as a carrier or tribute payer. Principales sent maceguales on long missions to the tierra caliente for flowers and other supplies needed in community fiestas, and the maceguales' opportunities for personal profit in such missions must have been considerable. Viceroys continued for a time to issue licenses to merchants for distant journeys, in a continuation of the Aztec tradition. But the disruption of native society in the sixteenth century tended to break down the system of regulations and privileges affecting pochteca.[163]

From Huitzilopochco and Xochimilco—both important merchant towns of the pre-conquest period—Indian traders of the sixteenth century are known to have traveled to Oaxtepec, Toluca, and Oaxaca to buy fruit and other goods for sale in the city. Indian fruit buyers from Tenochtitlan and Tlatelolco were active as purchasers in Oaxtepec and Cuernavaca for the city's supply in the mid-century, and their wares included both Indian and Spanish fruit. The large poppies from the Ixtacalco chinampas were sold in Toluca and other parts of the interior for ecclesiastical festivals.[164] Indian journeys from Xochimilco in the 1580's are recorded to Zacatecas, Guanajuato, and Nueva Galicia for trade in Indian and Spanish clothing and other Spanish merchandise. The viceregal government authorized a number of Indians to use horses in such long-distance traffic, and by the later sixteenth century one could speak, as did Bernal Díaz, of a genuine class of Indian muleteers (*arrieros*).[165] But in time, and as Indians were further absorbed into the economic life of the colony, this special viceregal concern for native commerce also disappeared. In 1597 Indians were permitted to trade in all goods, except arms and Spanish silks, without limitation, and to maintain up to six horses as beasts of burden.[166] By the eighteenth century many Indians were working as arrieros, generally under private Spanish employers. In jurisdictions such as Zumpango, where a number of main routes converged, *arriería* was the common employment of the late colonial period.[167]

The history of Indian and Spanish merchants is one of progressive intermingling under Spanish domination. The earliest conception was of a separation of trade. Indians were exempted from the sales tax (alcabala) so long as their traffic was in native goods, and to this extent the separation of Indian and Spanish commerce was maintained—over the protests however of treasury officials—to the end of colonial times.[168] The early policy of separation had been advocated by Cortés, in opposition to the royal proposal for "free" commerce between Indians and Spaniards. It was expressed in a Mexico City cabildo rule of 1528, which held that no Spaniard might trade in any Indian market of the city or with any Indian in an area five leagues around the city.[169] But an economic system in which so much of the city's provision was supplied in small amounts by individual Indians opened the way for many kinds of coercion and interference, in defiance of the policy of separation. In the sixteenth century Spaniards, Negroes, and mulattoes bought from Indians and resold to Spaniards at increased prices. Greater profits could be secured if Indian carriers could be intercepted on their way to the city and their produce seized rather than purchased. Seizures of fish, fodder, frogs, rabbits, cacao, and other goods are reported. The practice is one of the most frequently mentioned, and frequently condemned, in all early legislation relating to the city's supply.[170] Even in a transaction that might now be regarded as entirely businesslike, the official Spanish view of the sixteenth century was one of suspicion of the *regatón* or middleman. Spaniards were forbidden to buy from Indians for resale as early as the 1520's, and the prohibitions were reiterated in specific reference to maize, birds, sandals, honey, feathers, clothing, eggs, vegetables, fruit, charcoal, and firewood.[171] The interceptions persisted, however, despite the rules, and markups by regatones were recorded of several hundred per cent and more.[172] Outside the capital, in places where no important markets for Spanish consumers were located, interference in Indian commerce necessarily took other forms, as in the intrusions into Indian fishing, duck hunting, and zacate production, and in the repartimientos or forced sales by corregidores. Thus the policy of separation could be justified as a mode of protection for both societies, but it was repeatedly violated in practice, even by the officials who were entrusted to uphold it.

The most important trade routes within the Valley were identical with those of pre-conquest times. But in time the road network came to be enlarged and modified in accordance with Spanish commercial interests. Eventually nine great routes, each with its special purpose and significance, linked the Valley with the external areas of New Spain. The Zacatecas and Pachuca roads to the north connected the capital with the mines of the Spanish colony. The Toluca road provided communication with Michoacan and the west. Two roads directly south, one to Cuernavaca and the other to Cuauhtla, connected with the southern Marquesado and tierra caliente and with the Pacific ports of Acapulco and Huatulco. Two direct routes to Puebla, one passing through the famous bandit town of Río Frío, gave communication with Veracruz, Atlixco Valley, Izucar, and Oaxaca. Finally, two other roads to the east, one via Tepetlaoztoc and Calpulalpan, the other via Otumba and Apam, provided additional connections with Jalapa and Veracruz.[173] Virtually all the city's supply not provided by the Valley itself came by one or another of these roads: merchandise from Europe via Veracruz; silver, cattle, hides, wool, grains, and other agricultural produce from the north; pigs from Apam, Calpulalpan, and Toluca; wheat from Atlixco and Tehuacan; maize from Toluca, Tepeaca, Ixtlahuaca, and Metepec; sugar from Cuernavaca and Izucar; indigo from Michoacan.[174] Such heavy traffic on the roads always had serious consequences for the Indian towns through which the routes passed. Even in the 1540's a hundred mule trains might be on the road between Veracruz and the capital at one time. Tacuba in the sixteenth century regularly housed three thousand horses for the transport of goods to and from Toluca. In the early seventeenth century three thousand mules entered the city daily, laden with wheat, maize, sugar, and other goods. And thousands of steers were regularly stationed in Tepozotlan on their way from the Chichimec ranges to the city's slaughterhouses.[175] A community such as Chiconauhtla was a crucial transportation center, crowded with wagon traffic from Zacatecas and Guanajato, as well as from Apam, Jalapa, Veracruz, and Mexico City.[176]

The one supply route over which Indians maintained a measure of control was the canoe route through Lakes Chalco and Xochimilco, which penetrated to the center of the city by the *acequia real* and terminated near the main plaza. This canal was the only water route into the city that remained open through colonial times, for it was the only one in which the water level remained high enough to support a steady traffic.[177] The pre-conquest canoe route that had connected Lakes Zumpango and Xaltocan with the

TRADE ROUTES

city had already become permanently blocked and impassable by the 1540's, and proposals to reopen it were never realized.[178] The waters of Lake Texcoco remained navigable, save in extremely dry years, during the sixteenth century. But in the early eighteenth century a canal for the transport of supplies had to be dug from San Lázaro at the eastern end of the city across the bed of the lake to Texcoco. And by the end of colonial times even this had become so shallow that canoe traffic could no longer pass, or could pass only with great difficulty, from Texcoco to Mexico City in the winter months.[179] By far the larger part of the canoe transport was to be found on the southern canal route, which was kept open by springs in the dry season and received water from streams and runoffs in the wet season. Hence towns such as Xochimilco, Chalco, and Ixtapalapa continued as commercial centers, while northern towns concentrated on other activities.[180]

It was precisely during the dry season that a major part of the canoe traffic served the city's needs, and few cities of the world were so bountifully supplied. From November to March the Mexico City colonial markets were provided with tomatoes, fresh chiles, calabashes, and other agricultural produce from the tierra caliente by the canoe route. The year-round traffic in flowers and fruits from the south depended on it. Indians in Huitzilopochco bought green fruit from the south, ripened it, and sold it in the city.[181] During the summer growing season the produce of the chinampas of Lake Xochimilco and the gardens of Tlaxpana just west of the city were sold in the urban markets from twenty-four to forty-eight hours after picking, and in Mexico City in the eighteenth century radishes and even turnips were regarded as food fit only for animals after the second day.[182] Many other commodities besides fresh food and flowers were standard items in canoe commerce. Stone, sand, maize, fodder, wheat, barley, wood, lime, bricks, and sugar were usual cargoes. Wheat flour from Atlixco Valley was drawn by horses only as far as Ayotzingo and from there shipped by canoe to the city.[183]

The largest transport canoes of the colonial period were boats of fifty feet or more in length with capacities of several tons.[184] The minimum length was about fourteen feet.[185] They were uniformly of wood, cut from a single trunk, with a square bow and shallow draft. A skilled Indian carpenter of Xochimilco could make a canoe in about a week. Oars and poles were used to maneuver them.[186] Much of the transport took place at night, so that the heat of the day might be avoided. Boats laden with fruits, flowers, vege-

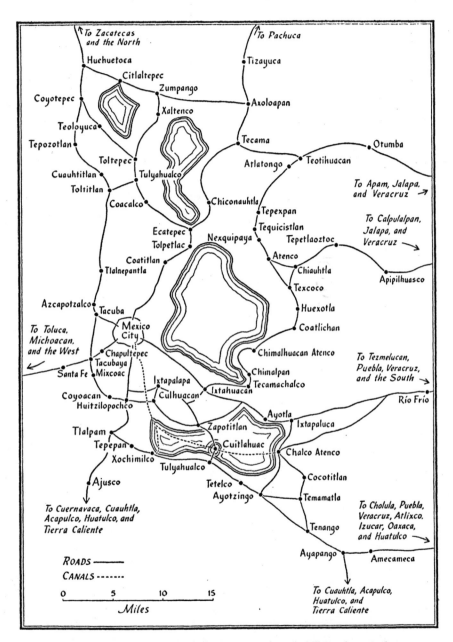

Map 10. Main roads and canals, seventeenth and eighteenth centuries.

tables, fish, fowl, and other produce entered the city at sunrise, and south-bound canoes left late on Thursday to arrive at the great Chalco Atenco market at daybreak on Friday.[187] Huitzilopochco, Mexicalzingo, Chalco Atenco, Xochimilco, Ayotzingo, and Tetelco were the principal embarkation points, depending on the materials to be transported and their point of origin. From any one of these locations goods could be carried in a single movement and unloaded near the Palacio in the center of the city. The journey was one of six to eight hours from Ayotzingo.[188] It was necessarily a standard route, with little chance for deviation, for portions of the lakes were filled with thick reed growths through which avenues fifteen to forty feet wide were cut for canoe transport. In late colonial times one such canal extended from the eastern part of Lake Chalco to Cuitlahuac, turned north in Lake Xochimilco, and joined the acequia real south of Culhuacan. Another proceeded north from Xochimilco, joining the acequia real at the same point. The cleaning of the canals and the removal of the encroaching tule were constant problems, generally solved by apportioning the task among the Indian towns along the route. When this was neglected the weed-choked canals much hampered the traffic, as in 1635, when four to five days, rather than the normal one day, were required for the trip.[189] The total number of canoes was estimated at 100,000 to 200,000 in the conquest period. In the seventeenth century the number of canoes entering the city was reported at more than a thousand per day. Presumably more accurate counts in the eighteenth century indicate that from 70 to 150 canoes were then entering the city each day, and a record of 1777 gives 26,246 canoe loads arriving in the city in that year.[190]

All this was possible because Indians retained their ancient skills as boatmen, and because Spaniards, who thought of transportation in connection with animals and wagons, rarely saw fit to learn the technique. Spaniards, however, owned and operated the *embarcaderos,* the stations for canoe loading in Lakes Chalco and Xochimilco, which were profitable properties managed after the manner of haciendas.[191] Independent Indian boatmen of the towns along the canal carried loads at prearranged prices, and transport activity provided an important occupation for the people of such towns. Canoe transport was less expensive than overland transport for hacendados and other Spaniards, and at various times Indians sought to take advantage of their situation by raising freight rates. An increase in charges from six reales to two pesos for the trip from Ayotzingo in the 1560's, and a similar increase from six reales to two and one-half pesos for the much shorter trip from Mexicalzingo in the 1630's, brought immediate Spanish complaints.[192] The normal price for the full trip from Chalco had risen to three and one-half pesos by the eighteenth century.[193] Spaniards in turn attempted to coerce the canoe operators, to detain the canoes for their own advantage, and in other ways to exploit the carriers. In the seventeenth century corregidores and others occasionally sought to establish canoe monopolies or to tax the traffic illegally. But on the whole, Indian boatmen remained free carriers to a surprising degree. In general, each trip required a special negotiation, and though standardized rates remained current for long periods, we have remarkably little evidence of systematic compulsion by Spaniards, of peonage or extortion, or of other kinds of exploitation in the use of Indian labor.[194]

In all, the location of towns with respect to routes, their traditions of craftsmanship, and their agricultural supply were factors that determined community success or failure in adapting to the economic conditions of the colony. Although it is quite true that all Indian towns were in a depressed economic state in the late colonial period, this was nevertheless a time of change in the fortunes of individual towns. Intricate combinations of circumstances brought relative prosperity to some communities and degradation to others. In several notable instances large and centrally located towns changed from an affluent condition to one of abject depression. The most conspicuous case is Texcoco, which in the early sixteenth century was a great city rivaling Tenochtitlan, but of which an eighteenth-century observer could say only that "the town is ruined now for lack of commerce."[195] Tacuba, the third city of the Aztec confederation, developed no industry and was overwhelmed by Spanish intrusion soon after the conquest; by the late eighteenth century it was a small suburban town with a population of hacienda peones, suppliers of wood and stone, gatherers of saltpeter, muleteers, pottery makers, and pulque sellers.[196] Coyoacan suffered a similar decline as an independent economic site; its concentration upon the masons' and builders' trades released it from dependence upon its own agriculture, but it never diversified its crafts. Cuauhtitlan was located on one of the great routes, but for Indians this meant deterioration rather than stimulation; although its pottery industry was preserved, it came to be celebrated as a backward and crime-ridden town, lacking in community pride. The whole of the Ecatepec region suffered as a result of its tequisquitl soils.[197] Its agriculture was limited and its people were impoverished.

The over-all pattern operating here appears to have been dominated in large part by drought. Spaniards of the eighteenth century attributed the decline of Tlatelolco to the process of desiccation and the alkalization of its soil. The Indians of Ixtapalapa possessed a large open pasturage area, but by 1790 not a single plant was growing on it. Otumba had the early advantages of its great artificial water supply, and it was an important pueblo, as an eighteenth-century Spaniard stated, so long as it had water. By the late colonial period, with the loss of its cochineal industry and the failure of its water, Otumba was a town of broken walls and ruins, "the driest and most depopulated in the country."[198]

Other towns, particularly those in the south where water remained abundant, did not decline so markedly. Huitzilopochco remained a small, wealthy Indian community in the eighteenth century, advantageously situated to profit from the capital markets. It supported a variety of local industries—salt and basket manufacture, fishing, pottery making—and its people were merchants trading in the city. It was essentially a commercial town, occupying a midway location between the tierra caliente and the city's markets.[199] Likewise Xochimilco retained its chinampa agriculture and its tradition of commerce; it was closely linked by canal with Tenochtitlan, and its lands did not attract Spanish exploitation. Although it was a large town, it successfully retained an Indian character. And in addition to its continuing chinampa agriculture, Xochimilco was perhaps the only late colonial community of the Valley of which it could be said that the majority of its adult male population were oficiales.[200]

A surprising sixteenth-century adaptation was made by Xaltocan, a community extremely well situated to exploit the lacustrine industries. The Indians of Xaltocan at the end of the sixteenth century gathered and sold quantities of salt and lime. From the lake reeds they made an industry of petate manufacture, and in the water they fished and hunted ducks and other birds, while the lakeshores provided tequisquitl for soap and dye making. They had fertile lands for dry farming as well as chinampas. "Industry and trade promote general prosperity," read the official congregación report of 1599. Fresh water came to Xaltocan from the springs of Ozumbilla, and wells provided ample drinking water. To the south of the town agricultural land was irrigated. The montes were several miles distant, but the inhabitants used horses to carry wood for fuel or burned dried maize stalks and zacate. The chinampas produced maize more abundantly than any others of the region, and it was a maize that matured rapidly and could be harvested while maize elsewhere was being killed by frosts. When surrounding towns suffered shortages their inhabitants came to Xaltocan for maize.[201] But these conditions did not last. By the eighteenth century the town's best lands were lost, and those that remained were too swampy for agriculture. The Indians had to rent maize fields from neighboring towns, and all the industries declined.[202]

Other towns made astonishing recoveries in late colonial times. Tepetlaoztoc, for example, attached itself to the profitable mule-carrier trade beginning in the mid-eighteenth century, and by the 1780's, with a population of 150 families, the community had forty-five mule stables and hostelries for the pack trains, each worth 2,000 pesos or more. In a single generation old houses were restored, new ones built, and an active trade established. The wealth of Tepetlaoztoc, according to a report of the late eighteenth century, was not concentrated in a few hands but was distributed throughout the population, and nudity, hunger, and misery were unknown.[203]

CHAPTER XIII

The City

In the Valley of Mexico the conquistadores established one *ciudad de españoles,* Mexico, or as it was known for a time, Mexico-Tenochtitlan. The decision to found the city on the site of the ruined Aztec capital was Cortés's own, and it prevailed against a contrary majority opinion of his followers.[1] The decision meant that the city would always be dangerously exposed to flood, that its environs would be swamp lands, that it would face unusual problems of water supply and commodity provision, and that relations with Indians on the island site would be of exceptional intimacy. For Indians, the site of the colonial capital required unique adjustments in labor and tribute. City life promoted miscegenation and the non-agricultural trades. City influences merged at all points with the myriad other forces that affected native peoples.

Spanish municipal authority, having at first asserted an enormous jurisdiction, was legally confined in 1539 to a radius of fifteen leagues.[2] In reality, its jurisdiction was confined to a still smaller area surrounding the city, for within the fifteen leagues the existing cabeceras, with their sujetos, were declared exempt from the capital city's control.[3] The exemption did not apply, of course, to viceregal and audiencia authority, which centered in the city and reached far beyond its limits. The viceroy and audiencia could demand Indian labor from any community in the Valley for the city's public works and could freely regulate relations between the city and the towns. But the corregidor and the municipal Spanish cabildo were dependent in such matters upon viceregal and audiencia favors. Although the Spanish cabildo repeatedly protested against the limitation of its powers, at times proposing alternative schemes such as making the corregidores of the surrounding jurisdictions alcaldes in the city government, it became progressively less effective through the colonial period. In the seventeenth century it was still citing the fifteen-league rule as the basis of its territorial demands. But because the cabildo was designed for the community of white colonists, its authority over Indians was always restricted and in doubt.[4]

In the environs of the city the Spanish cabildo's chief concern was not with the fifteen leagues assigned to it but rather with the maintenance of its ejidos—areas claimed as common or municipal properties outside the settled area and including the traditional Spanish *dehesas* or tracts for common pasturage.[5] The ejido boundaries were originally fixed by Nuño de Guzmán in the 1520's, and they underwent frequent revisions and confirmations, principally under audiencia direction.[6] Important ejido sections were located in the Guadalupe and Tenayuca areas, toward Coyoacan, and in other regions to the north, south, and west of the city.[7] The early problems related to the maintenance of ejido lands against Indian and private Spanish intrusion. Even after the original ejido survey the cabildo frequently found itself confronted with Indian occupation and Indian agriculture inside the limits. As the city expanded and increased in population, as larger numbers of cattle, pack trains, and animals for slaughter were required, and as the need for an extensive ejido property therefore increased, the lands themselves were reduced by cabildo thefts and by assignments of property to individuals.[8] The search for additional territories again brought the city into conflict with Indian communities in the late sixteenth century. North of Tlatelolco, native peoples were discovered to have moved the ejido boundaries in their own property interests. Indian houses and maize plantations within the ejidos were ordered destroyed, and the capital city's accumulated claims were confirmed in the early seventeenth century by the oidor Juan de Quesada y Figueroa.[9]

In the late seventeenth century the municipal cabildo undertook again to extend its ejidos, notably into the territories of Ixtapalapa, Ixtacalco, and other Indian communities to the south. New conditions of strife had now developed, for the native population had also begun to increase, and some of the former lake area could be used as pasture.[10] In the early eighteenth century the oidor Juan Díaz de Bracamonte resurveyed the ejidos and restored some of the ancient boundary markers, stimulating another series of disputes with Indian towns.[11] In typical instances the Indian towns were required to demonstrate their titles in sudden and peremptory orders. Those unable to do so argued title by immemorial possession or insisted on the necessity of occupation for community livelihood and payment of tributes. Occasionally the challenged communities were able to produce native mapas or títulos or viceregal grants dating from the sixteenth century. Legal suits were brought by the city against the communities of San Andrés, Ticoman, Tola, Coatlayuca, Mexicalzingo, and Chapultepec, and the remarkable fact is that all these Indian communities successfully defended themselves in court against the city's attack.[12]

The classic case occurred between the city and the Indian community of Tlatelolco, which was renting ejido lands to the Spanish proprietor of the hacienda of Santa Ana Aragón. Because the hacienda's occupation was at stake, the issue received special attention and ultimately came before the Council of the Indies in Spain. Both the audiencia and the Council of the Indies decided that the lands were ejidos and hence incapable of sale or rent by the Spanish cabildo, but that the Indians of Tlatelolco might properly enjoy their use and with special license might rent them to third parties. The outcome thus justified Tlatelolco's rental to the hacendado. The case illustrates how earnestly the lawyers of the eighteenth century sought to interpret traditional Indian common lands in terms of Spanish municipal land law—as capable of rental or sale, as requiring special dispensation, as property of the municipality, or as *concesión real*.[13] The failure of the eighteenth-century city to enlarge its territories indicates again the weakness of municipal authority in relation to other powers of the Spanish state.

Inside the city, the first Spaniards began by marking off the central portion, an area of some thirteen blocks in each direction, as the zone of white occupation. The region immediately surrounding this *traza* then comprised the colonial Indian community of San Juan Tenochtitlan, which consisted of the outer portions of the original four Indian barrios: Santa María Cuepopan (Tlaquechiuhcan) to the northwest; San Sebastián Atzacualco (Atzacualpa) to the northeast; San Pablo Zoquipan (Teopan, Xochimilco) to the southeast; and San Juan Moyotlan to the southwest. Each of the four was L-shaped at one of the four corners of the interior traza, and each necessarily gave up a portion of its territory to the Spanish center. The traza was symmetrically laid out with streets flanking rectangular blocks. Though some modifications in its size and internal form were made, its orderly plan always contrasted with the irregular disposition of streets in the Indian wards, and its monumental public and private buildings stood in equally sharp contrast to the Indians' adobe houses. The four barrios continued to

FORMA Y LEVANTADO DE LA CIUDAD DE MEXICO

Por la correspondencia de los numeros de Señan en esta Copia los conventos y casas señaladas.

N.º 1. Conventos de el Carmen
N.º 2. N.ra S.ra Agustin
N.º 3. S.to Domingo
N.º 4. S.t Pedro y S.ta Comp.ª
N.º 5. Mercenarios
N.º 6. Vot.ª el Carmen

Suma 18.

y una de Franc.te Diego, S.ta Maria, Sn. Pedro
S.t Agustin, S.t Diego, S.t Buenaventura, el Cruz
y otros S.t Domingo y S.ta Cat.l
Casa profesa, la Concep.ta el Hospicio y Cuna nombrada
N.ra S.ra d.la merced y N.ra S.ra de Belem.
y S.ta Ramon N.ra Montserrat

N.º 7. Monsas.
N.º 8. Hospitales.
N.º 9. Parroquias
N.º 10. Colegios

Suma 4.

A. Palacio R.l
B. Cathedral.
C. Casa de Cabildo.
D. Casa Arzp.l
F. Universidad.
G. Alameda.

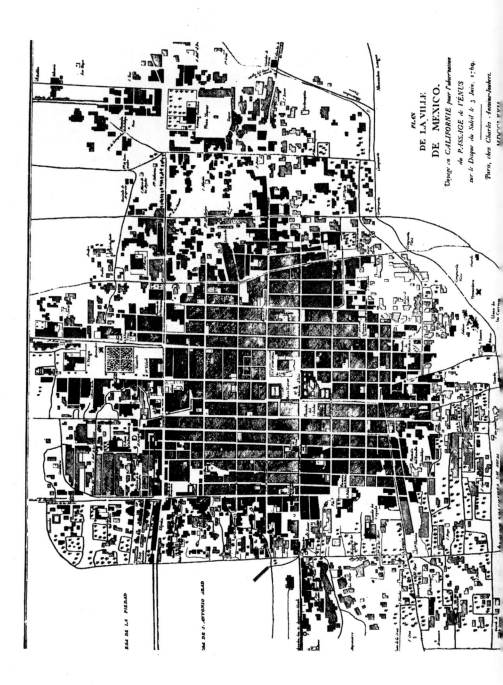

PLAN
DE LA VILLE
DE MEXICO.

Voyage en CALIFORNIE pour l'observation
du PASSAGE de VÉNUS
sur le Disque du Soleil le 3 Juin 1769.

Paris, chez Charles Antoine Jombert.

MDCCLXXII.

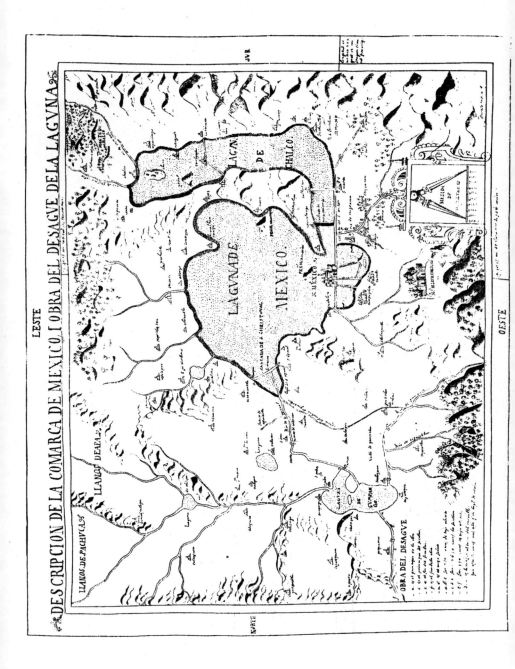

DESCRIPCION DE LA COMARCA DE MEXICO, I OBRA DEL DESAGVE DE LA LAGVNA

be subdivided into lesser units—also called barrios—and many of these lesser units retained their locations and native names through the colonial period.[14] At the northern end of the island bordering Santa María and San Sebastián was the distinct Indian cabecera of Santiago Tlatelolco, likewise divided into barrios, and separated from Tenochtitlan by the canal called Tezontlalli.[15]

San Juan Tenochtitlan and Santiago Tlatelolco, generally called partes or parcialidades of the total city, had separate Indian gobernadores and separate Indian cabildos throughout colonial times. By the middle years of the sixteenth century, Indian alcaldes were alternating among the Tenochtitlan barrios in the system of rotational representation based upon the surviving four-part division. Beneath the main four parts the lesser barrios were governed by tepixque, merinos, mandones, and similar officers, precisely as in other Indian communities.[16] In both parcialidades, and again as in other towns, the barrio subdivisions had functional meanings for community organization. When the Indians of Tenochtitlan complained to Spanish authorities about excessive demands by the sixteenth-century Indian governments, the particulars of the complaint were specified barrio by barrio. When the Indian governments undertook to organize labor for community tasks or for the construction of buildings for Spaniards, the work was subdivided among the lesser barrios. And when the Indian governments exacted tribute from the Indians of Tenochtitlan and Tlatelolco, the allotments and procedures of collection were similarly organized in accordance with the barrio subdivisions.[17]

Both San Juan Tenochtitlan and Santiago Tlatelolco, as cabeceras, also had jurisdiction over a number of estancias located outside the urban area. We have commented above on some of the most distant of these.[18] But each also had a large number of other estancias that were located closer to the city. These possessions originated in the pre-conquest period, and many of them are precisely mentioned in the documents of Indian imperialism as Aztec conquests, as possessions of Montezuma, as calpixqui locations, or in other ways. Some were subdivided and shared between Tenochtitlan and Tlatelolco, and within Tenochtitlan some were affiliated with one or another of the four barrios. The estancias, like the barrios, performed functional roles in the Indian governments, and like the estancias of other cabeceras they were liable to the tribute and labor demands of their cabeceras in Indian service.[19]

Spanish civil government paid little attention to this complex Indian organization. But the ecclesiastical government immediately recognized the Indian subdivisions and organized the missionary church in accordance with them. Under the direction of Cortés and Fray Pedro de Gante, in the first post-conquest years, each of the four Indian parts of Tenochtitlan became a distinct ecclesiastical unit.[20] With the establishment of the church, or chapel, of San José, adjoining the monastery of San Francisco inside the traza, the four Indian barrios emerged as visitas of San José, under Franciscan supervision.[21] Their iglesias de visita were San Juan (Baptista), Santa María de la Redonda, San Sebastián, and San Pablo. Since Tlatelolco was a separate Franciscan cabecera de doctrina, all the larger Indian subdivisions of the city were directly reflected in the early ecclesiastical structure.

To the extent that was practicable the Franciscans in Tenochtitlan and Tlatelolco also included within their visita jurisdictions the extra-urban estancias of the two parcialidades. San José at first ministered to Popotla, Ixtacalco, Ticoman, Tetecpilco, and other estancias of Tenochtitlan. The most distant visitas of San José were Santa Marta and Los Reyes on the mainland to the southeast, both of which were Tenochtitlan estancias.[22] The Franciscans in Tlatelolco maintained a visita connection at some distance with Santa Clara Coatitlan, one of the claimed Tlatelolco sujetos in dispute with the encomendero of Ecatepec.[23] Numerous other estancias of the two parcialidades were too distant for such visitation, but the examples mentioned suggest that here as elsewhere an effort was made in the early years to equate native cabecera-sujeto jurisdictions with the ecclesiastical organization.

In both Indian government and ecclesiastical organization, however, the relationship progressively broke down. By late colonial times a number of the sujetos of Tenochtitlan and Tlatelolco—Guadalupe, Ixhuatepec, Atlayauhtla (Santa María Magdalena Salinas), San Antonio de las Huertas, Popotla—had become pueblos with their own gobernadores.[24] In Tenochtitlan new alcaldes were introduced from Romita, La Piedad, Mixiuhca, Ticoman, and other subdivisions.[25] In Tlatelolco the number of alcaldes had increased to more than twenty by late colonial times. They represented individual barrios or small groups of barrios. Several were alcaldes of "pueblos" which were further subdivided into barrios but which retained allegiance and subordinate status to Tlatelolco, without separate gobernadores.[26] The various parcialidad controls over the distant estancias were gradually abandoned. Tlatelolco lost authority over Tepetlacalco, Coatepec, San Pablo de las Salinas, Xaloztoc, Ozumbilla, Tolpetlac, Xoloc, and other possessions.[27] The most distant estancias, those of Chalco province, were given up in the late eighteenth century, as we have seen.[28] A large number of sujetos to the south of the city, beginning with Nativitas (Tepetlatzinco) and Ixtacalco, and including Los Reyes, Santa Marta, and Ixtahuacan to the southeast, were transferred to the Mexicalzingo jurisdiction.[29] In the early nineteenth century Tenochtitlan still retained a tribute-collection authority over Xalpa, Chalmita, San Lucas Tepetlacalco, and Popotla, but the communities themselves fell under the political jurisdiction of the intendant of Tacuba.[30] Save for these four, the tribute jurisdiction of Tenochtitlan and Tlatelolco was reduced to a small area bounded by San Antonio de las Huertas to the west, Ixhuatepec to the north, the Peñon de los Baños to the east, and Nalverte and Santa Ana (Zacatlamanco) to the south. And even within this area some semi-independent communities with gobernadores existed.[31]

Beginning in the late sixteenth century ecclesiastical dependence upon the original Indian form similarly broke down. The first critical issue arose in the 1560's and 1570's, when the status of San José and the four barrio churches became the subject of Franciscan-secular dispute. In the interests of the secular clergy, Archbishop Alonso de Montúfar interpreted the four divisions as separate parishes and the Franciscan solution as a step toward combining four parishes into one.[32] Seculars sought to minister to the four churches. Strife broke out between Franciscans and Indians on one side and the secular clergy on the other.[33] San Pablo was transferred to the seculars and then to the Augustinians. San Sebastián was given first to the Carmelites and then in 1607 to the Augustinians. Santa María de la Redonda was assigned to the Franciscans as a separate cabecera de doctrina. Hence by the early seventeenth century only San Juan remained as a visita under San José.[34] Meanwhile two new doctrinas for Indians, Santa Cruz Coltzinco and Mixtecos, were founded. The former, in the east central part of the city between San Sebastián and San Pablo, extended into the traza as far as San Agustín. The latter had no definite boundaries, but it ministered, from Santo Domingo, to the Indian immigrants in various parts of the city.[35] When San Pablo was transferred to the Augustinians its extra-urban estancias remained as Franciscan visitas. But the visitas as a whole were reduced in number with the continuous establ hment of new cabeceras de doctrina.

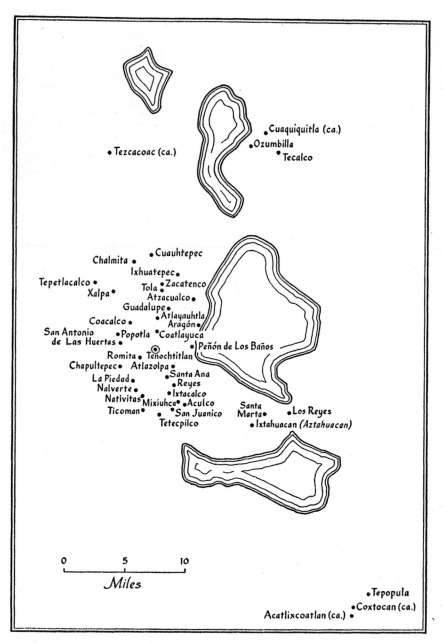

Map 11. Tenochtitlan sujetos, to the late eighteenth century.

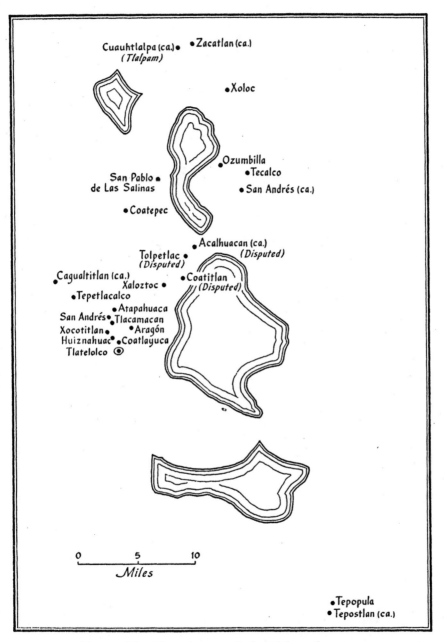

Map 12. Tlatelolco sujetos, to the late eighteenth century.

Coatlayuca, a sujeto of Tenochtitlan and former visita of San José, became a visita of Tlatelolco. Santa Marta became a distinct cabecera de doctrina with Los Reyes as its visita. Tetecpilco and Ticoman were attached to the separate doctrina of Mexicalzingo and then to Nativitas Tepetlatzinco.[36] In Tlatelolco, the Franciscans came into conflict with the parishes established for Spaniards. The church of Santa Catalina, in San Sebastián Atzacualco between the traza and Tlatelolco, was made the center of a parish that nominally included all of San Sebastián and half of Tlatelolco, while the remainder of Tlatelolco became attached to the parish of La Veracruz.[37] Coatitlan ceased to be a Tlatelolco visita and was attached to the Ecatepec ecclesiastical jurisdiction.[38] Thus by the early seventeenth century the distant visitas had been eliminated and the city was divided into three parroquias for Spaniards and seven for Indians, with their areas in some instances overlapping.[39]

It would be possible to trace the history of the ecclesiastical jurisdictions in Tenochtitlan and Tlatelolco in much greater detail. But the essential fact is that the various changes of the late sixteenth and early seventeenth centuries represented departures from the original Indian organization and corresponded directly to subsequent changes in the city's population. The influx of new Indian peoples, including non-Nahuatl speakers, was reflected in the doctrina of Mixtecos.[40] The progressive miscegenation, the spread of non-Indian populations outside the traza, and the penetration of the traza itself by native peoples were represented in the other ecclesiastical changes. At first it had been ruled that no Spaniard could live north of the traza in Santa María, San Sebastián, or Tlatelolco, and in 1528 all grants there were revoked. Thirty years later, however, the Spanish cabildo successfully defended its authority to assign properties outside the traza, and Indian and Spanish dwellings became steadily more interspersed. Many Spaniards lived in San Juan and San Pablo and the other Indian areas. The first episcopal usurpation of San Pablo and San Sebastián was intended to serve a resident Spanish population in those areas. The Cathedral parish included Indians, and the Indian parishes included Spaniards by the 1570's. The intrusion of Veracruz upon Tlatelolco in the 1560's was designed to accommodate Spanish, mestizo, and mulatto inhabitants. In the seventeenth century the doctrina of Santa María extended into the northwestern sector of the traza as far as the Cathedral. Even in the sixteenth century it could be argued that the Santa Catalina and Veracruz parishes, ostensibly for Spaniards, applied to Indians as well.[41] As would be expected, the ecclesiastics of the Indian areas in the city were unanimous in condemning the confusion of jurisdictions and populations.[42]

In the late seventeenth century, following disorders in the city, efforts were again made to separate Indian from non-Indian inhabitants. Urban regulations of the 1690's redefined the limits of the Spanish center, forbade Indians to establish residences there, and required native immigrants to return to their original communities.[43] Subsequently some of these same rules were repeated.[44] But the failure of all such efforts was expressed by the new subdivisions, ecclesiastical and secular, of the late eighteenth century. In the 1770's, with the secularization of San José, three new parishes were created. Their boundaries on the edges of the city were fixed essentially by the boundaries of the surviving Indian barrios, but all the parishes included Spaniards, Indians, and others, without ethnic separation.[45] The equivalent secular divisions were revised several times in the late eighteenth century, most notably in the creation of eight major and thirty-two minor wards in 1782. The wards, like the parishes, followed the boundary lines of some of the original Indian barrios, but other barrios were subdivided and regrouped and in general the effort was made to organize the city in a rational eighteenth-century form. The regulations spoke, as had preceding regulations, of a separation of Indian peoples in the city for ecclesiastical and tribute purposes. But the new system, once established, did nothing further to separate Indians from other inhabitants.[46]

The number of Indians in the city is a matter of fairly consistent record from the 1560's on, and our previous comments concerning the problems of interpreting population figures for the Valley as a whole apply with equal or greater force to the figures for the city. What many students would like to know, and what no one does know, is the size of the Indian population at the time of the conquest. It is at least possible that Tenochtitlan-Tlatelolco was the largest city of the occidental world in 1519. The upper limit of serious early estimates is found in the writings of Las Casas, who asserted that the Aztec capital contained over 50,000 houses, over 200,000 householders (*vecinos*), and a total population over 1,000,000.[47] Many other estimates, made from the sixteenth century to the present, might be cited.[48] Counts made in the early 1560's recorded a tributary population of between 18,000 and 21,636, with the latter figure representing the more careful count. The total population was counted at 75,665. In the most specific figures (1562),

Tenochtitlan was given a total of 45,335 and Tlatelolco a total of 30,330, with ratios respectively of 1 to 3.49 and 1 to 3.50 between tributaries and total population.[49] If we suppose a total Indian population of approximately 80,000 in 1560, and if we suppose the population of 1519 to have been three to five times that of 1560, a conquest population between about 250,000 and 400,000 would be indicated. No European city was so large as this in 1519.[50] It should be noted, however, that ratios of decline applicable to other communities may not be relevant to the city, which had been besieged with special intensity during the conquest and which received an unusual influx of Indian peoples from other areas during the colonial period. A Spaniard stated in 1534 that the urban Indian population was then still increasing. The oidor Vasco de Puga observed in the early 1560's that the number of Indians in the city had not declined at all to that date.[51]

Apart from temporary aberrations—as in the flood crisis of the early 1630's, when the tributary population dropped to an estimated 600—figures for the colonial Indian population of Tenochtitlan and Tlatelolco indicate, as one would expect, a decline from the 1560's to the middle seventeenth century and a rise thereafter. As in some other communities, the eighteenth-century rise was broken in the plague years beginning in 1736.[52] Figure 17 records what seem to be the most reliable statistical data, apart from the severe flood years, on urban Indian populations of the colonial period. The counts themselves should not be accepted unreservedly, for we know from many convincing commentaries of the difficulties of census-taking in the city's disorganized conditions. To the extent that they may be regarded as reliable, the figures indicate population movements of quite different orders for Tenochtitlan and Tlatelolco. In Tenochtitlan the eighteenth-century rise is fully evident, while in Tlatelolco one can hardly speak of a late colonial increase at all.

It is probable that the essential cause of this difference relates to aridity, and that here as elsewhere Indians tended to migrate from the arid regions. The depopulation of Tlatelolco was directly attributed in the late seventeenth century to the movement of Indians to Tenochtitlan. By the late eighteenth century it was quite evident that the most populous barrios were those nearest the water, notably to the southeast. In Tlatelolco as well as in the adjacent Santa María and San Sebastián sectors of Tenochtitlan, all once highly populous regions, the late colonial period was one of widespread desiccation. A Spanish resident in the late eighteenth century characterized all

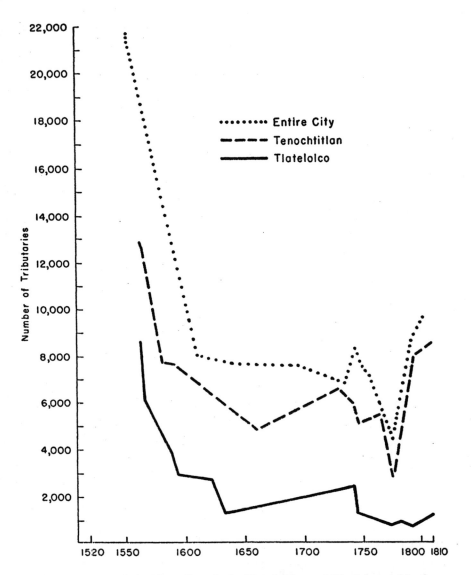

Figure 17. Recorded Indian tributaries in Tenochtitlan and Tlatelolco, and in the entire city, through the colonial period. Sources: see Appendix VI.

the northern portions of the city as *casi despoblados,* and stated that only vestiges of the earlier chinampas remained in the eastern parts of San Sebastián.[53] Thus drought and depopulation affected not only Tlatelolco but the northern parts of Tenochtitlan as well. Within Tenochtitlan, in the short span of fifteen years in the late eighteenth century, the barrios of San Juan to the west and Santa Cruz to the east became drought-ridden and sterile.[54]

We lack equivalent figures on the changes in the urban white population, largely because whites were not subject to tribute. Numerous contemporary estimates, however, suggest that the white increase was a steady one and that a total of about 70,000 was reached at the end of colonial times. There were temporary losses, as in the exodus during the floods of the late 1620's and early 1630's and in the epidemic of 1736–39, which affected whites as well as Indians.[55] But as with white population elsewhere in the Valley, no long-term declines took place. The same may probably be said for the city's Negro, mulatto, and mestizo populations, figures for which are even less reliable than for the whites. Mestizo children were sufficiently numerous to arouse comment as early as 1533. Mestizos were estimated at 2,000 and mulattoes at 1,000 about 1560.[56] Figures given for these classes in the mid-colonial period—on the order of 40,000 and 50,000—appear unreliable and exaggerated, perhaps because the mixed classes tended to concentrate in the sectors of heaviest white population.[57] The Revillagigedo census of the early 1790's, the first systematic count of all classes of the city's population, recorded a total of 26,451 that were neither white nor Indian. Humboldt, who knew the census figures, supposed that the total population of the city about 1800 stood at 135,000, and that of these the mestizo population accounted for some 26,500 and the mulatto for 10,000.[58] On the whole, it appears likely that the Indian population of the city outnumbered the Spanish by ten to one in the middle sixteenth century, that whites outnumbered Indians by more than two to one in the late eighteenth century, and that Indians approximately equaled the intermediate classes at the end of colonial times.[59] It is true that colonial peoples possessed only rough and pragmatic criteria for identifying an individual's affiliation with one group or another. Moreover, the success of some Indians in passing as mestizos in order to avoid tribute liability was well recognized in the city.[60]

The urban white population appears to have changed in inverse ratio to the attempts made at Indian Hispanization. In the sixteenth century, when

TABLE 27
Estimates of White Population in Mexico City

Date[a]	Number	Unit	Source
1525	150	houses	CDIAI, XIII, 77.
1550*	2,000	vecinos	López de Gómara, *Historia*, II, 106.
1557	1,500	households	Hakluyt, *The Principal Navigations*, IX, 355 (Robert Tomson).
1560*	3,000	houses	Latorre, *Relaciones geográficas*, p. 104.
1560*	8,000	men	Latorre, *Relaciones geográficas*, p. 104.
1569	5,000 to 6,000	men (?)	NCDHM (1941), II, 4.
1570	3,000	vecinos	López de Velasco, *Geografía y descripción*, p. 189.
1572	5,000 to 6,000	houses	Hakluyt, *The Principal Navigations*, IX, 380 (Henry Hawks).
1581*	4,000	vecinos	ENE, XV, 50.
1581*	8,000	men	ENE, XV, 50.
1585*	3,000+	vecinos	CDIHE, LVII, 174.
1600*	12,000 to 15,000	total (?)	Champlain, "Brief discovrs des choses," p. 41.
1610*	7,000	households (?)	Torquemada, *Monarchia indiana*, I, 299.
1612*	15,000+	total (?)	Vázquez de Espinosa, *Compendium and Description*, p. 156.
1625	30,000 to 40,000	total (?)	Gage, *A New Survey*, p. 122.
1629	20,000	families	*Memoria histórica . . . del desagüe* I, 132.
1646	8,000+	families (?)	Díez de la Calle, *Memorial*, p. 110.
1742*	50,000+	families	Villa-señor y Sánchez, *Theatro americano*, I, 35.
1790	52,706	total (except ecclesiastics and troops)[b]	"Noticias de Nueva-España en 1805," p. 8. Humboldt, *Political Essay*, I, 254.
1802*	67,500	total	Humboldt, *Political Essay*, II, 62.

[a]Asterisks indicate approximate dates.
[b]The number of ecclesiastics in the city is given as 8,166 in the census of 1790. See "Noticias de Nueva-España en 1805," p. 8. For numbers of troops see the tables in McAlister, *The "Fuero militar,"* Appendix I.

Spaniards were few and Indians many, serious efforts at Indian education were made. Later, when Indian population declined, these attempts were abandoned. The two most important early educational institutions for Indians were those mentioned above—San José in Tenochtitlan and the Colegio de Santa Cruz in Tlatelolco. At San José, established by Pedro de Gante in the first years following the conquest, instruction was given in reading, writing, singing, and the mechanical arts, as well as in Christian doctrine. Indians were taught to make paintings, images, retables, and other ornaments for Christian churches of the towns, and carpentry, shoemaking, smithing, and other trades were also taught. The school had some five hundred pupils in its early period, and Gante remained its leading figure for some fifty years.[61] The Colegio de Santa Cruz, which opened under Franciscan direction in the mid-1530's with about sixty Indian pupils, was an institution devoted more exclusively to humanistic learning.[62] The students, aged ten to twelve, were sons of caciques and principales and were drawn from many areas of the colony.[63] The teachers included not only Franciscan friars but also learned Indians, most notably Antonio Valeriano, who taught grammar at the colegio before serving as gobernador of Tenochtitlan in the 1570's.[64] Latin, logic, philosophy, and theology were taught. The school was supported by rural properties granted by Viceroys Mendoza and Velasco, and by properties in the city bequeathed by Indians.[65] It was an important cultural institution in the mid-sixteenth century, and among its productions were the Nahuatl-Latin herbal of Juan Badianus and a part of the textual and pictorial corpus of Sahagún.[66]

The decline of educational institutions in the city during the late sixteenth century and after may be taken as symptomatic of the subsequent Spanish neglect of formal Indian teaching. The Colegio de Santa Cruz never fulfilled the original hope that it would serve as a seminary for an Indian clergy. When the ecclesiastical council of 1555 forbade the creation of an Indian priesthood the colegio lost one of the principal reasons for its existence.[67] Latin, logic, philosophy, and theology were dropped from its curriculum.[68] Viceroys after Luis de Velasco failed to support it, and efforts were made to divert its income to other recipients. The annual royal grant of 300 ducados to the San José school similarly lapsed and both schools were in danger of extinction by 1570. In the early seventeenth century the Colegio de Santa Cruz was reduced to an elementary school for pupils from Tlatelolco itself. Its buildings fell into decay, and its faculty later in the century consisted of only two persons teaching reading and writing.[69] Proposals to restore its original character in the eighteenth century came to nothing. Only vestiges of its former buildings remained at the end of colonial times.[70]

Other institutions in the city dedicated to the welfare of Indians were always limited both in number and in influence. The Jesuit Colegio de San Gregorio had only seventeen Indian students in the 1590's, shortly after its foundation, and some of these were diverted to the labor gangs of the repartimiento system. In 1728 it had only fourteen pupils, and after the Jesuit expulsion in the 1760's it ceased to function.[71] The Colegio Seminario de la Metropolitana, founded in the late seventeenth century, offered sixteen scholarships in the early eighteenth century, of which four were for sons of caciques, and a colegio and convent for daughters of Indian caciques were established in the eighteenth century.[72] Efforts to educate mestizos were confined almost entirely to the Colegio de San Juan de Letrán, founded in the mid-sixteenth century. The institution offered instruction in Christian doctrine, reading, writing, grammar, and additional subjects, including the begging of alms. In 1579 only eighty mestizo students were in attendance, and most of these left at the end of their first year.[73] The Hospital Real de Indios, the most enduring of the institutions for non-whites, had eight wards, two doctors, and two surgeons in the eighteenth century, and an average of about three hundred patients. It was a hospital not in the instructional sense of Quiroga's Santa Fe, but exclusively for the cure of the sick. Its continued existence, while other institutions for Indians failed, may be explained by the fact that it was maintained by the Medio Real in Indian tribute.[74]

Apart from the decay of the formal instructional institutions, Spanish neglect of the Indian population of the city is documented in numerous ways. Frequent commentaries refer to the untaught, unsettled, and criminal character of the city's mixed population, its "pueblo bajo" of Indians, Negroes, mestizos, and mulattoes. Murder was reported to be a daily occurrence during the late sixteenth century.[75] Pitched battles between the Indians of Tlatelolco and those of the adjacent Tenochtitlan barrio of Santa María were traditional annual events.[76] In the eighteenth century the number of homicides was reported to have increased, and the Spanish government specified severe punishment for Indians who carried arms.[77] Spaniards spoke repeatedly in late colonial times of the vile, vicious, fetid, homeless, and unclothed population of the city, living in filth and disease and drunkenness. Humboldt estimated in the first years of the nineteenth century that ten or fifteen thousand of the city's inhabitants were sleeping in the open. The extreme urban squalor aroused repeated comment, in conjunction with observations on the depressed state of Indians and mestizos.[78] It is clear from the accounts that urban poverty in the seventeenth and eighteenth centuries had a special character, distinct from that of the towns and countryside, and that large portions of the late colonial city were slums.

On two occasions the urban masses rose in revolt against the Spanish government.[79] The first uprising, in 1624, occurred at a time of high maize prices and of sharp disputes between the viceroy and the archbishop. A crowd of Indians and mestizos stormed the viceregal palace, denounced the viceroy as a heretic, and in other ways demonstrated partisanship for the archbishop.[80] The second uprising, in 1692, also came at a time of high prices and was even more violent. It resulted in damage to the Spanish casas de cabildo, the viceregal palace, the jail, and other buildings. Indians were reported to have planned the revolt over a period of three months and to have selected a native king to lead them, their intention being to burn the city and slaughter the Spaniards as they fled from the houses. The Indian leaders were executed, and in both instances the disturbances were quickly suppressed.[81]

Efforts by Spaniards to organize the city's native population were directed primarily toward securing labor and tribute. Until 1564 the Indian population paid no tribute in money or in material goods to Spanish authorities, their tribute obligation being regarded as commuted to labor service for the city's need.[82] In the earliest period a substantial part of this service was devoted to the individual governors of the Spanish state. All the first heads of state—Cortés, Estrada, Nuño de Guzmán, Ramírez de Fuenleal, Antonio de Mendoza—received the direct service of the Indians of Tenochtitlan and Tlatelolco.[83] Through the sixteenth century, in an extension of this early service, Indians of the city were required to supply firewood, fodder, and water for the personal use of the viceroy and other royal officials. As in the "servicios" of supply to which other communities were liable, these provisions were paid for, but always at sub-market prices, and the payments were made not to the Indian workers but to the alguaciles in charge of the levies.[84]

A more productive form of Indian organization was devoted to the construction of buildings. Apart from private residences, many of which were built with early encomienda labor, the major building operations of the sixteenth century were the monasteries of Santo Domingo and San Agustín, the Franciscan chapel of San José, the Cathedral, the Hospital Real, the casa de fundación, and the casa real.[85] Relatively little major new building was begun in the late sixteenth century, but many existing structures required repair, and the constant sinking of the heavy buildings meant that new floors had to be laid and pillars and doorways elevated. The hundred-year labor on the second Cathedral began in the 1560's, with an extensive underground foundation to hold the massive structure in place.[86]

Other undertakings related to causeways, street pavements, canals, bridges, and the supply of water. The original Aztec causeways, connecting the city with Guadalupe to the north, Tacuba to the west, and Mexicalzingo and Coyoacan to the south, remained the principal causeways of the colonial period, but they were continually modified, strengthened, and repaired. The longest, San Antonio Abad directly south of the main plaza, was measured at 7,000 varas in the seventeenth century. The widest, San Cosme, connecting the city with Tacuba, measured fourteen varas across.[87] In the later colonial period several new approaches to the city were constructed, notably a road in the southeast to Los Reyes and beyond.[88]

The city's internal avenues had originally consisted both of raised streets and of canals, but in the colonial period the balance was sharply changed in favor of streets, and the change required extensive labor in the carrying and placement of earth fill. A large part of the work of conversion took place in the sixteenth century. It was a continuous operation, however, and was still being carried on at the end of the colonial period.[89] The paving of streets, accomplished most successfully with the globular stones from the Río de Tacubaya called *tenayucas,* gradually overcame the dust and mud of the central portions of the city.[90]

Canal labor involved not only the filling of canals to make streets but the regular maintenance of those canals that were permitted to remain. In periods of low water the levels of the canals receded alarmingly. When rainy seasons came late the muddy canal bottoms were malodorously exposed, and canoes were unable to navigate.[91] Even in periods free from drought or flood the accumulated sewage and other fill of the canals required removal, both to facilitate canoe traffic and to minimize the danger of future flood.[92] The main canal of the colonial period entered the city from Mexicalzingo and approached the traza on its eastern side, where a spur led directly to the Plaza del Volador and the Plaza Mayor. It was by this route that goods could come by water from Lakes Chalco and Xochimilco to the center of the city. Other major canals crossed the city from west to east along the north edge of the traza, between Tenochtitlan and Tlatelolco, just south of the Tlatelolco plaza, and in a curving route through the southern part of the traza. Many minor canals also remained in the eighteenth century, particularly in the four Indian barrios outside the traza. The main canals flowed into Lake Texcoco through sluices in the San Lázaro dike. All canals were crossed by bridges, and these also required constant maintenance and repair.[93]

Drinking water for the city was brought from springs some distance away. The canal waters, although "fresh" as regards salinity, were always polluted by wastes. Water was available under the city at a depth of four or five feet, and houses regularly had shallow wells for household uses, but it was not a potable supply.[94] The original Aztec aqueduct of the mid-fifteenth century from the Chapultepec springs had been broken by the Spaniards during the conquest and required rebuilding for Spanish and Indian use. This was accomplished with Indian labor in the 1520's and 1530's, but when Chapultepec water proved insufficient in the 1560's and 1570's efforts were undertaken to supplement it with water from sources in the Culhuacan-Huitzilopochco region and from much more distant sources in Santa Fe and Cuauhximalpan to the west.[95] A provisional aqueduct from Santa Fe was built in the 1570's, but work on a more durable construction continued into the seventeenth century.[96] In its completed form this was a magnificent aqueduct, consisting of approximately a thousand arches from Chapultepec to the center of the city, passing through La Verónica, Tlaxpana, and San Cosme, delivering water at the Puente de Mariscala (near the present Teatro Nacional), and in constant need of cleaning, maintenance, and repair. To it in the late eighteenth century was added a supply from the Desierto de Leones, both this and the Santa Fe water entering the city by the same aqueduct. Chapultepec water entered the city by a second aqueduct, under fairly continuous construction from the sixteenth to the eighteenth centuries. It also had some thousand arches and terminated in the Salto del Agua. The colonial city did not use the waters of Xochimilco and Lerma, the principal sources of modern supply.[97]

In spite of these large-scale operations, at no time were all parts of the city equally supplied with potable water. A vast Indian laboring force built the various aqueducts mainly for the Spanish sections of the city. The preconquest aqueduct had supplied a tank in Tlatelolco as well as Tenochtitlan, and its reconstruction in the first post-conquest years temporarily supplied both parcialidades. In 1532 there were four water outlets in the plaza of the

Spanish traza, others in the markets of Tlatelolco and Tenochtitlan, and still others in Spanish houses.[98] Water was brought to the Indian market in San Juan (near the Salto del Agua) and to the barrio of San Pablo, farther east, about 1575. These still were provided with water in the 1590's, but with the depletions of the late sixteenth century Tlatelolco was cut off from the Chapultepec supply, and the inhabitants of the northern part of the city had to depend on drinking water from the wells and canals. Another undertaking of the 1590's, therefore, was the construction of a new aqueduct from Azcapotzalco to Tlatelolco.[99] But this also functioned only temporarily, and during large parts of the seventeenth century Tlatelolco had no drinking water, a fact that is surely related to its progressive depopulation. Water was again made available to Tlatelolco in 1688, but in the eighteenth century this again failed.[100] Occasionally additional Indian quarters of the city were connected with the system in the eighteenth century. At the end of the colonial period, in spite of the huge constructions that had been undertaken, the aqueduct from Huitzilopochco was in ruins, Tlatelolco had no water, the original springs in Chapultepec were no longer being used, and the main water supply was frequently interrupted.[101]

At all stages of these various enterprises—buildings, causeways, streets, canals, and water supply—Indian labor was recruited by repartimiento. The officials in charge were variously the viceroy and his subordinates, the obrero mayor of the city's public works, special urban jueces repartidores, the Indian gobernadores of Tenochtitlan and Tlatelolco, and the Indian mandones and other barrio officials. Tenochtitlan and Tlatelolco were separate subdivisions in the early labor drafts, each with its juez repartidor.[102] In the early period Tenochtitlan and Tlatelolco alternated in the service for Viceroy Mendoza.[103] In the second half of the sixteenth century, with the establishment of the jueces and of percentage quotas, both parcialidades became liable to the organized repartimiento and, as in other towns, repartimiento labor for Spaniards functioned side by side with the native coatequitl for Indian officials and the communities.[104] Laborers were conducted by merinos, alguaciles, and others from the local barrios to the jueces repartidores and by them assigned to employers. Unlike the agricultural repartimiento, the urban drafts always classified workers in the two categories of skilled and unskilled workers, the former called oficiales, and the latter at first called maceguales and later generally called jornaleros or peones. Oficiales were principally carpenters and masons and were in great demand by Spanish employers.[105] In the 1570's Tenochtitlan and Tlatelolco were each expected to give 300 Indians in monthly rotation, of whom 240 were to be peones and 60 to be oficiales. From this labor pool the viceroy, the members of the audiencia, and other royal officers were entitled to draw as many workers as they wished for personal services; the Chapultepec aqueduct was to receive 50; the Monjas de la Concepción 30; the Dominicans 80 for the building of their monastery and 12 for regular services; and other recipients numbers in accordance with preassigned quotas.[106] Because the original liability of the city's Indians to labor in the maintenance of causeways, aqueducts, and streets was in lieu of tribute liability, no wages were paid in these tasks until the 1550's.[107]

Like the agricultural repartimiento, the urban repartimiento suffered from the depopulations and other disorders of the late sixteenth and early seventeenth centuries. In 1563 the Indian government of Tenochtitlan was already experiencing difficulties in meeting its quotas, both in the labor for Indian operations and in that for the public works.[108] Condemned criminals and slaves were put to work on the public works in the middle sixteenth century. Tenochtitlan, which was to provide 300 workers per month in 1572, was actually furnishing only 200 or 250. In 1590 the barrio of San Sebastián was required to give 30 carpenters and 30 masons but had only 23 carpenters and 25 masons to give.[109]

To compensate for the dearth of urban workers, the repartimiento recruited Indians from other towns of the Valley. This was actually a tradition from the earliest times, for Cortés had once assigned to the city six lakeside towns—Ixtapalapa, Huitzilopochco, Mexicalzingo, Culhuacan, Cuitlahuac, and Mixquic. Most of these were later reassigned to private encomenderos, but the city managed to retain Ixtapalapa as its putative encomienda town in the later sixteenth century.[110] Thus for a time the city was able to use Ixtapalapa laborers as other encomenderos were using the Indians of their encomiendas.[111] In special assignments under viceregal authority other communities were also expected to supply Indians for urban tasks. In the 1560's Texcoco, Chalco, and Tacuba jurisdictions were ordered to give two to three hundred workers apiece for weekly labor on the Cathedral, Santo Domingo, San Agustín, and other tasks.[112] As one might expect, such drafts competed with quotas already given for agriculture, and in the later sixteenth century the urban and the agricultural repartimientos were simultaneous drafts, drawing workers from each other. In the 1570's the town of Coyoacan was temporarily excused from its agricultural repartimiento obligations to send

200 Indian carpenters, masons, painters, and other workers for the casas reales. In the 1580's some 50 workers were diverted from the Texcoco quota in the agricultural repartimiento to work on the city's pavements. At the end of the sixteenth century the labor quotas of a number of towns—Cuauhtitlan, Tepetlaoztoc, Tenayuca, Tizayuca—were raised from four to five per cent, the additional one per cent being applied to the public works of Mexico City. Hence in many special cases, based commonly upon separation from the agricultural drafts in the sixteenth and early seventeenth centuries, the city received workers from every part of the Valley. The viceroy's inclination was always to shift repartimiento tasks from one place to another as individual and institutional demands were brought to his attention.[113]

As in agricultural repartimiento also, pressures in urban repartimiento induced irregularities, coercion, and illegal manipulations of the conditions of employment. The Indian gobernadores of Tenochtitlan and Tlatelolco connived with Spanish employers to sentence Indian debtors to obrajes and other enterprises, outside of repartimiento. Within repartimiento, repartidores yielded to extreme viceregal and audiencia demands for Indian masons, carpenters, tailors, smiths, candlemakers, and servants, and to the requests of other royal officials for skilled and unskilled workers. Laborers were taken from the Chapultepec aqueduct and privately turned over to individual employers. Indians worked and were not paid. The monasteries, churches, and private persons with licenses for woodcutting (notably in the montes of Chalco province) sold the licenses to contractors, who exploited and defrauded the Indian woodcutters. Repartidores made preferential assignments, favoring some employers with oficiales and full quotas, ignoring other employers, and holding workers for special purposes. Private employers sequestered workers and hired them out for profit, to the point at which the viceroy in the early seventeenth century allowed the public works authorities of the city to offer advanced wages in an official and competing system of peonage.[114]

Labor obligation was held to be the justification for the early tribute exemption of the Indians of the city. But one must remember that the native governments of Tenochtitlan and Tlatelolco, like those of other communities, had traditionally been supported in the pre-Spanish period by contributions from Indians and that this intra-Indian taxation was at no time included in the exemption.[115] The early colonial records of intra-Indian tribute indicate continued contributions of fish, frogs, salt, fowl, petates, and other goods for the gobernador and community.[116] The tribute was increased to two reales by Spanish order in 1549, and applied both to the Indian government and to the support of ecclesiastics, and although this was the equivalent of similar tributes in other towns it aroused immediate Indian opposition in the city. Several Indians were hanged in the middle sixteenth century for their refusal to pay it.[117] In the 1550's and early 1560's the tax was collected in the form of one-half real, or one-half real and ten cacaos, every eighty days (as in the original Aztec system) to make a total of between two and two and one-half reales per tributary per year.[118] The exemption thus applied only to the additional tribute for the Spanish government, and it continued to be justified in terms of the urban Indians' labor on the public works.

The city's exemption from normal tribute received criticism in the royal interest as early as the 1530's, and in the 1540's an ineffective assessment was proposed, at 4,000 pesos per year.[119] An inquiry made by the oidor Alonso de Zorita disclosed that the Indian government in Tlatelolco was already collecting more tribute than would have been paid to the royal treasury, and that it had taken over 50,000 pesos in advance.[120] A royal order requiring full tribute payment in the city was then issued in 1551. But the definitive regulation was made only in 1564 under the stimulus of the royal investigator Jerónimo de Valderrama.[121] Tributaries of Tenochtitlan and Tlatelolco were required for the first time to pay one peso and one-half fanega of maize apiece per year, with half payment by half-tributaries, widows, widowers, bachelors, and spinsters. Because the city was not a producer of maize, commutation of the maize payment at three reales per half-fanega was permitted.[122] Renewed Indian resistance took the form of open rebellion in both Tenochtitlan and Tlatelolco, with an attempt on the life of the gobernador. Some fifty Indians were captured and the gobernador, alcaldes, and regidores of Tenochtitlan were jailed for their failure to collect the tax and maintain order. Indians stoned the community house of Tenochtitlan, and in Tlatelolco the collectors were stoned and further imprisonments followed.[123]

The urban tribute nevertheless went into effect, and thereafter Indians of the city paid a tribute roughly equivalent to that of Indians elsewhere. Of the maize tribute or its equivalent in money, one-third was intended for the public works of the city and two-thirds for the community treasuries of Tenochtitlan and Tlatelolco and for the support of clergy. This meant, in effect, that each full tributary paid eleven reales per year, of which eight went to the crown, two to the Indian government, and one to the Spanish city.[124] The amounts were computed with absolute precision in the late sixteenth century. In the assessment made for Tenochtitlan in 1580, the 7,871 tributaries were to give 7,871 pesos in regular tribute and 2,951 pesos, 5 reales, for the community and public works. Of the latter amount, 1,967 pesos, 6 reales, was for the Indian treasury and 983 pesos, 7 reales, went to the Spanish cabildo for public works.[125] Half-tributaries gave 5½ reales, of which 4 were for the royal treasury, one for the community and one-half for the public works. The Spanish cabildo thus received a regular income, from which materials might be purchased and salaries paid for its pavements, canals, aqueducts, and other projects.[126]

In the sixteenth and seventeenth centuries the Indian governments had authority over the procedures of tribute collection as in other towns. The total amount was assessed on the basis of population counts, and the native governments of the two parcialidades were held liable for annual payments of this amount until a new assessment was made. Collections were arranged by barrios, and the merinos and other barrio officers were the actual collectors of tribute.[127] The Mixteca and Zapoteca populations in the city, the Tarascan and Chichimeca groups, and the "nación Meztitlan," each had its alguacil in charge of collection.[128] We have commented above on Códice Valeriano, the remarkable tribute record of a Tenochtitlan barrio in 1574, where the systematic Indian collection is carefully set forth in a pictorial and Nahuatl report. Códice Valeriano indicates full tributary payments of eleven reales per year, with four reales paid in each of the first two four-month periods, and three reales in the third. Separate sections cover the half-tributaries, and notes by the collectors relate to special circumstances such as deaths and changes from one category to another.[129]

From the start the Indian governments experienced difficulties in making collections. As elsewhere, the population counts fell rapidly out of date in a declining population, and the dead and absent had to be paid for by the present and living. Lists of tributaries were inaccurately compiled and often included duplications and names of persons totally unknown.[130] Because servants and workers in Spanish houses and employees of obrajes were difficult to reach, the Indian government yielded responsibility for tribute of persons in these classes to Spanish collectors. Accordingly for a time Spanish alguaciles appeared as tribute collectors under the presumptive authority of

Indian gobernadores. At a later time Indian collectors were again made responsible for private servants and obraje workers, and although the collectors were empowered to enter private Spanish houses, these tributary classes remained in large part beyond control.[181] Gobernadores in the seventeenth century used extortionist methods, sequestered receipts, misrepresented and falsified the tribute record, demanded double payments, and used many kinds of coercion.[182] Arrears developed from the earliest periods. Collectors and payers of tribute, as well as Indian gobernadores, alcaldes, and regidores, were repeatedly jailed by the Spanish state for failure to provide the full sum.[133]

In other jurisdictions it was customary for corregidores, at the time of taking office, to obtain security and bond for tribute delivery. But corregidores in the city successfully resisted this procedure, and instead the Indian gobernadores themselves were required, after the early seventeenth century, to secure bonds in Tenochtitlan and Tlatelolco. The bondsmen included Spaniards and mestizos as well as Indians, and the bonds were offered in a formal contract of obligation. A list of 1674 shows sixteen bondsmen, of whom thirteen were Spaniards and mestizos and three were Indians, the amounts being on the order of 500 to 1,000 pesos apiece.[134] Thus each gobernador was held responsible for tribute from his parcialidad and if the amount collected proved to be not enough he and the bondsmen were held liable from their own funds. Houses and other properties of gobernadores, alcaldes, regidores, and bondsmen were sequestered in lieu of payment. Ability to obtain security became one of the criteria for candidacy to the gobernador's office in Tenochtitlan and Tlatelolco, and it proved increasingly difficult to find non-Indians willing to jeopardize their properties in this way.[135]

Arrears continued despite arrests and bondsmen. In the early eighteenth century the city's arrears amounted to about 25,000 pesos in ordinary tribute, plus about 5,000 more for the Medio Real de Fábrica and the Servicio Real. In the forty years prior to 1735, the amount collected in city tribute was less than the assessed amount by about 350,000 pesos. Scarcely one-third of the amount owed was actually received.[136] Faced with a desperate situation, the Spanish government in the early eighteenth century began to remove portions of tribute control from the Indian authorities. In 1713 the gobernador of Tlatelolco no longer had charge of normal tributes or Servicio Real. His authority was limited to the so-called *pensión* or tribute destined for the city's public works. In the 1720's collection was suspended entirely, and finally the Spanish government determined to rent out the collection privilege to private Spanish bidders. The rental system went provisionally into effect in 1736, was given up because of the plague of that year, began again in 1743, and continued for about forty years.[137]

The mid-eighteenth century, while the rental system was in effect, was a time of extreme disorder in tribute procedure. Each full tributary now theoretically owed twelve reales annually. But the tributary lists were drawn up by congregating Indians in the public places of Tenochtitlan and Tlatelolco, and the lists therefore included only those persons whom the respective Indian governments could round up. Moreover, the lists specified names and ages only, giving no further identification by way of residence or profession. The tributary population itself continued to be of impermanent location as individuals shifted from house to house and from barrio to barrio. The large numbers of vagabonds or transients, who formed a substantial part of the tributary population, were described as "almost imaginary" for tribute purposes. Names and professions were changed. Tributaries lied about their marital status and their position on the matrícula.[138] Indians claimed to be mestizos or descendants of caciques, and tribute collectors had no way to prove their status. About eight hundred prominent Spanish urban families maintained household staffs of five or more Indian tribute payers each, and the 6,000 pesos of tribute that these persons represented proved to be virtually impossible to collect. Collectors, like others, found it difficult to tell one tributary from another, for Indians had similar names and wore similar clothing and to European eyes they all looked alike. Efforts to count the numerous employees of the royal cigar factory in the city were frustrated by the factory directors, who saw the effort as an interference. Arrest proved ineffective and too expensive a punishment.[139]

Notwithstanding these confusions, tribute rental resulted at first in an increased income for the royal treasury, for the renters paid the treasury directly. But few persons were willing to serve as tribute collectors, and occasionally no one bid for the position at all. The expenses were considerable, for subordinate staffs had to be paid, receipts for payment printed, and other running expenses met. Nearly all renters suffered personal losses, and an additional disadvantage was the active hatred, the "almost universal persecution," to which they were subjected by the tributary community. In 1776, when the new assessment for Tenochtitlan showed a decline in the number of tributaries, the Spanish administration adopted a policy of deceit by withholding this information and renting the collection on the basis of the former assessment of 1765. Thus the collector paid for the collection privilege an amount substantially larger than the tributary list allowed him to collect. In 1782 the administration abandoned the rental system altogether and made the Indian governments again responsible.[140]

The last years of tribute collection in the city are abundantly documented. Barrio records, the early nineteenth-century equivalents of Códice Valeriano, now in a thoroughly Hispanized form, show the numbers of tributaries, the amounts paid, and the distinction between married and single persons. As elsewhere, women were now exempt, the Indian alcaldes and other collectors took a fraction of the income as salary, and receipts were issued for payment. A number of the working papers of alcaldes have survived, with their lists, notes, tables, and arithmetical jottings.[141] Despite the intendancy laws requiring payment at seventeen reales, Indian tributaries in the city paid thirteen reales in the late colonial period, with half payments by single persons.[142] New rules required weekly payments, and provided that salary withholdings of one real per week be made by employers. Tributary lists were arranged not only by location in the Indian barrios but by obrajes, places of employment, professions, and the labor force of the tobacco factory.[143] Viceroy Revillagigedo pointed with pride to the 12,550 pesos collected in 1793, stating (not quite accurately) that in previous years scarcely one-half this amount had been received. The truth is that not once between 1790 and 1809 was the full amount of the assessment actually collected.[144] The three gobernadores of Tlatelolco of 1805, 1806, and 1807 were jailed for arrears. Accumulated tribute arrears in the eighteenth century exceeded 100,000 pesos.[145]

As in other Indian communities, the tributes in Tenochtitlan and Tlatelolco represented only one aspect of community finance. The Indian governments of the parcialidades received income not only from intra-Indian tribute but also from property rentals and sales, and from other sources. The two governments owned and rented pulquerías, pasture lands, and a number of urban and rural holdings in the eighteenth century, from all of which they derived a regular annual income.[146] The expenses of the city governments included salaries of officeholders and of the maestros de escuela, community lawsuits, construction and repair of buildings, fiestas, and purchases of goods. Their finances in the eighteenth century involved thousands of pesos while other communities operated in tens and hundreds. At the same time that the governments owed huge amounts in tribute arrears and maintained the indebtedness on their books, they made bequests of thousands of pesos to the crown.[147]

By the late sixteenth century the Indian government had lost nearly all its original authority over commerce and other areas of economic life within the city. Regulation of markets and supplies had fallen wholly to Spaniards, and the Spanish state had assumed control over both the white and the Indian economies, as well as over the intermediate exchanges that affected both. A major change in urban Indian commerce during the sixteenth century was the decline of the Tlatelolco market and the concentration of the main exchanges in Tenochtitlan. The Tlatelolco plaza was still attracting native buyers and sellers to a number estimated at 20,000 in the middle 1550's. But by the early seventeenth century an observer could say of the Tlatelolco market that "it means less for what it is than for the memory of what it was."[148] The San Juan market near the southwest corner of the traza was equally large and continued to be used extensively while the Tlatelolco market declined.[149] But the new Indian market of San Hipólito, created in the 1540's, usurped much of the traffic from both. San Hipólito attracted Spaniards and Indians from all parts of the Valley in the late sixteenth and seventeenth centuries.[150] The central plaza likewise served as a market, and the secondary plazas of Tenochtitlan, especially the Plaza del Volador, became market areas as well.[151]

All these markets operated to some degree on a daily schedule, as the Tenochtitlan and Tlatelolco markets had in pre-conquest times. The daily markets of the colonial city, however, dealt largely in foodstuffs, and regular market areas were assigned weekly.[152] The orderliness of the Indian markets, which had so impressed the first Spaniards, had broken down in San Hipólito by the 1560's, and the Indian markets suffered disarrangement after the Spanish manner.[153] The efforts of the sixteenth century to confine sellers of chickens, fruit, atole, and other foods to the plazas were unsuccessful, and in the seventeenth century Indians were permitted to sell foods freely in or out of the plazas. In late colonial times Spaniards, Indians, and mestizos were helter-skelter in the markets. Stalls, no longer limited to the marketplaces, were scattered throughout the city. Indians trafficked in goods from house to house and hawkers roamed everywhere.[154]

Two basic products of Indian consumption, pulque and maize, were especially subject to Spanish controls in the city economy.[155] The provision of pulque was unregulated at first and Indians and others manufactured, bought, and sold it freely. Spanish regulation thereafter took a number of forms, including absolute prohibition after the tumult of 1692 and restrictions on the number of taverns in more normal times.[156] The authorized taverns increased from twelve in the sixteenth century to forty-five in the eighteenth century.[157] But many special licenses were also issued for Indian sales of miel de maguey and pulque in the markets, outside of the specified taverns. The real control, of course, fell into the hands of the hacendados of the Valley, such as the Conde de Regla and the Conde de San Bartolomé de Xala. Tremendous profits could be made from the sale of pulque; in the late colonial period consumption in the city amounted to some seventy-five gallons per person per year.[158]

The fertile areas of the city's outskirts were never sufficient to provide maize for urban needs. No evidence has yet come to light of any system of agricultural landholding in the city corresponding to the calpullalli of the towns. Instead, all known urban properties were privately held, and they were used far more as residential sites than as cultivated plots.[159] Maize was grown by Indians within the city limits in the chinampas, but the chief yield here was the immature ears called *elotes* rather than the developed grain.[160] The irrigated areas to the south of the city, along the main canal, and the fertile region west of the city, in Tlaxpana and San Antonio de las Huertas, were intensely productive agricultural zones, but their produce consisted more of legumes than of maize. Many Indians in the city had no knowledge of agriculture whatever. They customarily bought maize in surrounding towns at harvest time, and occasionally the parcialidades were relieved of a portion of their repartimiento obligations so that people might go out into the towns for maize purchases.[161] The recurrent shortages in the city's maize supplies gave rise to that series of regulations to which we have referred, including the rule that corregidores were to transmit maize from the towns to the city, and the rule that Indians were to sow ten varas as part of their tribute obligation.[162] The shifting relations between the urban market and the producing towns made the city's maize supply one of the most attractive areas of the whole colony for financial speculation. As early as 1550 both Spaniards and Indians were reported to be hoarding maize for higher prices in the city, and in the seventeenth and eighteenth centuries the hacendados, the Spanish cabildo, the corregidor, and even sometimes the oidores and viceroy, were active profiteers in maize provision.[163] Consumption in the city exceeded 150,000 fanegas per year in the late colonial period, divided about equally between animals (especially pigs) and humans.[164]

The first formal institution for the regulation of urban maize supplies and prices was the pósito, established in the late 1570's but in effect operating before that in miscellaneous purchases and sales of maize by the Spanish cabildo.[165] With the creation of this, and the related alhóndiga, the city was given priority in the purchase of maize paid in royal tribute, beginning with the harvest of 1578. The measure originated in a time of crisis, for harvests of the immediately preceding years had been meager and the most serious of the sixteenth-century epidemics had barely abated. The remedial efforts in the first years were regarded as successful,[166] but the city's continued annual purchase was justified even in years of abundance as a means of preventing maize from falling into the hands of middlemen and speculators. The cabildo was authorized to buy royal tribute maize in an area extending fourteen leagues on all sides (this included the whole of the Valley of Mexico), but by 1582 it was contending that this was not enough, and it requested, and received, similar privileges in Tlaxcala, Cholula, and other areas.[167] The cabildo willingly entered into heavy debt in maize purchases, hoping to recoup from municipal sales, and itself became a speculator in the market. By 1594 the pósito was being supplied by purchases from Guanajuato and even more distant places. Such remote transactions were governed by transportation costs, the differences in regional prices, the quality and durability of the maize, the present and expected harvests, and the speculative acumen of the city's cabildo. The cabildo sometimes found itself with large quantities obtained from previous harvests at high prices only to be compelled to sell these at low prices in order to compete with market exchanges. In years of scarcity, when tribute maize even from the enlarged area was insufficient and when communities fell into arrears in their payments, the cabildo found itself necessarily dealing with the speculators themselves, who were the only ones with sufficient maize to supply the city.[168]

An important difference between the economy of the city and the economy of the towns relates to those Indians who became artisans in the crafts of Spanish urban society. The sixteenth-century record refers to a huge number of such crafts and in effect confirms the statement of a Spaniard of 1569 that there was then no trade in the city that Indians had not learned.[169] The full list includes sword makers, glove makers, glass workers, saddlers, bell makers, blacksmiths, and tailors.[170] By the end of the first colonial generation Indians were manufacturing doublets, waistcoats, breeches, and all Spanish garments.[171] Though imitative, these first-generation Indian craftsmen appear to have been remarkably positive and eager, and it may be suggested that the disciplines of pre-conquest craftsmanship were such as to encourage ingenuity in novel circumstances. Of special interest in this connection is the ideal of affirmation and creativity marking the criteria of good workmanship for the informants of Sahagún. The Indian artisan was to be well taught in his trade, according to Sahagún's record. But he was also to be "skillful," "ingenious," "imaginative," "vigorous," "deft," "lively," and "of good judgment." The poor craftsman, on the other hand, was described not only in terms suggestive of want of skill and the intent to defraud, but also as lacking enthusiasm, "sluggish," "dull," "coarse," and "lazy."[172] It should be added that a strong economic motive likewise encouraged craftsmanship among the Indians of the city. By the mid-century skilled Indian embroiderers and silver workers were making as much as a peso per day, or more than the best paid gobernadores outside the city. Carpenters were making four reales per day in the early 1560's, and masons three, while peones were making only one real.[173]

In the original Indian craftsmanship of Tenochtitlan and Tlatelolco, as in that of some other large communities of the Valley, each person and family worked at a particular skill, and specializations were handed down through families from generation to generation.[174] Groups of artisans had lived together in the barrios of the pre-conquest city.[175] The noteworthy fact for the colonial period is that even in the congested and disorganized conditions described above this family tradition and local specialization persisted.

This does not mean that all individuals in a barrio pursued an identical occupation, but that one or several activities predominated to a greater extent than free choice or normal distribution would have allowed. The external barrios of Tlatelolco in the 1790's provide a case in point. A census by professions in the barrios of Cimatlan and San Francisco Tequipec indicates clearly that the occupations of Cimatlan concentrated on the painting and metalworking arts while those of Tequipec concentrated on the masons' trades. Among other external barrios of Tlatelolco, Xocotitlan contained large numbers of salt manufacturers; Atlampa depended on duck hunting and petate making; about seventy per cent of the population of San Salvador de las Huertas were gardeners; Atepetlatl contained masons and salt producers; Atenco was a community of spinners; shoemakers and button makers comprised a large part of Apahuascan, and hat makers of Atecocoleca.[176] These concentrations meant that in some instances Indian congregations and cofradías were made up of persons of identical occupation, but, as we have observed, this does not appear to have been a primary or essential feature of Indian cofradía formation.[177]

Indian craftsmanship from the start received the full approval of the Spanish state. The king, the viceroy, and the missionaries all undertook to encourage mechanical arts among Indians.[178] A rule of the early colony, frequently reiterated later, was that Indians might use their skilled trades with full freedom, and viceregal authority of the middle sixteenth century often supported native craftsmen against interference by Spaniards.[179] Later the encouragement of Indian trades was justified as a means of eliminating vagabondage and idleness.[180] Among the Spanish craftsmen, however, the actual experience of Indian competition was less welcome. When Indians learned to make hats and saddles and similar articles, Spaniards found themselves no longer in control of the production of these items, and they were obliged to resort to new methods. They could lower their prices to meet the competition and suffer a financial loss. They could interfere illegally in Indian production, entering Indian houses, confiscating goods, and preventing Indian sales by force.[181] They could themselves purchase the native products for resale at Spanish prices, or, by more complex systems of farming out or providing material, they could in effect hire the Indian craftsmen.[182] Finally, they could meet the rivalry as their predecessors in Spain had met the rivalry of Jews, Moors, and other classes—by organizing craft guilds. Each of these responses was in fact made by Spanish craftsmen in the first few post-conquest generations, but the formation of craft guilds was the most effective and organized reaction and the one that earned the most durable position in the economy of the city.[183]

For a time in the sixteenth century it appeared that Indian organizations approximating guilds might be created to oppose the Spanish guilds. Indeed, the original Indian craft barrios in some ways resembled, and thus offered precedents for, urban Indian guilds. The native lace makers in the city in 1551 were sufficiently organized to make a common appeal to the viceroy in protest against Spanish lace makers who entered their houses, seized their goods, and molested them in other ways.[184] Among the candle makers in Tlatelolco, procedures of examination and supervision by an Indian inspector were in operation in 1551, precisely as in the guilds of Spaniards. Systems of apprenticeship and examination leading to viceregal licenses for itinerant trade or for establishing shops were in effect for other Indian crafts.[185] The Indian shoemakers of the city in 1560 were organized as a formal body of craftsmen with designated shops, and one of their number served as examiner, with judicial powers. Their economic problems closely paralleled those of the Spanish shoemakers, for Indians who were not official craftsmen intruded on their market with inferior shoes and sold them outside of the designated shops.[186] In the 1560's the Indian tailors of the city were sufficiently numerous and well-organized to interfere in an election dispute and exert political influence in Indian government.[187]

The exclusion of such Indian craft groups from the Spanish guilds was a policy expressed in several viceregal and guild statements, to the effect that none of the specified regulations for manufacture was to apply to Indian craftsmen. The point was made regarding the silk makers' guild in 1556, the painters' and gilders' guild in 1589, and the hat makers' guild in 1592, and it was surely implied in a number of other guild regulations, for it followed a general order of the crown.[188] The purpose here was to maintain Indian economy free from Spanish interference, and the result was to create an atmosphere favorable to the development of distinct native craft organizations.

The final result, however, was not two competing guild systems but the incorporation of native labor within the Spanish guilds. Already in the 1540's certain guilds, including the saddlers and the embroiderers, had undertaken to bring native oficiales within the processes of guild examination. The embroiderers ruled unequivocally in 1546 that no Indian could be an embroiderer without passing the examination, and the ruling successfully received viceregal confirmation in 1547.[189] The saddlers provided stalls and oficial status to native craftsmen who passed the examination, their stated purpose being to eliminate the inferior workmanship of those who were not oficiales.[190] It is especially interesting to observe the progressive changes in guild regulations. In silk making, Indians could still spin thread in their homes with their own silk and reels without being liable to guild control, but only white guild members were allowed to hire native workers, and in doing so they were permitted in 1576 to give examinations to Indians.[191] The leather tanners extended the examination procedures to include Indians in 1565 on the grounds that the Spanish oficiales were too few in number. And in 1568 the carpenters' guild, with viceregal approval, required examinations for Indian oficiales in carpentry.[192]

It is evident that the purpose of some of these regulations was not the elimination of independent Indian activity per se but rather the control of non-guild Spaniards who were hiring or farming out work to Indians in competition with the guild.[193] Especially as Indian artisans ceased to be independent workers the guilds sought to control them in order that other Spaniards could not. For those guilds that developed no such controls, the problem persisted for a long time. The shoemakers still had no effective examination procedure for Indians in 1629 and they continued to suffer the combined opposition of unlicensed Spanish and native makers of shoes. The unlicensed shoemakers worked together with inexpensive materials. They took advantage of the law that allowed Indians to sell freely in the city markets, and their sales were not confined to the legal shoe shops. The guilds were thus undersold by Indians who worked for non-guild whites and who sold their shoes in markets where guild shoes could not be sold. It is interesting that the guild in this case felt itself capable of withstanding normal Indian competition, which amounted to four or five pairs of shoes per Indian seller, with sales confined to the markets of San Juan, San Hipólito, and Tlatelolco. The complaint was directed against the much larger quantity produced by shop methods under Spanish direction outside the guild. The matter was serious enough to result in the closing of about a hundred of the city's 150 licensed shoe shops in the late 1620's.[194]

In some cases the guilds of the seventeenth and eighteenth centuries reacted against urban miscegenation, taking refuge in an insistence on ethnic purity and on the quality of professional white craftsmanship. The regulations of the painters' guild specified in 1686 that all apprentices were to be Spaniards. The ordinances of the makers of gold and silver wire in 1665 required that only Spaniards could submit to examination, "for it would not be right for any other to be examined in so noble an art." The dyers boasted in 1685 that their guild consisted entirely of Spaniards and that no examinations were permitted for Indians, mulattoes, or mestizos. The smiths and veterinarians, seeking to retain some of the dignity that Hispanic tradition associated with horsemanship, asserted in the early eighteenth century that all apprentices were to be "Spaniards, pure and without stain, as demonstrated through presentation of their baptismal records, for ours is a noble profession."[195]

But in the complexities of the city's late colonial economy such ethnic distinctions could not be consistently upheld. Some guilds explicitly admitted qualified Indians, Negroes, mulattoes, and mestizos to all offices, including that of inspector, while others formally prohibited them only from the rank of master. A common eighteenth-century phrase referred to the "maestros y indios" of a given craft.[196] But Indian maestros were recognized in many crafts,[197] and a guild policy of exclusion had become self-defeating and unenforceable in late colonial society. Far more characteristic of that society than the cautious rules of the Spanish craft guilds was the mixed labor force of the royal tobacco factory, founded in 1769, which numbered between six and nine thousand and consisted of men and women, Indians, and all mixed classes.[198]

Conclusion

The Black Legend provides a gross but essentially accurate interpretation of relations between Spaniards and Indians. The Legend builds upon the record of deliberate sadism. It flourishes in an atmosphere of indignation, which removes the issue from the category of objective understanding. It is insufficient in its awareness of the institutions of colonial history. But the substantive content of the Black Legend asserts that Indians were exploited by Spaniards, and in empirical fact they were.

We have not commented in detail on the conquest itself, a separate subject, already much studied. The conquest has a bearing here not for its military events but for its consequences, and the over-all consequence of conquest was the condition of Spanish domination and Indian subjugation. Aztec peoples could not confront Spaniards as a unified nation, with diplomacy and negotiation. Conquest destroyed Aztec nationalism and fixed adjustments at a local level. Nearly everything that could be called imperial in Aztec affairs came to an end. If Aztec society be thought of as a graduated complex of progressively more inclusive units, from the family and calpulli at one end to the total empire at the other, it becomes evident that conquest eliminated all the more comprehensive structures while it permitted the local and less comprehensive ones to survive.

The demarcation or cut-off point was the jurisdiction of the tlatoani. This became the cabecera, the essential unit of the early colonial period, on which encomienda, the missionary church, cacicazgo, and tribute and labor exactions directly depended. The cabecera won out over alternative organizing principles of greater or lesser range. One may suppose that this followed in part from the role of the tlatoani in Indian society, a role that was repeatedly affirmed in the events of pre-conquest history. But it was the consequence also of relations between Spaniards and Indians. Conceivably a differently ordered Spanish rule might have made the tribe rather than the cabecera the essential colonial unit. An opposite type of Spanish power might have settled upon the calpulli. We can glimpse some such alternative forces at work in the various readjustments and modifications made upon the standard cabecera, as when repartimiento reinvoked the tribal groups or when non-tlatoani towns were granted in encomienda and allowed to become cabeceras.

The most evident changes in Indian society occurred during the first forty or fifty years. This was the time when Indian peoples, or some of them, met the Spanish influence part way and reached positive degrees of cultural accord. The mid-sixteenth century has a special interest in the history of humanistic tutelage, with the community of Santa Fe, the Gante school, and above all the Colegio of Santa Cruz in Tlatelolco. One can speak here of a cultural florescence for upper-class Indians, and we may cite again the remarkable Badianus Herbal, a systematic catalogue of plants, classified in a European tradition, painted in an Indian style, its glosses written in Nahuatl by one learned native commentator and translated into Latin by another. The herbal was composed in 1552, and it seemed to give promise, thirty years after the conquest, of a combined culture, with enduring Indian values enriched by a European admixture.

The total possible range of Indian reaction at this time was relatively extensive. Because two complicated societies were intermeshing, opportunities for new combinations continually arose. It is in the sixteenth century that we find the most diverse individual incidents and the most unsettled conditions in both societies. But the long-term tendencies were toward the solutions of the seventeenth and eighteenth centuries, and the scope of Indian response became more limited. As the Indian population was reduced in size, Spanish controls became fixed and the traditional leaders lost power. Colonial law only partially reacted to what occurred, and local customs acquired a greater force than law. After the sixteenth century few individuals stand out in either society, and the history becomes one of localized groups. The seventeenth and eighteenth centuries have a peculiarly leaderless quality, as if all alternative solutions had been discarded.

Neither society was at first unified in its response to the conditions proffered by the other. Indians were at first divided between those who coop-

erated and those who resisted, and between the upper class and the maceguales. Both lines of division tended to disappear. But the geographical divisions in Indian society remained. The patterns of subordination, however
uniform in their abstract characteristics, were locally bounded. Cabecera
jurisdictions, encomiendas, and haciendas were discrete manifestations of
localism effectively preventing a consolidation of Indian interests. All native
conduct was so confined. No two towns were ever capable of uniting in
organized resistance. The common qualities of Indian towns were insufficient bases for concerted action.

   In Spanish society friars and encomenderos were the main conflicting parties of the early period. The friars, almost alone among Spaniards, were
guided by principles of Christian humanitarianism. It could be argued that
even they exploited native peoples in their coercive indoctrination and their
extirpation of pagan practices. Yet their effort as a whole may be distinguished from that of other Spaniards. What happened was that the spiritual component of Hispanic imperialism disappeared or concentrated its
energies elsewhere. Its effect for Indians was confined to the early period.
The church ceased to be active in Indian defense as ecclesiastics adopted the
methods and attitudes of civilian colonists. Churchmen could oppose encomienda in part because they were prohibited from becoming encomenderos,
but ecclesiastical condemnation of latifundium would have meant condemnation of an institution that was essential to ecclesiastical wealth and power.
There were many other divisions, of course, within Spanish society, but
none of them bore directly upon Indian life or livelihood. Thus the creoles
despised the peninsulares, but the issue between them was not native welfare, and in some degree what they were disputing over was Indian spoils.

   Tribute, labor, and land were the most clearly defined categories of Spanish demand. The three were differentiated in the colonial period, and the
legal instruments were different in each case. Tribute and labor were state-
controlled after the mid-sixteenth century, and their consequences for Indian society, however serious, were less severe than in the case of land. Tribute and labor were periodically adjusted to population changes, and the extreme Spanish requirements were confined to the earliest times. Moreover,
tribute and labor were already familiar types of pre-conquest exaction, and
the degree of change between the one period and the other has often been
overstated by critics of the Spanish regime.

Spanish usurpation of land has received less attention, probably because it followed the conquest by some years and did not occupy a major position among the Las Casas accusations. It occurred gradually, through many individual events over a long period, and phenomena that take place in this way lack the dramatic appeal of cataclysms like conquest. So deficient is the Black Legend with regard to land that until recently historians were interpreting hacienda as a direct outgrowth of encomienda. Only in our own time has this fundamental error been corrected, most effectively through the work of Silvio Zavala.

It is often said, with an implication of significance, that the lands of America were the property of the crown of Castile. But the point is at best legalistic, and for Indian history it is immaterial. The crown played an insignificant role either in fostering or in inhibiting latifundia. Legal possession of land by the crown did not mean that land usurpation, too, was a state-controlled enterprise. It was private and frequently illegal, though the state came to tolerate it and to profit from it through the devices of denuncia and composición. That it did not occur immediately is probably less the result of legal restriction than of sheer numbers of Indian people and the universality of Indian occupation of land. A prerequisite was available land, and this was not present when the Spaniards first came. Encomienda was therefore an appropriate institution for the early years. But with Indian depopulation, land became accessible, and when it became accessible, it was usurped.

One consequence of the historical concern with selected Black Legend themes is a weakness in our knowledge of hacienda history. The sections of this book that deal with hacienda make some contribution to the subject, but they suffer from inadequate information and lack a secure conceptual frame. Hacienda, perhaps more than any other single colonial topic, still needs systematic investigation, not alone in the Valley of Mexico but in all areas. We cannot now confidently compare our documented examples of Valley of Mexico hacienda with the institution in other regions, and until we can the Valley conditions will remain imperfectly defined. Our evidence, as the reader will have noted, suggests only a limited role for peonage, but this may be an aberration of the particular instances cited. We have suggested some possible explanations, supposing the accuracy of the observation itself, but it must be emphasized again that these are conjectural and await further demonstration. My own feeling is that the hacienda is a crucial institution, that for various reasons its study has been slighted, and that we would be well advised to make a concerted effort toward solving the historical problems that it raises.

With respect to land there can be no doubt that the hacienda came to be the dominant mode of control. In the tempo of its history it contrasts with tribute and labor. The extreme Spanish demands for tribute and labor occurred early, before much land was transferred to Spanish possession. This transfer, on the other hand, took place on a large scale only in the late sixteenth century and after, when private exploitation of tribute and labor had already been brought under state control. In a sense, land represented a new avenue of exploitation for Spaniards, after other avenues were blocked. But the hacienda combined its essential control of land with secondary controls over labor and tribute, and the result was the most comprehensive institution yet devised for Spanish mastery and Indian subordination. If there appeared, as we have thought, some benign features of hacienda, these are explicable in terms of the total matrix within which hacienda developed. Human character tends toward benevolence as well as toward cruelty, and the hacienda could afford certain kinds of benevolence that would have been incongruous with the harsher, more superficial, less subtle coercions of encomienda. Thus the hacendado could appear as the protector and advocate of his Indians against outside pressures. The encomendero was intended by law to play this same role, but he never did.

That land was important to Indians is obvious. Some of the most intimate and revealing documents of all Indian history are the native títulos for community land possession. The títulos were an Indian response to Spanish usurpation and Spanish legalism. Their purpose was to integrate community opposition against alienation. They speak only sparingly, or not at all, of conquest, tribute, and labor. They see the essential threat to community existence where in fact it lay, in Spanish seizures of land.

There had been seizures of land before the conquest, as in the "lands of Montezuma," but these had been accommodated within Indian practices of land disposition. The difference is one of degree. Moreover, the pre-conquest period, so far as we know, offers no comparable situation of population change. When Indian society seemed headed for extinction, in the late sixteenth and early seventeenth centuries, its practical need for land likewise diminished, and Indian gobernadores and others became the accomplices of Spaniards in the transfer of titles. When the population began to increase in the late seventeenth and eighteenth centuries the need for land correspondingly increased. But by then it was too late. Land transfer was cumulative in a way that tribute and labor exactions were not. Every increase in Indian population in the late colonial period meant an additional number that could not be incorporated in the traditional calpulli tenure, or could be incorporated only with a corresponding strain on other community institutions. The available land was hacienda land, and the new population could now be incorporated within colonial society only through the mediation of hacienda. When the hacendado authorized the towns to rent some of his lands or gave permission to individuals to occupy huts on the hacienda properties, both the hacendado and the Indian beneficiaries could regard the act as one of benevolence. All surrounding conditions were accepted as normal. An aristocracy had been created through innumerable acts over generations of time. Even if there had been an inclination to assign blame, there was no one to accuse, for no one was responsible. The institution and the ethos of the institution dominated all its members. A conquistador who killed or an encomendero who overcharged could be convincingly criticized on moral grounds, but similar criticism appeared excessive when turned against the hacendado, who had inherited most of his lands and played a paternalistic role in a society he had not created.

Given this kind of pressure, the original distinctions between cabeceras and sujetos became less meaningful and were progressively abandoned. The sharp disputes of the sixteenth century over sujeto affiliation disappeared in the eighteenth century. Each community confronted the hacienda as a separate entity. Law characteristically abetted the hacendado while it enacted meaningless rules concerning 500- and 600-vara measurements. Congregación was seriously and sincerely interpreted as a program in the Indian interest. Traditional Indian resources were insufficient to meet a force of such magnitude and long duration. The Indian community could regroup, assign new or reduced tlalmilli plots, and continue to function. But not all its members made the same decision at the same time. Gobernadores sold land to haciendas or usurped them for themselves. Caciques might become hacendados. Maceguales joined the peones or fled to the city.

The Indian community was further beset by a series of demands not comprehended in the three classifications of tribute, labor and land. Most of these were designed to extract from its economy the increment remaining beyond minimum subsistence. Ecclesiastical fees fall in this category, as do

the forced sales in corregimiento and the usurpations of produce. The political officials' handbook of 1777 openly declared the corregimiento of Chalco to be worth thirty times the corregidor's salary, a statement that suggests
the extent of precedented extra-legal exploitation by officials appointed to
uphold the law.

Variations occurred from area to area in the timing and intensity of these
processes. Tacuba was an early victim. Xaltocan prospered for a time and
yielded in the seventeenth century. Tepetlaoztoc made a late recovery based
not on land but on a pack-train commerce. Chalco province attracted powerful hacendados and became an area of extreme land pressures. By contrast,
Xochimilco lacked the kind of land that attracted hacendados and by a coincidence of circumstances maintained its craft economy and chinampa agriculture throughout the colonial period. Tenochtitlan and Tlatelolco, which
lacked land from the start, remained virtually immune from the struggle
against the hacienda. But Tenochtitlan made a more viable economic adjustment than Tlatelolco, which suffered progressively from drought, emigration, and neglect.

What we have studied is the deterioration of a native empire and civilization. The empire collapsed first, and the civilization was fragmented in
individual communities. Some creativity appeared in the early stages of
change, but the process as a whole could not be called a creative one for
Indians. The community proved to be the largest Indian social unit capable
of survival, and it survived in spite of manifold and severe stresses. The
cofradía and the fiesta were enlisted to support it. Indians in general yielded
to Spanish demands, protesting only in rare instances of community resistance. The civilization became infused with Hispanic traits at many points,
but it retained an essential Indian character, partly through the conviction
of its members, partly because it was depressed to a social status so low that
it was given no opportunities for change. One of the earliest and most persistent individual responses was drink. If our sources may be believed, few
peoples in the whole of history were more prone to drunkenness than the
Indians of the Spanish colony.

Appendixes

Encomiendas of the Valley of Mexico

ACOLMAN

Before 1529 this community and its sujetos were taken from the initial holdings of Pedro Núñez, Maestro de Roa, and reissued to the conquistador Pedro de Solís (Barrasa) as compensation for an affront by Cortés.[1] Officially regarded as the first holder, Pedro de Solís retained the encomienda until his death in the 1560's.[2] It was then inherited by his son, Francisco de Solís (Orduña), who held it to about 1610.[3] References of the period 1618 to 1639 indicate the possessor both as Francisco de Solís Orduña y Barrasa and as Francisco de Solís y Barrasa, presumably in the third life.[4] Francisco de Solís y Barrasa died about 1640, leaving a son of the same name, and it is probable that this son became the fourth holder. The seventeenth-century records of crown payments to ecclesiastics provide evidence that the encomienda was still extant in 1678.[5]

AXAPUSCO

Axapusco was one of the few non-cabeceras of the Valley of Mexico to be assigned distinct encomienda status. It was a sujeto of Otumba, with which it maintained strained relations, and was held in conjunction with other communities outside the Valley by the first holder, Francisco de Santa Cruz.[6] He possessed the encomienda through the 1540's and into the 1550's.[7] By 1560 it had been inherited by his son Alvaro de Santa Cruz, who retained it to 1569.[8] About 1570, with the death of Alvaro de Santa Cruz, it reverted briefly to the crown.[9] Thereafter, with Toltitlan in the Valley and some others outside the Valley, it was reassigned to Luis de Velasco the younger, later Marqués de Salinas, who had requested encomienda privileges in 1564.[10] Luis de Velasco, as viceroy of Peru, still held the encomienda in 1597.[11] In 1565 Axapusco was declared a cabecera (in an order granting it market privileges), and in the seventeenth century the Indians of Axapusco were arguing that the community had never been a sujeto of Otumba.[12] Reversion to the crown took place by 1603, and the Marqués de Salinas received other grants (see in this Appendix Azcapotzalco and Toltitlan). All known references to the status of Axapusco in the later colonial period indicate that it remained crown property through the seventeenth and eighteenth centuries.[13]

AZCAPOTZALCO

This encomienda, situated near Tenochtitlan, was initially held by the conquistador Francisco de Montejo.[14] Its tenure came under attack after the New Laws because Montejo was an official of the crown. Montejo's argument that Azcapotzalco had been granted to him as a special reward by Cortés proved of no avail, and the king ordered in 1550 that Azcapotzalco be placed under the crown.[15] Montejo died in 1553, and before the royal order could take effect the encomienda passed to his daughter Catalina and her husband, Alonso Maldonado. The Council of the Indies explicitly sanctioned Catalina's possession in 1557.[16] Maldonado was killed in a shipwreck in the early 1560's, and the widow, Catalina, held the encomienda through the 1560's and 1570's and until her death, sometime after 1582.[17] In the early seventeenth century Azcapotzalco was held with Toltitlan in a new assignment by Luis de Velasco II, who is said to have received there the cedula of his second viceregal appointment in 1607. Luis de Velasco II received the title of Marqués de Salinas in 1609, returned to Spain in 1611 to become president of the Council of the Indies, and died in 1617.[18] The Marqués de Salinas heir continued to hold the encomienda in the 1620's, 1630's, and 1640's, and in 1671 it was pending settlement with Toltitlan on behalf of the Marqués de San Román.[19] The latter died shortly before 1703, and all his tribute income thereupon reverted to the crown.[20] But the tributes of Azcapotzalco were reassigned to defray the expenses of the grants to the Montezuma descendants. In 1786 the tributes of 217 Azcapotzalco Indians were being paid to the Montezuma heiress, Teresa de Oca y Montezuma.[21]

CHALCO

Cortés originally assigned the rich province of Chalco to himself. Its possession was disputed by Nuño de Guzmán and others, and in 1524 Cortés unsuccessfully requested confirmation of his claim from the monarchy.[22] His enemies, including Nuño de Guzmán, seized Chalco province and its tributes during the 1520's, when Cortés was in Honduras, and again when

Cortés was in Spain.[23] The province of Chalco was not included in Cortés's Marquesado grant of 1529 and for several years its status was in doubt. About 1533 it was declared a royal province by decision of the audiencia.[24] Chalco tributes were being assigned to the Dominican order in the late 1530's for monastery construction.[25] From the middle sixteenth century the maize tributes of Chalco were designated for the Marquesado, in recompense for Tehuantepec. The payments related continually to Tenango and Chimalhuacan, with the provision that when these were insufficient to meet the quota the tributes of other towns would be similarly applied.[26] The tax was both paid in maize and (more frequently) commuted to money, and at various times it applied to a large number of Chalco communities, including Tlalmanalco, Chimalhuacan, Amecameca, Ecatzingo, Chalco Atenco, and Tenango.[27] Money tribute from the Chalco jurisdiction was assigned to the descendants of Pedro Montezuma in late colonial times.[28]

CHICOLOAPA

Separated from Coatlichan, which would otherwise have been its cabecera, Chicoloapa was granted initially by Cortés and again, in 1528, by the provisional governor Alonso de Estrada.[29] Its first holder was the medical doctor and first *protomédico* of Mexico, Pedro López.[30] It was inherited by his son, Gaspar López, in 1550–51 and held by him until after 1580.[31] The encomienda appears to have escheated to the crown prior to 1597 with the expiration of the second life and the known failure of the succession.[32] Records of the seventeenth century refer to Chicoloapa as a continuous crown possession.[33]

CHIMALHUACAN ATENCO

Chimalhuacan Atenco, with Ixtapaluca, was granted to the conquistador Juan de Cuéllar Verdugo by Cortés, and his possession was confirmed by Alonso de Estrada in 1528.[34] He renounced it, probably in an illegal sale. While Cuéllar and his sons received a royal pension, the new holder of Chimalhuacan Atenco, at a price of 3,000 pesos, became the professor of grammar Blas de Bustamante.[35] Regarded in his turn as the first holder, Bustamante held the property to about 1570.[36] It was inherited before 1580 by his son Gerónimo de Bustamante.[37] The third holder in the new series was the daughter of Gerónimo de Bustamante and Ana de Meneses, María de Bustamante.[38] Her husband was Felipe de la Cueva, but the relation between this couple and the seventeenth-century encomendero, Nuño de Villavicencio, remains unclear. The latter is recorded as encomendero in 1628.[39] The crown was already holding part of the encomienda in 1658.

Full formal escheatment occurred in 1670, Nuño Núñez de Villavicencio being the last encomendero.[40] As crown property in the eighteenth century, however, tribute from Chimalhuacan Atenco was designated for the encomienda of the Spanish Conde de Cifuentes.[41]

COYOACAN

Coyoacan, together with Tacubaya and their sujetos, was the principal holding of Cortés in the Valley of Mexico. Cortés's holdings were disputed, but he was confirmed in permanent possesssion for himself and his descendants as Marqués del Valle in 1529. He died in Spain in 1547. The Marquesado was inherited by his son Martín Cortés, the second Marqués del Valle. In the 1560's a proposed exchange of Coyoacan and Tacubaya (and Oaxaca) for Toluca Valley was interrupted by the Avila-Cortés conspiracy.[42] Following suppression of the conspiracy, Martín Cortés was exiled from the colony and died in Madrid in 1589. The sequestered encomienda was restored in 1574. The third Marqués del Valle, Fernando Cortés Ramírez de Arellano, died without issue in Madrid in 1602. Succession passed to his brother, Pedro Cortés Ramírez de Arellano, who returned to Mexico and with whose death in 1629, also without issue, the direct male line came to an end. The heirs of Cortés and bearers of the Marqués title in later colonial times were the Duques de Terranova and the Duques de Monteleone. The family genealogy is the subject of abundant record.[43]

CUAUHTITLAN, ZUMPANGO, XALTOCAN, ET AL.

Cuauhtitlan was united in a single composite encomienda with Zumpango, Xaltocan, Huehuetoca, Coyotepec, Toltepec, Teoloyuca, and other communities of the northern lake region. The cabecera pattern in this encomienda has been discussed above.[44] Cortés originally granted the encomienda to the conquistador Alonso de Avila (Dávila). To avoid personal rivalries with him Cortés immediately sent him to Spain with Aztec treasure for the monarchy. He was captured by the French, spent some time in a French prison, and subsequently went to Yucatan with Montejo. Efforts were made by Alonso de Estrada, as governor, to assign the tributes of Zumpango and Xaltocan to the Dominicans in Mexico City. But the crown provided for the protection of the encomienda during the absence of Alonso de Avila, and this order came to his brother, Gil González de Avila (Benavides), in Mexico, who proceeded to hold the encomienda in Alonso de Avila's name and with his permission. Alonso de Estrada then aided Gil González de Avila in a secret plan to take the encomienda from Alonso de Avila. Alonso de Avila died shortly after returning from

Yucatan, and through the connivance of the audiencia the encomienda remained "illegally" in the possession of Gil González de Avila, against the contrary demands of the royal fiscal.[45] The audiencia proposed in 1531, and the monarchy approved in 1532, a plan to remove Zumpango from this encomienda so that it could furnish lime for city building.[46] But the proposal did not take effect. With regard to the legality of the total holding, the viceroy favored Gil González de Avila against the royal fiscal, a circumstance that hostile observers connected with the financing of entertainments for the viceroy's sister at the time of her marriage.[47] The ensuing judicial dispute engendered strong feelings, and the audiencia's decision was appealed to the Consejo de Indias.[48] González de Avila nevertheless remained encomendero through the 1530's and until 1544, when Alonso de Avila the younger, son of Gil González de Avila and Leonor de Alvarado, inherited on the death of Gil González de Avila.[49] Gil González de Avila was later regarded as the first holder.[50]

The monarchy again ruled ineffectively in 1561 that Zumpango was to be put under the crown.[51] Alonso de Avila Alvarado retained the encomienda to the middle 1560's although the claim of the monarchy remained active.[52] On August 3, 1566, both Alonso de Avila Alvarado and his brother, Gil González de Benavides the younger, were executed as leaders of the Avila-Cortés conspiracy. On the same day all the towns of the encomienda reverted to the crown.[53]

Tributes were immediately paid to the monarchy. But in the seventeenth and eighteenth centuries royal tributes from this source were designated for the descendants of Pedro Montezuma, the Condes de Montezuma and Marqueses de Tenebrón, to Nicolás Pérez de Zamora (see Tizayuca and Tepozotlan), and to other recipients, in order to defray additional mercedes that had no connection with the original Cuauhtitlan encomienda.[54]

CUITLAHUAC

In the 1520's Cortés assigned Cuitlahuac as one of the propios of the city, and Alonso de Estrada sought to assign some or all of its tributes to the Dominicans in the city.[55] Neither of these early dispositions persisted. The first private holder, Juan de Cuevas, escribano mayor de minas, received Cuitlahuac by exchange with the viceroy at an unknown date sometime before 1544. He held it for more than twenty years.[56] In the later 1560's it was inherited by his son, Alonso de Cuevas, and held by him at least to 1606.[57] In 1628–29 the encomienda was in the possession of Josephe de Cuevas, possibly the third holder and the son of Alonso. A decade later the possessor was Alonso de (la) Cueva(s), but other records of the 1630's indicate tribute payments to Miguel de Cuevas Dávalos and Sebastián de Cueva(s).[58] Cuitlahuac is known to have been still in encomienda in 1658. The date of its escheatment to the crown, probably after 1678, is still to be discovered.[59]

CULHUACAN

Culhuacan was another of the towns first granted by Cortés to the city of Mexico for its propios.[60] Culhuacan was granted about 1525 to Cristóbal de Oñate, who held it for more than forty years.[61] In the 1560's Cristóbal de Oñate was implicated in the encomenderos' conspiracy. He was sent to Spain, returned for trial, and executed in 1568.[62] His wife, Catalina de Salazar, was the sister of Juan Velázquez de Salazar, encomendero of Tepetlaoztoc.[63] His son, Fernando (Hernando) de Oñate, inherited the encomienda as the second possessor and held it at least to 1597 and probably to 1604 or after.[64] Notices of the seventeenth century record Fernando de Oñate as encomendero in 1628 and as the last encomendero prior to the royalization of about 1659, but it is likely that these names refer not to the second holder but to the heir or heirs in the third or fourth generation.[65]

ECATEPEC

Sixteenth-century copies of Cortés's original statement (1527), if authentic, demonstrate that Cortés first held Ecatepec for himself and in 1527 assigned it to Leonor Montezuma, daughter of Montezuma, in *dote* and *arras*.[66] Later copies of the same document, perhaps through a scribe's error, often refer to the recipient as Marina or Mariana.[67] The extant texts mention Acalhuacan, Coatitlan, and Tizayuca (Tecoyuca) as sujetos of Ecatepec, included in the grant.[68] Interrogated on this point in the 1530's, Cortés deposed that he was certain that he had assigned Ecatepec to Leonor but that he was not certain that Coatitlan had been included.[69] The matter was of significance, for the subject communities were in dispute recurrently until the seventeenth century between the encomienda interests and the Indian governments of Tenochtitlan and Tlatelolco, particularly the latter.[70] Moreover, Tizayuca was separated from this encomienda and royalized in 1531.[71]

A second disputed feature concerned perpetuity. The texts of 1527 state that the Indians of Ecatepec were granted in dote and arras "para siempre jamás." Cortés later testified that he had simply granted an encomienda.[72] Subsequent encomenderos argued that in this case, unlike others, tenure was perpetual and that this would have been the case even without Cortés's assignment, since the area was of Leonor's patrimony in the Indian system of possession.[73] This argument was presented to offset the counterclaim that Cortés had lacked authority to issue such a grant.

In any case, the assignment was made to Leonor for her marriage to the conquistador Juan Paz (Páez).[74] After his death she married another Spaniard, Cristóbal de Valderrama, who, as her husband, was regarded as the first possessor, and who held the encomienda until his death in 1537.[75] The mestiza daughter of Leonor Montezuma and Cristóbal de Valderrama was Leonor de Valderrama y Montezuma, and her husband, the Spaniard Diego Arias de Sotelo, became the encomendero in the second life. He held the encomienda after his wife's death and to about 1568, when he was exiled as a consequence of the encomenderos' conspiracy.[76]

Their son and principal heir, Fernando Sotelo de Montezuma, became the encomendero in the third life. But another son, Cristóbal de Sotelo Valderrama, disputed the possession before the audiencia, which decided in favor of Fernando in 1588.[77] References of the 1580's give Fernando as the possessor.[78] Cristóbal, frequently charged with abuses in his relations with the Indians of the encomienda, was denied entry into Ecatepec by viceregal order in 1591.[79] But in 1593 the two brothers made an agreement whereby Cristóbal would receive one-third of the encomienda and Fernando two-thirds—one-third for himself and one-third for his sister, Ana de Sotelo, who had become a nun and renounced her "share." The agreement met the approval of the audiencia, and the two were regarded as co-encomenderos.[80] Cristóbal married Juana de Heredia Patiño and died intestate in 1607, his one-third remaining in his widow's possession with a payment of 11,000 pesos. Diego Sotelo Montezuma and Juan Sotelo Montezuma, sons of Fernando, sold Fernando's two-thirds in 1618 to Fernando Bocanegra for 9,660 pesos. Fernando Bocanegra in turn sold these two-thirds in 1624 for 10,000 pesos to Cristóbal de la Mota Ossorio de Portugal, who continued to hold them until his death. Cristóbal de la Mota Ossorio de Portugal, however, never paid the 10,000 purchase price of 1624. The real agreement was fulfilled when he married Manuela de Avalos, niece of Fernando Bocanegra, the dowry being computed in these terms, and no money changed hands. After her death, without issue, Cristóbal de la Mota Ossorio de Portugal retained the two-thirds for himself. He likewise bought the other third from Lorenzo Patiño de Varga, heir of Juana de Patiño, in 1662.[81] His possession, though legally indefensible, was supported by his powerful status as *secretario de cámara* of the audiencia.[82]

In 1681, after the death of Cristóbal de la Mota Ossorio de Portugal, his widow, Leonor de Zúñiga y Ontiveros, was formally accused of illegal possession. The charge depended partly on the illegal sales (encomiendas were normally alienable only through inheritance or renunciation) and partly on the questionable authority of Cortés's grant of a permanent encomienda. The Council of the Indies, however, decided in her favor in 1682.[83] She died in 1706. Later in the eighteenth century the tributes of this holding, though collected by the alcalde mayor in the name of the king, were distributed among her heirs.[84]

HUEYPOXTLA

Hueypoxtla, with its two distant estancias Tianquistonco and Tlacuitlapilco, was first divided between Antón Bravo and Pedro de Valencia (Pedro Valenciano).[85] Each remained encomendero of his respective portion in the 1540's. But by the early 1550's the double encomienda had been inherited, in the one part by the son of Antón Bravo, also Antón (Antonio) Bravo, and in the other by María Garao (García, Guercio), the daughter of Pedro de Valencia. Her successive husbands, Juan de Manzanárez, Dr. Frías de Albornoz, and perhaps Dr. Ambrosio de Bustamante, appear with her as encomenderos in records from the 1550's to the 1580's.[86] She is known to have been still living about 1597. Antón Bravo is known to have been still living about 1604 and to have left a son of the same name.[87] The encomienda persisted at least to 1658.[88] But there is evidence that Hueypoxtla tributes were being assigned to the Conde de Montezuma in 1647–48.[89]

HUITZILOPOCHCO (CHURUBUSCO)

In the 1520's Cortés assigned Huitzilopochco both as one of the propios of the city and, presumably somewhat later, as an encomienda to the conquistador Bernardino Vásquez de Tapia. At the latter's request Cortés then exchanged it for Huamuxtitlan in Guerrero, so that the encomienda remained vacant.[90] It was under the crown in the late 1520's and at least to 1536.[91] Vásquez de Tapia then successfully reacquired it as the first holder. Although the title was ostensibly transferred about 1541 to his recently married niece, Bernardino Vásquez de Tapia himself was regarded as the possessor through the 1540's and through most of the 1550's.[92] After his death about 1559 Huitzilopochco was inherited successively by his son and grandson, both of whom were likewise named Bernardino Vásquez de Tapia.[93] The son still held the property in the first years of the seventeenth century.[94] A Bernardino Vásquez de Tapia, possibly the grandson, was serving as encomendero in 1639–40.[95] In the eighteenth century Huitzilopochco tributes were granted to the encomienda of the Conde de Cifuentes.[96]

IXTAPALAPA

Immediately following the conquest Cortés assigned six towns—Ixtapalapa, Huitzilopochco, Mexicalzingo, Culhuacan, Cuitlahuac, and Mixquic —as propios of the city.[97] In 1525 the city requested confirmation of this

grant from the king, stating that the six towns were still then in its service.[98]
But in the period following 1525 five of these towns were lost to the city,
principally through encomienda grants to private individuals. These five
were Huitzilopochco, Mexicalzingo, Culhuacan, Cuitlahuac, and Mixquic,
and in 1529 the city requested the return of these communities to its service
as before.[99] Only Ixtapalapa remained from the original assignment. In 1564
the Spanish cabildo gave its opinion that Ixtapalapa had been in encomienda
to the city since conquest times.[100] Records of the 1530's and later indicate
that the city government did indeed understand itself to be not only the
possessor of a grant of propios but the corporate encomendero of the community of Ixtapalapa. The city used Ixtapalapa labor, received Ixtapalapa
tribute, and appointed and paid the salary of the Ixtapalapa cleric.[101] Finally
in 1582 the royal and viceregal government required the city to show its
titles for Ixtapalapa. This the cabildo was unable to do, and Ixtapalapa became crown property on December 23, 1582.[102]

IXTAPALUCA

The original grant of Ixtapaluca and Chimalhuacan Atenco by Cortés
to Juan de Cuéllar was confirmed by Alonso de Estrada in 1528.[103] Cuéllar
renounced Chimalhuacan Atenco but remained the encomendero of Ixtapaluca until his death, probably in 1551.[104] The encomienda then passed to
his widow, probably Ana Ruiz, and his minor son, Andrés de Cuéllar. Ana
Ruiz was married again, to Domingo de las Nieves.[105] Andrés de Cuéllar
held the encomienda in the second life in the 1550's and died without issue
before 1565.[106] On his death a younger brother, Martín de Cuéllar, illegally
inherited. Martín de Cuéllar retained the encomienda through the 1560's
and to 1574 when it was placed under the crown. The escheatment was the
consequence of a decision by the Consejo de Indias in 1573, upholding the
royal fiscal's position that the younger brother could not be the legal encomienda heir.[107] Martín de Cuéllar by royal compensation received 300
ducados from Xumiltepec tributes annually for the remainder of his life.
In 1575, despite the opposition of the fiscal, the property was reassigned to
Luis de Velasco the younger, in whose hands it remained in 1597. He died
in 1617, but the latter part of the encomienda history remains unknown.[108]

MIXQUIC

Mixquic was one of the towns granted by Cortés to the city before 1525,
and about 1527 Alonso de Estrada offered its tributes to the Dominicans.[109]
After this it was held by Bartolomé (Antonio) de Zarate. He renounced it
before 1550 so that it might be granted en dote to his daughter, Ana de Za-

rate, who became the wife of Gil Ramírez de Avalos.[110] It was listed as in the crown in 1536.[111] Gil Ramírez de Avalos was granted the encomienda by Viceroy Mendoza, but with the death of his wife, and with his own departure for Peru, the royal fiscal claimed the encomienda for the crown.[112] In the 1560's it nevertheless passed to the son of Gil Ramírez de Avalos and Ana de Zarate, also named Gil Ramírez de Avalos.[113] Presumably after his death the encomienda was reassigned to Luis de Velasco in the late sixteenth century, and in the seventeenth century it remained in his heirs, bearers of the titles Marqués de Salinas and Marqués de San Román.[114] The Marqués de San Román of the late seventeenth century died shortly before 1703, and all his tribute income therefore reverted to the crown. But in another assignment, effective in the early eighteenth century, thirty tributaries of Mixquic were granted to the Condes de Cifuentes.[115]

OTUMBA

Cortés first took Otumba for himself, successfully disputed the possession of Matienzo and Delgadillo, and installed Martín Cortés (a different person from the heir and second Marqués del Valle) as his tribute collector.[116] Although Cortés requested an official grant of Otumba from the crown, it fell outside the Marquesado established in 1529.[117] It was placed in the crown in November 1531, and not reassigned.[118] Otumba tributes, however, were still being assigned to Cortés in 1536.[119] In late colonial times tributes from the Otumba jurisdiction were applied to the 2,500-peso mayorazgo of the Condesa de Montezuma and to other annuities of the Montezuma family.[120]

OXTOTICPAC

Like Axapusco, Oxtoticpac was a sujeto of Otumba, separately granted in encomienda. It was held with Tlalistaca and Tlanalapa, communities falling just outside the Valley of Mexico to the northeast. Oxtoticpac was in service to Cortés during the early years when Cortés held Otumba. After he gave up Otumba, Oxtoticpac was taken by Diego de Ocampo (Docampo), later regarded as the first holder.[121] This may have been in recompense for Ocampo's loss of Tepetlaoztoc. In the 1540's Ocampo's tenure was questioned and he was unable to produce a legitimate title to Oxtoticpac. He still held it however in 1545. With his death and with a royal merced en dote it was inherited by his illegitimate daughter, the wife of Juan Velázquez Rodríguez.[122] In the 1560's Oxtoticpac was held by Juan Velázquez Rodríguez, and at the end of the century by Alonso Velázquez, presumably his son.[123] It had reverted to the crown at least by 1675.[124] But tributes from Oxtoticpac appear to have been granted to the Conde de Montezuma in 1647.[125]

TACUBA

Of all the encomiendas of the Valley of Mexico, Tacuba has the most intricate history. This circumstance derives in part from the encomienda's duration (Tacuba was a "perpetual" grant, like Ecatepec and the Marquesado del Valle),[126] in part from its various subdivisions and disputed successions, and in part from its situation within a complex group of mercedes issued to the descendants of Montezuma. Tacuba may first have been assigned to Montezuma's son and principal heir, Pedro Montezuma. In 1526, or before, Cortés assigned it instead to Tecuichpo or Isabel, daughter of Montezuma and Tecalco, as dote and arras on the occasion of her marriage to Alonso de Grado.[127] Instead of Tacuba, Pedro Montezuma received Tula, a community to the north of the Valley of Mexico and one that therefore does not receive attention in this listing.[128] Cortés's statement of the Tacuba grant, made in 1526, and many other formal references to it, speak of it as a permanent inheritance.[129] Isabel Montezuma had been the "wife" of Cuauhtemoc, and after Cuauhtemoc's death in 1525 she married sequentially and in the church Alonso de Grado, Pedro Gallego, and Juan Cano.[130] She was also the concubine of Cortés, by whom she had one daughter.[131] By Alonso de Grado she had no sons. By Pedro Gallego she had one son, Juan de Andrade (Gallego) Montezuma. By Juan Cano she had three sons and two daughters.[132] Alonso de Grado died in 1526–27. Pedro Gallego died about 1531. Isabel herself died in 1550 or 1551. Juan Cano died in Seville in 1572.[133]

The encomienda accompanied each of Isabel's marriages, although it was briefly taken by the audiencia in 1530.[134] Pedro Gallego was regarded as the encomendero during the period of his marriage, and Juan Cano was regarded as the encomendero from the time of his marriage until after the death of Isabel.[135] But Isabel's death and her will occasioned a series of disputes and the disruption of the tenure. The principal conflict—between her eldest son, Juan de Andrade, and her widower, Juan Cano—foreshadowed later conflicts between the Andrade and Cano families. Juan de Andrade argued that the property belonged to him, as the eldest son and heir, and that it had been held by his father, Pedro Gallego. The case was initially decided in favor of Juan de Andrade, but it was subsequently appealed by Juan Cano. After it appeared that the encomienda would be divided in a compromise settlement and in accordance with Isabel's will, both sides appealed, each demanding the entire amount.[136] These two claims were further disputed by Diego Arias de Sotelo (see Ecatepec in this Appendix), who regarded his mother-in-law, Leonor, as the true heir of Montezuma.[137] The solution was the rejection of the Arias de Sotelo claim and the division of the Tacuba estate.

In the 1560's the encomenderos were Juan de Andrade, Juan Cano, and the sons of Isabel and Juan Cano, namely Gonzalo Cano and Pedro Cano.[138] Two other offspring of Isabel and Juan Cano—Isabel Cano the younger and Catalina Cano—renounced their successions in favor of their father and their brothers.[139] But the whole made a six-part division. María Cano, daughter of Pedro Cano, claimed her father's sixth of the estate in the 1570's but the audiencia assigned her only one-twelfth, as half of Catalina's portion, and then undertook to take this from her and assign it to her uncle.[140] The failure of Pedro Cano's inheritance meant that in the second generation of the Cano family only Gonzalo Cano and Juan Cano Montezuma were successful heirs. Juan Cano Montezuma moved to Spain, married Elvira de Toledo, and initiated the families of Toledo Montezuma, Carbajal, and Vivero, which, from the late seventeenth century on, bore the titles Conde de Enjarada and Duques de Abrantes and Linares. Gonzalo Cano married Ana de Prado Calderón, from which marriage there developed eventually three branches: the Cano Montezuma family, deriving from the son, Juan Cano Montezuma y Prado; the Raza Cano Montezuma family, deriving from the first marriage of the daughter, María de Cano Montezuma, to Gerónimo Agustín de Espinosa; and the Andelo (Augdelo, Angdelo) Cano Montezuma family, stemming from María's second marriage, to Antonio Andelo Cano Calderón. The families mentioned were the main heirs of the subdivisions of the encomienda of Tacuba as it ultimately came to be established. Their history is a source for intricate genealogical study, with remarriages, legitimate and illegitimate claimants, and numerous lawsuits over succession.[141]

All these families, as well as the Juan de Andrade descendants and the Pedro Montezuma descendants, were the recipients also of additional mercedes granted by the crown, in some cases as reward for services, in others in recognition of Montezuma's capitulation, in still others by exchange for encomienda relinquishment. The mercedes were money grants, annuities, or rentas, issued in perpetuity or for a stated number of lives, and based upon designated tribute-paying encomiendas, undesignated vacant encomiendas, tribute income from stated jurisdictions, other royal income, or some department of the royal treasury. In the 1530's and 1540's Juan Cano had been active in requesting such grants, continually arguing that Isabel Montezuma had been deprived of most of her patrimony (as daughter of Montezuma) and that the Tacuba encomienda represented only a small fraction of what was properly hers, and his.[142] Gonzalo Cano had requested an enormous merced of 50,000 ducados.[143] The monarchy's principal response to these importunities was the series of grants of 1590, assigning smaller but substantial amounts to Gonzalo Cano and to the numerous offspring of Juan de Andrade.[144] As various mayorazgos were established these and similar annuities through colonial times, side by side with the Tacuba encomienda, supported the heirs of Montezuma. It should be noted that the grants of 1590 went chiefly to the Andrade Montezuma family, while the Tacuba encomienda, after the death of Juan de Andrade about 1577,[145] was confined within the branches of the Cano Montezuma family. These likewise received annuities, but at least at first in lesser amounts than the Andrade Montezuma family and the descendants of Pedro Montezuma received.[146]

Cortés's statement of 1526 listed Yetepec, Huizquilucan, Chimalpan, Chapulmaloyan, Azcapotzaltongo, Xilotzingo, Ocoyoacac, Catepec, Telasco, Guatuzco, Coatepec, and Tlazala as included in the Tacuba grant to Isabel, and he identified each of these as a sujeto of Tacuba. Cortés added that other sujetos of Tacuba had been assigned to other Spaniards and that he was refraining from granting them to Isabel pending the king's decision.[147] Variant spellings and copyists' changes complicate the task of identifying these towns. A partial check is obtained from the Memorial de los Pueblos, the native sixteenth-century Tacuba document listing sujetos of Tacuba and indicating those in encomienda to Juan Cano. The Memorial lists Huizquilucan (Vitzquillocan), Chimalpan (Chipalman), Chapulmaloyan, Azcapotzaltongo (Atzcapotzalco), Xilotzingo, and Telasco (Tlallachco?) as sujetos, and it states that Ocoyoacac and Coatepec (Couatepec), in the Juan Cano encomienda, no longer recognized Tacuba (i.e., as cabecera).[148] By the end of colonial times three of the former sujetos—Huizquilucan, Xilotzingo, and Tlazala—were no longer regarded as sujetos and were separately listed as pueblos in the encomienda. A second sujeto, San Bartolomé Naucalpan—not listed in the documents cited because it had been part of Huizquilucan—had also become separated and was recorded as a distinct pueblo.[149] Yetepec and Catepec have not been identified. Huizquilucan is separately documented as a Tacuba estancia and easily identified as modern San Martín Huizquilucan.[150] Chimalpan is known as a mountain and town (San Francisco Chimalpan del Monte) within the términos of Tacuba in numerous colonial documents.[151] Chapulmaloyan is documented independently as a Tacuba sujeto in the sixteenth century.[152] Azcapotzaltongo is repeatedly documented as a Tacuba sujeto and is a modern town.[153] Xilotzingo is surely not the separate Valley of Mexico encomienda (see Xilotzingo in this Appendix), nor is it the Santa Ana Xilotzingo near Lerma, both of which are also mentioned in the Memorial de los Pueblos. It is probably the Santa Ana Xilotzingo located southwest of Azcapotzaltongo, and if so it is also listed elsewhere as a Tacuba sujeto in the sixteenth century.[154] Telasco is perhaps to be identified as Tlallachco, requested by the gobernador of Tacuba in 1552, and as modern Atarasquillo.[155] Tlazala was demonstrably a Tacuba sujeto and is probably to be identified as the modern town of Tlaxcala, southwest of Azcapotzaltongo.[156] It will be remembered that Tacuba and Teocalhueyacan engaged in a dispute over Xilotzingo and Tlazala in the sixteenth century.[157]

Other communities listed in the Memorial de los Pueblos as in service to Juan Cano—Tepehuexoyucan, Cuappanohuayan, Capulhuac—were separately granted, in Isabel's will of 1550, to Gonzalo Cano. They were situated outside the Valley of Mexico to the southwest, and despite partially parallel histories they were unrelated to the Tacuba encomienda. Ocoyoacac, likewise outside the Valley to the southwest, differs from these in that it was included in Cortés's 1526 statement and in the Tacuba grant to Isabel. In spite of this, Cortés granted it later as a separate encomienda, to Antonio de Villagómez, who held it through his life. Juan Cano brought suit concerning Ocoyoacac in the 1530's; the crown's fiscal claimed it for the king in 1540; and it was finally restored to Isabel.[158] Because of these events the status of Ocoyoacac—as a normal terminable encomienda, or as a grant in perpetuity like the remainder of Tacuba—was in doubt. Isabel bequeathed it separately (Cuiacaque) to Gonzalo Cano in her will of 1550. It had the status of a distinct cabecera, and colonial references frequently indicate it as a holding independent from Tacuba.[159]

TECAMA

Seemingly separated from its cabecera, Tlatelolco, Tecama was assigned by Cortés about 1522 to the conquistador Juan González Ponce de León.[160] He died about 1540 and the encomienda was inherited by his son Juan Ponce de León. Juan Ponce de León held the property to 1552.[161] As the son-in-law of Hernando de Herrera, *relator* of the audiencia, Juan Ponce de León was in a position to exploit the encomienda, abuse its inhabitants, and resist the visitador Diego Ramírez. The case was pending in early 1552; and in early 1554, possibly without knowledge of Juan Ponce de León's death, the crown ordered the visita to proceed.[162] Juan Ponce de Léon was murdered, possibly by Bernardino de Bocanegra, in 1552. His wife, Catalina, was exiled. His three children, Luis, Juan, and María, were all minors. The royal fiscal argued successfully that with the murder two lives had been completed and that the encomienda should revert to the crown in accordance with the New Laws.[163] Viceroy Velasco ruled the escheatment in 1554, an order that was upheld on appeal by the Council of the Indies in 1558.[164] Tecama tributes were thereupon directed to the crown, but the children of Juan Ponce de Léon received lifetime annuities in compensation.[165]

TENAYUCA AND COATEPEC

It appears likely that the placement of Tenayuca in the crown in 1532 was the result of the death of its first holder, Cristóbal Flores.[166] In 1537 the crown ordered Viceroy Mendoza to assign encomiendas to the treasurer, Juan Alonso de Sosa, and Tenayuca in the Tepaneca zone and Coatepec in the Acolhua zone were two of the towns chosen in fulfillment of this order.[167] Sosa's wife, Ana de Estrada, the daughter of Alonso de Estrada, was the sister of the encomendero of neighboring Teocalhueyacan.[168] Cortés used the assignment of Tenayuca and Coatepec as one of his accusations against Mendoza.[169] The New Laws were announced in Mexico in March 1544, and in April the audiencia ruled the escheatment of this encomienda to the crown, since it was being held by a royal officer.[170] In 1564, after the death of Juan Alonso de Sosa, his sons entered a formal petition for restoration, but the petition was denied in 1570 by the Council.[171] The two towns remained under the crown.[172]

TENOCHTITLAN

Salazar and Chirinos, as factor and veedor, assigned the city to the crown about 1525. After their imprisonment "se lo tornaron a quitar a Su Magestad."[173] The reference is probably to Cortés and his party, but no private individual could have held Tenochtitlan for more than a brief period in the 1520's, and after the 1520's it was always understood to be in the crown. Its labor and tribute are discussed in Chapter XIII.

TEOCALHUEYACAN

Teocalhueyacan was originally a sujeto of Tacuba and was granted with the Tacuba assignment to Isabel Montezuma at the time of her marriage to Alonso de Grado. In the time of Isabel's marriage to Pedro Gallego, about 1528, the community was requested by Alonso de Estrada and his wife María (Marina) de la Caballería. Cortés thus separated it from Tacuba and assigned it to them as a distinct encomienda, a circumstance that facilitated its elevation to cabecera rank.[174] María de la Caballería has sometimes been confused with Marina, the consort of Cortés and the wife of Juan Jaramillo.[175] After Alonso de Estrada's death, in 1530, María de la Caballería remained as encomendero into the 1540's and until her death in 1551.[176] The encomienda was then inherited by Luisa de Estrada, daughter of María de la Caballería and Alonso de Estrada and widow of Jorge de Alvarado.[177] This Luisa de Estrada is not to be confused with the Luisa de Estrada who was the daughter of Francisco Vázquez de Coronado and who married Luis Ponce de León.[178] She held the encomienda to about 1570, save for an interval about 1563, when it was briefly held as a crown possession.[179] The son of Luisa de Estrada and Jorge de Alvarado, also named Jorge, married the daughter of the conquistador Angel de Villafañe. Juan de Villafañe, whose relationship to the family remains still in doubt, was the encomendero of the 1570's and in 1580.[180] Angel de Villafañe, grandson of Jorge de Alvarado and great-grandson of Alonso de Estrada, was encomendero by 1597, the encomienda now being generally referred to as Tlalnepantla.[181] He continued at least to 1629.[182] In 1653, after the encomienda had reverted, its income was made part of an annuity to Ana Enríquez de Cabrera, the mother of the viceroy Duque de Albuquerque. She died in 1658 and the merced was inherited by Baltasar de la Cueva Enríquez. The grant terminated in 1668.[183] In the eighteenth century annuities were made from this source to the Marquesa de Santa Cruz, the Duquesa de Albuquerque, and to others.[184] Because Tlalnepantla was still a composite community consisting of Tenayuca (under the crown) and Teocalhueyacan, and because an annuity was very similar to an encomienda, the statement could be made in 1724 that Tlalnepantla was partly in the crown and partly in encomienda to the Marquesa de la Conquista.[185]

TEOTIHUACAN

Teotihuacan was assigned by the royal officials about 1525 to the conquistador Francisco de Verdugo.[186] It was inherited before the late 1540's by his daughter, Francisca Verdugo, wife of Alonso de Bazán.[187] On the deaths of Francisca Verdugo and Alonso de Bazán, both about 1564, their first son Antonio Velázquez de Bazán was absent and the encomienda was assigned to the second son, Andrés de Bazán. When Andrés died three lives were completed and the encomienda reverted to the crown, but Viceroy Velasco received its tributes by special merced in the late 1560's.[188] The Consejo de Indias then assigned it to Antonio Velázquez de Bazán, who held it at least to 1597.[189] Antonio Velázquez de Bazán was the husband of María de Castro, daughter of the Conde de Lemos.[190] The heir of the fourth generation was their son, Rodrigo Velázquez de Castro y Bazán, who arrived from Spain about 1603 and maintained this encomienda, together with a number of others, at least to 1620.[191] The encomienda reverted to the crown before 1658, the last possessor being Josefa Bazán y Castro.[192] After royalization tributes of the Teotihuacan jurisdiction were designated to finance mercedes to the Montezuma family.[193]

TEPETLAOZTOC

Cortés held Tepetlaoztoc and took tributes from it for three years. It was then held for one year by Diego de Ocampo before being transferred in mid-1527 to Miguel Díaz de Aux. The governor Alonso de Estrada brought accusations against Díaz de Aux for his severe treatment of the Indians of the encomienda, sentenced him to perpetual exile from the colony, and gave Tepetlaoztoc to the factor Gonzalo de Salazar in 1528.[194] Miguel Díaz de Aux disputed the transfer unsuccessfully in the early 1530's.[195] Gonzalo de Salazar, actually the fourth, was regarded as the first holder.[196] In the early 1550's the Indian community brought suit against him for tribute excesses and other illegal exploitation. Part of the Indian testimony took the form of a pictorial record of abuses, which has been reproduced under the modern title *Códice Kingsborough* and which records details of the encomienda history to the 1550's.[197] Gonzalo de Salazar died about 1553. Juan Velázquez de Salazar, son of Gonzalo de Salazar, inherited the encomienda and held it from the 1550's through the remainder of the century.[198] Like his father, he was sued by the Indian community for various irregularities.[199] Juan Velázquez de Salazar probably died shortly before 1612, when the Montezuma heir Pedro de Tesifón was granted an annuity of 1,000 ducados in perpetuity, with additional annuities to his brothers. These payments were administered in part through the tributes of Tepetlaoztoc, which was in "encomienda" to Pedro de Tesifón and his brothers in 1628 and in the middle seventeenth century, and to his heirs after that.[200] The Montezuma heirs of the eighteenth century received one peso per day from Tepetlaoztoc tributes.[201]

TEPEXPAN

Tepexpan, often mentioned in conjunction with its distant estancia Temascalapa, was first assigned about 1522 to Jerónimo de Medina.[202] Some later lists include Maestro de Roa as an early Tepexpan encomendero, possibly as a consequence of intermingling jurisdictions of Acolman and Tepexpan.[203] The grant to Jerónimo de Medina was confirmed by Alonso de Estrada and by Luis Ponce de León as governors in the later 1520's, and by the audiencia in 1530.[204] In 1538 Jerónimo de Medina made a *renunciación en dote* to his daughter, Inés de Vargas, who became the wife of Juan Baeza de Herrera, secretary of the audiencia and inventor of mining machinery. The latter, together with his wife and children, were the encomenderos in the 1540's and to about 1552, when he died.[205] It remained in his widow and children and later in his eldest son, Jerónimo de Baeza (Vaca) de Herrera.[206] In the 1560's, taking advantage of Temascalapa's efforts to free itself from Tepexpan, the royal fiscal unsuccessfully argued that Temascalapa tributes should be paid to the crown. The audiencia ruled in 1552 that Temascalapa was a sujeto of Tepexpan. On appeal by the Indian community of Temascalapa, this case came before the Council of the Indies in the 1560's, and the judgment again was unfavorable to Temascalapa.[207] The encomienda was still in the possession of Jerónimo de Baeza de Herrera in 1597. He and his wife, Mariana de la Marcha, had fifteen sons and daughters, of whom ten (including four sons) were still living about 1604.[208] Royalization occurred at some time before 1678.[209]

TEPOZOTLAN

The first holder of Tepozotlan, Juan de Ortega, died in 1546 and the encomienda immediately reverted to the crown.[210] It remained crown property for the remainder of the colonial period, but some of its tributes were assigned to the heirs of Alvaro Pérez de Zamora, the encomendero of Mazatlan.[211]

TEQUICISTLAN

Tequicistlan, frequently listed with its sujeto Totolzingo, was first divided between the crown and the conquistador, Juan de Tovar.[212] About 1555 the encomienda half was inherited by his son (Juan) Hipólito de Tovar.[213] The encomienda is listed under the names Juan and Juan Hipólito until 1600, and it is possible that more than one person is indicated in these notices.[214] Juan Hipólito de Tovar died in 1600 and the encomienda half was listed as vacant and ready for reassignment in 1604.[215] Juan Cano Montezuma, one of the Tacuba encomenderos, had been granted an annuity of 1,000 pesos in 1590, and in 1604 the viceroy ruled that part of this income was to be drawn from the vacant half of Tequicistlan. Thus seventeenth-century notices record Tequicistlan as in encomienda in one-half and under the crown in the other half.[216]

TEQUIXQUIAC

Tequixquiac was divided into two encomiendas, one held by Martín López, the builder of the brigantines in the conquest, the other by his companion Andrés Núñez.[217] Andrés Núñez died before 1543 and his encomienda half descended to his daughter and her husband Gonzalo Portillo. A variant record substitutes Diego Gutiérrez as the encomendero of the second half and as the father-in-law of Gonzalo Portillo, but a viceregal notice of 1543 records Gonzalo Portillo's own testimony that the father-in-law was Andrés Núñez, to whom Cortés granted the original encomienda share.[218] Martín López died about 1575.[219] His son, Martín López Osorio (Ossorio), inherited the encomienda share. The son was survived in 1591 by his widow, Beatriz de Ribera, and their son, also named Martín López Osorio.[220] The latter held the encomienda share in the third life in the 1590's and in the early seventeenth century.[221] Gonzalo Portillo held the other half to 1569 and presumably longer, although this part of the encomienda was reissued in a new grant later in the century to Francisco Tello de Orosco.[222] Both parts of Tequixquiac appear to have been still in encomienda in 1666.[223] In 1675 in a new grant tributes from Tequixquiac were assigned to the Marqués de Ariza, and these were still being paid in the eighteenth century.[224]

TEXCOCO

With respect to encomienda, Texcoco was a "province" including Texcoco itself and four adjacent cabeceras, Huexotla, Coatlichan, Chiauhtla, and Tezayuca, each with its sujetos. Texcoco sought unsuccessfully to reduce all four to sujeto status.[225] About 1522 Cortés assigned Texcoco to the crown, but he immediately reversed this decision, put Tlaxcala under the crown, and took Texcoco for himself.[226] In 1524 Cortés sought to obtain royal authority for his possession, but this was forthcoming only in a general and provisional endorsement of Cortés's holdings, pending royal investigation.[227] In 1525, when Cortés was in the south, Salazar and Chirinos assigned Texcoco to the crown, but after their imprisonment in early 1526 Cortés again held it for himself.[228] Members of the audiencia seized Texcoco while Cortés was in Spain.[229] Cortés preserved at least an informal possession in early 1529,[230] but Texcoco was not included in the Marquesado grant of July of that year, and this clearly implied its imminent loss. The second audiencia formally placed Texcoco in the crown in March 1531.[231] Cortés continued to receive tributes from Texcoco at least to 1536.[232] But this must have come to an end by 1541, because in that year, following a royal order, Viceroy Mendoza assigned Texcoco tribute and Texcoco labor (at a wage) to the Augustinians for their church and monastery in the city.[233]

TEZONTEPEC

Not all early notices clearly distinguish between the Tezontepec in the northeastern corner of the Valley and the Tezontepec outside the Valley to the northwest near Misquiahuala. The former is sometimes designated in colonial documents as Tezontepec de Pachuca, since it fell within the Pachuca corregimiento.[234] It was first granted in encomienda to Rodrigo de Baeza.[235] Viceroy Mendoza assigned it on Baeza's death to his son Baltasar de Obregón, but in such a way that one-third of the proceeds were designated for the widow. The audiencia later deprived her of this portion, and the full encomienda fell to Baltasar de Obregón.[236] He held it in the 1540's and at least to 1564.[237] After 1564, on his death, it was inherited by his son, also named Baltasar de Obregón, who held it at least to 1573.[238] The community appears to have escheated to the crown and to have been reassigned to Francisco Tello de Orozco between 1573 and 1597.[239] A grandson of the first Baltasar de Obregón, also named Baltasar de Obregón, was living in Puebla, dispossesssed of the encomienda, in the early seventeenth century.[240] Tezontepec de Pachuca was listed as in the possession of the crown again in 1658.[241]

TIZAYUCA

Tizayuca appears to have been a sujeto of Ecatepec originally held with its cabecera by Cortés and later granted to Leonor Montezuma.[242] This may also be the Tizayuca that was granted to Manuel de Guzmán about 1525 by Peralmíndez Chirinos and Gonzalo de Salazar and taken again by Cortés after he returned from the south in 1526.[243] The assignment of Ecatepec to Leonor then may have occurred shortly after this.[244] But Tizayuca was put in the crown by the second audiencia in April 1531.[245] With Tolcayuca it was unsuccessfully requested by the Indian ruler of Ecatepec and later gobernador of Tenochtitlan, Diego Huanitzin (Panitzin) in 1532.[246] Pedro Núñez unsuccessfully requested it in 1555, and subsequent notices record its retention in the crown.[247] The Suma de Visitas indicates Tizayuca as a divided community, half under the crown and half in encomienda to Alonso Pérez de Zamora, but this is probably a reference to the communities of Tizayuca and Tolcayuca together. Tolcayuca, north of the Valley of Mexico, and frequently associated with Tizayuca (both were seemingly former estancias of Ecatepec), remained half under the crown and half in encomienda to the Pérez de Zamora heirs to the seventeenth century.[248]

TLATELOLCO

Cortés at first assigned Tlatelolco for the crown. Later he gave it in encomienda to Diego de Ocampo. It may have been while Diego de Ocampo was serving as Cortés's agent in Spain that Cortés assigned Tlatelolco for himself.[249] We do not know when Tlatelolco was formally royalized, largely because as an exempt community (to 1565) it does not figure in the early records of tribute. But its status as a crown town was virtually assumed by the Marquesado grant of 1529.

TOLTITLAN

Cortés granted Toltitlan to Bartolomé de Parales, the first holder, as a reward for services.[250] In the early 1540's, after Perales's death, a question of inheritance arose involving Perales's sons, his widow Antonia Hernández, and his widow's second husband, Juan de Moscoso. The issue was resolved following the death of the principal son and heir, and Juan de Moscoso succeeded in winning the encomienda.[251] Antonia Hernández died about 1564, and Juan de Moscoso died about 1569. There were no other heirs, and the encomienda escheated to the crown.[252] But by a special merced, Luis de Velasco the younger was allowed to receive its tributes, and this was regarded as an encomienda privilege with Axapusco and Azcapotzalco. The encomienda thus reverted to the first life.[253] Luis de Velasco died in Spain in 1617. The encomienda was inherited by his son, the second Marqués de Salinas, and in 1671, with Azcapotzalco, it was pending settlement for the Marqués de San Román.[254] The Marqués de San Román died shortly before 1703 and all his tribute income reverted to the crown.[255]

XILOTZINGO

Xilotzingo was first held by the conquistador Martín Vásquez.[256] He died by 1550 and his son, Francisco Vásquez (Laynes), the second holder, died by 1560.[257] The encomienda was then held by the widow and sons of Francisco Vásquez.[258] It remained in the family at least to 1597, when it was held by Matías Vásquez Laynes, presumably in the third life.[259] Xilotzingo was listed as vacant in 1604, evidently as a consequence of the holder's recent death.[260] Later in the seventeenth century Xilotzingo tributes were assigned to the Montezuma heirs.[261]

XOCHIMILCO

Xochimilco was granted to the conquistador Pedro de Alvarado.[262] The first audiencia introduced tribute-takers in Xochimilco about 1529 to ensure collections for fines levied against Alvarado.[263] In a bargain with Francisco de Montejo, Alvarado later agreed to trade Xochimilco and some other possessions for the governorship of Honduras and Higueras.[264] But Alvarado died in 1541, before this transaction was completed. His wife Beatriz de la Cueva also died in 1541, and because there were no encomienda heirs,

Xochimilco reverted to the crown.[265] A claim for succession seems to have been made through Jorge de Alvarado, brother of Pedro de Alvarado, and through the wife of Jorge de Alvarado, Luisa de Estrada, the encomendero of Teocalhueyacan.[266] But though coveted by others it remained a royal possession.[267] By special grant to Cortés, part of the Xochimilco tributes were designated for the Marquesado del Valle, and this continued in the seventeenth and eighteenth centuries.[268]

Cabeceras and Sujetos

The cabeceras and sujetos shown in Map 3 are listed here, together with sample documentary citations for the sujeto status. Sujetos situated close to their cabeceras, sujetos that cannot now be located and mapped, and some others are omitted. Dates are of all periods, but they concentrate in the middle and late sixteenth and early seventeenth centuries.

ACOLMAN

Atlatongo: PNE, VI, 210 (1580).
Chiapa: AGI, Justicia, leg. 208, no. 4, 2nd pag., fol. 216v (ca. 1566). ENE, XVI, 90 (ca. 1570). AGI, Indiferente general, leg. 1529, fol. 205v (ca. 1570). PNE, VI, 210 (1580).
Ixtlahuaca: PNE, VI, 210 (Tuchatlauco, 1580). PCR, Varios papeles, vol. 2, fols. 78r ff. (1582).
Nopaltepec: PNE, VI, 210 (1580).
Quauhtlapechco: PNE, VI, 210 (1580).
Tenextlacotla: PNE, VI, 210 (1580).
Tepetitlan: PNE, VI, 210 (1580).
Tlaxinca: PNE, VI, 210 (1580).
Xometla: PNE, VI, 210 (1580).
Zacatepec: ENE, XVI, 90 (ca. 1570). AGI, Indiferente general, leg. 1529, fol. 205v (ca. 1570).

AMECAMECA

Atlauhcan (Atlauhtla): BAGN, ser. 2, II, 23 (1599).
Nexapan: BAGN, ser. 2, II, 29 (1599).
Panohuayan: AGN, Mercedes, vol. 7, fol. 299r (1564).

AZCAPOTZALCO

Tilhuacan: AGN, General de parte, vol. 2, fol. 153v (1580); Indios, vol. 4, fol. 6v (1589).

CHIAUHTLA

Tlalticahuacan (Tlaltevacan): *El libro de las tasaciones,* p. 171 (1566).

CHICOLOAPA

Huatongo (Coatongo): PNE, VI, 40, 82 (1580).

CHICONAUHTLA

CHIMALHUACAN ATENCO

Aticpac: PNE, VI, 41 (1580).
Atlapulco: PNE, VI, 40 (1580).
Chimalpan: PNE, VI, 40 (1580).
Huiznahuac: PNE, VI, 40 (1580).
Mizcuitlan: PNE, VI, 40 (1580).

CHIMALHUACAN CHALCO

Ecatzingo: AGN, Mercedes, vol. 6, fol. 243v (1563). AGI, Contaduría, leg. 729, fols. 26r ff. (1628).
Mamalhuazacan: ENE, VII, 260 (1554).
Tepetlixpa: ENE, VII, 260 (1554).

CITLALTEPEC

COATEPEC

Acuauhtla: PNE, VI, 40 (cabecera, 1580).
Xocoatlaco: PNE, VI, 39 (1580).

COATLICHAN

Cuauhtlalpa: PNE, VI, 82 (1580). AGN, General de parte, vol. 2, fol. 143r (1580).

COYOACAN

Mixcoac: AGN, Hospital de Jesús, vol. 278, exp. 6 (Santo Domingo, 1620); vol. 382, exp. 38 (1807).
San Bernabé: AGN, Hospital de Jesús, vol. 278, exp. 6 (1620).
San Gerónimo: AGN, Hospital de Jesús, vol. 278, exp. 6 (1620).
Santa Lucía: AGN, Hospital de Jesús, vol. 278, exp. 6 (1620).
Santa Ursula: AGN, Hospital de Jesús, vol. 278, exp. 6 (1620).
Tizapan: AGN, Hospital de Jesús, vol. 278, exp. 6 (1620).
Tlalpam (San Agustín de las Cuevas): AGN, Hospital de Jesús, vol. 266, exp. 7, fols. 42v et passim (1607); vol. 278, exp. 5, fols. 3r ff. (1619).
Tlaltenango: AGN, Hospital de Jesús, vol. 278, exp. 6 (1620).

CUAUHTITLAN

Coyotepec: AGN, Mercedes, vol. 6, fols. 14v–15r (1563); vol. 8, fol. 214r (1565).
Huehuetoca: AGN, Mercedes, vol. 3, fol. 340v (1551). NCDHM (1941), II, 16 (ca. 1569).
Teoloyuca: MNM, Colección franciscana, leg. 190, fols. 11r, 14r (1562).
Toltepec: AGN, Mercedes, vol. 9, fols. 161v–162r (1567). PNE, III, 33 (ca. 1569).

CUITLAHUAC

Santa Catarina (Cuauhtli-Itlacuayan): AAMC, no. 25, p. 996 (1561).
Tulyahualco: AAMC, no. 25, p. 1002 (1561).
Zapotitlan: AAMC, no. 25, p. 997 (1561).

CULHUACAN

ECATEPEC

Coacalco: AGN, Mercedes, vol. 6, fol. 165r–165v (1563). PNE, VI, 171 (1580).
Coatitlan: AGI, Justicia, leg. 159, ramo 5 (disputed with Tlatelolco, 1527).
Tolpetlac: CDIAI, XLI, 142–44 (disputed with Tlatelolco, 1537). PNE, III, 29–31
(ca. 1569).

HUEXOTLA

San Bernardino: AGN, General de parte, vol. 2, fol. 63r (1579); Indios, vol. 3, fol.
154r–154v (1591).

HUEYPOXTLA

Tezcatepec: García Pimentel, *Descripción*, p. 88 (1569).
Tianquistonco: PNE, I, 110 (ca. 1548). García Pimentel, *Descripción*, p. 88 (1569).
Tlacuitlapilco: PNE, I, 110 (ca. 1548). García Pimentel, *Descripción*, p. 88 (1569).

HUITZILOPOCHCO, IXTAPALAPA, IXTAPALUCA,
MEXICALZINGO, MIXQUIC

OTUMBA

Ahuatepec: AGN, Mercedes, vol. 1, fol. 84r (1542); vol. 7, fol. 40r (1563). FHT, I,
87 (1576); III, 59–60 (1587).
Axapusco: PNE, III, 83 (ca. 1569).
Oxtoticpac: PNE, III, 83 (ca. 1569).
Tlamapa: PNE, III, 83 (ca. 1569). AGN, Indios, vol. 2, fol. 25r–25v (1582).
Xaltepec: PNE, III, 83 (ca. 1569).
Xamilililpa: AGN, Indios, vol. 2, fols. 24v–25r (1582).

TACUBA

Azcapotzaltongo: AGN, Mercedes, vol. 7, fol. 295r–295v (1564); vol. 8, fol. 127r
(1565).
Cepayautla: AGN, Mercedes, vol. 8, fol. 173r (1565). García Pimentel, *Descripción*,
p. 164 (1569). AGN, General de parte, vol. 2, fol. 156r (1580). Cf. FHT, II, 279–80
(Cepa, Autla, 1580).
Chimalpan (Chipalman): ENE, XIV, 118 (ca. 1560).
Ciuhtepec: ENE, XIV, 118 (ca. 1560). García Pimentel, *Descripción*, p. 163 (1569).
AGN, General de parte, vol. 2, fol. 156r (1580). Cf. FHT, II, 279–80 (Auhtepec,
1580).
Cuauhximalpan: ENE, XIV, 118 (ca. 1560).

Huizquilucan: ENE, XIV, 118 (ca. 1560). AGN, Mercedes, vol. 8, fol. 138r (1565); Indios, vol. 1, fols. 86v–87v (1580). FHT, III, 27–28 (1587).
Tecamachalco: ENE, XIV, 118 (ca. 1560).
Tlazala: AGI, Justicia, leg. 165, no. 2 (1562).
Tototepec (Los Remedios): AGN, Indios, vol. 1, fols. 86v–87v (1580). FHT, III, 27 (1587).
Xilotzingo: AGN, Mercedes, vol. 5, fol. 20v (1560); fol. 95v (1560). ENE, XIV, 118 (ca. 1560). AGI, Justicia, leg. 165, no. 2 (1562).

TACUBAYA

TECAMA

Axoloapan: AGN, Mercedes, vol. 1, fol. 49v (1542); vol. 4, fol. 313r–313v (1556). García Pimentel, *Descripción,* p. 58 (1569). AGN, General de parte, vol. 2, fol. 262r (1580).

TENANGO

Ayotzingo: AGI, Indiferente general, leg. 1529, fol. 155v (1571).
Pahuacan: AGI, México, leg. 665, cuad. 2, fol. 99r (1603).
Quautzotzongo: AGI, México, leg. 665, cuad. 2, fols. 97v, 107r ff. (before 1603).
Tepopula: AGN, Mercedes, vol. 5, fol. 4r (1560).
Xochitepec: AGI, México, leg. 665, cuad. 2, fol. 97v (before 1603).

TENAYUCA (see TLALNEPANTLA)

TENOCHTITLAN

Coxtocan: PNE, III, 18 (1570). AGI, México, leg. 665, cuad. 2, fol. 98r–98v (1603).
Cuaquiquitla (Cuauhtlihuizca): AGN, Mercedes, vol. 13, fol. 196r–196v (San Francisco, 1585).
Ixtahuacan (Aztahuacan): PNE, III, 18 (1570).
Los Reyes: PNE, III, 18 (1570). Durán, *Historia,* I, 32 (ca. 1579).
Ozumbilla (Ozumba): AGN, Mercedes, vol. 9, fols. 171v–172r (1567).
Santa Marta: Durán, *Historia,* I, 32 (ca. 1579).
Tecalco (Tecalca): AGN, Mercedes, vol. 7, fol. 329v (1564). AGI, Indiferente general, leg. 1529, fol. 206r (ca. 1570).
Tepetlacalco: Caso, "Los barrios antiguos," p. 24 (1586).
Tepopula: AGN, Indios, vol. 9, fols. 41r–41v (1618), 64v–65r (1619).
Tetecpilco: BM, Add. 13,994, fols. 220r ff. (1637). AA, Tierras y ejidos, leg. 1, no. 4065, exp. 19, fol. 7r (1708).

TEOCALHUEYACAN (see TLALNEPANTLA)

TEOTIHUACAN

Aticpac: PNE, VI, 210 (1580).
Coatlan: PNE, VI, 210 (1580).

TEPETLAOZTOC

TEPEXPAN

Atlanmaxac: PNE, VI, 209 (1580).

Atocpan: AGI, Justicia, leg. 208, no. 4, sep. pag., fol. 11r–11v (1530). PNE, VI, 209 (1580).

Maquixco: AGI, Justicia, leg. 208, no. 4, sep. pag., fol. 11r–11v (1530). García Pimentel, *Descripción*, pp. 56–57 (1569). PNE, VI, 209 (1580).

Santa Ana: García Pimentel, *Descripción*, p. 57 (1569).

Tecalco: AGI, Justicia, leg. 208, no. 4, sep. pag., fol. 11r–11v (1530). García Pimentel, *Descripción*, p. 57 (1569).

Temascalapa: AGI, Justicia, leg. 208, no. 4, sep. pag., fol. 11r–11v (1530). AGN, Mercedes, vol. 2, fols. 323v–324r (1544); vol. 7, fol. 18r–18v (1563). García Pimentel, *Descripción*, p. 56 (1569). PNE, VI, 209 (1580).

Teopancalco: AGI, Justicia, leg. 208, no. 4 (1566). García Pimentel, *Descripción*, p. 56 (1569). PNE, VI, 209 (1580).

Zacualuca: AGI, Justicia, leg. 208, no. 4, sep. pag., fol. 11r–11v (1530). PNE, VI, 209 (1580).

TEPOZOTLAN

Tepoxaco: AGN, Mercedes, vol. 5, fol. 255r (1561); vol. 9, fol. 177r (1567); vol. 12, fols. 13v–14r (1583); vol. 14, fol. 452r (1589).

Xoloc: AGN, Mercedes, vol. 13, fol. 9r–9v (1583).

TEQUICISTLAN

Totolzingo: PNE, I, 198 (ca. 1548). AGI, Indiferente general, leg. 1529, fol. 206r (ca. 1570). PNE, VI, 209 (1580). AGN, Mercedes, vol. 15, fols. 250v–251r (1590).

TEQUIXQUIAC

San Sebastián: AGN, Mercedes, vol. 13, fol. 244v (1586).

TEXCOCO

Atenco: AGN, Indios, vol. 4, fol. 204r (1590).

Calpulalpan: NCDHM (1941), II, 12 (ca. 1569). FHT, I, 108–9, 137 (1576).

Mazapa: FHT, I, 137 (1576).

Soltepec: Cervantes de Salazar, *Crónica*, p. 592 (ca. 1560).

TEZAYUCA

Acopolco: FHT, II, 304–5 (1580).

TEZONTEPEC

TIZAYUCA

Huitzila: García Pimentel, *Descripción*, p. 54 (1569).

TLALMANALCO

Chalco Atenco: PNE, I, 105 (ca. 1548). AGN, Mercedes, vol. 4, fol. 312r (1556). NCDHM (1941), II, 11 (ca. 1569). AGN, Indios, vol. 1, fol. 99v (1580).

Contla: BNP, no. 30, fol. 9v (1564).

Cuauhtlalpa: AGN, Mercedes, vol. 7, fol. 19v (1563). BNP, no. 30, fol. 9v (1564).
Temamatla: AGN, Congregaciones, vol. 1, fol. 132r (1581); Indios, vol. 4, fols. 13v–14r (1589); General de parte, vol. 6, fol. 194v (1602).

TLALNEPANTLA (TENAYUCA and TEOCALHUEYACAN)

Calacoayan: PNE, III, 32 (ca. 1569).
Tizapan: PNE, III, 32 (ca. 1569).
Xocoyahualco: PNE, III, 31 (San Gerónimo, ca. 1569).

TLATELOLCO

Coatepec: Fernández and Leicht, "Códice del tecpan," pp. 260 ff. (1576). Villa-señor y Sánchez, *Theatro americano*, I, 77 (formerly, i.e., before the middle eighteenth century). Barlow, "Tlatelolco como tributario," p. 201.
Coatitlan (Santa Clara): CDIAI, XLI, 143 (Ayatitcla, disputed with Ecatepec, 1537).
Ozumbilla (Ozumba, Atzompan): CDIAI, XLI, 144 (1537). Fernández and Leicht, "Códice del tecpan," p. 261 (1576). FHT, VII, 55–56, 62–64 (1634).
San Pablo de las Salinas: Villa-señor y Sánchez, *Theatro americano*, I, 77 (formerly, i.e., before the middle eighteenth century).
Tecalco: PNE, I, 199 (ca. 1548). ENE, XVI, 92 (ca. 1570). AGI, Indiferente general, leg. 1529, fol. 206r (ca. 1570). Fernández and Leicht, "Códice del tecpan," pp. 260 ff. (1576).
Tepetlacalco: AGN, Mercedes, vol. 1, fol. 46r (1542). Fernández and Leicht, "Códice del tecpan," pp. 260 ff. (1576). Villa-señor y Sánchez, *Theatro americano*, I, 77 (formerly, i.e., before the middle eighteenth century).
Tepopula: Fernández and Leicht, "Códice del tecpan," p. 260 (1576). AGN, Tierras, vol. 2825, exp. 6, fols. 1r ff. (1788).
Tolpetlac: CDIAI, XLI, 143 (disputed with Ecatepec, 1537). Fernández and Leicht, "Códice del tecpan," pp. 260 ff. (1576). FHT, VII, 55–56, 62–64 (1634).
Xaloztoc: Fernández and Leicht, "Códice del tecpan," pp. 260 ff. (1576). AGN, Congregaciones, vol. 1, fols. 101v–102r (1604).
Xoloc: CDIAI, XLI, 144 (1537). AGN, Mercedes, vol. 1, fol. 162r–162v (1542). García Pimentel, *Descripción*, p. 58 (1569). Fernández and Leicht, "Códice del tecpan," pp. 260 ff. (1576). FHT, VII, 55–56, 62–64 (1634).

TOLTITLAN

XALTOCAN

Acuitlapilco: PNE, VI, 170 (1580). AGN, Tierras, vol. 1584, exp. 1, fol. 5r (1599).
Atenango: PNE, VI, 170 (1580). AGN, Tierras, vol. 1584, exp. 1, fol. 5r (1599).
Atocan: PNE, VI, 170 (1580). AGN, Mercedes, vol. 17, fol. 99r (1591); Tierras, vol. 1584, exp. 1, fol. 5r (1599).
Ecatitlan: PNE, VI, 170 (1580). AGN, Tierras, vol. 1584, exp. 1, fol. 5r (1599).
Miltengo: PNE, VI, 170 (1580). AGN, Mercedes, vol. 14, fol. 5v (1587); Tierras, vol. 1584, exp. 1, fol. 5r (1599).
Nestlalpa: AGN, Mercedes, vol. 9, fol. 38r (1567). PNE, VI, 170 (1580). AGN, Mercedes, vol. 13, fols. 171v–172r (1585); Tierras, vol. 1584, exp. 1, fol. 5r (1599).

XILOTZINGO

XOCHIMILCO

Milpa Alta: NCDHM (1941), II, 10 (ca. 1569). AGN, Indios, vol. 9, fol. 81r (1619).
San Bartolomé: AGN, General de parte, vol. 6, fol. 165v (1602).
San Francisco: AGN, Indios, vol. 6 (1), fols. 65v–66r (1592).
San Gerónimo: AGN, Mercedes, vol. 1, fol. 210v (1542).
Tecomitl: CDIHE, LVII, 230–31 (1586).
Tepepan: Vetancurt, *Chronica,* p. 86 (in reference to ca. 1560). "Testamento de María Alonso," p. 203 (1623).

ZUMPANGO

San Sebastián: García Pimentel, *Descripción,* p. 94 (1569). PNE, III, 35 (1569).
Santiago: García Pimentel, *Descripción,* p. 94 (1569). PNE, III, 35 (1569).

Political Jurisdictions

In Chapter IV we have discussed and mapped the corregimientos, alcaldías mayores, and subdelegaciones of the Valley of Mexico. The boundaries of these, as shown on Map 5, require further comment and citation. No comparable map is known from any colonial period. Maps of the Valley were occasionally drawn in the sixteenth and seventeenth centuries, but no known map provides the boundaries of political jurisdictions until the late colonial period. Of the main jurisdictions of the Valley we have maps of the late eighteenth century for Xochimilco, Coyoacan, Tacuba, Cuauhtitlan, Citlaltepec, Teotihuacan, Otumba, and Coatepec.[1] About half of these maps show the precise boundaries. The remainder locate the towns in an unbounded area. For two other jurisdictions—Texcoco and Ecatepec—there exist census lists of towns of the late eighteenth century in the absence of the equivalent maps.[2] Both census lists and maps are lacking in the jurisdictions of Chalco, Mexicalzingo, and the city of Mexico. But a large quantity of other documentation of the late colonial period may be applied to these jurisdictions, and the approximate boundaries are quite fully ascertainable even for the areas whose maps show no boundaries.[3]

The regulations for intendants (1786) required that every jurisdiction possessing a corregidor or alcalde mayor be governed by a subdelegado, and no boundary changes are known to have occurred with the establishment of intendancies.[4] There exists a late colonial map of the intendancy of Mexico, but it fails to show the boundaries of the internal subdelegaciones.[5] The first known map of the Valley to show political subdivisions in a single portrayal is the map of Tomás Ramón del Moral in 1828–29. By this time, however, a considerable number of changes had occurred and the map is not useful for a reconstruction of the colonial boundaries.[6]

The titles of the jurisdictions, as given below, are those commonly used, but it should be noted that names of other principal towns were sometimes substituted for them.

CHALCO

The jurisdiction included the Chalco province of the conquest period, to which were attached in the sixteenth century the cabeceras of Cuitlahuac, Mixquic, and Ixtapaluca. References to these additions as falling within Chalco province represent a colonial extension of the original meaning of Chalco.[7] The jurisdiction contained a number of estancias of Tenochtitlan and Tlatelolco—Santiago Tepopula, Santos Reyes Acatlixcoatlan, San Juan Coxtocan, Santiago Tepostlan, La Asumpcion—not all of which can be precisely mapped.[8] We have no census map of the late eighteenth century, but a list of towns for 1770 and a list of haciendas for 1773 yield a jurisdiction that appears to coincide closely with modern Chalco boundaries. The northern border was mapped in the eighteenth century as the border shared with the Coatepec jurisdiction.[9]

XOCHIMILCO

Scarcely any changes occurred in the boundaries of the Xochimilco jurisdiction through the entire colonial period. The sixteenth-century corregimiento is known to have extended to Tulyahualco, Ixtayopa, and Tecomitl on the east, and to a point between Tepepan and Tlalpam on the west, and to have included Milpa Alta and some other towns of the jurisdiction shown in Map 5.[10] There exists a colonial map of the jurisdiction and a list of communities, both of the late eighteenth century.[11]

MEXICALZINGO

The jurisdiction of the 1570's contained the four Culhua cabeceras— Mexicalzingo, Ixtapalapa, Culhuacan, and Huitzilopochco—and the Tenochtitlan sujetos Santa Marta and Los Reyes. These remained, but in the very late colonial period a number of additional sujetos of Tenochtitlan in the Ixtacalco region (shown on Map 5 under Mexico) were added to the jurisdiction.[12] For Mexicalzingo we have no integral or complete list of communities for any period, and there is no map.

COATEPEC

The corregimiento of the 1570's included Coatepec, Chimalhuacan Atenco, and Chicoloapa, with a southern boundary falling between Aticpac and

Los Reyes and between Acuauhtla and Ixtapaluca.[13] The same boundaries, either exactly or almost exactly, were retained to late colonial times. For the late period there exist a list of communities and an excellent map showing boundaries.[14] All the communities of the late eighteenth century are identifiable as modern towns.

TEXCOCO

The jurisdiction originally included Teotihuacan and a large area to the north, but it had been reduced by the late 1570's through the creation of the separate jurisdiction of Teotihuacan.[15] The southern boundary corresponded to the northern boundary of Coatepec and is therefore mapped for the later period. To the east the Texcoco jurisdiction extended in the sixteenth century about three leagues beyond Calpulalpan, outside the Valley. These boundaries on the south and east remained, exactly or approximately, until the end of the colonial period.[16] By the early eighteenth century, however, a considerable modification had been made in the northern boundary, with the removal of Acolman from Teotihuacan and its attachment to the Texcoco jurisdiction.[17] The change meant that the distant northern estancias of Acolman, north of the Teotihuacan corregimiento, were likewise attached to the Texcoco jurisdiction. This northern enclave, remaining in the 1790's, consisted of Ixtlahuaca, Zacatepec, and Chiapa; the haciendas of Las Pintas, La Presa, and Dolores; the rancho of Coayuca; and some other communities.[18] For the late period we have two full lists of the communities of this jurisdiction but no map.[19]

OTUMBA

The corregimiento limits depended always upon the original organization of the cabecera of Otumba and its sujetos, both undisputed and disputed. Sixteenth-century records indicate that the jurisdiction extended on the east as far as Tepayuca, and this fact suggests an unchanged boundary through the colonial period.[20] A full toponymic record is contained in the congregación account of 1603, which lists some sixty place names.[21] The comparable list and map for the late eighteenth century show a jurisdiction that was completely or virtually identical.[22]

TEOTIHUACAN

The area of 1580, recently separated from Texcoco, included the cabeceras of Acolman, Tepexpan, Tequicistlan, and Teotihuacan, and their intermixed sujetos.[23] With the removal of Acolman to the Texcoco corregimiento, the new southern border of the jurisdiction came close to Teotihuacan itself. Since Tepexpan, Tequicistlan, and Totolzingo remained in the Teotihuacan jurisdiction, the change created a narrow corridor to the lake. The boundary was regarded as unnatural by a Teotihuacan official of the late eighteenth century, who pointed out that the hacienda of La Cadena lay very close to Teotihuacan but fell under Texcoco jurisdiction, while Tepexpan, several leagues south of La Cadena, fell under Teotihuacan jurisdiction. Meanwhile Ixtlahuaca, far to the north, was still under Texcoco.[24] The eighteenth-century record includes a full list of communities and a map.[25]

COYOACAN

The Coyoacan jurisdiction differed from all others in the Valley in that the power of political appointment fell to Cortés and his heirs of the Marquesado. The jurisdiction coincided with the Marquesado portion of the Valley: Coyoacan, Tacubaya, and their sujetos. A number of the sujetos were later separately listed as cabeceras or pueblos.[26] In the 1570's, 1580's, and 1590's, following the encomenderos' conspiracy, Coyoacan and Tacuba were temporarily combined as a single jurisdiction under the crown.[27] The southern boundary of Coyoacan between Tlalpam and Tepepan corresponded with the western boundary of Xochimilco. To the north the late colonial boundary ran south of Huizquilucan and probably coincided, exactly or approximately, with the western boundary of the modern Distrito Federal from the Huizquilucan area to Tecamachalco. Chapultepec fell within the area but remained a sujeto of San Juan Tenochtitlan in the eighteenth century.[28] We have both a list of towns and a map showing boundaries for the late colonial period.[29]

TACUBA

Except during the period of combination with Coyoacan, the southern boundary of this jurisdiction coincided with the northern boundary of Coyoacan. This boundary is recorded on the eighteenth-century map of Coyoacan. The northern boundary of the Tacuba jurisdiction fell in the sixteenth century between Azcapotzaltongo and Tepoxaco and ran south of Toltitlan.[30] In the eighteenth century, however, both Tepoxaco and Toltitlan were included within the Tacuba jurisdiction.[31] For the late eighteenth century we possess a full list of place names and a map.[32]

CUAUHTITLAN

Jurisdiction over Zumpango was shared between the corregidor of Cuauhtitlan and the corregidor of Citlaltepec in 1569.[33] The southern border of the Cuauhtitlan jurisdiction was identical with the northern border of the Tacuba jurisdiction, and it underwent the changes noted above relating to Tepoxaco and Toltitlan. The northern border may have approximated in part the present boundary between the states of Mexico and Hidalgo, but it should be noted that the hacienda of Dolores, now in Hidalgo, fell in the Cuauhtitlan jurisdiction in the colonial period. Villa-señor y Sánchez, in the middle eighteenth century, listed Xaltocan both in this jurisdiction and in Citlaltepec.[34] The communities are named and mapped in the records of the late eighteenth century.[35]

ECATEPEC

The jurisdiction of the late sixteenth century included the cabeceras of Chiconauhtla, Ecatepec, Tecama, and Xaltocan, with their sujetos.[36] The principal subsequent change was the removal of Xaltocan. The area contained a fairly large number of estancias of Tenochtitlan and Tlatelolco, including Ozumbilla, Xaloztoc, Tolpetlac, and Xoloc, over which the two parcialidades gradually lost control.[37] We have no eighteenth-century map of the jurisdiction, but three lists of towns of the late eighteenth century are extant.[38]

CITLALTEPEC

The jurisdiction of the late sixteenth century included the three cabeceras of Citlaltepec, Tequixquiac, and Zumpango, although for a time Zumpango was transferred to, or shared with, Cuauhtitlan.[39] Xaltocan was listed in the mid-eighteenth century in both Cuauhtitlan and this jurisdiction. We have the list of towns and the accompanying map of the late eighteenth century.[40]

MEXICO CITY

The corregimiento was not fully established until the 1570's, and for a time in the eighteenth century no corregidores were appointed.[41] The jurisdiction included the urban portions of the city itself and the nearby sujetos of Tenochtitlan and Tlatelolco. Popotla, though under the tribute-collection authority of the Indian gobernador of Tenochtitlan, fell administratively in the corregimiento of Tacuba in the late seventeenth century. It was attached to the corregimiento of Mexico in the eighteenth century. Continuous losses to neighboring jurisdictions occurred. In the late colonial period additional estancias in the south were transferred to the Mexicalzingo jurisdiction.[42]

PACHUCA

The sixteenth-century area included a number of towns north of the Valley of Mexico in the direction of Pachuca. Tizayuca and Tezontepec were the southernmost cabeceras of the jurisdiction in the sixteenth century and remained so in the eighteenth century.[43] Other parts of the area fell outside the Valley of Mexico.

HUEYPOXTLA

A central area north of the Valley of Mexico comprised the jurisdiction of Hueypoxtla in the sixteenth century.[44] In the eighteenth century the area was combined with Atitlaquia and Misquiahuala, to make a single large jurisdiction.[45] Hueypoxtla alone falls within the limits of this study.

An incidental comment may be made concerning subsequent boundaries of the independence period, which depended in part upon the corregimiento-subdelegado boundaries of the late colonial period and in part upon departures from colonial tradition made in the interests of nineteenth-century efficiency. The most notable manifestation of the latter was the creation of a geometrically circular Distrito Federal in 1824, with its center in the plaza of Mexico City and extending for a radius of two leagues in all directions.[46] In the 1820's and after, the organizations by states, prefectures, partidos, districts, municipalities, and municipios came into being, with far more frequent boundary changes than in the colonial period. Calpulalpan and its area were transferred to Tlaxcala in the 1860's.[47] In the late nineteenth century, nevertheless, a number of vestiges from the colonial jurisdictions persisted, such as the eastern boundary of the distrito of Cuauhtitlan, the northern boundary of the distrito of Texcoco, and the western boundary of the prefecture of Xochimilco. In the twentieth century discernible similarities may still be noted between the southern delegaciones of the Distrito Federal and the colonial Xochimilco corregimiento. The peculiar irregularities of the Mexico-Hidalgo state line which still exist in the region of Tizayuca and Ixtlahuaca are traceable directly to the colonial corregimientos and, still earlier, to the situation of Acolman and its distant sujetos in the period prior to the conquest.

Epidemics

The following is a tabulation of the principal epidemics in the colonial history of the Valley of Mexico. Bibliographical citations are selective, especially toward the end of the period, for the late epidemics are fully treated in the forthcoming study by Donald Cooper, cited here in manuscript. The term *matlazahuatl* is perhaps translatable as typhus or yellow fever, and *fiebre* commonly has the same meaning. *Hueyzahuatl* (great zahuatl) and *zahuatl tepiton* (small zahuatl) may refer to different intensities of the same epidemic or to distinct diseases. The former may be smallpox (*viruelas*) and the latter measles (*sarampión*). *Totonqui* is fever or anything hot and *matlaltotonqui* may be pleurisy. *Tlatlacistli* is a disease like catarrh or influenza, accompanied by coughing. The Spanish term *paperas* presumably indicates a form of mumps, and *tabardillo* is an unidentified pestilential fever. The phrase *dolores de costado* commonly means pneumonia. *Garrotillo* is perhaps best rendered as croup. But all such specific identifications remain questionable in a historical context. The common Nahuatl term *cocoliztli* probably refers to general sickness or plague and not to any specific illness.

1520–21. Viruelas, hueyzahuatl, brought by a Negro carrier; accompanied by sores (*lepra*) and mange (*sarna*) over the entire body. Díaz del Castillo, *Historia*, I, 525. López de Gómara, *Historia*, I, 291–92. Motolinía, *Memoriales*, pp. 18, 234. Motolinía, *History*, p. 38. Sahagún, *Historia general*, II, 41, 485. PNE, VI, 227. Mendieta, *Historia*, p. 514.

1531. Zahuatl, sarampión, viruelas, zahuatl tepiton. Motolinía, *Memoriales*, pp. 18, 234. Motolinía, *History*, p. 38. Chimpalpahin, *Annales*, p. 11. Mendieta, *Historia*, p. 514.

1532. Viruelas and zahuatl in Chalco and all Mexico. Chimpalpahin, *Annales*, p. 227. AAMC, no. 8, p. 473.

1538. Viruelas. *Codex Telleriano-Remensis*, fol. 45v.

1545–48. Great pestilence, cocoliztli, with high mortality; bleeding in nose and eyes;

occasionally dated from 1544 rather than 1545; identified by Humboldt as matla-zahuatl. *Cartas de Indias,* p. 331. Puga, *Provisiones,* fol. 102v. *Codex Telleriano-Remensis,* fol. 46v. *Histoire de la nation mexicaine,* p. 91. AAMC, no. 8, p. 474; no. 13, p. 646. Chimalpahin, *Annales,* p. 243. Humboldt, *Political Essay,* I, 117.

1550. Paperas in Tacuba and elsewhere, with many deaths. AAMC, no. 15, p. 687. *Codex Telleriano-Remensis,* fol. 47v.

1558. Death and famine. *Codex Telleriano-Remensis,* fol. 48v.

1559. Pestilence with symptoms like those of 1544 (1545) and 1576. *Cartas de Indias,* p. 331.

1563–64. Zahuatl, sarampión, matlaltotonqui, in Huitzilopochco, Amecameca, and elsewhere; nearly half the population of Chalco is reported to have died within a year and a half. Chimalpahin, *Annales,* p. 257. *Histoire de la nation mexicaine,* p. 104. AAMC, no. 15, p. 689. ENE, X, 59. Valderrama, *Cartas,* p. 45. AGN, Mercedes, vol. 7, fols. 276v, 287v–288r, 305r–305v.

1566. Cocoliztli; 800 deaths in the colony. AAMC, no. 13, p. 646.

1576–81. Great cocoliztli, affecting all Indian peoples but only a few Spaniards; date of origin variously reported; large number of deaths; the symptom most frequently mentioned is nosebleed; various terminal dates given in the late 1570's, but reported in the *Actas de cabildo* as not yet completed in 1581. Dávila Padilla, *Historia,* pp. 638 ff. *Histoire de la nation mexicaine,* p. 117. Sahagún, *Historia general,* II, 486. AAMC, no. 6, pp. 378–80; no. 13, pp. 637, 648; no. 14, p. 670; no. 15, p. 697; no. 24, p. 987. Cavo, *Historia de México,* pp. 229–30. *Cartas de Indias,* p. 331. Chimalpahin, *Annales,* pp. 288, 290, 292, 297. Cabrera y Quintero, *Escudo de armas,* pp. 124–25. Vetancurt, *Chronica,* p. 130. "Relación de Tequisquiac, Citlaltepec y Xilocingo," p. 293. AC, VIII, 474–75.

1587–88. Cocoliztli, mentioned in general and among Indians in the city. AAMC, no. 6, p. 389. AC, IX, 221, 225. AGN, General de parte, vol. 3, fol. 174r–174v.

1590. Tlatlacistli, with many deaths. "Anales de San Gregorio Acapulco," p. 119.

1592–93. Tlatlacistli, sarampión, cocoliztli; mortality among children. Chimalpahin, *Annales,* p. 14. "Unos anales coloniales de Tlatelolco, 1519–1633," p. 176.

1595–97. Sarampión, paperas, tabardillo; widespread sickness, extending as far as Guatemala, but with relatively few deaths; of varying duration in different towns. *Histoire de la nation mexicaine,* p. 133. AC, XII, 235. *Moderación de doctrinas,* pp. 16–17. Mendieta, *Historia,* p. 515.

1601–2. Cocoliztli, lasting eight months to June 1602, in Xochimilco. AGN, General de parte, vol. 6, fol. 156r–156v.

1604–7. Cocoliztli, sarampión, diarrhea; in Chalco and the Acolhua area, and in Tepozotlan, especially among Otomí; high mortality. Chimalpahin, *Annales,* pp. 15–16. AAMC, no. 15, p. 707; no. 18, p. 780. FHT, VI, 89–90. Alegre, *Historia de la Compañía de Jesús,* I, 445.

1613. Cocoliztli. AAMC, no. 14, p. 672.

1615–16. Sarampión and viruelas, in Mexico City; especially between January and March of both years. AC, XXI, 340, 344. Cisneros, *Sitio,* fol. 124v.

1627. Illness among Indians in Mexico City, as a secondary effect of flood. AC, XXVI, 174.

1629–31. Cocoliztli with many deaths in all areas; Azcapotzalco, Chimalhuacan, Teotihuacan, Texcoco specifically mentioned. FHT, VI, 448 ff., 497 ff. Cepeda and Carrillo, *Relación,* fol. 41v. Cavo, *Historia de México,* p. 305. AAMC, no. 14, p. 674.

1633–34. Cocoliztli and severe cough called *chichimeca,* with many deaths. AAMC, no. 13, pp. 654–55; no. 14, p. 675.

1639. Sarampión with many deaths. AC, XXXI, 343. AAMC, no. 13, p. 657; no. 14, p. 675.

1641–42. Illness and death associated with drought; cocoliztli with nosebleed. Cabrera y Quintero, *Escudo de armas,* p. 125. AC, XXXII–XXXIII, 228, 302, 318, 358 ff. AAMC, no. 13, p. 658; no. 14, p. 676. Vetancurt, *Chronica,* p. 131.

1651. Pestilence of chills and fevers among Indians in Mexico City. Guijo, *Diario,* p. 202.

1653. Viruelas and other illnesses, associated with drought. Guijo, *Diario,* p. 242.

1659. Sarampión, with many deaths. AAMC, no. 13, p. 663.

1663. Great pestilence of viruelas, tabardillo, and other diseases; both Spaniards and Indians affected; associated with drought. Guijo, *Diario,* pp. 513–14. Cabrera y Quintero, *Escudo de armas,* p. 125.

1667–68. Sickness associated with drought, notably in the spring of each year; catarrh, dolores de costado, tabardillo, and many deaths. Cabrera y Quintero, *Escudo de armas,* p. 125. Robles, *Diario,* I, 36, 57.

1678. Viruelas, in May. Robles, *Diario,* I, 239–40. Cabrera y Quintero, *Escudo de armas,* p. 125.

1692–97. Severe sarampión, with many deaths; pestilence in Mexico City in September 1692; fiebre, matlazahuatl, tabardillo, great mortality. AAMC, no. 14, pp. 678–80. Rivera, *Diario curioso,* p. 100. Cabrera y Quintero, *Escudo de armas,* p. 129.

1705. Illness and death associated with drought, in May. AC, XXXVIII–XLII (2), 400.

1711. Tabardillo, viruelas, dolores de costado, garrotillo, associated with drought, in Mexico City and the countryside, in May. AC, XLIII–XLVII (2), 86.

1714. Fiebre; 14,000 Indian deaths in the colony. Cabrera y Quintero, *Escudo de armas,* p. 129.

1720. Illness associated with drought. AC, LI–LIII, 51.

1727–28. Sarampión, especially in Mexico City, ending by January 1728. Alegre, *Historia de la Compañia de Jesús,* III, 233–34. León, "Bibliografía," no. 4, p. 13.

1731. Matlazahuatl in Huitzilopochco in September and October. Navarro de Vargas, "Padrón," pp. 569, 594–95.

1734. Viruelas, in August. Sedano, *Noticias de México,* II, 203. León, "Bibliografía," no. 4, p. 481.

1736–39. Severe epidemic of matlazahuatl, beginning in Mixcoac or Tacuba and spreading to Mexico City; disappeared in some localities by the summer of 1737 but continued in others to 1739; chills followed by headache, stomach-ache, high fever, nosebleed, and death; more severe among Indians than Spaniards; regarded by contemporary authorities as the same disease as that of 1576; a large number of details recorded. Alegre, *Historia de la Compañia de Jesús,* III, 262 ff. Cavo, *Historia de México,* pp. 418 ff. León, "Bibliografía," no. 4, p. 656. Sedano, *Noticias de México,* II, 56–57. AAMC, no. 18, p. 754. Cabrera y Quintero, *Escudo de armas, passim.* Alzate, *Gacetas de literatura,* II, 273. AGN, Tributos, vol. 11, exp. 13. AGI, México, leg. 2774, fol. 161r. Humboldt, *Political Essay,* I, 117. Orozco y Berra, *Historia de la dominación,* IV, 63 ff.

1748. Viruelas. Sedano, *Noticias de México,* II, 203.

1761–64. Viruelas, matlazahuatl. Sedano, *Noticias de México*, II, 203. Gálvez, *Informe general*, p. 89. Fonseca and Urrutia, *Historia*, I, 435. SLSF, Zúñiga y Ontiveros, "Efemérides." Humboldt, *Political Essay*, I, 111–12. Cooper, "Epidemic Disease," pp. 71 ff.

1768. Severe sarampión, in Mexico City. SLSF, Zúñiga y Ontiveros, "Efemérides." Cooper, "Epidemic Disease," p. 79.

1768–69. Severe sarampión and fiebre; deaths among children afflicted with cough; in Mexico City. SLSF, Zúñiga y Ontiveros, "Efemérides." Alzate, *Gacetas de literatura*, IV, 52. Cooper, "Epidemic Disease," p. 79.

1772–73. Matlazahuatl; illness and depopulation in Santa Marta, Los Reyes, the southern shore of Lake Texcoco, Tlatelolco, and related areas. SLSF, Zúñiga y Ontiveros, "Efemérides." Alzate, *Gacetas de literatura*, II, 121; IV, 156, 421.

1778. Epidemic causing over 2,000 tributary deaths in Xochimilco. AGN, Padrones, vol. 29, fol. 3r–3v.

1779–80. Sarampión, viruelas, beginning in the fall of 1779 and continuing into 1780. Humboldt, *Political Essay*, I, 111–12. Gómez, *Diario curioso*, pp. 67, 73. MNM, Colección antigua, T.4, 63. Sedano, *Noticias de México*, II, 203. Cooper, "Epidemic Disease," pp. 80 ff.

1784–87. Epidemic, dolores de costado, and other illnesses. Gómez, *Diario curioso*, pp. 175, 180–81. Cooper, "Epidemic Disease," pp. 98 ff.

1793. Chicken pox, in Mexico City and surrounding towns. Cooper, "Epidemic Disease," pp. 121 ff.

1797. Viruelas, in Mexico City and the towns. Cook, "The Smallpox Epidemic of 1797." Cooper, "Epidemic Disease," pp. 119 ff.

1806–10. Fiebres, especially in towns adjacent to Mexico City. López Sarrelangue, *Una villa mexicana*, pp. 128–29.

Agricultural Conditions and Maize Prices

The following list is a compilation of agricultural conditions and maize prices in the Valley of Mexico. Months and locations within the Valley are listed when known or significant. We include materials from AAMC and similar sources only sparingly, since locations are dubious and dates are frequently in error. Tribute commutations at 9 reales per fanega, preferential sales to royal officers, and fractions of reales are not recorded. We omit from this tabulation a number of sixteenth-century prices already recorded in Borah, *Price Trends*, pp. 53 ff., some of which are however included in Figure 13.

1525. 8 reales per fanega. AC, I, 48.

1526. 3 reales per fanega in ventas, i.e., Texcoco and Calpulalpan. AC, I, 83.

1528. Heavy rains; maize fields ruined. Motolinía, *History*, p. 129.

1530 (ca.). 4 reales per fanega. CDIHE, I, 529.

1541. Severe early frosts causing loss of maize and wheat. Motolinía, *Memoriales*, p. 231.

1543. Drought, frosts, shortages of wheat and maize in November and December, famine. *Histoire de la nation mexicaine*, p. 91. AC, V, 18, 19, 55. *Il manoscritto messicano vaticano 3738*, fol. 91r (93r).

1544. Shortages of wheat and maize in July after frosts of 1543. AC, V, 18, 19, 55. See also CDIHIA, I, 105.

1545. Shortages of wheat and maize in January. AC, V, 77.

1547–51. Rise in price of maize from one real to 8 reales per fanega. AGI, Patronato, leg. 181, ramo 20.

1547–57. Rise in price of maize from one-half real to 12 reales per fanega. CDIHE, XXVI, 345.

1550. Shortages of maize and wheat, April, Mexico City. AGN, Mercedes, vol. 3, fols. 25v–26r.

1551. Shortages of maize and wheat in Mexico City through most of the year, but an abundant new crop in 1551; maize 3 reales per fanega, November, Mexico City. AC, V, 290, 293; VI, 37.

1554. 4 to 5 reales per fanega, September. *Información sobre los tributos*, pp. 29 ff.

1557. Locust plague; 10 reales per fanega. "Unos anales coloniales de Tlatelolco, 1519–1633," p. 171. AAMC, no. 24, p. 985. CDIHE, XXVI, 347.

1558. Locusts, frosts, shortages. *Histoire de la nation mexicaine,* p. 99. *Codex Telleriano-Remensis,* fol. 48v.

1559. Locusts in April; 4 to 6 reales per fanega. *Histoire de la nation mexicaine,* p. 100. BAGN, VIII, 185.

1561. 3 reales per fanega, Chalco. ENE, IX, 93. See also ENE, XIV, 116.

1562. 4 reales per fanega, March, Mexico City; loss of maize, September. *Sobre el modo de tributar,* p. 94. *Histoire de la nation mexicaine,* p. 104.

1563. 4, 5, 6, 8, 10, 12 reales per fanega. CDIAI, IV, 446. CDIHIA, I, 366.

1564. 6 reales per fanega in Tlatelolco; 8 reales per fanega in Xochimilco. ENE, XV, 71. Valderrama, *Cartas,* p. 64. *Sobre el modo de tributar,* p. 125.

1568. 6 to 10 reales per fanega. ENE, XI, 40.

1569. 3 to 8 reales per fanega. AHH, Tributos, leg. 225, exp. 1. ENE, XI, 8, 40. Borah, *Price Trends,* pp. 55–57.

1570. 3 reales per fanega. AHH, Tributos, leg. 225, exp. 1. Borah, *Price Trends,* pp. 57–58.

1573. Shortages of maize and wheat, Mexico City. AC, VIII, 47, 59.

1576. Drought, prolonged heat in October, limited yields. *Cartas de Indias,* p. 331. AC, VIII, 362. Cf. Chimalpahin, *Annales,* p. 288.

1577. Continuous rains from April to November, fields excessively wet, harvests small. Dávila Padilla, *Historia,* p. 641. AC, VIII, 362.

1579. Great famine, maize shortages; 12 and 16 reales per fanega in Amecameca and Otumba; prospects for a larger harvest from the 1579 crop. AGN, Indios, vol. 1, fols. 69v–70r, 83v. *Histoire de la nation mexicaine,* p. 120. AC, VIII, 403–4.

1580. 8, 10, 12, 16, 18 reales per fanega in Azcapotzalco, Tlalmanalco, Acolman, and other towns. AGN, Indios, vol. 1, fols. 88v ff.; General de parte, vol. 2, fol. 153r–153v.

1581. 12 reales per fanega in Tlalmanalco in April; 8 reales per fanega in Tlalnepantla in July. AGN, Indios, vol. 1, fols. 132r–133r, 136r–137r.

1583. 10 reales per fanega, Otumba, February. AGN, Indios, vol. 1, fol. 123v. See also AC, VIII, 628–29.

1587. Rains came late, in July; famine in Mexico City in September; 10 reales per fanega, Mexico City, November. FHT, III, 32, 47–48, 58. AGN, General de parte, vol. 3, fols. 174r–174v, 213v.

1588. 10 reales per fanega, Mexico City, January. AGN, General de parte, vol. 3, fol. 213v.

1590. Continuous heavy rains, injurious to wheat. FHT, III, 96.

1591. Early rains, followed by drought, June. FHT, III, 201–2.

1592. Locusts in May. "Anales de San Gregorio Acapulco," p. 119. AAMC, no. 13, p. 637.

1594. Drought and frosts; 11–12 reales per fanega, Mexico City. AC, XII, 9, 96. AAMC, no. 10, p. 537.

1597. Drought and frost; 10 reales per fanega, Mexico City, March; drought to mid-August; harvest poorer than expected. AC, XII, 363–64; XIII, 100. Cabrera y Quintero, *Escudo de armas,* p. 125. Vetancurt, *Chronica,* p. 130.

1598. Shortages of wheat and maize, Mexico City; 10 to 18 reales per fanega, Mexico City, March and April. AC, XIII, 100, 102, 176, 185. AGI, México, leg. 24, ramos 1, 3.

1599. Rains delayed in spring; early frosts in autumn; 6 to 20 reales per fanega. FHT, IV, 354, 369–70. AGN, General de parte, vol. 5, fol. 122v. AGI, México, leg. 24, ramo 2. AC, XIII, 296, 311, 335, 371; XIV, 30.

1600. Heavy rains but scant harvests; 18 reales per fanega. FHT, IV, 460. AC, XIV, 53, 62. AGI, México, leg. 24, ramo. 3.

1601. Year of abundance; plentiful maize harvests everywhere; maize price fell from 14 to 12 to 10 reales per fanega. AGI, México, leg. 24, ramo 4. AC, XIV, 198, 286, 287.

1602. 18 reales (?) per fanega. Chimalpahin, *Annales*, p. 15.

1603. 24 reales per fanega, Teoloyuca. AGN, Congregaciones, vol. 1, fols. 11v–12r.

1604. Maize desiccated. AAMC, no. 15, p. 708. Chimalpahin, *Annales*, p. 15.

1605. 10 reales per fanega, Mexico City, October. AC, XVI, 173.

1606. Rains in July; early harvests, Chalco, November. FHT, VI, 9, 92.

1609. Limited harvest and short supplies. AC, XVII, 305–6.

1610. 7, 10 reales per fanega, Mexico City. AC, XVII, 523, 540.

1615. Shortage of maize and wheat, November; 9 reales per fanega, December, Mexico City. Banco nacional, *Publicaciones*, III, 18. AC, XXVII, 102–3.

1616. Late rains, drought, and extreme shortages; 9 reales per fanega, Mexico City, January; Cavo speaks of prices as high as 7 and 8 pesos (56–64 reales) per fanega in this year. Vetancurt, *Chronica*, p. 130. Cabrera y Quintero, *Escudo de armas*, p. 125. Banco nacional, *Publicaciones*, III, 18. Cisneros, *Sitio*, fol. 11v. FHT, VI, 300–301. AC, XX, 254. Cavo, *Historia de México*, p. 281.

1617. Abundance of maize and wheat. Banco nacional, *Publicaciones*, III, 18.

1618. Drought in July. AC, XXII, 136–37.

1619. 24 reales per fanega. AA, Barrio Lorenzot, 432 (743), fol. 121v.

1620. Drought; great shortage of wheat bread; maize 22 reales per fanega, Coyoacan. AC, XXIII, 145; XXIV, 78–79. AGN, Hospital de Jesús, vol. 278, exp. 1, fol. 1r.

1621. Drought; serious maize shortages; 22–40 reales per fanega. AC, XXIV, 78–79, 82–83. *Documentos relativos al tumulto*, II, 51–62. AGN, Hospital de Jesús, vol. 278, exp. 1, fol. 8v; exp. 5, fols. 3r ff.

1622. 16, 18 reales per fanega. AC, XXIV, 242–43, 265.

1624. Most severe drought yet known, June. AC, XXV, 145.

1627. Rains; abundant year. AC, XXVI, 171.

1629. 20 reales per fanega, Coyoacan. AGN, Hospital de Jesús, vol. 278, exp. 10, fol. 1r.

1630. 20 reales per fanega, Coyoacan. AGN, Hospital de Jesús, vol. 278, exp. 10, fol. 2r.

1633. 16 reales per fanega, Coyoacan. AGN, Hospital de Jesús, vol. 278, exp. 10, fol. 25r.

1638. Abundance (wheat) and moderate prices, January. AC, XXXI, 180.

1639. Drought. AC, XXXI, 343–46. AAMC, no. 13, p. 658; no. 14, p. 675.

1641. Extreme drought; failure of spring rains; maize rose from 8 or 9 reales per fanega to 18 or 20 reales in May and June, Mexico City. AC, XXXII, 228. AAMC, no. 14, p. 676. Vetancurt, *Chronica*, p. 131. Cabrera y Quintero, *Escudo de armas*, p. 125.

1642. Drought and famine; continued shortages of maize; 27, 28, 32, and 40 reales per fanega. AC, XXXIII, 293, 301, 358 ff. AGN, Hospital de Jesús, vol. 325, exp. 5, fol. 39r. Cabrera y Quintero, *Escudo de armas*, p. 125.

1643. Maize at continuously high prices; 32 to 40 reales per fanega, Xochimilco. AGN, Hospital de Jesús, vol. 325, exp. 5, fol. 39r.

1644. 32 reales per fanega, Xochimilco. AGN, Hospital de Jesús, vol. 325, exp. 5, fol. 39r.

1653. Drought in June. Guijo, *Diario*, p. 482. Cabrera y Quintero, *Escudo de armas*, p. 125. Vetancurt, *Chronica*, p. 131.

1661. Drought to June, followed by early autumn frosts; great shortages; maize rose to 28 reales per fanega. Guijo, *Diario*, pp. 459–60, 472–73. AAMC, no. 18, p. 792. Vetancurt, *Chronica*, p. 131.

1662. Continued shortages; 29 reales per fanega. Guijo, *Diario*, p. 482.

1663. Great drought, heat, famine; frosts in late spring; maize extremely dear. Guijo, *Diario*, pp. 513–14. Cabrera y Quintero, *Escudo de armas*, p. 125. Vetancurt, *Chronica*, p. 131.

1667. Drought in May and June. Robles, *Diario*, I, 36, 40. Cabrera y Quintero, *Escudo de armas*, p. 125.

1668. Drought in June. Robles, *Diario*, I, 57. Cabrera y Quintero, *Escudo de armas*, p. 125. Vetancurt, *Chronica*, p. 131.

1673. Maize shortage and high prices. Cavo, *Historia de México*, p. 338.

1675. 9, 20, 24 reales per fanega. AGN, Bienes nacionales, vol. 174, exp. 1675.

1676. 9, 20, 24 reales per fanega. AGN, Bienes nacionales, vol. 174, exp. 1675.

1678. Drought until June. Robles, *Diario*, I, 239, 241. Cabrera y Quintero, *Escudo de armas*, p. 125.

1680. 9 to 24 reales per fanega. AGN, Tierras, vol. 1598, exp. 2; Bienes nacionales, vol. 174, exp. 1680.

1682. 6 reales per fanega in numerous towns. AGI, Contaduría, leg. 773, no pag.

1686 (1685?). Drought until June. Cabrera y Quintero, *Escudo de armas*, p. 125. Vetancurt, *Chronica*, p. 131.

1689. 5 reales per fanega. AGN, Tierras, vol. 1672, exp. 1, fols. 96v, 104r.

1691. Heavy rains; losses in all crops; wheat disease; limited harvests. CDIHE, LXVII, 396. AGI, Patronato, leg. 226, ramo 18, fols. 6v ff.

1692. Extreme shortages; famine; maize rose from 17 to 28 reales between March and June. Cabrera y Quintero, *Escudo de armas*, p. 126. Robles, *Diario*, II, 257. Leonard, *Don Carlos de Sigüenza*, pp. 236 ff. AGI, Patronato, leg. 226, ramo 20, fols. 7r–8v.

1694. Shortage of maize, Mexico City. Robles, *Diario*, II, 312.

1695. Drought; frosts in September; great shortages of maize. Robles, *Diario*, III, 15, 50. AAMC, no. 14, p. 679.

1696. Maize extremely scarce through the year; 40 reales per fanega in April and August. Robles, *Diario*, III, 44, 50. AAMC, no. 14, p. 679. *Disposiciones complementarias*, I, 359.

1697. Continued serious shortages; 32 reales per fanega. AAMC, no. 14, p. 680. NYPL, Rich, no. 39. CDIHIA, IV, 343. Gemelli Carreri, *Las cosas más considerables*, p. 137.

1698. 16 reales per fanega, Axapusco. AGN, Tierras, vol. 1466, final pag., fol. 1v.

1700. 16 reales per fanega, Axapusco. AGN, Tierras, vol. 1466, final pag., fol. 5r.

1701. 16 reales per fanega, Axapusco. AGN, Tierras, vol. 1466, final pag., fol. 7r.

1702. Drought in June. AC, XXXVIII–XLII (1), 277–79.

1705. Drought in May. AC, XXXVIII–XLII (2), 400.

1708. 12, 13, 14 reales per fanega, Chalco and Mexico City. AGN, Vínculos, vol. 45, fol. 33r. AGI, México, leg. 781, fol. 137r.

1709. 16 reales per fanega, Chalco and Mexico City. AGN, Vínculos, vol. 45, fol. 33r. AGI, México, leg. 781, fol. 140r.

1710. 13 reales per fanega in Chalco; 20 reales per fanega in Mexico City, but 24, 28, and 32 in surrounding towns. AGN, Vínculos, vol. 45, fol. 33r. AGI, México, leg. 781, sep. pag., fol. 2v.

1711. Drought; 11 reales per fanega. AC, XLIII–XLVII (2), 86. AGN, Vínculos, vol. 45, fol. 33r.

1712. 16 reales per fanega, Chalco. AGN, Vínculos, vol. 45, fol. 33r.

1713. Drought and shortages; reduced harvests of Chalco maize; 24 reales per fanega. AC, XLIII–XLVII (2), 213. AGN, Vínculos, vol. 45, fol. 33r.

1714. 12 reales per fanega, Chalco. AGN, Vínculos, vol. 45, fol. 33v.
1719. 8, 16 reales per fanega. AGN, Tierras, vol. 1466, final pag., fol. 34v. AC, XLVIII–L (2), 192.
1720. Drought in June. AC, LI–LIII, 52.
1721. 8 reales per fanega, Mexico City. AC, LIV, 30.
1722. 8 reales per fanega, Mexico City. AC, LIV, 30.
1723. 11, 12 reales per fanega, Mexico City. AC, LIV, 29–30, 49.
1727. 18 reales per fanega, Coyoacan. AGN, Hospital de Jesús, vol. 319, exp. 27, fol. 71r; vol. 333, exp. 2, fols. 64v–65r.
1728. 8, 16 reales per fanega, Tlalmanalco and San Agustín de las Cuevas. AGN, Tierras, vol. 1923, exp. 6, fol. 39r; Hospital de Jesús, vol. 319, exp. 30, fol. 1r.
1729. 9 reales per fanega, Tlalmanalco. AGN, Tierras, vol. 1923, exp. 6, fol. 41r.
1730. 8, 12, 13, 14 reales per fanega, Tlalmanalco and Mexico City. AGN, Tierras, vol. 1923, exp. 6, fol. 48r. Banco nacional, *Publicaciones,* III, 4.
1731. 8 reales per fanega, Tlalmanalco. AGN, Tierras, vol. 1923, exp. 6, fol. 50r.
1732. 8 reales per fanega, Tlalmanalco. AGN, Tierras, vol. 1923, exp. 6, fol. 52r.
1734. 8 reales per fanega, Tlalmanalco. AGN, Tierras, vol. 1923, exp. 6, fol. 56r.
1741–42. Reduced harvests; 20 to 24 reales per fanega, Mexico City. AA, Pósito y alhóndiga, vol. 1, exp. 22, fol. 1r.
1743. 9 to 20 reales per fanega, Mexico City. AA, Pósito y alhóndiga, vol. 1, exp. 27, fols. 1r ff.
1744. 7 reales per fanega, Mexico City. AA, Pósito y alhóndiga, vol. 1, exp. 29, fol. 1v.
1747. Heavy rains; 12 to 20 reales per fanega. Cuevas Aguirre y Espinosa, *Extracto de los autos,* p. 5. AA, Pósito y alhóndiga, vol. 1, exp. 30, fols. 1r ff. AGN, Tierras, vol. 1466, final pag., fols. 60r–61r.
1748. 12 to 16 reales per fanega. AA, Pósito y alhóndiga, vol. 1, exp. 31, fols. 2r ff.
1749. Great drought and early frosts in interior and north; less severe in the Valley of Mexico; 22, 24 reales per fanega, Mexico City. Bentura Beleña, *Recopilación sumaria,* I, 5th pag., 67. *Documentos para la historia económica,* II, 56. AA, Pósito y alhóndiga, vol. 1, exp. 32. Cavo, *Historia de México,* pp. 437–38.
1750. 26 reales per fanega, Mexico City. AA, Pósito y alhóndiga, vol. 1, exp. 33.
1751. 8 reales per fanega, Tlalmanalco. AGN, Tierras, vol. 1923, exp. 1, fol. 45r.
1752. Rains and plenty. Castro Santa-Anna, *Diario,* I, 23.
1753. 6 reales per fanega, Tlalmanalco. AGN, Tierras, vol. 1923, exp. 1, fol. 45r.
1754. 7 reales per fanega, Tlalmanalco. AGN, Tierras, vol. 1923, exp. 1, fol. 45r.
1755. Drought in June; 11 reales per fanega, Tlalmanalco. Castro Santa-Anna, *Diario,* II, 132. AGN, Tierras, vol. 1923, exp. 1, fol. 45r.
1756. 8 reales per fanega, Tlalmanalco. AGN, Tierras, vol. 1923, exp. 1, fol. 45r.
1757. 6 to 7 reales per fanega, Tlalmanalco. AGN, Tierras, vol. 1923, exp. 1, fols. 45r, 78r.
1758. 9 reales per fanega, Tlalmanalco. AGN, Tierras, vol. 1923, exp. 1, fol. 45r.
1760. 15 to 28 reales per fanega, Tlalmanalco and Mexico City. AGN, Tierras, vol. 1923, exp. 1, fol. 45r. AA, Pósito y alhóndiga, vol. 1, exp. 44, fol. 2r. Banco nacional, *Publicaciones,* III-B, 24 ff.
1761. 9 reales per fanega, Tlalmanalco. AGN, Tierras, vol. 1923, exp. 1, fol. 45r.
1762. Abundant rains; 6 reales per fanega, Tlalmanalco. SLSF, Zúñiga y Ontiveros, "Efemérides." AGN, Tierras, vol. 1923, exp. 1, fol. 45r.
1763. Abundant rains; 8, 9 reales per fanega, Tlalmanalco and Mexico City. SLSF,

Zúñiga y Ontiveros, "Efemérides." AGN, Tierras, vol. 917, exp. 1, fol. 17v; vol. 1923, exp. 1, fol. 45r. AA, Pósito y alhóndiga, vol. 1, exp. 22, fol. 1r.

1764. Drought, but not severe enough to cause shortages; 6 reales per fanega, Tlalmanalco. SLSF, Zúñiga y Ontiveros, "Efemérides." AGN, Tierras, vol. 1923, exp. 1, fol. 45r.

1765. Early drought followed by sufficient rains; 6 to 18 reales per fanega in various towns. AGN, Tierras, vol. 917, exp. 1, fol. 29r; vol. 1923, exp. 1, fol. 49v. AA, Pósito y alhóndiga, vol. 1, exp. 52, fols. 1r ff. SLSF, Zúñiga y Ontiveros, "Efemérides." AH, Libro en que se Acientan los autos de cavildos, fol. 4r.

1766. Abundant rains; 8 to 14 reales per fanega in various towns. SLSF, Zúñiga y Ontiveros, "Efemérides." AH, Libro en que se Acientan los autos de cavildos, fol. 5v. AGN, Tierras, vol. 917, exp. 1, fol. 29r; exp. 4, fol. 21r.

1767. 10 to 12 reales per fanega, Tlatelolco. AGN, Tierras, vol. 917, exp. 3, fols. 14r ff.

1768. Drought and rain out of season; disease in wheat; shortages of all grains; 8 to 14 reales per fanega in various towns. Alzate, Gacetas de literatura, IV, 51–52. AGN, Tierras, vol. 917, exp. 3, fols. 18r ff. AH, Libro en que se Acientan los autos de cavildos, fol. 9r. BM, Add. 17,561, fols. 72r, 77v.

1769. Shortages of wheat and frijoles, but sufficient maize; 9 reales per fanega. Alzate, Gacetas de literatura, IV, 102. SLSF, Zúñiga y Ontiveros, "Efemérides." BM, Add. 17,561, fol. 72r.

1770. Drought; disease in wheat; reduced harvests; 9 to 12 reales per fanega. AH, Libro en que se Acientan los autos de cavildos, fol. 14v. SLSF, Zúñiga y Ontiveros, "Efemérides." BM, Add. 17,561, fols. 72r, 78r.

1771. Rainy season delayed; rains intermittent; frost in mid-October before maize reached maturity; wheat plentiful but shortages of maize; 8 to 16 reales per fanega. SLSF, Zúñiga y Ontiveros, "Efemérides." AH, Libro en que se Acientan los autos de cavildos, fol. 18r. BM, Add. 17,561, fols. 72r, 78r. AGN, Tierras, vol. 991, exp. 4.

1772. Drought in June; excessive rains in August and September; 12 to 22 reales per fanega in various towns. AA, Pósito y alhóndiga, vol. 2, exp. 62, fol. 1r. AH, Libro en que se Acientan los autos de cavildos, fol. 20r. SLSF, Zúñiga y Ontiveros, "Efemérides." BM, Add. 17,561, fols. 72r ff.

1773. Drought; frost in May; only immature ears harvested in some areas; 8 to 15 reales per fanega in various towns. AA, Pósito y alhóndiga, vol. 2, exp. 65, fol. 4r. AH, Libro en que se Acientan los autos de cavildos, fol. 21v. AGN, Tierras, vol. 1109, exp. 3, fol. 2v. SLSF, Zúñiga y Ontiveros, "Efemérides." BM, Add. 17,561, fol. 78r.

1774. 14 to 19 reales per fanega, Mexico City. BM, Add. 17,561, fols. 72r ff.

1775. 8 to 14 reales per fanega, Papalotla and Mexico City. AA, Pósito y alhóndiga, vol. 2, exp. 67, fols. 13r ff. PCR, folder 75. BM, Add. 17,561, fols. 72r, 78r.

1776. 8 to 13 reales per fanega, Chalco, Huehuetoca, Chimalhuacan Atenco, Mexico City. BM, Add. 17,651, fols. 72r, 78r. AGN, Tierras, vol. 1109, exp. 3, fol. 13v. AA, Pósito y alhóndiga, vol. 2, exp. 73, fol. 2v. AH, Libro en que se Acientan los autos de cavildos, fol. 29r.

1777. 7 to 10 reales per fanega, various towns. BM, Add. 17,651, fols. 72r, 78r. AGN, Tierras, vol. 1109, exp. 2, fol. 13v. PCR, folder 81. AA, Pósito y alhóndiga, vol. 2, exp. 74, fol. 28r.

1778. Drought in June; 7 to 10 reales per fanega in various towns. Gómez, Diario curioso, p. 45. AA, Pósito y alhóndiga, vol. 2, exp. 79, fols. 8r, 16r. PCR, folder 86. AGN, Tierras, vol. 1109, exp. 3, fol. 14r. BM, Add. 17,561, fols. 72v, 78r.

1779. Drought in June; 8 to 11 reales per fanega, Mexico City, Chimalhuacan Atenco, Huehuetoca. Gómez, *Diario curioso*, p. 67. AH, Libro en que se Acientan los autos de cavildos. BM, Add. 17,561, fols. 72v, 78v. AGN, Tierras, vol. 1109, exp. 3, fols. 10r ff.

1780. Drought and frosts; 9 to 19 reales per fanega in various towns. AH, Libro en que se Acientan los autos de cavildos. PCR, folder 89. BM, Add. 17,561, fol. 72v.

1781. 16 to 24 reales per fanega. PCR, folder 92. AH, Libro en que se Acientan los autos de cavildos. BM, Add. 17,561, fols. 72v, 78v.

1782. 14 to 16 reales per fanega, Mexico City and Molino de Flores. PCR, folder 95. BM, Add. 17,561, fols. 72v, 78v.

1783. 11 to 14 reales per fanega, Mexico City and Huehuetoca. BM, Add. 17,561, fol. 72v. AH, Libro en que se Acientan los autos de cavildos.

1784. 6 to 15 reales per fanega, Mexico City and Huehuetoca. AA, Pósito y alhóndiga, vol. 2, exp. 86, fols. 1v ff. AH, Libro en que se Acientan los autos de cavildos. BM, Add. 17,561, fol. 72v.

1785. Rainy season delayed; drought in May; almost all maize destroyed by severe frost, August 27; shortages began in September; sharp increase in price in last months of the year, from 16 reales up; highest recorded price is 40 reales per fanega. Gómez, *Diario curioso*, p. 207. Bentura Beleña, *Recopilación sumaria*, II, 1. Alzate, *Gacetas de literatura*, IV, 390. *Gazetas de México, compendio de noticias*, I, 411 ff.; VIII, 18. AGN, Tributos, vol. 2, exps. 5–7; Intendentes, vol. 33, fol. 160r. PCR, folder 105.

1786. Continued shortages and high prices; "año de hambre"; 32 to 48 reales per fanega; abundant harvest late in the year. AGN, Tributos, vol. 2, exp. 7, fol. 5v. BM, Add. 17,561, fol. 73r. Alzate, *Gacetas de literatura*, II, 133. *Gazetas de México, compendio de noticias*, III, 344.

1787. 28 reales per fanega, Mexico City; abundant harvest. BM, Add. 17,561, fols. 76v ff. *Gazetas de México, compendio de noticias*, III, 344.

1788. 9 to 16 reales per fanega, Mexico City and Huehuetoca. BM, Add. 17,561, fols. 74v ff. *Gazetas de México, compendio de noticias*, III, 174. AH, Libro en que se Acientan los autos de cavildos.

1789. Abundance of wheat and maize. *Gazetas de México, compendio de noticias*, III, 369, 403.

1791. 12 to 24 reales per fanega, various towns. AGN, Vínculos, vol. 55, exp. 2, sep. pag., fol. 2r–2v. Alzate, *Gacetas de literatura*, II, 241. AH, Libro en que se Acientan los autos de cavildos.

1792. 9 to 12 reales per fanega, various towns. AH, Libro en que se Acientan los autos de cavildos. AGN, Vínculos, vol. 55, exp. 2, sep. pag., fol. 2v.

1793. 12, 17 reales per fanega. AH, Libro en que se Acientan los autos de cavildos. AGN, Vínculos, vol. 55, exp. 2, sep. pag., fol. 3r.

1794. 12, 24 reales per fanega. AH, Libro en que se Acientan los autos de cavildos. AGN, Vínculos, vol. 55, exp. 2, sep. pag., fols. 3r, 19v.

1795. 16 to 24 reales per fanega. AH, Libro en que se Acientan los autos de cavildos. AGN, Vínculos, vol. 55, exp. 2, fol. 19v.

1796. 8 to 13 reales per fanega. AGN, Civil, vol. 217, exp. 4, fol. 1r. AH, Libro en que se Acientan los autos de cavildos.

1797. 11 to 24 reales per fanega. AGN, Civil. vol. 217, exp. 4, fols. 2r, 6r. AH, Libro en que se Acientan los autos de cavildos.

1798. 8 to 22 reales per fanega. AGN, Civil, vol. 217, exp. 4, fols. 3r, 7r. AH, Libro en que se Acientan los autos de cavildos.

1799. 21 reales per fanega. Huehuetoca. AH, Libro en que se Acientan los autos de cavildos.

1800. 17 to 20 reales per fanega, Huehuetoca. AH, Libro en que se Acientan los autos de cavildos.

1801. 16 reales per fanega, Huehuetoca. AH, Libro en que se Acientan los autos de cavildos.

1802. 16 reales per fanega, Huehuetoca. AH, Libro en que se Acientan los autos de cavildos.

1803. 24 reales per fanega, Huehuetoca. AH, Libro en que se Acientan los autos de cavildos.

1804. 14 reales per fanega, Huehuetoca. AH, Libro en que se Acientan los autos de cavildos.

1805. 12 reales per fanega, Huehuetoca. AH, Libro en que se Acientan los autos de cavildos; Libro en que se asientan los cabildos (Purificación).

1806. 12 reales per fanega, Huehuetoca. AH, Libro en que se asientan los cabildos (Purificación).

1807. 16 reales per fanega, Huehuetoca. AH, Libro en que se asientan los cabildos (Purificación).

1809. 24 reales per fanega. *Correo seminario,* I, no. 2, 15.

Population Figures

Figure 3 charts population changes in the Coyoacan jurisdiction, Milpa Alta, and Otumba; the figures given there are derived from the following sources:

Coyoacan Jurisdiction

1567: 5,902 (ENE, XI, 5 ff.)
1570: 5,200 (López de Velasco, *Geografía y descripción*, p. 194)
1597: 3,975 (ENE, XIII, 35, 40)
1607: 3,500 (AGN, Hospital de Jesús, vol. 266, exp. 7, fol. 42v)
1618: 3,019 (AGN, Hospital de Jesús, vol. 266, exp. 7, fol. 35r)
1632: 2,045 (AGN, Hospital de Jesús, vol. 278, exps. 5, 10)
1644: 1,781 (Miranda, "La población indígena," p. 187)
1692: 2,168 (Miranda, "La población indígena," p. 187)
1727: 3,345 (AGN, Hospital de Jesús, vol. 319, exp. 27, fol. 71r)
1736: 3,430 (AGN, Hospital de Jesús, vol. 302, exp. 1, fol. 78r)
1742: 2,948 (Villa-señor y Sánchez, *Theatro americano*, I, 69 ff.)
1763: 2,887 (AGN, Tributos, vol. 2, exp. 1)
1789: 3,011 (AGN, Tributos, vol. 37, exp. 6, fol. 8r)
1794: 3,220 (AGN, Hospital de Jesús, vol. 279, exp. 26, fol. 1r–1v)
1797: 3,268 (AGN, Tributos, vol. 16, exp. 13)
1799: 3,722 (AGN, Tributos, exp. último, fol. 4r)

Milpa Alta

1586: 2,500 (AGI, México, leg. 287)
1619: 1,712 (AGN, Indios, vol. 9, fols. 80v–81v)
1640:   830 (FHT, VII, 357)
1659:   654 (AGI, Contaduría, leg. 751)
1670:   566 (AGI, Contaduría, leg. 763)
1742:   730 (Villa-señor y Sánchez, *Theatro americano*, I, 166)
1795: 1,033 (AGN, Clero regular y secular, vol. 39, exp. 2, fol. 21r)

Otumba

1591: 387 (AGN, Indios, vol. 3, fol. 187v)
1603: 262 (AGN, Congregaciones, vol. 1, fol. 31v)

1623:   282 (*Moderación de doctrinas*, p. 44)
1644:   132 (AGN, Tributos, vol. 25, exp. 7, fols. 74r–74v)
1675:   132 (AGI, Contaduría, leg. 768. AGN, Tierras, vol. 1726, exp. 1, fol. 27r)
1700:   169 (AGN, Tributos, vol. 11, exp. 5)
1717:   230 (AGN, Tributos, vol. 25, exp. 7, fol. 64r)
1742:   406 (Villa-señor y Sánchez, *Theatro americano*, I, 144)

Figure 17 shows in graph form a series of statistics for the Indian tributary population of the city. Where figures for Tenochtitlan and figures for Tlatelolco are simultaneous or nearly so, their sum is shown as the tributary population for the whole city. At other times our sources provide figures for the whole city without indicating the division between Tenochtitlan and Tlatelolco. In these instances the combined graphs for the two parts do not always equate with the graph for the city as a whole, and this may be attributed both to defects in the statistics and to the uneven periodicity of the recorded numbers.

As explained in Chapter XIII the subject communities of Tenochtitlan and Tlatelolco were progressively reassigned to other jurisdictions. The population graphs should therefore be viewed with the understanding that the area to which they apply became smaller through time. This was especially the case in the eighteenth century. Our data are not so precise that we are able to compensate for this change statistically, and the figures are simply shown as given.

In several instances the figures are not furnished directly by the sources but derived from tributary assessments. This is especially true of the later figures, where the original data sometimes occur as pesos assessed rather than as numbers of tributaries. Thus the tributaries for the whole city for 1736, 1748, 1754, and 1775 are computed on the basis of twelve reales per tributary, and those for Tlatelolco in 1810 are computed on the basis of thirteen reales per tributary. Several of the figures for the seventeenth century are computed from the records of Servicio Real payments, at four reales per tributary. The dates, figures, and sources of Figure 17 are the following:

Tlatelolco

1562:   8,665 (*Sobre el modo de tributar*, p. 77)
1562 (ca.): 8,312 (ENE, XV, 71–73)
1565:   6,154 (*El libro de las tasaciones*, pp. 515–16)
1588:   3,959 (*Moderación de doctrinas*, p. 49)
1592:   3,000 (ca.) (AC, X, 171)
1623:   2,896 (*Moderación de doctrinas*, p. 49)
1634:   1,480 (AGN, Indios, vol. 12 (1), fols. 83v–84v)
1658:   1,510 (AGI, Contaduría, leg. 751, Servicio Real)
1742:   2,500 (ca.) (Villa-señor y Sánchez, *Theatro americano*, I, 59)
1744:   1,346 (BM, Eg. 1798, fol. 8v)

1775: 987 (BNM, ms. no. 439, fol. 471v)
1780: 999 (López Sarrelangue, "Los tributos de la parcialidad," p. 186.)
1790: 867 (AGN, Tributos, vol. 37, exp. 6, fol. 8r)
1810: 1,790 (AHH, Tributos, leg. 224, exp. 8, fol. 11r)

Tenochtitlan

1562: 12,971 (*Sobre el modo de tributar*, p. 77)
1563 (ca.): 12,866 (ENE, X, 1–3)
1580: 7,871 (AGI, México, leg. 748, sep. pag., fol. 19r)
1590: 7,652 (AGI, México, leg. 748, sep. pag., fol. 20r)
1659: 4,940 (AGI, Contaduría, leg. 751, Servicio Real)
1729: 6,636 (Léon, "Bibliografía," no. 4, p. 90)
1742: 5,900 (ca.) (Villa-señor y Sánchez, *Theatro americano*, I, 59)
1746: 5,028 (BM, Eg. 1798, fol. 8v)
1765: 5,626 (BNM, ms. no. 439, fol. 471v)
1775: 3,413 (BNM, ms. no. 431, fol. 471v)
1793: 8,026 (AGN, Tributos, vol. 37, exp. 6, fol. 8r)
1809: 8,624 (AHH, Tributos, leg. 224, exp. 8, fol. 8r)

Entire City

1562: 21,636 (*Sobre el modo de tributar*, pp. 77–78)
1563 (ca.): 21,178 (ENE, X, 1–3; XV, 71–73)
1610 (ca.): 8,000 (ca.) (Torquemada, *Monarchia indiana*, I, 299)
1644: 7,631 (Miranda, "La población indígena," p. 188)
1692: 7,631 (Miranda, "La población indígena," p. 188)
1736: 6,786 (BNM, ms. no. 439, fol. 460v)
1742: 8,400 (ca.) (Villa-señor y Sánchez, *Theatro americano*, I, 59)
1748: 8,049 (BNM, ms. no. 439, fol. 460v)
1754: 7,262 (BNM, ms. no. 439, fol. 461r)
1775: 4,400 (BNM, ms. no. 439, fol. 471v)
1793: 8,893 (AGN, Tributos, vol. 37, exp. 6, fol. 8r)
1800 (–1801): 9,672 (AGN, Tributos, vol. 43, exp. último, fol. 4r)

Abbreviations
Notes
Glossary
Bibliography

Abbreviations

AA   Archivo del Antiguo Ayuntamiento, Mexico City.

AAMC   Anales antiguos de México y sus contornos. José Fernando Ramírez, comp. 2 vols. MNM, Colección antigua, 32–273, 32–274.

AC   *Actas de cabildo de la ciudad de México.* Title varies. 54 vols. Mexico, 1889–1916.

AGI   Archivo General de Indias, Seville.

AGN   Archivo General de la Nación, Mexico City.

AGT   Archivo General, Tlaxcala.

AH   Archivo Parroquial, Huehuetoca.

AHH   Archivo Histórico de Hacienda, Mexico City.

BAGN   *Boletín del Archivo general de la nación,* I (1930) et seq.

BLMM   Mexican Manuscripts, Bancroft Library, University of California, Berkeley.

BM   British Museum, London.

BNM   Biblioteca Nacional, Mexico City.

BNMa   Biblioteca Nacional, Madrid.

BNP   Bibliothèque Nationale, Paris.

CDHM   *Colección de documentos para la historia de México.* Joaquín García Icazbalceta, ed. 2 vols. Mexico, 1858–66.

CDIAI   *Colección de documentos inéditos, relativos al descubrimiento, conquista y organización de las antiguas posesiones españolas de América y Oceanía, sacados de los archivos del reino, y muy especialmente del de Indias.* Title varies. 42 vols. Madrid, 1864–84.

CDIHE   *Colección de documentos inéditos para la historia de España.* Martín Fernández Navarrete and others, eds. 112 vols. Madrid, 1842–95.

CDIHIA   *Colección de documentos inéditos para la historia de Ibero-América.* Title varies. 14 vols. Madrid, 1927–32.

CDIU   *Colección de documentos inéditos, relativos al descubrimiento, conquista y organización de las antiguas posesiones españolas de ultramar.* 25 vols. Madrid, 1885–1932.

CDMNC   Centro de Documentación del Museo Nacional, Chapultepec, Mexico City.

ENE   *Epistolario de Nueva España 1505–1818.* Francisco del Paso y Troncoso, ed. 16 vols. Mexico, 1939–42. *Biblioteca histórica de obras inéditas,* ser. 2.

FHT   *Fuentes para la historia del trabajo en Nueva España.* Silvio A. Zavala and María Castelo, eds. 8 vols. Mexico, 1939–46.

HSA   Hispanic Society of America, New York.

MNM   Archivo Histórico, Museo Nacional (de Arqueología, Historia y Etnología), Mexico City.

NCDHM   (1886–92) *Nueva colección de documentos para la historia de México*. Joaquín García Icazbalceta, ed. 5 vols. Mexico, 1886–92.

NCDHM   (1941) *Nueva colección de documentos para la historia de México*. Joaquín García Icazbalceta, ed. 3 vols. Mexico, 1941.

NLAC   Newberry Library, Ayer Collection, Chicago.

NYPL   New York Public Library.

PCR   Papeles de los Condes de Regla, Washington State University, Pullman.

PNE   *Papeles de Nueva España*. Francisco del Paso y Troncoso, ed. 9 vols. Madrid and Mexico, 1905–48.

SLSF   Sutro Library, San Francisco.

UMCL   Clements Library, University of Michigan, Ann Arbor.

UT   University of Texas, Austin.

Notes

1. The geological history of the Valley of Mexico has been the subject of a large number of studies. See the recent summaries and bibliographies in Mooser, White, and Lorenzo, *La cuenca de México*.

2. Forests are described by the conquistadores and by Spaniards of the later sixteenth century. See the remarks of the anonymous conqueror in CDHM, I, 389; Motolinía, *History*, p. 206; López de Gómara, *Historia*, II, 105; and the comments of Pomar in NCDHM (1941), III, 56.

3. The terms are not universally accepted. Readers will find a number of variant titles in the literature, as well as alternatives to the chronological system presented here. The literature on the pre-conquest period is summarized, with bibliographies, in Vaillant, *Aztecs of Mexico*; Krickeberg, *Altmexikanischen Kulturen*; Tolstoy, *Surface Survey*; Wolf, *Sons of the Shaking Earth*; Cook de Leonard, *Esplendor del México antiguo*; and Jiménez Moreno, "Síntesis de la historia precolonial." For a comprehensive recent bibliography, see also Wauchope, *Ten Years*.

4. The principal statement is De Terra, Romero, and Stewart, *Tepexpan Man*. See also Aveleyra Arroyo de Anda and Maldonado-Koerdell, "Association of Artifacts with Mammoth," and Heizer and Cook, "New Evidence of Antiquity of Tepexpan."

5. The most detailed accounts are those of Vaillant: *Excavations at El Arbolillo, Excavations at Zacatenco, Early Cultures of the Valley of Mexico*, and *Aztecs of Mexico*.

6. The pioneer study of Teotihuacan is Gamio, *La población del valle de Teotihuacan*, which has now been supplemented by a large number of subsequent investigations. On the fall of the Classic civilization see Olivé and Barba, "Sobre la disintegración de las culturas clásicas."

7. The Post-Classic is the subject of an extensive literature. See, in addition to the works listed in note 3, Orozco y Berra, *Historia antigua*; Barlow, *The Extent of the Empire of the Culhua Mexica*; Soustelle, *La vie quotidienne*.

8. For radiocarbon dating see Wauchope, "Implications of Radiocarbon Dates." The written and pictorial sources are to be systematically treated in the forthcoming *Handbook of Middle American Indians*.

9. Apenas, "The 'Tlateles' of Lake Texcoco." Mooser, White, and Lorenzo, *La cuenca de México*, pp. 29–46. Sears, "El análisis de polen." Sears, "Palynology in Southern North America." Sears's conclusions depend upon the principle that an increase in the growth of oak trees indicates an increase in moisture and that low percentages of oak pollen and high percentages of pine pollen mean a moisture deficiency. He finds the Formative (Archaic) and the Post-Classic (Nahua) to have been relatively moist periods separated by a long dry period. See Sears, "Palynology in Southern North America"; Sears, "The Interdependence of Archaeology and Ecology," p. 116. On the

other hand, Sokoloff and Lorenzo, "Modern and Ancient Soils," find a progressive change from pluvial to moderately pluvial to seasonally arid.

10. The connection is suggested, with various degrees of development, in Sears, "Pollen Profiles"; Sears, "Palynology in Southern North America"; Sears, "The Interdependence of Archeology and Ecology," p. 116; Palerm, "The Agricultural Basis," p. 35; Deevey, "Limnological Studies," p. 232; Tolstoy, *Surface Survey*, pp. 70, 72.

11. Population in the Valley of Mexico is discussed in Chapter VI. Note that Cook, *Soil Erosion*, pp. 33, 82, computes 346 per square mile for the Teotihuacan area at the time of the conquest, and 1,245 per square mile in the Tepeaca region.

12. S. F. Cook presents evidence for an ecological explanation of the fall of Teotihuacan in "The Interrelation of Population, Food Supply, and Building," pp. 47–48.

13. We examine the Desagüe in Chapter IX. Post-colonial operations are interestingly described in González Navarro, "México en una laguna." See also the appropriate portions of *Memoria histórica . . . del desagüe.*

14. Cosío Villegas and others, *Historia moderna de México, la república restaurada, la vida social*, pp. 116–19.

15. The sparsely populated upper slopes of today abound in surface potsherds that give evidence of a heavy former occupation. The phenomenon has been frequently commented upon, e.g., by Wolf and Palerm, "Irrigation in the Old Acolhua Domain," p. 273, and Gamio, "Restos de la cultura tepaneca," p. 238. For the Lake Xaltocan movement see AGN, Tierras, vol. 1584, exp. 1, fols. 7r ff.

16. An exception, and a remarkable work on the interrelations of history and environment in the Valley, is Beltrán, *El hombre y su ambiente*. See also the interesting summary of Aschmann, "The Subsistence Problem," and the revealing study of Cook on the area to the north of the Valley, "The Historical Demography and Ecology of the Teotlalpan." The only systematic modern survey and bibliography of American Indian history after white contact is Armillas, *Program of the History of American Indians, Part II*.

17. The connection was succinctly summarized by Viceroy Luis de Velasco in 1595: "Las dos repúblicas de que este reino consiste, de españoles e indios, tiene(n) entre sí en lo que es su gobierno, aumento y estabilidad, gran repugnancia y dificultad porque la conservación de aquélla siempre parece que es la opresión y destrucción de ésta." *Advertimientos generales*, p. 47.

CHAPTER II

1. There exists a large bibliography on the migrations. See Vaillant, *Aztecs of Mexico*, pp. 92–93, for a tabular summary of some of the main tribes and texts. The migration narratives of the Mexica are tabulated through a correlation of toponyms in Acosta Saignes, "Migraciones de los mexica," fac. p. 180.

2. The rivalry and the sense of glorification in the antiquity of the legend are expressed in the Historia de los Mexicanos por sus Pinturas, for Texcoco and other towns. See NCDHM (1941), III, 219.

3. Tribal histories are recorded in numerous colonial texts by Indians, Spaniards, and mestizos. Bibliographical guides to this material are also to be included in the

forthcoming *Handbook of Middle American Indians*. An authoritative modern summary of the tribal histories is Jiménez Moreno, "Síntesis de la historia precolonial."

4. The view that the Otomi were the original inhabitants may be found in Dorantes de Carranza, *Sumaria relación*, pp. 3–4, and Chavero, *Pinturas jeroglíficas*, II, 31. Correctives are Mendizábal, "Los otomies no fueron los primeros pobladores," and Carrasco Pizana, *Los otomies*, pp. 241 ff. Modern archaeology has brought to light a long pre-Otomi history.

5. On this point see Clavigero, *Historia antigua*, I, 206–7.

6. BAGN, XVIII, 218.

7. Ixtlilxochitl, *Historia*, pp. 42 ff. Barlow, "El Códice Azcatitlan," p. 111. Torquemada, *Monarchia indiana*, I, 83. See the list of towns subordinate to Xaltocan in the letter of Pablo Nazareo, ENE, X, 125–26. The subject is treated thoroughly in Carrasco Pizana, *Los otomies*, pp. 257 ff.

8. *Códice Chimalpopoca*, pp. 24 ff., 34. Carrasco Pizana, *Los otomies*, pp. 266 ff.

9. Ixtlilxochitl, *Relaciones*, pp. 105, 135–38. Ixtlilxochitl, *Historia*, pp. 42, 77–78. Motolinía, *History*, p. 31.

10. Carrasco Pizana, *Los otomies*, pp. 32 ff., gives the names of a number of Otomi locations in the Valley from various sources.

11. Cortés, *Cartas*, II, 2. Cf. Aguilar, *Historia*, p. 98, where they are described under Tacuba, presumably because of the location of those he saw.

12. Sahagún, *Historia general*, I, 1. *Códice Ramírez*, p. 22. Cervantes de Salazar, *Crónica*, pp. 369, 371. López de Gómara, *Historia*, I, 266; II, 41. For Cortés's usage see Cortés, *Cartas*, I, 182, and CDIAI, XXVI, 6–7.

13. Chimalpahin, *Diferentes historias*, pp. 41–43. The term is also related to Teoculhuacan, the supposed origin of the migration. See NCDHM (1941), III, 6–7, 241–42, 244. The subject is discussed by Palacios, "¿De donde viene la palabra México?," pp. 497–98, and Barlow, "Some Remarks," pp. 345–49.

14. Carrasco Pizana, *Los otomies*, p. 249, adjusts the dating of the migration in accordance with the recommendations of Jiménez Moreno. Mexica subjection to the Culhuaque is treated in a number of texts, e.g., *Códice Chimalpopoca*, p. 22, and Torquemada, *Monarchia indiana*, I, 89 ff. The duration of the Culhua control is variously recorded. Compare *Anales de Tlatelolco*, p. 41, with Historia de los Mexicanos por sus Pinturas in NCDHM (1941), III, 226.

15. *Anales de Tlatelolco*, p. 46. NCDHM (1941), III, 267 ff. *Códice Chimalpopoca*, pp. 27–30.

16. Ixtlilxochitl, *Historia*, p. 151. "Culhuacan," p. 172. Alvarado Tezozomoc, *Crónica mexicayotl*, p. 119.

17. On Acamapichtli see the compilation of sources in García Granados, *Diccionario biográfico*, I, 4 ff. For the Culhua Tecuhtli title see, e.g., Ixtlilxochitl, *Historia*, p. 154.

18. The original Tizapan has been associated with the region known as El Olivar, west of Coyoacan and north of the modern community of Tizapan. See Gómez de Orozco, "Apuntes," p. 473, and Vaillant, *Aztecs of Mexico*, pp. 89, 272. But this would appear to be the result of a homonymic confusion. Sixteenth-century texts identify Tizapan as a fuente and estancia of Culhuacan. See NCDHM (1941), III, 226, 266. *Histoire de la nation mexicaine*, p. 37, and the Cuauhtemoc ordinance in Rendón, "Ordenanza," p. 29, refer to Tizapan Culhuacan. *Códice Ramírez*, p. 32, and, more precisely, Durán, *Historia*, I, 32, place Tizapan near the foot of the cerro of Culhuacan.

Hence it would appear that the Tizapan that was the home of the Mexica was much closer to the lake than the Tizapan associated with Coyoacan.

19. Sahagún, *Historia general*, I, 406 ff.; II, 25 ff.

20. Sahagún, *Einige Kapitel*, p. 486. Cf. Sahagún, *Historia general*, III, 39 (Coyoacan for Culhuacan). See also Alvarado Tezozomoc, *Crónica mexicana*, p. 274.

21. Durán, *Historia*, I, 364, 405. There exist some indications of a much larger "Culhua" territory in an earlier period. Chimalpahin speaks of Xochimilco, Cuitlahuac, Mixquic, Coyoacan, Ocuilan, and Malinalco as subjects of the Culhuaque in the seventh and ninth centuries. Chimalpahin, *Das Memorial breve*, pp. 3, 5. But here neither the dating nor the relation to the later Culhuaque is clear. Moreover, alliance rather than subjugation may be intended. See the discussion of the Nahuatl terminology and other relevant points in Zimmermann, *Das Geschichtswerk*, pp. 28, 72.

22. Aguilar, *Historia*, pp. 58 ff. Durán, *Historia*, I, 10. Chimalpahin, *Annales*, II, 22. Ixtlilxochitl, *Relaciones*, pp. 257, 316. Torquemada, *Monarchia indiana*, I, 149 ff. Alvarado Tezozomoc, *Crónica mexicana*, pp. 69 ff. *Códice Chimalpopoca*, pp. 37, 50–51, 66. Three of the subdivisions went to Tenochtitlan and one to Tlatelolco.

23. Related documents are the Títulos de las Tierras de los Indios de Cuitlahuac in AAMC, no. 25 (see especially pp. 996–97, 1002); BNM, ms. no. 1312; and MNM, Documentos sueltos, ser. 2, leg. 88, nos. 11–12. See also *Códice Chimalpopoca*, p. 62. An interesting nineteenth-century list of place names is Herrera y Pérez, "Tlahuac," pp. 294 ff.

24. Durán, *Historia*, I, 10. Ixtlilxochitl, *Historia*, p. 70.

25. Chimalpahin, *Annales*, p. 78. ENE, X, 118. Barlow, "El Códice Azcatitlan," pp. 119–20. Sources for the Mexica conquest of Mixquic are tabulated in Kelly and Palerm, *The Tajín Totonac*, pp. 282, 288 ff.

26. Durán, *Historia*, I, 10–12, 112–13. Barrios named Olac and Tepetenchi appear to make a connection between the Xochimilca and the Morelos area. See ENE, VIII, 238. Dorantes de Carranza, *Sumaria relación*, p. 5, comments on the Xochimilca extension to Acapetlahuaca, identified with Atlixco. Numerous other indications might be cited.

27. Latorre, *Relaciones geográficas*, p. 29. PNE, VI, 285.

28. Aguilar, *Historia*, p. 98.

29. PNE, VI, 9. *Historia tolteca-chichimeca*, p. 101. *Códice Chimalpopoca*, p. 66. Torquemada, *Monarchia indiana*, I, 89 ff. *Anales de Tlatelolco*, p. 52. *Codex Mendoza*, III, fol. 2v.

30. Ixtlilxochitl, *Relaciones*, pp. 257, 316. Torquemada, *Monarchia indiana*, I, 148 ff. *Códice Ramírez*, pp. 73 ff. Alvarado Tezozomoc, *Crónica mexicana*, pp. 62 ff. *Códice Chimalpopoca*, p. 47. *Codex Mendoza*, III, fol. 6r.

31. PNE, VI, 55, 66. Ixtlilxochitl, *Historia*, p. 70. Chimalpahin, *Annales*, p. 74.

32. *Códice Chimalpopoca*, p. 23. PNE, VI, 9.

33. Ixtlilxochitl, *Historia*, p. 196. Barlow, "El Códice Azcatitlan," pp. 121–23. Torquemada, *Monarchia indiana*, I, 151 ff. *Códice Chimalpopoca*, pp. 29, 32–33. Chimalpahin, *Annales*, pp. 8, 71. *Codex Mendoza*, III, fols. 4v ff.

34. Chimalpahin, *Annales*, pp. 7 ff., 113 ff. *Códice Chimalpopoca*, pp. 32–33, 53, 67. Alvarado Tezozomoc, *Crónica mexicana*, pp. 81 ff. *Códice Ramírez*, pp. 79 ff. Torquemada, *Monarchia indiana*, I, 151 ff., 158, 161, 163. Durán, *Historia*, I, 137 ff. Ixtlilxochitl, *Historia*, p. 196, speaks of the Mexica conquest of the Chalca in the reign of Itzcoatl. For the tribute history see ENE, VII, 260–61.

35. PNE, VI, 55, 66, 70 ff.

36. Cortés, *Cartas*, I, 193, 207. López de Gómara, *Historia*, II, 20. Díaz del Castillo, *Historia verdadera*, I, 547. Ocuituco, in modern Morelos, was identified in 1560 as within Chalco province (BAGN, XI, 209), but this represents an extension of the usual meaning of Chalco. This identification may have come about because the corregidor of Chalco was for a time in the middle sixteenth century the justicia in Ocuituco. See BAGN, X, 258. The Suma de Visitas lists Ocuituco as a bordering community, i.e., outside Chalco. See PNE, I, 105.

37. On the Otomi connection and the migration see Carrasco Pizana, *Los otomíes*, pp. 14 ff., 249 ff. Durán, *Historia*, I, 11. If Tlalnepantla was a wholly colonial foundation, the statement is of course weakened. Durán adds a sixth town, which may be Coyoacan. On the Crónica X see Barlow, "La crónica 'X'."

38. Sahagún, *Einige Kapitel*, p. 445. Alvarado Tezozomoc, *Crónica mexicana*, pp. 16–17. Durán, *Historia*, I, 41, 48. *Códice Ramírez*, pp. 38–39, 48.

39. Evidence concerning Mexica tribute to Azcapotzalco in this period is cited by Chapman, *Raíces y consecuencias de la guerra*, pp. 34, 101.

40. *Códice Chimalpopoca*, pp. 123, 129, 131–32, 134. NCDHM (1941), III, 229. Ixtlilxochitl, *Historia*, pp. 83 ff., 103–4. Torquemada, *Monarchia indiana*, I, 108 ff. A map of the extent of Tepaneca power is provided in Carrasco Pizana, *Los otomíes*, p. 271.

41. Ixtlilxochitl, *Historia*, pp. 107 ff. Ixtlilxochitl, *Relaciones*, pp. 158 ff. *Códice Chimalpopoca*, pp. 35 ff. Torquemada, *Monarchia indiana*, I, 117 ff. Chapman, *Raíces y consecuencias de la guerra*.

42. Ixtlilxochitl, *Historia*, pp. 153 ff. Torquemada, *Monarchia indiana*, I, 143 ff. On the establishment of the alliance see Barlow, "La fundación de la triple alianza," pp. 147–55. The Memorial de los Pueblos is published in ENE, XIV, 118 ff. *Códice Osuna*, pp. 250–53, provides a glyphic list of Tepaneca towns. On this subject see Gibson, "The Tepanec Zone," which is scheduled for publication in the near future.

43. As the term Culhua was sometimes used in error for Acolhua, so Acolhua was used in error for Culhua. See Torquemada, *Monarchia indiana*, I, 260, 289. When the king in 1522 addressed Cortés as governor and captain-general of New Spain, he identified the area as "Aculvacan é Uloa"—presumably Acolhuacan and Culhua (Mexica). See CDIHE, I, 97.

44. Carrasco Pizana, *Los otomíes*, pp. 254–55.

45. Ixtlilxochitl, *Historia*, p. 103. PNE, VI, 66. Chimalpahin, *Diferentes historias*, p. 17. Alvarado Tezozomoc, *Crónica mexicayotl*, p. 81. Durán, *Historia*, I, 12. *Codex Telleriano-Remensis*, fol. 32r. See also NCDHM (1941), III, 268, where Amtlicha is a misreading of Coatlicha(n).

46. Ixtlilxochitl, *Historia*, pp. 83 ff. Torquemada, *Monarchia indiana*, I, 108 ff. Chapman, *Raíces y consecuencias de la guerra*.

47. Chimalpahin, *Annales*, pp. 132, 184. Sahagún, *Historia general*, II, 45. "Anales de Tula," p. 12. The amenities of Acolhua life are described, and perhaps exaggerated, in Ixtlilxochitl, *Historia*, pp. 173 ff., 209 ff., *et passim*.

48. Ixtlilxochitl, *Historia*, pp. 167 ff. Ixtlilxochitl, *Relaciones*, pp. 234 ff. See also the commentary on Mapa Quinatzin in Boban, *Documents pour servir*, I, 234 ff. I have discussed this subject in my article "Llamamiento general," pp. 3 ff.

49. PNE, VI, 219. All of the last four, according to information gathered in each in the late sixteenth century, had been independent communities until his period. See PNE, VI, 210–11, 221, 227, 231. They had, of course, been liberated from Tepaneca control only recently.

50. The *Pintura de México* is published in Ixtlilxochitl, *Historia*, pp. 258 ff. For the geographical extent of the Acolhua region see Gibson, "Llamamiento general."

51. The suffix "tzin" in names such as Coanacochtzin is honorific, and it might as reasonably be attached to many other names, e.g., Cacamatzin. I have used it indiscriminately, more or less in accordance with the usage of the sources.

52. Ixtlilxochitl, *Historia*, p. 329. Torquemada, *Monarchia indiana*, I, 220.

53. This narrative is taken from Torquemada, *Monarchia indiana*, I, 220–27. Note, however, that Torquemada may be confusing events of the years just prior to the conquest with events of 1519–22. Compare the division between Ixtlilxochitl and Coanacochtzin in 1522 indicated in Ixtlilxochitl, *Relaciones*, p. 387.

54. Durán, *Historia*, I, 16 ff. NCDHM (1941), III, 218 ff. The history is recorded in a large number of additional sources.

55. Mexica conquests are frequently recorded in the literature. The most systematic analysis of the relevant documentation is Kelly and Palerm, *The Tajín Totonac*, pp. 264 ff.

56. Sahagún, *Einige Kapitel*, p. 445.

57. This subject is discussed in more detail in Chapters III, IV, V, and XIII, and the appropriate citations will be found in the notes to those chapters.

58. "Relación de Zempoala," p. 30.

59. The nine peoples listed represent the principal ethnic divisions of the late precolonial period. It should be noted, however, that on the fringes of the Valley several peripheral or vestigial groups were to be found and that in some instances, perhaps in more instances than our sources record, these infringed upon the Valley itself. Chichimeca speakers are reported in Epazoyuca, in a statement that clearly distinguishes Chichimeca from Otomi. See "Relación de Zempoala," p. 35. Ocuiltec was spoken in Ocuilan, southwest of the Valley, and Mazahua and Matlatzinca were spoken to the west. In the middle sixteenth century Cervantes de Salazar stated that six languages were spoken in Tacuba: Otomi, Guata, Mazahua, Chuchumé, Chichimeca, and Nahuatl. See Cervantes de Salazar, *Crónica*, p. 33.

60. *Códice Xolotl, passim.*

61. For various migrations see *Al severo tribunal*, pp. 3–4. PNE, VI, 41–42. NCDHM (1941), III, 235. The remark of the conquistador is in ENE, VII, 33.

62. E.g., Durán, *Historia*, I, 341.

63. Durán, *Historia*, I, 353.

64. Durán, *Historia*, I, 386. For the aqueduct, see Lizardi Ramos, "El manantial y el acueducto de Acuecuexco."

65. Ixtlilxochitl, *Relaciones*, p. 295. Ixtlilxochitl, *Historia*, pp. 70, 74–75. PCR, folder 9, fol. 1r. PNE, VI, 40. FHT, II, 304–5.

66. Motolinía, *Memoriales*, p. 296. Motolinía, *History*, p. 269.

67. *Códice Chimalpopoca*, pp. 24–25.

68. Ixtlilxochitl, *Historia*, p. 158. Our interpretation of Ixtlilxochitl's data differs substantially from Veytia's. Veytia believed the pre-conquest albarradón to have been the Mexica boundary on the east, and he placed the southern line between Ixtapalapa and Culhuacan, through Lake Chalco, and between Nativitas and Xochimilco—a virtual impossibility. To the north, Veytia located the line between Zumpango and Citlaltepec, whereas in reality both were Tepaneca towns. See Veytia, *Historia antigua*, III, 167–68. Ixtlilxochitl's Cuexomatl can be identified near Cuitlahuac. See AAMC, no. 25, p. 1001, and Herrera y Pérez, "Tlahuac," p. 295. His Río de Acolhuacan can be

identified as the Río de San Cristóbal (Ecatepec) from Torquemada, *Monarchia indiana*, I, 137. For Tequicistlan and the boundary, see Alvarado Tezozomoc, *Crónica mexicana*, p. 75. The Cerro de Xoloc, still called by this name, lies between Xaltocan and Tizayuca. Tototepec (Tututepec) is the Hidalgo town, northeast of Pachuca. It would appear that Veytia took Ixtlilxochitl's information and elaborated upon it by guesswork, neglecting to identify the locations. It may be noted that Pomar in 1582 placed the boundary between Texcoco and Mexico in the middle of Lake Texcoco, a location that does not agree with the interpretation given by Veytia. See NCDHM (1941), III, 5.

69. Ixtlilxochitl, *Historia*, p. 195. I have not identified the places mentioned in this boundary: Quauhtepetl, Ozelotepetl, and Coliuhcan hills and Huehué y Chocayan. The approximate location, however, can be determined from the facts that Soltepec, under Texcoco, bordered Tlaxcalan territory and that Tezmelucan, under Huejotzingo, was three leagues from a hill that marked the Acolhua boundary. See Cervantes de Salazar, *Crónica*, pp. 568, 592. It may be noted that in 1627 a site of Tlaxcala called Santiago Tejaloapan was identified as bordering certain lands of Texcoco called Tepomaxac. See AGT, 1627, no. 31, fol. 1r.

70. Thus Montezuma fixed the boundary of Chalco at Cocotitlan, Nepopohualco, and Oztoticpac. See *Códice Chimalpopoca*, p. 53. Cocotitlan is a community still existing between Chalco and Tlalmanalco. Nepopohualco may be the subject community of Totolapa in the southern part of Chalco province. See ENE, VIII, 236. Modern maps sometimes give the name Nepozualco. Several towns named Oztoticpac (Oxtoticpac) are known for the Valley, but none that would seem to fit a Chalco boundary.

71. AGN, Tierras, vol. 1 (1), fol. 40r–40v; vol. 1 (2), fol. 46r–46v. It is clear from the Azcapotzalco argument that the boundaries established were Tepaneca. It may be that the communities in question were assigned to Tlatelolco by the oidor Francisco de Ceynos in 1544. See AGN, Tierras, vol. 1 (1), fols. 40v–41r, 239r; vol. 1 (2), fols. 52r, 76v. This case is commented upon by Barlow, "Los caciques coloniales," pp. 552–56.

72. Cortés, *Cartas*, I, 187 ff. Díaz del Castillo, *Historia verdadera*, I, 553. Aguilar, *Historia*, p. 98. Cervantes de Salazar, *Crónica*, p. 612. López de Gómara, *Historia*, II, 8–9, 46. See also ENE, VII, 33–34, 261.

73. Cortés, *Cartas*, II, 2. CDIAI, XIII, 293. López de Gómara, *Historia*, II, 8 ff., 41. Sahagún, *Einige Kapitel*, p. 486. Díaz del Castillo, *Historia verdadera*, I, 551–54.

74. E.g., Chimalpahin, *Annales*, p. 188.

75. Ixtlilxochitl, *Relaciones*, pp. 387–88. Ixtlilxochitl, *Historia*, pp. 415, 420, *et passim*. Cortés, *Cartas*, I, 186 ff.; II, 1 ff. López de Gómara, *Historia*, I, 266 ff. Torquemada, *Monarchia indiana*, I, 225–26, *et passim*.

76. *Archivo mexicano*, I, 235. The exception is Ixtapalapa, which remained under the city's charge for a longer time. See Appendix I.

77. *Archivo mexicano*, I, 235. The spelling "Mezquique" undoubtedly refers to Mixquic, not to Mixcoac. See Appendix I, sc. Mixquic, note 109.

78. See Appendix III for these jurisdictions.

79. It is probable that the agricultural labor drafts of the period ca. 1550 to 1555 likewise depended upon the Indian tribal jurisdictions. But thus far we have very little documentation to demonstrate such a dependence. An even earlier precedent, but one presumably involving fewer workers, is to be found in the late 1530's and 1540's, with

the assignment of Chalco tribute, possibly including labor, to the Dominicans in the city, and of Acolhua (Texcoco) labor to the Augustinians. See Appendix I, sc. Chalco, Texcoco.

80. AGN, Mercedes, vol. 4, fols. 256v–257r.

81. AGI, Patronato, leg. 181, ramo 30.

82. NCDHM (1941), II, 9–10. PNE, III, 31. Vetancurt, *Chronica*, p. 72.

83. E.g., AGN, Congregaciones, vol. 1, fols. 19v–20r.

84. Late colonial examples are Texcoco and Toltitlan. See Vetancurt, *Chronica*, p. 51, and AGN, Indios, vol. 50, fols. 59r–60v.

85. AGN, Indios, vol. 6 (1), fol. 292v; vol. 17, fols. 234v–235v. Vetancurt, *Chronica*, p. 43. Over 2,000 persons were said to have moved from Xochimilco to Mexico City within one and one-half years in the early seventeenth century. See FHT, VI, 253–54.

86. Gemelli Carreri, *Las cosas más considerables*, pp. 141–42.

87. Most of these are listed in the bibliography under author or title. For Crónica X see Barlow, "La crónica 'X.'" Mapa Quinatzin and Codex Boturini are described and reproduced in a number of texts. See Radin, "The Sources and Authenticity," pp. 11–12, 19; Pls. 1–11, 16–17. Bibliographies and commentaries on these and related materials will appear in the forthcoming *Handbook of Middle American Indians*.

CHAPTER III

1. The phrase is from Soustelle, *La vie quotidienne*, p. 20.

2. Las Casas, *Apologética historia*, p. 120. The statement was borrowed by Torquemada, *Monarchia indiana*, I, 247.

3. The first Spaniards used the designation ciudad indiscriminately to refer to large communities such as Cuauhtitlan and Acolman as well as to those that became formal ciudades. Cortés, *Cartas*, I, 186, 197, 219; II, 48. Las Casas, *Apologética historia*, pp. 130–31. Cervantes de Salazar, *Crónica*, pp. 624, 630, 632. I do not know when Tenochtitlan was granted the ciudad title. It received arms as a city in 1523. Texcoco appears to have been granted the ciudad title twice, in 1543 and again in 1551. For these grants see CDIAI, VIII, 18, 28, 34, 36. CDIU, XXII, 102–3. Peñafiel, *Colección de documentos*, sec. 7, pp. 3–4. AGN, Padrones, vol. 43, fol. 4r–4v. NLAC, 1121, fol. 43r–43v.

4. Viñas y Mey and Paz, *Relaciones*, I, 38, 48, 104, 120, 129, 148, 183, 197, 204; II, 341, *et passim*.

5. E.g., by Antonio Cortés for Tacuba. CDIHIA, I, 194.

6. Coats of arms were granted to pueblos, such as Azcapotzalco (CDIU, XXII, 104) and to villas, such as Coyoacan (*Nobilario de conquistadores*, pp. 282–83), as well as to ciudades, such as Xochimilco (*Nobilario de conquistadores*, p. 298). Communities accorded formal ciudad status were very frequently referred to, through negligence, as pueblos. See, for example, AGN, General de parte, vol. 1, fol. 151v.

7. Viñas y Mey and Paz, *Relaciones*, I, 216, 256, 323, *et passim*.

8. See examples in Viñas y Mey and Paz, *Relaciones*, I, 38, 48, 221.

9. Larger divisions within what appeared to be single communities might be termed partes or parcialidades, as Tenochtitlan and Tlatelolco in Mexico City. See Chapter XIII.

10. Thus the inhabitants of Seville are identified by collación—Santa María, San Juan, San Vicente, and others—in *Documentos americanos . . . Sevilla, passim*.

11. E.g., ENE, IV, 90, concerning the city of Mexico. *Proceso inquisitorial*, p. 28, relates the term to Texcoco.

12. See Durán's distinction between American and Spanish usage in the late sixteenth century. Durán, *Historia*, I, 42. Collación appears in records of Indian testimonies of 1666 in Vera, *Informaciones*, pp. 40 ff. But so thoroughly did the world disappear from the Mexican vocabulary that the nineteenth-century editor of Ixtlilxochitl's writings was unable to interpret the phrase "barrios y calaciones." Ixtlilxochitl, *Relaciones*, p. 235.

13. Note the use of the term estancia in the Laws of Burgos of 1512. See Simpson, *Studies in the Administration of the Indians*, I. It appears very early in the Valley of Mexico. See AC, I, 12 (1524).

14. CDIU, X, 110. Similar observations are made by colonists in CDIAI, XIII, 236, and AGI, México, leg. 24, ramo 1 ("aldeas, which over here they call sujetos," 1598).

15. Thus Ixtacalco appears as an "estancia y barrio" of Tenochtitlan in AGN, Indios, vol. 3, fol. 62v. Minor instances of confusion between barrios and estancias may be noted in García Pimentel, *Descripción*, *passim*, and in PNE, VI, 39 ff., *et passim*. In the geographical relation of Chiconauhtla, Tecama, Xaltocan, and Ecatepec, all sujetos are called barrios. See PNE, VI, 167 ff.

16. Examples may be found in Navarro de Vargas, "Padrón," p. 566, and BNM, ms. no. 2449, fol. 53r.

17. Examples may be found in AGN, Mercedes, vol. 7, fols. 19v, 64v, 70v; vol. 13, fols. 36v–37r, 173v; vol. 18, fol. 317r–317v; and in numerous other documents.

18. This might have meant including the Culhuaque, Cuitlahuaca, and Mixquica under the Mexica. The Chalca and Xochimilca might have been included under the Acolhuaque or the Mexica. Note that the letter of Antonio Cortés in ENE, XVI, 72, speaks of only three cabeceras in this way. The letter, by the cacique of Tacuba, reflects a derivative Triple Alliance point of view.

19. Thus in Mixquic in 1570 the five barrios constituted the cabecera. See AGI, Indiferente, leg. 1529, fol. 155r.

20. Contrast Bandelier's emphatic statement (in italics in the original) that "no office whatever, no kind of dignity, was, among the Mexicans, transmissible by inheritance." Bandelier, "On the Art of War," pp. 116–17. Bandelier's point is a technicality. In practice, as many particular dynastic histories demonstrate, a tlatoani was the son or some other relative of the preceding tlatoani.

21. Note that Sahagún sometimes uses the term tlatoani in a broader sense, to include any of a number of Indian officials. See, e.g., Sahagún, *Einige Kapitel*, p. 567.

22. The letter of Ramírez de Fuenleal in 1532, in CDIAI, XIII, 236, is one example among many.

23. Thus colonists spoke retroactively of pre-conquest cabeceras and sujetos. ENE, XIV, 148. CDIAI, II, 44; XIII, 236. Navarro de Vargas, "Padrón," p. 586.

24. A royal order of 1538 forbade this use of the term señor, but the order was countermanded in 1541. See CDIU, X, 399; XXI, 328. See in addition Chamberlain, "The Concept of the Señor Natural."

25. See Alegría, "Origin and Diffusion of the Term 'Cacique,'" pp. 313–15. In the same way, Indians sometimes referred to the viceroy as tlatoani. See Peñafiel, *Colección de documentos*, sec. 7, pp. 25, 42.

26. The colonial official who seems to have understood most clearly the various problems of cabecera determination was Ramírez de Fuenleal. See CDIAI, XIII, 236–37, 253–54.

27. The areas listed are those of the tribes described in Chapter II, with the exception of the Otomi, who had no tribal area in 1519.

28. Note, however, that Coyoacan had a Spanish cabildo briefly following the conquest and pending the establishment of government in the city of Mexico.

29. Dynastic sources for Tenochtitlan are summarized in García Granados, *Diccionario biográfico*, III, 429. For the other topics relating to Tenochtitlan see the fuller discussion in Chapter XIII.

30. García Granados, *Diccionario biográfico*, III, 433, presents a tlatoani tabulation for Tlatelolco. See especially *Anales de Tlatelolco*; Barlow, "Los caciques de Tlatelolco"; Barlow, "Los caciques precortesianos de Tlatelolco."

31. The suppression of the rebellion is described in some detail in Ixtlilxochitl, *Historia*, pp. 251 ff.; Alvarado Tezozomoc *Crónica mexicayotl*, pp. 117 ff.; Torquemada, *Monarchia indiana*, I, 176 ff.; Alvarado Tezozomoc, *Crónica mexicana*, pp. 186 ff. See also McAfee and Barlow, "Anales de la conquista de Tlatelolco," pp. 326 ff. The statement that Tlatelolco had no more señores after this defeat is to be found in Sahagún, *Historia general*, II, 38; *Codex Telleriano-Remensis*, fol. 36v; Torquemada, *Monarchia indiana*, I, 176; and other sources.

32. Alvarado Tezozomoc, *Crónica mexicayotl*, p. 121. Sahagún, *Vida económica de Tenochtitlan*, pp. 30–31. *Anales de Tlatelolco*, p. 6. Rendón, "Ordenanza," p. 28, lám. 10.

33. CDIAI, XLI, 142.

34. E.g., Bentura Beleña, *Recopilación sumaria*, I, 53, 82.

35. The debate of the 1570's provoked the argument, on the part of the anti-Franciscan party, that Tenochtitlan and Tlatelolco had been "una ciudad" in pre-Spanish times. See ENE, XI, 147 ff.

36. Torquemada, *Monarchia indiana*, I, 163. Chimalpahin, *Annales*, p. 98. Chimalpahin states that twelve years of cuauhtlatoani rule followed the death of Chimalpilli. Chimalpahin, *Annales*, pp. 136–37.

37. Torquemada, *Monarchia indiana*, I, 136. Chimalpahin, *Annales*, pp. 168, 191. See also *Códice Chimalpopoca*, p. 60.

38. At first glance this attribution of Ecatepec to the Mexica will appear a bold one. But Ecatepec was claimed by neither the Acolhuaque nor the Tepaneca, so far as we know, and the several early colonial statements that it was of Montezuma's patrimony carry much weight. See AGI, Justicia, leg. 124, no. 5, exp. 1; Fonseca and Urrutia, *Historia*, I, 464. Muriel, "Reflexiones," pp. 244–45. López de Meneses, "Tecuichpochtzin," p. 486. For the encomienda, see Appendix I. A problem remains concerning Tizayuca, which appears to have been subordinate to Ecatepec in the pre-conquest period. Cortés stated that Tizayuca (Tecoyuca) was a sujeto of Ecatepec and included in the encomienda. If the identification with Tizayuca is correct, it would appear that Tizayuca is to be included within the Mexica area, though not as a tlatoani site. We consider it below in connection with the Acolhua area, for it was a calpixqui location under Nezahualcoyotl. See Table 2. Tolcayuca appears to fall in the same category, but it is located north of our Valley boundary. I do not understand why Ecatepec should appear as a conquered town as late as the rule of Tizoc in the 1480's. See the sources listed in Kelly and Palerm, *The Tajín Totonac*, p. 302.

39. Names of the two dynasties are listed by Barlow, "Los tecpaneca," p. 286.

40. AGN, Mercedes, vol. 4, fols. 202r, 244r; General de parte, vol. 3, fol. 75r; Indios, vol. 17, fol. 289v. See the Historia de los Mexicanos por sus Pinturas, in NCDHM (1941), III; 228: "siempre ha habido allí dos señores y agora los hay." Miguel Barrios comments on the persistence of Mexica and Tepaneca groups in Tilhuacan to the

twentieth century. Barrios E., "Tecpanecos y mexicanos," pp. 287–88. This community was a colonial sujeto of Azcapotzalco. See AGN, General de parte, vol. 3, fol. 75r.

41. Alvarado Tezozomoc, *Crónica mexicana*, p. 530. Chimalpahin, *Annales*, pp. 191, 237–38. Torquemada, *Monarchia indiana*, III, 150.

42. See Chapter II, notes 20 and 21.

43. NCDHM (1941), III, 250. Crónica X evidence is provided by Durán, *Historia, Códice Ramírez*, and Alvarado Tezozomoc, *Crónica mexicana, passim*. For Tezozomoc, see *Códice Chimalpopoca*, p. 63. The Culhuacan dynasty is tabulated to the middle fourteenth century in García Granados, *Diccionario biográfico*, III, 414–15.

44. *Códice Chimalpopoca*, p. 63. The Ixtapalapa dynasty is also tabulated in García Granados, *Diccionario biográfico*, III, 423.

45. E.g., Chimalpahin, *Annales*, pp. 171 ff.

46. *Códice Chimalpopoca*, p. 63.

47. Zumpango and Citlaltepec had stronger tlatoani traditions than Huehuetoca. Thus Zumpango and Citlaltepec, but not Huehuetoca, are included in the Memorial de los Pueblos. See Table 1. For references to the dynasty of Zumpango see Torquemada, *Monarchia indiana*, I, 82, 84; *Códice Chimalpopoca*, p. 54. The geographical relation of Citlaltepec gives Ecatototzin as the conquest ruler. "Relación de Tequisquiac, Citlaltepec y Xilocingo," p. 297. For Aztatzontzin and his rule over the communities mentioned, see *Códice Chimalpopoca*, p. 63.

48. This subject is discussed in greater detail in Chapter IV and in Appendix I, sc. Cuauhtitlan.

49. Alvarado Tezozomoc, *Crónica mexicayotl*, p. 102, indicates a ruler, and Tacubaya (Tlaçuivayan) is included in the Memorial de los Pueblos (ENE, XIV, 119) in a way that would seem to indicate the existence of a tlatoani.

50. Statements contrary to Cortés's argument, and to the effect that Tacubaya was a sujeto of Coyoacan or that both together formed a single pueblo, may be found in CDIAI, XII, 560; XIII, 427; XIV, 334. These occur in the years immediately following Cortés's Marquesado grant (CDIAI, XII, 291, and CDIU, XVIII, 38). Cortés's motive is not wholly clear, but he was presumably committed to a defense of the original list against audiencia attack. Moreover, if he could establish Tacubaya as a cabecera he might conceivably assign additional sujetos to it and thus increase his holdings.

51. The Memorial de los Pueblos (ENE, XIV, 118 ff.) does not state explicitly that the towns were cabeceras or that they had tlatoque. But tlatoque are clearly implied in the contrast that the Memorial de los Pueblos expresses between these towns and others that had no señor and that were ruled only by mayordomos and principales. Note also the striking similarity with the comparable Acolhua list in Motolinía, *Memoriales*, pp. 353 ff., where the matter is made quite explicit.

52. For the Mexica intervention in Tenayuca see above, note 41. The antiquity of the dynasty is well documented. See, e.g., *Anales de Tlatelolco*, p. 21, Ixtlilxochitl, *Relaciones*, p. 476. Fifteenth-century rulers are indicated, e.g., in Torquemada, *Monarchia indiana*, I, 157 ff.; *Códice Chimalpopoca*, pp. 42, 47; Alvarado Tezozomoc, *Crónica mexicayotl*, p. 134. For the cacique's statement of 1561, see ENE, XVI, 73.

53. It might be argued also that Santa Fe was a Spanish-founded cabecera in the Tepaneca zone. But Santa Fe was a special case under the influence of Vasco de Quiroga, and it never truly fitted the cabecera-sujeto pattern.

54. Those mentioned are the tlatoque of Texcoco, Coatlichan, Huexotla, Chiconauhtla, Acolman, Otumba, and Teotihuacan. *Códice Chimalpopoca*, pp. 61, 63.

55. These tabulations have been made by García Granados, *Diccionario biográfico*, III, 410, 421–22, 427. Others of the Acolhua towns would lend themselves to similar tabulations.

56. See below, notes 86 ff.

57. Ixtlilxochitl, *Relaciones*, p. 234. Ixtlilxochitl, *Historia*, pp. 168–69. The same sources indicate that he established calpixque in Texcoco itself (where he retained the tlatoani position) and in Cempoala and other locations outside the limits of our area. The two Ixtlilxochitl passages appear contradictory with respect to Coatepec and Ixtapaluca, one stating that a single calpixqui in Tetitlan collected tributes from these two towns, the other stating that each had a calpixqui. See also Motolinía, *Memoriales*, pp. 353–56; *Códice Chimalpopoca*, pp. 64–65; and Mapa Quinatzin (Boban, *Documents pour servir*, I, 219–42, and Atlas, Pls. XI, XII). The connections among these are discussed in Gibson, "Llamamiento general," pp. 3 ff.

58. Tizayuca appears to have been a sujeto of Mexica Ecatepec with an Acolhua calpixqui. See above, note 38, and Appendix I, sc. Ecatepec, Tizayuca.

59. Lack of evidence prevents a thorough clarification of the condition of Coatepec. The geographical relation speaks of the four communities as cabeceras, but this may be an aberrant usage and without significance. Tetitlan, as we have said, may have been a calpixqui location for Coatepec and Ixtapaluca. The joint rule in Coatepec at the time of the Spanish arrival appears to have been in a military tradition from the fifteenth century. It is possible that the former connection with Chalco relates to a multiple tlatoani rule. The incomplete data derive from PNE, VI, 40, 50–52, 55.

60. The "señores" are mentioned in Durán, *Historia*, I, 347, although this evidence might be criticized. Moreover, it is not always possible to distinguish the two towns named Tezontepec. The geographical relation of Tequicistlan states that it was a pueblo por sí until subjugated by Montezuma I and Nezahualcoyotl. PNE, VI, 226–27, 229.

61. For Chicoloapa, see PNE, VI, 80, 82–83. We mention Tecama here although we have no evidence that it was truly an Acolhua town. Barlow, noting the extended jurisdiction of Tlatelolco to the north, suggested that this jurisdiction might have included Tecama. See Barlow, "Tlatelolco como tributario," p. 201. A hint occurs in a record of 1637, which comments casually on the extension of the Tlatelolco jurisdiction to Tlalnepantla and Tecama. See AGN, Desagüe, vol. 4, fol. 105r. We know that Tlatelolco jurisdiction came close to Tecama, but we cannot be certain that it ever included it. See Chapter XIII. The many colonial references to Tecama are partly to be explained by its assignment as a separate encomienda, but they contrast peculiarly with the limited pre-conquest data. And why was it separately assigned in encomienda?

62. See the Xochimilco letter of 1563 in CDIAI, XIII, 296–97, 300.

63. Examples of the three kinds of reference may be seen in AGN, Mercedes, vol. I, fols. 15r, 145v; vol. 4, fol. 78r; General de parte, vol. I, fol. 124r; vol. 2, fols. 37v, 116r. A Nahuatl will of 1588 refers to Tepetenchi both as a cabecera (in Spanish) and as a tlaxilacalli (i.e., calpulli or barrio). See AGN, Vínculos, vol. 279, exp. I, fols. 6r ff. The viceroy in 1562 stated, apparently erroneously, that the "pueblo" of Xochimilco was divided among four señores. See *Sobre el modo de tributar*, p. 27.

64. *Códice Chimalpopoca*, p. 63. Mayehuatzin is indicated as of the "shore" of Cuitlahuac, but this would fit with Atenchicalcan ("rose bush on the edge of the water").

65. FHT, I, 55–56. Documents of 1579 speak of Atenchicalcan as a barrio. See BNM, ms. no. 1312, fols. 38v, 39v, 40r, 40v. Olivera Sedano, "Cuitlahuac," p. 299, equates the four cabeceras with the names of modern barrios.

66. Chimalpahin, *Annales*, pp. 86, 124–25, 153. Kirchhoff, "Composición étnica," p. 298.

67. Chimalpahin, *Annales*, pp. 154 ff. AGI, México, leg. 665, cuad. 2, fols. 97r ff.

68. PNE, I, 105; VI, 58. ENE, IX, 44; X, 23, 60. AGN, General de parte, vol. 2, fol. 55r; Mercedes, vol. 7, fol. 299r; Indios, vol. 3, fol. 183r; Tierras, vol. 994, 6th pag., fols. 3v, 11r. Two modern students have been successful in locating some of these subdivisions of Amecameca. See Cook de Leonard and Lemoine V., "Materiales para la geografía histórica," p. 290, fig. 2.

69. Four cabeceras of Chalco are indicated in ENE, III, 91; IX, 44; X, 23. AGN, Mercedes, vol. 7, fol. 51v. *Sobre el modo de tributar*, p. 26. The five parts of Amecameca are termed cabeceras in a document of 1597. AGN, Tierras, vol. 994, 6th pag., fol. 1r. A variant occurs in the Suma de Visitas, which states that the four cabeceras were Tlalmanalco, Chimalhuacan, Amecameca, and Chalco Atenco. PNE, I, 105. But Chalco Atenco was commonly understood to be a sujeto of Tlalmanalco. See AGN, Indios, vol. 1, fol. 99v; Mercedes, vol. 4, fol. 312r. AGI, Contaduría, leg. 729, pp. 24 ff. NCDHM (1941), II, 11. A document of 1564 assigns only three cabeceras to Chalco, i.e., Tlalmanalco, Tenango, and Chimalhuacan. See *Sobre el modo de tributar*, p. 66. A notice of 1551 indicates Tenango and Tepopula(-Amilco) as two cabeceras and Tepostlan (Tepustlan) as a third. See AGN, Mercedes, vol. 3, fol. 327v. The cabecera attribution is aberrant, though it occurs again in a notice of 1552. See NLAC, 1121, fols. 120v–121r. This is probably the Tepostlan where Montezuma maintained a calpixqui (see *Codex Mendoza*, III, fol. 41r). Barlow, *The Extent of the Empire of the Culhua Mexica*, p. 74, identifies it as the Tepoztlan near Cuernavaca, but AGN, Mercedes, vol. 3, fol. 327v, shows a Tepostlan near Tenango-Tepopula in Chalco province.

70. Examples may be seen in AGN, Indios, vol. 1, fol. 16r–16v; vol. 3, fol. 154r–154v.

71. See AGI, Justicia, leg. 159, ramo 5; leg. 164, no. 2, fols. 50r ff.

72. The subject is treated in Chapter X. Note, however, that Montezuma and principales in general held widely scattered properties, some of which were termed estancias. See NCDHM (1941), III, 255; ENE, X, 120 ff.; *Códice Kingsborough*, fol. 209v.

73. AGI, Indiferente, leg. 1529, fol. 155r.

74. See García Pimentel, *Descripción*, p. 88.

75. García Pimentel, *Descripción*, pp. 163–64. ENE, XIV, 118. Villa-señor y Sánchez, *Theatro americano*, I, 231–32, mentions a third, Coapatengo. The two towns are misnamed as three, Autepec (Auhtepec), Cepa, and (y) Autla, in FHT, II, 279–80, from AGN, General de parte, vol. 2, fol. 156r. Barlow, *The Extent of the Empire of the Culhua Mexica*, p. 33, cites García Pimentel, *Descripción*, pp. 163–64, to the effect that Ciuhtepec and Cepayautla were sujetos of Teotenango. But this applies only to ecclesiastical visitation, and the *Descripción* states unequivocally that they were sujetos of Tacuba.

76. García Pimentel, *Descripción*, pp. 58, 91. ENE, XVI, 92. Villa-señor y Sánchez, *Theatro americano*, I, 77. AGN, Mercedes, vol. 1, fol. 162r; Indios, vol. 12 (1), fol. 83v.

77. AGN, Indios, vol. 12 (1), fol. 83v; Congregaciones, vol. 1, fols. 101v–102r; Tierras, vol. 2825, exp. 6, fols. 1r ff. AGI, México, leg. 665, cuad. 2, fol. 98v.

78. AGN, Tierras, vol. 2825, exp. 6, 2nd pag., fols. 3r, 5r.

79. PNE, III, 18, 25. Vetancurt, *Chronica*, p. 88. Durán, *Historia*, I, 32. AGN, Indios, vol. 9, fols. 41r–41v, 64v–65r. AGI, México, leg. 665, cuad. 2, fol. 98r.

80. *Codex Mendoza*, III, fols. 17v, 20r, 21v. BNP, no. 419, doc. 1, fols. 16v–23r. AGN, Tierras, vol. 1586, exp. 1, fols. 64r ff.; Indios, vol. 9, fols. 64v–65r.

81. ENE, IX, 140–42; XVI, 72. AGI, Justicia, leg. 1029, no. 10.
82. The subject receives more detailed attention in Chapter IV.
83. ENE, XIV, 118; XVI, 71–74. AGI, Justicia, leg. 1029, no. 10. I have dealt with this subject more fully in the article "The Tepanec Zone," which is soon to be published.
84. The Tacuba campaign mentioned Teocalhueyacan (ENE, XIV, 118), but we have no evidence that Tacuba seriously sought to recover it.
85. AGI, Justicia, leg. 165, no. 2; leg. 1029, no. 10. The case was complicated by the fact that both Tacuba and Teocalhueyacan were in encomienda, and by the fact that Teocalhueyacan had been separated from Tacuba's own jurisdiction. See Chapter IV and Appendix I, sc. Tacuba, Teocalhueyacan. Both Tlazala and Xilotzingo were included in the Tlalnepantla congregación of 1603, and by the end of the colonial period both had become separate pueblos, no longer sujetos but still within the encomienda of Tacuba. See AGN, Congregaciones, vol. 1, fol. 47r; Tributos, vol. 7, exp. 16, fol. 4r.
86. Orozco y Berra, Historia antigua, II, 201–3. Orozco y Berra, "Tlacopan y Texcoco," pp. 508–9. See the striking similarity in wording between the Texcoco argument in Motolinía, Memoriales, pp. 353 ff., and the Tacuba argument in ENE, XIV, 118 ff. Both campaigns included the statement that 123 towns paid joint tribute in the Aztec empire. See CDIHIA, I, 193–94; Peñafiel, Colección de documentos, sec. 7, pp. 9–10.
87. Motolinía, Memoriales, p. 353. See the statement of Pomar in NCDHM (1941), III, 5, and the statement of Hernando Pimentel in ENE, XVI, 75.
88. See the interesting reaction of the Spanish cabildo of Mexico City, that this constituted a disservice to the crown. AC, VI, 44.
89. NCDHM (1941), III, 5. Coatlichan and Huexotla were among the principal Acolhua capitals prior to the Triple Alliance. See, e.g., Ixtlilxochitl, Historia, pp. 103–4. For the common encomienda see Appendix I, sc. Texcoco. The towns are indicated as sujetos of Texcoco in, e.g., AGN, Mercedes, vol. 7, fol. 131v; vol. 15, fol. 22r.
90. Proceso inquisitorial, p. 30. AGN, Mercedes, vol. 2, fol. 179r; vol. 3, fol. 333Ar.
91. AGN, Mercedes, vol. 3, fol. 333Ar; vol. 4, fols. 250r–252r; vol. 6, fol. 231v; vol. 7, fol. 292r–292v.
92. NCDHM (1941), III, 5. FHT, VI, 433.
93. AGI, Justicia, leg. 164, no. 2, fols. 50r ff.; leg. 208, no. 4, sep. pag., fol. 11r–11v.
94. NLAC, 1121, fols. 52v–53r, 119v–120r. AGI, Justicia, leg. 164, no. 2, fols. 40r ff., 50r ff.
95. AGI, Justicia, leg. 164, no. 2, fols. 1r ff., 119r ff.; leg. 208, no. 4, fols. 73r ff., 216r–216v, 250v. AGN, Mercedes, vol. 7, fols. 18r–18v, 147r, 148r; vol. 84, fol. 120r–120v.
96. AGN, Indios, vol. 4, fol. 73r; vol. 20, fol. 53r.
97. Examples may be seen in CDIAI, XIII, 297; AGN, Mercedes, vol. 5, fols. 288v–289r; vol. 6, fol. 165r.
98. NCDHM (1886–92), IV, 11–12, 118–19; V, 110. FHT, II, 279–80. Advertimientos generales, pp. 26, 49. AGN, Indios, vol. 17, fols. 151v–152r, 212v–214v.
99. As Mendieta stated in 1591, Indians were so inclined toward lawsuits and divisions that if all separatist factions had their way every man's house would be a cabecera. See NCDHM (1886–92), V, 109.
100. NCDHM (1941), III, 50. A map of the type indicated may be seen in Gamio, La población del valle de Teotihuacan, I (2), lám. 142, fac. p. 384. The curate's remark is in Navarro de Vargas, "Padrón," p. 573.
101. AGN, Indios, vol. 6 (1), fol. 142r. The affected towns were probably former

sujetos of Tacuba that had been attached to Tlalnepantla, a circumstance that gave additional justification to the Tacuba claim. See ENE, XIV, 118.

102. AGN, Congregaciones, vol. 1, fol. 74r. Navarro de Vargas, "Padrón," pp. 583–84.

103. In the seventeenth-century congregaciones, Indians who had moved to or near haciendas were exempted from the orders of removal that affected their former communities. Examples from the Valley of Mexico may be seen in AGN, Congregaciones, vol. 1, fols. 83r–83v, 94v–95r.

104. Data relating to the Mexico City division, in imitation of Madrid, are abundant in eighteenth-century documentation. See especially Bentura Beleña, *Recopilación sumaria*, I, 5th pag., p. 88; II, 26 ff. For the divisions in greater or lesser degrees in Ecatepec, Tecama, Chiconauhtla, and other Indian towns, see AGN, Padrones, vol. 6, fols. 315r, 316v, 318r; vol. 12, fol. 143r; vol. 18, fol. 308r.

105. Examples may be studied in AGN, Padrones, vol. 6, fol. 321v, *et passim*.

106. Villa-señor y Sánchez, *Theatro americano*, I, 231 ff.

107. Thus Santa María Ozumbilla and other sujetos of Tlatelolco were regarded as subordinate to Chiconauhtla (Ecatepec) in government (justicia) and to Tlatelolco in tribute, in the 1630's. See AGN, Indios, vol. 12 (1), fols. 83v–84v. In the eighteenth century Santa Marta and Los Reyes were similarly subject to Mexicalzingo jurisdiction while they continued to pay tributes to Tenochtitlan. See Villa-señor y Sánchez, *Theatro americano*, I, 61–62. San Mathías Ixtacalco and Santa María Magdalena Atlayauhtla (Las Salinas) became partially separate from Tenochtitlan, and San Francisco Xocotitlan partially separate from Tlatelolco. The three towns had distinct *propios*, but separate records and treasuries were achieved only in 1780. See AGN, Tierras, vol. 1058, exp. 4, fols. 1r ff.

108. AGN, Tierras, vol. 2825, exp. 6, fols. 1r ff. Bentura Beleña was oidor and a judge of the Juzgado General de Indios. See Bentura Beleña, *Recopilación sumaria*, II, 199 ff.

109. Vetancurt, *Chronica*, p. 72. NCDHM (1941), II, 9–10. PNE, III, 31.

110. Alvarado Tezozomoc, *Crónica mexicana*, p. 530, refers to Montezuma's placing of his son Acamapich in Tenayuca. *Códice Chimalpopoca*, p. 63, gives Montezuma as the Tenayuca ruler. For cabecera status in the sixteenth century see NCDHM (1941), II, 10.

111. There exist occasional notices of a chief (Sahagún, *Einige Kapitel*, p. 517) and a cacique (Fernández del Castillo, "Don Pelayo y la virgen," p. 467) in Teocalhueyacan, but they are vague and possibly garbled. Seler's term Häuptling appears to have no basis in Sahagún's Nahuatl. Accounts of the conquest of Teocalhueyacan do not seem to comment on a tlatoani. The supposed cacique, named Ce Cuauhtli, and also known as Juan de Tovar and Juan del Aguila, may have been simply a tequitlato of Los Remedios. See Boturini Benaduci, *Catálogo*, pp. 85–86. This personage is frequently mentioned in the miraculous literature (see, e.g., Vera, *Tesoro guadalupano*, pp. 97, 141 ff.), but his true identity remains in doubt.

112. For these various usages see ENE, XVI, 73; NCDHM (1941), II, 10; AGI, Patronato, leg. 181, ramo 21, fol. 4v; AGN, General de parte, vol. 2, fols. 206v, 228v, 287r.

113. For these histories, see Appendix I.

114. AGN, General de parte, vol. 2, fols. 206v–207v; Clero regular y secular, vol. 103, 2nd pag., fol. 1r.

115. FHT, III, 36. The peculiar situation gave rise to some misleading interpreta-

tions. Santa María Tepetlacalco, in three notices of 1580, appeared as a parte of Tena-yuca, an estancia of Tlalnepantla, and a sujeto of Teocalhueyacan. See AGN, General de parte, vol. 2, fols. 212r, 273r, 287r. A notice of 1560 spoke of the "pueblo" of Xilo-tzingo, "subject to Tacuba of the cabecera of Teocalhueyacan" (AGN, Mercedes, vol. 5, fol. 20v), a confusing phrase that suggests the dispute over Tlazala and Xilotzingo.

116. Villa-señor y Sánchez, *Theatro americano*, I, 77. AGN, Congregaciones, vol. 1, fol. 47r.

117. Vetancurt, *Chronica*, p. 72. AGN, Congregaciones, vol. 1, fol. 48v.

118. AGN, Congregaciones, vol. 1, fols. 46v ff. Included in the congregación were several towns that had been claimed by Tacuba in its petition of the middle sixteenth century. See ENE, XIV, 118 ff.

119. These included Santiago Tlazala and Santa Ana Xilotzingo. See AGN, Pa-drones, vol. 6, fols. 246r ff.

120. Vetancurt listed sixteen Spanish haciendas producing maize and wheat in the area in the late seventeenth century. See Vetancurt, *Chronica*, p. 72. For an account of their relations with Indians see FHT, VII, 152.

121. Villa-señor y Sánchez, *Theatro americano*, I, 75–76.

122. AGN, Indios, vol. 50, fols. 2r–6r. The Indian government of Teocalhueyacan was now the government of the "parcialidad de Otomies" of Tlalnepantla. See AGN, Clero regular y secular, vol. 103, 2nd pag., fols. 1r ff.

123. Villa-señor y Sánchez, *Theatro americano*, I, 77. AGN, Padrones, vol. 6, fols. 145r ff.; Tierras, vol. 1533, exp. 1, 2nd pag., fols. 1r–151r.

124. The new terminology is clearly reflected in the reports of the late eighteenth century in AGN, Padrones.

CHAPTER IV

1. For general treatments of encomienda see Chamberlain, "Castilian Backgrounds"; León Pinelo, *Tratado de confirmaciones reales*, fols. 1r ff.; Solórzano y Pereira, *Política indiana*, pp. 130 ff.; Zavala, *La encomienda indiana*; Simpson, *The Encomienda in New Spain*. Relevant laws are summarized in *Recopilación de leyes*, II, 249 ff. (Lib. VI, títs. 8 ff.). Property and possession are distinguished in *Las siete partidas*, II, 370 (Part. III, tít. 2, ley 27). Dominium denotes absolute ownership. For the various legal meanings of señorío, see *Las siete partidas*, III, 133 (Part. IV, tít. 25, ley 2).

2. CDIAI, II, 103–4; XII, 213 ff. ENE, IV, 19; X, 114. García Icazbalceta, *Don Fray Juan de Zumárraga*, II, 172. AGI, Justicia, leg. 164, no. 2, fols. 50r ff. CDIU, XXI, 333. Encinas, *Cedulario*, II, 185–86.

3. CDHM, I, 472 ff. Cortés, *Cartas y relaciones*, p. 328.

4. Conquistadores are listed in ENE, XIV, 58–60, 148–55, and CDHM, I, 431–36. For the encomenderos, see Appendix I.

5. Salazar and Chirinos seemingly assigned Tenochtitlan to the crown about 1525. After their imprisonment in 1526 it was taken from the crown, presumably by Cortés himself, who had just returned to the city from his Honduras expedition. CDIAI, XXVIII, 323–25.

6. CDIAI, XII, 279; XXVIII, 175. Cortés, *Cartas y otros documentos*, pp. 32–33. *Archivo mexicano*, I, 204. *Documentos inéditos relativos a Hernán Cortés*, p. 347.

7. *Documentos inéditos relativos a Hernán Cortés*, p. 346. *Archivo mexicano*, I, 204. *El libro de las tasaciones*, pp. 481–83. *Sobre el modo de tributar*, p. 97. Compare the

remarks of Pomar on these towns after they had become separated from the Indian jurisdiction of Texcoco, NCDHM (1941), III, 5.

8. CDIAI, XII, 539; XXVII, 85; XXVIII, 323–24. ENE, I, 141. *Nuevos documentos relativos a los bienes*, pp. 1 ff., 27 ff., 63 ff.

9. See the cabildo's strongly worded petition against Cortés in 1529. AC, II, 10 ff.

10. CDIHE, I, 105–8. CDIAI, XII, 291, 381 ff.; XIII, 237 ff. CDIU, XVIII, 38.

11. Suárez de Peralta, *Noticias históricas*, p. 129.

12. CDIAI, XXVI, 379–80. The controversy over the method of counting is summarized by Suárez de Peralta, *Noticias históricas*, pp. 142–43.

13. In secret instructions, the crown permitted the removal of Coyoacan and Tacubaya from the Marquesado, at the discretion of the second audiencia and depending upon the requirements of the city. In fact, the audiencia declared Cortés's possession to be prejudicial to the city, but Cortés kept the two towns. See CDIAI, XIII, 427; XIV, 334.

14. Cortés arrived back in New Spain in the midsummer of 1530. See CDIHE, I, 32. For the subsequent controversies and the solutions reached, see *Nuevos documentos relativos a los bienes*, pp. 63 ff.; ENE, III, 91; VIII, 149–50; *El libro de las tasaciones*, p. 481; CDIAI, XII, 330 ff.; BAGN, VII, 220; Ternaux Compans, *Voyages, relations et mémoires*, XVI, 157.

15. ENE, VII, 261, 263. AGI, Contaduría, leg. 825 (1), fols. 306r ff. See Appendix I, sc. Chalco.

16. CDIU, IX, 299 ff. León Pinelo, *Tratado de confirmaciones reales*, fol. 4v.

17. *Archivo mexicano*, I, 235.

18. BAGN, VIII, 188. ENE, IV, 62–63.

19. AGN, Mercedes, vol. 2, fol. 331r–331v. CDIHE, XXVI, 336.

20. *Leyes y ordenanzas*, fol. 6v.

21. Puga, *Provisiones*, fols. 100v–101r. AC, V, 162–63. AGN, Mercedes, vol. 1, fol. 129r. CDIU, X, 322–29. CDIAI, VIII, 25.

22. For the population loss, see Chapter VI. The order of 1549 is published in Puga, *Provisiones*, fols. 172r (173r) ff. On this subject see Miranda, *El tributo indígena*, pp. 103 ff.

23. See the remarks of Zorita in CDIAI, II, 104. Culhuacan and Ixtapalapa had received no tasaciones by 1552. ENE, VI, 130.

24. *El libro de las tasaciones*, p. 58. ENE, VI, 136.

25. Scholes, *The Diego Ramírez Visita*.

26. E.g., the contract between Bernardino Vásquez de Tapia and the Indians of Huitzilopochco in 1554. Boban, *Documents pour servir*, I, 387–89, and Atlas, no. 27.

27. Viceroy Mendoza stated that he devoted two mornings each week to Indian cases, and the king ordered the audiencia in 1551 to continue the practice. CDIAI, VI, 489–90. CDIHIA, VIII, 13.

28. *El libro de las tasaciones*, pp. 149–50. Good colonial statements on the conspiracy may be found in Torquemada, *Monarchia indiana*, I, 629 ff.; Suárez de Peralta, *Noticias históricas*, pp. 189 ff.; Cavo, *Historia de México*, pp. 206 ff. The full modern study is Orozco y Berra, *Noticia histórica de la conjuración*. An interesting feature of the conspiracy is the attention it received in Indian annals and codices: e.g., Códice Aubin (*Histoire de la nation mexicaine*, p. 107); AAMC, no. 13, p. 636; Mapa de Tepexpan (see Boban, *Documents pour servir*, I, 266–67); the Diario of Chimalpahin (BNP, no. 220, p. 98); Chimalpahin, *Annales*, pp. 276–77; and Códice de Juan Bautista (MNM, Colección Gómez de Orozco, no. 14, pp. 133–34).

29. An encomenderos' statement of 1597 asserted that three-quarters of the original encomiendas had reverted and were at an end. ENE, XIII, 11.

30. Encomienda practice in Hispaniola may be studied in CDIAI, I. For the derivative Mexican practice see Miranda, *El tributo indígena*, p. 52.

31. AGN, Hospital de Jesús, leg. 293, exp. 123, fol. 2r.

32. See the tabulation by García Granados, *Diccionario biográfico*, III, 412, from data of the Anales de Cuauhtitlan.

33. *Códice Chimalpopoca*, p. 63, and facsimile, p. 64. Sahagún, *Historia general*, III, 39.

34. *Códice Chimalpopoca*, pp. 19, 21, 35–36, 52.

35. García Granados, *Diccionario biográfico*, III, 438, tabulates the early rulers. Others figure in the commentary of Pablo Nazareo, ENE, X, 124–25. The rule was interrupted for a long time, according to the Anales de Cuauhtitlan (*Códice Chimalpopoca*, p. 50). Note that Xaltocan figures as a calpixqui location, not a tlatoani location, under Nezahualcoyotl, in Table 2.

36. *Códice Chimalpopoca*, p. 26.

37. An Indian gobernador is mentioned as of 1565. See *El libro de las tasaciones*, p. 658.

38. E.g., CDIHIA, I, 100. AGN, Mercedes, vol. 3, fol. 105v. Orozco y Berra, *Noticia histórica de la conjuración*, 2nd pag., p. 4.

39. AGN, Mercedes, vol. 3, fols. 340v–341r. García Pimentel, *Descripción*, pp. 258 ff.

40. Note that Tacuba possessed sujetos outside the Valley of Mexico that were separately granted in encomienda. The Tacuba sujetos are referred to in the Memorial de los Pueblos and the Antonio Cortés letter of 1561. See ENE, XIV, 118; XVI, 71–74. The towns are mapped and discussed in Gibson, "Llamamiento general," and Gibson, "The Tepanec Zone."

41. See Chapter III, note 61.

42. See Appendix I, sc. Ecatepec, Tizayuca.

43. PNE, VI, 82–83.

44. See Appendix I, sc. Oxtoticpac.

45. AGI, Justicia, leg. 165, no. 2, fols. 52r ff.

46. Ramírez de Fuenleal stated in 1532 that in some instances Spaniards with cabeceras in encomienda preferred that these be known as estancias, "para disminuir lo que tienen y dar á entender que es poco." See CDIAI, XIII, 254. No examples are known from the Valley of Mexico.

47. In the case of Tizayuca, the separation from Ecatepec, the separation from the Cortés holdings, and the royalization of 1531 comprised a series of events that virtually assured cabecera status. The crucial factor here may have been less the placement in encomienda than the subsequent royalization.

48. ENE, XIV, 118. AGI, Justicia, leg. 165, no. 2. The dispute concerned Tlazala and Xilotzingo. See Chapter III, notes 84 and 85.

49. A brief pre-conquest dynasty is tabulated by García Granados, *Diccionario biográfico*, III, 426. It will be recalled that Oxtoticpac was a calpixqui location—i.e., not a tlatoani location—under Nezahualcoyotl. See Table 2.

50. PNE, III, 83. Oxtoticpac appears to have had an Indian gobernador in 1599, and it was indicated as a cabecera in the congregación of 1603. FHT, IV, 263–64. AGN, Congregaciones, vol. 1, fol. 32v. But we need more information concerning relations between Oxtoticpac and Otumba.

51. AGN, Mercedes, vol. 8, fol. 51r. FHT, VII, 143, 187–88; 310–11. AGI, Justicia, leg. 134, no. 1. The lack of a tlatoani tradition in Axapusco may be related to the false cacique records of CDHM, II, 1–24.

52. The role of encomienda in reducing multiple cabeceras to single cabeceras is uncertain, and lack of evidence prevents any clear judgment. But it seems probable that encomienda hastened this process, e.g., in Cuitlahuac.

53. It may be noted in this connection that Cortés wanted to enumerate the sujetos of his Marquesado towns, because he feared that the audiencia would deny that some were sujetos. See CDIAI, XII, 555 ff.

54. PNE, I, 110. El libro de las tasaciones, pp. 205–6. García Pimentel, Relación, pp. 166, 175, 179. ENE, IX, 29.

55. An example occurs in the dispute between Tepexpan and Temascalapa, to which we have referred above. The royal fiscal, anxious to increase royal revenues, argued in 1566 that Temascalapa was a cabecera, that it was therefore not a legitimate part of the Tepexpan encomienda, and that it should hence revert to the crown and pay its tribute to the royal treasury. The encomendero's argument, against this, undertook to demonstrate that Temascalapa was a true estancia of Tepexpan, properly within the encomienda. The interesting dispute is documented in AGI, Justicia, leg. 208, no. 4.

56. The Coyoacan-Huitzilopochco controversy is documented in CDIHIA, I, 177–78, and AGN, Mercedes, vol. 4, fols. 216v–218r. The Coyoacan-Xochimilco conflicts are documented in CDIAI, XII, 295; XLI, 135–36, and ENE, III, 27–28.

57. It should not be supposed that all Marquesado boundary claims arose from Indian dispute. In 1564, on the eve of the encomenderos' conspiracy, the second Marqués del Valle claimed a jurisdiction for Coyoacan that included the city's western houses and lands. See AC, VII, 182.

58. Some interesting but enigmatic Tlalpam material published by Rivera Cambas, México pintoresco, II, 436, suggests that a Tepaneca faction in Tlalpam had recognized Xochimilca rule.

59. We have too little information concerning this Nuño de Guzmán and audiencia grant. It may have been intended as a confirmation of land properties. It was disqualified, in any case, by the second audiencia in 1531, and the gobernador and other Indian leaders of Tlatelolco were required to return the disputed area to the encomienda. See AGI, Justicia, leg. 123, no. 2.

60. ENE, X, 113.

61. AGI, Justicia, leg. 123, no. 2.

62. CDIAI, XLI, 144. CDIHIA, I, 84.

63. García Pimentel, Descripción, p. 58. Fernández and Leicht, "Códice del tecpan," pp. 260 ff. PNE, I, 199. ENE, XVI, 91–92. AGN, Mercedes, vol. 1, fol. 162r; vol. 7, fol. 329v; vol. 9, fol. 171v; Indios, vol. 12 (1), fols. 83v–84v; Tierras, vol. 2825, exp. 6, 2nd pag., fols. 1r ff. AGI, Indiferente, leg. 1529, fol. 206r.

64. AGI, Justicia, leg. 124, no. 5, exp. 4, fols. 3r ff. For additional copies, some of which identify the recipient as Marina or Mariana, see Appendix I, sc. Ecatepec.

65. AGI, Justicia, leg. 124, no. 5. See the letter of Diego Huanitzin, later to be gobernador of Tenochtitlan, in Ternaux Compans, Voyages, relations et mémoires, VIII, 264. The letter is dated 1532, and it requests Tizayuca and Tolcayuca as sujetos of Ecatepec. See also the Tlatelolco letter of 1537, which accuses the Ecatepec encomendero of usurping Coatitlan (Ayatitcla) and Acalhuacan. CDIAI, XLI, 142–44.

66. See AGI, Justicia, leg. 159, no. 5.

67. Ponce de León appeared before the Spanish cabildo on July 4, 1526. He died the same month. See AC, I, 90–91, 94, 98. Torquemada, *Monarchia indiana*, I, 597, states that Ponce de León entered Mexico on June 2, 1526.

68. Full documentation on these cases involving Ecatepec may be found in AGI, Justicia, leg. 124, no. 5, and leg. 159, no. 5. For the further history of the encomienda see Appendix I, sc. Ecatepec.

69. NCDHM (1941), II, 9. PNE, III, 29–30. *El libro de las tasaciones,* pp. 139–40. FHT, VII, 62–64 (Santa Clara).

70. See the labor demands in the tecpan construction of the 1570's in Fernández and Leicht, "Códice del tecpan," pp. 260 ff. AGN, Indios, vol. 12 (1), fols. 83v–84v.

71. AGI, Justicia, leg. 123, no. 2. See also the incident of ca. 1522 in which Cortés sought to grant Otumba and thirty-three other towns to the Indian leader Ixtlilxochitl but was dissuaded by the argument that the communities were already in the Indian leader's possession. Ixtlilxochitl, *Relaciones,* p. 387.

72. PNE, I, 199. Cook and Simpson accordingly list Tecalco (Teacalco) as in encomienda to the caciques of Mexico. Cook and Simpson, *The Population of Central Mexico,* p. 201. But there is no more justification for listing Tecalco in this way than for listing any estancia of any cabecera.

73. Ternaux Compans, *Voyages, relations et mémoires,* VIII, 262 ff.

74. Muriel, "Reflexiones," p. 243. BNM, ms. no. 46, fols. 299v–300r. AGN, Historia, vol. 4, exp. 4, fols. 37v ff. López de Meneses, "Tecuichpochtzin," p. 473. Prescott, *History of the Conquest of Mexico,* III, 446 ff., contains the document.

75. Zavala, *La encomienda indiana.* Zavala, *De encomiendas y propiedad territorial.* Simpson, *The Encomienda in New Spain.* Miranda, *El tributo indígena.* Miranda, "La función económica del encomendero."

76. The statement of the Indians of Xochimilco occurs in CDIAI, XIII, 293–94. But Montejo the younger appears to have used Indians from his father's encomienda in Azcapotzalco for the conquest of Yucatan as late as 1541. Chamberlain, *The Conquest and Colonization of Yucatan,* p. 211.

77. CDIHIA, I, 191. ENE, VII, 102.

78. *Documentos inéditos relativos a Hernán Cortés y su familia,* pp. 343 ff. Ternaux Compans, *Voyages, relations et mémoires,* XVI, 157.

79. Cervantes de Salazar, *Crónica,* p. 317.

80. See Simpson, *The Encomienda in New Spain,* pp. 1 ff.

81. ENE, VI, 135.

82. CDIAI, II, 245, 255, 257. AGN, Mercedes, vol. 3, fol. 330r.

83. CDIAI, XXVII, 26.

84. See, e.g., Cuevas, *Historia de la iglesia,* I, 433–34.

85. CDIHIA, I, 187–89. ENE, VI, 126 ff.; XVI, 40 ff. *Archivo mexicano,* I, 134, *et passim.* AGN, Mercedes, vol. 4, fol. 40r. AGI, Justicia, leg. 134, no. 1. CDIU, XXII, 56 ff.

86. On these subjects see *El libro de las tasaciones;* Scholes, *The Diego Ramírez Visita;* Miranda, *El tributo indígena.* Tribute and labor receive further attention in Chapters VIII and IX.

87. The extraordinarily full documentation on this encomienda is to be found principally in *Códice Kingsborough* and AGI, Justicia, leg. 108, no. 4; leg. 117, no. 5; leg. 151, no. 1; leg. 159, no. 2. A major study of this encomienda is in preparation by John Glass.

88. On Díaz de Aux, see Gardiner, *Naval Power*, pp. 136–37. Salazar was described in 1531 as the principal enemy of Cortés. He is credited with the extravagant statement that Charles V was a heretic for favoring such a traitor as Cortés. Quite apart from his activity as an encomendero, a very full record remains of his intrigues and manipulations of power, which were so extreme that Zumárraga could say of him in 1529 that he was the cause of all the colony's troubles. Ternaux Compans, *Voyages, relations et mémoires*, XVI, 49, 155. CDIAI, XIII, 176.

89. A tribute tasación was made ca. 1543 by Pedro Vásquez de Vergara. AGN, Mercedes, vol. 2, fols. 209v–210r. It appears possible that Códice Vergara (BNP, nos. 37–39) and Códice de Santa María Asunción (BNM; microfilm in CDMNC, rollo 4, exp. 2; see Carreño, "Manuscritos," p. 17) are documents surviving from his inquiries. Both are signed by Vergara.

90. AGI, Justicia, leg. 151, no. 1; leg. 159, no. 2.

91. AGI, Justicia, leg. 151, no. 1; leg. 159, no. 2. ENE, IX, 25. AGN, Mercedes, vol. 4, fols. 146v ff., 257r. For repartimiento, see Chapter IX. The community had once before complained of ill treatment, in accusation against Miguel Díaz de Aux in 1527. See AGI, Justicia, leg. 108, no. 4, fol. 2r.

92. Hanke and Millares Carlo, *Cuerpo de documentos*, pp. 39–63.

93. An exception is the conduct of Cristóbal de Valderrama in Ecatepec in 1593. See AGN, Indios, vol. 6 (1), fol. 168r–168v.

94. The list of those that terminated in accordance with the New Laws includes Axapusco, Toltitlan, Azcapotzalco, Chicoloapa, and Tecama. Some of these, however, were reassigned. ENE, XIII, 8 ff., contains a list of those in the second life in the 1590's. See Appendix I.

95. The fear that Indians would attack the city continued to be expressed for more than a generation after the conquest. See PNE, III (supl.), 35, 155–56. Characteristic arguments for perpetuity are numerous in the sources. Cuevas, *Documentos inéditos*, pp. 109–10. AGI, Indiferente, leg. 1624. ENE, XI, 113–23; XIII, 4 ff. AC, V, 162–63; VI, 227; VII, 325 ff. Gómez de Cervantes, *La vida económica*, pp. 81 ff.

96. AGN, Reales cédulas, duplicados, vol. 6, fols. 112v–113v. Torquemada, *Monarchia indiana*, I, 615. AC, XXX, 209. León Pinelo, *Tratado de confirmaciones reales*, fol. 21v. For material on encomienda succession see also CDIU, XXII, 46 ff.; Encinas, *Cedulario*, II, 200 ff.; Puga, *Provisiones*, fols. 136v–137r; León Pinelo, *Tratado de confirmaciones reales*, fols. 14v ff.; Solórzano y Pereira, *Política indiana*, pp. 192 ff.; *Recopilación de leyes*, II, 279 ff. (Lib. VI, tít. 11); AGI, México, leg. 26, ramo 2; Zavala, *La encomienda indiana, passim*.

97. See Appendix I for relevant instances in the Valley of Mexico. On the late colonial encomienda in general, see AGI, México, leg. 636; Indiferente, leg. 1612.

98. We adopt this terminology partly to avoid confusion with the alcaldes, and despite the fact that alcalde mayor came to be the common term after the early period. There can be no doubt that differences were recognized between corregidores and alcaldes mayores in the sixteenth century. See, e.g., AGN, Ordenanzas, vol. 1, fol. 84v, where an order is applied to corregidores, or, where corregidores were lacking, to the alcaldes mayores in whose jurisdictions the corregimientos fell. See also BAGN, X, 258–60, in which the corregidor of Chalco was made justicia in Totolapa and other communities, with the explanation that some of these had corregidores but should have justicias. Simpson, *The Encomienda in New Spain*, p. 191, states that the corregidor governed a town whereas an alcalde mayor governed a province. An example

in the Valley might be Antonio Delgadillo in 1563, who was alcalde mayor of Pachuca and corregidor of Tizayuca. See AGN, Mercedes, vol. 6, fol. 140v. But there are so many exceptions to this rule that we must call it generally inapplicable to the history of the Valley of Mexico. On the origin and continuation of the distinction, see also Miranda, *Las ideas y las instituciones políticas*, p. 122.

99. For the earlier history of corregimiento in Spain, see Albi, *El corregidor*.

100. E.g., AC, II, 96. CDIHIA, I, 20, 45 ff. CDIU, XXIII, 153.

101. See commentary and citations in Simpson, *The Encomienda in New Spain*, pp. 102 ff. Corregidores are mentioned in a royal order of 1528 (Puga, *Provisiones*, fol. 9v) and are mentioned further as having been introduced into some of the Marquesado towns while Cortés was still in Spain—i.e., in early 1530 or before. See above, note 14. CDIAI, XIII, 21.

102. E.g., CDIHIA, I, 101. CDIAI, VII, 534 ff.

103. BAGN, X, 258–60. Fonseca and Urrutia, *Historia*, I, 536. CDIU, XXIII, 153.

104. Encinas, *Cedulario*, III, 18. Simpson, *The Encomienda in New Spain*, p. 85.

105. BAGN, VII, 191, *et passim*. An arithmetical or copying error may slightly affect the statement concerning Huitzilopochco and Mixquic.

106. NCDHM (1941), III, 3. AGN, Mercedes, vol. 14, fols. 66v, 366r–366v; vol. 15, fols. 4v–5r, 84v–85r, 142v ff., 203v–204v, 210r–210v; vol. 16, fols. 275v–276r; vol. 17, fols. 8r–8v, 191v–192v, 223r–223v; vol. 19, fols. 11r–12r, 100r–100v.

107. AGN, General de parte, vol. 1, fol. 135r; Mercedes, vol. 10, fols. 106r–106v, 204r, 205v–206r; vol. 13, fols. 78v–79r.

108. AGN, Mercedes, vol. 23, fol. 27r–27v.

109. BAGN, VIII, 189. There is a slight confusion in this text concerning the distribution between corregidor and alguacil. See *Sobre el modo de tributar*, p. 85. For additional examples of food, goods, and services paid to corregidores see ENE, VIII, 148 ff.; *El libro de las tasaciones, passim*.

110. E.g., in Mexicalzingo, ENE, VIII, 148.

111. CDIU, XXI, 273, 279. The Chalco conversion is explained in BAGN, VIII, 197, and *Sobre el modo de tributar*, pp. 85–86. For other similar conversions see BAGN, VII, 537 ff.; AGN, Mercedes, vol. 4, fol. 372r.

112. See the Texcoco example of 1587 in FHT, III, 4–5.

113. In practice, tenientes appear to have been little other than alguaciles under a different name. Both performed essentially a police function. See Gómez de Cervantes, *La vida económica*, p. 92. Some corregimientos of the Valley had alguaciles while others had tenientes, and the same officer sometimes was designated by both titles. See BAGN, VII, 221–22, 540–41; VIII, 189.

114. Examples of appointment by various authorities and further data are documented in AGN, General de parte, vol. 1, fol. 196r–196v; vol. 2, fols. 26v–27r; vol. 6, fol. 217v; Mercedes, vol. 6, fol. 251r. See also AC, XXX, 210.

115. This "year" (año) might, however, mean a period of sixteen months. See, e.g., AGN, General de parte, vol. 4, fol. 157r. For instances of substitute rule by tenientes, see AGN, Mercedes, vol. 7, fols. 207v–208r; General de parte, vol. 5, fol. 178v.

116. An example of alternation occurs in Teotihuacan. FHT, II, 360–61, 366. Division between a superior and a subordinate capital, with the teniente in the latter, occurs in eighteenth-century Chalco. See Villa-señor y Sánchez, *Theatro americano*, I, 64.

117. E.g., PNE, VI, 173, 195.

118. For the general history of the intendancy, see Fisher, *The Intendant System,* and Navarro García, *Intendencias en Indias.*

119. Bentura Beleña, *Recopilación sumaria,* II, sep. pag., v–vii, xxxix. AHH, Tributos, leg. 225, exp. 29. AGN, Tierras, vol. 1412, exp. 5, fol. 11v.

120. It was Humboldt's observation in the early nineteenth century that, far from constituting a reform, the intendancy system brought greater evils than the system it displaced, for the reason that the subdelegados did not have fixed salaries. Humboldt, *Political Essay,* I, 195.

121. *Instrucciones que los vireyes de Nueva España dejaron* (1873), II, 362. AGN, Civil, vol. 169, 2nd pag., p. 224; Hospital de Jesús, leg. 329, exp. 2. Alcaldes mayores and corregidores were again abolished in 1811. See *La constitución de 1812,* II, 93.

122. Chalco: AGN, Mercedes, vol. 3, fol. 25v. Xochimilco: *El libro de las tasaciones,* p. 305. Mexicalzingo: AGN, Mercedes, vol. 4, fol. 323r–323v. Texcoco: Peñafiel, *Colección de documentos,* 7th sec., p. 5. Coatepec: AGN, Mercedes, vol. 4, fol. 153r–153v. Cuauhtitlan (juez de comisión): AGN, Tierras, vol. 13, exp. 4, fols. 297r, 299r, 311r. Otumba: AGN, Mercedes, vol. 3, fols. 25v–26r. Mexico: NCDHM (1892), V, 248. Tacuba: AGN, Mercedes, vol. 84, fols. 27r, 33v.

123. FHT, I, 108–9; II, 363. AGN, Mercedes, vol. 5, fol. 94r; vol. 6, fol. 140v; Indios, vol. 2, fol. 99v. "Relación de Zempoala," pp. 29 ff.

124. For these and other changes, see Appendix III.

125. See Chapter III, note 107.

126. These solutions and other particularities of the corregimiento boundaries are discussed in more detail in Appendix III.

127. Cuevas, *Documentos inéditos,* pp. 246 ff.

128. Bentura Beleña, *Recopilación sumaria,* I, 38 ff.

129. The variety of tasks may be seen in the detailed notices of AGN, Indios and Mercedes.

130. On procedure in tribute collection, see Chapter VIII.

131. García Pimentel, *Descripción,* p. 63.

132. Characteristic criminal records of seventeenth-century Coyoacan are in AGN, Hospital de Jesús, leg. 278, exp. 2, and exp. 7, fols. 3r ff.

133. CDIHIA, I, 20. This was probably an exaggeration. There occur several instances in Valley history in which Indians requested to be transferred from encomienda to crown status. AGI, Justicia, leg. 151, no. 1, sep. pag., fol. 18v; leg. 1029, no. 10. ENE, VI, 209; X, 113. We know of no instance in which crown Indians requested to be transferred to encomienda.

134. BNP, no. 30. Boban, *Documents pour servir,* I, 400–403.

135. The Magariño case is documented in Códice Cuevas, AGI, Mapas (México), leg. 9. The accompanying text is in AGI, Patronato, leg. 181, ramo 21. See "Algunos documentos," pp. 129 ff.

136. In theory, in the seventeenth and eighteenth centuries no corregidor was to leave office until he had undergone a residencia of thirty days. See Bentura Beleña, *Recopilación sumaria,* I, 90. Examples of Valley residencias may be studied in AGI, Escribanía de cámara, leg. 228, exp. 7; leg. 229, exp. 6; leg. 232, exp. 1; leg. 237, exp. 2.

137. E.g., AGI, Escribanía de cámara, leg. 175, exp. 3.

138. AGI, Patronato, leg. 181, ramo 21; Mapas (México), leg. 9.

139. AGI, México, leg. 24, ramo 1. See also on this subject Valderrama, *Cartas,* pp. 62, 205 ff.

140. CDIHE, CIV, 360–62. MNM, Documentos sueltos, ser. 2, leg. 88, no. 5. García and Pereyra, *Documentos inéditos,* VII, 71. AGI, Escribanía de cámara, leg. 232, exp. 1.

141. Puga, *Provisiones,* fol. 176r–176v. Bentura Beleña, *Recopilación sumaria,* I, 43. AGI, México, leg. 748.

142. AGN, Ordenanzas, vol. 1, fol. 84r–84v. CDIHIA, I, 188. ENE, VI, 127. MNM, Documentos sueltos, ser. 2, leg. 88, no. 5.

143. See *Aranzeles de los tribunales.*

144. Bentura Beleña, *Recopilación sumaria,* I, 38.

145. AGN, Clero regular y secular, vol. 103, 2nd pag., fols. 1r–3r.

146. CDIHIA, I, 188. García and Pereyra, *Documentos inéditos,* VII, 71.

147. Bentura Beleña, *Recopilación sumaria,* I, 39–43; 2nd pag., 17–18. *Cedulario americano,* pp. 317–18.

148. BAGN, II, 816. FHT, VI, 317–18. BM, Add. 18,204, fol. 8v.

149. AGN, Civil, vol. 1690, exps. 1, 2, 3.

150. BNM, ms. no. 466, fol. 57r.

151. The guidebook, entitled "Yndize comprehensibo de todos los Goviernos corregimientos y Alcaldias mayores que contiene la Gobernacion del Virreynato de Mexico," is without catalogue number in the manuscript collection of NYPL.

CHAPTER V

1. *Recopilación de leyes,* I, 1 ff. (Lib. I, tít. 1 ff.). Puga, *Provisiones,* fols. 21r, 34r.

2. *Concilio III provincial mexicano,* pp. 20–21. On the baptismal controversy see Mendieta, *Historia,* pp. 269 ff.; Torquemada, *Monarchia indiana,* III, 152 ff.

3. There were great conflicts among the orders, the archbishop of Mexico wrote in 1556, not over which would take the most care in conversion but over which would have the largest number of places and provinces under its control. Montúfar, "Carta del arzobispo," p. 341.

4. On the missionary movement and conversion in sixteenth-century Mexico in general see the classic work of Ricard, *La "conquête spirituelle" du Mexique.* The history of each sixteenth-century convento and convento site is summarized in Kubler, *Mexican Architecture.* An exception to the generalization concerning Franciscan priority is Ecatepec, which was first Dominican and then ceded to the Franciscans.

5. CDIAI, VI, 489. The provincial council of 1585 permitted Indians to become ecclesiastics under particular conditions. See *Concilio III provincial mexicana,* pp. 41–42. A rule of 1697 permitted "indios mestizos" to be clerics. *Disposiciones complementarias,* I, 101–3. See on this subject García Icazbalceta, *Carta a José María Vigil,* p. 12; Ricard, *La "conquête spirituelle" du Mexique,* pp. 273 ff.; Phelan, *The Millennial Kingdom,* pp. 132–33. See also the argument of Ribadeneyra y Barrientos, *Manual compendio,* p. 273.

6. CDIAI, XXVI, 141. CDIU, XXI, 157. *Cartas de Indias,* p. 56. NCDHM (1941), II, 5, 55 ff.

7. All Franciscan monasteries, and perhaps all Dominican and Augustinian monasteries as well, regularly maintained such schools in the sixteenth century, as did the single Jesuit establishment outside the capital, at Tepozotlan. NCDHM (1941), II, 5–6. NCDHM (1886–92), IV, 176. PNE, VI, 64. Torquemada, *Monarchia indiana,* III, 111. Alegre, *Historia de la Compañía de Jesús,* I, 193–94; II, 386–87.

8. This and other educational institutions in the city are discussed in Chapter XIII.

9. The regulations of Santa Fe are published in *Don Vasco de Quiroga*, pp. 243–67. The intellectual comparison between Quiroga and More has been developed particularly by Zavala, *La "Utopia" de Tomás Moro* and *Ideario*.

10. See, in addition to the works cited in the preceding note, Ricard, *La "conquête spirituelle" du Mexique*, pp. 192 ff.; Kubler, *Mexican Architecture*, I, 12–13, 225–26; Phelan, *The Millennial Kingdom*, p. 128; Martin, *Los vagabundos*, pp. 140 ff. For hostile criticism, see AC, III, 41; ENE, III, 84. The foundation was a success, at least in the sense that the community survived through the colonial period. The statement of Grijalva, *Crónica*, fols. 15v ff., that it at one time contained a population of 300,000 appears much exaggerated. López de Velasco, *Geografía y descripción*, p. 194, recorded only 150 families ca. 1570. The community maintained an isolated existence, free from tribute, throughout the seventeenth and eighteenth centuries, and it was regarded as a special town under the direct protection of the king. Only in 1790 after the establishment of the intendancy did secular authority question its tradition of tribute exemption. In 1790 Santa Fe was still called a hospital, and it was governed by one Indian gobernador, one alcalde, one regidor, one alguacil mayor, and three topiles, all elected by Indian voters. The contador of the late eighteenth century did not know if it belonged to Tacuba, Coyoacan, or Michoacan jurisdiction. See AGN, Tierras, vol. 191, exp. 6, fols. 1r ff., 7v ff., 12r. A general impression of the late colonial period falsely assigned it to the Bishopric of Valladolid. See Navarro y Noriega, *Catálogo de los curatos*, pp. 51–52.

11. The conclusion of one Aztec calendrical cycle was noted, but no New Fire ceremony was held, in 1559. See Sahagún, *Historia general*, I, 407.

12. See Mendieta, *Historia*, pp. 107–8, and Sahagún, *Historia general*, I, 129, 628 ff. These are samples from a huge literature.

13. Aztec "character" was far from being wholly committed to those qualities of militarism for which it is famous. Its ethical ideal, in the interpretation of Jacques Soustelle, tended toward pacifism, serenity, and personal humility. Soustelle, "Apuntes sobre la psicología," pp. 497–502.

14. See Lamb, "Religious Conflicts," pp. 526–39. On confession, see the interesting observations of Suárez de Peralta, *Noticias históricas*, pp. 31–32. Modern Indian misunderstandings of Christianity in a Valley town are reported in Madsen, "Christo-Paganism," and Madsen, *The Virgin's Children*.

15. Ruiz de Alarcón, "Tratado." Serna, "Manual de ministros." The latter is also published in CDIHE, CIV, 1–267.

16. Navarro de Vargas, "Padrón," pp. 559 ff. AGN, Civil, vol. 270, exp. 1. Moxó, *Cartas mejicanas*, pp. 215 ff.

17. Motolinía, *History*, pp. 154, 275 ff. See the discussion of Motolinía and the "Golden Age" of the Mexican church in Phelan, *The Millennial Kingdom*, p. 40. The Sahagún quotation is from his Psalmodia Christiana (1583), in García Icazbalceta, *Bibliografía mexicana*, p. 382. See also Sahagún's remarks on the decline of Indian Christianity and the missionary spirit in Sahagún, *Historia general*, II, 244 ff., 247.

18. Thus López de Velasco, *Geografía y descripción*, pp. 194 ff., uses the term doctrina, while Navarro y Noriega, *Catálogo de los curatos*, uses the term curato.

19. The phrase cabecera de doctrina was the common one. Cabeza might be used in the same sense, or in the sense of the capital of a religious province. See, for example, Ojea, *Libro tercero*, p. 1. Usage was not uniform.

20. NCDHM (1941), II, 10–12. AGI, México, leg. 287; Contaduría, leg. 729, fols. 24r ff.

21. Others were Oxtoticpac, Axapusco, and Teocalhueyacan. For the cabeceras de doctrina as of ca. 1570 see Table 7. Tecama, a visita of Augustinian Acolman, was the cabecera of a doctrina with a convento by 1604. García Pimentel, *Descripción*, p. 92. AGN, Congregaciones, vol. 1, fols. 19r, 91v.

22. The cabecera status of these three is documented in NCDHM (1941), III, 4–5; PNE, VI, 167–68, 209.

23. An example is Ecatepec. See the summary of its sixteenth-century history in Kubler, *Mexican Architecture*, II, 458.

24. ENE, XVI, 89–92. AGI, Patronato, leg. 182, ramo 44, fol. 2r; Indiferente, leg. 1529, fols. 205r–206v.

25. García Pimentel, *Descripción*, pp. 92, 95. PNE, III, 28–29, 30. AGI, México, leg. 665, cuad. 2, fol. 98r. ENE, XVI, 91–92.

26. It is obvious that the statement of Cook and Borah, in *The Indian Population of Central Mexico 1531–1610*, p. 12, that "parish boundaries coincided with the political boundaries of the towns," cannot be applied to the Valley of Mexico boundaries discussed above. Cook and Borah recognize small exceptions, and the situation in the Valley of Mexico may have been unusual.

27. A number of visitas were abandoned and their hermitas destroyed in the congregaciones of the late sixteenth and early seventeenth centuries. See AGI, México, leg. 122. The most specific evidence for the Valley of Mexico relates to the area of Tenango. See AGI, México, leg. 665, cuad. 2, fols. 97 ff.

28. NCDHM (1886–92), IV, 11–12, 118–19, 131, 217. CDIAI, IV, 456–57. Zorita, *Historia*, pp. 501–3.

29. In Guadalupe a cleric had charge of five sujetos of Tenochtitlan and Tlatelolco in 1570. See PNE, III, 28–29. The doctrina de clérigos at Tizayuca included a medley of Indian community types, with visitas in several jurisdictions, towns both in encomienda and in the crown, and sujetos of Tepexpan, Tlatelolco, and Tecama. García Pimentel, *Descripción*, pp. 54 ff.

30. García Pimentel, *Descripción*, p. 65. The degrees of justification depend upon cabecera status. To summarize what we have already stated on this point: Tizayuca, Santa Fe, and Guadalupe were originally non-tlatoani communities; Huehuetoca and Zumpango shared the tlatoani of Cuauhtitlan but were understood to be distinct señoríos; Tizayuca, a separate encomienda, had become an undisputed cabecera and was surely beyond argument by 1570; Zumpango's connection with Cuauhtitlan was recalled by the Indian annalist of the Anales de Cuauhtitlan (1570), but Zumpango's cabecera status could hardly be seriously questioned.

31. NCDHM (1941), II, 16.

32. García Pimentel, *Descripción*, pp. 261, 263. PNE, III, 37 ff. The terminology of the report is of special interest. Tizayuca, Tepozotlan, Hueypoxtla, and Huehuetoca were described as cabeceras, though by normal criteria of this period Huehuetoca, lacking a gobernador, remained a sujeto of Cuauhtitlan. The secular clergy admitted the dispute with Cuauhtitlan but supported the Huehuetoca side. See García Pimentel, *Descripción*, pp. 55, 82, 88, 258 ff. The phrase "pueblo por sí" was customarily and in normal usage synonymous with cabecera, and its application to Teoloyuca and Coyotepec represented a presumably deliberate distortion.

33. García Pimentel, *Descripción*, p. 88. Cf. PNE, VI, 28.

34. See the observation of Ciudadreal in CDIHE, LVIII, 233. Vetancurt, *Chronica,* p. 62. On the Chalco dispute see Chimalpahin, *Annales,* pp. 233 ff. By the 1740's Ayapango had been transferred to the nearest doctrina, that of Dominican Amecameca, and the issue was finally resolved by its elevation to parochial status, with a set of its own visitas, by order of 1769. Villa-señor y Sánchez, *Theatro americano,* I, 66–67. BNM, ms. no. 2449, fol. 55r.

35. The sujetos of Otumba were not all undisputed, however. For Atocpan see Vetancurt, *Chronica,* p. 89.

36. See note 24. AGN, Congregaciones, vol. 1, fols. 59v–60r. Zacatepec became a visita of Tezontepec. See Villa-señor y Sánchez, *Theatro americano,* I, 158–59.

37. The map of cabeceras de doctrina and visitas is derived from a variety of seventeenth-century sources. Vetancurt, *Chronica,* gives a systematic listing of late seventeenth-century Franciscan visitas. AGN, Congregaciones, vol. 1, lists a number of others for the early seventeenth century, and *Moderación de doctrinas* gives some for 1623.

38. Royal orders on this subject are dated 1749, 1753, 1757, and 1766, in Bentura Beleña, *Recopilación sumaria,* I, 5th pag., p. 165. See the interesting letter of the viceroy in 1755. *Instrucciones que los vireyes de Nueva España dejaron* (1867), pp. 41–43.

39. The doctrinas (curatos) of the early nineteenth century are listed in Navarro y Noriega, *Catálogo de los curatos,* pp. 13 ff., and in "Noticias de Nueva-España en 1805," pp. 9–16.

40. Chimalpahin, *Annales,* pp. 11–12, 231, 233 ff. AGN, Mercedes, vol. 7, fol. 299r–299v.

41. Torquemada, *Monarchia indiana,* I, 638–39. Zorita, *Historia,* p. 512. Ricard, "Documents pour l'histoire des franciscains," pp. 231–32.

42. NCDHM (1941), I, 86 ff. CDIHE, LVII, 215. Torquemada, *Monarchia indiana,* III, 320 ff. Mendieta, *Historia,* pp. 347 ff. Similar cases of Indian loyalty relating to Cuauhtitlan and Xochimilco may be found in Mendieta, *Historia,* pp. 323 ff., 327 ff.

43. Vetancurt, *Chronica,* p. 142.

44. *Instrucciones que los vireyes de Nueva España dejaron* (1867), p. 42.

45. *Cartas de Indias,* p. 95. CDIAI, II, 82.

46. Montúfar, "Carta del arzobispo," p. 341. Ricard, "Documents pour l'histoire des franciscains," pp. 228 ff. NCDHM (1886–92), IV, 110.

47. NCDHM (1886–92), V, 87. AGI, Indiferente, leg. 1529, fol. 155v. Torquemada, *Monarchia indiana,* III, 280–81.

48. López de Velasco, *Geografía y descripción,* pp. 193 ff. The archbishop of Mexico in an anti-Mendicant letter of 1556 mentioned doctrinas in which two friars ministered to 100,000 persons. Montúfar, "Carta del arzobispo," p. 340.

49. García and Pereyra, *Documentos inéditos,* XV, 225–26. *Moderación de doctrinas, passim.*

50. Numbers of clergymen in the late sixteenth century are recorded in the account of Ponce's travels, in CDIHE, LVII–LVIII. Numbers in the Franciscan conventos as of 1586 are in AGI, México, leg. 287. For numbers of Augustinians in 1573 see AGI, Patronato, leg. 182, ramo 44. The seventeenth-century clergy are documented in AGN, Congregaciones, vol. 1; AGI, México, leg. 326; *Moderación de doctrinas;* and other sources. AGI, Contaduría, legs. 657 to 840, consist of treasury records from the early sixteenth to the middle eighteenth centuries, and through the record of royal payments to non-encomienda clergymen the number in most towns may be easily figured.

For the late colonial clerical population of Mexico City see "Noticias de Nueva España en 1805," p. 8.

51. Montúfar, "Carta del arzobispo," pp. 340–41. NCDHM (1886–92), IV, 4.

52. Compendio histórico del concilio III, I, 69 ff. See also NCDHM (1886–92), IV, 155–56, for rules for friars ca. 1570.

53. García Pimentel, Descripción, pp. 53 ff., 66 ff., 81 ff., 87 ff., 91 ff., 224 ff., 258 ff.

54. E.g., CDIHE, LVII, 501. Cartas de Indias, pp. 196 ff.

55. Proceso inquisitorial, pp. x, 2 ff., 82 ff., et passim. Procesos de indios, pp. 109 ff., 115 ff. AGN, Inquisición, vol. 23, no. 1, fols. 1r ff.; vol. 38 (1), no. 4, fols. 9r ff.

56. ENE, XI, 148 ff.

57. NCDHM (1886–92), IV, 112. For other evidence of beatings, whippings, imprisonment, branding, and additional punishment of Indians by friars, see NCDHM (1886–92), V, 8–9; NCDHM (1941), II, 59; Carreño, Un desconocido cedulario, p. 132; CDIAI, IV, 496; Champlain, "Brief discovrs des choses," pp. 64–65; ENE, XI, 164, 169; AC, II, 68; García Pimentel, Descripción, pp. 62, 93.

58. NCDHM (1886–92), IV, 61, 115–16. AC, II, 68. García and Pereyra, Documentos inéditos, XV, 139–40.

59. NCDHM (1886–92), IV, 110, 114; V, 8–9.

60. García y Pereyra, Documentos inéditos, XV, 139–40. Seventeenth-century examples may be seen in Otumba and Tlalnepantla. FHT, VII, 227–28. AGN, Civil, vol. 270, exp. 1, fols. 93r ff.

61. Sedano, Noticias de México, I, 34. León, "Bibliografía," no. 4, pp. 292–93.

62. AGN, Civil, vol. 1686, exp. 1, fol. 4v.

63. AGN, Clero regular y secular, vol. 201, fols. 3r–6v.

64. E.g., CDIAI, IV, 496, 516. Encomenderos argued that friars forbade Indian service in the encomiendas and that they beat Indians who performed such service. AC, II, 68. Zorita stated that Indian rulers had been strictly obeyed in the pre-conquest period but that by his own time this had diminished since Indians lacked rulers whom they could fear and respect. CDIAI, II, 37, 40.

65. NCDHM (1941), I, 4. See also the comments on this passage in Kubler, Mexican Architecture, I, 157, and Phelan, The Millennial Kingdom, pp. 82 ff.

66. Pérez de Rivas, Corónica y historia religiosa, I, 55–56. Alegre, Historia de la Compañía de Jesús, I, 64–65. Decorme, La obra de los jesuítas, I, 250.

67. Grijalva, Crónica, fol. 50r. Cartas de Indias, p. 170. Chimalpahin, Annales, pp. 11–12.

68. AGN, Mercedes, vol. 5, fols. 3r–3v, 5v–6r, 240r; vol. 7, fol. 318v. NLAC, 1121, fols. 45r ff. NCDHM (1941), II, 5.

69. AGN, Inquisición, vol. 75, no. 12, fols. 55r–64r.

70. Pérez de Rivas and other Jesuit historians present the donation as a voluntary one. See note 66. Our earliest indication of the donation is by Pérez de Rivas, about seventy years after the event. He states that 3,000 workers were given and that the church was built within three months. These figures fit the repartimiento statistics, for 300 workers per week, furnished for ten weeks, would be tantamount to 3,000 workers. It is likely that the workers were not given from Tacuba alone but rather from the Tacuba repartimiento jurisdiction (see Chapter IX). We may be reasonably sure of this, since the orders were issued to the Indian officials of Mexico City, Texcoco, Chalco, and Tacuba, and each of these four was to provide 300 (raised from 200) laborers. See AGN, Mercedes, vol. 5, fols. 3r–3v, 5v–6r, 240r.

71. NCDHM (1886–92), IV, 119–20. García Pimentel, *Descripción*, p. 95.

72. The account is taken from the Títulos de Santa Isabel Tola, published in Peñafiel, *Colección de documentos,* sec. 1, pp. 11–12.

73. CDIAI, IV, 521. AGN, Clero regular y secular, vol. 37, final pag., fols. 17r ff. García Pimentel, *Descripción, passim.* In the middle eighteenth century the Franciscan convento in Tlatelolco received the service of two Indian sacristans, two topiles, two kitchen helpers, two laundresses, and one portero who also cared for the stables. See AGI, México, leg. 727, exp. 1. For the occasional salaries, notably for cantores, see AGN, Indios, vol. 1, fols. 4v–5r, 88v–89v, *et passim.* In Xochimilco the "capitán y maestro de la capilla" and the two alguaciles who aided in weddings each received eight pesos per year in the 1560's. See *Sobre el modo de tributar,* p. 111.

74. See citations in Chapter VIII, note 22. For the Indian attitude here see CDIAI, XIII, 300.

75. Las Casas, *Apologética historia,* p. 368.

76. See the charges against the Augustinians at Acolman in the early seventeenth century. FHT, VI, 114–15.

77. Instances of encomendero payments to clergymen may be seen in AGN, Indios, vol. 2, fols. 91v, 205v, 215v; Mercedes, vol. 6, fols. 2v–3r. An example of a division of payment between encomendero and crown, in Tizayuca, is documented in García Pimentel, *Descripción,* p. 60.

78. AGN, Mercedes, vol. 6, fol. 321r–321v. NLAC, 1121, fols. 168r, 193r. NCDHM (1886–92), IV, 54. ENE, XVI, 89. CDIAI, IV, 454. Salaries of the secular clergy are recorded for the sixteenth century in García Pimentel, *Descripción,* pp. 60, 70, 90–91, 225, 266. As with labor, it was possible to divert some encomienda tribute to the church. See the offer of Alonso de Estrada, reported by Dávila Padilla, *Historia,* p. 44, to provide the Dominicans with fish from Cuitlahuac, Mixquic, Zumpango, and Xaltocan. Félix de Peñafiel, the curate of Tequixquiac in 1569, received a salary of 180 pesos de minas, or approximately 275 pesos de oro común. At four reales per fanega, a normal price for maize in 1569, the royal maize quota was the equivalent of about twenty-five pesos. Hence, although Peñafiel stated that he could not support himself on his salary, and although he justified his tolerance of non-Christian practices accordingly, he was receiving a substantially larger salary than the royal quota granted. See García Pimentel, *Descripción,* p. 70.

79. AGI, Contaduría, leg. 768 (A); leg. 773; leg. 788, ramo 3; México, leg. 326. See *Moderación de doctrinas, passim.*

80. NLAC, 1476, fols. 24r ff.

81. AGN, Congregaciones, vol. 1, fol. 57r.

82. NCDHM (1886–92), IV, 1, 6. ENE, VIII, 70 ff.; X, 18–21; XVI, 62. PNE, III (supl.), 56 ff. Montúfar, "Carta del arzobispo," pp. 345, 349. Cuevas, *Documentos inéditos,* pp. 163 ff.

83. NCDHM (1886–92), IV, 131–32. AGI, Justicia, leg. 158, no. 3.

84. CDIU, XX, 191–93. Puga, *Provisiones,* fol. 149r. NCDHM (1886–92), IV, 16–17, 131. CDIAI, IV, 492. Few properties, of course, moved from Spanish to Indian possession. But some lands became exempt from tithe even in Spanish possession, on the principle that they had been exempt when under Indian possession. This reversed the criterion. See *Compendio histórico del concilio III,* pp. 230–31. Many Indian maize transactions were liable to tithe despite the supposed exemption of native goods. See, for example, AGN, Tierras, vol. 1923, exp. 1, fols. 49v–50v, 78r; Fonseca and Urrutia,

Historia, III, 136 ff., 202. See also for tithe in relation to early tribute payments ENE, XI, 5 ff.; XIV, 116–17; XV, 92–93.

85. See Puga, *Provisiones*, fol. 88v; García and Pereyra, *Documentos inéditos*, XV, 21–24.

86. Lorenzana, *Concilios provinciales*, p. 131. For Huitzilopochco see CDIHIA, I, 178. The practice was probably related to the Indian support of corregidores in civil visitas.

87. This topic is amply documented for a large number of towns. It receives more precise treatment in Chapter VIII.

88. *Cartas de Indias*, p. 170. Chimalpahin, *Annales*, pp. 11–12. Grijalva, *Crónica*, fol. 50r.

89. E.g., Lorenzana, *Concilios provinciales*, pp. 130 ff.

90. CDIAI, IV, 514–15. Montúfar, "Carta del arzobispo," pp. 352–53.

91. The subject is considered in Chapter VIII.

92. Examples of these practices or commentary upon them may be found in AGN, Civil, vol. 270, exp. 1, fols. 93r ff.; *Instrucciones que los vireyes de Nueva España dejaron* (1867), p. 252; NCDHM (1886–92), IV, 131–32.

93. AGN, Clero regular y secular, vol. 39, exp. 2; Civil, vol. 2092, exp. 6, fols. 1r, 3r–4v. Ocaranza, *Capítulos*, I, 293.

94. NCDHM (1886–92), IV, 6.

95. AGI, México, leg. 727, exp. 1. Ocaranza, *Capítulos*, I, 293.

96. NCDHM (1886–92), IV, 215. AC, VIII, 579. Zorita, *Historia*, p. 505. ENE, X, 174–75.

97. CDMNC, rollo 10, exp. 5, fols. 6r ff. Mendieta, *Historia*, pp. 421 ff. Torquemada, *Monarchia indiana*, III, 218. NCDHM (1886–92), IV, 54, 181. NCDHM (1941), I, 180; II, 5. Grijalva, *Crónica*, fol. 17r–17v.

98. Lorenzana, *Concilios provinciales*, pp. 130–32.

99. *Compendio histórico del concilio III*, pp. 72–73.

100. PNE, III, 18.

101. AGN, General de parte, vol. 3, fol. 225r–225v. CDIHE, XXVI, 163–64.

102. BLMM 135, fols. 186v ff. Alegre, *Historia de la Compañía de Jesús*, II, 386–87.

103. Alegre, *Historia de la Compañía de Jesús*, II, 386–87. The Indian statement, however, should not in itself be regarded as proof that the Jesuits were charging no fees.

104. Ocaranza, *Capítulos*, I, 273–74, 292–93. BLMM 135, fols. 249r ff. AGI, México, leg. 727, exp. 1. *Aranzel para todos los curas*, pp. 4–6.

105. *Aranzel para todos los curas*, p. 7. Examples for Otumba, Oxtoticpac, and Axapusco may be found in *Documentos para la historia económica*, V.

106. Ocaranza, *Capítulos*, I, 275. López Sarrelangue, "Los tributos de la parcialidad," pp. 156–57. López Sarrelangue, *Una villa mexicana*, pp. 232 ff. AGI, México, leg. 727, exp. 1. MNM, Colección antigua, 339, refers to the income of a Xochimilco cofradía as tlapohualli. For the translation see Molina, *Vocabulario*, sc. tlapoalli.

107. E.g., BNM, ms. no. 165, fol. 6r. CDMNC, rollo 10, exp. 5, fol. 7r.

108. FHT, VI, 402–3. CDMNC, rollo 10, exp. 5, fols. 1r ff. AGN, General de parte, vol. 2, fol. 212r.

109. FHT, VI, 586. AGN, Tierras, vol. 152 (1), exp. 2; Padrones, vol. 12, fol. 144r–144v.

110. E.g., lands belonging to the Franciscan conventos in Tepepan and Atlapulco are listed in Ocaranza, *Capítulos*, I, 261. Cf. Chevalier, *La formation des grands domaines*, p. 310.

111. AGI, México, leg. 727, exp. 1. Gómez de Cervantes, *La vida económica*, pp. 185–86. CDIAI, VI, 185.

112. The extremes are given in Ocaranza, *Capítulos*, I, 294, with Tlatelolco receiving 4,444 pesos and San Antonio de las Huertas receiving 62 pesos. The "Noticias de Nueva-España en 1805," pp. 9 ff., lists the income of all parishes as of ca. 1800 with higher figures.

113. E.g., in Huitzilopochco before 1569. See García Pimentel, *Descripción*, p. 227.

114. AGN, Clero regular y secular, vol. 16, exp. 1, fol. 49r. The Indian cofradías in Franciscan communities are enumerated in Vetancurt, *Chronica*. There is no systematic listing for other towns.

115. Vetancurt, *Chronica*, pp. 41 ff., 74, 88.

116. In an información of 1749 relating to Santiago Tlatelolco the Franciscans made a special point of the assertion that membership in the cofradías had been free and voluntary and that no one had been compelled to serve as mayordomo. The assertion clearly implies that coercion was not entirely unknown elsewhere. See AGI, México, leg. 727, exp. 1.

117. For the ceremonies of the cofradías of San José in Mexico City see Vetancurt, *Chronica*, pp. 41–42. A mixed cofradía of Spaniards and Indians in the sixteenth century is illustrated in Coatepec. PNE, VI, 64. A mestizo cofradía is exemplified in Coyoacan in the eighteenth century. AHH, leg. 120, exp. 4, fol. 12r. The indios mixtecos maintained a cofradía in the convento of Santo Domingo in the city. See BLMM, 135, fol. 140r.

118. AGN, Clero regular y secular, vol. 103, 9th pag., fol. 1r.

119. The cofradía records are in MNM, Colección antigua, no. 339, fols. 1r ff., 151r ff.

120. AGN, Clero regular y secular, vol. 16, exp. 1, fols. 25r ff.

121. AGN, Clero regular y secular, vol. 16, exp. 1, fol. 41r.

122. AGN, Tierras, vol. 1109, exp. 3, fol. 17r. For another example see AGN, Tierras, vol. 1084, exp. 5, fol. 3r.

123. AGN, Tierras, vol. 1109, exp. 3.

124. AGN, Hospital de Jesús, vol. 120, exp. 4, fol. 7r; Tierras, vol. 1084, exp. 5, fols. 3r ff.; vol. 1518, exp. 1, fols. 24v–25r. *Al severo tribunal*, pp. 81–82. López Sarrelangue, *Una villa mexicana*, pp. 229–30, 236, 239. CDMNC, rollo 10, exp. 5, fols. 23r ff.

125. The Huitzilopochco documentation will be found in AGN, Tierras, vol. 1702, exp. 4.

126. See Carrera Stampa, *Los gremios mexicanos*, p. 88.

127. Gálvez, *Informe general*, p. 38.

128. An interesting case in point is a dispute between Xochimilco Indians and Spaniards during the seventeenth century over the privilege of carrying the Host in the procession of Holy Week. The dispute developed into a conflict between the Indian community as a whole and a cofradía of Spaniards. See CDMNC, rollo 10, exp. 5, fols. 9r ff.

129. Torquemada, *Monarchia indiana*, III, 220 ff. For particular descriptions of

fiestas see CDIHE, LVII–LVIII, *passim*; Vetancurt, *Chronica*, *passim*. See also Garibay K., "Un cuadro real," p. 223, and Madsen, "Christo-Paganism," pp. 134–35.

130. García Pimentel, *Descripción*, p. 64. Zorita, *Historia*, p. 408.

131. Paz, "Todos Santos," pp. 22–27.

132. Colonial examples in Ayotzingo, Toltitlan, Tlatelolco, Tulantongo, San José,
and other locations are mentioned. Villa-señor y Sánchez, *Theatro americano*, I, 67,
77, 157. Vetancurt, *Chronica*, pp. 52, 67. "Unos anales coloniales de Tlatelolco, 1519–
1633," p. 185. León, "Bibliografía," no. 4, p. 78. Castro Santa-Anna, *Diario*, I, 68–69.
BNM, ms. no. 20058/18, fol. 2r. Cabrera y Quintero, *Escudo de armas*, pp. 124 ff.

133. Oroz, Mendieta, and Suárez, *Relación*, pp. 123 ff. Chimalpahin, *Annales*, pp.
223–24, 228, 230, 300–301. Mendieta, *Historia*, pp. 594 ff. Motolinía, *History*, pp. 185
ff. CDIHE, LVIII, 234–35. Torquemada, *Monarchia indiana*, III, 392 ff. Dávila Padilla, *Historia*, pp. 705–6. Mendizábal, "El santuario," pp. 521–27.

134. Franco, *Segunda parte*, pp. 556 ff. Carreño, *Fr. Domingo de Betanzos*, pp.
53, 233–34.

135. CDIHE, LVII, 107. Sahagún, *Historia general*, II, 481.

136. Cuevas, *Album histórico guadalupano*, is the fullest effort to document the
apparition in 1531. Failure to prove the 1531 date, of course, should not be construed
as proof that the date was not 1531.

137. *Cartas de Indias*, p. 310. *Información que el arzobispo de México Don Fray
Alonso de Montúfar mandó*, *passim*.

138. *Información que el arzobispo de México Don Fray Alonso de Montúfar mandó*,
pp. 5, 15, 36, 113.

139. AC, XVI, 422. Cabrera y Quintero, *Escudo de armas*, p. 129. León, "Bibliografía," no. 4, p. 63. Grijalva, *Crónica*, fols. 81v ff. Fernández del Castillo, "Don Pelayo
y la virgen," pp. 461 ff.

140. The literature on this subject is immense. For bibliography, see Vera, *Tesoro
guadalupano*; Montejano y Aguiñaga, *Notas para una bibliografía guadalupana*;
Compendio histórico del concilio III, III, 191 ff. Testimonies and other evidence relating to authenticity may be found in Vera, *Informaciones*; Cuevas, *Album histórico
guadalupano*; Cabrera y Quintero, *Escudo de armas*, pp. 321 ff. A remarkably full
eighteenth-century account is Florencia, *La estrella del norte*. The first systematic
criticism occurs in García Icazbalceta, *Carta acerca del origen*. Many historical notices
appear in seventeenth- and eighteenth-century sources. A complete history remains to
be written.

141. Examples of Indian wills illustrating this may be consulted in AGN, Hospital
de Jesús, vol. 120, exp. 4, fols. 7r, 25r; vol. 333, exp. 1, fols. 10v–11v, 14r–14v; Tierras,
vol. 2, exp. 6, fols. 49r ff.; vol. 994, 5th pag., fols. 37r ff. BAGN, XXV, 67–69.

142. An example is the false history of the Chapultepec church building, purportedly
of 1521–23, made up of partial records and erroneous dates. See BNP, no. 277. The similarity with the migration myths, discussed above, and other kinds of false record,
discussed later, is obvious.

143. Cabrera y Quintero, *Escudo de armas*, p. 150.

144. Navarro de Vargas, "Padrón," p. 559.

145. AGN, Clero regular y secular, vol. 103, 9th pag., fols. 2r ff. Gómez, *Diario
curioso*, pp. 225–26.

146. The most detailed studies of this subject in the modern Valley are by William
Madsen. See again his "Christo-Paganism" and *The Virgin's Children*.

CHAPTER VI

1. Ecclesiastical counts and tribute counts might actually depend upon the same data. See, for example, Bentura Beleña, *Recopilación sumaria*, I, 62.

2. AGI, México, leg. 26, ramo 1; leg. 323. CDIAI, IV, 448; VI, 166. CDIHE, XXI, 548. AC, VI, 493.

3. AGN, Hospital de Jesús, leg. 329, exp. 2, fols. 2r ff. García Pimentel, *Descripción*, p. 85.

4. BNM, ms. no. 451, fols. 291v–292r. BNP, no. 145. NYPL, Rich, no. 39. FHT, VII, 286–87. In two nearby towns a difference of one-half real in tribute might mean that one decreased in population while the other increased. See the testimony in *Sobre el modo de tributar*, p. 45.

5. An estimate of the year 1771 supposed a total tributary population of 600,000 while the tributary census recorded 397,900. See Gálvez, *Informe general*, p. 87. The Revillagigedo census was believed to be low by one-seventh. See "Noticias de Nueva-España en 1805," p. 4. See also Humboldt, *Political Essay*, I, 97–99, on this subject.

6. CDIAI, II, 104–5; VI, 183. NCDHM (1886–92), IV, 213. Bentura Beleña, *Recopilación sumaria*, I, 2nd pag., 18–19. PNE, VI, 29. Navarro de Vargas, "Padrón," pp. 557 ff. *Advertimientos generales*, p. 24. Alegre, *Historia de la Compañía de Jesús*, II, 181. *Memoria histórica . . . del desagüe*, I, 132. Alzate, *Gacetas de literatura*, II, 51–52. The refinements of the conception of divine punishment as the cause of population decline are treated in Phelan, *The Millennial Kingdom*, pp. 88 ff.

7. For examples see FHT, I, 91–92; ENE, X, 59; Alegre, *Historia de la Compañía de Jesús*, I, 445; AGN, Mercedes, vol. 7, fols. 276v, 287v–288r, 305r–305v; Padrones, vol. 29, fol. 3r–3v.

8. AC, XXXI, 343; XLIII–XLVII (2), 86; LI–LIII, 52. Guijo, *Diario*, p. 8. Alzate, *Gacetas de literatura*, II, 121–23. Chimalpahin, *Annales*, p. 292. The pattern was far from uniform, however. Dávila Padilla, *Historia*, p. 638, states that the epidemic of 1576 began in the spring and continued through the summer and beyond.

9. Sticker, "Die Einschleppung Europäischer Krankheiten." Cook, "The Incidence and Significance of Disease," pp. 320 ff.

10. In the plague of 1576 the viceroy distributed instructions on methods of cure to all affected towns, the principal method being prompt bleeding. See *Cartas de Indias*, p. 331. NCDHM (1941), III, 52. In the epidemic of 1595 one of the foremost needs was for barberos to perform bleedings. See AC, XII, 235. Inoculation was used in the epidemic of 1797. See Cook, "The Smallpox Epidemic of 1797," pp. 937–69. The eighteenth-century epidemics are the subject of an important study, soon to be published, by Donald B. Cooper.

11. The two lists are published in ENE, IX, 2 ff., and BAGN, XI, 195 ff. Cf. Cook and Simpson, *The Population of Central Mexico*, pp. 4–5.

12. AGI, Indiferente, leg. 1529, fols. 205r–206v. ENE, XVI, 88–93. PNE, III, 32–33, 82–83.

13. Compare the López de Velasco figures of Table 7, for example, with 2,762 for Tlalnepantla (PNE, III, 31–32) and 2,157 for Ecatepec (PNE, III, 29–31).

14. Thus there existed no count of the Otomi population of Tepozotlan in López de Velasco's time. See García Pimentel, *Descripción*, p. 85.

15. Table 10 shows a total of 117,270, without Hueypoxtla, Tizayuca, and Santa Fe. López de Velasco assigns 7,230 to these three, not all of whom, however, would fall within the Valley of Mexico as we define it. His figure for Mexico City may be com-

pared with Figure 17. Total population may be computed by the factor 2.8, the factor determined by Borah and Cook, *The Population of Central Mexico in 1548*. We use the López de Velasco figures in the above computation because these alone include all jurisdictions. Note, however, that the doctrinas were still in process of formation. The danger in using mixed sources without identifying the jurisdictions is illustrated in Cook and Simpson, *The Population of Central Mexico*, pp. 50–59. They use figures for the entire "province" of Texcoco rather than for the city of Texcoco alone. They confuse Coatitlan and Cuauhtitlan, and in effect they list Milpa Alta twice, since Milpa Alta was a sujeto of Xochimilco and its figures are separable from Xochimilco figures only if one computes population by ecclesiastical jurisdiction. My intention in making these remarks is to clarify a point and not to condemn the important pioneering work of Cook and Simpson.

16. CDIAI, II, 104; XIII, 298. NCDHM (1941), I, 39. Valderrama, *Cartas*, pp. 148, 269.

17. Cook and Simpson, *The Population of Central Mexico*, p. 38, suppose a loss of approximately sixty per cent from the conquest to 1565. Borah and Cook show that this depends upon a misunderstanding of the Suma de Visitas and conclude that the highland population declined by about eighty per cent between 1532 and 1568. Borah and Cook, *The Population of Central Mexico in 1548*. Cook and Borah, *The Indian Population of Central Mexico 1531–1610*, p. 52.

18. For the highland area as a whole the Cook-Borah calculations yield a decline of about twenty-seven per cent from 1568 to 1580. Cook and Borah, *The Indian Population of Central Mexico 1531–1610*, p. 52.

19. Gómez de Cervantes, *La vida económica*, p. 137. Torquemada, *Monarchia indiana*, I, 307.

20. The figures relate respectively to Chimalhuacan, Chicoloapa, and Tizayuca. PNE, VI, 67, 80–81. CDIAI, IX, 208.

21. The special tribute called Servicio Real is particularly useful for such conversion, for unlike most other assessments it was uniform for all areas and separately recorded. It was a tax of four reales per tributary per year. Hence twice the number of pesos assessed in Servicio Real gives the number of tributaries in the tribute record of any town.

22. The seventeeth-century materials begin with AGI, Contaduría, leg. 699, and continue for about 100 legajos.

23. A small sample cannot resolve the general question of the date of lowest population, but it can indicate that towns differed considerably from one another. On the basis of the half-real paid for the Cathedral, José Miranda favors the 1620's as the period of lowest population for the whole colony. See Miranda, "La población indígena," p. 185. Alzate, who reported a low point in the epidemic of the 1730's, was wholly mistaken or was speaking only of a period of his own recent past. Alzate, *Gacetas de literatura*, II, 273.

24. The latter were Coyoacan and Tacubaya with their sujetos. In the course of time San Agustín de las Cuevas and Cuajimalpa became cabeceras, with population statistics separately recorded. The figures for all four towns are uniformly included in the Coyoacan jurisdiction graph in Figure 3.

25. Borah and Cook, *The Population of Central Mexico in 1548*, pp. 75 ff., 102. The change in tributary status in the sixteenth century is well documented for the

Valley of Mexico. But we know of no Valley document on this subject comparable to the great text relating to Huejotzingo, in BNP, no. 287.

26. Mexico City yields a ratio of 1 to 3.5 between tributaries and total Indian population in 1800. The various ratios are capable of almost limitless computation and refinement in the great amount of colonial data on these subjects. Our ratios for the late eighteenth century are calculated from the data of AGN, Tributos, vol. 43, final exp., fol. 4r–4v, the results for the Valley of Mexico intendancies being the following factors: Chalco, 4.06; Citlaltepec, 4.79; Coatepec, 4.37; Coyoacan, 4.19; Cuauhtitlan, 4.70; Ecatepec, 4.97; Mexicalzingo, 4.54; Mexico, 3.55; Otumba, 5.03; Tacuba, 5.11; Teotihuacan, 5.79; Texcoco, 4.32; Xochimilco, 4.34. These factors are based on tributary counts made after the introduction of the intendancies, but with the pre-intendancy definition of "tributary." They are thus directly comparable with the 2.8 factor of the late sixteenth century. The dates of the counts range from 1797 to 1803.

27. The total population of the Valley in 1808 was recorded at ca. 400,000. BNP, no. 205, fol. 3r. The difference of 125,000 is to be attributed to the non-Indian population, more than half of which was located in Mexico City. See Humboldt, *Political Essay*, I, 254.

28. Sample figures for the sixteenth century are to be found in García Pimentel, *Descripción*. Interesting figures for the Xochimilco jurisdiction in the eighteenth century are in AGN, Padrones, vol. 29, fol. 3r. In Mexico City in the late eighteenth century the ratio of Indian men to Indian women was 100 : 128. Humboldt, *Political Essay*, I, 254.

29. In Mexico as a whole in the late nineteenth century one-half of the infants born alive failed to survive their first year. See the discussion in González Navarro, *La vida social*, pp. 47 ff. In Teotihuacan in the early twentieth century three-quarters of the deaths occurred in infancy. See Gamio, *La población del valle de Teotihuacan*, I (1), xxiv.

30. See the remarks of Clavigero on longevity. Clavigero, *Historia antigua*, IV, 66. Instances of Indians aged over 100 and up to 132 may be found in Vera, *Informaciones*, pp. 23, 29, and *Gazetas de México, compendio de noticias*, I, 44, 291; VII, 17. But in Chimalhuacan in the late sixteenth century the oldest persons were said to be aged 45 to 50. PNE, VI, 76.

31. Humboldt, *Political Essay*, I, 256–57. BNP, no. 205, fol. 2v.

32. This is clear wherever the record provides data on numbers of Indians and numbers of mestizos. See lists for the Ecatepec jurisdiction in BN, ms. no. 451, fols. 294r ff., and for the Xochimilco jurisdiction in AGN, Padrones, vol. 29, fol. 3r. The city of Texcoco had 571 Indian families and 541 non-Indian families in 1786. AGN, Padrones, vol. 43, fol. 6v.

33. Occasional marriages are recorded between Indian men and Spanish women. See AGN, Civil, vol. 1271, exp. 4; Indios, vol. 10, cuad. 3, fols. 87v–88r. Even eighteenth-century records reveal few formal marriages between Indians and non-Indians. Thus the Ecatepec jurisdiction of 1781 shows 1,848 Indian men married to Indian women and only 95 Indian men married to "otras castas." See BNM, ms. no. 451, fol. 297r–297v.

34. The terms pardo and coyote had other ethnic meanings also. Zambo does not appear to have been widely used in the Valley of Mexico. On the refinements of terminology in word lists and in the genre scenes, see Humboldt, *Political Essay*, I, 243

ff.; "Cuadros de mestizos del Museo de México," pp. 237–48; León, *Las castas del México colonial*; Torres Quintero, *México hacia el fin del virreinato*, pp. 11 ff.; Blanchard, "Les tableaux de métissage," pp. 59–66; Blanchard, "Encore sur les tableaux de métissage," pp. 37–60; Aguirre Beltrán, *La población negra*, pp. 175 ff.; Rosenblat, *La población indígena*, pp. 277–84, 285–87.

35. The balcarrotas were the long locks worn by Indians on either side of the face. Indians in the city, and occasionally elsewhere, did wear short hair. See Ojea, *Libro tercero*, p. 8, and PNE, VI, 56. In pre-conquest times it was considered ignominious to wear short hair. ENE, XV, 65. UT, TxU-A, pp. 410–14. Clavigero, *Historia antigua*, II, 362. For the wearing of Indian clothing by mestizos, mulattoes, and Negroes, see AGN, Ordenanzas, vol. 1, fol. 75r.

36. BNM, ms. no. 15, fol. 18v.

37. AGN, Mercedes, vol. 2, fol. 268v; vol. 4, fol. 186r–186v.

38. Evidence for Tlatelolco, Coyoacan, Cuitlahuac, Tacubaya, and other towns in the environs of the city may be found in AGN, Mercedes, vol. 3, fols. 105r, 218r–218v, 227v, 285v–286r; vol. 5, fols. 76v–77r; vol. 6, fols. 176v–177r, 182v–183r, 184r–184v; vol. 7, fols. 305v–306r; General de parte, vol. 1, fol. 241r; vol. 2, fol. 69r. See also NLAC, 1121, fol. 34r.

39. E.g., AGI, Justicia, leg. 159, no. 1. CDIHIA, I, 187. ENE, VI, 118. NCDHM (1886–92), IV, 133. The Marqués del Valle letter of 1563 speaks of the evil mestizos and mulattoes, who "cover the land." CDIAI, IV, 459. Later concentration points included especially the key locations on the caminos reales, such as Cuauhtitlan. See AGN, Padrones, vol. 4, fol. 239v. For regulations concerning mestizos, mulattoes, and Negroes see Martin, *Los vagabundos*, pp. 91 ff.

40. Thus in the 1540's and the 1550's Indian alcaldes and alguaciles in Mexico City and in the towns were authorized to apprehend Negro, mulatto, and mestizo intruders and to deliver them to the audiencia jail or to other Spanish custody. See AGN, Mercedes, vol. 3, fol. 105r; vol. 4, fol. 186r–186v; vol. 5, fols. 76v–77r. Spanish government here could not quite countenance the arrest of Spaniards by Indians, but Indian communities were invited to take a prenda in instances of comparable intrusion by whites and to summon Spanish alguaciles del campo. See AGN, Mercedes, vol. 5, fols. 76v–77r.

41. AGN, Mercedes, vol. 2, fols. 90v–91r.

42. Encinas, *Cedulario*, IV, 341. *Recopilación de leyes*, II, 212 (Lib. I, tít. 3, leyes 21–23).

43. Viceroy Enríquez's comments on this subject are in CDIHE, XXVI, 378. For later rules see AGN, Indios, vol. 6 (1), fols. 277v, 303r. The caciques' remarks are published in NCDHM (1886–92), IV, 132.

44. AGN, Mercedes, vol. 4, fols. 92r, 93v. It appears likely that the mesones or hospicios maintained by Indian communities in the sixteenth and early seventeenth centuries for lodging white travelers were in some degree responses to the demands for ethnic separation. These began as Indian enterprises, but they came to be auctioned out or rented to Spaniards (e.g., in Xochimilco, Amecameca, and Tenango. See *Sobre el modo de tributar*, pp. 108, 114; BAGN, ser. 2, II, 19; AGI, México, leg. 665, cuad. 2, fol. 97v). Towns such as Tlatelolco, Cuauhtitlan, and Texcoco had such hospicios. They were still extant but no longer used for the lodging of white travelers in the late seventeenth century. See BAGN, IX, 25.

45. *Cedulario americano*, pp. 319–22.

46. A similar attempt to establish civil schools in the late sixteenth century failed because no provision was made for financing. The viceroy in 1598 commented that salaries of teachers were small, that almost all applicants for teaching posts were mestizos and Negroes, and that they exploited rather than taught the students. AGI, México, leg. 24, ramo 1. *Recopilación de leyes*, II, 193 (Lib. VI, tít. 1, ley 18). The law of 1691 for the establishment of schools and the employment of maestros in the Spanish language is published in *Cedulario americano*, pp. 444–46. But the principal foundations were in the eighteenth century. See AGI, México, leg. 1238, no. 120.

47. Royal and viceregal orders, municipal ordinances, and miscellaneous Spanish commentary from the sixteenth century on made repeated reference to the program of Spanish speech. García and Pereyra, *Documentos inéditos*, XV, 106–8. Encinas, *Cedulario*, IV, 339. AC, VII, 11–12. *Disposiciones complementarias*, I, 101–3. Lorenzana, *Cartas pastorales*, pp. 91–100, 143–52. *La administración de D. Frey Antonio María de Bucareli*, I, 177 ff. AGI, México, leg. 24, ramo 1. BNM, ms. no. 437, fol. 463r. General data on the policy are provided by Edmundo O'Gorman in BAGN, XVII, 163–71.

48. See, for example, AGN, General de parte, vol. 1, fols. 164r, 196r–196v, 216v.

49. See examples in AGN, Clero regular y secular, vol. 103, 10th pag., fol. 6r; Hospital de Jesús, vol. 120, exp. 6, fol. 2r; vol. 333, exp. 1, fol. 6r. AA, Tierras y ejidos, vol. 2, no. 4066, exp. 26, fols. 19v ff.

50. AGN, Clero regular y secular, vol. 201, 1st pag., fols. 2v ff.

51. AGN, Hospital de Jesús, vol. 120, exp. 6, fol. 2r; vol. 333, exp. 1, fol. 6r. AGI, México, leg. 66r, sep. pag., fols. 3v ff. BAGN, IX, 12.

52. A good example from Tecama appears in AGI, Justicia, leg. 159, no. 1.

53. AHH, Tributos, leg. 225, exp. 29.

54. See statements connecting Indian class status and literacy, e.g., in NCDHM (1886–92), IV, 176, and Díaz del Castillo, *Historia verdadera*, II, 559.

55. AGN, Mercedes, vol. 8, fol. 95v. BNM, ms. no. 439, fol. 464v. BAGN, X, 235–36. Puga, *Provisiones*, fols. 159v–160v. *Gazetas de México, compendio de noticias*, I, 414–15. Studies of Indian vagabondage are Martin, *Los vagabundos*, pp. 125 ff., and Zavala, "La libertad de movimiento," pp. 103–63.

56. See, for example, AHH, Tributos, legs. 224–25.

57. CDIAI, VI, 505–6. *Recopilación de leyes*, II, 192 (Lib. VI, tít. 1, ley 12). AGN, General de parte, vol. 1, fol. 124v; Indios, vol. 17, fols. 234v–235r; Mercedes, vol. 7, fols. 40v–41r, 292v–293r.

58. Motolinía, *Memoriales*, pp. 313–14. CDIAI, II, 50. Las Casas, *Apologética historia*, p. 559. PNE, VI, 29. Durán, *Historia*, II, 226. Torquemada, *Monarchia indiana*, I, 166; II, 549–50. Sahagún, *Historia general*, I, 324; II, 242. For an example of drunkenness in pre-conquest ceremony see *Codex Magliabecchiano*, fol. 48v. For various pre-conquest practices see Martín del Campo, "El pulque," pp. 5–23, and Gonçalves de Lima, *El maguey y el pulque*.

59. *Compendio histórico del concilio III*, II, 70. Suárez de Peralta, *Noticias históricas*, p. 20. See also NCDHM (1886–92), IV, 247. *Instrucciones que los vireyes de Nueva España dejaron* (1867), pp. 8–9, 117. Motolinía, *History*, p. 45. AC, V, 25.

60. García Pimentel, *Descripción*, p. 64 *et passim*.

61. Encinas, *Cedulario*, IV, 349. AC, IV, 134. Bentura Beleña, *Recopilación sumaria*, I, 2nd pag., 5. *Recopilación de leyes*, II, 197–98 (Lib. VI, tít. 1, ley 37). In 1539 drunken

Indians were to be punished with 100 public lashings for the first offense. See Carreño, *Un desconocido cedulario*, p. 133.

62. Guijo, *Diario*, p. 541. Sales were again forbidden in the city following the uprising of 1692. AGI, Patronato, leg. 226, ramo 17, fols. 2r ff. See also Robles, *Diario*, II, 257, 264–65.

63. Zorita acutely noted that Indians became drunkards at the time when caciques lost power. See CDIAI, II, 51.

64. An apparent justification for some leniency in the prohibitions was the continued medicinal use of pulque. See, for example, *Compendio histórico del concilio III*, II, 69.

65. See the statement of Pomar in NCDHM (1941), III, 28. The personal effects of an Indian leader in Coatepec in 1537 included two Indian balls. *Procesos de indios*, p. 38.

66. See Cabrera y Quintero, *Escudo de armas*, pp. 76–77. Ocaranza, *Capítulos*, pp. 265–69. Spanish authority adopted a most ambivalent attitude toward the volador. Dances and a volador ceremony were permitted in 1571 on the celebration of the fiftieth anniversary of the conquest. The city's Spanish cabildo ordered a volador ceremony for a viceregal reception in 1595. Orozco y Berra, *Historia de la dominación*, II, 258. AC, XII, 223. In 1597, dances and Indian drum music were permitted during the daytime, but the volador was prohibited. See AGI, México, leg. 24, ramo 1. Durán, *Historia*, II, 225 ff., has an interesting section on dances, including the volador. A volador is recorded in Xochimilco in 1591. AGN, Indios, vol. 5, fol. 207r–207v. Accidents in volador ceremonies are recorded, e.g., in 1611 and 1644. See Franco, *Segunda parte*, p. 339, and Rosa y Saldívar, "Un inventario," p. 258. On the volador in general, see Tudela, "El 'volador' mejicano," and Larsen, "Notes on the Volador."

67. AGN, Civil, vol. 194, exp. 3, fols. 1r–2r.

68. Indian dances were frequently required by Spanish authorities in order to provide an exotic or colorful character in Spanish ceremonies. See, for example, AC, XXXII–XXXIII, 447. Commentaries on Indian dances, from various points of view, are contained in Cervantes de Salazar, *Crónica*, pp. 38–39; Motolinía, *Memoriales*, pp. 339 ff.; Lorenzana, *Concilios provinciales*, pp. 146–47; AGN, Indios, vol. 6 (1), fol. 116v; Hospital de Jesús, vol. 333, exp. 1, fol. 14r–14v.

69. Lorenzana, *Concilios provinciales*, p. 147. We do not know to what extent the prohibition was effective.

70. Pomar comments on Indian incest rules in NCDHM (1941), III, 26. A cacique's shift from polygamy to monogamy in the early period is recorded in Chimalpahin, *Annales*, pp. 212–14. See also Motolinía, *Memoriales*, pp. 123 ff.

71. See ENE, VII, 297; XI, 161; Chimalpahin, *Annales*, pp. 261–62; AGN, Mercedes, vol. 4, fols. 163r–163v, 321r–321v.

72. A statement relating to Chicoloapa in PNE, VI, 84, observes that Indians in the pre-conquest period did not marry until the ages of 25 (women) and 30 (men). The implication might be that in 1579, when this statement was made, the ages at marriage were lower. A contrary assertion is to be found in Encinas, *Cedulario*, IV, 322, and *Recopilación de leyes*, II, 226 (Lib. VI, tít. 5, ley 7), that pre-conquest Indians married at the age of 12 and that in the colony they were postponing marriage until the ages of 25 and 30 in order to avoid tribute payment. A royal law of 1581 asserted that encomenderos were compelling early marriages in order to increase tributes. See *Recopilación de leyes*, II, 190 (Lib. VI, tít. 1, ley 3). It should be noted that the contador

general in 1814 computed the number of married persons under age 16 to be 16.27 per thousand in New Spain and only 1.23 per thousand in Spain, and that he attributed this difference in part to Indian custom. See Navarro y Noriega, "Memoria sobre la población," p. 289.

73. CDIAI, II, 124.

74. The subject is treated by Zorita, in CDIAI, II, 52 ff.; Las Casas, *Apologética historia*, pp. 572 ff.; Part III of *Codex Mendoza*; and a number of other sources.

75. Manufacture of adobes by women is documented in 1561 in AGN, Tierras, vol. 1 (1), fol. 6r. Gómez de Cervantes reported on his experience in Indian court cases, that Indian men brought their women to the trials to answer questions, and that as a judge he had asked an Indian man his name, only to have the wife answer. Gómez de Cervantes, *La vida económica*, p. 135.

76. PNE, VI, 48.

77. E.g., AH, Bautismos de indios del año de 1590. Examples from AH are reproduced in González, "¡ Huehuetoca," pp. 183 ff.

78. AGN, Vínculos, vol. 279, exp. 1, fol. 10r.

79. AGN, Indios, vol. 1, fol. 16r–16v, *et passim*. The territorial unit, the cult and temple, the control over lands, the craft specialization, and the tribute and labor organization were all characteristic of the pre-conquest calpulli in its pre-conquest form. For various interpretations of the pre-conquest calpulli see Bandelier, "On the Social Organization," pp. 583 ff.; Moreno, *La organización política y social,* pp. 45 ff.; Monzón, *El calpulli*; Katz, *Die sozialökonomischen Verhaltnisse*, pp. 107 ff. Bandelier's views are now for the most part discredited.

80. AGN, General de parte, vol. 2, fols. 37v, 165r–165v, 282r–282v.

81. E.g., AGN, Civil, vol. 1344, fol. 15r–15v.

82. CDIAI, II, 31. The relation of the calpulli to endogamy and exogamy in marriage is currently being studied by Pedro Carrasco, whose detailed analysis of the marriage records of Chiauhtla, near Texcoco, has recently been published. See Carrasco, "El barrio y la regulación del matrimonio."

83. Rentero and terrazguero are Spanish terms, referring to attributes of serfdom. Mayeque is presumably a derivative plural of the Nahuatl *maitl,* hand, and it is related to *tlalmaitl,* farmhand. Molina, *Vocabulario,* sc. tlalmaitl, defines tlalmaitl as labrador or gañán. Zorita (CDIAI, II, 95) and others use Spanish plurals in the form mayeques and tlalmaites. Ramírez Cabañas, "Los macehuales," pp. 122–23, observes how infrequently the term mayeque occurs in sixteenth-century texts.

84. Motolinía, *Memoriales,* pp. 108, 319–20, 324.

85. E.g., Vasco de Quiroga, in CDIAI, X, 389 ff.

86. CDIAI, XLI, 110.

87. Díaz del Castillo, *Historia verdadera,* I, 321. Sahagún, *Historia general,* I, 56. Durán, *Historia,* II, 219 ff. Ixtlilxochitl, *Historia,* p. 188. Ixtlilxochitl, *Relaciones,* pp. 256–57. CDIAI, X, 389 ff.; XIII, 57 ff. Torquemada, *Monarchia indiana,* I, 231; II, 563 ff. *Don Vasco de Quiroga,* pp. 298–99. For Indian slavery in general see Bosch García, *La esclavitud prehispánica*; Soustelle, *La vie quotidienne,* pp. 100 ff.

88. Icaza, "Miscelánea histórica," p. 50. CDIAI, VI, 509. ENE, IV, 28.

89. ENE, IV, 28; VI, 47–49, 123–24; VIII, 145–46, 182–84; XVI, 58.

90. Motolinía, *History,* pp. 144–45. Motolinía, *Memoriales,* p. 108. CDIHIA, I, 219. BAGN, VI, 192.

91. Tribute is the subject of a separate chapter of this book. We may point out here,

however, that the exemption indicates Spanish dependence upon Indian systems of tribute collection through the middle sixteenth century.

92. On the delivery of non-slaves as slaves to Spaniards, see Motolinía, *History*, p. 42; ENE, XVI, 60; CDIAI, XIII, 55–61. For labor, see Chapter IX.

93. CDIHIA, I, 172, 177. ENE, VI, 119. AGI, Justicia, leg. 151, no. 1, fols. 70v ff. There are some errors in the original computations and we have adjusted the raw data in standard ways. The changes are minor.

94. FHT, III, 72. The class had disappeared in Hueypoxtla by 1579. See García Pimentel, *Descripción*, p. 89.

95. CDIAI, II, 31. Indians sometimes used the term tlatoani in reference to ranking Spaniards (e.g., Chimalpahin, *Annales*, pp. 225, 231), and Spaniards sometimes, but rarely, used the term cabeza for cacique (e.g., AGN, Indios, vol. 3, fol. 183r).

96. The literature contains a large documentation on this subject. See CDIAI, II, 24–25; Durán, *Historia*, I, 97 ff.; Las Casas, *Apologética historia*, pp. 173 ff.; López de Gómara, *Historia*, II, 227 ff. See also Alcocer, *Apuntes*, pp. 73 ff., and Soustelle, *La vie quotidienne*, pp. 64 ff.

97. See Chapter VII, notes 11, 30, and 37.

98. Numerous notices relate to Indian voyaging. Ternaux Compans, *Voyages, relations et mémoires*, VIII, 262–63; XVI, 87–88. *Anales de Tlatelolco*, pp. 10–12. Herrera, *Historia general*, II (Dec. III), 287. CDIU, X, 118. For prohibitions see *Recopilación de leyes*, II, 192–93 (Lib. VI, tít. 1, ley 16).

99. AGN, Mercedes, vol. 4, fol. 215v; vol. 5, fol. 63v; General de parte, vol. 1, fols. 81v, 224v, 226v.

100. Cortés, *Cartas*, II, 108–9. Alcocer, *Apuntes*, pp. 77–78. CDIAI, II, 201–2.

101. PNE, VI, 62, 78. MNM, Colección antigua, T2-57, fol. 9v. AGN, Hospital de Jesús, vol. 333, exp. 1, fols. 10v–11v, 14r–14v, 25r–25v.

102. AGN, Indios, vol. 3, fol. 63r; vol. 50, fol. 17v; Congregaciones, vol. 1, fols. 8v–9r, 86v.

103. CDMNC, rollo 10, exp. 5, fols. 4r ff. Lists of possessions of the early sixteenth century may be compared with lists and wills of the seventeenth and eighteenth centuries. *Procesos de indios*, pp. 38, 84. AGN, Tierras, vol. 2, exp. 6, fols. 47r ff.; vol. 994, 5th pag., fols. 37r ff.; 81v, 102r ff.; Hospital de Jesús, vol. 333, exp. 1, fols. 10v ff., 25r–25v. BNM, ms. no. 165, fols. 2r ff., 10r–10v. MNM, Colección antigua, T2-57, fols. 9r–10v. The will of Antonio Vejarano, the informant of Sahagún, is in MNM, Colección antigua, T2-57, fols. 11r–14r.

104. *Procesos de indios*, p. 99. Chimalpahin, *Annales, passim*.

105. See also Chimalpahin's statements of ancestry, e.g., in *Annales*, pp. 294 ff. Mapa Reinisch (BNP, no. 99) illustrates the care with which Indians kept genealogical records.

106. CDIAI, IV, 449. Ixtlilxochitl, *Relaciones*, p. 445.

107. García and Pereyra, *Documentos inéditos*, XV, 123. ENE, VII, 297. Ternaux Compans, *Voyages, relations et mémoires*, VIII 257–58. CDIAI, IV, 450. Valderrama, *Cartas*, p. 137, comments on 300 supposed principales in two cabeceras of Chalco province. After examination it was discovered that about thirty of these were legitimate principales.

108. See examples in Gibson, "The Aztec Aristocracy."

109. AGN, Tierras, vol. 1788, exp. 7, fols. 27r, 29r.

110. CDIAI, II, 90, 102. AGN, Mercedes, vol. 8, fols. 159v–160r. See also AGN, Mer-

cedes, vol. 8, fols. 105v–106r; General de parte, vol. 2, fol. 267r; Indios, vol. 9, fol. 15r–15v.

111. AGN, Mercedes, vol. 3, fols. 214v–215r; Indios, vol. 1, fols. 69v–70r, 84v–85r, 136v.

112. The records occur in AGN, Vínculos, vol. 279, exp. 1.

113. See AGN, Hospital de Jesús, vol. 120, exp. 5, fol. 31r.

114. *Códice Chimalpopoca*, p. 63. Alvarado Tezozomoc, *Crónica mexicayotl*, pp. 131–34.

115. "Información del señor," pp. 354, 356 ff. Alvarado Tezozomoc, *Crónica mexicayotl*, p. 134. Chimalpahin, *Annales*, p. 208.

116. Chimalpahin, *Annales*, pp. 210, 280. AC, I, 210; II, 4.

117. CDHM, II, 87, 311.

118. *Documentos inéditos relativos a Hernán Cortés*, pp. 355 ff. "Información del señor," pp. 354–55.

119. *Cedulario heráldico*, no. 129. Fernández del Castillo, *Apuntes*, pp. 23–24. Fernández de Recas, *Cacicazgos*, pp. 53–54.

120. His wife was Mencia de la Cruz, mentioned in her son's will. AGN, Vínculos, vol. 242, exp. 1, fols. 9v–10r. Fernández del Castillo, *Apuntes*, p. 29. AGN, Tierras, vol. 1735, exp. 2, fols. 64r ff.

121. AGN, Tierras, vol. 1735, exp. 2, fols. 27r ff., 67r. Fernández del Castillo, *Apuntes*, pp. 25–26.

122. Chimalpahin, *Annales*, p. 210. AC, I, 210; II, 4. "Información del señor," p. 354. AGN, Mercedes, vol. 2, fols. 268v, 322r; vol. 4, fol. 216v.

123. AGI, Justicia, leg. 152, no. 1. AGN, Mercedes, vol. 4, fols. 2r, 216v. Fernández del Castillo, *Apuntes*, pp. 12, 31. Fernández del Castillo, "Hernán Cortés y el Distrito federal," p. 539. See also AGN, Tierras, vol. 1735, exp. 2, fol. 11r.

124. Chimalpahin, *Annales*, p. 280. AGN, Vínculos, vol. 242, exp. 1, fols. 6r ff.

125. AGN, Tierras, vol. 1735, exp. 2, fol. 9r; Vínculos, vol. 242, exp. 1, fols. 11v ff., 37r ff. Chimalpahin, *Annales*, p. 290. The genealogy is confused by Fernández del Castillo, *Apuntes*, p. 32.

126. AGN, Tierras, vol. 1735, exp. 2, fols. 11r, 16r, 81r; Indios, vol. 1, fol. 135r; vol. 6 (1), fol. 242r. AC, X, 114.

127. AGN, Tierras, vol. 1735, exp. 2, fol. 3r–3v; vol. 2001, exp. 1, *passim*.

128. AGN, Vínculos, vol. 241, exp. 5, fols. 1r ff.; vol. 242, exp. 1, fols. 90r ff.; Hospital de Jesús, vol. 120, exp. 5; vol. 302, exp. 6. Fernández del Castillo, *Apuntes*, pp. 165–66. Some of the documentation is summarized by Fernández de Recas, *Cacicazgos*, pp. 54 ff.

129. Chimalpahin, *Annales*, pp. 254 ff. AGN, Mercedes, vol. 7, fol. 299r; vol. 19, fol. 277r–277v; Indios, vol. 3, fol. 183r; Tierras, vol. 994, 6th pag. BNP, no. 26.

130. Details of this history may be found in AGN, Tierras, vols. 994, 995; 1828, exp. 1.

131. AGN, Hospital de Jesús, vol. 302, exp. 7, fols. 4r ff. See also AGN, Indios, vol. 6 (1), fols. 101v, 102v; vol. 50, fols. 46v–48v.

132. AGN, Tierras, vol. 994, *passim*; Indios, vol. 15, cuad. 1, fol. 77r; vol. 50, fols. 10r–11r.

133. AGN, Mercedes, vol. 7, fols. 317r–317v, 355r; Tierras, vol. 994, 5th pag., fols. 37r ff.; vol. 1828, exp. 1, fols. 1r ff.; Hospital de Jesús, vol. 120, exp. 6, fol. 2v. Cf. the phrase of Alvarado Tezozomoc, *Crónica mexicayotl*, p. 56: "cihuapilli Mestiza." AGN,

Civil, vol. 1344, fol. 28v. For the legal prohibition of mestizo caciques see the rule of 1576 in *Recopilación de leyes*, II, 246 (Lib. VI, tít. 7, ley 6).

134. For example, in Tacuba in 1769. AGN, Clero regular y secular, vol. 130, exp. sin número, fols. 3v–4v.

135. A list of such communities, principally in the seventeenth and eighteenth centuries, includes the following: Santa Isabel Tula (Peñafiel, *Colección de documentos*, sec. 1, p. 4. BNP, no. 222, fol. 2r); Guadalupe (AA, Tierras y ejidos, vol. 2, no. 4066, exp. 36, 'fol. 106v); Los Remedios (AC, LI–LIII, 50. BAGN, VII, 377–78. Fernández de Recas, *Cacicazgos*, pp. 103 ff.); San Miguel, near Cuauhtitlan (Cuevas, *Album histórico guadalupano*, p. 130); Tlazala (AGN, Civil, vol. 270, exp. 1); Tecalco (AGN, Indios, vol. 22, fols. 98r–99v, 112r–113r); Xochitepec (AGI, México, leg. 665, cuad. 2, fol. 164r); Teoloyuca (AGN, Vínculos, vol. 272, exp. 3). See also the interesting documents concerning the cacicazgo of Oxtoticpac, in AGN, Tierras, vol. 1726, exp. 1.

136. AGN, Vínculos, vol. 240, exp. 10, fols. 7r ff.

137. AGN, Tierras, vol. 1466, exp. 1. CDHM, II, 1–24. Note that J. F. Ramírez accepted the authenticity of part of this material (CDHM, II, x ff.), and that Bandelier, "On the Distribution and Tenure of Lands," pp. 432–33, regarded the Axapusco merced as the oldest document executed by Europeans on Mexican soil.

138. AGN, Tierras, vol. 1466, exp. 1, 3rd pag., fols. 12v ff. For other false cacicazgo papers see the supposed cedula of 1551 to the Texcoco caciques in Boban, *Documents pour servir*, I, 213–15, and the Austria y Montezuma papers in BNP, no. 419, fols. 1r ff.

139. An example of serious investigation is AGN, Tierras, vol. 1726, exp. 1. An example of perfunctory inquiry is AGN, Indios, vol. 22, fols. 98r–99r, 112r–113r.

140. See the remarks of Vetancurt, *Chronica*, p. 142, and Humboldt, *Political Essay*, I, 179.

141. AGN, Tierras, vols. 994–95.

142. AGN, Clero regular y secular, vol. 130, exp. sin número, fol. 5r. *Nobilario de conquistadores*, pp. 253–55. CDIHIA, I, 194. *Códice Chimalpopoca*, p. 63.

143. CDIHIA, I, 193–94. ENE, XVI, 71–74.

144. Alegre, *Historia de la Compañía de Jesús*, I, 64–65. Pérez de Rivas, *Corónica y historia religiosa*, I, 55–56. Alvarado Tezozomoc, *Crónica mexicayotl*, p. 169. Vetancurt, *Chronica*, p. 70. Grijalva, *Crónica*, fols. 81v ff.

145. AGN, Clero regular y secular, vol. 130, exp. sin número, *passim*.

146. Humboldt, *Political Essay*, I, 179.

147. Alamán, *Historia de México*, V, 440 ff. See also Mier, *Escritos inéditos*, p. 382.

CHAPTER VII

1. CDIHIA, I, 193–94. ENE, IX, 140–42; XVI, 64–66, 71–74, 74–75. NCDHM (1886–92), IV, 128–36. See Chapter III, notes 18, 81 ff.

2. In this usage the terms gobernador and juez gobernador are synonymous.

3. E.g., AC, I, 211.

4. E.g., AGN, Mercedes, vol. 2, fols. 268v, 322r. FHT, I, 137. It is absent in those cabeceras in which the cacique inheritance terminated early—e.g., Coatepec, where Cortés named the first colonial gobernador, Francisco Yolictzin, and where the successors of the gobernador achieved office by local Indian election and viceregal confirmation. See PNE, VI, 52–53. Ramírez de Fuenleal stated in 1532 that Spaniards were referring to the tlacuchcalcatl (one of the ranking officers under Montezuma) as gobernador. CDIAI, XIII, 254.

5. PNE, VI, 72–73.
6. AGN, Mercedes, vol. 4, fol. 244r.
7. CDIAI, VI, 501 ff.
8. The Tenochtitlan succession following Montezuma, as well as the successions in Texcoco and Tacuba, deserve a more extensive discussion and documentation than is appropriate here. The essential problem is one of reconciling discrepancies among various texts, particularly the native annals. The difficulties diminish in the middle sixteenth century and after, with the appearance of additional, securely dated documents. Our citations are intended to be representative, not exhaustive.
9. Evidence from a number of sources is reviewed by Eulalia Guzmán, who believes that Montezuma was deliberately killed by Cortés. Cortés and others reported that Montezuma was killed by Indians. See Cortés's statement and the Guzmán analysis in Cortés, *Relaciones*, I, 434 ff., 452 ff.
10. Cortés, *Cartas*, I, 183. Sahagún, *Historia general*, II, 41. López de Gómara, *Historia*, II, 222. Chimalpahin, *Annales*, p. 192. Alvarado Tezozomoc, *Crónica mexicayotl*, pp. 159–60. Cervantes de Salazar, *Crónica*, pp. 555, 578. Ixtlilxochitl, *Relaciones*, pp. 450–51.
11. Cervantes de Salazar, *Crónica*, p. 555. Chimalpahin, *Annales*, pp. 206–7. *Anales de Tlatelolco*, p. 9. *Histoire de la nation mexicaine*, pp. 148–50. Cortés, *Cartas*, II, 33 ff., 157 ff. Díaz del Castillo, *Historia verdadera*, I, 510; II, 341. Alvarado Tezozomoc, *Crónica mexicayotl*, p. 143. There is strong evidence that Cuauhtemoc executed Montezuma's son and that he married Montezuma's daughter in order to "legitimize" his succession. See NCDHM (1941), III, 277; López de Gómara, *Historia*, II, 222; Oviedo y Valdés, *Historia general y natural*, III, 549.
12. BNP, no. 419, fol. 146r–146v. Alvarado Tezozomoc, *Crónica mexicayotl*, pp. 165–66. Chimalpahin, *Annales*, pp. 207, 266. A summary of biographical data on Tlacotzin is provided by Alcocer, *Apuntes*, pp. 77–78.
13. Chimalpahin, *Annales*, pp. 195, 266–67. Alvarado Tezozomoc, *Crónica mexicayotl*, p. 167. *Histoire de la nation mexicaine*, p. 88. CDIAI, XLI, 110. Ternaux Compans, *Voyages, relations et mémoires*, XVI, 177.
14. Sahagún, *Historia general*, II, 42. Chimalpahin, *Annales*, pp. 222, 226–27, 233. Ternaux Compans, *Voyages, relations et mémoires*, VIII, 265–66. Alvarado Tezozomoc, *Crónica mexicayotl*, p. 168. *Histoire de la nation mexicaine*, p. 151. AGN, Inquisición, vol. 38 (1), no. 4, fol. 5v. AGI, Justicia, leg. 123, no. 2.
15. Chimalpahin, *Annales*, pp. 144, 195, 237–38, 267. Alvarado Tezozomoc, *Crónica mexicayotl*, pp. 136, 168–69. Ixtlilxochitl, *Historia*, p. 260. AGI, Justicia, leg. 123, no. 2. Peñafiel, *Colección de documentos*, sec. 1, p. 15. BNP, nos. 41–45, fol. 13v. Earlier Spanish use of the term gobernador is seen in 1533, in AC, III, 52.
16. Ternaux Compans, *Voyages, relations et mémoires*, VIII, 264–65. Alvarado Tezozomoc, *Crónica mexicayotl*, pp. 141–42. BNP, nos. 41–45, fol. 13v. Chimalpahin, *Annales*, pp. 241, 250, 267. Ixtlilxochitl, *Historia*, p. 260. AC, V, 294.
17. AGN, Mercedes, vol. 3, fol. 44r–44v; vol. 4, fols. 35v, 57v, 256v; vol. 84, fols. 27v, 46r–46v. NLAC, 1121, fol. 211r–211v. BNP, nos. 41–45, fol. 14r. *Histoire de la nation mexicaine*, pp. 95 ff. "Anales de San Gregorio Acapulco," p. 111. Chimalpahin, *Annales*, pp. 252, 255. BNP, no. 220, pp. 96–97.
18. *Códice Osuna*, pp. 75–76, 128, 165–66. See the Túmulo Imperial of Cervantes de Salazar, in García Icazbalceta, *Bibliografía mexicana*, p. 180. "Anales de San Gregorio Acapulco," pp. 112–13. BNP, no. 220, p. 97. Chimalpahin, *Annales*, pp. 252, 256. ENE, IX, 140–42. Alvarado Tezozomoc, *Crónica mexicayotl*, pp. 170, 173. In my article "Ro-

tation of Alcaldes," p. 221, I cite the Codex Aubin (*Histoire de la nation mexicaine*, p. 98) as indicating the beginning of the rule of Cristóbal de Guzmán on January 6, 1556. I now believe that this should be read as indicating January 6, 1557.

19. AGN, Mercedes, vol. 7, fol. 202v. Chimalpahin, *Annales*, pp. 259, 264, 268. "Anales de San Gregorio Acapulco," p. 114. Alvarado Tezozomoc, *Crónica mexicayotl*, pp. 174–75. *Códice Osuna*, p. 107. *Histoire de la nation mexicaine*, p. 155. See the account of his marriage in office in Garibay K., "Un cuadro real," p. 233. The death of Luis de Santa María Cipac is one of the themes of UT, G–42.

20. AGN, Mercedes, vol. 4, fols. 35v, 57v. Chimalpahin, *Annales*, p. 252.

21. Alvarado Tezozomoc, *Crónica mexicayotl*, pp. 174–75. Chimalpahin, *Annales*, p. 273.

22. Garibay K., "Un cuadro real," p. 230. Alvarado Tezozomoc, *Crónica mexicayotl*, pp. 175–76. *Histoire de la nation mexicaine*, p. 156. Chimalpahin, *Annales*, p. 278. The event is recorded in the annals of Jiménez's town, Tecamachalco. See Peñafiel, *Colección de documentos*, 6th sec., p. 43.

23. Alvarado Tezozomoc, *Crónica mexicayotl*, pp. 171, 176. *Histoire de la nation mexicaine*, pp. 114, 156. Peñafiel, *Colección de documentos*, sec. 6, p. 55. Sahagún, *Historia general*, I, 3. Torquemada, *Monarchia indiana*, I, 607; III, 114–15.

24. Alvarado Tezozomoc, *Crónica mexicayotl*, p. 171.

25. *Histoire de la nation mexicaine*, pp. 115, 156. AGN, Indios, vol. 3, fol. 119r; vol. 9, fol. 132v. Chimalpahin, *Annales*, p. 313. AAMC, no. 13, p. 639. BNM, ms. no. 1312, fols. 47r–49r. García and Pereyra, *Documentos inéditos*, XII, 173.

26. Ixtlilxochitl, *Relaciones*, p. 258. Ixtlilxochitl, *Historia*, p. 329. Sahagún, *Historia general*, II, 45. Díaz del Castillo, *Historia verdadera*, I, 295–96. Cervantes de Salazar, *Crónica*, pp. 270, 381. Torquemada, *Monarchia indiana*, I, 459. Las Casas, *Apologética historia*, p. 568. Alvarado Tezozomoc, *Crónica mexicayotl*, p. 123. NCDHM (1941), III, 232.

27. Díaz del Castillo, *Historia verdadera*, I, 295 ff., 488 ff.; II, 3. Chimalpahin, *Annales*, pp. 188, 192. Cervantes de Salazar, *Crónica*, pp. 270, 366 ff. Alvarado Tezozomoc, *Crónica mexicayotl*, p. 148. Cortés, *Cartas*, I, 90 ff. Torquemada, *Monarchia indiana*, I, 184, 469 ff. *Procesos de residencia*, pp. 3, 35–36, 65. "Anales de Tula," p. 12.

28. Cortés, *Cartas*, I, 186–87. Cervantes de Salazar, *Crónica*, pp. 371 ff., 572–73. Díaz del Castillo, *Historia verdadera*, I, 365, 369, 545. López de Gómara, *Historia*, I, 266, 341–42. Torquemada, *Monarchia indiana*, I, 471 ff.

29. Aguilar, *Historia*, pp. 89, 91. Cortés, *Cartas*, I, 179 ff. Motolinía, *Memoriales*, p. 265. Sahagún, *Historia general*, II, 45. Sahagún, *Einige Kapitel*, p. 571. *Códice Ramírez*, p. 188.

30. Aguilar, *Historia*, p. 91. CDIAI, XXIX, 56. Ixtlilxochitl, *Relaciones*, pp. 403 ff. Sahagún, *Historia general*, II, 45. Torquemada, *Monarchia indiana*, I, 184, 222 ff., 433 ff., 575. Chimalpahin, *Annales*, pp. 206–7. NCDHM (1941), III, 277. See the Cano report in Oviedo y Valdés, *Historia general y natural*, III, 549. *Anales de Tlatelolco*, p. 9. Cf. López de Gómara, *Historia*, II, 122–23, 143–45. Motolinía, *Memoriales*, p. 265, states that Coanacochtzin died a natural death on the Honduras expedition.

31. The evidence becomes confused here. *Anales de Tlatelolco*, p. 67. Sahagún, *Historia general*, II, 45. Mapa Tlatzin in Aubin, *Mémoires sur la peinture*, pp. 65–69. CDIAI, XXVII, 389, 525; XXVIII, 295. *Archivo mexicano*, I, 208. Cortés, *Cartas*, II, 1–2, 63. Díaz del Castillo, *Historia verdadera*, I, 369. Chimalpahin, *Annales*, p. 209.

32. Sahagún, *Historia general*, II, 45–46. CDIAI, XII, 538. *Procesos de indios*, p. 40. AGI, Justicia, leg. 128, no. 1. AAMC, no. 3, p. 267.

33. Chimalpahin, *Annales,* p. 226, states that Carlos acceded in 1531, but this appears to be contradicted by the more persuasive evidence of AGN, Inquisición, vol. 2, no. 10, fol. 262v. See also NCDHM (1941), III, 4; Chimalpahin, *Annales,* p. 239; AGN, Inquisición, vol. 2, no. 10, fols. 253r ff., 259v.

34. Motolinía, *Memoriales,* pp. 265–66. Chimalpahin, *Annales,* pp. 240, 261. Ixtlilxochitl, *Relaciones,* p. 444. Sahagún, *Historia general,* II, 46. Torquemada, *Monarchia indiana,* I, 167; II, 348. NCDHM (1941), III, 59. ENE, IV, 129; IX, 140–42; XVI, 74–75. García Icazbalceta, *Bibliografía mexicana,* p. 180. Peñafiel, *Colección de documentos,* sec. 7, pp. 3–4, 6–8, 9–10. CDIHIA, II, 315–16. MNM, Documentos sueltos, ser. 1, leg. 23, no. 55. AGN, Mercedes, vol. 1, fol. 160v; vol. 4, fols. 250r ff., 257r. AGI, Justicia, leg. 1029, no. 10.

35. McAfee and Barlow, "The Titles of Tetzcotzinco," pp. 120, 122. AGN, Mercedes, vol. 1, fols. 160v, 250r ff. García Icazbalceta, *Bibliografía mexicana,* p. 180. ENE, IV, 129.

36. E.g., FHT, I, 91.

37. *Códice Chimalpopoca,* p. 63. Ixtlilxochitl, *Historia,* p. 404. Sahagún, *Einige Kapitel,* p. 571. López de Gómara, *Historia,* II, 123, 144. Díaz del Castillo, *Historia verdadera,* II, 341. Cortés, *Cartas,* II, 157 ff. Oviedo y Valdés, *Historia general y natural,* III, 549. Chimalpahin, *Annales,* pp. 206–7. *Anales de Tlatelolco,* p. 9. Alvarado Tezozomoc, *Crónica mexicayotl,* p. 165. NCDHM (1941), III, 277.

38. AC, I, 180–81. AA, Tierras y ejidos, vol. 2, no. 4066, exp. 38, fol. 5r–5v. AGN, Inquisición, vol. 2, no. 10, fol. 271v; Mercedes, vol. 2, fol. 49r.

39. AGI, Justicia, leg. 1029, no. 10. CDIHIA, I, 194. Cf. Alvarado Tezozomoc, *Crónica mexicayotl,* pp. 169 ff. García Icazbalceta, *Bibliografía mexicana,* p. 180. AA, Tierras y ejidos, vol. 2, no. 4066, exp. 38, fol. 22r. *Nobilario de conquistadores,* p. 253. AGN, Mercedes, vol. 3, fol. 22r; vol. 4, fols. 257r, 343r; vol. 8, fol. 159v.

40. AGN, Mercedes, vol. 8, fol. 214v.

41. Antonio Cortés's will of 1574 is recorded in BNP, no. 115. AGN, Mercedes, vol. 10, fols. 71v–72r; General de parte, vol. 1, fol. 107r. FHT, II, 317–18. AAMC, no. 10, pp. 523–24.

42. AAMC, no. 15, p. 704. Gibson, *Tlaxcala,* pp. 94, 98 ff., 101–2, 107.

43. AGN, Indios, vol. 9, fol. 9r. Peñafiel, *Colección de documentos,* sec. 7, pp. 14 ff. Gamio, *La población del valle de Teotihuacan,* I (2), 540–41.

44. *Histoire de la nation mexicaine,* p.157. FHT, IV, 442–43. AGN, Indios, vol. 6 (1), fols. 78r, 97r, 137r, 170v, 171v, 261r, 279r, 311v, 314r.

45. E.g., ENE, VII, 263. Las Casas, *Apologética historia,* p. 554. NCDHM (1941), III, 285. CDIAI, XIII, 254–55.

46. ENE, XIV, 146–47.

47. An example is Aguirre Beltrán, "El gobierno indígena," pp. 282–83 *et passim.* Aguirre Beltrán believes that the alcaldes and regidores of the colonial towns were the old calpulli functionaries with new names, the "teachcauh" becoming alcaldes and the tequitlatos becoming regidores. He regards the essential transition as one of nomenclature. See also Chávez Orozco, *Las instituciones democráticas.* The conclusions of neither of these two writers apply to the Valley of Mexico.

48. The earliest positively identified alcaldes occur in the late 1530's in Texcoco. See AGN, Inquisición, vol. 2, no. 10, fols. 254v–255r. CDIAI, VI, 502.

49. Torquemada, *Monarchia indiana,* I, 511. Cortés, *Cartas,* II, 108–9. See above, note 12.

50. AGN, Mercedes, vol. 2, fol. 91v.

51. *Histoire de la nation mexicaine*, p. 92. Translation is lacking in the Aubin edition but is provided by McAfee and Barlow, "La segunda parte," p. 162. See also the related documents, Códice Cozcatzin, BNP, nos. 41–45, fol. 13v, and the Títulos de Santa Isabel Tola in Peñafiel, *Colección de documentos*, sec. 1, p. 15.

52. *Códice Osuna*, p. 81. *Histoire de la nation mexicaine*, p. 92. Chávez Orozco, *Las instituciones democráticas*, p. 6. BNP, nos 41–45, fols. 13v–14r. Peñafiel, *Colección de documentos*, sec. 1, p. 15.

53. For the evidence and further explanation of this system see Gibson, "Rotation of Alcaldes," pp. 212–23.

54. Puga, *Provisiones*, fols. 40r, 77r. CDIU, X, 53–54.

55. Archivo municipal, Puebla, Cartilla vieja, fol. 54r. The Spanish cabildo in Mexico City proposed a cabildo of 24 members, of whom 18 would be white and 6 Indian. The 6 Indian members would be drawn partly from Tenochtitlan and partly from Tlatelolco. See AC, VI, 492–93; VII, 11.

56. *Códice Osuna*, pp. 122 ff. MNM, Colección Gómez de Orozco, no. 14. AGN, Indios, vol. 4, fol. 54r.

57. ENE, XV, 164.

58. CDIAI, X, 372–73.

59. *Disposiciones complementarias*, I, 152–54. Bentura Beleña, *Recopilación sumaria*, I, 42; 4th pag., 206. AGN, Indios, vol. 9, fols. 35v–36r.

60. García Pimentel, *Descripción*, pp. 67, 91.

61. See above, note 25. Vera, *Informaciones*, pp. 40 ff.

62. See examples in AGN, Civil, vol. 1429, *passim*.

63. See examples for Temascalapa and Texcoco in AGN, Mercedes, vol. 2, fol. 323v; Indios, vol. 12 (1), fol. 132r–132v.

64. Accounts of these elections may be found in FHT, VII, 227–28; AGI, México, leg. 748, fols. 11r ff.; AGN, Civil, vol. 1429, exp. 3, fols. 1r–16r; Hospital de Jesús, fol. 333, exp. 27.

65. AGN, Indios, vol. 50, fol. 25r–25v; Hospital de Jesús, vol. 319, exp. 15, fols. 14v–15r; vol. 329, *passim*; vol. 333, exp. 32, fol. 31r; Civil, vol. 1429, *passim*; Tierras, vol. 191, exp. 6, fols. 2r ff.

66. AGN, Indios, vol. 5, fol. 92v; vol. 9, fols. 35v–36r. Bentura Beleña, *Recopilación sumaria*, I, 5th pag., 206. *Disposiciones complementarias*, I, 152–54.

67. BNM, ms. no. 437, fol. 463r. Bentura Beleña, *Recopilación sumaria*, II, 191. BAGN, XVII, 165–67.

68. In the intendancy ordinances in the late eighteenth century Spanish-speaking Indians were to be preferred, not required, in the holding of offices. See Bentura Beleña, *Recopilación sumaria*, II, sep. pag., ix.

69. Vera, *Informaciones*, pp. 15–17. AGN, Indios, vol. 12 (1), fol. 115r; vol. 17, fols. 289r–290v, 308r.

70. AGN, Civil, vol. 1344, fols. 15r ff.

71. AGN, Indios, vol. 12 (1), fol. 132r–132v.

72. AGN, Tierras, vol. 1735, exp. 2, fol. 76r.

73. AGN, Indios, vol. 17, fol. 234v.

74. AGN, Civil, vol. 1344, fol. 42r; Hospital de Jesús, vol. 329, exp. 2.

75. AGN, Hospital de Jesús, vol. 319, exp. 15, fols. 17r–18r; Civil, vol. 1344, fol. 2r; vol. 1529, exp. 3, fol. 3r–3v.

76. AGN, Hospital de Jesús, vol. 319, exp. 15; vol. 333, exp. 27, fols. 1r ff.; Civil, vol.

1429, *passim*; Indios, vol. 50, fols. 249v–250v. *Códice Osuna,* pp. 13 ff. The Códice de Juan Bautista records an interesting case in Tenochtitlan after the failure of the "legitimate" dynasty. Here the candidacy of the former alcalde Pedro Dionisio was rejected on grounds of immorality. The passage is translated by Garibay K., "Un cuadro real," p. 230.

77. AGN, Civil, vol. 1344, fol. 2r; vol. 1429, exp. 3, fol. 2r–2v; Indios, vol. 50, fols. 59r–60v.

78. Palafox y Mendoza, *Virtudes del indio,* pp. 38–39. See also AGN, Civil, vol. 1344, fol. 31v. Cf. Bentura Beleña, *Recopilación sumaria,* II, sep. pag., viii–ix.

79. See, e.g., the election of 1734 in Tacubaya, AGN, Hospital de Jesús, vol. 333, exp. 29.

80. AGN, Civil, vol. 1429, *passim.*

81. AGN, Indios, vol. 12 (1), fol. 120r–120v; vol. 18, fol. 506r; vol. 50, fols. 25r–25v, 249r–250v.

82. AGN, Indios, vol. 6 (2), fol. 206r. AGI, Justicia, leg. 159, no. 2.

83. FHT, VII, 227–28. AGN, Civil, vol. 1344, fols. 5r–5v, 47r ff.; Hospital de Jesús, vol. 329, exp. 2, *passim*; vol. 333, exp. 29, fol. 3r; Tierras, vol. 1466, exp. 1, fols. 2r ff.

84. E.g., AGN, Tierras, vol. 2825, exp. 6, 2nd pag., fol. 1v.

85. Las Casas, *Apologética historia,* p. 568. Torquemada, *Monarchia indiana,* II, 361. ENE, VIII, 112. AGN, Hospital de Jesús, vol. 329, exp. 2.

86. NLAC, 1476, fol. 12r. AGN, Civil, vol. 1344, *passim.* Barlow, "Dos documentos," p. 110. Gamio, *La población del valle de Teotihuacan,* I (2), 540. Peñafiel, *Colección de documentos,* 7th sec., pp. 14–15. AGN, Hospital de Jesús, vol. 319, exp. 15, fols. 14v–15r; Indios, vol. 2, fol. 86r; vol. 6 (1), fol. 250r–250v; vol. 50, fols. 249r–250v.

87. CDIHIA, I, 181.

88. Thus in 1538 an Indian agent of Tenochtitlan and Tlatelolco was in Valladolid consulting with Spanish lawyers concerning the estancias claimed by the Ecatepec encomienda interests. See AGI, Justicia, vol. 124, no. 5, exp. 3. See also AGI, Justicia, vol. 123, no. 2.

89. AGN, Mercedes, vol. 5, fol. 67r–67v.

90. See, e.g., AGN, General de parte, vol. 1, fol. 129v. Presumably the corregimiento court had jurisdiction in more serious offenses, but we cannot yet make a purely legal distinction between the types of crime appropriate to the one and those appropriate to the other.

91. E.g., García Pimentel, *Descripción,* p. 63.

92. Examples may be seen in BNP, nos. 29, 112, 114; NLAC, 1121, fol. 113v; and numerous other sources.

93. AGN, Mercedes, vol. 4, fol. 163r–163v. CDIAI, VI, 509.

94. AGN, Mercedes, vol. 2, fols. 263r, 264r, 270r.

95. See NCDHM, I, 22.

96. FHT, I, 137. Chimalpahin, *Annales,* pp. 244–45. AGN, Indios, vol. 2, fol. 86r; vol. 4, fol. 237v; Mercedes, vol. 84, fols. 17r–17v, 47r, 52v, 69r–69v, 71r–71v; General de parte, vol. 2, fol. 189r–189v. *Códice Osuna,* pp. 47 ff.

97. *Códices indígenas,* no. 31.

98. E.g., BNP, nos. 29, 112, 114.

99. Mayordomos of various types are documented in AGN, Indios, vol. 1, *passim*; General de parte, vol. 2, fol. 53r; Tierras, vol. 1780, exp. 5. See also BNP, no. 30, fol. 12r; *Códice Osuna,* pp. 81 ff.

100. Durán, *Historia,* II, 223. Torquemada, *Monarchia indiana,* II, 544–45. ENE, XIV, 146–47. Alvarado Tezozomoc, *Crónica mexicana,* pp. 234, 299, 347. CDIAI, II, 26 ff., 87.

101. CDIAI, II, 30. CDIHE, IV, 198–99. Torquemada, *Monarchia indiana,* II, 544–45. ENE, XIV, 146–47. Motolinía, *Memoriales,* p. 306. On the inheritance of calpulli offices see Durán, *Historia,* II, 223. Waterman, "Bandelier's Contribution," p. 259, lists, with some duplication, seventeen titles applied to the achcacauhtin by various writers.

102. ENE, XIV, 147. Calpixqui, presumptively "house-guard," is defined by Molina, *Vocabulario,* as *mayordomo.*

103. ENE, VI, 158; XIV, 147. Alvarado Tezozomoc, *Crónica mexicana,* p. 353. NCDHM (1886–92), V, 86 ff. Surviving records of localities outside the Valley of Mexico—e.g., Huejotzingo (BNP, no. 387) and Tlaxcala (Gibson, *Tlaxcala,* pp. 119–20)—suggest that the units of 20, 100, etc. actually contained only rough approximations of these numbers.

104. ENE, VI, 158. See also NCDHM (1886–92), V, 86 ff. This is not the case however in the Huejotzingo and Tlaxcala documents cited in note 103. I have found no comparable data on this subject for any of the communities of the Valley of Mexico. See however the viceregal reform in Coyoacan, cited in note 110.

105. AGN, General de parte, vol. 2, fol. 204r–204v; Tierras, vol. 13, exp. 4, fol. 320v. Ixtlilxochitl, *Relaciones,* p. 445. BAGN, ser. 2, II, 22 ff. Thus the Códice de Jaun Bautista refers to "tepixque tlaxilacalpan," or barrio guardians, in Tenochtitlan in 1564. See MNM, Colección Gómez de Orozco, no. 14, p. 63.

106. FHT, VI, 222–23. García Pimentel, *Descripción,* pp. 85, 89, 95, 258, 262. Durán, *Historia,* II, 223. Chimalpahin, *Annales,* p. 225. *Codex Telleriano-Remensis,* fol. 45v. CDIU, XXI, 323. Puga, *Provisiones,* fols. 40r, 77r. BAGN, ser. 2, II, 22 ff. Villa-señor y Sánchez, *Theatro americano,* I, 58. AGN, Indios, vol. 1, fols. 84v–85r, 136v. The term *tapia* (e.g., AGN, Mercedes, vol. 1, fol. 126v) is probably a corruption of the Nahuatl *tlapia,* guard or custodian of something.

107. Torquemada, *Monarchia indiana,* I, 544–45. Villa-señor y Sánchez, *Theatro americano,* I, 58. NCDHM (1886–92), V, 86. Sahagún, *Historia general,* I, 322, makes a similar connection between the achcacauhtin and the alguaciles, and many additional equivalences are recorded.

108. AGN, Indios, vol. 1, fols. 83v–84r, 99r–102r. The five tequitlatos are recorded in the estancia of San Martín, subject to Tlalmanalco. The Tizayuca indicated here was a sujeto of Otumba. For Huehuetoca see García Pimentel, *Descripción,* p. 258.

109. AGN, Mercedes, vol. 5, fol. 312r. The centurions in Xochimilco were called merinos. See *Sobre el modo de tributar,* pp. 108, 110.

110. AGN, General de parte, vol. 2, fol. 204r–204v.

111. AGN, Indios, vol. 6 (1), fols. 290v, 292v. The persistence of tlayacanque is well documented in Tacuba and its sujetos in 1580. See AGN, Indios, vol. 1, fols. 86v–87v. The records relating to the distribution of excess maize, in AGN, Indios, vol. 1, provide our fullest data on the local political nomenclature in the late sixteenth century.

112. CDIAI, VI, 502. *Cartas de Indias,* p. 56. Torquemada, *Monarchia indiana,* III, 280–81. NCDHM (1941), II, 59. Durán, *Historia,* II, 223.

113. AGN, Indios, vol. 1, fols. 16r–16v, 35r ff., 83v–84r. AA, Tierras y ejidos, leg. 2, no. 4066, exp. 36, fol. 63r.

114. AGN, Indios, fol. 136v, *et passim,* García Pimentel, *Descripción,* pp. 62, 85, 89. Durán, *Historia,* II, 233, states that the señores of towns still had groups of noble cantores in the pre-conquest manner, in the later sixteenth century.

115. *Compendio histórico del concilio III*, III, 256, 257.

116. AGN, Mercedes, vol. 4, fols. 214v–215r.

117. *Sobre el modo de tributar*, p. 108. AGN, General de parte, vol. 2, fol. 42r. FHT, II, 193, 199. Similar practices continued into the seventeenth century. See the example of Acolman in 1618. AGN, Indios, vol. 7, fol. 166v.

118. AGN, Indios, vol. 10 (1), fol. 17v.

119. *Sobre el modo de tributar*, p. 114. AGN, Indios, vol. 6 (1), fol. 262r; vol. 6 (2), fol. 240r.

120. E.g., *Ordenanzas del trabajo*, pp. 45–46. Zorita, *Historia*, p. 408.

121. AGN, Indios, vol. 1, *passim*. UT, G-42.

122. Instances are recorded in AGN, Civil, vol. 1688, exp. 1, and *Códice Osuna*, pp. 13 ff.

123. Bentura Beleña, *Recopilación sumaria*, II, sep. pag., xxxix. AHH, Tributos, vol. 225, exp. 29. AGN, Tierras, vol. 1412, exp. 5, fol. 11v.

124. AGN, Mercedes, vol. 3, fols. 74v, 327v–328v.

125. AGN, Mercedes, vol. 1, fols. 145v, 210v; vol. 4, fols. 98v–99r; vol. 7, fols. 75v–76r. NLAC, 1121, fols. 211r–211v, 348r ff. Vetancurt, *Chronica*, p. 56. Note that our only evidence for a multiple governorship after 1555 is a viceregal order of 1563 addressed to the "gobernadores" of Xochimilco. If the viceroy was misinformed, or if this represents an error from some other cause, our statement becomes untenable.

126. See Chapter VI, note 129.

127. Vetancurt, *Chronica*, p. 72. AGN, Indios, vol. 6 (1), fols. 208v–209r; Clero regular y secular, vol. 103, 2nd pag., fols. 1r ff.

128. AGN, Mercedes, vol. 2, fol. 270r; vol. 3, fol. 218r–218v; vol. 7, fol. 230r; Indios, vol. 7, fol. 144r–144v.

129. AGN, Tributos, vol. 2, exp. 7, fols. 7v–8r; Mercedes, vol. 4, fols. 202r, 244r; Tierras, vol. 2, exp. 1, fol. 4r; exp. 4, fol. 30r; vol. 1084, exp. 5, fol. 2v; General de parte, vol. 3, fol. 75r; Clero regular y secular, vol. 130, exp. sin núm., fol. 45r. AGI, Contaduría, leg. 729, sep. pag.; leg. 768 (A).

130. AGN, Indios, vol. 17, fols. 289v–290v.

131. See Chapter III, note 91.

132. AGN, Mercedes, vol. 4, fols. 250r ff.; vol. 7, fol. 292r–292v.

133. Very full documentation on the disputes between Tepexpan and Temascalapa may be found in AGI, Justicia, leg. 164, no. 2, and leg. 208, no. 4. For the viceregal rulings and other details see also AGN, Mercedes, vol. 2, fols. 323v–324v; vol. 7, fol. 18r–18v; vol. 84, fol. 120r–120v.

134. Examples may be found in AGN, Indios, vol. 50, fols. 288v–290r; Mercedes, vol. 4, fols. 250r ff.; vol. 6, fol. 231v; vol. 7, fol. 292r–292v.

135. AA, Tierras y ejidos, vol. 2, no. 4066, exp. 36, fol. 93r. AGN, Indios, vol. 50, fols. 249r–250v; Hospital de Jesús, vol. 329, exp. 2, *passim*.

136. AGN, Hospital de Jesús, vol. 333, exp. 27, fol. 7r. MNM, Colección antigua, T2-58, fol. 19v. Some of these changes occur in the sixteenth century in a few towns. See AGN, Indios, vol. 1, fol. 135r; Mercedes, vol. 10, fols. 96v–97v.

137. AGN, Indios, vol. 50, fol. 47v.

138. Xochimilco in the late eighteenth century continued to elect one alcalde for Tecpan, one for Tepetenchi, and one for Olac, but in addition to these three traditional alcaldes Xochimilco elected thirteen other alcaldes. See AGN, Civil, vol. 1344, fols. 1r ff.

139. AGN, Hospital de Jesús, vol. 329, exp. 2, no pag.; Padrones, vol. 47, fols. 39r ff. AHH, Tributos, leg. 225, exp. 29, no pag. Throughout the seventeenth and eighteenth

centuries there occurred a tendency to abandon the Indian office-holding titles and to adopt Spanish ones in the lower grades. By the end of the colonial period, though the titles topil, tepixqui, and tequitlato were still fairly widely used, other Nahuatl designations were more rare, and the preference in most community governments favored such Spanish titles as mayordomo, mandón, alguacil, fiscal, and merino. For examples of the persisting Nahuatl titles in the seventeenth and eighteenth centuries see AGN, Indios, vol. 12 (1), fol. 38r–38v; Civil, vol. 1429, *passim*. See also AA, Tierras y ejidos, leg. 2, no. 4066, exp. 36, fol. 63r.

140. See the Títulos de Santa Isabel Tola in Peñafiel, *Colección de documentos*, sec. 1, p. 15. *Códice Osuna*, pp. 87, 114. AGN, Mercedes, vol. 3, fols. 327v–328r.

141. Cervantes de Salazar, *Crónica*, p. 303. Cervantes de Salazar, *Life in the Imperial and Loyal City*, p. 62. Torquemada, *Monarchia indiana*, II, 555. Alvarado Tezozomoc, *Crónica mexicayotl*, pp. 172 ff. Fernández and Leicht, "Códice del tecpan," pp. 243 ff.

142. The rules of 1553 are recorded in NLAC, 1121, fols. 348r ff. The Indian report of 1561 makes a precise connection between the ciudad status and the appropriate constructions. See AGN, Mercedes, vol. 5, fol. 312r.

143. AC, LI–LIII, 187–88.

144. Bentura Beleña, *Recopilación sumaria*, I, 3rd pag., 50; 4th pag., 60; II, 202. AGN, Civil, vol. 225, exp. 5, fol. 4v.

145. Nuttall, "Las tres casas," pp. 588–91, summarizes earlier publications on the Coyoacan casa de comunidad and jail. For the remnants of the water supply in the eighteenth century see Alzate, *Gacetas de literatura*, II, 113.

146. AGN, Padrones, vol. 4, fol. 239v; Tierras, vol. 566, exp. 4, fol. 1r; vol. 1518, exp. 1, fols. 23v, 24v.

147. AGN, Indios, vol. 6 (1), fol. 226v.

148. Palafox y Mendoza, *Virtudes del indio*, pp. 37 ff.

149. Navarro de Vargas, "Padrón," pp. 559, 577. The episodes are described with convincing circumstantial detail.

150. AGN, Hospital de Jesús, vol. 333, exp. 29, fols. 13v–14r.

CHAPTER VIII

1. Cortés, *Cartas*, I, 85 ff. Díaz del Castillo, *Historia verdadera*, I, 380 ff. Miranda, *El tributo indígena*, pp. 45 ff.

2. At a later time, Spanish political theory made much of a formal remission of tribute authority by Montezuma, which was said to have been voluntarily executed through a public scribe in the presence of Spanish and Indian witnesses. Fonseca and Urrutia, *Historica*, I, 412. Maniau Torquemada, *Compendio*, p. 10.

3. See CDIAI, XXVII, 23.

4. The Matrícula de Tributos, or its allied document *Codex Mendoza*, has generally been understood as an incomplete listing of the tribute-paying towns in Aztec imperialism. My hypothesis is rather that it is a record of the calpixqui locations under Montezuma, and hence, within limits, not incomplete.

5. The Hernando Pimentel lists are published by Orozco y Berra, *Historia antigua*, II, 201–3. See also Orozco y Berra, "Tlacopan y Texcoco," pp. 508–9, and the Hernando Pimentel letter of 1562 in ENE, XVI, 74–75. The Tacuba counterparts are published in ENE, XIV, 118–22; XVI, 71–74. The materials are discussed in my articles, "Llamamiento general" and "The Tepanec Zone."

6. The towns are listed in *Codex Mendoza*, III, fols. 17v, 20v. The Indian arguments are documented in AGI, Justicia, leg. 123, no. 2; leg. 124, no. 5; leg. 159, no. 5.

7. Miranda, *El tributo indígena*, p. 48, points out the close parallel between this passage and the words of Zorita (in the edition cited in the present work, CDIAI, II, 104).

8. Zorita in CDIAI, II, 33.

9. Cuevas, *Documentos inéditos*, p. 230. The parallel phrase of Zorita is in CDIAI, II, 104.

10. ENE, VII, 261, 263.

11. *Archivo mexicano*, I, 209, 241, 269; II, 218–19. *Documentos inéditos relativos a Hernán Cortés*, XXVII, 351 ff. CDIAI, XII, 531 ff.; XXVII, 25, 33, 40 ff.

12. *Nuevos documentos relativos a los bienes, passim*. CDIAI, XIII, 113, 142. ENE, I, 141 ff.; VI, 135–36; XVI, 40–47.

13. Oviedo y Valdés, *Historia general y natural*, III, 535–36.

14. ENE, III, 81–82; VII, 296. Ternaux Compans, *Voyages, relations et mémoires*, VIII, 256. MNM, Colección franciscana, 190, fols. 11r, 16r ff. In Xochimilco in 1561 the salaries of the Indian political officers were reported as amounting to 300 pesos, while the tributes demanded by the Indian government were reported at over 20,000 pesos. See *Sobre el modo de tributar*, pp. 114, 127.

15. Montúfar, "Carta del arzobispo," p. 353. MNM, Colección franciscana, 190, fols. 10r ff. CDIHE, XXVI, 378. CDIAI, IV, 518. ENE, VI, 128, 295 ff.; VII, 265. AGN, Mercedes, vol. 4, fols. 153r–153v, 163r–163v; vol. 6, fol. 331r–331v; vol. 8, fol. 202r–202v.

16. AC, VI, 494. Montúfar, "Carta del arzobispo," p. 353. CDIAI, IV, 518.

17. *Disposiciones complementarias*, I, 96–97. Puga, *Provisiones*, fols. 135r, 140v ff. CDIAI, VI, 503. CDIU, X, 254; XXI, 280 ff. CDIHIA, VIII, 339.

18. An example of pre-conquest tribute to a local tlatoani may be seen in Teotihuacan. Guzmán, "Un manuscrito," pp. 93–94. This edition is preferable to Chavero, "Teotihuacan," pp. 431–63. See also *Información sobre los tributos*, pp. 61 ff. Tributes to caciques in the mid-sixteenth century are exemplified in Coyoacan. Fernández del Castillo, *Apuntes*, p. 25. See also Guzmán, "Un manuscrito," pp. 97 ff.

19. Guzmán, "Un manuscrito," pp. 97 ff. Zorita, *Historia*, p. 408.

20. See examples in AGN, Indios, vol. 1, fols. 16v, 44v–45r, 69v–70r; Tierras, vol. 994, 6th pag., fol. 15r.

21. On the exemption of caciques and principales, see CDIAI, IV, 444–45; XIII, 254–55, 299–300. ENE, VII, 264.

On the exemption of those paying to private Indian recipients, see the following: ENE, VII, 262. CDIAI, II, 25, 89–90, 92, 95, 101; IV, 361. CDIHIA, I, 218. CDHM, II, 120–21. *Sobre el modo de tributar*, p. 97.

On exemption of the aged and infirm, see: CDIAI, II, 92, 120; XII, 255–56. Valderrama, *Cartas*, p. 69.

On the exemption of children living with their families, see CDIAI, II, 91–92. CDIAI, XIII, 256. But compare the remarks of Vasco de Puga in ENE, X, 34, where it is suggested that persons under fourteen years were taxed in the Indian system in Xochimilco.

Exemption of merchants is mentioned in ENE, VII, 297. But it is most likely that merchants commonly did pay tribute in the Indian system, the tribute being the cloth, feathers, precious stones, and other objects of their merchandise. See the remarks of Zorita in CDIAI, II, 88, 93, 97.

Regarding the exemption of craftsmen, Ramírez de Fuenleal stated in 1532 that in some locations the pintores, serving as scribes, were exempted. See CDIAI, XIII, 255. But craftsmen were likewise tribute payers in the Indian system. See Zorita's remarks on this subject in CDIAI, II, 88, 93, 97.

22. CDIAI, II, 92; IV, 361; XIII, 255–56. ENE, VII, 297. Valderrama, *Cartas*, pp. 59, 69. Other pre-conquest classes reported as having been exempt from tribute were the mandones, war heroes, orphans, widows, and poor. There is some indication that these were also exempt in early colonial tribute, and this would appear a likely contingency in view of the continued Indian control over tribute collection. See CDIAI, II, 92, 120; XIII, 255–56. Numbers of persons exempt from tribute are sometimes given in the Suma de Visitas (PNE, I) and in later reports (e.g., García Pimentel, *Descripción*, pp. 259 ff.).

23. Miranda rejects the evidence indicating that tributes might be graduated in accordance with land allotments. See Miranda, *El tributo indígena*, pp. 32–33. To me, on the other hand, the evidence appears quite convincing, not only for the pre-conquest period in Chalco and Texcoco and elsewhere, but also and continuously in the colonial period. CDIAI, IV, 443; VI, 167, 169. CDIHE, IV, 200. ENE, VII, 262. NCDHM (1941), III, 9. *Información sobre los tributos*, pp. 62 ff. *Códice Mariano Jiménez*, fols. 3v–4r. It is clear, however, that pre-conquest tributes, graduated in accordance with land holdings, did not apply to all towns. See, e.g., *Información sobre los tributos*, p. 62.

24. The evidence is from a document of 1561. *Sobre el modo de tributar*, pp. 106–7.

25. *Sobre el modo de tributar*, pp. 111–12.

26. MNM, Colección franciscana, 190, fols. 10r ff. García Pimentel, *Descripción*, pp. 64–65, *et passim*. FHT, I, 72. AGN, Mercedes, vol. 84, fol. 118r–118v.

27. For the pre-conquest periodization of payment, see *Información sobre los tributos*, pp. 30 ff. Barlow, "The Periods of Tribute Collection," pp. 152–54.

28. The most fully documented example of a town's tribute as of ca. 1550 relates to Utlaspa, just north of the Valley of Mexico, pictorially recorded in *Códice Mariano Jiménez*. Evidence for tribute procedure in the Valley of Mexico to the mid-sixteenth century may be found in *El libro de las tasaciones* and in the Suma de Visitas (PNE, I), as well as in a number of individual town notices in BAGN, VII, 191 ff. (Huitzilopochco, Mixquic, Mexicalzingo, Chiconauhtla, Tenayuca, Texcoco, Chalco, Otumba), 537 ff. (Mexicalzingo, Coatepec, Chalco, Otumba); VIII, 188 ff. (Xochimilco, Chalco, Texcoco, Acalhuacan); XI, 204 ff. (many towns); CDIAI, XII, 333–34 (Otumba, Chalco, Texcoco); CDIHIA, I, 167 ff. (Culhuacan, Mexicalzingo, Huitzilopochco); ENE, III, 91 (Chalco); IV, 128–30 (Texcoco); VI, 117–19 (Huitzilopochco); VIII, 148–50 (Mexicalzingo, Coatepec, Chalco, Otumba); X, 23 ff. (Tlalmanalco, Tenango, Xochimilco, Mexico, Chimalhuacan, Tlalmanalco, Tenango), 59 (Amecameca); XI, 6 ff. (Coyoacan, Tacubaya); XIV, 116 ff. (Chalco, Texcoco, Xochimilco, Mexico). There is some duplication in these listings.

29. See Mendoza's remarks on the occasions for introducing new tasaciones, in CDIAI, VI, 503.

30. CDIAI, IV, 443–44; VI, 167; XIII, 236. ENE, VII, 260–61. Oviedo y Valdés, *Historia general y natural*, III, 537.

31. A document of one of the Otumba estancias, dated as late as 1563, refers to "sementeras de su magestad" from which royal tributes were paid. See AGN, Mercedes, vol. 6, fols. 313v–314r. We cannot document continuity in the actual lands so employed from the time of Montezuma to the time of royal or encomienda tribute in any

instance in the Valley of Mexico. But continuity is unequivocally stated in certain towns outside the Valley of Mexico (e.g., Acayuca and Chachoapam, *El libro de las tasaciones,* pp. 3, 166–67), and it may reasonably be supposed in at least some instances in the Valley as well.

32. See the cases of Tlalmanalco in 1556 and of Nonoalco and Ahuatepec, sujetos of Otumba, in 1563. AGN, Mercedes, vol. 4, fol. 312r; vol. 7, fol. 40r–40v.

33. *El libro de las tasaciones,* pp. 305–6. The particular tasación was made in 1556 and was not changed until 1564. See also the statement of 1562: "Todos ayudan a beneficiar el tributo que dan a Vuestra Majestad, que es cinco mil fanegas de maíz." *Sobre el modo de tributar,* p. 28. For Texcoco the comparable amount was 8,000 fanegas, but this included Huexotla, Chiauhtla, Tezayuca, and probably Coatlichan. See Chapter III, note 89, and *El libro de las tasaciones,* pp. 481–82.

34. Spanish provisions for poor and good harvests are exemplified in the case of Citlaltepec in 1564. See *El libro de las tasaciones,* p. 646. Indian derramas for paying deficits in poor harvest years are documented for Tlalmanalco in 1556. See AGN, Mercedes, vol. 4, fol. 312r.

35. The process is documented for a large number of towns in *El libro de las tasaciones, passim.* The change in Xochimilco, dated 1564, followed upon Indian refusal to cultivate lands for royal tribute. See AGN, Mercedes, vol. 6, fol. 207r–207v, for the refusal, and *El libro de las tasaciones,* p. 306, for the change. See also Zorita, *Historia,* pp. 408 ff., and Zorita's further remarks on the difficulties created by this change, in CDIAI, II, 100.

36. It followed upon royal orders for the conversion of commodity payments to payments in gold and silver or for a reduction in the variety of commodity payments. CDIU, X, 247. *Disposiciones complementarias,* I, 131. A royal ruling is specifically cited in the 1556 tasación of Texcoco. ENE, IV, 129. *El libro de las tasaciones,* pp. 481–82.

37. BAGN, VII, 539–40. ENE, IV, 129. CDIHIA, I, 196–97. ENE, IX, 2 ff., lists the various goods paid in encomienda in 1560 and their values.

38. See, e.g., AGI, Contaduría, leg. 729, sep. pag., fols. 11r ff.; leg. 788, ramo 2.

39. CDIHE, XXVI, 345–47. AC, VII, 181. PNE, III (Supl.), 37–38, *et passim.* AGI, Patronato, leg. 181, ramo 20.

40. For various data on sales of tribute goods see BAGN, VII, 186; ENE, XIV, 116; CDIU, XXIV, 94–95; and especially the very full financial record of AHH, Tributos, leg. 225, exp. 1.

41. Thus some 400 Indian "hijosdalgos" (i.e., principales) and persons serving in the churches in Xochimilco were required to pay tributes to the Indian community ca. 1553, but not yet to Spaniards. See CDIAI, XIII, 299–300. In 1564, despite Indian protest, "every married man" as well as widows, widowers, bachelors, and spinsters became liable in tribute payment to Spaniards. *El libro de las tasaciones,* p. 306.

42. Miranda, *El tributo indígena,* pp. 133–38.

43. NCDHM, IV, 135. CDIAI, II, 102, 120–21; IV, 361. ENE, VII, 264; X, 34. Cuevas, *Documentos inéditos,* p. 226. On the Spanish theory of just exemption from tribute see Solórzano y Pereira, *Política indiana,* pp. 92 ff. On the exemption of the Indians of Santa Fe, see León, *Documentos inéditos,* p. 40. Caciques were however generally exempted, by a royal order of 1572. *Recopilación de leyes,* II, 230 (Lib. VI, tít. 5, ley 18). The relatives of caciques were often also exempted by special viceregal license. See, e.g., AGN, Indios, vol. 2, fol. 85r.

44. *El libro de las tasaciones, passim.* The arrangements for half-tributaries appear to have derived from Spanish practices and not from pre-conquest Indian exemptions. This history is not wholly clear, but note that in sixteenth-century Spain two widows might be counted as one vecino. See, e.g., Viñas y Mey and Paz, *Relaciones*, I, 42.

45. A transitional schedule in Xochimilco required payments four times per year. See *Sobre el modo de tributar,* pp. 111–12. For the standard payments by tercios see *El libro de las tasaciones, passim.* An example of private debt repaid in four-month periods in 1542 may be seen in AC, IV, 275.

46. An example of the phrase may be seen in the Zumpango tasación of 1565 in *El libro de las tasaciones,* p. 659. Note, however, that the possession of land by an aged, blind, poor, or crippled person might eliminate the exemption, for such possession was regarded as an indication that the disability was a minor one. See, e.g., the Tlatelolco regulation of 1564 in *El libro de las tasaciones,* p. 516. It is interesting that Zorita states that such persons were exempted in the pre-conquest period even if they were landholders. See CDIAI, II, 92. Practice in this probably also varied from community to community. A sixteenth-century variant is indicated in *Sobre el modo de tributar,* pp. 95, 101, where the bachelor remaining under dominio paternal gave one-quarter of a full tribute payment and was regarded as a quarter tributary.

47. *Cartas de Indias,* p. 307. See also the argument against "personal tribute" (i.e., the uniform head tax without regard to property) in CDIAI, VI, 166 ff.

48. *Sobre el modo de tributar,* pp. 105–6.

49. *Cartas de Indias,* p. 308.

50. Continued Indian apportionment by landholding appears clearly in the Marqués del Valle letter of 1563, in CDIAI, IV, 445. In Xochimilco in the 1560's principales paid one-half fanega of maize while maceguales paid one-quarter fanega. See Puga's letter of 1564 in ENE, X, 34. Graduated tributes by land, by houses, and even by the fertility of the soil are indicated in *Sobre el modo de tributar,* pp. 95, 98, 102.

51. E.g., CDIAI, VI, 166 ff.

52. See examples in PNE, III, 14, 17.

53. ENE, X, 34. AGN, Mercedes, vol. 4, fol. 153r–153v. AGI, Justicia, leg. 151, no. 1, fols. 70v–71r, 74r–74v. CDIAI, II, 121.

54. The first Spanish counts for the city of Mexico in the early 1560's exempted youths of twelve and under. *Sobre el modo de tributar,* p. 44. But later rules forbade collection from any under fourteen. See, e.g., AGN, Indios, vol. 6 (1), fol. 75v.

55. ENE, X, 34. *El libro de las tasaciones,* pp. 149–50, *et passim.* An example of Indian disregard of the distinction between those living with their parents and those living separately may be seen in Tecama. See AGN, Mercedes, vol. 4, fol. 153r–153v.

56. The rule is not wholly clear. Presumably the king intended it to apply to both men and women while the distinction between whole and half tributaries continued. See Encinas, *Cedulario,* IV, 322. The text in *Recopilación de leyes,* II, 226–27 (Lib. VI, tít. 5, ley 7), adds a maximum of fifty years and reduces the minimum age to eighteen. These provisions may stem from the later enactment of 1618. Cf. Miranda, *El tributo indígena,* p. 141.

57. An example is the 1559 tasación for Acalhuacan in BAGN, VIII, 205–6.

58. Examples of payments of one and one-half reales to the communities, not all however in addition to the peso paid to the crown or encomendero, may be examined in ENE, X, 21–24; AGN, Indios, vol. 1, fols. 107r–108r, 111v–112r, 113v–114r, *et passim.* See also the 1565 rule for Culhuacan, where each tributary had paid one and

one-half reales for the community and contributed to a planting for the gobernador, and where the new ruling raised the payment to two reales and eliminated the planting. *El libro de las tasaciones,* p. 156. The identification of gubernatorial and community funds in this instance is noteworthy. See also BAGN, VIII, 204; Zorita, *Historia,* pp. 409–10. A number of examples of tribute division between community and crown or encomendero, some with arithmetical errors, may be examined in *El libro de las tasaciones.* Other tributes of the 1560's however continued in an earlier form. See, e.g., Citlaltepec in 1563, where payments to the comunidad still included chickens, cacao, fuel, mantles, petates, and the produce of common planting of maize, chile, and beans. The list is in AGN, Mercedes, vol. 7, fols. 54v–55r.

59. *El libro de las tasaciones,* pp. 59, 206, 308, 508, 542.

60. This remarkable document is BNP, no. 376.

61. The original rule of 1577 is recorded in Bentura Beleña, *Recopilación sumaria,* I, 54. A similar and earlier rule may be noted in Xochimilco in 1558, where each oficial and macegual was required to work a field of five by ten brazas or a chinampa of one by ten brazas. See *Sobre el modo de tributar,* pp. 106, 109.

62. In Texcoco Indian craftsmen were not excused, though they for a time refused to contribute. See AGN, General de parte, vol. 2, fol. 111r–111v. We have no record of any attempt to enforce the rule in Mexico City.

63. The phrase "en quadro" in the order of 1577 is presumably to be applied both to the ten-vara and to the five-vara measurements. See Bentura Beleña, *Recopilación sumaria,* I, 54.

64. There can be no doubt that subsequent references to this rule, including references by the audiencia itself, indicated brazas rather than varas. FHT, II, 296. AGN, Indios, vol. 1, fols. 113v, 137r; vol. 5, fol. 340v; Tierras, vol. 1923, exp. 1, fol. 23v. AGI, México, leg. 24, ramo 1. Bentura Beleña, *Recopilación sumaria,* I, 40. *Recopilación de leyes,* II, 222 (Lib. VI, tít. 4, ley 31). Ten brazas, as normally understood, would be the equivalent of twenty varas, and this equation is specifically made with reference to these plantings in AGN, Tierras, vol. 1923, exp. 2, fol. 49r. If the original intention was in fact ten varas, the effect would be to quadruple the size of each tributary's payment. A reference in AC, VIII, 578, raises the amount still further, to fifty brazas.

65. These confusions become evident from the record of land distribution in Tlalmanalco in 1764. Here the ten brazas were assigned to peones after the manner of calpullalli and by barrios. A barrio of twenty-six peones was assigned 1,040 varas, or forty varas per peón, but it is not clear if this represents a two-dimensional, a peripheral, or some other measurement. See AGN, Tierras, vol. 1923, exp. 2.

66. AGN, Indios, vol. 1, fols. 111v–112v. I have rounded the figures to eliminate fractions.

67. Fonseca and Urrutia, *Historia,* I, 519 ff., provides the legal history of this tax.

68. AC, XI, 189. Gómez de Cervantes, *La vida económica,* pp. 119–20. The event is mentioned, and a chicken illustrated, in *Histoire de la nation mexicaine,* p. 133, under the year 1595—a fact that would seem to indicate only a gradual enforcement after the original order of 1592. Torquemada's assertion that the abolition occurred early in the rule of Viceroy Conde de Monterrey is incorrect and is specifically denied by the Conde de Monterrey himself. Torquemada, *Monarchia indiana,* I, 653. *Advertimientos generales,* pp. 76–77. Chickens received in tribute were both sold to the public and granted to religious and charitable institutions. See AGN, General de parte, vol.

5, fols. 1r, 86v, 91r, 105v. AGI, México, leg. 24, ramo 4. AGN, Reales cédulas, duplicados, vol. 69, fol. 242v. *Recopilación de leyes,* II, 236 (Lib. VI, tít. 5, ley 42).

69. The cedula is dated 1591 but collection of the Servicio Real began in 1592. NCDHM (1886–92), V, 116 ff. Fonseca and Urrutia, *Historia,* I, 418–19. Chimalpahin, *Annales,* p. 14. AC, XI, 18. See also AAMC, no. 10, p. 504; no. 15, p. 703. *Recopilación de leyes,* II, 228–29 (Lib. VI, tít. 5, ley 16).

70. Fonseca and Urrutia, *Historia,* I, 536 ff. Bentura Beleña, *Recopilación sumaria,* I, 3rd pag., 232. Maniau Torquemada, *Compendio,* pp. 75 ff. Díez de la Calle, *Memorial,* pp. 126–27.

71. For the alcabala see Bentura Beleña, *Recopilación sumaria,* I, 55, 77, and Fonseca and Urrutia, *Historia,* II, 5 ff.; III, 176. Viceregal permission was sometimes given to Indian authorities for the collection of extra tributes in order to make up deficits of past years. See, e.g., the case of Xochimilco in 1620 in AGN, Indios, vol. 9, fols. 100v–101r.

72. Bentura Beleña, *Recopilación sumaria,* I, 77–78. Fonseca and Urrutia, *Historia,* I, 417–18. CDIHE, XXVI, 387. *Recopilación de leyes,* II, 227 (Lib. VI, tít. 5, ley 8).

73. The number of bondsmen per jurisdiction varied considerably. In the 1790's the number ranged from one in the jurisdiction of Coyoacan to eleven in that of Chalco. See the interesting materials of AGN, Tributos, vol. 16, exp. 13.

74. E.g., in Acolman, AGN, Tributos, vol. 25, exp. 7, fols. 64r ff.; in Tepexpan, AGN, Tierras, vol. 1649, exp. 2.

75. AGI, Contaduría, leg. 788, ramo 3. AGN, Tierras, vol. 1649, exp. 2; Hospital de Jesús, vol. 156, exp. 8, fols. 4v ff.; vol. 325, exp. 5, fols. 24r ff. Fonseca and Urrutia, *Historia,* I, 422 ff. The nine-real conversion followed upon a number of instances of fraud. E.g., in Tepozotlan persons to whom the tribute maize was entrusted refused to take it on time, permitted it to spoil, and then collected in money at high prices. See AGN, Indios, vol. 3, fol. 68r–68v. Moreover, when harvests were poor Indian communities not only had less to eat but had to pay more for maize to give in tribute. See AGN, Congregaciones, vol. 1, fol. 11v. The uniform nine-real value followed upon a rule of 1627. See AGN, Reales cédulas, duplicados, vol. 9, fols. 75r–76r.

76. AGN, Tierras, vol. 1649, exp. 2; Hospital de Jesús, vol. 120, exp. 6, fols. 1r ff.; vol. 319, exp. 12, fols. 26r ff.

77. AGN, Tributos, vol. 25, exp. 7, fol. 64r; Hospital de Jesús, vol. 319, exp. 12, fols. 26r–27r.

78. CDIHE, XXI, 520. Puga, *Provisiones,* fol. 102v. Alzate, *Gacetas de literatura,* IV, 102. Cavo, *Historia de México,* p. 233. AGN, Indios, vol. 50, fols. 2r ff.; General de parte, vol. 2, fol. 211v; Tributos, vol. 11, exp. 13. On the other hand, Indian officers were sometimes jailed for their failure to deliver tributes in the most severe crises, as in the flood of 1630 in Mexico City and the plague of 1736. See AGN, Hospital de Jesús, vol. 302, exp. 1, fols. 1v ff.; Indios, vol. 12 (1), fols. 77r–78r.

79. Bentura Beleña, *Recopilación sumaria,* I, 62–63.

80. FHT, VI, 503–4, 549–52; VII, 419–20, 435–36. On the forms for tribute reporting and the classifications of tributaries, see Bentura Beleña, *Recopilación sumaria,* I, 3rd pag., 39; AGN, Tributos, vol. 3, exp. 2, fols. 43r ff.; vol. 15, exp. 2, fols. 7r ff.

81. AGN, Hospital de Jesús, vol. 266, exp. 7, fols. 8r, 29r; vol. 278, exp. 10, fols. 9r ff.; vol. 319, exp. 28, fol. 1r; vol. 325, exp. 5, fol. 2r. For collection procedure in the Coyoacan jurisdiction see AGN, Hospital de Jesús, vol. 382. Maize tributes to the Marqués del Valle were paid by Chimalhuacan Chalco, Tlalmanalco, Amecameca, Ecatzingo,

Chalco Atenco, Xochimilco, Milpa Alta, Atocpan, Tenango Tepopula, Ayapango, and other communities. See AGN, Hospital de Jesús, vol. 156, exp. 1.

82. Bentura Beleña, *Recopilación sumaria*, I, 54–55. AGI, Contaduría, leg. 729, fols. 34r ff. AC, XXV, 67–68.

83. AC, VIII, 362 ff.; XXXIV, 3 ff. AGI, México, leg. 24, ramos 2–3.

84. AGN, Civil, vol. 1271, exp. 4; Hospital de Jesús, vol. 333, exp. 2, fol. 18r–18v. FHT, VI, 513–14.

85. AGN, Tributos, vol. 23, exp. 5, fols. 1r ff.; Hospital de Jesús, vol. 302, exp. 7, fol. 24r; vol. 382, exp. 38. See the varieties of procedure in delivery to Spanish authority in AGI, Contaduría, leg. 735, fols. 12r ff.; leg. 825 (1), *passim*. See also the various data on tribute collection in the Ecatepec jurisdiction in AGN, Padrones, vol. 47, fols. 161v ff.

86. Printed receipts are preserved in AGN, Hospital de Jesús, exp. 24. More often receipts were issued in manuscript. See the evidence for the Otumba jurisdiction in the 1790's, where printed receipts were issued for Otumba itself and manuscript receipts elsewhere. *Documentos para la historia económica*, V, 26.

87. The continued relationship between the size of the tribute payment and the size of the land allotment is clearly expressed in testimonies taken in Coyoacan in 1731. See AGN, Hospital de Jesús, vol. 156, exp. 6, fols. 3r ff.

88. *Recopilación de leyes*, II, 226–27 (Lib. VI, tít. 5, ley 7). Gálvez, *Informe general*, p. 87. In some notices the upper limit was not mentioned, and it is probable that the number of persons exempted for old age was smaller than the number of persons over fifty years. Thus in Tacubaya in 1727 of 349 persons otherwise liable only one was exempted for old age. León, "Bibliografía," no. 4, p. 90. AGN, Hospital de Jesús, vol. 319, exp. 12, fols. 21v–22r.

89. AGN, Tributos, vol. 11, exp. 5, fols. 5r ff.; Hospital de Jesús, vol. 319, exp. 12, fol. 21v; vol. 329, exp. 2, fol. 9r.

90. The tribute matrícula in Ecatepec in 1781 was an elaborate form with eleven categories: caciques, widows and spinsters, reserved, Indian women married to mulattoes, absentees of both sexes, children, young men about to become tributaries, Indian men married to Indian women, Indian men married to absentees and other castas, Indian bachelors and widows, and the total of the last three. See BNM, ms. no. 451, fol. 294r. It thus foreshadowed the post-intendancy form.

91. The official rule was that both a cacique and his eldest son were exempt from tribute. See Bentura Beleña, *Recopilación sumaria*, I, 3rd pag., 40; BNM, ms. no. 482, fol. 85v.

92. AA, Tierras y ejidos, leg. 1, no. 4065, exp. 20, fols. 14r–15r.

93. *Instrucciones que los vireyes de Nueva España dejaron* (1867), p. 88. Fonseca and Urrutia, *Historia*, I, 434. The proposal to exempt widows was already made in the sixteenth century. See *Sobre el modo de tributar*, p. 33. Moreover, a *Recopilación* law of 1618 exempts women. *Recopilación de leyes*, II, 230 (Lib. VI, tít. 5, ley 19).

94. Bentura Beleña, *Recopilación sumaria*, I, 3rd pag., 39, 43.

95. Bentura Beleña, *Recopilación sumaria*, II, sep. pag., xlii–xliii. BNM, ms. no. 451, fol. 290r.

96. AGN, Tributos, vol. 3, exp. 2, fols. 43r ff.; vol. 43, exp. último, fol. 4r–4v.

97. *Instrucciones que los vireyes de Nueva España dejaron* (1867), p. 122. *Instrucciones que los vireyes de Nueva España dejaron* (1873), II, 360.

98. BNM, ms. no. 451, fols. 287r ff., 300r.

99. Bentura Beleña, *Recopilación sumaria*, I, 3rd pag., 16. Fonseca and Urrutia, *Historia*, I, 525 ff.

100. AGN, General de parte, vol. 5, fol. 266v. BAGN, XIV, 423 ff. Bentura Beleña, *Recopilación sumaria*, I, 43; 4th pag., 204. León, "Bibliografía," no. 1, pp. 158 ff. Maniau Torquemada, *Compendio*, pp. 78–79. *Instrucciones que los vireyes de Nueva España dejaron* (1867), p. 32. Full data on the Medio Real del Hospital may be found in AGI, México, leg. 2774, *passim*, and in Fonseca and Urrutia, *Historia*, VI, 199 ff.

101. BNM, ms. no. 451, fol. 291r. Bentura Beleña, *Recopilación sumaria*, II, sep. pag., xlii. The same ordinances fixed the payment for Negroes and mulattoes at twenty-four reales, payable at eighteen years of age for both married and single persons. Bentura Beleña, *Recopilación sumaria*, II, sep. pag., xliii. In the Ecatepec jurisdiction, where a full tributary's payment had been only thirteen reales per year, the intendancy order would have meant an increase of four reales per year. Here the various intendancy changes would have meant an annual tribute increment of 1,089 pesos for the entire jurisdiction. For a full accounting of the pre-intendancy figures here see BNM, ms. no. 451, fols. 287r–300v.

102. Bentura Beleña, *Recopilación sumaria*, I, 3rd pag., 48. Fonseca and Urrutia, *Historia*, I, fac. 450. The figures should not be understood as absolutely accurate. The table of Fonseca and Urrutia contains some internal inconsistencies and probably other errors. Maniau Torquemada, *Compendio*, pp. 10–11, gives a total range in New Spain between twelve and twenty-four reales. Gálvez, *Informe*, p. 92, gives the range between eight and twenty-four reales. It is noteworthy that Viceroy Conde de Revillagigedo in 1792 ordered the tribute in Mexico City to continue at thirteen reales per year despite the intendancy rules. See BNM, ms. no. 466, fol. 279r.

103. AGN, Hospital de Jesús, vol. 278, exp. 6, fol. 5v; vol. 319, exp. 12, fols. 30r ff; vol. 333, exp. 10, *passim*. Maniau Torquemada, *Compendio*, p. 10, and Humboldt, *Political Essay*, I, 87, both state that the tribute in 1601 amounted to thirty-six reales per tributary per year. If so, this would represent the high point. But we have no evidence that official levies ever rose this high in the Valley of Mexico.

104. AGN, Tierras, vol. 191, exp. 6, fols. 1r ff.

105. AGI, Justicia, leg. 164, no. 2, fols. 50r ff., 119r ff.; leg. 165, no. 2, fols. 232r ff.; leg. 208, no. 4, fol. 229r.

106. Sixteenth-century cases pertaining to this subject, relating to Huexotla, Texcoco, and Tecama, may be examined in AGN, General de parte, vol. 1, fol. 108v; vol. 2, fols. 63r–63v, 143r.

107. AGN, Tributos, vol. 2, exp. 4. In the double cabecera, Azcapotzalco, on the other hand, the sixteenth-century custom was to divide the estancias' contributions to the cabecera in such a way that the Mexica portion and the Tepaneca portion received equal amounts. See AGN, General de parte, vol. 3, fol. 75r. This of course relates to intra-Indian tributes and the "sobras de tributos," not to Spanish tribute collection.

108. AGI, Contaduría, leg. 735, fols. 12r ff. AGN, Tributos, vol. 25, fol. 74r.

109. AGN, Tierras, vol. 1649, exp. 2.

110. E.g.., Bentura Beleña, *Recopilación sumaria*, I, 92.

111. NCDHM (1886–92), IV, 183. AGN, Hospital de Jesús, vol. 329, exp. 2, fols. 2r ff., 8r ff.; Tributos, vol. 6, exp. 22. Indians were technically free to move from one community to another, but they were required to pay in full the year's tribute in the original location, and they incurred the risk of double assessment. See, e.g., FHT, VI, 253–54. See Zavala, "La libertad de movimiento," pp. 103–63.

112. BNM, ms. no. 439, fol. 465; ms. no. 451, fols. 291v–292r.

113. García and Pereyra, *Documentos inéditos*, VII, 71. Bentura Beleña, *Recopilación sumaria*, I, 3rd pag., 16, 41–42, 45; 5th pag., 207. Fonseca and Urrutia, *Historia*, I, 526 ff.

114. Bentura Beleña, *Recopilación sumaria*, I, 15–16; 5th pag., 232. Gómez de Cervantes, *La vida económica*, p. 134.

115. AGN, Indios, vol. 12 (1), fol. 51v; Hospital de Jesús, vol. 319, exp. 15, fol. 20v.

116. AGN, Hospital de Jesús, vol. 278, exp. 10, fols. 1r ff., 9r ff., 25r; vol. 325, exp. 5, fols. 10r ff.; Indios, vol. 3, fols. 68r–68v, 69r.

117. AGN, Tributos, vol. 22, exp. 17, fols. 14v–15r.

118. AGN, General de parte, vol. 2, fols. 295v–296r, 301v; Indios, vol. 2, fols. 100r–100v, 133r–133v, 135v–136r, 138r.

119. AGN, Hospital de Jesús, vol. 325, exp. 5, fols. 42r ff. The ten-vara plantings were still maintained in Tlalmanalco in the late eighteenth century, while in nearby Xochitepec each tributary was contributing one and one-half reales to the caja. AGN, Tierras, vol. 1923, exp. 1. *Al severo tribunal*, p. 81.

120. AGN, Mercedes, vol. 10, fols. 243r–244r.

121. Examples in Tenayuca and Chicoloapa are documented in AGN, Mercedes, vol. 7, fol. 274r; Tierras, vol. 1811, exp. 1, fol. 27r.

122. CDIAI, IV, 443. AGN, Indios, vol. 21, fol. 180v; vol. 50, fols. 21v–22v.

123. *Al severo tribunal*, pp. 34–35. AGI, Contaduría, leg. 763 (A), "Servicio Real," 1671.

124. AGN, Hospital de Jesús, vol. 120, exp. 6, fol. 2v.

125. *Documentos para la historia económica*, V, 14–15, 17. See also AGN, Tierras, vol. 1466, exp. 1, fols. 86r ff., for the earlier eighteenth century.

126. Bentura Beleña, *Recopilación sumaria*, II, sep. pag., xvi. AGN, Hospital de Jesús, vol. 120, exp. 6, fol. 3r–3v.

127. AGN, Tierras, vol. 2, exp. 4, fols. 23r ff.; vol. 1466, exp. 1, 4th pag., fols. 3v–4r; vol. 1702, exp. 4, fol. 95r; Hospital de Jesús, vol. 130, exp. 6, fol. 3r–3v; Tributos, vol. 24, exp. 8, fol. 3r. *Documentos para la historia económica*, V, 1 ff.

128. Navarro de Vargas, "Padrón," p. 595. *Al severo tribunal*, pp. 101, 103 ff.

129. CDIU, XXI, 327.

130. Encinas, *Cedulario*, IV, 325.

131. Bentura Beleña, *Recopilación sumaria*, I, 3rd pag., 4. But at various times other officials were authorized, or required, to be key holders, including escribanos, regidores, and mayordomos. *El libro de las tasaciones*, p. 483, *et passim*. AGN, Hospital de Jesús, vol. 319, exp. 12, fol. 26r. Bentura Beleña, *Recopilación sumaria*, I, 54; II, sep. pag., xvi. In Azcapotzalco in 1555 the Mexica gobernador was to hold one key, the Tepaneca gobernador another, and the alcaldes the third. See AGN, Mercedes, vol. 4, fol. 202r. Later the two governments maintained separate cajas. See AGN, Tierras, vol. 2, exp. 4, fol. 23r.

132. E.g., for Ixtacalco and other towns in AGN, Tierras, vol. 1058, exp. 4, fols. 2r ff.; for Huitzilopochco in AGN, Tierras, vol. 1702, exp. 4, fols. 9v ff.; for Coyoacan in AGN, Hospital de Jesús, vol. 333, exp. 2, fols. 6r ff.; for Axapusco in AGN, Tierras, vol. 1466, exp. 1, final pag.; for Tlalmanalco in AGN, Tierras, vol. 1923, exps. 5–6.

133. Bentura Beleña, *Recopilación sumaria*, I, 39.

134. E.g., AGN, Tierras, vol. 566, exp. 4, fol. 4r–4v; AA, Aguas Tacubaya y Otros Pueblos, leg. 1, no. 55, exp. 1, fols. 4v ff.

135. The various investments of the towns of Chalco jurisdiction of 1769 are recorded in AGN, Tierras, vol. 1518, exp. 1, fols. 22r ff. The list indicates what would be expected, that towns with funds to loan were relatively rare. On the other hand, substantial sums might be involved. Cuitlahuac in 1769 had 4,846 pesos invested in a mortgage loan yielding five per cent. Occasionally the record indicates also town income from speculation in the eighteenth-century lottery. See AGN, Padrones, vol. 6, fol. 317v.

136. Numerous examples may be found in *El libro de las tasaciones, passim.*

137. Montúfar, "Carta del arzobispo," pp. 352–53.

138. AGN, General de parte, vol. 1, fol. 130v.

139. *Al severo tribunal,* p. 57. AGN, Congregaciones, vol. 1, fols. 117v–118r. Similar lands, with income used for ecclesiastical expenses, are documented in Ayapango, Amecameca, and other towns. See AGN, Tierras, vol. 1518, exp. 1, fols. 23r ff.

140. E.g., AGN, Tierras, vol. 1466, exp. 1, final pag.; vol. 1923, exp. 6.

141. See the order in *La administración de D. Frey Antonio María de Bucareli,* II, 177 ff. Bentura Beleña, *Recopilación sumaria,* I, 5th pag., 209–10. For an act of payment to the maestro de escuela see AGN, Tierras, vol. 1058, exp. 4, fol. 8v. Mixquic and Tepopula are examples of towns that assigned particular lands, the income from which (by land rental or sale of the produce) was used to pay the maestro de escuela. See AGN, Tierras, vol. 1518, exp. 1, fols. 22v, 25r.

142. Bentura Beleña, *Recopilación sumaria,* II, sep. pag., xviii–xix. *Documentos para la historia económica,* V, 45 ff.

143. AGN, Tierras, vol. 1702, exp. 4, fols. 99v–100r. CDIAI, IV, 360, 442, 515. García Pimentel, *Descripción,* pp. 64, 225–26. Encinas, *Cedulario,* IV, 325. Zorita, *Historia,* p. 408.

144. E.g., to six specified days in Xochimilco. *Sobre el modo de tributar,* p. 110.

145. See the examples of the towns of the Otumba jurisdiction in *Documentos para la historia económica,* V.

146. E.g., Tacubaya, ENE, XI, 9–11; Mexicalzingo, AGN, Mercedes, vol. 8, fol. 222v.

147. ENE, XI, 106.

148. AGN, General de parte, vol. 1, fol. 152r, documents the permission to use force. Ca. 1614 Buenaventura de los Reyes, a cacique of Tlaxcala, was named by the viceroy as gobernador of Mixquic and specifically charged with the settlement of tribute arrears. By 1618 he had accomplished this to the viceroy's satisfaction. See AGN, Indios, vol. 7, fol. 144r–144v.

149. Fonseca and Urrutia, *Historia,* I, 422. A maize tribute debt in Texcoco was converted by the audiencia into a money debt of 1,700 pesos ca. 1598. See AC, XIII, 319.

150. AC, XX, 253–54; XXIII, 244. Payments for arrears were constantly demanded together with payments of amounts currently due. See AGI, Contaduría, leg. 729, fols. 30r ff.

151. AGN, Indios, vol. 9, fol. 168v; Civil, vol. 169, exp. 3, 2nd num. no. 69; Tributos, vol. 16, exp. 13.

152. AGI, Contaduría, leg. 763, *passim.* AGN, Indios, vol. 12 (1), fols. 77r–78r, 172v–173r; Hospital de Jesús, vol. 319, exp. 13, fol. 30r; exp. 15, fols. 23r ff. PCR, "Escriptura de obligacion que hisieron los naturales de Tescuco," fol. 2r.

153. AGN, Indios, vol. 12 (1), fols. 172v–173r; Hospital de Jesús, vol. 319, exp. 13, fol. 29r; exp. 16, *passim.*; vol. 325, exp. 5, fols. 11r ff.

154. A gobernador of Coyoacan held office for seventeen years, left office owing 7,000

pesos, collected and paid 5,200 pesos during the next five years, and was then ordered to complete the payment within eight days. AGN, Hospital de Jesús, vol. 319, exp. 18, fol. 1r.

155. AGN, Indios, vol. 12 (1), fols. 77r–78r.

156. Bentura Beleña, *Recopilación sumaria,* II, sep. pag., xxxix. A large number of records showing computations and receipts of the one per cent salary may be seen in AAH, Tributos, leg. 225, exp. 29. The salaries were paid to the collectors, who were in some instances alcaldes rather than gobernadores.

157. Examples may be seen in AGN, Hospital de Jesús, vol. 120, exp. 6, fols. 1r ff.; Tierras, vol. 1702, exp. 4, fols. 1r ff.

158. AGN, Hospital de Jesús, vol. 329, exp. 2, fols. 1v–2r, 6v–7r; vol. 333, exp. 1, fol. 6r.

159. In the 1620's and 1630's Xochimilco and Coyoacan each owed over 10,000 pesos in back tributes. See AGN, Hospital de Jesús, vol. 278, exp. 10, fols. 37v–38r. AC, XXIII, 243. See also AC, XXVII, 69.

160. AGN, Tributos, vol. 2, exps. 1, 5–8, *passim. Instrucciones que los vireyes de Nueva España dejaron* (1867), p. 86. Crises sometimes brought special exemptions and dispensations from Spanish authority, as in the epidemic years 1736–38, when tribute collection in some areas failed completely. But some of the gobernadores were jailed anyway. See AGN, Tributos, vol. 11, exp. 13; Hospital de Jesús, vol. 302, exp. 1, fols. 1v ff., 67r. Unscrupulous gobernadores sometimes announced a condition of crisis and a state of arrears so that they might be allowed to collect additional tributes. See AGN, Indios, vol. 50, fols. 81r–82r.

161. Tribute income by decades from 1600 to 1790 is tabulated in Fonseca and Urrutia, *Historia,* I, 450. Income and expenses in the various ramos as of 1794 are tabulated in "Estado de las rentas," p. 407.

162. Fisher, *Champion of Reform,* pp. 70–71, 74.

163. AGN, Tributos, vol. 23, exp. 14, fols. 8r, 12r ff.

164. AGN, Tierras, vol. 1412, exp. 5, fol. 11r–11v. *La constitución de 1812,* II, 87.

CHAPTER IX

1. See Chapter X.

2. Zorita's comments are in CDIAI, II, 105. On Indian chanting and singing during the rebuilding of Tenochtitlan see Motolinía, *History,* p. 42.

3. See the remarks of Cristóbal de Molina, in AC, XXIII, 244–45.

4. A cedula of 1522 permitted the Spanish "rescate" of Indians who were already slaves in Indian society. See AA, Barrio Lorenzot, nos. 439–40 (746–47), I, fol. 2r. The delivery of non-slaves as slaves is documented in Motolinía, *History,* p. 42, and CDIAI, XIII, 57 ff. See also ENE, XVI, 60. Ramírez de Fuenleal's remark occurs in CDIAI, XIII, 256.

5. ENE, I, 56 ff. Zavala, "Los esclavos indios," is a summary history of Spanish enslavement of Indians in Mexico.

6. *Disposiciones complementarias,* I, 77–78. FHT, III, 4–5. CDIAI, IV, 521. *Cartas de Indias,* p. 170. CDIHIA, I, 133. These citations are illustrative only; the subjects receive more detailed attention elsewhere in this book.

7. Many persons searched for gold and silver in the Valley of Mexico through the colonial period, but no deposits were found. See BNM, ms. no. 455, fol. 168v. There

were occasional salt and sulphur mines. Vetancurt, *Chronica*, p. 89. See Chapter XII.

8. Many commentators refer to the large number of Indian workers in the building of the city. See, e.g., Motolinía, *History*, p. 41; Castillo, *Fragmentos*, p. 107.

9. AGI, Justicia, leg. 124, no. 5, exp. 1; leg. 164, no. 2; leg. 165, no. 2. Fernández and Leicht, "Códice del tecpan." AGN, General de parte, vol. 1, fols. 124v, 172v.

10. E.g., in Tacubaya, AGN, Hospital de Jesús, vol. 279, exps. 41–42.

11. AGN, General de parte, vol. 3, fol. 75r; Indios, vol. 4, fols. 204r–205v. BNP, no. 30, fols. 8r ff. AGI, Justicia, leg. 152, no. 1, fols. 1r ff.

12. *Recopilación de leyes*, II, 286 ff. (Lib. VI, tít. 12, leyes 6 ff.). AC, II, 63; IX, 28. Puga, *Provisiones*, fol. 34r. CDIAI, XLI, 149–51.

13. CDIAI, XLI, 149–51. CDIU, X, 175–77. Encinas, *Cedulario*, IV, 304–6, 308–10. Torquemada, *Monarchia indiana*, III, 255. Puga, *Provisiones*, fols. 89r, 105r–106v, 200v–201v.

14. By 1538 the viceroy was in a position to grant free permission for the city's supply of native goods by tamemes, except by the route from Veracruz, which was to be traversed by animal pack trains. See AC, IV, 134.

15. AC, XV, 111–13. Part of the Spanish argument favoring the use of tamemes placed the responsibility on Indian society. Spaniards asserted that the custom was so established in Indian life that it could not be eradicated, and that Indians preferred to carry goods themselves even where an abundance of animals existed. See Mendoza's remarks in ENE, XVI, 29–36, and Cervantes de Salazar, *Crónica*, p. 26. The remarks contain some truth, but there can be no doubt that Spaniards exploited Indians as carriers.

16. Puga, *Cedulario*, fols. 172r–173r. CDIU, XXI, 270–71, 273, 279.

17. AC, VI, 227–28; VII, 9. Labor was still the only form of tribute exacted by Spaniards in the city. See AC, VI, 195; VII, 8. See also Chapter XIII.

18. Suárez de Peralta, *Noticias históricas*, pp. 164–65.

19. See Chapter X.

20. On the terminology see León Pinelo, *Tratado de confirmaciones reales*, fol. 5v.

21. Theoretical aspects of repartimiento, and the justification in terms of public utility, are discussed in Solórzano y Pereira, *Política indiana*, pp. 55 ff.

22. I have discussed the pre-conquest rotations in my article "Llamamiento general," pp. 2 ff. For the rotational service to Viceroy Mendoza, which alternated between inhabitants of Tenochtitlan and inhabitants of Tlatelolco in five-day and twenty-day shifts, see Aiton, *Antonio de Mendoza*, pp. 36, 49; Aiton, "The Secret Visita," p. 19.

23. Alamán, *Disertaciones*, I, 304 ff. CDIAI, XXVI, 166 ff.

24. Chimalpahin, *Annales*, p. 251. CDIHIA, I, 209.

25. CDIHIA, I, 209–10. *Códice Osuna*, pp. 193, 275. *Histoire de la nation mexicaine*, p. 96. AC, VI, 191–92. AGN, Mercedes, vol. 4, fols. 256v ff.

26. CDIAI, II, 115.

27. *Histoire de la nation mexicaine*, p. 96. CDIAI, II, 115. Chimalpahin, *Annales*, pp. 251–52. *Códice Osuna*, pp. 123 ff. Torquemada, *Monarchia indiana*, I, 192, 618. *Memoria histórica . . . del desagüe*, I, 59 ff. Both the pre-conquest dike and the dike of 1555–56 are illustrated on the mapa attributed (erroneously) to Alonso de Santa Cruz. See Apenas, *Mapas antiguos*, lám. 2.

28. Notices of the dimensions vary. See Cepeda and Carrillo, *Relación*, fol. 4r; Ojea, *Libro tercero*, p. 1; AGI, Patronato, leg. 181, ramo 30.

29. CDIHIA, I, 209–10. *Códice Osuna*, pp. 123–24.

30. AC, VI, 191–92. CDIAI, II, 114–15. *Memoria histórica* . . . *del desagüe*, I, 59 ff. AGN, Mercedes, vol. 4, fols. 256v ff.

31. The problem of repartimiento justification, with particular reference to agriculture, is discussed by Solórzano y Pereira, *Política indiana*, pp. 55 ff.

32. These are estimates of the mid-sixteenth century. See Chapter XIII, Table 27.

33. AGN, Mercedes, vol. 3, fols. 97v ff. There is evidence, however, that some form of agricultural repartimiento was already functioning by this date. The text speaks of workers already being given. Pedro Vásquez de Vergara later testified that he had served as repartidor in agriculture under Viceroy Mendoza, and though the references may be to the few months remaining of Mendoza's term after July, 1550, this would not appear to be the most likely interpretation. See AGI, Justicia, leg. 164, no. 2, fols. 130r ff. Viceroy Mendoza's Instrucción to his successor implies a limited labor at the beginning but one that had been developed considerably by the time of his departure from office. See CDIAI, VI, 506–7. In official mercedes, the shift from Mendoza's rule to Velasco's rule occurred between October 4 and November 28, 1550. AGN, Mercedes, vol. 3, fols. 211v–212r. Cf. Schäfer, *El Consejo real*, II, 439. Torquemada, *Monarchia indiana*, I, 647, is surely in error in the statement that the repartimiento de panes was introduced in the period of Viceroy Velasco. The successor of Vásquez de Vergara in 1553 was an alguacil, Bartolomé, presumably an Indian or mestizo. See NLAC, 1121, fol. 286r.

34. AGN, Mercedes, vol. 3, fols. 25v–26r, 97v ff. NLAC, 1121, fol. 286r.

35. AGN, Mercedes, vol. 4, fol. 210r–210v.

36. AGN, Mercedes, vol. 4, fol. 183r–183v.

37. AGN, Mercedes, vol. 7, fols. 141r–141v, 217v–219r. The area of the repartimiento was larger, however, than the area we are identifying as the Valley of Mexico. See Map 7.

38. Procedures in the main agricultural repartimientos of the Valley of Mexico may be studied in the recorded instructions to repartidores: Azcapotzalco in 1576, FHT, I, 111–14; Azcapotzalco in 1580, FHT, II, 250–57; Tacubaya in 1587, FHT, III, 27–28; Tacuba in 1591, FHT, III, 176–77; Chalco in 1591, FHT, III, 204–5; Tepozotlan in 1604, FHT, V, 222–24.

39. E.g., AGN, Mercedes, vol. 7, fol. 305r–305v. FHT, VI, 388.

40. This at least was the salary of Andrés de Cabrera, beginning in 1560, for conducting the agricultural repartimiento. Mexico City was still the distribution point and Cabrera had received no salary previously. See AGN, Mercedes, vol. 5, fol. 29r. It is possible that larger salaries were granted to the jueces repartidores later in the century.

41. Gómez de Cervantes, *La vida económica*, p. 107.

42. An earlier scheduling, from Monday through Saturday, was abandoned ca. 1580. See FHT, I, 113, 130; II, 251, 384.

43. In a reform of 1599 payment was to be made at the repartimiento center on the day following completion of the work. See FHT, IV, 318–19.

44. Agricultural repartimiento was itself sometimes referred to as the "coatequitl de panes" and its labor as "tequio." See AGN, Indios, vol. 4, fol. 1r; FHT, IV, 318.

45. The clearest documentation relates to areas outside the Valley of Mexico. See AGN, General de parte, vol. 2, fol. 125r; vol. 5, fol. 19r.

46. This differentiation is clearly expressed in documents of Xochimilco. AGN, General de parte, vol. 1, fol. 124v; Indios, vol. 4, fol. 1r; vol. 9, fols. 80v–81v. Note also that in Xochimilco the services within Indian society were specified, or confirmed, by Span-

ish authority; stated numbers of persons brought fuel, served the principales, worked on the principales' casa, served as florists, fishers, doctors, tailors, etc. See *Sobre el modo de tributar*, pp. 108, 123–24.

47. The subject is treated in Chapter II.

48. The areas of Mexico (including Xochimilco), Texcoco, and Tacuba are first mentioned as repartimiento areas in 1550. See AGN, Mercedes, vol. 3, fol. 97v. The towns of three of the four provinces designated for flood labor in 1555—the provinces of Tenochtitlan, Texcoco, and Tacuba—are listed in AGN, Mercedes, vol. 4, fols. 256v–257r. The towns of three provinces in the agricultural repartimiento of 1555—the provinces of Texcoco, Tacuba, and Chalco—are listed in AGN, Mercedes, vol. 4, fols. 146v–147r.

49. The continuity received comment at the time. See the remark of Juan Bautista Pomar on the Acolhua connection, NCDHM (1941), III, 5. See also Hernández, *Antigüedades*, p. 112. Torquemada calls attention to the similar connection between the Tepaneca area and the colonial "llamamientos." Torquemada, *Monarchia indiana*, I, 144. For the meaning of llamamiento here and a more detailed examination of the phenomenon and its documentation see my two articles, "Llamamiento general," and "The Tepanec Zone."

50. FHT, II, 267–68, 277–78, 299–300; V, 182–83. In January 1604, one Spanish faction requested that the repartimiento center be in Tepozotlan while another requested that it be in Cuauhtitlan. See FHT, V, 198–99.

51. Documentation on these late repartimiento centers may be found in FHT, VI, 437–38, 589–90; Cepeda and Carrillo, *Relación*, 2nd pag., fol. 41r; AGN, Desagüe, vol. 3, 2nd pag., fols. 75v–76r, 129v–130r, 132r–132v.

52. AGN, Indios, vol. 6 (1), fols. 200v–201v. NCDHM (1886–92), IV, 134, 183 ff. FHT, VI, 437–38, 443–44.

53. NCDHM (1941), I, 167. AGN, Indios, vol. 2, fol. 189r–189v.

54. AGN, General de parte, vol. 2, fols. 125v, 204r–204v; vol. 5, fol. 19r; Indios, vol. 6 (1), fol. 261v; vol. 9, fols. 64v–65r.

55. AGN, Indios, vol. 12 (1), fols. 83v–84v, 152r. FHT, IV, 353–54.

56. E.g., 200 workers from the Tacubaya jurisdiction in the Valle de Toluca, FHT, VI, 77.

57. A large number of documentary notices pertain to this subject. See, e.g., AC, XI, 43; AGN, Mercedes, vol. 5, fol. 3r–3v; Indios, vol. 4, fol. 204r; FHT, III, 13–14.

58. AGN, Ordenanzas, vol. 1, fol. 52v.

59. FHT, IV, 378–79.

60. Gómez de Cervantes, *La vida económica*, pp. 111 ff. *Sobre el modo de tributar*, p. 103. FHT, III, 37–38; VI, 293–94. AGN, General de parte, vol. 6, fol. 175r–175v; Mercedes, vol. 4, fol. 56r; Indios, vol. 4, fols. 1r, 70v, 97v; vol. 9, fols. 80v–81v.

61. FHT, II, 208; IV, 498; VI, 101–2. Valderrama, *Cartas*, p. 60. Gómez de Cervantes, *La vida económica*, pp. 116–17.

62. Thus the servicio of fodder was abolished and the servicio of stone reduced in the first quarter of the seventeenth century. See AC, XVIII, 94; AGN, Indios, vol. 9, fols. 80v–81v.

63. FHT, I, 112; II, 253. The terms sencilla and dobla, however, do not appear to have been commonly used until near the end of this thirty-year period.

64. AGN, Mercedes, vol. 7, fol. 141r–141v.

65. AGN, Indios, vol. 4, fols. 115r, 205r–205v, 214r–214v; vol. 5, fol. 328r; vol. 6 (1),

fols. 200v, 221v–222v; vol. 9, fols. 80v–81v. The ten per cent dobla became common after 1590. See FHT, III, 96 ff.

66. AGN, Indios, vol. 9, fol. 74r–74v.

67. León Pinelo, *Tratado de confirmaciones reales*, fol. 5v, in the early seventeenth century, reported the Mexican repartimiento percentages at two per cent and ten per cent. This was the most common combination, but it was not the only one.

68. FHT, III, 47–48, 80–81, 96, 201–3, 206–7; IV, 286, 354.

69. FHT, III, 32, 186–87; IV, 265–66, 275–76. The Viceroy Marqués de Villamanrique informed his successor in 1590 that he had abolished the four per cent sencilla and concentrated the entire draft in the two ten per cent dobla periods, after discounting one-third as *impedidos*. He stated that although doblas amounted to twenty weeks per year no single town was liable for more than ten weeks. *Advertimientos generales*, p. 25. But it is difficult to reconcile these assertions with the recorded repartimiento rules.

70. FHT, IV, 275–76.

71. FHT, IV, 354, 369–70, 478–79; V, 1, 23, 107, 168–69, 198 ff.

72. FHT, VI, 295–96, 322–23.

73. For examples of arrears, which amounted to some 500 laborers within an eight-month period in Texcoco in 1617, see FHT, VI, 300–1, 313–14. For a case of threatened arrest and imprisonment see AGN, General de parte, vol. 6, fol. 156r–156v.

74. FHT, VI, 444–45, 613. Gómez de Cervantes, *La vida económica*, p. 106. NCDHM (1886–92), IV, 133.

75. FHT, I, 45, 119–20; VI, 299–300, 388; *et passim*.

76. Gómez de Cervantes, *La vida económica*, pp. 106 ff. NCDHM (1886–92), V, 20 ff. Mendieta, *Historia*, pp. 519 ff. BAGN, IX, 173 ff. Cuevas, *Documentos inéditos*, pp. 354–85.

77. AGN, Indios, vol. 8, fols. 2r ff., contains the full statistical accounting. The records may be related to the viceregal inquiry into disorders in the Chalco repartimiento, involving the historian Fernando de Alva Ixtlilxochitl. See Peñafiel, *Colección de documentos*, sec. 7, pp. 16 ff.

78. The bibliography of the cedula is compiled by Silvio Zavala and María Castelo in FHT, V, vi–vii.

79. FHT, V, xvi–xvii, 71 ff.

80. FHT, V, 88–90, 136–38. The Indian laborers now had a free choice, the viceroy declared, the only compulsion being that required to make them assemble in the plaza.

81. FHT, VI, 195–96.

82. AC, XV, 103, 106. FHT, VI, 115–16, 220–21, 295–96.

83. FHT, VI, xxi–xxii, xxx–xxxi, xlii–xliv, 394–97, 616 ff.

84. Thus Chiconauhtla and other towns remained liable for the repartimiento in the vertientes of Pachuca. AGN, Indios, vol. 12 (1), fols. 83v–84v. The principal form in which repartimiento continued was the Desagüe.

85. These statements were made by labradores and they may well be exaggerations. But the tendency that they indicate is indisputable. See FHT, VI, 562–63, 588–90.

86. The main exception relates to the Presa de Acolman and the removal of the town of Acolman to higher ground in the seventeenth century. See Castillo, "La inundación de Acolman," pp. 549 ff.

87. See Viceroy Velasco's report to the king in September 1555. *Memoria histórica . . . del desagüe*, I, 68–69.

88. The Nezahualcoyotl albarradón extended in a north-south direction for a distance of about ten miles between Atzacualco and Ixtapalapa on the east side of the city, thus protecting Tenochtitlan from the flood waters of Lake Texcoco. Torquemada, *Monarchia indiana*, I, 157 ff., 192–93. Alvarado Tezozomoc, *Crónica mexicana*, pp. 384 ff. *Memoria histórica . . . del desagüe*, I, 37 ff. Many other sources refer to these events.

89. AC, XXIII, 242–44.

90. Cepeda and Carrillo, *Relación*, fols. 4v ff. *Memoria histórica . . . del desagüe*, I, 59 ff. AGI, Patronato, leg. 181, ramo 30.

91. ENE, IX, 216–17. PNE, III (supl.), 39–40.

92. AC, VIII, 417, 419, 428. *Memoria histórica . . . del desagüe*, I, 73–74.

93. Torquemada, *Monarchia indiana*, I, 310. Humboldt, *Political Essay*, II, 91. AGN, Desagüe, vol. 3, fol. 1v. AC, XVII, 93 ff.; XXVI, 173.

94. Much of its stone had been taken for city building and private purposes. See AC, XXIII, 243; XXIV, 28–30.

95. AGN, Desagüe, vol. 3, fols. 1v ff. *Memoria histórica . . . del desagüe*, I, 9. Gamio, *La población del valle de Teotihuacan*, I (2), 368 ff. Castillo, "La inundación de Acolman."

96. Cepeda and Carrillo, *Relación*, fols. 6v ff. Maza, *Enrico Martínez*, pp. 99 ff.

97. Cobo, *Obras*, I, 472. Humboldt, *Political Essay*, II, 94. AC, XXV, 125–26. For statements on the length of the tunnel see Cepeda and Carrillo, *Relación*, fol. 1v; *Memoria histórica . . . del desagüe*, I, 128; AC, XXX, 173. See also various Desagüe maps in Apenas, *Mapas antiguos*. The statement of CDIHE, XXI, 448, giving the tunnel's length as over 20,000 varas, appears to confuse the length of the tunnel with the length of the whole Desagüe canal.

98. Statements on the depth approximate seventy varas. CDIHE, XXI, 449–50. *Memoria histórica . . . del desagüe*, I, 128. Cobo, *Obras*, II, 472.

99. Humboldt, *Political Essay*, II, 95. Pferdekamp, "Enrico Martínez," pp. 423 ff. *Memoria histórica . . . del desagüe*, I, 93 ff.

100. Cepeda and Carrillo, *Relación*, fols. 18r–19r, 21r–21v. AC, XXX, 173 ff. Humboldt, *Political Essay*, II, 93–94.

101. Cepeda and Carrillo, *Relación*, fol. 1v. Cobo, *Obras*, II, 472.

102. Humboldt, *Political Essay*, II, 97–98, effectively summarizes the deficiencies in the construction, and the subsequent plans.

103. Cepeda and Carrillo, *Relación*, sep. pag., fol. 1r. *Memoria histórica . . . del desagüe*, I, 113–14. BNM, ms. no. 450, fols. 361v ff. Humboldt, *Political Essay*, II, 98–99. AC, XXIV, 280.

104. AC, XXIV, 280. Cepeda and Carrillo, *Relación*, sep. pag., fol. 3v.

105. Cepeda and Carrillo, *Relación*, sep. pag., fol. 16r. *Memoria histórica . . . del desagüe*, I, 121 ff. CDIHE, XXI, 453.

106. AGN, Desagüe, vol. 3, fols. 8v ff. AC, XXVI, 170, 174, 238–39. CDIHE, XXI, 453.

107. BNM, ms. no. 450, fol. 363r. NYPL, Rich, no. 39. BNMa, 18660/2, fol. 4v. AC, XXVII, 138 ff., 146, 192; XXX, 173. Cepeda and Carrillo, *Relación*, fol. 1r. Franco, *Segunda parte*, pp. 452 ff.

108. BNMa, 18660/2, fol. 5r. AC, XXVII, 185. Cobo, *Obras*, II, 470. BNM, ms. no. 450, fol. 363v. Cepeda and Carrillo, *Relación*, sep. pag., fol. 8r. The main plaza, the Cathedral, the viceregal palace, the Plaza del Volador, and all of Tlatelolco however remained dry, for they were on higher ground. Vetancurt, *Chronica*, p. 121.

109. AC, XXX, 174.

110. CDIHE, XVI, 454. Humboldt, *Political Essay*, II, 94, 109. It is noteworthy that the viceroy, audiencia, and entire city gave thanks for the supposed completion of the Desagüe in 1675. See Robles, *Diario*, I, 176.

111. Gemelli Carreri, *Las cosas más considerables*, p. 97. AC, XXV, 125–26. Humboldt, *Political Essay*, II, 126.

112. Torquemada, *Monarchia indiana*, I, 728. AGN, Desagüe, vol. 2, fols. 1r ff.; vol. 3, fols. 9v–10v; vol. 4, fol. 11r. CDIHE, XXI, 454.

113. The 1609 records are in AGN, Desagüe, vol. 1, *passim*. See also AGN, Desagüe, vol. 3, fols. 8v, 15v. Some communities, e.g., Ecatepec and Chiconauhtla, requested Desagüe labor in order to be freed from other repartimientos. See *Memoria histórica . . . del desagüe*, I, 112.

114. AGN, Desagüe, vol. 2, fols. 1r–26r. It will be remembered that the Tepozotlan and Tacubaya jurisdictions were the remnants of the former Tepaneca labor area on the west side of the lakes; Tacuba, while itself on the west side, was the repartimiento capital for the eastern towns, those of the former Acolhua labor area.

115. AGN, Desagüe, vol. 3, fols. 9v, 15r.

116. AGN, Desagüe, vol. 3, 2nd pag., fols. 75v–76r, 129v–130r, 131v–132v.

117. Enrico Martínez had justified the practices, stating that Indian labor was always coerced and that Indians had to be compelled even to work their own fields. *Memoria historica . . . del desagüe*, I, 112.

118. AGN, Desagüe, vol. 5, 2nd pag., fols. 3r ff.

119. AGN, Desagüe, vol. 4, fols. 105r, *et passim*. Humboldt, *Political Essay*, II, 127.

120. AGN, Desagüe, vol. 2, 2nd pag., fols. 5r ff.

121. AGN, Desagüe, vol. 3, fols. 9v–10v, 15r–19r.

122. AGN, Desagüe, vol. 3, 3rd pag., fols. 2032r ff.; vol. 4, fol. 11r; vol. 5, 2nd pag., fols. 3r ff. At least several of these, however, had given workers in small numbers before this.

123. AGN, Desagüe, vol. 3, 2nd pag., fols. 75v–76r. Cepeda and Carrillo, *Relación*, 2nd pag., fol. 41v.

124. Motolinía, *Memoriales*, p. 184. AGN, Mercedes, vol. 3, fol. 178r. CDHM, II, 85. Aiton, *Antonio de Mendoza*, p. 111. Aiton, "The Secret Visita," p. 13.

125. *Legislación del trabajo*, pp. 49 ff., 68 ff. Bentura Beleña, *Recopilación sumaria*, II, 298 ff. Dusenberry, "Woolen Manufacture," is an exceptionally informative article on this subject.

126. *Legislación del trabajo*, p. 71. AGI, México, leg. 26, ramo 1.

127. AGI, México, leg. 26, ramo 1. AC, XV, 114. By the late eighteenth century the manufacturing establishments in Texcoco were commonly known as *fábricas*. They were engaged in the manufacture of cloth, underclothing, and hats. See AGN, Padrones, vol. 43, fol. 8r.

128. *Legislación del trabajo*, pp. 49 ff., 68 ff. Bentura Beleña, *Recopilación sumaria*, II, 298 ff. BNM, ms. no. 439, fol. 224r, 466r–466v. AGN, Indios, vol. 2, fols. 40v–41r. One of the most interesting and informative of all surviving documents concerning obrajes is the "Visita a los obrajes de paños en la jurisdicción de Coyoacan 1660" in BAGN, XI, 33–116. The inspecting oidor moved through the obraje of Melchor Díaz de Posadas from one room to another, questioning the workers and receiving direct reports from them of present and past conditions. Some had been kept in the obraje against their will and some had not been outside for years. Evidence of beatings and other ill treatment was disclosed. Several workers had been killed. Other obrajes were

also visited, and conditions in some were more mild. The document contains abundant information on the workers, their labor, the technology of the obrajes, salaries, and other conditions.

129. BNM, ms. no. 439, fol. 224r.

130. Hakluyt, *The Principal Navigations*, IX, 421, 459.

131. AGI, México, leg. 644, *passim*. *Legislación del trabajo*, p. 70. Aiton, "The Secret Visita," p. 13. FHT, V, 81.

132. BAGN, IV, 17–18. AGI, México, leg. 24, ramo 4; leg. 644, *passim*. *Instrucción del virrey Marqués de Croix*, p. 63.

133. *Legislación del trabajo*, pp. 70–72.

134. FHT, VI, 323–24. BNM, ms. no. 439, fol. 224r. *Legislación del trabajo*, pp. 49, 72. Bentura Beleña, *Recopilación sumaria*, II, 298–99. AGI, México, leg. 644, *passim*. *La administración de D. Frey Antonio María de Bucareli*, II, 251 ff.

135. This is the estimate of the Spanish cabildo in Mexico City in 1602. It may be somewhat exaggerated. See AC, XV, 114.

136. See AC, XV, 113–15. The order of 1601 requiring Negro workers is published in numerous sources, e.g., *Documentos para la historia económica*, XI, 18 ff. But the order was never obeyed and later cedulas permitted Indian laborers in obrajes again. See Bentura Beleña, *Recopilación sumaria*, II, 298.

137. E.g., AGN, Mercedes, vol. 4, fol. 119v.

138. AGN, Indios, vol. 3, fols. 1v–2r. FHT, VI, 455–56.

139. "Los Indios son fáciles en recibir dineros, y obligarse por ellos, y siendo mucha cantidad, quedan casi en esclavonia." Bentura Beleña, *Recopilación sumaria*, I, 2nd pag., 77.

140. BNM, ms. no. 439, fol. 224r. *Legislación del trabajo*, pp. 68 ff.

141. BAGN, VI, 195–96.

142. *Códice Osuna*, p. 258. See Plate IX.

143. *Compendio histórica del concilio III*, II, 69. *Legislación del trabajo*, pp. 68, 71. *Advertimientos generales*, pp. 32–33.

144. *Cedulario americano*, pp. 379–81. *Legislación del trabajo*, p. 69.

145. AGI, México, leg. 644, *passim*. Bentura Beleña, *Recopilación sumaria*, II, 303.

146. *La administración de D. Frey Antonio María de Bucareli*, II, 251 ff. Bentura Beleña, *Recopilación sumaria*, II, 303. BNM, ms. no. 439, fol. 224r. AGI, México, leg. 644, *passim*. *Panaderías, tocinerías*, and other urban economic enterprises received convict labor, though commonly for lesser crimes, and in other ways resembled the obrajes. FHT, V, 82; VI, 323–24. AGN, Inquisición, vol. 215, no. 8, fols. 17r, 18r–18v. AGI, México, leg. 644, *passim*. *La administración de D. Frey Antonio María de Bucareli*, II, 264. For additional material on these subjects see Dusenberry, "Woolen Manufacture"; Carrera Stampa, "Los obrajes"; Carrera Stampa, "El obraje novohispano"; *Documentos para la historia económica*, XI.

147. AGN, Indios, vol. 2, fol. 161r–161v.

148. FHT, IV, 263–64, 362–63, 453; V, xiv, 244–45; VI, 94. *Ordenanzas del trabajo*, pp. 60–61.

149. *Ordenanzas del trabajo*, pp. 60–61. FHT, V, 216–17; VI, 94.

150. FHT, VI, 139–40, 184. AGN, Indios, vol. 3, fol. 115r; General de parte, vol. 4, fol. 131v.

151. FHT, VI, 299–300.

152. FHT, VI, 410–11, 562–63.

153. It is interesting that in the aftermath the Spanish cabildo of Mexico City could

ascribe an increase in the price of wheat to the abolition of repartimiento. The argument asserted that the abolition of repartimiento had so reduced Indian labor in the haciendas that the labradores had become destitute and production had fallen alarmingly. See AC, XXX, 176, 185. This argument could apply, however, only to those haciendas that still depended upon repartimiento in 1632, and we know that a severe labor crisis affected such haciendas prior to the abolition. It would appear that the cabildo exaggerated the consequences of abolition, much as Suárez de Peralta exaggerated the consequences of the prohibition of labor as a form of encomienda tribute. See note 18.

154. FHT, VI, 410–11; VI, 455–56. AGN, Indios, vol. 9, fol. 19r; vol. 13, fols. 75r–76v.

155. *Códice Osuna*, pp. 182 ff. ENE, II, 190–91.

156. Grijalva, *Crónica*, fol. 50r. Puga, *Provisiones*, fols. 172r–173r. This is computed on the basis of thirty-four maravedís per real. See the royal order of 1538 that the real in the Indies was to be of thirty-four maravedís and no more. CDIU, X, 401–2.

157. CDIU, XXI, 267. Puga, *Provisiones*, fols. 172r–173r. NLAC, 1121, fol. 286r. *Cartas de Indias*, p. 95.

158. But it should be noted that the Indians of Chalco in 1554 were reported to be receiving only eight maravedís per day in these tasks. See ENE, VII, 261.

159. CDIU, XXI, 267. This is seemingly the wage referred to by Zorita, i.e., two and one-half or three reales per week. CDIAI, II, 116. A wage of two-fifths real per day for peones and five-sixths real per day for oficiales is recorded in 1555. AGN, Mercedes, vol. 4, fols. 190v ff. The wage of one-half real per day for peones and one real per day for oficiales is known to have been in effect in 1560 (AGN, Mercedes, vol. 5, fol. 3r–3v), 1561 (*Sobre el modo de tributar*, p. 37), 1563 (AGN, Mercedes, vol. 7, fols. 198v ff.), 1565 (AGN, Mercedes, vol. 8, fol. 66v), 1572 (AGN, Inquisición, vol. 75, no. 12, fols. 55v, 56r, 64r), and 1576 (FHT, I, 113). For criticism of the one-half real daily wage as inadequate, see NCDHM (1886–92), V, 26–28; *Compendio histórico del concilio III*, II, 47.

160. The wage of three-quarters real for peones is recorded in 1564. *Códice Osuna*, pp. 113–14. Valderrama, *Cartas*, p. 61. The same sources indicate one to one and one-half reales for oficiales. But a provision of 1578 granting Indians who guarded animals a wage of four reales every eight days could be interpreted as signifying four reales for a six-day week, or two-thirds real per day. See *Ordenanzas del trabajo*, p. 29. Four reales per week are mentioned also in connection with labor in Citlaltepec in 1580. See FHT, II, 370–71. Viceroy Velasco later stated that he had raised the peones' wage from four to six reales per week (*Advertimientos generales*, p. 48), and according to this evidence we should suppose the wage of two-thirds real per day to have persisted to ca. 1590. The viceroy stated also that he had raised the oficiales' wage from one real to two reales per day, and this would indicate that the oficiales' wage remained constant from 1553 to ca. 1590.

161. Viceroy Marqués de Villamanrique stated in 1590 that he had ordered a wage of one real (for peones) in repartimiento in some instances. His successor stated that he had raised the wage for peones from two-thirds of one real to one real, and the oficiales' wage from one real to two reales per day. *Advertimientos generales*, pp. 26, 48. The notices thus suggest several enactments about 1590. The wage of one real per day for peones is further documented in particular assignments of 1590–91. See FHT, III, 91, 96, 155. But Gómez de Cervantes, ca. 1599, continues to speak of a peón's wage in repartimiento as one-half real per day. The oficiales' wage he gives correctly as two reales per day. Gómez de Cervantes, *La vida económica*, p. 104.

162. The increase in 1603 amounted to one-half real or food, at the peón's option. The order of 1610 however assumed the standard peón's wage to be still one real per day. See *Ordenanzas del trabajo,* pp. 48–50, 52–53. The order of 1610 applied specifically to the agricultural repartimiento. The wage of two reales per day for peones in 1629 relates to the urban repartimiento. See FHT, VI, 437–38.

163. Food was in addition to this. *Sobre el modo de tributar,* pp. 43, 110. Valderrama, *Cartas,* p. 62.

164. *Sobre el modo de tributar,* pp. 43, 110. NCDHM (1886–92), IV, 185.

165. An Indian peón who joined the urban repartimiento voluntarily in 1572 earned one real per day, and an oficial who did the same earned four reales per day. AGN, Inquisición, vol. 75, no. 12, fols. 56r, 64r. This was twice the normal repartimiento wage for peones at this time, and four times the normal repartimiento wage for oficiales. Much depended upon the particular skill or profession of the oficial. In the 1560's and 1570's, carpenters and masons were making three reales per day, while silversmiths were making eight. Others earned four and six, and the lowest earning was two. NCDHM (1886–92), IV, 185. *Sobre el modo de tributar,* p. 20. By ca. 1600 masons and carpenters were earning four reales (plus food) per day, while tailors, shoemakers, and others were receiving six or eight. But oficiales sometimes had to serve as peones in the repartimiento. See Gómez de Cervantes, *La vida económica,* pp. 104–5. The same income, six to eight reales per day, is indicated for these oficiales, as well as for masons and carpenters, in Mexico City in 1629. FHT, VI, 437–38. It is noteworthy that the highest incomes recorded for Indian oficiales, eight reales or one peso per day, did not change from the 1560's to 1629.

166. This was in addition to food. AGN, Hospital de Jesús, vol. 278, exp. 1, fol. 2r.

167. AGN, Indios, vol. 6 (2), fol. 67v.

168. AGI, México, leg. 26, ramo 1.

169. These sums were in addition to food. NCDHM (1886–92), IV, 134. BAGN, IX, 179. NCDHM (1941), I, 166. FHT, VI, 443–44. *Sobre el modo de tributar,* p. 50.

170. *Compendio histórico del concilio III,* II, 45. AGN, Mercedes, vol. 8, fol. 106r; General de parte, vol. 2, fols. 42r, 53r.

171. *Códice Osuna,* p. 259. CDIAI, II, 114.

172. *Memoria histórica . . . del desagüe,* I, 80, 100–1. Torquemada, *Monarchia indiana,* I, 729. AGN, Desagüe, vol. 1, *passim*; vol. 2, 4th pag., fols. 1r ff.; vol. 3, fols. 15r ff.; vol. 4, *passim*; vol. 5, fols. 1r ff; 2nd pag., fols. 3r ff.

173. This was in addition to food. AGI, México, leg. 644.

174. AGN, Tierras, vol. 917, exp. 5, fols. 7r ff.; vol. 991, exp. 4; Vínculos, vol. 55, exp. 1; exp. 2, fols. 1r ff.

175. PCR, folder 109. *Legislación del trabajo,* pp. 156–57. AGN, Vínculos, vol. 55, exp. 2; Tierras, vol. 991, exp. 4.

176. PCR, folders 88, 105, 109. AGN, Hospital de Jesús, vol. 279, exp. 41; Tierras, vol. 566, exp. 4, fol. 123r. Alzate, *Gacetas de literatura,* III, 73. Peones in the hacienda of Molino de Flores demanded a wage of two and one-half reales per day, for the first time, in December 1779. PCR, folder 88.

177. AGN, Hospital de Jesús, vol. 279, exp. 41; Tierras, vol. 566, exp. 4, fols. 12r–13r. PCR, folder 109. Oficiales' wages ranged up to six reales in the labor on the Santuario de Nuestra Señora de Guadalupe in 1794, but this amount was achieved by only one of sixteen workers. See *Documentos para la historia económica,* III, 157. See also the interesting case in the hacienda of Mazapa, in the Texcoco jurisdiction, in 1790. Here an Indian carpenter normally received a wage of four reales per day, but because of the

abundance of oficiales this was reduced by one-half real, and the mayordomo threatened to reduce the wage by an additional one-half real. See AGN, Civil, vol. 1686, exp. 45.

178. By a rule of 1656 an Indian laborer assigned to his creditor for debt was to receive three reales per day (or six, if he were an oficial) in the discharge of the debt. See Bentura Beleña, *Recopilación sumaria*, I, 57. But there is no evidence that the wage of three reales per day became common for peones before the nineteenth century. Only occasionally is this wage recorded in the late eighteenth century. *Documentos para la historia económica*, III, 157 ff., 161 ff. AGN, Vínculos, vol. 233, exp. 8, fols. 111r ff.

179. NCDHM (1886–92), IV, 64. ENE, VII, 261. FHT, I, 111 ff.; VII, 416. *Ordenanzas del trabajo*, pp. 48–50, 52–53. BAGN, II, 491. *Advertimientos generales*, p. 26. AGN, Mercedes, vol. 5, fol. 3r–3v; vol. 7, fols. 198v ff.; Desagüe, vol. 1, *passim.*; vol. 3, fols. 14r ff.; Hospital de Jesús, vol. 278, exp. 1, fol. 2r.

180. In the early period Indians supplied their own food. NCDHM (1886–92), IV, 133–34. In the early seventeenth century workers in the urban repartimiento were offered an option of one real per day with food or one and one-half reales without. *Ordenanzas del trabajo*, pp. 48–50. Torquemada, *Monarchia indiana*, I, 729, states that the workers in the Desagüe labor of the early seventeenth century received no food. But in general in the later sixteenth century and during the remainder of the colonial period both food and wages were provided. Gómez de Cervantes, *La vida económica*, p. 104. *Advertimientos generales*, p. 26. *Memoria histórica . . . del desagüe*, I, 61–63, 100, 128. AC, VI, 191 ff. BAGN, II, 491. CDIHIA, I, 210. AGN, Hospital de Jesús, vol. 278, exp. 1, fol. 2r; vol. 279, exp. 41; Desagüe, vol. 1, *passim*; vol. 2, 7th pag.

181. AA, Pósito y Alhóndiga, vol. 2, no. 3695, exp. 91. AGN, Tierras, vol. 991, exp. 4. A document of exceptional interest is AGI, México, leg. 2096, sep. pag., fols. 94v ff., containing the testimonies of hacendados in Chalco province concerning their tiendas and the values of their daily sales.

182. Examples may be seen in AGN, Tierras, vol. 70, exp. 8, fols. 17r ff.; vol. 991, exp. 4; Vínculos, vol. 55, exp. 2.

183. PCR, folder 105 (March 30, 1785).

· 184. We cannot state unequivocally that debt labor "began" in the obrajes. It was, however, a recognized obraje technique by 1590 (AGN, Indios, vol. 3, fols. 1v–2r), and the legislation of 1595 demonstrates that a full repertory of debt-labor devices on the part of the obrajeros was recognized before the end of the sixteenth century. Bentura Beleña, *Recopilación sumaria*, I, 2nd pag., 75 ff.

185. FHT, VI, 324–25. *Legislación del trabajo*, pp. 50, 70 ff. Bentura Beleña, *Recopilación sumaria*, II, 299 ff.

186. Bentura Beleña, *Recopilación sumaria*, II, 300. Carrera Stampa, "Los obrajes," pp. 557–58. Indian workers frequently did not know the amount of their indebtedness or the conditions of service that debt required. In the seventeenth century debts of forty or fifty pesos were not uncommon in the obrajes. Workers died in debt and their sons were impounded for labor in discharge of the fathers' debts. *Legislación del trabajo*, p. 73. BNM, ms. no. 439, fol. 224r. *Documentos para la historia económica*, XI, 57.

187. Bentura Beleña, *Recopilación sumaria*, I, 55. AGI, México leg. 24, ramo 4 (viceroy to king, December 22, 1600). Cf. Borah, *New Spain's Century of Depression*, pp. 38–39, 56–57.

188. *Legislación del trabajo*, pp. 69–70. Bentura Beleña, *Recopilación sumaria*, I, 2nd pag., 76–77.

189. The limits appear to have varied from one to twenty-four pesos. *Ordenanzas*

del trabajo, pp. 45–46. Bentura Beleña, *Recopilación sumaria*, I, 2nd pag., 77; 3rd pag., 15; II, 195. *Legislación del trabajo*, p. 51. Zavala, "Orígenes coloniales del peonaje," pp. 729, 741 ff. BNM, ms. no. 439, fol. 224r.

190. *Legislación del trabajo*, p. 69. Bentura Beleña, *Recopilación sumaria*, I, 56. FHT, VI, 372–73.

191. AC, XXIII, 243–44.

192. Bentura Beleña, *Recopilación sumaria*, I, 2nd pag., 77 ff.; II, 196–97.

193. Bentura Beleña, *Recopilación sumaria*, II, 195. An adjustment of the debt had to be made, however, before employment could be legalized at another hacienda.

194. Alzate mentions a hacienda in Chalco province employing 300 laborers in the wheat harvest alone. Alzate, *Gacetas de literatura*, IV, 392. See also note 198, below, concerning Los Portales.

195. AGN, Tierras, vol. 964, exp. 3, fols. 8r ff.; vol. 2034, cuad. 7, fol. 6r–6v.

196. AGN, Tierras, vol. 991, exp. 4.

197. AGN, Tierras, vol. 964, exp. 3, fol. 8r–8v.

198. AGN, Tierras, vol. 2034, cuad. 7, fols. 6r, 8r–9v.

199. Five pesos then constituted a legal limit in salary advances. Bentura Beleña, *Recopilación sumaria*, II, 196. *Documentos para la historia económica*, II, 70–71.

CHAPTER X

1. Zorita in CDIAI, II, 25 ff., 100 ff., *et passim*. Cortés in CDIAI, IV, 443 ff. Puga in ENE, X, 34 ff. Anonymous account in ENE, XIV, 145 ff. Ixtlilxochitl, *Historia*, pp. 169–71. Torquemada, *Monarchia indiana*, II, 545 ff. I am in general agreement with the summary of these sources in Kirchhoff, "Land Tenure," pp. 353 ff. Kirchhoff, like other modern writers on Aztec land tenure, corrects and modifies the misconceptions of Bandelier, "On the Distribution and Tenure of Lands." The same applies to Freund, "Agrarrecht und Katasterwesen," pp. 24 ff.; Katz, "Die sozialökonomischen Verhältnisse," pp. 33 ff.; and Caso, "La tenencia de la tierra," with which I am also in agreement.

2. AA, Tierras y ejidos, vol. 1, no. 4065, exp. 20, fol. 24v. BN, ms. no. 1312, fols. 36r ff. BNMa, 20417/29, fol. 6r. Humboldt, *Political Essay*, II, 124. Orozco, *Legislación y jurisprudencia*, II, 741. Foster, *Culture and Conquest*, p. 57. Bowman, "The Vara de Burgos." The common usage can be tested in passages that refer to measurable distances in terms of varas, e.g., from the Cathedral to San Antón, 1,440 varas (*Documentos relativos al tumulto*, III, 405–6), and the elevation of the Valley of Mexico above sea level, 2,550 varas (Alzate, *Gacetas de literatura*, II, 269). Both these records are sufficiently accurate to indicate that the vara used was .84 meters.

3. AGN, Mercedes, vol. 1, fol. 76r. AA, Tierras y ejidos, vol. 2, no. 4066, exp. 38, fol. 28r–28v. BNM, ms. no. 1312, fol. 36r.

4. PNE, I, 113, 198–99. Fernández del Castillo, *Apuntes*, p. 12. AGN, Mercedes, vol. 4, fol. 217r. It is worth noting that Molina lists four Nahuatl words meaning braza (cemmatl, cenmitl, cenyollotli, cemmatzotzopaztli) depending on the Indian measurement from elbow to hand, from shoulder to hand, etc. See Molina, *Vocabulario*, fol. 21r. Brazas from the foot to the extended hand are frequently mentioned both in Indian measurement and in Spanish measurement derived from Indian practice. See PNE, III (supl.), 200; *El libro de las tasaciones*, pp. 12, 540; FHT, VI, 382–83. A braza

equal to one and one-half Spanish brazas, or three varas, is mentioned in Texcoco and Temascalapa. AGI, Justicia, leg. 208, no. 4, fol. 254r. PCR, "Títulos de las tierras . . . Vatán," fol. 35r. Indian forms of measurement were studied by Brinton in *The Lineal Measures,* but the subject needs systematic restudy based on records of colonial lands.

5. CDIAI, II, 105; IV, 444; VI, 167. ENE, X, 35. Oviedo y Valdés, *Historia general y natural,* III, 537. Román y Zamora, *Repúblicas de Indias,* I, 120.

6. The cedula followed upon a suggestion of Zumárraga and Betanzos. Puga, *Cedulario,* fol. 90r.

7. CDHM, II, 171. Las Casas, *Apologética historia,* p. 373.

8. It is possible that there was some continuity in particular cases. At a later time the church acquired lands in the manner of other property owners. A characteristic act of cofradía donation of land is recorded in PNE, VI, 64. See also AGN, Tierras, vol. 1109, exp. 3, *passim.* There is no indication in these instances of a connection with the pre-conquest temple lands.

9. On Montezuma's lands and common labor see CDIAI, II, 32; IV, 444; VI, 167; Oviedo y Valdés, *Historia general y natural,* III, 537. Zorita (CDIAI, II, 32) makes it clear that other rulers of the Triple Alliance observed the same system, and Pomar implies the same for Nezahualcoyotl. See NCDHM (1941), III, 9. Lands called Itonal or Ytunales seem to have been of a similar type but used for the supply of military forces. Ixtlilxochitl, *Historia,* p. 170. AGI, Indiferente general, leg. 1624. Guzmán, "Un manuscrito," p. 97. Chevalier, *La formation des grandes domaines,* p. 16.

10. CDHM, II, 171. CDIAI, XIII, 257.

11. Indians of Otumba were required in 1531 to make "the plantings that they used to make," and the reference may be to pre-conquest plantings. See ENE, VIII, 149–50. See also Chapter VIII, note 31, for communities outside the Valley of Mexico. Otumba was required to plant 2,000 brazas in 1531, and this is the largest single dimension known in Spanish tribute; but the single figure is not sufficient to provide an estimate of the true size.

12. *El libro de las tasaciones,* pp. 12, 156. CDIHIA, I, 173, 179. ENE, VI, 118. The Acolman braza is specified. The others are not. Cf. the 1554 contract of Huitzilopochco, BNP, no. 27. See Boban, *Documents pour servir,* I, 387–89, and *Atlas,* no. 27.

13. *El libro de las tasaciones,* pp. 173, 588.

14. *El libro de las tasaciones,* pp. 587–88.

15. Texcoco was required to provide 26,000 fanegas, then 16,000 fanegas, then 8,000 fanegas. For the 8,000 fanegas, "hagan y beneficien de común las sementeras que fueren convenientes y necesarias." Similar arrangements may be noted for Xochimilco, Tenayuca, and other towns. *El libro de las tasaciones,* pp. 35, 392, 481–82.

16. CDIAI, II, 106; XIII, 257.

17. Ixtlilxochitl, *Historia,* p. 170. Torquemada, *Monarchia indiana,* II, 546.

18. Ixtlilxochitl, *Historia,* p. 170. CDIAI, II, 90.

19. Guzmán, "Un manuscrito," pp. 95, 97. AGI, Justicia, leg. 159, no. 2. See also the legends of the reverse side of Códice García Granados, illustrated in Barlow, "El reverso del Códice García Granados," lám. G-3.

20. CDIAI, XIII, 257. CDIHIA, I, 218–19. AGN, Tierras, vol. 13, exp. 4, fols. 303v ff.; Mercedes, vol. 7, fol. 355r. The cacique Cocopin in Tepetlaoztoc and his descendants had "pueblos y estancias" named Mazahuacan, Caltecoya, Tlacoyoca, and others, each of which made a planting of 400 brazas "en cuadra" as tribute. The tributes are specifically designated as having been "para su recámara." Some were in areas, e.g., Chalco

province, outside the sujetos of Tepetlaoztoc. See *Códice Kingsborough,* fol. 209v.

21. The tecpan and dwellings of the cacique and principales were located on this land. See AGI, Justicia, leg. 159, no. 2.

22. The original notice reads 200 by 200 brazas for the gobernador, 100 by 100 brazas for each alcalde, 80 by 80 brazas for each regidor, and 100 by 100 brazas for the mayordomo. But later additions to the text suggest that each of these "brazas" was of two ordinary brazas. *Códice Mariano Jiménez,* fols. 1r–2v.

23. ENE, VIII, 234–39.

24. These possibilities are brought out in testimonies concerning Cuauhtitlan lands in the 1550's. See AGN, Tierras, vol. 13, exp. 4, fols. 303v ff. The lands in question measured 400 by 200 brazas and were probably tecpantlalli.

25. Guzmán, "Un manuscrito," pp. 100–101. We deduce the audiencia's decision from the text of the document, but it is not stated explicitly and the deduction may be in error. Notice, however, that Francisco Verdugo Quetzalmamalictzin, cacique of Teotihuacan, bequeathed both tecpantlalli and pillalli to his wife and daughter in his will of 1563. UMCL, Clements 100, Phillipps, 13685, fol. 38. BNP, no. 243, fols. 2r–9r, 11r–13v; no. 244.

26. *Códice Kingsborough,* fol. 210v. AGI, Justicia, leg. 159, no. 2.

27. Confusions or disputes concerning the proper identification of lands may underlie the controversies in Cuitlahuac in 1579 and in Tizayuca in 1565. AGN, General de parte, vol. 2, fol. 48v; Mercedes, vol. 7, fol. 77v. Note that Zorita affirms the continued existence of tlatocamilli ca. 1555. CDIAI, II, 90.

28. AGN, Mercedes, vol. 4, fols. 2v–3r; vol. 84, fol. 38v. A statement expressing Spanish alarm at the Indian abandonment of agriculture may be found in CDIHE, XXVI, 345 ff.

29. *Códice Mariano Jiménez,* fol. 5r. AGN, Mercedes, vol. 7, fols. 54v–55r. The original Utlaspa measurements were given as 800 by 400 and 400 by 400 brazas, but again this "braza" was of two ordinary brazas.

30. E.g., AGN, Tierras, vol. 1923, exp. 2, fols. 35v ff.

31. AGN, Mercedes, *passim.* The characteristic viceregal grant forbade the Indian community to sell (vender), exchange (trocar), or alienate (enajenar) the property granted. But towns felt free to rent such properties.

32. See Chapter VIII.

33. Sheepherding as a communal activity in the Indian towns may reflect not simply a form of economic Hispanization but also a response to epidemic, for sheepherding required less labor than agriculture and it utilized, and therefore protected, community lands abandoned through depopulation.

34. The records of AGN, Mercedes, are summary statements of grants. The full procedure is recorded in other documents, e.g., BNM, ms. no. 1312, fols. 35r–41r.

35. ENE, VII, 262. Ixtlilxochitl, *Historia,* p. 170, distinguishes pillalli from tecpillalli, describing the latter as belonging to "unos caballeros, que se decían de los señores antiguos." The name tecpillalli suggests a form of pillalli associated either with the tecpan or with the tetecuhtin. See CDIAI, II, 24–25. Torquemada also distinguished two types of pillalli, one belonging to the descendants of the reyes and señores, populated by terrazgueros, and salable; the other belonging to the "nobles" honored for valor, without terrazgueros, and not salable. Torquemada, *Monarchia indiana,* II, 545–46. These notices are not satisfactorily related to the conditions of the colonial period, and it is likely that the distinctions involved in them failed to survive the first post-

conquest years. Monzón argues that pillalli was included within calpullalli and finds the notion of their separation "casi imposible." Monzón, *El calpulli*, p. 41. Here we take the opposite view.

36. *Códice Ramírez*, p. 75. Dorantes de Carranza, *Sumaria relación*, p. 3. PNE, III, 229. Torquemada, *Monarchia indiana*, I, 164. The Itzcoatl distributions of land, both in the city and in other communities, are documented with many interesting details in Códice Cozcatzin, BNP, nos. 41–45.

37. Torquemada, *Monarchia indiana*, I, 162–63. Guzmán, "Un manuscrito," p. 93 ff. ENE, VII, 262. Cuevas, *Documentos inéditos*, p. 229.

38. E.g., CDIAI, II, 10, 89–90.

39. NCDHM (1941), III, 255, 277–78.

40. *Procesos de indios,* pp. 41, 45, 46. AGN, Tierras, vol. 13, exp. 4, fol. 320r.

41. Guzmán, "Un manuscrito," pp. 94–95. AGI, Justicia, leg. 208, no. 4, fol. 229r.

42. Orozco y Berra, "Tlacopan y Texcoco," p. 508. AGN, Tierras, vol. 13, exp. 4, fol. 320r.

43. See, e.g., NCDHM (1941), I, 23, and the statement of Cortés in Chimalpahin, *Annales,* p. 198.

44. CDIAI, XIII, 257–58. Cortés, *Cartas,* II, 108–9. CDIHIA, I, 218–19.

45. *Códice Kingsborough,* fol. 214r. AGN, Tierras, vol. 13, exp. 4, fol. 320r.

46. E.g., ENE, V, 62–63. Isabel did receive the encomienda of Tacuba, as has been said. For the particular communities involved in this grant see Appendix I.

47. A large number of such appeals and related documents are known. Puga, *Provisiones,* fol. 111r–111v. ENE, VI, 123; X, 113. NCDHM (1886–92), IV, 133. AC, VI, 44. Ternaux Compans, *Voyages, relations et mémoires,* VIII, 261–69. In some instances the history of these lands may be traced with some precision. Thus Xocoyoltepec was a location in Chalco province listed in Codex Mendoza, presumably as a calpixqui location under Montezuma. Chimalpahin tells us that it was cultivated for Axayacatl and later for his brother and successor Tizoc. It descended then to Tezcatlpopoca, son of Tizoc, and was taken from the son of Tezcatlpopoca, Diego Tehuetzquiti, when the Spaniards came. Its return was then the subject of a petition by Diego Tehuetzquiti in 1532. *Codex Mendoza,* III, fol. 41r. Chimalpahin, *Annales,* pp. 144, 146, 250, 267. Alvarado Tezozomoc, *Crónica mexicayotl,* p. 142.

48. Puga, *Provisiones,* fol. 111r–111v. CDIAI, XIII, 295–96.

49. Seizure of lands by other Indians operated in some measure to facilitate Spanish usurpation, for it could be argued that such lands did not properly belong to their possessors. See, e.g., CDIHIA, XIII, 332 ff., 340.

50. CDIAI, IV, 450. CDIHIA, I, 218–19. AGN, Tierras, vol. 13, exp. 4, fols. 300r ff.

51. AGN, Indios, vol. 9, fols. 64v–65r. The recipients included one Spaniard. We do not know how he came to be involved, but it is conceivable that he did so through simple purchase.

52. E.g., agricultural and pastoral grants in AGN, Mercedes, vol. 2, fol. 113r; vol. 6, fols. 221v–222r; *et passim*. A characteristic grant of pasture land to a principal of Amecameca in 1594 confirmed his possession of an estancia de ganado menor (ca. three square miles) but required him to introduce 2,000 head on it within a year and to maintain no fewer than 2,000 head for four consecutive years, under penalty of loss of the land. AGN, Tierras, vol. 994, 3rd pag., fol. 1r. A characteristic agricultural grant to four principales of Coatepec in 1590 confirmed their possession of two caballerías (ca. 211 acres) but required them to cultivate the larger part. As in grants to commu-

nities, sale, exchange, or other alienation was forbidden. AGN, Vínculos, vol. 244, exp. 1, fols. 4v ff.

53. These remarks on seventeenth-century cacicazgo are drawn from a number of records relating especially to the Mendoza cacicazgo in Tlatelolco and to the Páez de Mendoza cacicazgo in Amecameca. AGN, Tierras, vols. 994–95; vol. 1586, exp. 1; vols. 1592–94.

54. AGN, Vínculos, vol. 233; Tierras, vols. 994–95.

55. AGN, Indios, vol. 50, fol. 17v; Padrones, vol. 18, fol. 310r. See also BAGN, XXV, 70.

56. Abundant evidence may be found in AGN, Tierras, vol. 1586, exp. 1; vol. 1598, exp. 1; vol. 1653, exp. 8; vol. 1726, exp. 1; vol. 1735, exp. 2.

57. E.g., Ixtlilxochitl, *Historia*, p. 170. ENE, VII, 262.

58. Ixtlilxochitl, *Historia*, p. 170.

59. AGN, Tierras, vol. 1518, exp. 1, fols. 22r ff.; vol. 1923, exp. 1, fols. 20r ff. CDIAI, II, 26. CDIHE, XXVI, 346. The word milpa, however, applied not simply to an individual plot in the calpullalli but to any plot, e.g., the land cultivated for an Indian officer or a cultivated plot on a hacienda. CDIAI, II, 91. PCR, folder 101 (June 4, 1784). This use of the term repartimiento should not be confused with the labor institution described in Chapter IX.

60. Molina defines tlalmilli as "tierras, o heredades de particulares, q̄ estan juntas en alguna vega &c." Molina, *Vocabulario*, sc. tlalmilli.

61. CDIHE, IV, 198. CDIAI, II, 26–27. Ixtlilxochitl, *Historia*, p. 170. ENE, XIV, 145. Torquemada, *Monarchia indiana*, II, 545.

62. CDIAI, II, 27–29. CDIHE, IV, 198–99; VI, 167.

63. See the list given by Cortés in CDIHE, IV, 199–200.

64. CDIAI, II, 28; VI, 167. CDIHE, IV, 198–99.

65. AGN, General de parte, vol. 2, fol. 196r; Tierras, vol. 1109, exp. 3; vol. 1584, exp. 1, fol. 53v. CDIU, XXI 340.

66. AGN, General de parte, vol. 2, fols. 37v, 282r–282v. For similar migrants in Coyoacan see AGN, Mercedes, vol. 84, fols. 53v–54r.

67. AGN, General de parte, vol. 2, fols. 91r, 142r. MNM, Colección franciscana, no. 190, fol. 11r. Valderrama, *Cartas*, pp. 47, 68.

68. AGN, Mercedes, vol. 84, fol. 38v.

69. AGN, Tierras, vol. 1584, exp. 1, fols. 7r, 53v, 112v.

70. Alienation of maceguales' lands by principales, alguaciles, and others is recorded in AGN, General de parte, vol. 2, fols. 55r–55v, 91r; Mercedes, vol. 2, fol. 239v. For distributions of lands by gobernadores to maceguales see AGN, Hospital de Jesús, vol. 120, exp. 6, fol. 4r; *Al severo tribunal*, p. 83. An instance of gubernatorial usurpation of maceguales' lands is recorded in AGN, Indios, vol. 50, fols. 81r–82r. Sale or rental of community properties is documented in CDIAI, IV, 443; AGN, Hospital de Jesús, vol. 120, exp. 6, fols. 2r ff.; General de parte, vol. 2, fols. 55r–55v, 196r; vol. 3, fols. 235v–236r. There may have been some pre-conquest precedent for the sale of common lands. Our information on this, however, is slight. See ENE, VII, 262. The sale of common lands by gobernadores, alcaldes, and principales continued in the seventeenth century, although it was forbidden by law. See Bentura Beleña, *Recopilación sumaria*, I, 41.

71. CDIAI, VI, 167–69. See Chapter VIII, note 23.

72. CDIHE, IV, 200.

73. *Códice Mariano Jiménez*, fols. 3v–4r. I have doubled the dimensions, since each "braza" here contained two ordinary brazas.

74. Códice Vergara is in BNP, nos. 37–39. Códice Santa María Asunción is in BNM, and a microfilm of it may be consulted in CDMNC, rollo 4, exp. 2. See Carreño, "Manuscritos," pp. 12 ff. For purposes of illustration the plots were depicted in these two codices as approximately equivalent in size, but the measurements attached to each indicate a wide variation. There is some evidence that the two documents may be parts of the same original. Although a Valley of Mexico provenience is not yet demonstrated, both may be from Tepetlaoztoc. Both are signed by Pedro Vásquez de Vergara, and AGN, Mercedes, vol. 2, fols. 209v–219r, shows that he was ordered to go to Tepetlaoztoc in 1543. Fragments VI and VIII of the Humboldt Collection show similar land measurements. See Seler, "Mexican Picture Writing," pp. 190 ff., 200 ff.

75. AGN, Tierras, vol. 1702, exp. 4, 2nd pag., fols. 6v ff.

76. The Xaltocan documents are in AGN, Tierras, vol. 1584, exp. 1, fols. 120v ff. The fact that family size is indicated in the two codices mentioned and in the Xaltocan documents as well suggests that some effort was made to equate family size with the amount of land assigned. It is also possible that some of the disparities in size were in compensation for disparities in the agricultural quality of the land.

77. García Pimentel, *Descripción*, p. 89.

78. AGN, Mercedes, *passim*.

79. CDIAI, VI, 168. We cannot be certain of the date of this document.

80. NCDHM (1941), I, 18 ff. Motolinía, *History*, p. 269. Montúfar, "Carta del arzobispo," p. 352. AGN, Mercedes, vol. 1, fol. 84r; vol. 2, fol. 162r–162v. Many other instances are recorded in AGN, Mercedes, vols. 1–2.

81. BNM, ms. no. 1312, fols. 22r ff. Other documents of this type relating to Valley of Mexico towns include: "Anales de San Gregorio Acapulco," pp. 122 ff.; AAMC, no. 25; BNM, ms. no. 1312, fols. 8r ff.; Codex Kaska (HSA, HC 397/433/1–4), vol. 4, fols. 34r ff.; McAfee and Barlow, "The Titles of Tetzcotzinco."

82. E.g., to the oidor Lorenzo de Tejada, ENE, V, 34; to Cortés, CDIAI, XII, 376; CDIU, XVIII, 38 ff.

83. AC, I, 28, 59, 88.

84. CDIU, X, 69–70; XXII, 147, 156. ENE, II, 221, Puga, *Provisiones*, fol. 86r. Encinas, *Cedulario*, I, 65–66. AA, Tierras y ejidos, vol. 2, no. 4065, exp. 2. AC, II, 74, 113; VII, 43.

85. CDIU, XXII, 157–58, 163. AGN, Mercedes, *passim*.

86. AC, I, 28–29. CDIAI, XII, 279, 376 ff. *Archivo mexicano*, I, 60–62, 200 ff., *et passim*.

87. CDIAI, XIII, 25. AC, I, 18 ff.; II, 14–15. Cortés, *Cartas y relaciones*, pp. 554–55. *Archivo mexicano*, I, 235. ENE, III, 92.

88. AC, I, 163–64, 176, 205; III, 9, 114; VI, 36; VIII, 623; IX, 353. ENE, II, 220.

89. ENE, I, 140; V, 34; XV, 187 ff.; XVI, 73. CDIAI, XIII, 126; XVI, 552; XXIX, 327–28, 380 ff., 465 ff. CDHM, II, 120–21. Aiton, *Antonio de Mendoza*, pp. 93, 110, 113.

90. ENE, I, 129, 132. CDIAI, XIV, 334.

91. CDIAI, XIII, 25–26. CDHM, II, 56. Cortés, *Cartas y relaciones*, pp. 554–55. *Documentos inéditos relativos a Hernán Cortés*, XXVII, 355–57.

92. *Documentos inéditos relativos a Hernán Cortés*, pp. 355–57. CDIAI, XXIX, 380 ff.

93. *Documentos inéditos relativos a Hernán Cortés*, pp. 352, 353, 356.

94. See the comments in NCDHM (1941), I, 25; II, 9. ENE, XVI, 71–74.

95. AC, I, 18 ff., 28–29, 36, 205, *et passim*. ENE, I, 131.

96. AGN, Mercedes, vol. 4, fol. 122r; vol. 84, fol. 126v.

97. NCDHM (1941), I, 25; II, 9.

98. AC, I, 72–73, 176, *et passim*.

99. CDIAI, VI, 184–85. AGN, General de parte, vol. 2, fol. 196r.

100. CDIAI, VI, 184. ENE, V, 34. Aiton, *Antonio de Mendoza*, p. 113.

101. AGN, General de parte, vol. 2, fol. 212r; Mercedes, vol. 6, fols. 334v–335r. ENE, V, 34. CDIAI, XIII, 20.

102. AGN, Tierras, vol. 2, exp. 7. CDIAI, XXVII, 41. PCR, Recaudos de las tierras que vendió Simón Vanegas, *passim*.

103. AGN, Mercedes, vol. 1, fol. 49v; vol. 2, fol. 321r; vol. 6, fols. 21r, 24r, 314r–314v; vol. 8, fol. 83v; vol. 22, fols. 169r–170r; General de parte, vol. 4, fols. 46v–47r; Tierras, vol. 13, fol. 326r. FHT, VI, 103–4.

104. AGN, Mercedes, vol. 5, fols. 95v, 255r–255v; vol. 7, fol. 184r.

105. CDHM, II, 66. CDIAI, XI, 10.

106. AGN, Mercedes, vol. 5, fol. 295r–295v. As corregidor, Magariño conspired with a second party to request a valuable merced, conducted the negotiation in secrecy so that the true value of the lands would not be known, and falsely represented the lands as unoccupied. See AGI, Patronato, leg. 121, ramo 21, fols. 4r ff. See also AGN, Mercedes, vol. 8, fol. 163r–163v. Many other examples of political officials who were property holders within the areas of their jurisdictions might be cited.

107. BNMa, 20245/17; 20417/29. PCR, Reales provisiones, no. 133. AGN, Mercedes, vol. 7, fol. 246v. Gamio, *La población del valle de Teotihuacan*, I (2), 521–22. Bentura Beleña, *Recopilación sumaria*, I, 2nd pag., 69. Orders of 1574 and 1580 allowed for the rectangular forms shown in the table as well as for a single measurement (1,500 pasos de Salomón, i.e., 2,500 varas, for the estancia de ganado mayor; 1,000 pasos de Salomón, i.e., ca. 1,666 varas, for the estancia de ganado menor) in all directions from the house site. Bentura Beleña, *Recopilación sumaria*, I, 2nd pag., 62, 65. Hence the estancias are sometimes shown in circular, rather than rectangular, form. See PCR, Reales provisiones, no. 133 (where, however, the diameter is given as the radius and the total size therefore much enlarged); Galván Rivera, *Ordenanzas*, pp. 160 ff. See Orozco, *Legislación y jurisprudencia*, II, 758; Carrera Stampa, "The Evolution of Weights and Measures," pp. 19 ff. The term estancia was employed in the meaning of "farm" and in this sense an estancia might contain several estancias de ganado.

108. AGN, Mercedes, vol. 7, fol. 311r–311v; vol. 9, fol. 38r–38v, *et passim*. AGI, México, leg. 665, cuad. 4, fols. 58v ff. The conditions of the grants are discussed by Chevalier, *La formation des grands domaines*, pp. 66 ff.

109. AGN, Mercedes, *passim*. PCR, Varios papeles, vol. 1, exp. 1. Romero de Terreros, "Dos conquistadores," pp. 229–31.

110. PCR, Reales provisiones, no. 133.

111. AGN, Mercedes, vols. 1–35. These volumes contain grants to 1621 including, by my count, 646 grants in the Valley of Mexico.

112. The missing years, together with calculations for the amount of land granted in them, are given for Mexico as a whole in Simpson, *Exploitation of Land*, pp. 6 ff.

113. My count of the mercedes of the first thirty-five volumes of AGN, Mercedes, arrives at a figure slightly less than Simpson's for herding grants and about 16 per cent less than his for agricultural grants. Moreover, the area included is somewhat larger than his Region 13, the Valley of Mexico. See Simpson, *Exploitation of Land*, pp. 54–55. The discrepancy appears to be due less to errors in counting than to differ-

ences in categorization and interpretation. Some grants fall only partly within the Valley of Mexico. Although the grants are specifically recorded, the material is not easily reduced to exact figures. Simpson supposes a general encroachment beyond the grants involving three times the area granted. This, however, is impossible in the Valley of Mexico for it presumes an occupation in excess of the total land area.

114. Writing ca. 1555, Zorita remarked upon the "multitude" of Spanish agricultural properties and stated that this represented a change from conditions of ten to twenty years before. CDIAI, II, 116.

115. These and other comments in this paragraph upon the rate and distribution of land assignment are based upon the same thirty-five volumes of AGN, Mercedes.

116. CDIAI, VI, 183. Torquemada, *Monarchia indiana,* I, 305, 307.

117. CDIAI, XI, 10-11. AGN, Indios, vol. 2, fols. 148r, 161r-161v.

118. AGN, General de parte, vol. 1, fol. 98r; vol. 2, fols. 193v-194r.

119. AGN, Congregaciones, vol. 1, fols. 83r-83v, 94v-95r.

120. E.g., AGI, Justicia, leg. 159, no. 1.

121. AGN, Mercedes, vol. 1, fol. 101v; vol. 2, fol. 283v; vol. 3, fols. 25r, 114v ff., 288r. NLAC, 1121, fol. 62r-62v. Many other instances might be documented.

122. For an instance of water seizure see ENE, XV, 187. An instance of sale is recorded in Tacubaya in 1590, where the gobernador and other Indian authorities sold water rights to a Spanish property holder for agricultural irrigation. He paid thirty pesos and received rights to the water "para siempre jamás." In the process of legalization great efforts were made to demonstrate that the Indian community granted the rights voluntarily and not under compulsion. See AA, Aguas Tacubaya y otros pueblos, leg. 1, no. 55, exp. 1. For an eighteenth-century distribution of water, by *surcos, naranjas, dedos,* and other measurements, see León, "Bibliografía," no. 4, pp. 28-29. There exists a large documentation on the seizure, sale, distribution, and measurement of water.

123. E.g., AGN, Indios, vol. 5, fols. 153r, 182v.

124. AC, I, 79.

125. The normal period for such grazing was December 1 to March 31, but under special circumstances, as in 1591 when the prolonged growing season meant that crops were still green in early December, the initial date might be postponed. CDIU, XXII, 165 ff. Bentura Beleña, *Recopilación sumaria,* I, 2nd pag., 46. AC, IX, 353. AGN, Tierras, vol. 13, exp. 5, fol. 330v; Indios, vol. 3, fol. 20v; vol. 6 (2), fol. 32r.

126. CDIU, XXII, 165 ff. PCR, Reales provisiones, *passim.*

127. E.g., AGN, General de parte, vol. 6, fols. 194v-195r.

128. AGI, Justicia, leg. 159, no. 1. AGN, Tierras, vol. 13, exp. 5, fols. 326r ff. ENE, IV, 96.

129. AGN, Tierras, vol. 13, exp. 5, fol. 326r. Cobo, *Obras,* II, 471. FHT, III, 43-44. Gemelli Carreri, *Las cosas más considerables,* p. 108.

130. Bentura Beleña, *Recopilación sumaria,* I, 2nd pag., 59. CDIAI, IX, 209. AGN, General de parte, vol. 2, fols. 132v-133r.

131. AGN, Indios, vol. 2, fols. 167r, 237v; vol. 4, fol. 199v; Mercedes, vol. 7, fol. 33r; Congregaciones, vol. 1, fol. 100r-100v. Bentura Beleña, *Recopilación sumaria,* I, 2nd pag., 44. See also the interesting narrative of the "Anales de San Gregorio Acapulco," pp. 136 ff., where Indians, encouraged by a friar, burned the rancho of an intrusive Spanish herder.

132. AC, V, 63, 119. CDIAI, II, 29; VI, 506. CDIU, XXII, 211. AGN, Tierras, vol. 13, exp. 5, fol. 331r. Cervantes de Salazar, *Crónica,* p. 31.

133. Vetancurt, *Chronica,* p. 86.

134. AGN, Reales cédulas, duplicados, vol. 1, exp. 156, fol. 162r. CDIU, XXI, 336. AC, IV, 245.

135. AGN, Mercedes, vol. 4, fols. 2v–3r; vol. 84, fol. 38v.

136. From 1572 to 1585 this rule applied to sales over thirty pesos. But Spanish purchasers divided larger sales into smaller portions to evade the rule. Hence in 1585 the order reverted to its original form. AGN, General de parte, vol. 7, fols. 49v–50r; Tierras, vol. 74, exp. 5, fols. 11v–12v; vol. 2699, exp. 2, fol. 2r–2v; Indios, vol. 6 (1), fols. 252v–253r. *Recopilación de leyes,* II, 195–96 (Lib. VI, tít. 1, ley 27). Encinas, *Cedulario,* IV, 254–55. See on this subject, Gibson, *Tlaxcala,* pp. 86–87, 231–32.

137. Bentura Beleña, *Recopilación sumaria,* I, 41; 2nd pag., 113. A prohibition of all Indian land sales in the Chalco area was ordered in 1563. See AGN, Mercedes, vol. 7, fol. 208v.

138. AA, Tierras y ejidos, leg. 2, no. 4066, exp. 29, fols. 12v ff. AGN, Tierras, vol. 2, exp. 6, fols. 34r ff.

139. AC, I, 174–75. CDIAI, VI, 506. AGN, Mercedes, vol. 5, fols. 181v–182r. AGI, Justicia, leg. 159, no. 1. NLAC, 1121, fols. 48r ff.

140. BNM, ms. no. 437, fols. 316r ff. Galván Rivera, *Ordenanzas,* pp. 192 ff. In Tepexpan the viceroy ruled in 1560 that no cattle might approach within one league of the town either during the *agostero* period (December 1 to March 31) or at any other time. A similar rule, but with a distance of one-half league, was applied to Xochimilco in 1561. See AGN, Mercedes, vol. 5, fols. 174v–175r, 255r. For other local restrictions upon the pasturage rule see AGN, Indios, vol. 5, fol. 310v; vol. 6 (2), fol. 203r.

141. See the particular application to Xaltocan, AGN, Mercedes, vol. 84, fol. 38v.

142. CDIAI, II, 28. Examples from various towns in the late sixteenth and seventeenth centuries may be seen in FHT, III, 18–19; AGN, General de parte, vol. 3, fol. 268v; Vínculos, vol. 244, exp. 1, fols. 35r ff., 51r ff. The term realengo here means unoccupied land.

143. Examples are documented in AGN, General de parte, vol. 2, fols. 196r, 212r; vol. 3, fol. 235v; Mercedes, *passim.*

144. E.g., AA, Tierras y ejidos, leg. 2, no. 4066, exp. 29, fols. 12v ff., describing numerous small land sales, unrecorded exchanges, trades made in punishment, sales in unknown amounts, etc.

145. See the example of Zumpango in AGN, General de parte, vol. 2, fol. 165r–165v.

146. Indeed, the visitador Jerónimo Valderrama asserted that most pueblos had changed their original sites by 1564. Valderrama, *Cartas,* pp. 47, 68. For the ecclesiastical connection see Lorenzana, *Concilios provinciales,* pp. 147–48; *Concilio III provincial mexicano,* pp. 25–26; Cervantes de Salazar, *Crónica,* p. 29; NCDHM (1886–92), V, 90 ff. Alegre, *Historia de la Compañía de Jesús,* I, 169. Secular, or combined secular and religious, interest is expressed in various royal and viceregal orders: Puga, *Provisiones,* fols. 203r–203v, 208v; Maza, *Código,* pp. 14–15, 18–19; García and Pereyra, *Documentos inéditos,* XV, 204–8; CDIAI, XXIII, 542–44. Examples of congregaciones in the Valley of Mexico from the 1530's through the mid-sixteenth century are BNP, no. 84, fols. 11r ff.; AGN, Mercedes, vol. 84, fols. 51v–52r; Chapa, *San Gregorio Atlapulco,* pp. 96 ff. For other rules concerning congregación, dating from a period prior to the conquest of Mexico, see CDIU, XXI, 314 ff., and *Recopilación de leyes,* II, 207–8 (Lib. VI, Tít. 3, ley 1). See also Simpson, *Studies in the Administration of the Indians,* II; Cline, "Civil Congregation." An interesting discussion of congregación, by Ernesto de la Torre, is published in BAGN, XXIII, 147–83.

147. See NCDHM (1886–92), V, 92.

148. Cuevas, *Documentos inéditos*, p. 115. AC, VII, 6, 181.

149. NCDHM (1941), I, 25.

150. AGN, Tierras, vol. 1584, exp. 1, fols. 3v, 93v ff. *Advertimientos generales*, p. 53. BAGN, ser. 2, II, 25 ff. On the other hand, fear was expressed lest congregated Indians become more susceptible to epidemic. See Dávila Padilla, *Historia*, p. 124.

151. AGN, Tierras, vol. 1584, exp. 1, fols. 33v ff.; General de parte, vol. 5, fols. 122v–123r.

152. Thus in the Xaltocan congregación of 1599 the names of all persons moved are recorded together with the amounts of land that each family head was to cultivate. AGN, Tierras, vol. 1584, exp. 1, 158r–163v. See also the record of the Tlalnepantla congregación, AGN, Congregaciones, vol. 1, fols. 48r ff.

153. AGI, México, leg. 122; leg. 665, cuad. 2, fols. 200r ff. Additional data on these subjects may be found in AGN, Congregaciones, vol. 1, *passim*.

154. See examples in the record of the Xaltocan congregación, AGN, Tierras, vol. 1584, exp. 1, fols. 40v, 44r, 47r, 63r ff.

155. A proposed congregación in this district in 1603 would have brought Mexica peoples of Zacatepec and other communities into association with Acolhua peoples. The two "have been great enemies, one with the other, since ancient times, and they still are today, and they have never agreed but have been divided." AGN, Congregaciones, vol. 1, fols. 19v–20r, 59v–6or. On rare occasions we find congregaciones made at Indian request; e.g., AGN, Mercedes, vol. 6, fol. 140v. And occasionally congregación brought opportunities for modifications in Indian tribute and service obligations, as when a sujeto of one cabecera was congregated with a sujeto of another. See the example of Azcapotzaltongo and the sujetos of Tlalnepantla in AGN, Indios, vol. 6 (1), fol. 142r.

156. AGN, Congregaciones, vol. 1, *passim*.

157. BAGN, ser. 2, II, 45–46. AGN, Tierras, vol. 1584, exp. 1, fol. 34v. AGI, México, leg. 665, cuad. 2, fols. 137v ff.

158. AGN, Tierras, vol. 1584, exp. 1; Congregaciones, vol. 1, fols. 30v ff., 46r ff. BAGN, ser. 2, II, 17 ff. AGI, México, leg. 665, cuad. 2, fols. 97r ff.

159. AGI, México, leg. 122, *passim*. AGN, Indios, vol. 6 (1), fol. 196r; Vínculos, vol. 244, exp. 1, fols. 16r ff. PCR, Varios papeles, vol. 2, fols. 78v–79r.

160. AGN, Indios, vol. 6 (2), fol. 181v. *Advertimientos generales*, p. 53.

161. AGI, México, leg. 665, cuad. 2, fols. 207v ff.

162. Bentura Beleña, *Recopilación sumaria*, I, 5th pag., 207. BNM, ms. no. 437, fols. 316r–318r; no. 488, fols. 24r–25v. See also AGN, Tierras, vol. 1122, exp. 2, fols. 5r–8r; Hall, *The Laws of Mexico*, pp. 63–68; Maza, *Código*, pp. 25–30; Galván Rivera, *Ordenanzas*, pp. 192–94, 195–97. These laws were frequently included in post-colonial codifications, for the reason that they explained, in part, the nineteenth-century concept of the *fondo legal*.

163. Bentura Beleña, *Recopilación sumaria*, I, 5th pag., 208. AGN, Tierras, vol. 1122, exp. 2, fols. 19r–20r.

164. AGN, Vínculos, vol. 244, exp. 1, fols. 171 ff. For laws on composición see Fonseca and Urrutia, *Historia*, IV, 399–400, and Orozco, *Legislación y jurisprudencia*, I, 46–53. See also McBride, *The Land Systems*, pp. 56 ff. For the texts of composiciones relating to various haciendas see PCR, Varios papeles, vol. 1, exp. 2, fols. 308r ff.; vol. 3, no. 18.

165. Numerous examples may be found in AGI, México, leg. 664, *passim*.

166. See AGN, Vínculos, vol. 244, exp. 1, fols. 1r ff.

167. See the interesting example of Mixcoac in AGN, Hospital de Jesús, vol. 318, exp. 6, fols. 5r ff.

168. E.g., AGN, Tierras, vol. 1653, exp. 8, fol. 55r–55v.

169. Cases illustrating these several Indian responses may be found in AA, Tierras y ejidos, leg. 2, no. 4066, exp. 26, fols. 6v, 8r; exp. 27, fol. 16v; exp. 29, fols. 5v–6r; exp. 33, fol. 9r.

170. See Codex Kaska in HSA, HC 397/433/1–4, vol. 3, fol. 63v. For the sale of documents see Navarro de Vargas, "Padrón," p. 573.

171. AGN, Tierras, vol. 2, exp. 5, fol. 7r. In the mid-eighteenth century the gobernador of Xochitepec produced 100 documents, of which all but one were declared to be forgeries. See below, note 197. The Techialoyan group comprises a separate subject, now being studied by Donald Robertson. His article, "The Techialoyan Codex of Tepotzotlán," explains the problem, illustrates the type, and provides a bibliography.

172. AGN, Tierras, vol. 2, exp. 3, fols. 32r ff. AGI, México, leg. 664. PCR, Varios papeles, vol. 1, exp. 2, fol. 318r.

173. PCR, Varios papeles, vol. 2, fols. 79r ff. AGN, Tierras, vol. 2, exp. 6, fols. 34r ff.; Vínculos, vol. 244, exp. 1, passim.

174. The Los Portales titles are in HSA, HC: NS3/29/1–3.

175. These records are respectively PCR, Varios papeles, vols. 1–3; and AGN, Vínculos, vol. 244, exp. 1.

176. For Xalpa see Romero de Terreros, Antiguas haciendas, pp. 23–35; Romero de Terreros, "Epigrafía," pp. 418–21. Some of the original grants are indicated in AGN, Mercedes, vol. 6, fols. 21r, 314r–314v.

177. NCDHM (1941), I, 25–26. PCR, Varios papeles, vol. 1, exp. 1. ENE, XVI, 73.

178. A systematic list by political jurisdiction, but with some jurisdictions missing, is available for the late eighteenth century in AGN, Padrones. The fullest supplementary guides to late colonial haciendas are in AGN, Tierras and AGN, Vínculos. These are unsystematic court records, but they provide useful lists for the reason that haciendas were very frequently involved in litigation.

179. AGN, Padrones, vol. 6, fols. 315v, 317r. Tauregui is referred to as a rancho in BNM, ms. no. 451, fol. 294r.

180. For various figures for estancias and caballerías see AGN, Tierras, vol. 1702, exp. 5, fols. 37v ff.; PCR, Varios papeles, vol. 1, exp. 1, fol. 12v. AC, VIII, 143 ff.

181. AGN, Padrones, vol. 6, fol. 317v.

182. Gazetas de México, compendio de noticias, I, 394; VI, 539.

183. AGN, Vínculos, vol. 244, exp. 1, fols. 115r ff. Gazetas de México, compendio de noticias, XII, 8.

184. La administración de D. Frey Antonio María de Bucareli, I, 433. León, "Bibliografía," no. 10, pp. 41–43. Romero de Terreros, El conde de Regla, pp. 131 ff. AGN, Tierras, vol. 2033, exp. 1.

185. San Xavier consisted of a tremendous number of discontinuous properties from the region of Acolman to Ixcuincuitlapilco and Epazoyuca far to the north of the Valley of Mexico. See PCR, Mayorazgo de Regla, vols. 3–4. PCR, Diligencias, fols. 10r ff., gives its boundaries as of 1777.

186. E.g., PCR, folder 78 (September 15, 1776) ff.

187. PCR, Varios papeles, vol. 1, exp. 2, fol. 514v.

188. AHH, Tributos, leg. 224, exp. 8, fols. 9r–11r. AGI, México, leg. 791. AC, XLVIII–L (1), 8. AGN, Civil, vol. 174, nos. 1, 10, 51.

189. *Al severo tribunal*, pp. 36–37.

190. See above, note 162. *Disposiciones complementarias*, I, 89–90. AGN, Hospital de Jesús, vol. 318, exp. 6.

191. PCR, Varios papeles, vol. 2, fols. 84r, 183v.

192. PCR, Varios papeles, vol. 2, fol. 82r. *Disposiciones complementarias*, I, 89–90.

193. *Al severo tribunal*, pp. 28–30. The community was on record with 229 tributaries, but about 75 of these were already missing in 1620. FHT, VI, 388–89.

194. AGI, México, leg. 665, cuad. 2, fols. 1r ff., 222v ff. FHT, VII, 149–50.

195. AGI, México, leg. 665, cuad. 2, fols. 201v ff., 205r ff., 249r ff.

196. AGI, México, leg. 664; leg. 665, cuad. 1, fols. 1r ff.

197. AGI, México, leg. 664. *Al severo tribunal*, pp. 48 ff.

198. The case is documented in PCR, Varios papeles, vol. 2, fols. 78r ff. The same series contains other and similar cases in the history of Santa Lucía, including Spanish-Indian land conflicts in Zumpango, Xaltocan, Tizayuca, and other communities.

199. AGN, Congregaciones, vol. 1, fol. 47v. AGN, Tierras, vol. 1533, exp. 1, fol. 29r; Padrones, vol. 6, fols. 145r ff.

200. AGN, Tierras, vol. 1533, exp. 1, fols. 1r ff., 13v ff., 28v ff.

201. AGN, Tierras, vol. 1535, exp. 1, fols. 9r–9v, 19r.

202. AGN, Tierras, vol. 1535, exp. 1, fols. 19r, 33r.

203. Villa-señor y Sánchez, *Theatro americano*, I, 163. AGN, Tierras, vol. 1811, exp. 1.

204. *Al severo tribunal*, pp. 61 ff.

205. See AGN, Tierras, vol. 1518, exp. 1, fols. 22r ff.

206. AGN, Tierras, vol. 1518, exp. 5; vol. 1934, exp. 1.

207. AGN, Tierras, vol. 1535, exp. 1, fol. 35r.

CHAPTER XI

1. Of the many tree varieties in the Valley of Mexico, these three (together with related types, such as the evergreen *ayauhquahuitl*, which resembles the common ocotl pine or cedar) receive most frequent mention in the sources as constituting the forest cover of the higher regions. See, e.g., Ojea, *Libro tercero*, p. 2. For a list of other trees derived from historical sources see Jacobs Muller, "Recursos naturales," pp. 13–14. There is a large literature on the dendrology of the Valley.

2. A number of additional Nahuatl words describe soil types or qualities. Those given here as well as some others are listed by Sahagún, *Historia general*, II, 476 ff.

3. See our comments above in Chapter X, note 74.

4. *The Badianus Manuscript*, Pl. III, p. 37, *et passim*.

5. The term tequisquitl seems to have been used at times in reference to any saline soils, but it has particular application to the soils impregnated with soda ash (sodium carbonate). Gálvez, *Informe general*, p. 79. Orozco y Berra, *Memoria para la carta hidrográfica*, p. 146. Basurto, *El arzobispado*, p. 204. Humboldt, *Political Essay*, II, 26; III, 467 ff. See Chapter XII, note 42.

6. The term tepetate was (and is) loosely applied to several distinct soils, of various degrees of infertility. AC, VIII, 143. BNM, ms. no. 455, fol. 154r–154v.

7. PNE, I, 25, 105, 110, 113, *et passim*. BAGN, ser. 2, II, 15 ff. BNM, ms. no. 455, fols. 205r ff.

8. Examples, principally from the 1920's and 1930's, are tabulated in Carlson, *Geography*, p. 406.

9. Reiche, *La vegetación en los alrededores de la capital*, pp. 8 ff. Ramírez, *La vegetación de México*, pp. 129 ff.

10. The process is described in Carlson, *Geography*, pp. 407–8, and other works on Mexican geography. Winter is also almost the only time when rain falls in the morning. The change occurs with the return of northern winds in the autumn, a phenomenon noted by Alzate in the eighteenth century. Alzate, *Gacetas de literatura*, II, 280.

11. Alzate, who wrote with perspicacity on these and related subjects, noted that summer rains fell normally after three P.M. Alzate, *Gacetas de literatura*, II, 310.

12. Reiche, *La vegetación en los alrededores de la capital*, p. 10. Ramírez, *La vegetación de México*, pp. 134–35. Alzate, *Gacetas de literatura*, II, 280, and IV, 53–61, describes the month-by-month rainfall of a typical year in the late eighteenth century and provides the temperature readings at four times each day from April to December, 1769. A day-by-day record of rainfall and other climatic phenomena from 1763 to 1773 is given in the "Efemérides" of Zúñiga y Ontiveros (SLSF).

13. Seasonal variations in temperature and moisture receive abundant comment in colonial sources. With regard to the differences in moisture between north and south, S. F. Cook has collected a number of notices relating to the aridity of the Teotlalpan, which includes the northern part of the Valley of Mexico. See Cook, *The Historical Demography and Ecology of the Teotlalpan*, pp. 19 ff. See also his map (p. 3).

14. See above, note 12. Indians identified a change in rainfall during the first colonial generation, asserting that the period of seasonal precipitation had diminished by half, from 60–80 days to 30–40 days, and locating the change at or near 1540. Cervantes de Salazar, *Crónica*, p. 10. PNE, VI, 43. The testimony is weakened by the facts of known pre-conquest drought (e.g., Chimalpahin, *Annales*, pp. 57–58) and by the longer wet seasons of later years.

15. AGI, México, leg. 665, cuad. 2, fols. 97r ff., 223r ff. Alzate, *Gacetas de literatura*, II, 43.

16. Alvarez, *Algunos datos*, pp. 144 ff. Motolinía, *History*, pp. 214–15.

17. *Histoire de la nation mexicaine*, p. 92. "Anales de San Gregorio Acapulco," p. 111. AC, VI, 131.

18. AC, VI, 131. PNE, III (supl.), 199 ff. Torquemada, *Monarchia indiana*, I, 300, 309.

19. The point may be appreciated through a comparison of the seventeenth-century maps with the Humboldt map, in Apenas, *Mapas antiguos*, láms. 17, 18, 19, 30. But in the dry seasons of the seventeenth and eighteenth centuries Lake Texcoco was so reduced that canoes could not travel between Texcoco and the capital. AA, Desagüe, leg. 1, no. 740, exp. 11, fol. 17r. Humboldt, *Political Essay*, II, 27. In June 1691, before the start of the rainy season, one could travel on foot or horseback from Texcoco to Mexico City. See Sigüenza's letter of 1692, in Leonard, *Don Carlos de Sigüenza*, p. 222. For a map showing the gradual modification of the lake surfaces see Lobato, "Meteorología de México," p. 88.

20. Relations between pre- and post-conquest erosion are discussed in Cook, *The Historical Demography and Ecology of the Teotlalpan*, pp. 52 ff.

21. Torquemada, *Monarchia indiana*, I, 309–10. Martínez, *Reportorio de los tiempos*, pp. 180–81. AC, XXV, 116.

22. The use of wooden estacas is indicated in the sixteenth century in CDIHE, LVII, 177. For the seventeenth and eighteenth centuries see Ojea, *Libro tercero*, p. 6, and Alzate, *Gacetas de literatura*, I, 398 ff. The subject is discussed in Alvarez, *Algunos datos*, pp. 160 ff., and Téllez Pizarro, *Estudio sobre cimientos*, pp. 10 ff.

23. Cobo, *Obras*, II, 469. Alzate, *Gacetas de literatura*, I, 400–401.

24. BNM, ms. no. 455, fol. 154v. Humboldt, *Political Essay*, II, 128. *Gazetas de México, compendio de noticias*, III, 403.

25. PNE, III (supl.), 39–40, 199–200. Torquemada, *Monarchia indiana*, I, 311.

26. AGN, Padrones, vol. 6, fol. 315r. Alzate, *Gacetas de literatura*, II, 52.

27. PNE, III, 67. Cervantes de Salazar, *Crónica*, p. 11. Robles, *Diario*, II, 77.

28. Alzate, *Gacetas de literatura*, II, 52. See our remarks on the differing rates of population change in Tenochtitlan and Tlatelolco in Chapter XIII.

29. Flooding of the Hacienda de Santa Ana Aragón in 1763 is noted in AGN, Tierras, vol. 917, exp. 1, fol. 17v. When the Conde de Regla took possession of the Hacienda de Santa Lucía in 1777 he had to do it by canoe because the hacienda was inundated. See AGN, Tierras, vol. 2034, cuad. 5, fol. 1v.

30. "Maize" is originally a Taino word. Nahuatl terms are *tlaolli, centli*, and others. See Molina, *Vocabulario*, sc. mayz, maiz.

31. Most of the advantages of maize have long been known. It is only recently, however, that maize has been rated so highly in nutritive quality. See Cravioto, "Nutritive Value of the Mexican Tortilla"; Aguirre Beltrán, "Cultura y nutrición." The older view that Mexican native diet, including maize, was of low nutritional value is expressed in Llamas, "La alimentación."

32. Relations between maize and pre-conquest calendrical ceremonial are revealed in accounts of monthly festivals, e.g., Sahagún, "Relación breve de las fiestas." Motolinía, *History*, pp. 67 ff., describes three such festivals, identifying the appropriate periods by the height of the maize plant. See also Kubler and Gibson, *The Tovar Calendar*.

33. NCDHM (1941), III, 49. "Relación de Zempoala," p. 38. Alzate, *Gacetas de literatura*, IV, 104. *Gazetas de México, compendio de noticias*, III, 190. AC, XII, 118. See Beltrán, "Plantas usadas en la alimentación."

34. AC, XII, 118; XLIII–XLVII (2), 78. AA, Pósito y alhóndiga, vol. 2, no. 3695, exp. 60, fol. 9r. BNMa, 2449, fol. 56r.

35. Alzate, *Gacetas de literatura*, II, 233–34.

36. Durán, *Historia*, II, 258. For continuing and developing superstitions in maize planting in the colonial period see Ruiz de Alarcón, "Tratado."

37. Alzate, *Gacetas de literatura*, IV, 102.

38. Clavigero, *Historia antigua*, II, 268–69. Gamio, *La población del valle de Teotihuacan*, I (2), 522. Sahagún's illustration is in his *Florentine Codex*, Book IV, Pl. 96. See Plate V.

39. From the time of Viceroy Mendoza the caballería (ca. 105 acres) was understood to contain twelve fanegas de sembradura of maize. This is the equivalent of ca. 8.8 acres per fanega de sembradura. The caballería was identified as an area of 1,104 by 552 varas; the fanega de sembradura of maize was an area of 276 by 184 varas. See BNMa, 20417/29, fol. 3r; Orozco, *Legislación y jurisprudencia*, II, 745; Carrera Stampa, "The Evolution of Weights and Measures," p. 19. Both Orozco and Carrera Stampa, by error, give the measurement 376 by 184 rather than 276 by 184 varas. For the equation of one fanega with 1.5 bushels, see below, note 48. With regard to the weight of maize, the United States government (for customs purposes) and the various states assign a minimum of 52 and a maximum of 56 pounds per bushel for shelled, and a minimum of 68 and a maximum of 72 pounds per bushel for husked, maize. We have computed the weight per fanega from these limits in shelled maize. The weight depends additionally, of course, upon size of kernels, moisture content, and other fac-

tors. Borah and Cook, *Price Trends*, p. 11, equate the fanega with approximately 100 pounds. Cook, *The Historical Demography and Ecology of the Teotlalpan*, p. 39, supposes a fanega to be 144 liters and a liter of maize to weigh 830 grams. This would be the equivalent of about 65 pounds per bushel, but it appears to overestimate the fanega by about 160 per cent. See note 48 on the size of the fanega. A common estimate of the United States corn belt is that one bushel contains approximately 100 ears, but this relates to the large modern ear.

40. Díaz del Pino, *El maíz*, p. 101. Five pounds per acre is the equivalent of approximately eleven acres per bushel.

41. Spaniards appear to have brought the term *coa* from Cuba, and in the Valley of Mexico they almost never used the Nahuatl term *huictli*. See Molina, *Vocabulario*, sc. victli.

42. E.g., AGN, General de parte, vol. 2, fol. 184v.

43. AA, Pósito y alhóndiga, vol. 2, no. 3695, exp. 91. Clavigero, *Historia antigua*, II, 268–69.

44. A statement of 1557 asserted that the larger part of Indian land was irrigated. CDIHE, XXVI, 348. Palerm, "La distribución del regadío," pp. 3–4, 9–10, 66, 70, lists locations in the Valley of Mexico with pre-conquest irrigation works, mainly from PNE. See also Palerm, "The Agricultural Basis," pp. 36–41; Palerm and Wolf, "El desarrollo del area clave"; Wolf and Palerm, "Irrigation in the Old Acolhua Domain." There remained remnant irrigated lands in Indian possession in the early seventeenth century, e.g., in Cuauhtitlan. See MNM, Colección antigua, T.2-57, fol. 12r; AGN, Congregaciones, vol. 1, fols. 93r–93v, 102r, 105v. Examples of Spanish usurpation of irrigation streams may be seen in NCDHM (1941), III, 53; ENE, XV, 187, 193. On the development of irrigated wheat see Chapter IX, note 69, and this chapter, note 126. Such irrigated wheat was raised almost entirely on the property of Spaniards, not Indians.

45. Irrigated maize was raised in the tierra caliente and in Michoacan, but hardly at all in the Valley of Mexico even in late colonial times. But by the late eighteenth century most wheat throughout the colony was irrigated. See Alzate, *Gacetas de literatura*, II, 234–35. *Gazetas de México, compendio de noticias*, II, 23 ff., 133–34. *Documentos para la historia económica*, II, 57. It will be remembered that we have dated the appearance of large-scale wheat irrigation in the Valley of Mexico in the late sixteenth century. See Chapter IX.

46. Motolinía, *History*, p. 270. López de Velasco, *Geografía y descripción*, p. 188. AA, Pósito y alhóndiga, vol. 2, no. 3695, exp. 91. Humboldt, *Political Essay*, II, 394–95, 413.

47. AGN, Tierras, vol. 995, *passim*.

48. Our calculations here regarding yield, as well as some other calculations of this chapter, depend upon the equation of the colonial fanega with ca. 1.5 United States bushels. In this I agree with the judgments of Molíns Fabrega, "El Códice mendocino," pp. 306–7, and Borah and Cook, *Price Trends*, p. 11, that the fanega was the approximate equivalent of 55 liters. (The two works differ somewhat, but from the present point of view inconsequentially, as to the exact amount.) The standard United States bushel is a measure of ca. 35.2 liters. It should be noted that some other students have supposed a much larger fanega. Carrera Stampa, "The Evolution of Weights and Measures," p. 15, lists the fanega at ca. 90 liters and 2.5 U.S. bushels. Anderson and Barlow, "The Maize Tribute," p. 416, regard 2.5 United States bushels as a con-

servative estimate for the fanega. (They err in equating 1.6 English bushels with over two United States bushels.) Cook, *The Historical Demography and Ecology of the Teotlalpan*, p. 39 (see above, note 39), equates the fanega with 144 liters (i.e., ca. four United States bushels), but this view is seemingly revised in the more recent *Price Trends*. See also Katz, *Die sozialökonomischen Verhältnisse*, p. 89. Historically there have been many fanegas, including a Paraguayan fanega of 288 liters. To me, a fanega approximating the fanega of Castile, or Seville, or Toledo (these range from 53.1 to 55.5 liters) seems most appropriate for the colonial Valley of Mexico. If this is incorrect, many of our other calculations of this chapter are likewise incorrect.

49. AGN, Tierras, vol. 1466, final pag.

50. AGN, Tierras, vol. 1923, exp. 1, fol. 78r. This is based on the carga of two fanegas. The common carga of the early period was one-half fanega. See *Códice Osuna*, pp. 182 ff., 264 ff.; AC, II, 58. Suárez de Peralta, *Noticias históricas*, p. 21, states that one-half fanega was the amount that an Indian could carry. By our calculations this would be about 40 pounds of maize. Depending on the commodity, the period, and the carrier, a number of other cargas are documented in the colonial period. The normal Spanish carga was four fanegas (BNMa, 20417/29, fol. 8r), and this carga is likewise occasionally mentioned in Mexico (e.g., BNM, ms. no. 465, fol. 278r, with reference to wheat flour in Mexico City in 1777). Cargas of three fanegas likewise receive occasional notice in the colony: with reference to maize in Mexico City in 1692 (AGI, Patronato, leg. 226, ramo 18, fol. 12v); with reference to maize in Mexico City in 1791 (Humboldt, *Political Essay*, II, 68). The city's pósito dealt in maize shipments from the interior of Mexico in 1692, figured in cargas of 2½ fanegas (AGI, Patronato, leg. 226, ramo 20, fol. 5v). The largest carga recorded appears to be of 8 fanegas, in reference to wheat flour carried by canoe in the eighteenth century (AHH, Temporalidades, leg. 106, exp. 7, fol. 2r). All these, however, are exceptional. The normal maize carga of the seventeenth and eighteenth centuries was the carga of two fanegas. For indications of this carga of two fanegas see AGI, México, leg. 781, fols. 11r, 126r ff.; AGN, Tierras, vol. 995, *passim*; BNM, ms. no. 465, fol. 278r; AA, Pósito y alhóndiga, vol. 1, no. 3694, exp. 27, fols. 2r–5r; *Gazetas de México, compendio de noticias*, III, 174.

51. On the making of tortillas see Champlain, "Brief discovrs des choses," p. 52; Cervantes de Salazar, *Crónica*, p. 14; AGI, México, leg. 2096, 1770, *passim*. Hand grinding freed Indian communities from the dependence on mills and water power, which were important factors in contemporaneous Spanish towns. See, e.g., Viñas y Mey and Paz, *Relaciones*, I, 5 ff.

52. Alzate, *Gacetas de literatura*, IV, 103, 385, 387. *Gazetas de México, compendio de noticias*, II, 146–47.

53. AGI, México, leg. 2096, 1770, *passim*. CDIHE, LVII, 103. Gemelli Carreri, *Las cosas más considerables*, p. 86. Cervantes de Salazar, *Crónica*, p. 307.

54. AGI, Patronato, leg. 226, ramo 19, fol. 9v; México, leg. 1238 (3), no. 315; leg. 2096, 1773–74. CDIHE, XXVI, 346. Ocaranza, *Capítulos*, p. 293. Alzate, *Gacetas de literatura*, II, 301–2.

55. CDIHE, XXVI, 346. Ocaranza, *Capítulos*, p. 293. Cervantes de Salazar, *Crónica*, p. 14. Gemelli Carreri, *Las cosas más considerables*, p. 141. PNE, VI, 197. AGN, Civil, exp. 1, fols. 79r ff.

56. Anderson and Barlow, "The Maize Tribute," p. 416. Cervantes de Salazar, *Crónica*, p. 14. Alzate, *Gacetas de literatura*, III, 84–85; IV, 106 ff. Hernández Xolocotzi, "Maize Granaries."

57. CDIAI, II, 97. CDIHE, XXVI, 346. AGI, Contaduría, leg. 786, *passim*.

58. NCDHM (1886–92), IV, 133–34. AGN, Desagüe, vol. 1, *passim*; vol. 2, 7th pag., fols. 1r ff.

59. *Memoria histórica . . . del desagüe*, I, 61. BAGN, II, 491. *Legislación del trabajo*, p. 156. *Documentos para la historia económica*, III, 62. AGN, Desagüe, vol. 2, 7th pag., *passim*.

60. The total area of the Valley of Mexico, ca. 75 by 40 miles, is the equivalent of ca. 3,000 square miles or 1,920,000 acres. If we suppose a conquest population of about 1,500,000, this means a little more than one acre per person. Discounting mountains and lakes, we may increase the density to one person per two-thirds acre. If 9 pounds of maize were planted per acre, a yield of 1:100 would be the equivalent of 900 pounds per acre, or somewhat over 7 fanegas per person per year.

61. AGI, México, leg. 2096. NYPL, Rich, no. 39. AA, Pósito y alhóndiga, vol. 2, no. 3695, exp. 91.

62. Borah and Cook, *Price Trends*, pp. 13–19. The commutation at 9 reales was continued in official transactions. But higher prices were sometimes charged also, e.g., 18 reales in Coyoacan in 1727. AGN, Hospital de Jesús, vol. 325, exp. 5, fols. 24r ff.; vol. 333, exp. 2, fols. 64v–65r.

63. Humboldt, *Political Essay*, IV, 13. Alzate, *Gacetas de literatura*, II, 241. AGN, Indios, vol. 1, fols. 96r–96v, 98r–99r. For similar differences see AGN, General de parte, vol. 2, fol. 153r–153v; AA, Pósito y alhóndiga, vol. 2, no. 3695, exp. 91.

64. AC, XII, 118. Alzate, *Gacetas de literatura*, III, 86. Humboldt, *Political Essay*, II, 130–31. Transportation costs at various periods are indicated in, e.g., AGI, Patronato, leg. 226, ramo 20, fols. 5r ff.; AGN, Tierras, vol. 1923, exp. 1, fol. 78r. The price of maize also depended in part upon the price of wheat. In the early 1690's the price of maize increased partly because wheat was stricken by blight and many persons who normally ate wheat bread had to depend instead upon maize. See "Copia de una carta," p. 73.

65. February was normally regarded as the month of lowest prices. See AC, LIV, 30.

66. AC, XXXII, 228.

67. A parallel may be found in wheat prices in Spain. See Giralt Raventos, "En torno al precio del trigo."

68. PCR, folder 89.

69. E.g., AC, XXVI, 174.

70. For dates of the appeal see Table 24. Los Remedios was made patron of the city by Viceroy Martín Enríquez, and the shrine on the hill called Tototepec, west of the city, was constructed by his order. Literature on Los Remedios is much less extensive than literature on Guadalupe. AC, XVI, 422. Cabrera y Quintero, *Escudo de armas*, pp. 110 ff. Fernández del Castillo, "Don Pelayo y la virgen."

71. See Guijo, *Diario*, pp. 514–16.

72. AAMC, no. 10, p. 537. The image was brought in May 1692, after poor crops and shortages, and was retained for three years, to March 1695. But 1695 proved to be a disastrous year with severe shortages in April and with frosts in September that created continued hardships through the summer of 1696. Robles, *Diario*, II, 248; III, 13, 50. *Disposiciones complementarias*, I, 359.

73. See *Gazetas de México, compendio de noticias*, III, 369.

74. For the pre-conquest frosts see *Anales de Tlatelolco*, p. 56; Chimalpahin, *Annales*, pp. 114–15; NCDHM (1941), III, 230; Clavigero, *Historia antigua*, I, 322. The

1541 frost is mentioned in Motolinía, *Memoriales*, p. 231. The 1695 frost is cited in Robles, *Diario*, III, 50. For the frost of 1785 see below.

75. Indeed, in the later colonial period a class of small-scale agricultural speculators called *pegujaleros* planted crops in May or June by preference. Alzate, *Gacetas de literatura*, IV, 422–23.

76. Robles, *Diario*, III, 50. A similar year was 1661, when a severe drought to mid-June was followed by early frosts in the autumn. The maize price rose sharply to 28 reales per fanega in late 1661 and to 29 reales per fanega in 1662. Likewise in 1771 rains began only in late June and plants were still immature when the first frosts came in October. Guijo, *Diario*, pp. 459–60, 472–73, 482. SLSF, Zúñiga y Ontiveros, "Efemérides."

77. Alzate, *Gacetas de literatura*, II, 133. *Gazetas de México, compendio de noticias*, I, 411. Frosts had continued through March in 1785 and the dry season had continued through May. Some of the first maize planting was destroyed in the spring and a second and late planting had to be made. See PCR, folder 105.

78. AGN, Tributos, vol. 2, exp. 5, fol. 105r. AA, Pósito y alhóndiga, vol. 2, no. 3695, exp. 91.

79. AA, Pósito y alhóndiga, vol. 2, no. 3695, exp. 91. *Gazetas de México, compendio de noticias*, I, 411.

80. AGN, Tributos, vol. 2, exp. 5, fol. 21r; exp. 6, fols. 5v ff. PCR, folder 105 (September 17, 1785).

81. AGN, Tributos, vol. 2, exp. 7, fol. 5v; Intendentes, vol. 33, fols. 16or ff. Sedano, *Noticias de México*, II, 3 ff.

82. AA, Pósito y alhóndiga, vol. 2, no. 3695, exp. 91. AGN, Tributos, vol. 2, exp. 7, fol. 5. *Documentos para la historia económica*, II, 56. Of entire towns it was reported that most inhabitants had died or fled. See AGN, Tributos, vol. 2, exp. 8 bis, fols. 4v ff., 8v.

83. *Gazetas de México, compendio de noticias*, I, 414–15. AGN, Tributos, vol. 2, exp. 5, fol. 21r, *et passim*. AA, Pósito y alhóndiga, vol. 2, no. 3695, exp. 91.

84. Bentura Beleña, *Recopilación sumaria*, II, 1 ff. *Gazetas de México, compendio de noticias*, II, 185 ff., *et passim*. Sedano, *Noticias de México*, II, 3 ff.

85. AGN, Bandos y ordenanzas, vol. 13, fols. 412r ff., 418r ff. Sedano, *Noticias de México*, II, 3 ff. AGI, México, leg. 1238 (3), no. 315. PCR, folder 105. Banco nacional, *Publicaciones*, IV. The disaster was not universal in Mexico. Supplies of maize and wheat remained high in parts of Michoacan. See *Gazetas de México, compendio de noticias*, II, 42. This is the crisis that Humboldt, *Political Essay*, II, 397, and McBride, *The Land Systems*, p. 11, as well as some other sources, misdate in 1784.

86. Gómez, *Diario curioso*, p. 207.

87. Rains began late in 1785. See PCR, folder 105; Bentura Beleña, *Recopilación sumaria*, II, 1. For other combinations of drought and frost see AC, XIII, 100; Robles, *Diario*, III, 50; Guijo, *Diario*, pp. 459–60, 472–73, 482.

88. *Cartas de Indias*, p. 331. But cf. the curious conflicting evidence of Chimalpahin, *Annales*, p. 288.

89. Alzate, *Gacetas de literatura*, IV, 51 ff., 102.

90. Robles, *Diario*, II, 236. *Carta de un religioso*, pp. 11–12. Castro Santa-Anna, *Diario*, I, 23. PCR, folder 75 (September 5, 1775). SLSF, Zúñiga y Ontiveros, "Efemérides," *passim*.

91. The word maguey is probably of Taino origin; *metl* is Nahuatl; *agave* is Greek.

92. The word pulque may be of Nahuatl origin, though the matter remains in doubt. See the discussion in Gonçalves de Lima, *El maguey y el pulque*, pp. 13–14.

93. CDIHE, LVII, 102.

94. On the nature and history of maguey see Segura, *El maguey*; Martín del Campo, "El pulque"; Gonçalves de Lima, *El maguey y el pulque*; Payno, "Memoria sobre el maguey."

95. AGN, Indios, vol. 50, fols. 284r–284v, 296r–298r. Puga, *Provisiones*, fol. 70r–70v, 169r. BNM, ms. no. 455, fol. 157v. AC, XXX, 174–75. BAGN, XVIII, 218–19. Durán, *Historia*, II, 240, states that pulque was a colonial invention, of Spaniards and Negroes, and that only the agua miel was known to pre-conquest peoples.

96. CDIHE, XXI, 446–47; LVII, 100 ff. Motolinía, *History*, pp. 272 ff. Motolinía, *Memoriales*, pp. 315 ff. CDHM, I, 382. Cervantes de Salazar, *Crónica*, p. 12. PNE, VI, 30. Dorantes de Carranza, *Sumaria relación*, pp. 120 ff.

97. The official Spanish view always accepted the Indian belief in the medicinal properties of pulque in mild form. See PNE, VI, 30; "Relación de Tequisquiac, Citlaltepec y Xilocingo," pp. 293, 307. BAGN, XVIII, 217; CDIHE, XXI, 447; CIV, 385. Bentura Beleña, *Recopilación sumaria,* I, 5th pag., 292.

98. AGN, Mercedes, vol. 6, fol. 286r. "Relación de Tequisquiac, Citlaltepec y Xilocingo," p. 293. PNE, VI, 172, 218, 225, 227, 236.

99. AGN, Indios, vol. 4, fols. 199v–200r.

100. BNM, ms. no. 455, fols. 205v, 207r–207v, 208r–208v. AGN, Padrones, vol. 4, fol. 239r; Indios, vol. 50, fols. 284r–284v, 296r–298r.

101. This late increase is documented in the Zumpango area in AGN, Historia, vol. 72, exp. 6, fol. 2r, and in the Teotihuacan area, because of the decrease in moisture, in Villa-señor y Sánchez, *Theatro americano*, I, 153. Villarroel, *México por dentro y fuera*, p. 132, comments upon the shift from grains to maguey in the environs of the capital in the late eighteenth century.

102. The history of this tax may be examined in Fonseca and Urrutia, *Historia*, III, 338 ff.; Bentura Beleña, *Recopilación sumaria*, I, 5th pag., 292; CDIHE, XXI, 447; CIV, 386; BNM, ms. no. 466, fols. 431r–432r; AGN, Bandos y ordenanzas, vol. 4, fol. 35r; vol. 9, fol. 365r; vol. 11, fol. 177r; vol. 20, fol. 161r.

103. This incident is related in AGN, Civil, vol. 100, exp. 5.

104. Miscellaneous references to the cultivation or utilization of these plants may be found in a number of colonial sources. AGI, México, leg. 665, cuad. 2, fol. 121r; Justicia, leg. 159, no. 1; Patronato, leg. 181, ramo 21, fol. 8r. Motolinía, *Memoriales*, pp. 327 ff. Cervantes de Salazar, *Crónica*, pp. 15–16, 307. CDIHE, LVII, 172. NCDHM (1941), III, 49, 58. *El libro de las tasaciones*, p. 11. AGN, General de parte, vol. 1, fol. 226v. *Información sobre los tributos*, pp. 29 ff. "Relación de Tequisquiac, Citlaltepec y Xilocingo," p. 295. BAGN, ser. 2, II, 19 ff.

105. For all Valley of Mexico tribute provinces except Chalco, Codex Mendoza indicates equal amounts of maize, frijoles, chia, and huauhtli, i.e., one troje of each per year per province. Chalco gave six trojes of maize, two of frijoles, and one each of chia and huauhtli. A tabular summary is given in Molíns Fabrega, "El Códice mendocino," p. 305.

106. Habas are documented in the towns of Chalco province in BAGN, ser. 2, II, 19 ff., and AGI, México, leg. 665, cuad. 2, fols. 98r ff. Cabbages, lettuce, radishes, and artichokes are mentioned in "Relación de Tequisquiac, Citlaltepec y Xilocingo," p. 307.

107. For tunas see NCDHM (1941), III, 57; PNE, VI, 67; BNM, ms. no. 455, fols.

157r, 162r ff.; AGN, Tierras, vol. 556, exp. 4, fol. 41r. For grape cultivation in Xochimilco see AGN, General de parte, vol. 2, fol. 56r.

108. AGN, Clero regular y secular, vol. 39, exp. 2, fols. 9r, 13r. BNP, no. 258, fol. 4v.

109. See Chapter XII, notes 135–37.

110. Alcocer, "Catálogo de los frutos comestibles." Urbina, "Plantas comestibles." Urbina, "Raíces comestibles."

111. For use of the word camellón see AGI, Indios, vol. 2, fol. 138r; BNM, ms. no. 165, fols. 1r ff.; no. 455, fol. 161r; AGN, Civil, leg. 1271, exp. 1, no. 9, fols. 79 ff.

112. Alzate, Gacetas de literatura, II, 383. AA, Fincas. Chinampas. Haciendas, vol. 1, no. 1084, exp. 1. Chinampas were characteristically rectangular. See, however, Fernández de Recas, Cacicazgos, p. 86, for a "chinampa redonda."

113. Willey and García Prada, "El embrujo de las chinampas," pp. 83–96, state that the chinampas never floated. Leicht, "Chinampas y almácigos flotantes," pp. 375–86, believes that almácigos may have floated but that chinampas did not. West and Armillas, "Las chinampas de México," believe that chinampas probably did not float. It is incorrect to assert, as Willey and García Prada do ("El embrujo de las chinampas," p. 84), that early observers say nothing of floating gardens and that Clavigero in the late eighteenth century was the first to inform a credulous posterity. Acosta, writing in the 1580's, spoke of the "sementera movediza en el agua . . . y se lleva de una parte a otra." Acosta, Historia natural y moral, pp. 533–34. Vetancurt in the seventeenth century clearly referred to portable gardens moving on the water. Vetancurt, Teatro mexicano, p. 33. Gemelli Carreri, also in the seventeenth century, described chinampas as pieces of land floating in the lake, easily moved on the water from place to place. Gemelli Carreri, Las cosas más considerables, p. 50. Ojea likewise referred to the chinampas as "vnos huertos mobibles." Ojea, Libro tercero, p. 3. In the eighteenth century Alzate commented on a floating island called El Bandolero, of the hacienda of San Isidro, which blew back and forth in the wind, and on which cows grazed. Alzate, Gacetas de literatura, II, 397–98. The Gaceta of 1734 describes floating gardens with considerable circumstantial detail. León, "Bibliografía," no. 4, pp. 437–38. Joachín Velázquez de León, an extremely well-informed observer of Indian life, stated in 1790 that Indians freely moved their chinampas from place to place. BNM, ms. no. 455, fol. 161r. Humboldt reported that floating chinampas still existed in the early nineteenth century, that they were towed or poled in the water, and that some bore houses. Humboldt, Political Essay, II, 75. Clavigero, Historia antigua, II, 266, speaks of chinampas towed from canoes. On the other hand, numerous descriptions of chinampas occur in the colonial period without mention of floating. See, e.g., CDIHE, LVII, 172–73; Torquemada, Monarchia indiana, II, 483. And the many evidences of the loss of chinampas under conditions of high or low water indicate clearly that the non-floating chinampa was known from the sixteenth century. AGN, Indios, vol. 2, fol. 138r. Torquemada, Monarchia indiana, II, 483. Alzate, Gacetas de literatura, II, 110. CDIHE, LVII, 173. Although West and Armillas, "Las chinampas de México," p. 165, state that floating chinampas were reported in the Cuitlahuac area in 1923, they conclude that the chinampas probably did not float.

114. Alvarado Tezozomoc, Crónica mexicayotl, pp. 37–38. Apenas, "The 'Tlateles' of Lake Texcoco," pp. 29–32.

115. Alzate, Gacetas de literatura, II, 110.

116. Apenas, "The Pond in our Backyard," p. 17.

117. For indications of the existence of chinampas in the environs of the city and in

such southern towns as Mexicalzingo, Coyoacan, Cuitlahuac, and Xochimilco, see BNP, no. 110, fols. 1r ff.; no. 112, fols. 2r ff. BNM, ms. no. 165. AA, Fincas. Chinampas. Haciendas, vol. 1, no. 1084, exp. 1; Tierras y ejidos, vol. 1, no. 4065, exp. 19, fol. 28r; AGI, Justicia, leg. 124, exp. 2; AGN, Civil, vol. 1271, exp. 1, fols. 79r ff.; Hospital de Jesús, vol. 120, exp. 4, fols. 3r–3v, 12r, 15r ff.; Indios, vol. 2, fol. 138r; Tierras, vol. 1908, exp. 1; Castillo, *Fragmentos,* p. 101; Alvarado Tezozomoc, *Crónica mexicana,* pp. 248, 279, 300, 313–14.

118. Alzate, *Gacetas de literatura,* II, 384, 390.

119. The techniques are described in detail in Alzate, *Gacetas de literatura,* II, 383 ff. Compare modern techniques as described in West and Armillas, "Las chinampas de México," pp. 167 ff.

120. CDIHE, LVII, 172. Cervantes de Salazar, *Crónica,* p. 14. PNE, VI, 194. Alzate, *Gacetas de literatura,* II, 384, 393 ff. AGN, Civil, vol. 1271, exp. 1, fols. 79 ff. Ojea, *Libro tercero,* p. 3.

121. Alzate, *Gacetas de literatura,* II, 236, 391 ff. CDIHE, LVII, 173. *Sobre el modo de tributar,* p. 106. In eighteenth-century Xochimilco Indian agriculturists used fertilizer from the bat caves of Ixtapalapa in chile production. See Alzate, *Gacetas de literatura,* II, 306.

122. Motolinía, *History,* p. 270.

123. Gemelli Carreri, *Las cosas más considerables,* p. 44, and a letter of the late seventeenth century in CDIHE, LXVII, 396, state that the temporal was harvested in October. But the schedules of the Valley of Mexico repartimientos show that harvests occurred customarily in November or December and occasionally as late as January. See FHT, III, 80 ff.; IV, 354, 369, 478; V, 168, 198; VI, 92.

124. See Foster, *Culture and Conquest,* p. 58.

125. FHT, III, 32, 186; IV, 265–66, 275–76; VI, 191–92, 223–24. Gemelli Carreri, *Las cosas más considerables,* p. 44, says that planting took place in October and harvesting in June. Harvesting of irrigated wheat sometimes took place as early as April. See AGI, México, leg. 24, ramo 1. *Gazetas de México, compendio de noticias,* II, 344.

126. FHT, III, 32, 186–87. Notices of the extent of irrigation in wheat agriculture vary according to the time and place. In 1598 a viceregal statement observed only that irrigation was "de alguna importancia" in Mexico. AGI, México, leg. 24, ramo 1. In 1604 the viceroy informed the king that in the areas about Tacuba and Tacubaya most wheat farming benefited from irrigation. AGI, México, leg. 26, ramo 1. In 1599 there were eighteen irrigated wheat haciendas in the Tacubaya repartimiento. In 1607 seventeen out of 114 labradores in the Tepozotlan repartimiento used irrigation. FHT, IV, 265–66. AGN, Tierras, vol. 70, exp. 8, fols. 17r–18r. Even in 1692 it was stated that the most abundant wheat harvest was the non-irrigated crop. CDIHE, LXVII, 396. And even in the eighteenth century Chalco province still had few irrigated haciendas. In 1734 an agrimensor for water supplies had to come to Chalco province from Mexico City "because there are not many irrigated haciendas in this province, and the labradores and vecinos here lack the necessary knowledge for measuring water supplies." AGI, México, leg. 664, fols. 25v–26r. The common view that Mexican wheat required irrigation (e.g., Chevalier, *La formation des grands domaines,* p. 58) thus cannot be uniformly upheld.

127. FHT, III, 47–48; IV, 286–87; V, 23; *et passim.*

128. CDIAI, VI, 492. NCDHM (1941), III, 59.

129. García and Pereyra, *Documentos inéditos,* XV, 117–18. AGN, General de parte, vol. 2, fol. 90r; Mercedes, vol. 3, fol. 349r; vol. 4, fols. 2v–3r, 27v, 368r.

130. AGN, Mercedes, vol. 7, fols. 217v–219r. The area included here was somewhat larger than the Valley of Mexico.

131. BNMa, 20417/29, fol. 3r. AC, VIII, 143. This fits with the modern Spanish fanega (for wheat), reported by Foster, *Culture and Conquest*, p. 57, as .64 hectares (1.5 acres). One fanega of wheat thus occupied about one-sixth the amount of ground that one fanega of maize occupied. Colonial notices on this point state that a given measure of maize required from four to ten times the amount of land that the same measure of wheat required. Cervantes de Salazar, *Crónica*, p. 14. AGN, Tierras, vol. 70, exp. 8, fol. 18v.

132. AGN, Tierras, vol. 70, exp. 8, fols. 17r–18r. The list includes 94 labores, but 4 of these planted no wheat. It omits 3 others that were not visited because they were too distant, and it omits 17 irrigated labores. A labrador near Acolman is known to have planted 500 fanegas of wheat and maize in 1607. FHT, VI, 115. This is the largest recorded planting of the Valley for the period.

133. AGN, General de parte, vol. 1, fols. 192r ff.; vol. 2, fols. 128r ff.

134. FHT, II, 299–300.

135. AGN, General de parte, vol. 4, fols. 29v ff.

136. AGN, Tierras, vol. 70, exp. 8, fols. 17r–18r.

137. AGN, General de parte, vol. 6, fols. 209v–210r.

138. AGN, Mercedes, vol. 3, fols. 25v–26r; vol. 4, fols. 2v–3r. See Chapter VIII.

139. AGN, Ordenanzas, vol. 1, fol. 36r–36v.

140. AC, XXVII, 188. By 1630 Indian towns were no longer able to supply the city sufficiently, the tribute maize of fourteen leagues in the city's environs was not enough, towns were defaulting on their payments of tribute maize, and the city was obliged to purchase maize elsewhere. See Chapter XIII.

141. The practice was prohibited in the eighteenth century. Bentura Beleña, *Recopilación sumaria*, II, 3. *Gazetas de México, compendio de noticias*, I, 413.

142. *Instrucciones que los vireyes de Nueva España dejaron* (1867), p. 305. AGI, Patronato, leg. 226, ramo 18, fol. 8r. *Documentos relativos al tumulto*, II, III. Alzate, *Gacetas de literatura*, II, 241. This subject, which we do not treat here in detail for the reason that it does not relate directly to Indian history, is one of the most abundantly documented economic subjects of the colonial period.

143. AC, XXXV, 6 ff. CDIHE, LXVII, 408. Robles, *Diario*, II, 257. AGI, Patronato, leg. 226, ramo 18, fol. 34r.

144. Alzate, *Gacetas de literatura*, II, 280–81; IV, 49 ff., 102.

145. It will be remembered that the Codex Mendoza evidence suggests a much larger pre-conquest maize tribute from Chalco province than from any other tribute area. See above, note 105.

146. These figures compare approximately with our computations for the size of wheat farms, above.

147. SLSF, Zúñiga y Ontiveros, "Efemérides," *passim*. Clavigero, *Historia antigua*, II, 269. PCR, folders 75 ff. BNMa, 2449, fol. 56r. Variations occurred in the irrigated maize plantations. These are occasionally noticed in the documentation as in the Hacienda de Los Portales (AGN, Tierras, vol. 2034, cuad. 7, fols. 6r ff.) and in Molino de Flores (PCR, folder 78). A different maize schedule is observed also in the upland cold areas, as in Ayapango, where the first plowing took place in August, the second in October, planting in March, and harvest in January. See BNMa, 2449, fol. 56r. This cycle of one and one-half years must have required crop rotation or fallow fields, although the point is not specified. For the normal schedule of operations see Table 25.

148. AGN, Tierras, vol. 1109, exp. 3, *passim*; vol. 1923, exp. 1, fols. 45r ff.; Hospital de Jesús, vol. 278, exp. 1, fol. 2r.

149. AGI, México, leg. 782, fols. 9r ff.; leg. 2096, sep. pag., fols. 94v ff. In times of shortage and need the city hired guards to ensure that the Indian paddlers were not delayed in the pulquerías along the route. AGI, Patronato, leg. 226, ramo 20, fol. 10r.

150. AGI, Patronato, leg. 226, ramo 18, fol. 4v. These were unusually large shipments and they should not be regarded as typical.

151. AGI, México, leg. 781, fol. 135r.

152. AA, Pósito y alhóndiga, vol. 1, no. 3694, exp. 22, fol. 2r; vol. 2, no. 3695, exp. 65, fol. 13r–13v. Villa-señor y Sánchez, *Theatro americano*, I, 68. Figures on maize consumption in the city vary markedly, and their interpretation is problematic. See, e.g., Villa-señor y Sánchez, *Theatro americano*, I, 36; San Vicente, "Exacta descripción," p. 36; Humboldt, *Political Essay*, II, 68.

153. Villa-señor y Sánchez, *Theatro americano*, I, 68.

154. BNP, no. 258. NYPL, "Yndize comprehensibo," *passim*.

155. Thus a high maize price such as that of 1789 induced some transfer from wheat to maize plantation and encouraged late speculative maize plantings at the risk of autumn frosts. *Gazetas de México, compendio de noticias*, III, 369.

156. AGN, Historia, vol. 72, exp. 6, fol. 2r.

157. AGN, Vínculos, vol. 55, exp. 1, fols. 1r ff.; Tierras, vol. 2033, sep. pag., fol. 12v. The figures for 1770 indicate a marked increase from those of the 1740's. See PCR, Varios papeles, vol. 1, exp. 2, fols. 522v–523v.

158. The series of letters is in PCR, folders 75 ff.

159. The weekly financial records of the early 1770's and many other data concerning the Hacienda de Santa Ana Aragón may be found in AGN, Tierras, vol. 991, exp. 4. Santa Ana is one of the most abundantly documented haciendas of the Valley. See especially its inventories of the 1760's and 1770's in AGN, Tierras, vol. 917; vol. 964, exp. 3.

CHAPTER XII

1. See, e.g., PNE, VI, 62, 78, 86. "Relación de Tequisquiac, Citlaltepec y Xilocingo," pp. 295–96, 307.

2. Descriptions of maceguales' houses in various sixteenth-century towns of the Valley may be found in PNE, VI, 62, 78, 85–86, 176, 197, 218, 225, 230, 236; NCDHM (1941), III, 62–63; "Culhuacan," p. 173. See also Cervantes de Salazar, *Crónica*, p. 29. For a description of houses in the eighteenth century see Alzate, *Gacetas de literatura*, I, 72. For straw roofs in the Valley of Mexico see "Relación de Tequisquiac, Citlaltepec y Xilocingo," pp. 295, 302, 307; AGN, Tierras, vol. 1584, exp. 1, fol. 12r–12v; BNP, no. 37–39, *passim*.

3. Thus Indians of Chimalhuacan Atenco, lacking montes, bought wood in Ixtapaluca and Coatepec. Indians of Tequicistlan obtained wood from the montes of Texcoco. PNE, VI, 197, 230.

4. Quarries of various types of stone are indicated in PNE, VI, 30; AGN, Mercedes, vol. 3, fols. 130v, 135v; León, "Bibliografía," no. 4, p. 588; Vetancurt, *Chronica*, 2nd pag. ("Tratado de la ciudad de México"), p. 2.

5. PNE, VI, 197.

6. AGN, Mercedes, vol. 3, fol. 140r–140v.

7. PNE, VI, 63, 78, 86. "Culhuacan," p. 173.

8. AGI, Patronato, leg. 181, ramo 38. PNE, III, 35. CDIAI, XLI, 136. CDIU, X, 131. AGN, Mercedes, vol. 3, fols. 105v–106r. AC, VI, 76. Cervantes de Salazar, *Crónica,* p. 603. CDHM, II, 175. García Pimentel, *Descripción,* pp. 71, 89, 96. *El libro de las tasaciones,* p. 205.

9. García Pimentel, *Descripción,* pp. 89, 91. AGN, Mercedes, vol. 4, fol. 37r. Villaseñor y Sánchez, *Theatro americano,* I, 89. Indian manufacture is described in Sahagún, *Historia general,* II, 226.

10. AGN, Tierras, vol. 1584, exp. 1, fol. 8r. García Pimentel, *Descripción,* p. 96. "Relación de Tequisquiac, Citlaltepec y Xilocingo," p. 301.

11. On the metate and molcajete see Blanchard, "Survivances ethnographiques." Sahagún, *Historia general,* II, 229, provides an account of baskets. Christian images, as well as chairs, are included among the furnishings of Indian houses in the description by Henry Hawks, in Hakluyt, *The Principal Navigations,* IX, 396. Torquemada listed grinding stones, jars, and petates and stated that Indian houses contained nothing further. Torquemada, *Monarchia indiana,* III, 235.

12. Clavigero states that candles were among the goods particularly welcomed by Indians on the arrival of the Spaniards. Clavigero, *Historia antigua,* II, 365. Professional Indian candlemakers and sellers of candles, depending upon an Indian market in the city and in the towns, appear in the documentation by 1543 and are frequently mentioned in texts of the mid-sixteenth century. AGN, Mercedes, vol. 2, fol. 206r; vol. 7, fol. 154r; General de parte, vol. 1, fol. 66v. In a statement of 1574 it was asserted that the making and selling of tallow candles were common practices among the Indians of the city. See AA, Barrio Lorenzot, vol. 2, no. 432 (743), fol. 6v. The use of ocotl torches is commented upon in the sixteenth century by Motolinía, *History,* p. 95. Ocotl was being sold in the Tlatelolco market in 1576. See AGN, General de parte, vol. 1, fol. 209r. It appears likely that both candles and torches continued to be used through the colonial period.

13. AGN, Tierras, vol. 1584, exp. 1, fol. 8r; Civil, vol. 1271, exp. 1, no. 9, fols. 79r ff. AGI, México, leg. 2096, 1770. "Relación de Tequisquiac, Citlaltepec y Xilocingo," p. 307.

14. Muñoz Camargo, *Historia,* p. 25. Shirts and trousers, taking the place of the *maxtlatl,* were in general use by 1580, and probably long before. UT, JGI-XXIV-8, fol. 2r. PNE, VI, 56, *et passim.* Ojea, *Libro tercero,* p. 9. CDIHE, LVII, 105–6. MNM, Colección antigua, T. 2–57, fol. 9r. Gómez de Cervantes, *La vida económica,* p. 135, speaks of the loincloth (venda) still in use in the late sixteenth century, but other sources generally do not.

15. *Legislación del trabajo,* p. 26. PNE, VI, 56, *et passim.* "Culhuacan," p. 172. CDIHE, LVII, 105–6. Ojea, *Libro tercero,* p. 9.

16. CDIHE, LVII, 105–6. Authorities differ as to whether the term huarache is of Taino or Japanese or some other origin.

17. AGI, México, leg. 24, ramo 1. Caciques and principales did wear Spanish clothing, completely or in part. See PNE, VI, 56, 84, *et passim.* ENE, XV, 66. AGN, Vínculos, vol. 244, exp. 1, fol. 129r.

18. The rebozo, or woman's shawl, which is so common a feature of modern Mexican dress, is occasionally mentioned in the eighteenth century, e.g., AGI, México, leg. 1238 (3), no. 368, but its widespread use appears to have developed principally in the nineteenth century. For additional data on Indian dress of various periods see CDIHE,

LVII, 105-6; Hakluyt, *The Principal Navigations*, IX, 395; Torquemada, *Monarchia indiana*, III, 234-35; Gemelli Carreri, *Las cosas más considerables*, pp. 72-73; Morales Rodríguez, "Costumbres y creencias," pp. 31 ff.

19. PNE, VI, 56, 235, *et passim*. Manufacture and sale of maguey cloth in the later sixteenth century are recorded in Hueypoxtla, Xilotzingo, and other communities. See García Pimentel, *Relación*, pp. 89, 91; Zorita, *Historia*, p. 115.

20. PNE, VI, 56, 229, 235. Hakluyt, *The Principal Navigations*, IX, 387. CDIHE, LVII, 104. Zorita, *Historia*, p. 115.

21. Mantles, both of henequen and of cotton, were pre-conquest tribute items recorded in Codex Mendoza and tabulated in Molíns Fábrega, "El Códice mendocino," p. 313. See also Zorita in CDIAI, II, 94; PNE, VI, 78, 85, 218, 225, 230.

22. On types of mantles see Borah and Cook, *Price Trends*, pp. 27 ff.

23. Clavigero, *Historia antigua*, II, 340, comments upon the retention of ceremonial mantles in the eighteenth century. For the reception of 1640 see Gutiérrez de Medina, *Viage de tierra, y mar*, fol. 36v.

24. AGN, Mercedes, vol. 3, fols. 293v, 319r. Fernández del Castillo, *Apuntes*, p. 26.

25. On Indian textile manufacture see Motolinía, *Memoriales*, p. 184; Suárez de Peralta, *Noticias históricas*, pp. 26 ff.; AGI, México, leg. 1238 (3), no. 368. For professional male Indian weavers see, e.g., AGN, Indios, vol. 3, fol. 41r.

26. PNE, VI, 56, 229. See also Ojea, *Libro tercero*, p. 9. Torquemada, *Monarchia indiana*, I, 611, states that Indians began to use woolen cloth in appreciable quantities in the 1530's and 1540's.

27. PNE, VI, 56.

28. See the statement by Río de la Losa in Orozco y Berra, *Memorial para la carta hidrográfica*, p. 182. For the chemical composition of Lake Texcoco and other waters see Peñafiel, *Memoria sobre las aguas, passim*; Hay, "Apuntes," p. 550.

29. See the interesting statement concerning the flooding of the salt grounds in the Tequicistlan area ca. 1542, PNE, VI, 230.

30. Humboldt, *Political Essay*, II, 76-77. Sahagún, *Historia general*, II, 230, mentions earthen containers (tinajas).

31. Brief sixteenth-century accounts of the salt-making process may be found in AA, Tierras y ejidos, vol. 2, no. 4066, exp. 38, fols. 17v-18r; Cortés, *Cartas*, I, 75; NCDHM (1941), III, 62; Cervantes de Salazar, *Crónica*, p. 272; PNE, VI, 176. See also Sahagún, *Historia general*, II, 229-30.

32. PNE, VI, 176. CDIHE, LVII, 178. Cervantes de Salazar, *Crónica*, p. 272. Torquemada, *Monarchia indiana*, I, 167, 450. Sahagún, *Historia general*, II, 230. Cortés, *Cartas*, I, 75. Gage, *A New Survey*, p. 95. In Tlalnepantla an Indian *salinero* offered to supply the church with an organ and a retablo. See Torquemada, *Monarchia indiana*, III, 219. For the derivative modern methods of salt extraction see Apenas, "The Primitive Salt Production," pp. 35-40.

33. BNMa, 20058/18, fol. 2r. García Pimentel, *Descripción*, p. 225. Cortés, *Cartas*, I, 75. López de Gómara, *Historia*, I, 207-8. Cuevas, *Historia de la iglesia*, I, 287-88. Torquemada, *Monarchia indiana*, I, 449-50. PNE, VI, 218, 236. López de Velasco, *Geografía y descripción*, p. 191, stated that over fifty lake towns depended upon the salt trade for their livelihood.

34. Thus Coatepec Chalco, Chimalhuacan Atenco, Teotihuacan, Tepexpan, and other towns lacked salt supplies and obtained salt from outside. See PNE, VI, 62, 77-78, 225, 236.

35. Salt was distributed to the Desagüe workers in the amount of one loaf to a little

more than one-half fanega of maize, and one loaf for every 50 workers each day. See AGN, Desagüe, vol. 2, 7th pag.; *Memoria histórica* . . . *del desagüe,* I, 100. For additional data on production, distribution, and sale of salt see Mendizábal, "Influencia de la sal," pp. 309 ff.

36. Cervantes de Salazar, *Crónica,* p. 272. Torquemada, *Monarchia indiana,* I, 450. Indian producers paid no alcabala, the implication being that only pure salt could be regarded as appropriately a Spanish commodity. See Gálvez, *Informe general,* p. 79. In an act of charity in 1605 impoverished Indians were permitted to sweep but not to dig the city's ejidos for tequisquitl. See AC, XVI, 45–46.

37. Zorita, *Historia,* p. 124. Clavigero, *Historia antigua,* II, 349 ff. See Ceballos Novelo, "El temazcal."

38. Soap may be made from caustic soda (sodium hydroxide) and animal fats. Caustic soda is made when soda ash (sodium carbonate) is treated with lime. We lack an early account of the soap-making process, but Humboldt, *Political Essay,* III, 467, provides some details for the late colonial period. For the sixteenth-century Texcoco and Xaltocan tequisquitl in soap manufacture see the statement of Pomar in NCDHM (1941), III, 55, and AGN, Tierras, vol. 1584, exp. 1, fol. 7v.

39. AGN, Tierras, vol. 1584, exp. 1, fols. 7v, 73v. Orozco y Berra, *Memoria para la carta hidrográfica,* pp. 154–55, comments upon the use of tequisquitl in the manufacture of dyes, bleaches, and soap in the nineteenth century.

40. NCDHM (1941), III, 55. CDIHE, LVII, 214. PNE, VI, 225. The essential ingredients of gunpowder were saltpeter, sulphur, and charcoal. The famous ascent of Popocatepetl by Cortés's men was to secure sulphur, not saltpeter. Spaniards made gunpowder in Teotihuacan and in Mexico City in the sixteenth century. Later manufacture centered in Chapultepec and Santa Fe. For the materials used and details of manufacture see BNM, ms. no. 439, fols. 346r–357v; ms. no. 455, fols. 114r ff.

41. AA, Desagüe, vol. 1, no. 740, exp. 16, fol. 4v. AGN, General de parte, vol. 5, fols. 299r ff. BNMa, 20058/18, fol. 2r.

42. The differences among sodium chloride or salt (sal), sodium carbonate or soda ash (sometimes called tequisquitl), and potassium nitrate or saltpeter (salitre) were clearly recognized in colonial times, although the terminology used was not always a precise one. In Mexicalzingo in the eighteenth century the distinction between sal and salitre made a division of labor between two Indian sujetos: Nativitas, which produced salitre, and San Simón, which produced sal. See BNMa, 20058/18, fol. 2r. The term salitre was sometimes used in reference to salt licks for cattle. See PCR, Reales provisiones. The various materials occurred in different concentrations in different regions, and this presumably gave rise to the regional specializations. Fractional evaporation of mixed solutions to yield a series of salts is a modern technique in the Valley of Mexico, but this practice cannot yet be documented for the colonial period. See Chapter XI, note 5.

43. Sahagún, *Historia general,* II, 370–71. Ojea, *Libro tercero,* p. 2. Alvarado Tezozomoc, *Crónica mexicana,* p. 425. Cervantes de Salazar, *Crónica,* p. 11. AGN, Tierras, vol. 1584, exp. 1, fol. 7v. PNE, VI, 77. Motolinía, *History,* p. 206. Torquemada, *Monarchia indiana,* I, 308: Viera, *Compendiosa narración,* p. 38. Clavigero, *Historia,* I, 148–49. The xohuilin was known also by such names as huili and joile. Varieties of pescado blanco are listed in Orozco y Berra, *Memoria para la carta hidrográfica,* p. 161.

44. Motolinía (*History,* p. 206), the Ponce text (CDIHE, LVII, 178), and Gage (*A New Survey,* p. 94) state erroneously that there were no fish in the salt lakes. Cf. Alzate, *Gacetas de literatura,* II, 109, and numerous other sources. For the fullest account

of the fish of the Valley of Mexico see Alvarez del Villar and Navarro G., *Los peces del valle de México.*

45. NCDHM (1941), III, 54. García Pimentel, *Descripción,* p. 96. "Relación de Tequisquiac, Citlaltepec y Xilocingo," p. 300. AGN, Indios, vol. 17, fols. 73v–74r; Tierras, vol. 1584, exp. 1, fol. 7v; Congregaciones, vol. 1, fols. 65v–66r. Vetancurt, *Teatro mexicano,* p. 34.

46. CDIHE, LVII, 171. Oviedo y Valdés, *Historia general y natural,* III, 528. See also "Relación de Tequisquiac, Citlaltepec y Xilocingo," pp. 300–301.

47. "Relación de Tequisquiac, Citlaltepec y Xilocingo," p. 301. AGN, Congregaciones, vol. 1, fols. 65v–66r.

48. CDIHE, LVII, 179. Borah and Cook, *Price Trends,* p. 83. Cortés, *Cartas,* I, 100.

49. AGN, Congregaciones, vol. 1, fols. 65v–66r. PNE, VI, 59. Ojea, *Libro tercero,* p. 2.

50. AGN, Tierras, vol. 1584, exp. 1, fol. 7v; Indios, vol. 2, fol. 139r; vol. 17, fols. 73v–74r; General de parte, vol. 1, fol. 226v; García Pimentel, *Descripción,* pp. 96, 225. FHT, II, 357–58. BNMa, 20058/18, fol. 2r. NCDHM (1941), III, 54. PNE, VI, 59, 176, 230. AGI, Patronato, leg. 181, ramo 20.

51. AGN, Indios, vol. 17, fols. 73v–74r.

52. FHT, I, 55–56. AGN, Indios, vol. 12 (1), fol. 186v; vol. 16, fols. 64v–65r; Tierras, vol. 1624, exp. 2, fols. 2r ff.; vol. 1780, exp. 7, fols. 118v ff.; vol. 1908, exp. 8, fols. 1r ff.

53. Alvarado Tezozomoc, *Crónica mexicayotl,* pp. 72–73, gives the Nahuatl names. For modern identifications see especially Deevey, "Limnological Studies," pp. 224 ff.

54. Sahagún, *Historia general,* II, 371–72. Alvarado Tezozomoc, *Crónica mexicana,* p. 425. PNE, VI, 59, 77. CDIHE, LVII, 178. BNMa, 20058/18, fol. 2r. NCDHM (1941), III, 55. Clavigero, *Historia antigua,* II, 353–54. BNM, ms. no. 455, fol. 208r–208v. Orozco y Berra, *Memoria para la carta hidrográfica,* pp. 150 ff. Poumarède, "Desagüe del valle de México," p. 472. Modern collection is described by Apenas, "The Pond in our Backyard," p. 18. Some earlier confusions on this subject are clarified by Deevey, "Limnological Studies," pp. 225–27.

55. NCDHM (1941), III, 55. Clavigero, *Historia antigua,* I, 149–50. Cervantes de Salazar, *Crónica,* pp. 21–22. Sahagún, *Historia general,* II, 371–72. Deevey, "Limnological Studies," pp. 224, 226.

56. See the account in Deevey, "Limnological Studies," p. 227, where Sahagún, Pomar, Hernández, and López de Gómara are cited in reference to tecuitlatl. But Deevey's reference to the contributions of López de Gómara to this subject, concerning threshing floors, should be modified, for López de Gómara in this as in a number of other matters obtained his information from others. See Motolinía, *Memoriales,* pp. 327–28, as well as Zorita, *Historia,* p. 114, and Cervantes de Salazar, *Crónica,* p. 307, all of whom mention threshing floors.

57. NCDHM (1941), III, 55.

58. Sahagún, *Historia general,* II, 343 ff. For an enumeration of the types of duck recognized by Indians in the nineteenth century, see Orozco y Berra, *Memoria para la carta hidrográfica,* pp. 147 ff.

59. Cortés, *Cartas,* I, 99 ff., mentions birds in the native market at the time of the conquest. See also Sahagún, *Historia general,* II, 230, on the sale of eggs.

60. Cervantes de Salazar, *Crónica,* pp. 304–5. CDIHE, LVII, 94. Motolinía, *History,* p. 91.

61. NCDHM (1941), III, 54. BNM, ms. no. 455, fol. 208r. PNE, VI, 197. UT, JGI-XXIV-8, fols. 1v–2v.

62. Cervantes de Salazar, *Crónica*, pp. 26–27. NCDHM (1941), III, 54. "Relación de Tequisquiac, Citlaltepec y Xilocingo," p. 301. Linné, "Bird Nets," pp. 122–30. Beyer, "La tiradera," pp. 220–22. Apenas, "The Pond in our Backyard," pp. 16, 18.

63. Gemelli Carreri, *Las cosas más considerables*, p. 74.

64. "Relación de Tequisquiac, Citlaltepec y Xilocingo," p. 301. García Pimentel, *Descripción*, p. 96. PNE, VI, 62, 175, 197. BNMa, 20058/18, fol. 2r.

65. AGN, Tierras, vol. 1058, exp. 4, fols. 79r ff.; vol. 1702, exp. 4, fols. 10r, 93r–93v.

66. Cervantes de Salazar, *Crónica*, p. 498. AGN, Civil, vol. 174, exp. 7, no. 84. Mendoza, "Un barrio prehispánico," p. 361. Caso, "Los barrios antiguos," p. 22.

67. Cervantes de Salazar, *Crónica*, p. 304. Gemelli Carreri, *Las cosas más considerables*, p. 73. Hakluyt, *The Principal Navigations*, IX, 387. CDIHE, LVII, 94. Torquemada, *Monarchia indiana*, II, 489. Sahagún, *Historia general*, II, 336 ff. Clavigero, *Historia antigua*, II, 327, speaks of the last feather artist known to him, living in Michoacan in the eighteenth century.

68. AGN, Indios, vol. 6(1), fols. 236v–237v. Cervantes de Salazar, *Crónica*, pp. 304–5. Zorita, *Historia*, p. 115. Torquemada, *Monarchia indiana*, I, 235; II, 557. For nineteenth- and twentieth-century methods of cannonading, directly derivative from the colonial, see Orozco y Berra, *Memoria para la carta hidrográfica*, p. 149; Villada, "Los anátidos del valle de México," pp. 153–54; Apenas, "The Pond in our Backyard," p. 18.

69. Cervantes de Salazar, *Crónica*, pp. 304–5. AGN, Indios, vol. 6 (1), fols. 236v–237v. Zorita, *Historia*, p. 115. Torquemada, *Monarchia indiana*, I, 235; II, 557. Alzate, *Gacetas de literatura*, II, 301. Viera, *Compendiosa narración*, p. 38, gives the city's consumption at over 6,000 per day in the eighteenth century, or more than 2,000,000 per year. For lower estimates of bird consumption in the nineteenth century see Villada, "Los anátidos del valle de México," p. 154; Almonte, *Guía de forasteros*, p. 293. On the relation of bird hunting and animal slaughter see Alzate, *Gacetas de literatura*, IV, 186.

70. Torquemada, *Monarchia indiana*, I, 235, 308; II, 557. Alzate, *Gacetas de literatura*, II, 123, 301.

71. Torquemada, *Monarchia indiana*, II, 557, stated that two items had disappeared or were disappearing in the early seventeenth century: tecuitlatl and "unos como limos." The references are probably to a single product, for Torquemada's presumptive sources, Motolinía, Cervantes de Salazar, Zorita, or López de Gómara, speak of "unos como limos" in ways that seem to signify only tecuitlatl. See above, note 56. In the twentieth century, after much questioning of informants, Apenas found that tecuitlatl was still remembered, but no longer used, in the vicinity of Chimalhuacan Atenco. Apenas, "The Pond in our Backyard," p. 18.

72. Alzate, *Gacetas de literatura*, II, 123. Cuvier, however, did recognize this instantly on seeing specimens of the axolotl brought by Humboldt more than half a century before. There is a large literature on the axolotl.

73. BNM, ms. no. 455, fols. 167v–168r. Sahagún, *Historia general*, II, 324. Cervantes de Salazar, *Crónica*, pp. 26–27. Pomar, in NCDHM (1941), III, 49, comments on the eating of deer meat, and Cervantes de Salazar, *Crónica*, p. 307, speaks of its sale in the Indian market.

74. AGN, General de parte, vol. 1, fol. 152r. Cervantes de Salazar, *Crónica*, p. 307. PNE, VI, 175. NCDHM (1941), III, 49. Alzate, *Gacetas de literatura*, IV, 186.

75. BNM, ms. no. 455, fol. 168r. Cervantes de Salazar, *Crónica*, p. 307. Durán, *Historia*, II, 219. Gómez de Cervantes, *La vida económica*, p. 136. See the interesting

remarks in Clavigero, *Historia antigua,* II, 278, concerning Indian skills in catching snakes.

76. NCDHM (1941), III, 62. The ocotochtli is described in Sahagún, *Historia general,* II, 326. The Códice de Tlatelolco shows a garment of what appears to be ocelotl skin in the mid-sixteenth century. Barlow calls it "piel de tigre." *Anales de Tlatelolco,* p. 110, and reproduction of the codex. Cervantes de Salazar, *Crónica,* p. 304. PNE, VI, 229.

77. BNM, ms. no. 455, fol. 167v. An interesting account of the tuzas may be found in Villa R., "Mamíferos silvestres," pp. 376 ff.

78. Cervantes de Salazar, *Crónica,* p. 27, states that 15,000 or 20,000 Indians were employed in the viceregal hunts of the mid-sixteenth century. A viceregal hunt is recorded in 1681 in Rivera, "Diario curioso," p. 51. Common Indian hunts for deer, coyotes, rabbits, and similar game are reported from the pre-conquest period as part of the ceremony of Quecholli, See Sahagún, *Historia general,* I, 211-12. No examples are known from the colonial period.

79. Sahagún, *Historia general,* II, 330. Alzate, *Gacetas de literatura,* IV, 188-89. A survey of the fauna of the Valley of Mexico, including fish, insects, reptiles, birds, and mammals, with special reference to those used by Indians, is given by Martín del Campo, "Productos biológicos," pp. 53 ff. On mammals see especially Villa R., "Mamíferos silvestres," pp. 269 ff.

80. Díaz del Castillo, *Historia verdadera,* I, 317. Gómez de Cervantes, *La vida económica,* p. 136. On turkeys see the interesting article of Cárcer Disdier, "Los pavos," pp. 89 ff.

81. Motolinía, *Memoriales,* p. 332. López de Gómara, *Historia,* II, 290. Zorita, *Historia,* p. 119. Oviedo y Valdés, *Historia general y natural,* III, 537.

82. Motolinía, *History,* p. 155. BAGN, VIII, 185. CDIHE, XXVI, 346-47. Borah and Cook, *Price Trends,* pp. 38, 79. AGN, Ordenanzas, vol. 1, fols. 30v-31r.

83. For evidence of Indian adoption of chicken raising see AGN, Mercedes, vol. 8, fols. 165v-166r; López de Gómara, *Historia,* II, 290; PNE, VI, 217, 229. García Pimentel, *Descripción,* p. 71. Viceroy Martín Enríquez sought to encourage Indian chicken raising by regulation of the price and by ordering that each Indian raise twelve hens and six turkeys every year. The order was repeated in 1617 but was not obeyed. AGN, Ordenanzas, vol. 1, fols. 30v-31r. Bentura Beleña, *Recopilación sumaria,* I, 2nd pag., 91. *Ordenanzas del trabajo,* pp. 58-60.

84. PNE, VI, 226, 230. NLAC, 1121, fol. 247r-247v. "Relación de Tequisquiac, Citlaltepec y Xilocingo," pp. 295, 307. AGN, General de parte, vol. 1, fol. 152r; Congregaciones, vol. 1, fols. 86v, 112v.

85. AA, Pósito y alhóndiga, vol. 2, no. 3695, exp. 91. AGN, Civil, vol. 1690, exp. 3, fol. 2v.

86. AGI, México, leg. 24, ramo 1, 1598. AGN, Indios, vol. 3, fol. 63r; vol. 22, fols. 98r-99v, 112r-113r; General de parte, vol. 1, fols. 115r, 166v; Congregaciones, vol. 1, fols. 8v-9r; Tributos, vol. 24, exp. 8, fol. 3r.

87. By the end of the sixteenth century Indian consumption of pork, mutton, and beef had been commented upon by a large number of authorities, including López de Gómara (*Historia,* II, 288), Juan de Pomar (NCDHM [1941], III, 49), and Gómez de Cervantes (*La vida económica,* p. 95). It received attention in the Spanish cabildo (AC, VI, 494) and the Relaciones geográficas ("Relación de Tequisquiac, Citlaltepec y Xilocingo," p. 305; PNE, VI, 217, 224, 227). It engaged the attention of the Desagüe

planners (BAGN, II, 491). By 1598 it could be said that the Indian taste for meat had become fixed and unalterable. See AGI, México, leg. 24, ramo 1, 1598. *Codex Magliabecchiano*, fol. 72v, makes an interesting connection, by way of taste, between the eating of pork and the eating of human flesh. On the continued use of dog meat, despite its high price in comparison with beef, see Durán, *Historia*, II, 218–19. Durán expresses the Spaniards' horror at this as at some other Indian foods.

88. Bentura Beleña, *Recopilación sumaria*, I, 2nd pag., 16–17.

89. CDIHE, XXI, 464–65; CIV, 380. CDIHIA, I, 45 ff. Gómez de Cervantes, *La vida económica*, pp. 94–95. Chevalier, *La formation des grands domaines*, pp. 114 ff., 128 ff. AC, VI, 494.

90. AGN, Ordenanzas, vol. 1, fol. 24r. Bentura Beleña, *Recopilación sumaria*, I, 24; 2nd pag., 53–54. Chevalier, *La formation des grands domaines*, p. 129.

91. AGN, General de parte, vol. 1, fol. 151v. By the early 1580's slaughterhouses were being allowed to function in Xochimilco, Texcoco, Coyoacan, Otumba, Tacuba, and Tlalmanalco. AGN, General de parte, vol. 2, fols. 132r–132v, 160v–161r, 233r. Bentura Beleña, *Recopilación sumaria*, I, 24.

92. CDIHE, LVII, 89. See also Durán, *Historia*, II, 219.

93. AGN, Mercedes, vol. 6, fols. 182v–183r. Torquemada, *Monarchia indiana*, III, 217. Vázquez de Espinosa, *Compendium and Description*, p. 169. Muñoz Camargo, *Historia*, pp. 276–77. Alzate, *Gacetas de literatura*, II, 301.

94. BAGN, ser. 2, II, 22 ff. Alzate, *Gacetas de literatura*, II, 109.

95. AGN, Congregaciones, vol. 1, fols. 19v–20r; Tierras, vol. 1584, exp. 1, fol. 6v. CDIAI, IX, 209. CDIHE, LVII, 108. PNE, VI, 27.

96. CDIHE, LVII, 230.

97. See, e.g., AGI, Justicia, leg. 159, no. 2.

98. AGN, Congregaciones, vol. 1, fol. 10r–10v. NLAC, 1121, fols. 232r–232v, 294r ff. Torquemada, *Monarchia indiana*, III, 532 ff. Vetancurt, *Chronica*, pp. 119–20. Valdés, "Fray Francisco de Tembleque," pp. 223–33. Valdés, *El padre Tembleque*. Romero de Terreros, *Los acueductos*, pp. 39 ff. Ricard, *La "conquête spirituelle" du Mexique*, pp. 176–77.

99. AGN, Tierras, vol. 566, exp. 4, fol. 1r; Padrones, vol. 12, fol. 143r. Alzate, *Gacetas de literatura*, II, 113, 450. Clavigero, *Historia antigua*, II, 334–35.

100. CDIHIA, I, 105–6. ENE, IV, 76–77.

101. AGI, México, leg. 24, ramo 1. CDIHE, LVII, 101. Humboldt, *Political Essay*, II, 400. AC, IV, 134; V, 275. Bentura Beleña, *Recopilación sumaria*, I, 2nd pag., 112. Encinas, *Cedulario*, IV, 349.

102. There exists a huge literature on intoxicant beverages, legal and illegal, on local specializations, and on the recipes for manufacture. See, e.g., AGI, México, leg 2324, and subsequent legajos; *Diccionario universal*, VIII, 354 ff.; BNMa, 19518; Villarroel, *México por dentro y fuera*, pp. 59 ff.; "Brevajes en la colonia"; Ramírez, *Adiciones*, I, 219 ff.

103. CDIHE, XXI, 465. AC, XXX, 195; XLVIII–L (1), 170–71.

104. Soconusco and other provinces paid tribute in cacao. See the tabulation in Molíns Fabrega, "El Códice mendocino," p. 310. The community of Tepexpan, in the Valley of Mexico, likewise was liable for cacao from Soconusco. See PNE, VI, 234.

105. Vázquez de Espinosa, *Compendium and Description*, p. 224. Thompson, "Notes on the Use of Cacao," p. 96. Borah and Cook, *Price Trends*, p. 36. Borah, *Early Colonial Trade*, p. 71.

106. AC, XXV, 206; XXX, 195. Coastal cacao plantations in Venezuela began in 1615 according to Vázquez de Espinosa, *Compendium and Description*, pp. 96–97.

107. ENE, VIII, 102. Borah, *Early Colonial Trade*, pp. 18, 24, 65, 71. CDIHE, XXI, 465. *Correo seminario*, I, no. 2, 9 ff.; no. 3, 20.

108. See the discussion and citations in Thompson, "Notes on the Use of Cacao," p. 99.

109. The Anonymous Conqueror mentions the use of cacao as a pre-Spanish beverage. CDHM, I, 380 ff. Motolinía, *Memoriales*, p. 315. Las Casas, *Apologética historia*, p. 559. Torquemada, *Monarchia indiana*, II, 558, comments upon the increased use. See also Bruman, "The Culture History of Mexican Vanilla," pp. 362, 366.

110. CDIHE, XXI, 465. AC, XXX, 195; XLVIII–L (1), 170–71.

111. Motolinía, *History*, p. 218. Zorita, *Historia*, p. 126. Champlain, "Brief discovrs des choses," p. 45. Alzate, *Gacetas de literatura*, I, 234 ff. A large number of recipes are recorded. Thompson, "Notes on the Use of Cacao," pp. 111 ff., provides a bibliography.

112. Motolinía, *History*, p. 218. Zorita, *Historia*, p. 126. AC, XXV, 206; XXXII, 229. CDIHE, XXI, 465. See Thompson, "Notes on the Use of Cacao," pp. 99–100, for sharp changes in price in the eighteenth century.

113. AC, XXVI, 343–44; XXX, 195, 201–2, 232–38; XXXII–XXXIII, 229; XLVIII–L (1), 170–71. CDIHE, XXI, 465.

114. Torquemada, *Monarchia indiana*, I, 147. A tabulation of barrios of Tenochtitlan, with their associated professions and deities, is given in Monzón, *El calpulli*, pp. 50–51.

115. Díaz del Castillo, *Historia verdadera*, I, 318, 388; II, 11. Sahagún, *Historia general*, II, 56–57. AGN, Indios, vol. 2, fol. 163v.

116. Clavigero, *Historia antigua*, II, 338. Villa-señor y Sánchez, *Theatro americano*, I, 77.

117. Dark clays workable by hand, mold, or wheel, and capable of hardening well in firing, were available in numerous locations. BNM, ms. no. 455, fol. 154r. García Pimentel, *Descripción*, p. 224. AGN, Tributos, vol. 2, exp. 7, fol. 5r–5v. Vetancurt, *Chronica*, p. 56.

118. Barlow, "El códice de los alfareros," pp. 5–8. BNP, no. 258, fol. 3r. Vetancurt, *Chronica*, p. 61. AGN, Padrones, vol. 4, fol. 239r. NYPL, "Yndize comprehensibo," fols. 17v–18r.

119. PNE, VI, 63, 78. AGI, Justicia, leg. 151, no. 1, fol. 70v.

120. AGN, Indios, vol. 2, fol. 139v; vol. 3, fol. 221r; Hospital de Jesús, vol. 329, exp. 2, fol. 10v. In 1603 the city requested Indians of Coyoacan as laborers in street paving, asserting that they were the most skilled. See AC, XV, 128. See also AA, Barrio Lorenzot, 433 (745), fols. 230r–231r.

121. Motolinía, *History*, p. 214. Motolinía, *Memoriales*, p. 184. CDIHE, LVII, 111. AGN, General de parte, vol. 2, fol. 111r–111v; Padrones, vol. 43, fols. 7v–8r. BNP, no. 258, fol. 4r.

122. Ixtlilxochitl, *Relaciones*, p. 455. CDIAI, XIII, 296. *Sobre el modo de tributar*, p. 107.

123. Vetancurt, *Chronica*, p. 56. *Sobre el modo de tributar*, pp. 106 ff.

124. Villa-señor y Sánchez, *Theatro americano*, I, 165–66. Vetancurt, *Chronica*, p. 56. BNM, ms. no. 455, fol. 207r.

125. Motolinía, *History*, p. 59. Motolinía, *Memoriales*, p. 331.

126. Gómez de Orozco, "El mercado de los perros." Sahagún, *Historia general*, I, 56. NCDHM (1941), III, 238, 280. Motolinía, *Memoriales*, p. 334.

127. See, e.g., ENE, I, 86.

128. Cortés, *Cartas*, I, 99 ff. Díaz del Castillo, *Historia verdadera*, I, 321 ff. CDHM, I, 392 ff. Motolinía, *Memoriales*, pp. 326 ff. López de Gómara, *Historia*, I, 236 ff. Las Casas, *Apologética historia*, pp. 181–82. Sahagún, *Historia general*, II, 211 ff. Cervantes de Salazar, *Crónica*, pp. 304 ff. See also Zorita, *Historia*, pp. 115 ff.; Cervantes de Salazar, *Life in the Imperial and Loyal City*, pp. 57–58.

129. Cortés, *Cartas*, I, 99–100. Díaz del Castillo, *Historia verdadera*, I, 321. Motolinía, *Memoriales*, pp. 326–27.

130. Cortés, *Cartas*, I, 101. Díaz del Castillo, *Historia verdadera*, I, 322–23. Cervantes de Salazar, *Crónica*, p. 308. Oviedo y Valdés, *Historia general y natural*, III, 528.

131. This may reflect the early seizure of objects of value by Spaniards.

132. BNP, no. 106, is a modern copy of a plan of an aboriginal market place, supposed by Aubin to refer to Mexico City. But we cannot be sure either of the provenience or of the date. The goods include both Indian and Spanish wares: petates, wheat bread, Spanish hats, etc. The document is described in Boban, *Documents pour servir*, II, 282–83.

133. Fernández del Castillo, *Apuntes*, pp. 26 ff.

134. AC, V, 63. CDIAI, XIII, 257. AGN, Indios, vol. 2, fols. 54v, 139r; Mercedes, vol. 5, fol. 294v. BNM, ms. no. 455, fol. 159r. "Relación de Tequisquiac, Citlaltepec y Xilocingo," p. 296.

135. CDIHE, XXVI, 346; LVII, 178. For an Indian record of fodder payments see *Códice Osuna*, pp. 209 ff. The servicio was terminated in 1611. See AC, XVIII, 94.

136. Gómez de Cervantes, *La vida económica*, p. 111. PNE, VI, 195, 197. CDIAI, VI, 493–94. CDIHE, LVII, 178. AGN, Civil, fol. 1271, exp. 1, no. 9, fols. 79 ff. "Culhuacan," p. 172. UT, JGI-XXIV-8, fol. 1v.

137. Gómez de Cervantes, *La vida económica*, p. 111. AA, Barrio Lorenzot, "Colección de ordenanzas," 433 (745), fol. 262r–262v.

138. BNM, ms. no. 455, fols. 162r ff. Villa-señor y Sánchez, *Theatro americano*, I, 143. AGN, Indios, vol. 5, fol. 174v.

139. Alzate, *Gacetas de literatura*, III, 288. BNM, ms. no. 455, fols. 162r ff. Some wild cochineal was to be found in the Xochimilco area in late colonial times. See NYPL, "Yndize comprehensibo," fol. 22r. On cochineal in general see Diguet, "Histoire de la cochenille"; Lee, "Cochineal Production and Trade"; Lee, "American Cochineal in European Commerce."

140. AGN, Mercedes, fol. 4, fol. 127v. Spaniards believed that Indian depopulation resulted in greater decrease in agriculture than in trade, and that former Indian agriculturists in the 1550's were turning in large numbers to commerce. ENE, VIII, 102. CDIU, XXI, 261.

141. Puga, *Cedulario*, fols. 142v–143r.

142. AGN, Mercedes, vol. 3, fol. 293r–293v. Puga, *Cedulario*, fol. 184r.

143. CDIAI, XIII, 255. ENE, XV, 164–65.

144. AGN, Mercedes, vol. 1, fol. 116r; vol. 5, fol. 223r–223v. Cervantes de Salazar, *Crónica*, p. 308. For the duties of the Spanish alguacil, which included arrest of criminals, enforcement of price regulations, enforcement of other market ordinances, night patrols, and control of drunkenness and disorder, see AGN, Mercedes, vol. 5, fol. 223r–223v.

145. Fernández del Castillo, *Apuntes*, pp. 26–27.

146. AGN, Tierras, vol. 566, exp. 4, fols. 4r–4v, 41r.

147. AGN, Hospital de Jesús, vol. 279, exps. 39–40.

148. Motolinía, *Memoriales*, p. 331. AGN, Mercedes, vol. 3, fol. 11r; vol. 7, fol. 114v; vol. 8, fols. 61v–62r, 233v. Sahagún, *Historia general*, I, 401.

149. AGN, General de parte, vol. 2, fol. 226r. Ixtlilxochitl, *Relaciones*, p. 57.

150. AGN, Mercedes, vol. 3, fol. 60r; Indios, vol. 5, fol. 279r; General de parte, vol. 2, fols. 40r, 116r, 139r–139v. The measurements were to apply to maize, chile, beans, tomatoes, and other foods sold in the markets.

151. Cortés, *Cartas*, I, 100, originally commented on the use of aboriginal measures by volume and the absence of aboriginal measures by weight in the city market of the conquest period. See also AC, VI, 493. In many other Indian transactions measurement by weight is lacking. A discussion of this subject may be found in BNP, no. 237.

152. E.g., Cervantes de Salazar, *Crónica*, p. 308. Alzate, *Gacetas de literatura*, IV, 415.

153. E.g., AH, Libro en que se Acientan los autos de cavildos, illustrates the Indian use of fanegas and cargas in the eighteenth century.

154. Torquemada, *Monarchia indiana*, I, 614. Cavo, *Historia de México*, p. 162. MNM, Colección antigua, T.2–57, fols. 11v–12r. AA, Fincas. Chinampas. Haciendas, vol. 1, no. 1084, exp. 1, fols. 3r, 9r–9v. The Spanish cabildo of the city expressed itself in 1551 as opposed to the coinage of silver and copper currency, in the belief that such currency aroused the cupidity of Indian peoples and encouraged them to shift from agriculture to commerce. See AC, V, 293.

155. CDIAI, II, 193–94. On methods of deceit involving cacao, see Sahagún, *Historia general*, II, 216–17.

156. The continued use of cacao as an exchange medium in the late colonial period is commented upon by Clavigero, *Historia antigua*, IV, 280, and Humboldt, *Political Essay*, III, 26.

157. AC, IV, 220; V, 289. NLAC, 1121, fols. 327v–328r. Gómez de Cervantes, *La vida económica*, p. 112. Gemelli Carreri, *Las cosas más considerables*, p. 44. Champlain, "Brief discovrs des choses," pp. 44–45. Gage, *A New Survey*, p. 112. For additional and later prices, and for the fluctuations in price, see Thompson, "Notes on the Use of Cacao," pp. 97 ff.

158. E.g., in cofradía payments, MNM, Colección antigua, 339, fols. 2r ff.

159. Cortés, *Cartas*, I, 90. NCDHM (1941), III, 238, 280. See the remarks of Durán, *Historia*, II, 218–19, on the continuing dog market at Acolman in the late sixteenth century.

160. Villa-señor y Sánchez, *Theatro americano*, I, 64, 163–64. Vetancurt, *Chronica*, pp. 79–80.

161. ENE, VIII, 102. CDIU, XXI, 261. AC, V, 293.

162. AGN, Mercedes, vol. 6, fols. 176v–177r.

163. García Pimentel, *Descripción*, p. 65. AGN, Mercedes, vol. 3, fol. 278r–278v, *et passim*. For the pochteca in pre-conquest society, see Acosta Saignes, *Los pochteca*.

164. AGN, Mercedes, vol. 3, fols. 278r–278v, 285r, 285v. Alzate, *Gacetas de literatura*, II, 395.

165. AGN, General de parte, vol. 2, fols. 148v, 291r; Mercedes, vol. 6, fol. 243r–243v. Díaz del Castillo, *Historia verdadera*, II, 561.

166. For the privilege of keeping the beasts of burden, however, each Indian had to cultivate 50 additional "brazas" of land for the community, i.e., 60 in all. See AGI, México, leg. 24, ramo 1.

167. AGN, Historia, vol. 72, exp. 6, fol. 2r.

168. Bentura Beleña, *Recopilación sumaria*, I, 55, 77; 3rd pag., 15. Humboldt, *Political Essay*, I, 186. A full legal history of this exemption may be found in *Documentos relativos al arrendamiento del impuesto o renta de alcabalas*, pp. 269 ff. See also Smith, "Sales Taxes," pp. 2 ff., 14.

169. CDIU, XX, 316. Cortés, *Cartas y relaciones*, p. 326. AC, I, 168.

170. AGN, Mercedes, vol. 3, fol. 218r–218v; vol. 5, fols. 180v–181r; vol. 6, fols. 176v–177r; General de parte, vol. 1, fol. 152r–152v. FHT, II, 357–58. AA, Barrio Lorenzot, "Colecsión de ordenanzas," 433 (745), fols. 285r ff.

171. AC, I, 168; II, 65–66; VI, 45; XXXVI, 296. AGN, Civil, vol. 75, exp. 9, fols. 1r, 5r. Bentura Beleña, *Recopilación sumaria*, I, 2nd pag., 9, 104–5; 5th pag., 294–95.

172. Gómez de Cervantes, *La vida económica*, p. 100. AGN, Mercedes, vol. 3, fols. 227v, 345v–346r.

173. No single source describes all the roads, or even all the main roads, of the Valley of Mexico. Our information is derived from a number of late colonial sources, principally concerning travel and trade. The main roads are, however, shown on some late colonial maps. See especially Apenas, *Mapas antiguos*. Robbers are mentioned in Río Frío at least by the 1660's. See Guijo, *Diario*, p. 483.

174. Cuevas Aguirre y Espinosa, *Extracto de los autos*, pp. 17 ff. Alzate, *Gacetas de literatura*, II, 245, 301. Villa-señor y Sánchez, *Theatro americano*, I, 162. AGI, Patronato, leg. 226, ramo 20, fol. 3r.

175. Motolinía, *History*, p. 204. Zorita, *Historia*, p. 193. Vázquez de Espinosa, *Compendium and Description*, p. 156. AGN, Mercedes, vol. 7, fol. 37r–37v.

176. AGN, General de parte, vol. 6, fol. 306r.

177. CDIHE, LVII, 172. Humboldt, *Political Essay*, II, 27. Maps of the canoe route south of the city may be found in AA, Desagüe, vol. 2, no. 741, exps. 65, 71; Historia de las inundaciones, vol. 1, no. 2272, fol. 75r.

178. Work began on the project to reopen this channel in the 1540's and was well advanced by 1550. But subsequent information suggests that it was never completed, or, if completed, in operation for only a short time. AGN, Mercedes, vol. 2, fol. 122v. CDIAI, VI, 493. NCDHM (1886–92), IV, 213.

179. NCDHM (1941), III, 54. León, "Bibliografía," no. 4, p. 369. Humboldt, *Political Essay*, II, 27, 129–30. AA, Desagüe, vol. 1, no. 740, exp. 11, fol. 17r.

180. AA, Desagüe, vol. 1, no. 740, exp. 16, fols. 3r ff.

181. Gemelli Carreri, *Las cosas más considerables*, p. 44. Villa-señor y Sánchez, *Theatro americano*, I, 67. Alzate, *Gacetas de literatura*, II, 297 ff. Navarro de Vargas, "Padrón," p. 586.

182. Alzate, *Gacetas de literatura*, II, 298–99. *El segundo conde de Revilla Gigedo*, p. 170. Clavigero, *Historia antigua*, IV, 133–34.

183. Gómez de Cervantes, *La vida económica*, p. 102. Cervantes de Salazar, *Crónica*, p. 304. Gemelli Carreri, *Las cosas más considerables*, p. 159. Villa-señor y Sánchez, *Theatro americano*, I, 62, 67. AGN, Mercedes, vol. 7, fols. 113v–114r; Indios, vol. 2, fol. 18v.

184. Ojea, *Libro tercero*, p. 3, mentions boats from 15 to 50 pies, or up to approximately 46 feet. Cobo, *Obras*, II, 469–70, speaks of canoes as large as the Capilla de la Congregación, which he identifies as 110 by 35 pies, or a length of about 100 feet and a width of 32 feet. This provides the largest known measurement, and it may be an exaggerated one. Canoes of the conquest period are reported with 60 men; if we suppose an average of 130 or 140 pounds per man this would give a load of about four

tons. Torquemada, *Monarchia indiana*, I, 460. The normal load in maize transport to the city was approximately 70 fanegas; estimating the fanega at 84 pounds, we arrive at a normal transport capacity of about three tons. See AGI, México, leg. 781, fol. 11r.

185. Ojea, *Libro tercero*, p. 3.

186. The preferred tree was the huiyametl, the spruce or hemlock. NCDHM (1941), III, 55. *Sobre el modo de tributar*, p. 107. López de Gómara, *Historia*, I, 235–36. Cisneros, *Sitio*, fol. 109v. León, "Bibliografía," no. 4, p. 437.

187. *Gacetas de México, compendio de noticias*, IV, 276. Vetancurt, *Teatro méxicano*, p. 33. Vetancurt, *Chronica*, pp. 79–80. Walton, *Present State*, pp. 297–98.

188. Villa-señor y Sánchez, *Theatro americano*, I, 62–63, 67. CDIHE, I, 195. AA, Desagüe, vol. 2, no. 741, exp. 44. AGN, General de parte, vol. 3, fol. 224r. BM, Add. 17,577, fol. 24r.

189. AA, Desagüe, vol. 2, no. 741, exps. 44, 71. Ojea, *Libro tercero*, p. 2. FHT, VI, 92–94.

190. López de Gómara, *Historia*, I, 235, gives 50,000 canoes in the city and 200,000 in the lakes, for the conquest or early post-conquest period. For later colonial figures see Ojea, *Libro tercero*, p. 3; Vázquez de Espinosa, *Compendium and Description*, p. 156. Sedano, *Historia de México*, I, 60; BNP, no. 262, fol. 26r; BNM, ms. no. 465, fol. 278r; Alamán, *Disertaciones*, III, 75.

191. See the notices of embarcaderos for sale, in *Gazetas de México, compendio de noticias*, I, 312; VIII, 24.

192. BNMa, 20058/18, fol. 2r. AGN, Mercedes, vol. 7, fol. 113v. FHT, VII, 3–4.

193. AHH, Temporalidades, leg. 106, exp. 7, fols. 2v ff.

194. AGN, Indios, vol. 2, fol. 224r–224v. FHT, VII, 13–15. See the series of boat records from the Jesuit haciendas of Chalco in the eighteenth century. AHH, Temporalidades, leg. 106, exp. 7.

195. Cortés, *Cartas*, I, 90. Villa-señor y Sánchez, *Theatro americano*, I, 156.

196. AGN, Padrones, vol. 6, fol. 146r–146v.

197. AGN, Padrones, vol. 6, fols. 239r–239v, 315r ff.

198. Alzate, *Gacetas de literatura*, II, 52, 121 ff. AGN, Padrones, vol. 12, fol. 143r–143v. Villa-señor y Sánchez, *Theatro americano*, I, 143–45.

199. García Pimentel, *Descripción*, p. 225. Navarro de Vargas, "Padrón," p. 586. Villa-señor y Sánchez, *Theatro americano*, I, 62–63.

200. Villa-señor y Sánchez, *Theatro americano*, I, 165–66. Vetancurt, *Chronica*, pp. 56 ff. AGN, Padrones, vol. 29, fols. 1r ff.

201. García Pimentel, *Descripcion*, p. 96. AGN, Tierras, vol. 1584, exp. 1, fols. 4v ff.

202. Villa-señor y Sánchez, *Theatro americano*, I, 84. See the observations of Garay, *El Valle de México*, p. 64, for the nineteenth century.

203. AGN, Padrones, vol. 43, fol. 10r–10v.

CHAPTER XIII

1. *Archivo mexicano*, I, 60 ff. CDIAI, XXVI, 420. López de Gómara, *Historia*, II, 104. Ojea, *Libro tercero*, pp. 5–6. Dorantes de Carranza, *Sumaria relación*, p. 3. Kubler, *Mexican Architecture*, I, 69–71, discusses the conditions and motives for the selection of the site.

2. CDIU, XXII, 147. AA, Barrio Lorenzot, 439 (746), fols. 68r–69v; Tierras y ejidos,

vol. 2, no. 4066, exp. 41, fols. 20v–22v. An earlier rule limited the city's jurisdiction to five leagues. ENE, II, 221. Puga, *Provisiones,* fol. 86r. AC, III, 85–86. CDIU, XXII, 147.

3. CDIU, XXII, 147–48.

4. AC, VII, 43; XXX, 208. AA, Tierras y ejidos, vol. 2, no. 4066, exp. 38, fol. 31v.

5. There are numerous indications that the city's ejidos were regarded as a pasturage. AC, II, 176. Bentura Beleña, *Recopilación sumaria,* I, 2nd pag., 2. AA, Tierras y ejidos, vol. 1, no. 4065, *passim;* vol. 2, no. 4066, *passim. Sobre el modo de tributar,* p. 31.

6. ENE, II, 220. For a summary history of the inspections and revisions, and texts of *mojonera* inscriptions, see AA, Tierras y ejidos, vol. 1, no. 4065, exp. 1; vol. 2, no. 4066, exp. 38. For the audiencia's authorization in assigning ejidos see AC, II, 86.

7. AC, II, 164, 167; VI, 36; VIII, 714. ENE, II, 220. Some precise boundaries of 1529 are recorded in AC, I, 205. For later boundaries see AA, Tierras y ejidos, vol. 1, no. 4065, exp. 4; exp. 6; vol. 2, no. 4066, exp. 41.

8. AC, II, 20, 97, 167; III, 9. AA, Tierras y ejidos, vol. 2, no. 4066, exp. 38, fols. 4r ff. Gómez de Cervantes, *La vida económica,* p. 183.

9. AC, VIII, 623; XIV, 108. AA, Tierras y ejidos, vol. 1, no. 4065, exp. 1; exp. 4; vol. 2, no. 4066, exp. 38, fols. 18v–19r, 29v.

10. AA, Tierras y ejidos, vol. 1, no. 4065, exp. 4; exp. 19, fol. 28r, *et passim;* vol. 2, no. 4066, exp. 26, fol. 8v.

11. AGN, Civil, vol. 225, exp. 5, fol. 1r. AA, Tierras y ejidos, vol. 1, no. 4065, exp. 1.

12. AA, Tierras y ejidos, vol. 1, no. 4065, exp. 19; exp. 20; vol. 2, no. 4066, exp. 26; exp. 29; exp. 33; exp. 36; exp. 38, fols. 27v–28v. See also the published testimonies of *Títulos principales,* pp. 16 ff., 49 ff., not all of which appear to be authentic.

13. AGI, México, leg. 791. AC, XLVIII–L (1), 106–7, 121–22; LIV, 228, 246.

14. The four quarters of the pre-conquest city receive frequent mention, e.g., in Alvarado Tezozomoc, *Crónica mexicana.* Ojea, *Libro tercero,* p. 7. León, "Bibliografía," no. 4, pp. 437–38. AGN, Civil, vol. 1271, exp. 4. Cossío, "Algunas noticias," pp. 6–9, lists subdivisions within the traza. Toussaint, Gómez de Orozco, and Fernández, *Planos de la ciudad.* Caso, "Los barrios antiguos." For modern survivals see Benítez, "Toponimia indígena de la ciudad," pp. 511–54.

15. *Documentos relativos al tumulto,* II, 415, 429. Vetancurt, *Chronica,* p. 67. Caso, "Los barrios antiguos," pp. 9, 48.

16. AGN, Civil, vol. 1271, exp. 4; Indios, vol. 4, fols. 192v–193r. BNM, ms. no. 165, fols. 2v, 8v. MNM, Colección Gómez de Orozco, no. 14, p. 63.

17. UT, G-30, illustrates tribute and complaint by barrios. For labor see *Códice Osuna,* pp. 122 ff.; Fernández and Leicht, "Códice del tecpan."

18. San Francisco Cuaquiquitla, San Pedro Tecalco, San Pedro Ozumba (Ozumbilla), Santa Ana Zacatlan, San Bartolomé Cuauhtlalpa, San Lucas Xoloc, and others. See Chapter III.

19. The extra-urban possessions of Tenochtitlan and Tlatelolco comprise a special subject on which I plan a separate publication. The problems require more technical kinds of documentary analysis than would be appropriate here.

20. Ricard, "Documents pour l'histoire des franciscains," p. 228. NCDHM (1941), II, 7.

21. Ricard, "Documents pour l'histoire des franciscains," pp. 227–30, 231. Torquemada, *Monarchia indiana,* III, 228.

22. Only the Christian names are given in PNE, III, 25–26, but the native names are

reconstructed fairly thoroughly by Paso y Troncoso. The Franciscans in Tenochtitlan also ministered to Mexicalzingo (San Marcos), which was a distinct cabecera, not a sujeto of Tenochtitlan. They could not reasonably claim as visitas Coxtocan and Tepopula, located far to the south in Chalco province. AGI, México, leg. 665, cuad. 2, fols. 97r ff.

23. NCDHM (1941), II, 8–9. See Chapter IV.

24. The communities had gobernadores in the late colonial period, but Tenochtitlan retained a degree of control over them nevertheless, particularly with respect to tribute collection. BNM, ms. no. 466, fol. 281v. AHH, Tributos, leg. 224, exp. 8, fols. 8v–10r; exp. 10. AGN, Civil, vol. 169, exp. 3, no. 25; Tributos, vol. 23, exp. 5.

25. AA, Tierras y ejidos, vol. 1, no. 4065, exp. 19, fols. 25r ff. AGN, Tributos, vol. 23, exp. 5.

26. AHH, Tributos, leg. 224, passim; leg. 225, exp. 26. AGN, Tributos, exp. 5; exp. 15.

27. AHH, Tributos, leg. 225, exp. 29. BNM, ms. no. 451, fol. 294r. Villa-señor y Sánchez, Theatro americano, I, 77.

28. See Chapter III, note 108.

29. AHH, Tributos, leg 225, exp. 29. AGN, Civil, vol. 169, exp. 3, no. 89.

30. AHH, Tributos, leg. 224, exp. 8, fol. 3v. For Xalpa, Chalmita, and Tepetlacalco see AGN, Civil, vol. 169, exp. 3, 2nd num., no. 9. For Popotla see AGN, Tierras, vol. 191, exp. 2, fol. 1r; Villa-señor y Sánchez, Theatro americano, I, 75.

31. AHH, Tributos, leg 224, exp. 8; exp. 10.

32. Ricard, "Documents pour l'histoire des franciscains," pp. 228 ff.

33. Ricard, "Documents pour l'histoire des franciscains," pp. 231–32. Torquemada, Monarchia indiana, I, 638 ff.

34. Torquemada, Monarchia indiana, III, 228. ENE, XII, 25, 35.

35. For the boundaries of Santa Cruz Coltzinco see BAGN, IX, 26–29. For Mixtecos see AGN, Indios, vol. 11, fols. 98v–101v.

36. For the extra-urban estancias of San Pablo see PNE, III, 18. The other changes are recorded in Vetancurt, Chronica, pp. 67–69, 88. Some reverison to a connection with the city occurred in the eighteenth century with the principle of anexos. In 1767, Acatlan, Ixtacalco, Tetecpilco, Nativitas (Tepetlatzinco), Mexicalzingo, Tequisquilapan, Chapultepec, and San Antonio de las Huertas were all anexos of San José. See AGI, México, leg. 727, exp. 2. Some of these we list as separate doctrinas in Chapter V.

37. ENE, XI, 163. PNE, III, 12 ff. BAGN, IX, 23 ff.

38. It was still listed under Tlatelolco in 1569. NCDHM (1941), II, 8–9. But it occurs immediately after this as a visita (Santa Clara) of Ecatepec. PNE, III, 30.

39. Documentos relativos al tumulto, II, 395 ff. Torquemada, Monarchia indiana, I, 301. Sedano, Noticias de México, II, 73 ff.

40. The presence of Mixteca, Zapoteca, Tlaxcalteca, and other peoples is frequently commented upon in the seventeenth century. See, e.g., AGN, Indios, vol. 17, fols. 234v–235v.

41. AC, I, 175; VI, 492; VIII, 21, 181. AA, Tierras y ejidos, vol. 2, no. 4066, exp. 30, fols. 17r–21r. Advertimientos generales, p. 52. NCDHM (1941), II, 7. PNE, III, 12 ff. BAGN, IX, 17. ENE, XI, 163.

42. BAGN, IX, 1–34. A cedula of 1629 ordered parroquia changes that were never effected. See BNP, no. 259, fols. 1r ff. For the ecclesiastical divisions of the early seventeenth century see Compendio histórico del concilio III, III, 231 ff., and Documentos relativos al tumulto, II, 395 ff. For those of 1692 see BAGN, IX, 1–34. Changes in the

eighteenth century are summarized in Cabrera y Quintero, *Escudo de armas,* and in Sedano, *Noticias de México.* The curatos of the late colonial period are listed in "Noticias de Nueva-España en 1805" and in AHH, Tributos, leg. 224, exp. 8. A general history is contained in Marroquí, *La ciudad de México,* III, 545 ff.

43. BAGN, IX, 2 ff. Robles, *Diario,* II, 263. AGI, Patronato, leg. 226, ramo 17, fols. 4r ff., 10r. AA, Barrio Lorenzot, vol. 445 (752), pp. 45–46.

44. For new demarcations of the traza in the eighteenth century see Carrera Stampa, "Planos de la ciudad," p. 319. An order of 1753 required Indians serving in Spanish houses in the city to return to their native jurisdictions. Castro Santa-Anna, *Diario,* I, 117–18. On the other hand, some arguments favored the continued residence of Indians in the urban area. See, e.g., AC, LIV, 28. An incomplete census record of the mid-eighteenth century indicates that the Spanish sector of the city was still predominantly Spanish, but with an occasional Indian householder and with numerous Indian servants. AGN, Civil, vol. 1496, *passim.*

45. Sedano, *Noticias de México,* II, 73–74. AHH, Tributos, leg. 224, exp. 8, fols. 2r ff., shows which barrios corresponded with which parroquias.

46. Bentura Beleña, *Recopilación sumaria,* II, 26 ff., contains abundant data on the cuartel system and its antecedents. For the proposal of 1753 see also Castro Santa-Anna, *Diario,* I, 119–20. Maps of the divisions of the later eighteenth century are described in Carrera Stampa, "Planos de la ciudad," pp. 360 ff. See especially the Villavicencio map, which Carrera Stampa reproduces in lámina XXVIII. The cuartel regulation permitted Indian maestros, and apprentices up to the age of fifteen, to retain residence in the city. See Bentura Beleña, *Recopilación sumaria,* II, 47. For the numbers involved in this exception as of 1809 see AHH, Tributos, leg. 224, exp. 8, fols. 7v–8r.

47. Las Casas, *Apologética historia,* p. 131.

48. See the discussion in Cook and Simpson, *The Population of Central Mexico,* pp. 30 ff.

49. The preliminary survey ca. 1561 found 18,000 tributaries in Tenochtitlan and Tlatelolco. The count, dated 1562, recorded 12,971 tributaries for Tenochtitlan and 8,665 tributaries for Tlatelolco, to make the total of 21,636 tributaries. The 21,178 tributaries (misprinted in two texts as 21,168 and 20,178), which are also recorded, depend upon slightly variant figures for both: 12,866 tributaries for Tenochtitlan and 8,312 tributaries for Tlatelolco. A notice of January 1564 states that the 8,312 tributaries of Tlatelolco were counted three years previously. *Sobre el modo de tributar,* pp. 20, 38, 44, 77, 93. Miranda, *El tributo indígena,* p. 134. ENE, X, 1–3; XV, 71–73. Valderrama, *Cartas,* p. 64. *Sobre el modo de tributar,* p. 77, gives the total population: 45,335 in Tenochtitlan; 30,330 in Tlatelolco; and 75,665 in all. Cook and Simpson, *The Population of Central Mexico,* p. 53, give 77,022, citing the document "Información para su magestad. . . ." The document is now published in *Sobre el modo de tributar,* pp. 91 ff.

50. See Mols, *Introduction à la démographie historique,* II, 504–5, 512–13. Mols's information suggests that four European cities—Paris, Naples, Milan, and Venice—had populations over 100,000 in the early sixteenth century and that none of these had reached the quarter-million mark.

51. ENE, III, 59, 64. *Sobre el modo de tributar,* p. 45.

52. FHT, VI, 619–21. See also AC, XXVII, 192. On the deaths in the city in 1736 and after see Cabrera y Quintero, *Escudo de armas,* p. 511; Sedano, *Noticias de México,* II, 56–57; León, "Bibliografía," no. 4, p. 656.

53. BAGN, IX, 25. Alzate, *Gacetas de literatura,* II, 52, 121, 275. See also the ex-

treme reductions entered, seemingly in a later hand, on the 1623 document published in Barlow, "Las ocho ermitas," pp. 187–88.

54. Alzate, *Gacetas de literatura*, II, 275; IV, 156.

55. Of ca. 20,000 Spanish families in the city it was said that only 400 remained in 1629 at the time of the great flood. *Memoria histórica . . . del desagüe*, I, 132. Cf. Humboldt, *Political Essay*, I, 111–12. Some exodus from the city also occurred in the period following its foundation. See ENE, III, 59, 64.

56. Puga, *Provisiones*, fol. 88r. See also AC, V, 180–81. Latorre, *Relaciones geográficas*, p. 104.

57. Gemelli Carreri, *Las cosas más considerables*, p. 42, stated in the late seventeenth century that the city contained approximately 100,000 inhabitants, of whom over half were Negroes and mulattoes. See also Villa-señor y Sánchez, *Theatro americano*, I, 35.

58. "Noticias de Nueva-España en 1805," p. 8. Humboldt, *Political Essay*, I, 97–98; II, 61–62.

59. Humboldt's estimate for ca. 1800 was 33,000 Indians and 67,500 whites. Humboldt, *Political Essay*, II, 62.

60. BLMM 135, fol. 89r. BAGN, IX, 20.

61. Gante's letter of 1529 is quoted in Cuevas, *Historia de la iglesia*, I, 159–61. Oroz, Mendieta, and Suárez, *Relación*, pp. 57–59. Ricard, "Documents pour l'histoire des franciscains," p. 231. NCDHM (1941), II, 5–6. NCDHM (1886–92), IV, 177. See the remarks on the Gante school and the further bibliography in Kubler, *Mexican Architecture*, I, 153; Weismann, *Mexico in Sculpture*, pp. 43, 196; and Robertson, *Mexican Manuscript Painting*, p. 43.

62. On the foundation see CDIAI, II, 204; *Cartas de Indias*, p. 169; García and Pereyra, *Documentos inéditos*, XV, 71–72; AGN, Mercedes, vol. 2, fols. 188v–189r; Mendieta, *Historia*, pp. 414 ff.; and other citations listed below.

63. Torquemada, *Monarchia indiana*, III, 113. NCDHM (1886–92), IV, 178; V, 243.

64. NCDHM (1886–92), IV, 178; V, 250 ff. Torquemada, *Monarchia indiana*, III, 114. García Icazbalceta, *Bibliografía mexicana*, p. 475. Gómez de Orozco, "Dos escritores indígenas," p. 128–30.

65. NCDHM (1886–92), IV, 178; V, 241 ff. AGN, Mercedes, vol. 4, fols. 45v–46r. Puga, *Provisiones*, fols. 186v–187r. López, "Inventario," pp. 35–36.

66. On the Tlatelolco manuscript production see Robertson, *Mexican Manuscript Painting*, pp. 155 ff. For the colegio in general there exists a substantial literature in addition to the works cited above. Sahagún, *Historia general*, II, 251 ff. Cervantes de Salazar, *Crónica*, p. 320. Cuevas, *Historia de la iglesia*, I, 386 ff. Steck, *El primer colegio de América*. Ocaranza, *El imperial colegio de indios*. Carreño, "El colegio de Tlatelolco," Zahar Vergara, "Fray Juan de Gaona." Ricard, *La "conquête spirituelle" du Mexique*, pp. 262 ff.

67. CDIAI, VI, 488–89. The council of 1585 ruled that Indians might not be admitted to the clergy except through "the greatest and most careful" process of selection (*Concilio III provincial mexicano*, pp. 41–42), but in practice the exception was almost completely disregarded. The matter is most fully studied by Ricard, *La "conquête spirituelle" du Mexique*, pp. 269 ff.

68. NCDHM (1886–92), IV, 178. Torquemada, *Monarchia indiana*, III, 115.

69. NCDHM (1886–92), IV, 178–80. Torquemada, *Monarchia indiana*, III, 115. Vetancurt, *Chronica*, p. 68.

70. León, "Bibliografía," no. 4, pp. 52, 84. BAGN, VI, 23–37. Sedano, *Noticias de México*, I, 98–100. Osores, *Historia de todos los colegios*, pp. 4 ff.

71. FHT, IV, 478. BNM, ms. no. 1312, fols. 47r ff. León, "Bibliografía," no. 4, p. 85. For efforts to reestablish the colegio in the late eighteenth century see Osores, *Historia de todos los colegios*, p. 47; *La administración de D. Frey Antonio María de Bucareli*, II, 183 ff.

72. León, "Bibliografía," no. 4, p. 84. BNM, ms. no. 437, fol. 463r. Sedano, *Noticias de México*, I, 101–2, 132.

73. Cuevas, *Historia de la iglesia*, I, 391 ff. Osores, *Historia de todos los colegios*, pp. 8 ff.

74. Bentura Beleña, *Recopilación sumaria*, I, 5th pag., 204. BM, Add. 17,564, fol. 84v. Fonseca and Urrutia, *Historia*, VI, 199 ff. Viera, *Compendiosa narración*, p. 65. The hospital at one time also received income from the labor repartimiento payments and from theatrical presentations. AGN, Indios, vol. 6 (1), fols. 263v–264r. *Advertimientos generales*, p. 74. Vázquez de Espinosa, *Compendium and Description*, pp. 161–62. See Fernández, "El hospital real de los indios."

75. AC, XIII, 115.

76. BAGN, III, 481 ff. CDIHIA, IV, 135. Torquemada, *Monarchia indiana*, I, 295. Cabrera y Quintero, *Escudo de armas*, p. 255, states that these came to an end as a result of the plague of the 1730's.

77. The punishment for an Indian caught carrying arms in the 1770's was 100 lashes and four years of service in the fort at Veracruz. Bentura Beleña, *Recopilación sumaria*, II, 58–61.

78. BNM, ms. no. 15, fols. 15r ff.; no. 439, fol. 469r. BLMM 135, fols. 129r ff. AGI, México, leg. 1238 (1), no. 74. *Instrucciones que los vireyes de Nueva España dejaron* (1867), pp. 6 ff. BM, Add. 18,204, fols. 4r ff. Humboldt, *Political Essay*, I, 235. *Gazetas de México, compendio de noticias*, IV, 158 ff. Bentura Beleña, *Recopilación sumaria*, II, 338 ff.

79. For a generation and more after the conquest the Spanish residents of the city lived in fear of Indian uprising. See the discussion in Kubler, *Mexican Architecture*, I, 77 ff. The only incident of the early period, however, was a planned and imperfectly executed Negro rebellion in 1537, which was speedily suppressed by the arrest of its leaders. The rebellion is commented upon in Chimalpahin, *Annales*, p. 237; *Codex Telleriano-Remensis*, fol. 45r; CDIAI, II, 198. Torquemada, *Monarchia indiana*, I, 610. Sigüenza spoke of the rebellion of 1537 as an Indian revolt, aided by Negroes. See BAGN, IX, 7. For later uprisings and planned uprisings by Negroes and mulattoes in the city see Querol y Roso, *Negros y mulatos de Nueva España*, pp. 8 ff.

80. *Documentos relativos al tumulto, passim*. NLAC, 1246. Guthrie, "Riots in Seventeenth-Century Mexico City," pp. 244 ff.

81. AGI, Patronato, leg. 226, contains 27 ramos on the uprising of 1692. Robles, *Diario*, II, 250 ff. AC, XXXV, 3 ff. *Carta de un religioso*. Leonard, *Don Carlos de Sigüenza*, pp. 110 ff., 210 ff. Guthrie, "Riots in Seventeenth-Century Mexico City," pp. 246 ff. Rivera, "Diario curioso," pp. 78–79.

82. *Cartas de Indias*, p. 170. CDIHIA, I, 133–34. ENE, IV, 90. AC, VI, 456; VII, 8.

83. CDHM, II, 100. Aiton, *Antonio de Mendoza*, pp. 36, 49. Aiton, "The Secret Visita," p. 19. See the remarks of Zumárraga in Cuevas, *Historia de la iglesia*, I, 254.

84. FHT, I, 21–22. CDHM, II, 100. Gómez de Cervantes, *La vida económica*, pp. 112 ff. *Sobre el modo de tributar*, p. 8. Códice Osuna contains many records of this service.

85. AGN, Mercedes, vol. 4, fols. 190v ff.; vol. 5, fols. 6r, 240r; vol. 7, fol. 133r–133v. ENE, IV, 90.

86. Ojea, *Libro tercero*, p. 7. Gage, *A New Survey*, p. 132. Vázquez de Espinosa, *Compendium and Description*, p. 157. Kubler, *Mexican Architecture*, II, 296, 513, 529. Chappe d'Auteroche, *A Voyage to California*, p. 41. For the Cathedral, see Toussaint, *La catedral de México*. There exist numerous works on the history of individual buildings in the city. A convenient summary is Orozco y Berra, *Memoria para el plano de la ciudad*.

87. *Sobre el modo de tributar*, p. 46. Cepeda and Carrillo, *Relación*, fols. 3v–4r.

88. The number and location of pre-conquest causeways remains a subject of some dispute. See Schottelius, "Wieviel Dämme." Materials on this subject are reviewed by Gardiner, *Naval Power*, pp. 35 ff. New evidence from cuts made in modern highway construction is provided by González Rul and Mooser, "La calzada de Iztapalapa." For the dimensions of the various colonial causeways see Cepeda and Carrillo, *Relación*, fols. 3v–4r. The road to the southeast is depicted on Humboldt's map, which is reproduced in Apenas, *Mapas antiguos*, lám. 30. For late repair and construction of causeways see BNM, ms. no. 466, fol. 174v. On the construction of the "calzada de tierra" to Guadalupe in the late eighteenth century see López Sarrelangue, *Una villa mexicana*, pp. 68 ff.

89. CDHM, I, 391. López de Gómara, *Historia*, II, 105–6. Hakluyt, *The Principal Navigations*, IX, 363. CDIHE, LVII, 177. Humboldt, *Political Essay*, II, 46.

90. AC, II, 194. CDIAI, VI, 493. FHT, III, 13–14. On pavement of the early seventeenth century, see Cisneros, *Sitio*, fols. 109v ff. On tenayucas see Villa-señor y Sánchez, *Theatro americano*, I, 76; *Códice Osuna*, pp. 143 ff. The use of flagstones in place of tenayucas in city paving began about 1770. See BNM, ms. no. 455, fol. 19r.

91. Torquemada, *Monarchia indiana*, I, 311. Gage, *A New Survey*, p. 120. Continuous testimonies from the sixteenth to the late eighteenth centuries refer to the filth and foul smells of the canals, in which garbage, sewage, and occasional dead bodies were thrown. *Códice Osuna*, p. 117. AC, I, 128; XIII, 335; XLVIII–L (2), 61. Gómez de Cervantes, *La vida económica*, p. 102. García Icazbalceta, *Bibliografía*, p. 240. Cuevas Aguirre y Espinosa, *Extracto de los autos*, pp. 36–37. Bentura Beleña, *Recopilación sumaria*, II, 339. BNM, ms. no. 466, fol. 172v.

92. Cuevas Aguirre y Espinosa, *Extracto de los autos*, p. 4. SLSF, Zúñiga y Ontiveros, "Efemérides."

93. Dimensions and routes of the canals are given in Cepeda and Carrillo, *Relación*, p. 4, and Cuevas Aguirre y Espinosa, *Extracto de los autos*, pp. 38 ff. The earliest canals are shown on the mapa attributed (erroneously) to Alonso de Santa Cruz. See the discussion in Linné, *El valle y la ciudad de México en 1550*, and in Toussaint, Gómez de Orozco, and Fernández, *Planos de la ciudad*, pp. 127 ff. Canals of the early seventeenth century are described in Cisneros, *Sitio*, fols. 109r ff. The eighteenth-century canals are shown on a number of maps reproduced in Carrera Stampa, "Planos de la ciudad." For the extension of the canal system to Guadalupe in the late eighteenth century see López Sarrelangue, *Una villa mexicana*, pp. 55 ff.

94. CDIHE, LVII, 177–78. Ojea, *Libro tercero*, p. 6. Alzate, *Gacetas de literatura*, II, 116.

95. Chimalpahin, *Annales*, pp. 128, 212. Cervantes de Salazar, *Crónica*, pp. 22–23, 300. *Histoire de la nation mexicaine*, pp. 88, 113. CDIAI, XIII, 234. CDIU, X, 236–37. AC, I, 128, 139; II, 43; VII, 442 ff.; VIII, 64, 139 ff. ENE, XI, 102.

96. AC, VIII, 64, 139 ff. *Histoire de la nation mexicaine*, p. 113. FHT, VI, 4–6, 192. López de Velasco, *Geografía y descripción*, p. 192. CDIHE, LVII, 27.

97. Gutiérrez de Medina, *Viage de tierra, y mar*, fol. 33v. AC, XXXII, 228. Franco, *Segunda parte*, p. 534. León, "Bibliografía," no. 4, p. 345. Villa-señor y Sánchez, *Theatro americano*, I, 72. Humboldt, *Political Essay*, II, 34. Orozco y Berra, *Memoria para la carta hidrográfica*, p. 84. Romero de Terreros, "Los acueductos de México" and *Los acueductos* are informative summary histories. See also Cossío, "Las aguas de la ciudad," pp. 33–52. Diego de Cisneros described the qualities of the waters from their various sources in the early seventeenth century. Cisneros, *Sitio*, fols. 68v ff.

98. Díaz del Castillo, *Historia verdadera*, I, 330–31. Cervantes de Salazar, *Crónica*, p. 300. CDIAI, XIII, 234.

99. "Unos anales coloniales de Tlatelolco, 1519–1633," p. 173. AC, VIII, 181; X, 171–72, 178; XII, 10. CDIHE, LVII, 232. Cisneros, *Sitio*, fol. 66v.

100. FHT, VIII, 61–63. Vetancurt, *Chronica*, p. 69. Alzate, *Gacetas de literatura*, II, 113–14. BNM, ms. no. 466, fol. 168r.

101. León, "Bibliografía," no. 4, p. 345. Alzate, *Gacetas de literatura*, II, 113–14. BNM, ms. no. 466, fols. 166r ff.

102. FHT, I, 97. AGN, Inquisición, vol. 75, no. 12, fols. 55r ff.

103. Aiton, *Antonio de Mendoza*, pp. 36, 49.

104. See, e.g., Fernández and Leicht, "Códice del tecpan."

105. AGN, Mercedes, vol. 4, fols. 190v ff.; vol. 5, fol. 3r–3v; vol. 7, fols. 198v–199r, 354v–355r; Inquisición, vol. 75, no. 12, fols. 55r, 56r, 64r.

106. AGN, Inquisición, vol. 75, no. 12, fols. 60r–66r. The urban labor draft of the 1570's was larger than that of the 1560's; Tenochtitlan was required in 1564 to give only 200 laborers, of whom 40 were to be oficiales. See AGN, Mercedes, vol. 7, fols. 354v–355r.

107. *Sobre el modo de tributar*, pp. 30, 32, 37. For the difficulties of earlier payment, in compliance with a royal order, see ENE, II, 190. The Spanish cabildo was still protesting the rule that the labor was to be recompensed in 1562. AC, VII, 8. Numerous details of urban labor to the middle 1560's may be found in *Códice Osuna*.

108. AGN, Mercedes, vol. 7, fols. 18or, 354r–355r.

109. AC, VI, 26, 44. AGN, Inquisición, vol. 75, no. 12, fols. 60r–61r; Indios, vol. 4, fols. 192v–193r.

110. *Archivo mexicano*, I, 97, 235. AC, II, 14–15. ENE, I, 83–84. See Appendix I, sc. Ixtapalapa.

111. E.g., AC, IV, 179–80; V, 260–61.

112. AGN, Mercedes, vol. 5, fols. 3r, 6r, 240r. *Sobre el modo de tributar*, p. 27.

113. AGN, Indios, vol. 4, fol. 204r; vol. 6 (1), fols. 221v–222r. FHT, III, 13–14. Numerous additional examples may be found in FHT and in AGN, Mercedes.

114. AGN, Indios, vol. 7, fol. 157r–157v; Inquisición, vol. 75, no. 12, fols. 55r ff. FHT, II, 335. NCDHM (1886–92), IV, 183, *Legislación del trabajo*, p. 91. AC, XV, 106.

115. Spanish writers frequently repeated the Indians' statement that they had paid no tribute to Montezuma in the pre-conquest period. Zorita, *Historia*, p. 434. *Sobre el modo de tributar*, pp. 29, 31, 45, 51, 52. Torquemada, *Monarchia indiana*, I, 624.

116. See UT, G-30.

117. *Histoire de la nation mexicaine*, p. 92. Peñafiel, *Colección de documentos*, sec. 1, p. 15. The hanging is illustrated in the Códice de Tlatelolco. See the comments of R. H. Barlow in *Anales de Tlatelolco*, p. 114.

118. *Códice Osuna*, pp. 73 ff. Zorita, *Historia*, p. 435. *Sobre el modo de tributar*, pp. 44, 51.

119. BAGN, VIII, 186–88. CDIHIA, I, 133.

120. *Sobre el modo de tributar*, pp. 21, 34.

121. *Sobre el modo de tributar*, pp. 8–9, 19 ff., 42. These passages explain the delay between 1552 and 1564. See also the important letter in Zorita, *Historia*, pp. 432–37. Some of the Spanish opposition to the urban tribute related not to tribute itself but to the fact that unrecompensed labor would no longer be given in place of tribute. BAGN, VIII, 186. Torquemada, *Monarchia indiana*, I, 624–25.

122. ENE, X, 1–3; XV, 71–73. Valderrama, *Cartas*, p. 64. For various alternative proposals concerning amount and procedure, made in the early 1560's, see *Sobre el modo de tributar*, pp. 21 ff.

123. See the account of the imposition of tribute in 1564 in the Códice de Juan Bautista, MNM, Colección Gómez de Orozco, no. 14, pp. 48 ff. "Unos anales coloniales de Tlatelolco, 1519–1633," p. 172. Valderrama, *Cartas*, pp. 160–61. Chimalpahin, *Annales*, p. 264, contains interesting data on the disrepute of the Indian gobernador of Tenochtitlan, who permitted the tribute to be imposed. See also NCDHM (1886–92), IV, 182. Torquemada, *Monarchia indiana*, I, 624–25, seems to depend in some degree on this document.

124. This accounts for the frequent references after 1564 to the "one real paid for bridges" or the "one real for repairs." It should be noted that this one real was a subdivision of the ordinary tribute, not an increment upon it. AC, VII, 228; VIII, 33; XII, 61, 94; XIV, 123, 130. Valderrama, *Cartas*, p. 64.

125. AGI, México, leg. 748, sep. pag., fol. 19r. A similar division for Tlatelolco in 1565 is recorded in *El libro de las tasaciones*, pp. 515–16.

126. NCDHM (1886–92), IV, 184. For a modification proposed by the Spanish cabildo in 1582 see AC, VIII, 578.

127. Names of the merinos, tepixque, alguaciles, and other tribute collectors of the barrios of the city, with amounts owed in 1636 and 1637, are recorded in AGN, Civil, vol. 1271, exp. 4. A similar document, BM, Add. 13,994, is published in Caso, "Los barrios antiguos," pp. 50 ff.

128. AGN, Indios, vol. 6 (1), fols. 290v ff.; vol. 23, fols. 64v–65v.

129. BNP, no. 376. See Chapter VIII and Plate VIII.

130. The original tasaciones of 1564 depended on counts made two to three years before (see note 49) and were still in effect ten years later. NCDHM (1886–92), IV, 183. AGI, México, leg. 748, sep. pag., fol. 45r–45v.

131. AGN, Indios, vol. 6 (1), fols. 35r, 221v; vol. 12, fol. 134v; vol. 15 (2), fol. 82r. FHT, VI, 236–38, 253–54.

132. AGN, Civil, vol. 1688, exp. 1, fols. 1r ff.

133. NCDHM (1886–92), IV, 184. MNM, Colección Gómez de Orozco, no. 14, p. 64. "Unos anales coloniales de Tlatelolco, 1519–1633," p. 181. AGN, Indios, vol. 10 (3), fol. 14v.

134. AGI, México, leg. 748 (1728); sep. pag., fols. 21r ff. AGN, Tributos, vol. 10, exp. 4, fols. 3r–3v, 12r–12v.

135. AGI, México, leg. 748 (1667); sep. pag., fol. 13v. AGN, Tributos, vol. 10, exp. 4, fols. 11r, 39r. In 1728 all the *fiadores* appear to have been Indians, a circumstance that was regarded as unfavorable from the point of view of the royal treasury because of the Indians' characteristic insolvency. See AGI, México, leg. 748 (1728).

136. AGI, México, leg. 748, sep. pag., fol. 64v. BNM, ms. no. 439, fol. 462r. BM, Eg. 1798, fol. 12v.

137. BAGN, XXV, 65. AGI, México, leg. 748, sep. pag., fol. 45r–45v. BNM, ms. no. 439, fol. 460v. BM, Eg. 1798, fol. 12r–12v.

138. BM, Eg. 1798, fols. 17v, 27r ff. BNM, ms. no. 439, fols. 463v–465v. The "vagos" were not necessarily itinerant people. They might be resident Indians originating elsewhere. See BAGN, IX, 20; BNM, ms. no. 439, fol. 471v; BM, Eg. 1798, fol. 18v.

139. BNM, ms. no. 439, fols. 465v ff. BAGN, IX, 24.

140. BNM, ms. no. 439, fols. 460v ff.; no. 455, fol. 215r. AGN, Tierras, vol. 1354, exp. 3, fols. 1r ff. Fonseca and Urrutia, *Historia*, I, 449.

141. BNM, ms. no. 466, fol. 282v. AHH, Tributos, legs. 224, 225.

142. AGN, Tributos, vol. 16, exp. 9; vol. 23, exp. 4. AHH, Tributos, legs. 224, 225. BNM, ms. no. 466, fols. 278r ff., 287r–287v. Indian half-tributaries had to pay 7 reales at first, but in October 1792 this was changed to 6½. Mulatto and other half-tributaries had to pay 12 reales by the revised rule.

143. BNM, ms. no. 466, fols. 280v ff. AHH, Tributos, leg. 225, exp. 8.

144. *Instrucciones que los vireyes de Nueva España dejaron* (1873), II, 359–60. AHH, Tributos, leg. 225, exp. 24.

145. AGN, Tributos, vol. 10, fols. 76r–76v, 146r–146v. AGI, México, leg. 748, sep. pag., fol. 64v.

146. Many of these are listed in AGN, Civil, vol. 169, exp. 3, and vol. 174, exp. 7.

147. AGN, Civil, vol. 169, exp. 3, no. 12; vol. 174, exp. 7, no. 45.

148. Cervantes de Salazar, *Life in the Imperial and Loyal City*, p. 62. Torquemada, *Monarchia indiana*, II, 555.

149. Cervantes de Salazar, *Crónica*, p. 303. Cervantes de Salazar, *Life in the Imperial and Loyal City*, p. 62. Sedano, *Noticias de México*, II, 9–10.

150. "Anales de San Gregorio Acapulco," p. 110. Cervantes de Salazar, *Crónica*, pp. 303–4. AGN, Mercedes, vol. 5, fols. 223r–223v, 294v. Sedano, *Noticias de México*, II, 9–10. Torquemada, *Monarchia indiana*, II, 555 ff. CDIHE, LVII, 180. Bentura Beleña, *Recopilación sumaria*, I, 2nd pag., 91.

151. CDIHE, LVII, 180. Cervantes de Salazar, *Life in the Imperial and Loyal City*, p. 41. Bentura Beleña, *Recopilación sumaria*, I, 2nd pag., 91. Sedano, *Noticias de México*, II, 9–10. BNM, ms. no. 466, fol. 185r–185v. BAGN, VI, 562 ff.

152. Motolinía, *History*, pp. 208–9. CDIAI, XIII, 59. López de Velasco, *Geografía y descripción*, pp. 191–92. Cervantes de Salazar, *Crónica*, p. 303. Torquemada, *Monarchia indiana*, II, 555 ff. AGN, Mercedes, vol. 5, fol. 223r–223v. CDIHE, LVII, 180. Hakluyt, *The Principal Navigations*, IX, 380. Vázquez de Espinosa, *Compendium and Description*, p. 156.

153. AGN, Mercedes, vol. 5, fol. 294v.

154. Bentura Beleña, *Recopilación sumaria*, I, 2nd pag., 6, 91, 92, 105. AA, Barrio Lorenzot, "Colecsion de ordenanzas," 432 (743), fol. 118r. BNM, ms. no. 466, fol. 185r. *El segundo conde de Revilla Gigedo*, p. 170.

155. A third product particularly subject to systematic controls was meat, an item of Indian diet but a less important one than pulque or maize. The subject is studied in Dusenberry, "The Regulation of Meat Supply."

156. For regulation of the late sixteenth century see AGN, Ordenanzas, vol. 1, fol. 74r. The 1692 prohibitions are documented in AGI, Patronato, leg. 226, ramo 17, fols. 2r ff. *Documentos relativos al tumulto*, I, 31, comments on illegalities and covert payments in pulquería regulation.

157. AC, VI, 249, 326–27; VII, 173. *Recopilación de leyes*, II, 197–98 (Lib. VI, tít. 1,

ley 37). Fonseca and Urrutia, *Historia*, III, 367, 376 ff. *La administración de D. Frey Antonio María de Bucareli*, I, 433 ff. BAGN, XVIII, 205 ff.

158. AGN, Indios, vol. 10, *passim*. *La administración de D. Frey Antonio María de Bucareli*, I, 433 ff. PCR, "Testamento del señor D. Manuel Rodriguez Saenz." For amounts of pulque received in the city in various years see BNM, ms. no. 465, fol. 278r; Sedano, *Noticias de México*, II, 104; Clavigero, *Historia antigua*, II, 360. Humboldt, *Political Essay*, II, 71.

159. The statement would not apply to the estancias of the city. The main native sources for this subject are Códice Cozcatzin (BNP, nos. 41–45) and its affiliates, the Títulos de tierras pertenecientes al pueblo de Santa Isabel Tola (Peñafiel, *Colección de documentos*, sec. 1) and the Colección Chavero IV and V, including the Códice de Ixhuatepec (Chavero, *Pinturas jeroglíficas*, II, 16 ff.). These indicate individual holdings of 10 or 20 by 200 or 400 varas or brazas, a very clear conception of the pre-conquest distribution by Itzcoatl, and usurpation by the Indian gobernadores of the sixteenth century. A large number of other colonial texts refer to private Indian landholding in the city. So far as we now know, none indicates the existence of calpullalli. The subject of urban landholding is one for which I plan a separate publication.

160. *Sobre el modo de tributar*, pp. 31, 52–53. Zorita, *Historia*, p. 436. AGI, Justicia, leg. 124, no. 5, exp. 2.

161. *El segundo conde de Revilla Gigedo*, p. 170. Vetancurt, *Chronica*, p. 88. FHT, VI, 437–38. Zorita, *Historia*, p. 436. *Sobre el modo de tributar*, pp. 31, 52. AGN, Indios, vol. 6(2), fol. 49r–49v.

162. CDIAI, VI, 507. AC, IV, 99; V, 143, 290; VIII, 578. See Chapter VIII.

163. AGN, Mercedes, vol. 3, fols. 25v–26r. *Documentos relativos al tumulto*, I, 51 ff.; II, *passim*.

164. The 150,000-fanega statement is made for the middle eighteenth century by Villa-señor y Sánchez, *Theatro americano*, I, 36. But the Gazeta of 1734 speaks of a consumption of over twice this amount, 328,500 fanegas. León, "Bibliografía," no. 4, p. 510. An intermediate figure, 288,192 fanegas, is given for 1777. BNM, ms. no. 465, fol. 278r. The animal consumption was reckoned at over 80,000 fanegas (40,000 cargas) in 1770 (AGI, México, leg. 2096) and at over 200,000 fanegas (300 cargas per day) in 1788 (*Gazetas de México, compendio de noticias*, III, 174).

165. AC, VIII, 47, 59, 725–30. Proposals for an alhóndiga had been made from the 1530's on. See AC, IV, 99; VII, 364; PNE, III (supl.), 38, 220–21. The viceroy later stated that the pósito began in 1571. AC, XXVI, 71.

166. AC, VIII, 362 ff.; XIV, 84–85. CDIHE, XXVI, 385.

167. AC, VIII, 362, 403–4, 420, 578, 619. AGN, General de parte, vol. 3, fol. 24r–24v.

168. AC, XII, 9, 13, 118, 363–64; XIII, 210. There exists an enormous documentation on the pósito and the alhóndiga, and on the whole history of maize provision in the city. See especially AC, XXVII, 102–4; XXXIV, 3–12, *et passim*; AGI, México, leg. 24, ramos 1–4; leg. 781; Patronato, leg. 226; AA, Pósito y alhóndiga. Lee, "Grain Legislation"; Guthrie, "Colonial Economy," pp. 107 ff.

169. PNE, III (supl.), 108.

170. Motolinía, *Memoriales*, p. 185. Motolinía, *History*, pp. 241–42. Torquemada, *Monarchia indiana*, II, 488; III, 208 ff. Hakluyt, *The Principal Navigations*, IX, 387. Díaz del Castillo, *Historia verdadera*, II, 559.

171. Motolinía, *History*, p. 242. AGN, Mercedes, vol. 3, fol. 348r–348v.

172. Sahagún, *Historia general*, II, 190 ff., 202.

173. *Sobre el modo de tributar,* pp. 20, 43.

174. The process whereby sons learned from their parents is illustrated in *Codex Mendoza,* III, fol. 7or.

175. Thus when Bernal Díaz recounted the Spaniards' visit of Tenochtitlan he described a continuous tour from one area of economic specialization and craftsmanship to another. Díaz del Castillo, *Historia verdadera,* I, 318–19.

176. AHH, Tributos, leg. 224, exps. 2, 3, 5, 6; leg. 225, exp. 27.

177. The connection between a particular religious form and a particular economic activity had antecedents in pre-conquest life, where labor was ritualistic and where professions had their special deities. Sahagún's Book I is a catalogue of Aztec deities: Yiacatecuhtli, worshiped by merchants; Napatecuhtli, worshiped by makers of reed mats; and others. Sahagún, *Florentine Codex,* Book I, The Gods, pp. 17, 20 ff. The connection received a certain additional impetus with the conversion to Christianity. The traditional Spanish guild was simultaneously a cofradía. Spanish tailors and hosiers had a cofradía in Mexico City ca. 1570. A similar institution by the Indian leather workers may have been wholly in imitation of Spaniards. PNE, III, 2. Carrera Stampa, *Los gremios mexicanos,* pp. 79 ff., 88, 336.

178. Puga, *Provisiones,* I, fol. 117r–117v. CDIAI, VI, 504.

179. E.g., AGN, Mercedes, vol. 3, fol. 348r–348v. In the early 1560's, when Indian tribute in the city received much attention, proposals were made for graduated tributes, with oficiales paying more than others. But such plans were rejected in favor of a uniform rate for all tributaries. See *Sobre el modo de tributar,* pp. 21, 32, 34.

180. AGN, Indios, vol. 6 (1), fol. 161r.

181. Motolinía, *History,* p. 242. AGN, Mercedes, vol. 3, fols. 244r–244v, 348r–348v, 354v–355r.

182. AA, Barrio Lorenzot, "Colecsion de ordenanzas," vol. 1, no. 431 (743), fol. 78r. To prevent such farming out, and to prevent middlemen's profits, rules were enacted forbidding guild members to purchase the work of Indian sculptors for sale. AA, Barrio Lorenzot, "Colecsion de ordenanzas," vol. 1, no. 431 (743), fol. 208r–208v. The intention was surely not to forbid all sales to Spaniards by Indian sculptors. See NLAC, 1121, fols. 171v–172r, for regulations concerning Indian makers of images in the 1550's. Cf. Weismann, *Mexico in Sculpture,* p. 201, after unpublished material of Manuel Toussaint. For similar rules concerning hats see AA, Artesanos–Gremios, vol. 1, no. 381, fol. 34r. For rules concerning shoes and other goods see AC, VI, 45.

183. The major work on colonial guilds is Carrera Stampa, *Los gremios mexicanos.* The principal collection of guild ordinances is Barrio Lorenzot, *El trabajo en México,* for which, however, we cite in this work the manuscript version in AA.

184. AGN, Mercedes, vol. 3, fol. 244r–244v. Note also that in the accusations recorded in 1564 the Indian *cordoneros* and tailors registered their complaints through Indian spokesmen. *Códice Osuna,* pp. 28 ff.

185. AGN, Mercedes, vol. 3, fol. 325v. CDIAI, VI, 504. AA, Barrio Lorenzot, "Colecsion de ordenanzas," vol. 1, no. 431 (743), fol. 326r.

186. AGN, Mercedes, vol. 5, fol. 43v. See the similar problem faced by Spanish shoemakers and Spanish hat makers. AA, Barrio Lorenzot, "Colecsion de ordenanzas," vol. 1, no. 431 (743), fols. 78r, 263v–264r.

187. The detailed Indian account occurs in the Códice de Juan Bautista. The passage is translated by Garibay K., "Un cuadro real," pp. 228–29.

188. AA, Barrio Lorenzot, "Colecsion de ordenanzas," vol. 1, no. 431 (743), fols.

57r, 75v–76r, 208r–208v; vol. 2, no. 432 (744), fol. 6v. *Legislación del trabajo*, p. 65. A number of other examples are documented in Carrera Stampa, *Los gremios mexicanos*, pp. 233 ff.

189. AA, Barrio Lorenzot, "Colecsion de ordenanzas," vol. 1, no. 431 (743), fols. 326r, 329r–329v.

190. AA, Barrio Lorenzot, "Colecsion de ordenanzas," vol. 1, no. 431 (743), fols. 20r, 246v. Examiners for Indian saddlemakers were to be chosen by the city and examinations were to take place before an alcalde of the city. Indians had learned the difficult art of saddlemaking in the early post-conquest years after stealing a saddle tree, analyzing its construction, and imitating it. See Motolinía, *History*, p. 242. Spaniards in the 1540's were discovered to be selling Indian-made saddles in the city, advertising them as importations from Spain. AA, Barrio Lorenzot, "Colecsion de ordenanzas," vol. 1, no. 431 (743), fol. 246r.

191. AA, Barrio Lorenzot, "Colecsion de ordenanzas," vol. 1, no. 431 (743), fols. 95v–98v. See the rules for Indian spinners of silk in 1563. AGN, Mercedes, vol. 6, fols. .33v ff. Borah, *Silk Raising*, pp. 35–36, interprets the rules of 1563 as legalizing Indian competition in a separate guild, where illegal discrimination could not stifle it. Borah further regards the 1576 regulation as providing additional liberation of Indians from white control. My interpretation would be that guild supervisors were taking control of an Indian production that had previously been declared free.

192. AA, Barrio Lorenzot, "Colecsion de ordenanzas," vol. 1, no. 431 (743), fols. 193r, 282r.

193. AA, Barrio Lorenzot, "Colecsion de ordenanzas," vol. 1, no. 431 (743), fols. 95v–98v, 183v, 208r–208v.

194. AA, Barrio Lorenzot, "Colecsion de ordenanzas," vol. 1, no. 431 (743), fols. 263v ff.

195. Carrera Stampa, *Los gremios mexicanos*, pp. 223–24. AA, Barrio Lorenzot, "Colecsion de ordenanzas," vol. 1, no. 431 (743), fols. 147v–148r, 332r.

196. Carrera Stampa, *Los gremios mexicanos*, pp. 226 ff. AA, Barrio Lorenzot, "Colecsion de ordenanzas," vol. 1, no. 431 (743), fols. 188r, 274r.

197. Indian maestros in various trades are documented in AGN, Indios, vol. 1, fol. 136v; Tributos, vol. 10, fol. 14r. AA, Tierras y ejidos, vol. 1, no. 4065, exp. 20, fol. 14r.

198. Gálvez, *Informe general*, p. 38. BNM, ms. no. 15, fols. 26v, 28r; ms. no. 466, fol. 178r. Viera, *Compendiosa narración*, p. 70.

APPENDIX I

1. Millares Carlo and Mantecón, *Indice y extractos de los protocolos*, I, 140. CDIAI, XXVI, 511. Dorantes de Carranza, *Sumaria relación*, p. 221. See also *Archivo mexicano*, I, 134.

2. *Relación de las encomiendas*, p. 16. ENE, VI, 128, 173; VII, 61; IX, 4; XVI, 36 ff. García Pimentel, *Relación*, p. 156. NLAC, 1121, fol. 169v. PNE, I, 25. *El libro de las tasaciones*, pp. 12–13.

3. García Pimentel, *Relación*, p. 156. ENE, XIII, 9, 39; XVI, 88. AGI, Patronato, leg. 182, ramo 44, fol. 2r. AGN, General de parte, vol. 2, fol. 61r. Guzmán, "Un manuscrito," pp. 100–101. PNE, VI, 210. FHT, III, 29; VI, 114–15. Dorantes de Carranza, *Sumaria relación*, p. 221. All these are named Francisco de Solís except the two that fall

latest in time, in 1604 and 1607. The name occurs in these as Francisco de Solís Orduña, but Dorantes de Carranza, *Sumaria relación*, p. 221, identifies this as the name of the son of Pedro de Solís. He appears to have been still living in 1609. See Cavo, *Historia de México*, p. 272.

4. FHT, VI, 360, 382. AGN, Indios, vol. 7, fol. 166v. AGI, Contaduría, leg. 735, fols. 24r ff.

5. AC, XXXII, 134 ff. AGI, Contaduría, leg. 768 (1678).

6. E.g., AGI, Justicia, leg. 134, no. 1. ENE, IX, 2. García Pimentel, *Relación*, p. 180. *Relación de las encomiendas*, p. 23.

7. AGI, Justicia, leg. 134, no. 1. AGN, Mercedes, vol. 1, fol. 96r–96v. ENE, XV, 212.

8. ENE, IX, 2. NCDHM (1941), II, 14. *Relación de las encomiendas*, p. 23.

9. *El libro de las tasaciones*, p. 308. García Pimentel, *Relación*, p. 180.

10. ENE, X, 48–49.

11. ENE, XIII, 10, 44.

12. AGN, Mercedes, vol. 8, fol. 51r–51v. FHT, VII, 143.

13. AGN, Congregaciones, fol. 33r. *Moderación de doctrinas*, p. 46. AGI, Contaduría, leg. 751 (1658).

14. García Pimentel, *Relación*, p. 157. ENE, IX, 7. *Relación de las encomiendas*, p. 25. *El libro de las tasaciones*, p. 57. Cuevas, *Historia de la iglesia*, II, 482.

15. AGI, Justicia, leg. 204, no. 2, ramo 3. CDIU, XXIV, 73.

16. Chamberlain, *The Conquest and Colonization of Yucatan*, p. 310. García Pimentel, *Relación*, p. 157. Cuevas, *Historia de la iglesia*, II, 482. ENE, VII, 201 ff.; IX, 7. *El libro de las tasaciones*, p. 58. AGI, Justicia, leg. 204, no. 2, ramo 3.

17. Chamberlain, *The Conquest and Colonization of Yucatan*, p. 310. García Pimentel, *Relación*, p. 157. *Relación de las encomiendas*, p. 25. ENE, X, 79–82. She is known to have been living in September 1582. See AC, VIII, 580.

18. Torquemada, *Monarchia indiana*, I, 756–57, 767. Cavo, *Historia de México*, pp. 269, 273. Alamán, *Disertaciones*, III, 22. Rubio Mañé, "Apuntes," pp. 91–92. Schäfer, *El Consejo real*, I, 352.

19. AGI, Contaduría, leg. 729, fols. 24r ff.; leg. 735, fols. 24r ff.; leg. 763 (1671).

20. AGI, Contaduría, leg. 816 (Tributos).

21. AGI, Vínculos, vol. 73, exp. 4, fol. 1r. NLAC, 1106, no. 22, shows a disbursement of Azcapotzalco tribute funds to the Conde de Montezuma in the middle seventeenth century.

22. CDIAI, XII, 279, 539. Cortés, *Cartas y otros documentos*, pp. 32–33. *Documentos inéditos relativos a Hernán Cortés*, p. 347.

23. CDIAI, XII, 539; XXVII, 85. ENE, I, 141; VII, 261, 263.

24. ENE, III, 91.

25. *Cartas de Indias*, p. 170. Chimalpahin, *Annales*, pp. 11–12.

26. Fonseca and Urrutia, *Historia*, I, 470. BAGN, XV, 582 ff. AGN, Hospital de Jesús, vol. 235; vol. 266, exp. 74.

27. AGN, Hospital de Jesús, vol. 156, exp. 1; exp. 8.

28. Fonseca and Urrutia, *Historia*, I, 456.

29. PNE, VI, 83. AGN, Hospital de Jesús, vol. 293, exp. 123, fol. 2r.

30. PNE, VI, 83. ENE, IX, 7. García Pimentel, *Relación*, p. 159. *Relación de las encomiendas*, p. 26. *El libro de las tasaciones*, p. 173. Dorantes de Carranza, *Sumaria relación*, p. 309. Two doctors of this name are known in sixteenth-century Mexico, this encomendero being the earlier. See García Icazbalceta, *Bibliografía*, pp. 229–30.

31. ENE, VI, 173; IX, 9; XV, 216. *El libro de las tasaciones,* p. 173. *Relación de las encomiendas,* p. 26. PNE, VI, 40, 48, 68, 79, 83.

32. ENE, XIII, 8 ff., 34 ff. Dorantes de Carranza, *Sumaria relación,* pp. 309–10.

33. Dorantes de Carranza, *Sumaria relación,* p. 309. AGI, Contaduría, leg. 729, fols. 25r ff.; leg. 735, fols. 12 ff., 24 ff.; leg. 751 (1658).

34. AGI, Justicia, leg. 218, no. 2, ramo 1, fol. 14v.

35. García Pimentel, *Relación,* p. 161. Aiton, "The Secret Visita," p. 17. PNE, VI, 78. ENE, XV, 155. CDIAI, XIV, 205. *Relación de las encomiendas,* p. 17. Dorantes de Carranza, *Sumaria relación,* p. 275.

36. Icaza, *Diccionario autobiográfico,* I, 213. ENE, XV, 212. AGN, Mercedes, vol. 4, fol. 56r; vol. 6, fol. 171r; vol. 7, fol. 16r. ENE, IX, 11. *Relación de las encomiendas,* p. 17. García Pimentel, *Relación,* p. 161.

37. Dorantes de Carranza, *Sumaria relación,* p. 274. PNE, VI, 40.

38. ENE, XIII, 35. Dorantes de Carranza, *Sumaria relación,* pp. 274–75.

39. Dorantes de Carranza, *Sumaria relación,* p. 274. AGI, Contaduría, leg. 729 (1628).

40. AGI, Contaduría, leg. 751 (1658); leg. 768 (1678, Data).

41. AGI, Contaduría, leg. 820 (1), fol. 50v; leg. 840 (1), fols. 279v–280r. For the grant to the Conde de Cifuentes see AGI, México, leg. 636, no. 7, and AGN, Historia, vol. 410, exp. 6.

42. AC, VII, 116. Orozco y Berra, *Noticia histórica de la conjuración.*

43. Conway, *The Last Will and Testament,* pp. 69 ff. Dorantes de Carranza, *Sumaria relación,* pp. 99 ff. Clavigero, *Historia antigua,* III, 317 ff. The principal unpublished source for Coyoacan and its area is AGN, Hospital de Jesús.

44. See Chapter IV, notes 32 ff.

45. Díaz del Castillo, *Historia verdadera,* II, 519–20, 546–47. Dávila Padilla, *Historia,* p. 44. ENE, IV, 21–23, 156. Dorantes de Carranza, *Sumaria relación,* p. 281. CDIHIA, I, 100, 109 ff.

46. CDIAI, XLI, 136–37. CDIU, X, 131.

47. CDIHIA, I, 109 ff.

48. Díaz del Castillo, *Historia verdadera,* II, 519–20, 546–47, 606. CDHM, II, 121–22. CDIHIA, I, 110.

49. CDIU, X, 131. AGI, Justicia, leg. 123, no. 2. CDIAI, XLI, 144. *Cartas de Indias,* pp. 716–17. Suárez de Peralta, *Noticias históricas,* p. 223. Icaza, *Diccionario autobiográfico,* I, 199–200. Dorantes de Carranza, *Sumaria relación,* p. 281. Orozco y Berra, *Noticia histórica de la conjuración,* 2nd pag., p. 33. AGN, Mercedes, vol. 2, fol. 277r. Orozco y Berra, *Noticia histórica de la conjuración,* p. 412, confuses the names and generations.

50. *Relación de las encomiendas,* p. 29.

51. CDIU, XXIV, 73.

52. PNE, I, 190. AC, VI, 76. AGN, Mercedes, vol. 4, fols. 213v–214r. *El libro de las tasaciones,* pp. 149–50, 658. Cervantes de Salazar, *Crónica,* p. 604. ENE, IX, 12–13; X, 113. PCR, Varios papeles, leg. 1, exp. 1, fol. 5r. *Relación de las encomiendas,* p. 29.

53. Orozco y Berra, *Noticia histórica de la conjuración,* pp. 50–51. *El libro de las tasaciones,* p. 149.

54. NCDHM (1941), II, 16. AGI, Contaduría, leg. 743; leg. 768; leg. 816; leg. 820 (2), fol. 370v; leg. 825 (1), fol. 422r.

55. *Archivo mexicano,* I, 235. AC, II, 14–15. Dávila Padilla, *Historia,* p. 44.

56. Aiton, "The Secret Visita," pp. 18–19. Dorantes de Carranza, *Sumaria relación,* p. 294. AGN, Mercedes, vol. 2, fol. 270r. ENE, IX, 8; XV, 212. *Relación de las encomiendas,* p. 16. Juan de Cuevas seems to have signed a document as escribano in 1566. See *El libro de las tasaciones,* p. 653.

57. García Pimentel, *Relación,* p. 159. PNE, VI, 68. NLAC, 1476, fols. 18r ff. UT, JGI-XXIV-8, fol. 2r. ENE, XIII, 8, 35. FHT, VI, 109.

58. AGI, Contaduría, leg. 729, fol. 46r; leg. 735, fols. 24r ff. NLAC, 1476, fols. 24r ff., 39r. Dorantes de Carranza, *Sumaria relación,* p. 295, states that the son and potential heir of Alonso de Cuevas ca. 1604 was Juan de Cuevas. We do not know what happened to him.

59. AGI, Contaduría, leg. 751 (1658). Our statement concerning 1678 derives from the fact that as of that date the crown was not yet paying the salary of the Dominican friar in Cuitlahuac. See AGI, Contaduría, leg. 768 (1678). See also NLAC, 1476, fol. 37r, concerning properties of Alonso de Cuevas e Davalos in Cuitlahuac in 1686.

60. AC, II, 14–15. *Archivo mexicano,* I, 235.

61. ENE, VI, 130, 173; XV, 216. *El libro de las tasaciones,* p. 156. CDIHIA, I, 167. NLAC, 1121, fol. 168r. *Relación de las encomiendas,* p. 19.

62. Bancroft, *History of Mexico,* II, 625–26. Orozco y Berra, *Noticia histórica de la conjuración,* 2nd pag., p. 281.

63. AGI, Justicia, leg. 151, no. 1, fol. 11r. Dorantes de Carranza, *Sumaria relación,* pp. 290, 315–16.

64. García Pimentel, *Relación,* p. 164. PNE, VI, 66. "Culhuacan," p. 171. ENE, XIII, 8, 35. Fernando de Oñate, the son of Cristóbal de Oñate, appears to have been alive in 1604. See Dorantes de Carranza, *Sumaria relación,* p. 315.

65. AGI, Contaduría, leg. 729, fols. 39 ff. *Mercedes y pensiones,* p. 53. Concerning the date ca. 1659, we know that Culhuacan was still in encomienda in 1658 and that it was in the crown in 1660. AGI, Contaduría, leg. 751 (1658). *Mercedes y pensiones,* p. 53.

66. AGI, Justicia, leg. 124, no. 5, exp. 4, fols. 3r ff.; leg. 159, ramo 5.

67. AGI, Escribanía de cámara, leg. 178, exp. 12 (1), fol. 7v; exp. 12 (2), fols. 1v–3r. Fonseca and Urrutia, *Historia,* I, 464. Muriel, "Reflexiones," p. 244. NYPL, Rich, no. 40, fol. 1r–1v. Her name was Leonor, according to the testimony of her son-in-law, Diego Arias de Sotelo. See ENE, IX, 169–70. López de Meneses, "Tecuichpochtzin," pp. 476–77, supposes that both names are correct and that one is appropriate to the period before her confirmation and the other to the period after. This, however, does not seem to explain why different copies of the same document refer to her by different names, and I therefore propose a copyist's error as the explanation.

68. Coatitlan is quite different from Cuauhtitlan, with which it has often been confused. Nor should it be confused with Coatlichan. Cf. Fonseca and Urrutia, *Historia,* I, 464. A more serious problem relates to Tizayuca, which commonly occurs in these texts in the form Tecoyuca. I have rejected the identification with the Tezayuca near Texcoco on two counts: (1) The Diego Huanitzin (Panitzin) letter of 1532 associates Tizayuca and Tolcayuca as sujetos of Ecatepec, an association that strongly supports an argument for the town that we refer to, in this work, as Tizayuca. See Ternaux Compans, *Voyages, relations et mémoires,* VIII, 264. See also the commentary under Tizayuca in this Appendix. (2) The community near Texcoco, referred to throughout this work as Tezayuca, was closely connected with the Texcoco encomienda. Given its history, it seems unlikely that it could have been claimed as an Ecatepec sujeto. See Texcoco in this Appendix. To me, the evidence seems fairly conclusive, although a linger-

ing doubt remains. The fact that both "Tizayuca" and "Tezayuca" were royalized in 1531 appears to be only a coincidence, and not an indication that the references are to the same town.

69. AGI, Justicia, leg. 124, no. 5, exp. 2.

70. CDIHIA, I, 83–84. AGI, Justicia, leg. 124, no. 5. See Chapter IV.

71. See Tizayuca in this Appendix.

72. AGI, Justicia, leg. 124, no. 5, exp. 2.

73. These arguments received expression even in administrative lists of encomiendas. See García Pimentel, *Relación*, p. 160, and *Relación de las encomiendas*, p. 27. The subject is discussed in Chapter IV.

74. AGI, Justicia, leg. 124, no. 5; leg. 159, ramo 5.

75. Fonseca and Urrutia, *Historia*, I, 464. Ternaux Compans, *Voyages, relations et mémoires*, VIII, 264. *El libro de las tasaciones*, p. 139. ENE, IX, 8. García Pimentel, *Relación*, p. 160. Alvarado Tezozomoc, *Crónica mexicayotl*, p. 126. CDIAI, II, 208. López de Meneses, "Tecuichpochtzin," shows that Páez died by 1529 and that Leonor married Valderrama by 1531.

76. Alvarado Tezozomoc, *Crónica mexicayotl*, p. 126. ENE, IX, 8, 169–70; XV, 211. *El libro de las tasaciones*, pp. 139, 178. BAGN, VIII, 205–6. AGN, Mercedes, vol. 5, fol. 95v; vol. 6, fol. 321r; Tierras, vol. 1 (2), fol. 90r. *Relación de las encomiendas*, p. 27. NCDHM (1941), II, 8–9, 16. Muñoz Camargo, *Historia*, p. 289. The genealogies are recorded in Alvarado Tezozomoc, *Crónica mexicayotl*, pp. 126–27, 154–55.

77. AGI, Escribanía de cámara, leg. 178, exp. 12 (1), fol. 7v.

78. AGN, Mercedes, vol. 13, fols. 212v–213r. AGI, México, leg. 287 (1586).

79. AGN, Indios, vol. 5, fol. 309r; vol. 6 (1), fol. 168r.

80. AGI, Escribanía de cámara, leg. 178, exp. 12 (1), fol. 7v. ENE, XIII, 40. Alvarado Tezozomoc, *Crónica mexicayotl*, p. 126.

81. Fonseca and Urrutia, *Historia*, I, 465. AGI, Escribanía de cámara, leg. 178, exp. 12 (1), fols. 1v, 3r, 7v–8r; exp. 12 (2), fols. 6r ff., 170r.

82. AGI, Contaduría, leg. 751 (1658); Escribanía de cámara, leg. 178, exp. 12 (1), fols. 1r ff.

83. Fonseca and Urrutia, *Historia*, I, 465. AGI, Escribanía de cámara, leg. 178, exp. 12 (1).

84. Fonseca and Urrutia, *Historia*, I, 464–65. AGI, Contaduría, leg. 820 (1), fol. 51v; leg. 820 (2), fol. 52r.

85. PNE, I, 110. *El libro de las tasaciones*, pp. 205–6. García Pimentel, *Descripción*, pp. 88 ff. García Pimentel, *Relación*, p. 166. *Relación de las encomiendas*, p. 32. ENE, IX, 16. Icaza, *Diccionario autobiográfico*, I, 205.

86. *El libro de las tasaciones*, pp. 205–6. *Relación de las encomiendas*, p. 32. PNE, I, 110; VI, 12. AC, VI, 76. ENE, IX, 16. García Pimentel, *Descripción*, p. 88. FHT, II, 363.

87. ENE, XIII, 9, 37. Dorantes de Carranza, *Sumaria relación*, p. 163. AGN, Congregaciones, vol. 1, fol. 57v.

88. AGI, Contaduría, leg. 751 (1658).

89. NLAC, 1106, no. 22.

90. AC, II, 14–15. ENE, IV, 19.

91. CDIHIA, I, 176. BAGN, VII, 191.

92. ENE, IV, 19–20; IX, 20. PNE, I, 174. CDIHIA, I, 175 ff. Scholes, *The Diego Ramírez Visita*, pp. 51 ff. Vázquez (Vásquez) de Tapia, *Relación*, p. 59. BNP, no. 27. Boban, *Documents pour servir*, I, 387–89, and *Atlas*, no. 27.

93. The will of the first Bernardino Vásquez de Tapia is dated September 8, 1558. See MNM, Colección antigua, T.3–61, fols. 28r ff. ENE, IX, 20; XIII, 9, 39. *Relación de las encomiendas*, p. 36. García Pimentel, *Relación*, pp. 171–72. AGN, Indios, vol. 2, fol. 215v. Dorantes de Carranza, *Sumaria relación*, pp. 167–68, 439. It would appear that the second Bernardino Vásquez de Tapia was born very late. In 1554, at the age of seventy, his father had no sons or daughters to succeed. See CDIHIA, XIV, 220.

94. Dorantes de Carranza, *Sumaria relación*, pp. 167–68.

95. AGI, Contaduría, leg. 735, fols. 24r ff.

96. This may have begun shortly after 1675 and it may have continued to about 1759. AGI, Contaduría, leg. 820 (1), fol. 51r; leg. 840 (1), fols. 279v–280r. AGN, Historia, vol. 410, exp. 6.

97. *Archivo mexicano*, I, 235.

98. ENE, I, 83–84.

99. AC, II, 14–15. Only for Mexicalzingo do we lack a record of an assignment in private encomienda. Mexicalzingo was placed in the crown in 1531. See *El libro de las tasaciones*, p. 239.

100. AC, VII, 198.

101. AC, II, 153; IV, 179–80; V, 260–61; VI, 399; VIII, 165, 224, 235, 270–71, 284, 317, 508, 570.

102. AC, VIII, 594, 619–20.

103. AGI, Justicia, leg. 218, no. 2, ramo 1, fol. 14v.

104. García Pimentel, *Relación*, pp. 161, 167. AC, II, 108. *Procesos de indios*, p. 41. *El libro de las tasaciones*, p. 587. ENE, VI, 173; IX, 14; XVI, 42–43.

105. ENE, XVI, 42–43. The document implies, but does not state explicitly, that Ana Ruiz was the widow. Ana Ruiz appears not to be the Indian woman from Texcoco, also named Ana, whom Juan de Cuéllar "first married," according to Díaz del Castillo, *Historia verdadera*, II, 524.

106. *El libro de las tasaciones*, p. 588. *Relación de las encomiendas*, p. 31.

107. García Pimentel, *Relación*, p. 167. *El libro de las tasaciones*, p. 588. AGI, Justicia, leg. 218, no. 2, ramo 1, fols. 11r, 42r ff.

108. AGI, México, leg. 28 (1579). PNE, VI, 47. ENE, XIII, 10, 37. Schäfer, *El Consejo real*, I, 352.

109. *Archivo mexicano*, I, 235. Dávila Padilla, *Historia*, p. 44. The references here are to Mezquique and Mezquic, surely meaning Mixquic and not Mixcoac. Equivalent spellings may be found in FHT, VII, 92, and *Relación de las encomiendas*, p. 43. Cf. Kubler, *Mexican Architecture*, I, 139–40.

110. ENE, IX, 31. *Relación de las encomiendas*, p. 43. García Pimentel, *Relación*, p. 170.

111. BAGN, VII, 191.

112. ENE, XV, 212. *Relación de las encomiendas*, pp. 43–44.

113. AGI, Indiferente general, leg. 1529, fol. 155r; Patronato, leg. 182, ramo 44, fol. 1r. García Pimentel, *Relación*, pp. 170–71.

114. ENE, XIII, 38. AGI, Contaduría, leg. 729, fols. 44r ff.; leg. 735, fols. 24r ff.; leg. 751 (Tributos).

115. AGI, Contaduría, leg. 816 (Tributos); leg. 820 (1), fol. 51r; leg. 820 (2), fol. 52v.

116. AGI, Justicia, leg. 134, no. 1. *Nuevos documentos relativos a los bienes*, pp. 63 ff. CDIAI, XII, 279. *Documentos inéditos relativos a Hernán Cortés*, pp. 346–47.

117. Cortés, *Cartas y otros documentos,* pp. 32–33. CDIAI, XII, 560–61.

118. ENE, VIII, 149–50. AGI, Contaduría, leg. 751 (1658).

119. BAGN, VII, 222.

120. AGI, Contaduría, leg. 820 (2), fols. 370v–371r. Fonseca and Urrutia, *Historia,* I, 456.

121. ENE, IV, 157. *Relación de las encomiendas,* p. 39. In ENE, IV, 157, it is implied that Diego de Ocampo had two sujetos of Otumba. If so, we do not know what the second sujeto was. The reference may be to Tlalistaca, which was not a sujeto of Otumba but which was sufficiently near to engage in land disputes with Ahuatepec, which was a sujeto of Otumba. See AGN, Mercedes, vol. 1, fol. 84r.

122. ENE, IV, 157; IX, 25. *Relación de las encomiendas,* p. 39.

123. ENE, IX, 25; XIII, 39. AGN, Mercedes, vol. 8, fol. 82r. NCDHM (1941), II, 14.

124. AGI, Contaduría, leg. 768 (1678, Servicio Real).

125. NLAC, 1106, no. 22.

126. ENE, XIII, 242.

127. ENE, XV, 137–39. Prescott, *History of the Conquest of Mexico,* III, 446–50. López de Meneses, "Tecuichpochtzin," pp. 473 ff. *Archivo mexicano,* II, 241 ff. CDIU, XVIII, 51. NYPL, Rich, no. 40, fols. 1v, 3v ff. BNM, MS no. 46, fols. 299v–300r. AGN, Historia, vol. 4, exp. 4, fols. 37v ff. AGI, Justicia, leg. 165, no. 2, fols. 52r ff. NLAC, 1168, no. 4, no. 7.

128. Tula and its estancias remained in Pedro Montezuma and later passed to his son, Diego Luis Montezuma, and to other descendants. NCDHM (1941), III, 255. ENE, XIII, 38. There exists an enormous documentation on this encomienda in AGI, Patronato, leg. 245, and in AGN, Vínculos, as well as in other sections of these same archives.

129. Cortés's statement is published in Prescott, *History of the Conquest of Mexico,* III, 446 ff., and in Muriel, "Reflexiones," pp. 241 ff. See also AGN, Historia, vol. 4, exp. 4, fols. 37v ff.; BNM, MS no. 46, fols. 299v–300r; NLAC, 1168, no. 7.

130. Oviedo y Valdés, *Historia general y natural,* III, 549. NCDHM (1941), III, 240 ff., 277. CDIAI, XXVII, 359; XXVIII, 45. Díaz del Castillo, *Historia verdadera,* II, 522. NYPL, Rich, no. 40, fol. 1v. NLAC, 1168, no. 4. CDIU, XVIII, 51. *Archivo mexicano,* II, 241, 244. García Pimentel, *Relación,* pp. 161–62.

131. López de Meneses, "Tecuichpochtzin," pp. 475–76. *Archivo mexicano,* II, 242 ff. NYPL, Rich, no. 40, fols. 3v–4v.

132. Ixtlilxochitl, *Historia,* pp. 306–7. Oviedo y Valdés, *Historia general y natural,* III, 549. García Pimentel, *Relación,* pp. 161–62. ENE, V, 62–63. NLAC, 1168, no. 4. López de Gómara, *Historia,* II, 221.

133. López de Meneses, "Tecuichpochtzin," pp. 475, 480, 489 ff., 495. CDIAI, XXVI, 424; XXVII, 359. NLAC, 1168, no. 4. AC, II, 67. NCDHM (1941), III, 277.

134. CDIU, XVIII, 43. López de Meneses, "Tecuichpochtzin," p. 478.

135. AC, II, 67. PNE, I, 291. CDIHIA, I, 194. ENE, IX, 11–12.

136. AGI, Justicia, leg. 181, fols. 202v ff. López de Meneses, "Tecuichpochtzin," pp. 489–94. NYPL, Rich, no. 40, fols. 2v–3v. Cuesta and Delgado, "Pleitos cortesianos," pp. 260–62.

137. NYPL, Rich, no. 40, fols. 3v–4v.

138. AGN, Mercedes, vol. 8, fol. 214v. García Pimentel, *Descripción,* pp. 230 ff. NCDHM (1941), II, 9. García Pimentel, *Relación,* pp. 161–6.

139. AGI, Justicia, leg. 181, exp. 1. López de Meneses, "Tecuichpochtzin," p. 492. López de Meneses, "Dos nietos," pp. 88, 94–96. AGN, Historia, vol. 4, exp. 4, fols. 37v ff.

140. AGI, Justicia, leg. 181, exp. 1. AGN, Historia, vol. 4, exp. 4.

141. There exists a huge documentation on this subject. See Fonseca and Urrutia, *Historia*, I, 455 ff.; Villa-señor y Sánchez, *Theatro americano*, I, 74; Ortega y Pérez Gallardo, *Historia genealógica*, II, 4–7; BNM, MS no. 455, fol. 216v; BNP, no. 258, fol. 12v. The genealogies and related documents receive massive attention in AGI, Indiferente general, leg. 1615; Patronato, leg. 245; numerous legajos of Justicia and Contaduría; and AGN, Vínculos.

142. See the Relación de la genealogía and the Origen de los mexicanos in NCDHM (1941), III, 240 ff., 256 ff. CDIU, XVIII, 51–52. ENE, V, 62–63. AGI, Patronato, leg. 181, ramos 8–9; leg. 245.

143. AGI, Patronato, leg. 245.

144. Fonseca and Urrutia, *Historia*, I, 259 ff.

145. See López de Meneses, "Tecuichpochtzin," p. 492; López de Meneses, "Dos nietos," p. 86.

146. See again for this the materials cited in note 141.

147. Prescott, *History of the Conquest of Mexico*, III, 449–50. AGN, Historia, vol. 4, exp. 4, fols. 37v ff. Muriel, "Reflexiones," pp. 241 ff. López de Meneses, "Tecuichpochtzin," pp. 473 ff. BNM, MS no. 46, fols. 299v–300r. See also the Antonio Cortés letter of 1566 in AGI, Justicia, leg. 1029, no. 10, and the testament of Antonio Cortés in BNP, no. 115. Cortés's reference to other Tacuba sujetos assigned in encomienda to Spaniards would apply to Teocalhueyacan in the Valley of Mexico, but probably not so early as 1526. See AGI, Justicia, leg. 165, no. 2, fols. 52r ff.

148. ENE, XIV, 118 ff.

149. Villa-señor y Sánchez, *Theatro americano*, I, 74. AGN, Tributos, vol. 7, exp. 16. Both Tlazala and Xilotzingo were ordered abandoned in the Tlalnepantla congregación in 1603. See AGN, Congregaciones, vol. 1, fol. 47r.

150. AGN, Mercedes, vol. 8, fol. 138r.

151. AGN, Mercedes, vol. 4, fols. 28r, 45r; vol. 9, fols. 191v–192r; vol. 13, fols. 93v–94r; Hospital de Jesús, vol. 344, exp. 1. Vetancurt, *Chronica*, p. 70.

152. AGN, Mercedes, vol. 8, fol. 153v.

153. AGN, General de parte, vol. 2, fols. 233v–234r; Indios, vol. 1, fols. 86v–87v; Mercedes, vol. 7, fol. 295r; vol. 8, fol. 127r.

154. AGN, Mercedes, vol. 5, fols. 20v, 95v.

155. CDIHIA, I, 194. Barlow, *The Extent of the Empire of the Culhua Mexica*, p. 35.

156. AGI, Justicia, leg. 165, no. 2, fols. 52r ff., 115r ff., 142v ff.

157. See Chapter III, note 85.

158. See citations in López de Meneses, "Tecuichpochtzin," pp. 481–82, 484. NYPL, Rich, no. 40, fols. 2r ff. AGI, Escribanía de cámara, leg. 178, exp. 12 (1), fol. 8r–8v.

159. AGI, Escribanía de cámara, leg. 178, exp. 12 (1), fol. 8r–8v. López de Meneses, "Tecuichpochtzin," pp. 492–93. García Pimentel, *Descripción*, p. 231. NYPL, Rich, no. 40, fols. 2v–3v. NLAC, 1168, no. 4, no. 7. AGI, Justicia, leg. 181, exp. 1 (1576).

160. For the possible connection with Tlatelolco see Chapter III, note 61. AGI, Justicia, leg. 204, no. 2, ramo 1. *El libro de las tasaciones*, p. 367. Icaza, *Diccionario autobiográfico*, I, 117–18. Dorantes de Carranza, *Sumaria relación*, p. 205.

161. AGI, Justicia, leg. 204, no. 2, ramo 1. AGN, Mercedes, vol. 1, fol. 49r; vol. 3, fol. 330r. Icaza, *Diccionario autobiográfico*, I, 117–18. ENE, VI, 133–37; XV, 211–12; XVI, 44–45. PNE, I, 198. *El libro de las tasaciones*, p. 368.

162. Puga, *Provisiones*, fol. 150v. ENE, VI, 128–29, 131–37.

163. AGI, Justicia, leg. 204, no. 2, ramo 1. Torquemada, *Monarchia indiana*, I, 620. Muñoz Camargo, *Historia*, p. 288.

164. AGI, Justicia, leg. 204, no. 2, ramo 1. *El libro de las tasaciones*, p. 367.

165. AGI, Patronato, leg. 182, ramo 44, fol. 2r; Contaduría, leg. 751 (1658); leg. 786B. AGN, Mercedes, vol. 5, fols. 105v–106r. Torquemada, *Monarchia indiana*, I, 620.

166. AGI, Justicia, leg. 208, no. 3. BAGN, VII, 204. CDIAI, II, 238. *El libro de las tasaciones*, p. 390.

167. AGI, Justicia, leg. 208, no. 3. CDIHE, XXVI, 336–37. CDIAI, II, 190. The third was Tonala. Cf. Icaza, *Diccionario autobiográfico*, II, 256–57.

168. Dorantes de Carranza, *Sumaria relación*, pp. 264, 289.

169. CDHM, II, 69.

170. ENE, IV, 81; XV, 92–93. AGN, Mercedes, vol. 2, fols. 300r ff., 331r–331v. CDIHE, XXVI, 336. AGI, Justicia, leg. 208, no. 3. *El libro de las tasaciones*, p. 390.

171. AGI, Justicia, leg. 208, no. 3.

172. AGI, Contaduría, leg. 751 (1658); leg. 768 (1678).

173. CDIAI, XXVIII, 324.

174. AGI, Justicia, leg. 165, no. 2, fols. 52r ff. ENE, XIV, 118. See Chapter III, notes 111 ff. Dorantes de Carranza, *Sumaria relación*, pp. 263, 289. García Pimentel, *Relación*, p. 182. *Relación de las encomiendas*, pp. 46–47.

175. CDIAI, XXVIII, 356, 405; XXXII, 444 ff.; XLI, 188 ff. López de Meneses, "El primer regreso," p. 75. Fernández del Castillo, "Alonso de Estrada," pp. 406 ff.

176. CDIAI, II, 194; XXXII, 444 ff. AGI, Justicia, leg. 213, no. 4, fol. 1r–1v. Puga, *Provisiones*, fol. 118v. AGN, Mercedes, vol. 1, fol. 132r. Icaza, *Diccionario autobiográfico*, I, 219–20. Cf. Fernández del Castillo, "Alonso de Estrada," pp. 403, 407.

177. *Relación de las encomiendas*, pp. 46–47. García Pimentel, *Relación*, p. 182. NCDHM (1941), II, 10. Jorge de Alvarado was dead by 1550. AGN, Mercedes, vol. 3, fol. 74v. Dorantes de Carranza, *Sumaria relación*, p. 264. Cf. Icaza, *Diccionario autobiográfico*, I, 103.

178. See Dorantes de Carranza, *Sumaria relación*, p. 279.

179. García Pimentel, *Relación*, p. 182. NCDHM (1941), II, 10. CDIHIA, I, 360. AGI, Justicia, leg. 213, no. 4; Patronato, leg. 181, ramo 21, fol. 4r. *Relación de las encomiendas*, pp. 46–47.

180. Martínez Cosío, *Los caballeros*, pp. 40–41. AGN, Mercedes, vol. 10, fol. 96v; General de parte, vol. 2, fol. 206v.

181. Dorantes de Carranza, *Sumaria relación*, pp. 196, 280, 451. ENE, XIII, 40.

182. AGI, Contaduría, leg. 729, fol. 44v.

183. *Mercedes y pensiones*, pp. 47 ff., 96.

184. *Mercedes y pensiones*, p. 144.

185. AGN, Indios, vol. 50, fols. 2r–6r. See also AGI, Contaduría, leg. 751 (1658); leg. 816 (Encomienda); 817 (Tributos); leg. 820 (1), fol. 56v.

186. CDIAI, XXVIII, 410. Cortés, *Cartas*, II, 129.

187. *Relación de las encomiendas*, p. 30. Icaza, *Diccionario autobiográfico*, I, 196–97. PNE, I, 113. CDIAI, VI, 493. ENE, VI, 173; VII, 61; IX, 14. NCDHM (1941), I, 87. Guzmán, "Un manuscrito," p. 99. Gamio, *La población del valle de Teotihuacan*, I (2), 501.

188. NCDHM (1941), I, 85; II, 13. García Pimentel, *Relación*, p. 163.

189. García Pimentel, *Relación*, p. 163. PNE, VI, 219. NCDHM (1941), III, 53. ENE, XIII, 9, 40. AGI, México, leg. 287 (1586).

190. Dorantes de Carranza, *Sumaria relación*, p. 107. CDIHE, IV, 237.

191. CDIHE, IV, 237. Dorantes de Carranza, *Sumaria relación*, p. 182. Lists of the encomiendas possessed by him in the period 1617–20 may be found in AGN, Indios, vol. 7, fol. 116v; vol. 9, fol. 139r–139v.

192. AGI, Contaduría, leg. 751 (1658); leg. 768 (1678).

193. Fonseca and Urrutia, *Historia*, I, 459–60.

194. *Códice Kingsborough*, fols. 215r ff. AGI, Justicia, leg. 108, no. 4, fols. 2r ff.

195. AGI, Justicia, leg. 108, no. 4; leg. 117, no. 5.

196. García Pimentel, *Relación*, p. 174.

197. The suit is recorded in AGI, Justicia, leg. 151, no. 1.

198. AC, VI, 145. ENE, IX, 25; XIII, 9, 41. NLAC, 1121, fol. 316r. *Relación de las encomiendas*, p. 40. AGN, Indios, vol. 3, fol. 41r. Dorantes de Carranza, *Sumaria relación*, pp. 289–90.

199. AGI, Justicia, leg. 159, no. 2.

200. Juan Velázquez de Salazar was still living in the early seventeenth century but had no male heirs. See Dorantes de Carranza, *Sumaria relación*, p. 290. Fonseca and Urrutia, *Historia*, I, 455–57. NLAC, 1106, no. 22. AGI, Contaduría, leg. 729, fol. 45v; leg. 735, fols. 24r ff.

201. Fonseca and Urrutia, *Historia*, I, 457.

202. AGI, Justicia, leg. 164, no. 2, fols. 50r ff. García Pimentel, *Relación*, p. 175. *Relación de las encomiendas*, p. 41. ENE, IX, 26.

203. E.g., AGI, Justicia, leg. 208, no. 4.

204. AGI, Justicia, leg. 164, no. 2, fols. 50r ff.; leg. 208, no. 4, sep. pag., fols. 11r–11v, 217v.

205. AGI, Justicia, leg. 208, no. 4, sep. pag., fol. 11v. *Relación de las encomiendas*, p. 41. García Pimentel, *Relación*, p. 175. Dorantes de Carranza, *Sumaria relación*, p. 298. AGN, Mercedes, vol. 2, fols. 323v–324r. PNE, I, 198. ENE, VI, 173; IX, 26; XV, 216.

206. ENE, IX, 26; XVI, 90. Dorantes de Carranza, *Sumaria relación*, p. 298. García Pimentel, *Relación*, p. 175. García Pimentel, *Descripción*, p. 56. PNE, VI, 231.

207. AGI, Justicia, leg. 208, no. 4.

208. ENE, XIII, 41. Dorantes de Carranza, *Sumaria relación*, pp. 298–99.

209. AGI, Contaduría, leg. 768 (1678).

210. *El libro de las tasaciones*, p. 415. NLAC, 1121, fol. 62r–62v. Millares Carlo and Mantecón, *Indice y extractos de los protocolos*, I, 65 ff., identifies the *bachiller* as Juan de Ortega.

211. BAGN, XI, 213. García Pimentel, *Descripción*, p. 82. AGI, Contaduría, leg. 729, fols. 34r ff.; leg. 743; leg. 768 (1678). *El libro de las tasaciones*, p. 227. Dorantes de Carranza, *Sumaria relación*, pp. 436–37. AGN, Indios, vol. 3, fol. 69r.

212. AGI, Indiferente general, leg. 1529, fol. 206r. García Pimentel, *Relación*, p. 179. *Relación de las encomiendas*, p. 42.

213. PNE, I, 198. ENE, IX, 29. BAGN, XI, 212.

214. ENE, IX, 29; XIII, 41; XVI, 91. BAGN, XI, 212. García Pimentel, *Relación*, p. 179. AGI, Indiferente general, leg. 1529, fol. 206r; Patronato, leg. 182, ramo 44, fol. 2r.

215. AGI, México, leg. 325.

216. AGI, México, leg. 325; Contaduría, leg. 751 (1658); leg. 763 (1671). *Moderación de doctrinas*, p. 64.

217. Gardiner, *Martín López*, pp. 56 ff.

218. Dorantes de Carranza, *Sumaria relación*, p. 385. ENE, IX, 26. García Pimentel,

Relación, p. 174. *Relación de las encomiendas,* p. 41. AGN, Mercedes, vol. 2, fols. 118v–119r.

219. Gardiner, *Martín López,* pp. 168–69.

220. Gardiner, *Martín López,* pp. 114, 152. FHT, III, 132–33; V, 206–7. Dorantes de Carranza, *Sumaria relación,* pp. 215–16.

221. ENE, XIII, 40; AGN, Indios, vol. 9, fol. 19r. MNM, Colección antigua, T.2–57, fol. 9r.

222. PNE, I, 207. ENE, IX, 26; XIII, 10. *Relación de las encomiendas,* p. 41. García Pimentel, *Descripción,* p. 72.

223. AGI, Contaduría, leg. 751 (1658); México, leg. 326 (1666).

224. AGI, Contaduría, leg. 768 (Espiritual); leg. 816 (Encomienda).

225. *Sobre el modo de tributar,* p. 97. *El libro de las tasaciones,* p. 482. NCDHM (1941), III, 5. Cervantes de Salazar, *Crónica,* p. 573. See Chapter III, note 89.

226. Cortés, *Cartas y relaciones,* p. 331. CDHM, I, 476. *Archivo mexicano,* I, 167, 204, 240, 269, 449; II, 140. CDIAI, XII, 264; XXVII, 22, 33, 40, 380, 512; XXVIII, 175.

227. CDIAI, XII, 279; XXVII, 85. Cortés, *Cartas y otros documentos,* pp. 32–33.

228. CDIAI, XXVIII, 323 ff. Mendieta, *Historia,* pp. 296–97. Torquemada, *Monarchia indiana,* III, 191.

229. ENE, I, 141. CDIAI, XXVII, 85.

230. *Archivo mexicano,* I, 167.

231. *El libro de las tasaciones,* p. 481.

232. BAGN, VII, 220.

233. Grijalva, *Crónica,* fol. 50r.

234. E.g., AGN, Indios, vol. 2, fol. 99v.

235. García Pimentel, *Relación,* p. 158. *Relación de las encomiendas,* p. 40. Dorantes de Carranza, *Sumaria relación,* pp. 310–11.

236. CDHM, II, 80. García Pimentel, *Relación,* p. 158.

237. Icaza, *Diccionario autobiográfico,* p. 199. PNE, I, 203. ENE, IX, 25; XV, 212. *Relación de las encomiendas,* p. 40.

238. PNE, III, 81–82. Dorantes de Carranza, *Sumaria relación,* p. 311. García Pimentel, *Relación,* p. 158. AGI, Patronato, leg. 182, ramo 44, fol. 2v.

239. ENE, XIII, 10. Identification of Tezontepec de Pachuca here may be made by comparison with ENE, XIII, 41.

240. Dorantes de Carranza, *Sumaria relación,* p. 311.

241. AGI, Contaduría, leg. 751 (1658).

242. See Chapter III, notes 38 and 58. See also Ecatepec in this Appendix.

243. CDIAI, XXVII, 154. There remains a possibility that the Manuel de Guzmán grant related to Tezayuca rather than Tizayuca. Both were royalized in 1531. See *El libro de las tasaciones,* pp. 471, 481.

244. Cortés specifically listed Tizayuca in the Ecatepec grant. For our reasons for identifying this as Tizayuca rather than Tezayuca see Ecatepec, note 68, in this Appendix.

245. *El libro de las tasaciones,* p. 471.

246. Diego Panitzin also accompanied Cortés on the expedition to the south. Ternaux Compans, *Voyages, relations et mémoires,* VIII, 264.

247. ENE, VIII, 35–36. *El libro de las tasaciones,* p. 472. García Pimentel, *Descripción,* p. 53. CDIAI, IX, 208.

248. PNE, I, 203–4. ENE, IX, 33; XIII, 41. *Relación de las encomiendas,* p. 45. García

Pimentel, *Relación*, p. 176. García Pimentel, *Descripción*, p. 55. *El libro de las tasaciones*, p. 523. CDIAI, IX, 208. AGI, Contaduría, leg. 751 (1658).

249. *Archivo mexicano*, I, 204, 240, 269; II, 140. AGI, Justicia, leg. 124, no. 5, exp. 2.
250. ENE, IX, 27. AGN, Mercedes, vol. 2, fol. 190r. García Pimentel, *Relación*, p. 181. *Relación de las encomiendas*, p. 41.
251. AGI, Justicia, leg. 131, no. 1. *Relación de las encomiendas*, p. 41. AGN, Mercedes, vol. 2, fols. 86r, 190r. ENE, IX, 27. *El libro de las tasaciones*, p. 530.
252. García Pimentel, *Relación*, p. 181. *El libro de las tasaciones*, pp. 542–43. García Pimentel, *Descripción*, p. 59. NCDHM (1941), p. 16.
253. ENE, XIII, 10, 41. García Pimentel, *Relación*, p. 181. NCDHM (1941), II, 16–17. *El libro de las tasaciones*, p. 539.
254. García Pimentel, *Relación*, p. 181. ENE, XIII, 41. Torquemada, *Monarchia indiana*, I, 756. AGI, México, leg. 287; Contaduría, leg. 729, fols. 24r ff.; leg. 763 (1671).
255. AGI, Contaduría, leg. 816 (Tributos).
256. *Relación de las encomiendas*, p. 49. García Pimentel, *Relación*, p. 174. ENE, IX, 37.
257. AGN, Mercedes, vol. 3, fol. 171r. PNE, I, 297. García Pimentel, *Relación*, p. 174. ENE, IX, 37. *Relación de las encomiendas*, p. 49.
258. ENE, IX, 37. *Relación de las encomiendas*, p. 49.
259. ENE, XIII, 43.
260. AGI, México, leg. 325.
261. NLAC, 1106, no. 22.
262. CDIAI, XIII, 293–94.
263. ENE, I, 146.
264. CDIAI, II, 245, 255, 257.
265. BAGN, VIII, 188–89. *El libro de las tasaciones*, p. 304.
266. Icaza, *Diccionario autobiográfico*, I, 103–4. Dorantes de Carranza, *Sumaria relación*, pp. 263–64.
267. See the request of Luis de Moscoso in 1543 in ENE, IV, 62–63.
268. AGN, Hospital de Jesús, vol. 156, exp. 1; exp. 8; vol. 325, exp. 5.

APPENDIX III

1. Xochimilco: AGN, Padrones, vol. 29, fol. 3r. Coyoacan: AGN, Padrones, vol. 6, fol. 1r. Tacuba: AGN, Padrones, vol. 6, fol. 145r. Cuauhtitlan: AGN, Padrones, vol. 4, fol. 240r. Citlaltepec: AGN, Historia, vol. 72, exp. 6, fol. 1r. Teotihuacan: AGN, Padrones, vol. 18, fol. 307r. Otumba: AGN, Padrones, vol. 12, fol. 142r. Coatepec: AGN, Padrones, vol. 3, fol. 1v. Each map is accompanied by a list of communities.
2. Texcoco: AGN, Padrones, vol. 14, fols. 190r–191v; vol. 43, fol. 5r–5v. Ecatepec: AGN, Padrones, vol. 6, fol. 319r–319v; vol. 47, fols. 1r ff. Another excellent list for Ecatepec is in BNM, MS no. 451, fols. 294r ff.
3. E.g., towns of the Chalco jurisdiction are listed in AGN, Tierras, vol. 1518, exp. 1, fols. 22r ff., and haciendas of the Chalco jurisdiction are listed in AA, Pósito y alhóndiga, vol. 2, exp. 65, fol. 13r. Some Mexicalzingo communities are recorded in AHH, Tributos, leg. 225, exp. 29.
4. Bentura Beleña, *Recopilación sumaria*, II, sep. pag., vii ff.
5. The intendancy map is reproduced in Navarro García, *Intendancias en Indias*,

lám. XII. For various full and partial lists of the subdelegaciones after the introduction of the intendancies see BAGN, II, 328 ff.; *Real ordenanza*; *El segundo conde de Revilla Gigedo*, pp. 25 ff.; Zúñiga y Ontiveros, *Calendario manual*, pp. 119 ff.; AGN, Tributos, vol. 16, exp. 13.

6. The Ramón del Moral map is reproduced in Apenas, *Mapas antiguos*, lám. 32.

7. AGN, General de parte, vol. 2, fols. 80v, 196r, 261r. BNM, MS no. 1312, fol. 35v. See also Chapter II, note 36.

8. AGI, México, leg. 665, cuad. 2, fol. 98r–98v. AGN, Indios, vol. 9, fol. 41r–41v; Tierras, vol. 2825, exp. 6, 2nd pag.

9. AGN, Tierras, vol. 1518, exp. 1, fols. 22r ff.; Padrones, vol. 3, fol. 1v. AA, Pósito y alhóndiga, vol. 2, exp. 65, fol. 13r.

10. AGN, Indios, vol. 3, fol. 196r; vol. 6 (1), fols. 65v, 322v. Tlalpam (San Agustín de las Cuevas) was usurped from Xochimilco by Coyoacan in the sixteenth century. See CDIAI, XIII, 295. Tepepan was established by Indians of Xochimilco to prevent intrusion by a Spanish landowner. See Vetancurt, *Chronica*, p. 86.

11. AGN, Padrones, vol. 29, fols. 3r ff.

12. PNE, VI, 193 ff. AGN, General de parte, vol. 1, fols. 36v–37r. Villa-señor y Sánchez, *Theatro americano*, I, 61–62. Durán, *Historia*, I, 32. AHH, Tributos, leg. 225, exp. 29.

13. PNE, VI, 39 ff.

14. AGN, Padrones, vol. 3, fols. 1v ff.

15. Thus the Texcoco jurisdiction to the 1570's included Teotihuacan and Temascalapa. NCDHM (1941), I, 86. Guzmán, "Un manuscrito," p. 99. García Pimentel, *Descripción*, p. 64.

16. FHT, I, 108–9. AGN, Mercedes, vol. 5, fol. 94r. For the sixteenth-century limits of Tlaxcala see Gibson, *Tlaxcala*, pp. 6 ff. Calpulalpan, Soltepec, and a number of other communities, all in the modern state of Tlaxcala, were within Texcoco jurisdiction in the colonial period. AGN, Padrones, vol. 14, fols. 190r–191v; vol. 43, fol. 5r–5v.

17. For the jurisdiction of Teotihuacan, including Acolman, in the late sixteenth century see PNE, VI, 209 ff. By 1709 Ixtlahuaca, a sujeto of Acolman, appears to be recorded in the Texcoco jurisdiction. See PCR, Varios papeles, vol. 2, fol. 78r. The dating of the change remains to be established more exactly.

18. AGN, Padrones, vol. 14, fols. 190r–191v; vol. 43, fol. 5r–5v. The three Indian towns, Zacatepec, Ixtlahuaca, and Chiapa, were former sujetos of Acolman. See AGI, Justicia, leg. 208, no. 4, 2nd pag., fol. 216v; Indiferente general, leg. 1529, fol. 205v; AGN, Congregaciones, vol. 1, fols. 19v–20r, 59v–60r; PCR, Varios papeles, vol. 2, fol. 78r; PNE, VI, 210; ENE, XVI, 90.

19. AGN, Padrones, vol. 14, fols. 190r–191v; vol. 43, fol. 5r–5v.

20. AGN, Indios, vol. 4, fols. 184v–185r.

21. AGN, Congregaciones, vol. 1, fols. 30v ff.

22. AGN, Padrones, vol. 12, fols. 142r ff.

23. PNE, VI, 209 ff.

24. AGN, Padrones, vol. 18, fol. 308r–308v.

25. AGN, Padrones, vol. 18, fols. 307r ff.

26. See AGN, Hospital de Jesús, vol. 329, exp. 2.

27. AGN, Mercedes, vol. 10, fols. 96v–97v; vol. 11, fols. 27v–28r, 49r–49v, 88v–89r, 104r–104v, 197v–198r; vol. 14, fols. 176r–176v, 181r–181v, 186v–188r; vol. 16, fols. 64v–65r.

28. AA, Tierras y ejidos, leg. 2, exp. 29, fol. 5r. For unexplained reasons Villa-señor y Sánchez, *Theatro americano*, I, 72-73, discusses Los Remedios under Coyoacan rather than under Tacuba.

29. AGN, Padrones, vol. 6, fols. 1r ff.

30. AGN, Indios, vol. 1, fol. 87v; vol. 3, fols. 30v, 154v; vol. 6 (1), fols. 4r, 14r; General de parte, vol. 1, fol. 98r; vol. 2, fols. 233v, 234r; Mercedes, vol. 8, fol. 127r. MNM, Colección franciscana, leg. 190, fol. 12r.

31. AGN, Indios, vol. 50, fols. 59r-60v; Padrones, vol. 6, fols. 196r ff., 201r ff. Villa-señor y Sánchez, *Theatro americano*, I, 77.

32. AGN, Padrones, vol. 6, fols. 145r ff.

33. García Pimentel, *Descripción*, p. 94.

34. Villa-señor y Sánchez, *Theatro americano*, I, 81, 84-85.

35. AGN, Padrones, vol. 4, fols. 240r ff.

36. PNE, VI, 167 ff.

37. AGN, Tierras, vol. 2825, exp. 6, 2nd pag.; Congregaciones, vol. 1, fols. 91r-91v, 101v-102r; Indios, vol. 12 (1), fols. 83v-84v; vol. 17, fols. 151v-152r, 212v. PNE, II, 34. FHT, VII, 62-64. What appears to have been the most northern of these estancias, Santa Ana Zacatlan, was probably in the Pachuca jurisdiction. Its location is identified one-half league west of Tizayuca. García Pimentel, *Descripción*, p. 58.

38. AGN, Padrones, vol. 6, fol. 319r-319v; vol. 47, fols. 1r ff. BNM, MS no. 41, fol. 294r.

39. AGN, Mercedes, vol. 12, fols. 56v, 209r-209v; vol. 13, fols. 244v-245r; vol. 19, fol. 137r-137v. García Pimentel, *Descripción*, p. 94. It will be noted that the "Relación de Tequixquiac, Citlaltepec y Xilocingo" does not include Zumpango in the late sixteenth century.

40. See above, note 34. The late colonial map and list are in AGN, Historia, vol. 72, exp. 6, fols. 1r ff.

41. *Instrucciones que los vireyes de Nueva España dejaron* (1867), p. 21. For a history of the office of corregidor in the city see Romero de Terreros, "Los corregidores de México," pp. 84 ff.

42. Vetancurt, *Chronica*, p. 70. León y Gama, "Descripción," p. 54. AHH, Tributos, leg. 225, exp. 29.

43. García Pimentel, *Descripción*, p. 63. AGN, Indios, vol. 2, fol. 99v; vol. 4, fol. 192r; General de parte, vol. 4, fols. 17v-18r. Villa-señor y Sánchez, *Theatro americano*, I, 145-47.

44. PNE, VI, 12 ff.

45. Villa-señor y Sánchez, *Theatro americano*, I, 138-41.

46. The circular district is mapped in Almonte, *Guía de forasteros*, fac. p. 288, and in the Ramón del Moral map, Apenas, *Mapas antiguos*, lám. 32.

47. These changes are the subject of abundant record in the nineteenth century. They are summarized in García Cubas, *Diccionario*, IV, 62 *et passim*.

Glossary

Acequia real. Main (royal) canal
Achcacauhtin. Subordinate officers of a calpulli or town
Agravio. Injury, offense
Ají. Chile
Albarradón. Dike
Alcabala. Sales tax
Alcalde. Judge and cabildo member
Alcalde mayor. Spanish official in charge of a district
Alcaldía mayor. District or jurisdiction of an alcalde mayor
Aldea. Village; small town
Alguacil. Constable
Alhóndiga. Municipal storehouse and grain market
Almud. One-twelfth of a fanega
Altepetl. Town
Altepetlalli. Town land
Amo. Master, proprietor
Ancianos. Elders
Anexo (anejo). Dependent church
Arancel. Ecclesiastical fee list
Arriería. Mule-train transport
Arriero. Muleteer
Arroyo. Small stream or stream bed
Asentista. Contractor
Asistencia. Dependent church
Atlatl. Throwing stick
Atole. Beverage made from maize
Audiencia. Court and governing body under the viceroy, or the area
  of its jurisdiction
Auto de fe. Auto-da-fé; act of ceremonial ecclesiastical sentencing,
  or the resulting punishment
Axolotl. Larval salamander
Balcarrotas. Indian hair style
Baldías. Vacant or public lands
Bando. Proclamation

Barranca. Ravine
Barrio. Town subdivision
Braza. Unit of measure; commonly two varas
Caballería. Unit of agricultural land; about 105 acres
Cabecera. Head town
Cabildo. Municipal council
Cacica. Female cacique
Cacicazgo. Estate or institution of cacique rule
Cacique. Indian chief or local ruler
Caja de comunidad. Community strongbox or treasury
Calabaza. Squash, gourd
Calmecac. Pre-conquest school
Calpixqui (pl. *calpixque*). Tax collector and administrative official
Calpullalli. Land belonging to a calpulli
Calpulli (pl. *calpultin*). Territorial unit or the group of families occupying it
Camellón. Chinampa
Cantores. Singers
Capilla. Chapel
Capitán. Captain
Carga. Load, generally of two fanegas
Carnicería. Slaughterhouse or meat market
Casa de rentero. Household of a subordinate or tenant
Casas de comunidad. Building for community government
Casas reales. "Royal houses"; the principal political building of a town
Cédula. Royal or other order
Celemín. Unit of dry measure; commonly one almud
Chía. Sage
Chinampa. Aquatic garden
Chinancalli. Calpulli
Choza. Hut
Cihuacoatl. "Snake woman," title of Aztec official
Cihuapilli. Female pilli
Ciudad. City
Coatequitl. Indian institution of labor assignment
Cobradores de tributos. Tribute collectors
Cofradía. Sodality
Colegio. College or school
Comal (*comalli*). Griddle
Compadrazgo. Relationship through godparents
Compadre. Godparent
Composición. Legalization of land title

Común. Community, or the total population of a community

Comunidad. Community

Concesión real. Royal concession

Congregación. Congregation or concentration of scattered populations

Contador. Accountant

Convento. Monastery

Corregidor. Spanish officer in charge of a district

Corregimiento. Institution, office, or jurisdiction of a corregidor

Coyote. Coyote; person of mixed Indian and Negro ancestry

Cuartel. Quarter or district of a town

Cuartillo. One-fourth, especially of an almud or a real

Cuauhtlatoani. Military ruler

Cubo. Unit of measure; bucket; vat

Curato. Parochial jurisdiction

Dehesa. Common pasture land

Denuncia. Accusation or statement of land claim

Derechos. Ecclesiastical or other fees

Derrama. Additional or unauthorized tribute

Desagüe. Drainage

Diezmo. Tithe

Dobla. Seasonal heavy agricultural labor in repartimiento

Doctrina. Doctrine; parochial jurisdiction

Ejido. Type of community land

Elotes. Immature maize ears

Embarcadero. Wharf, pier

Encomendero. Possessor of an encomienda

Encomienda. Grant of Indians, mainly as tribute payers, or the area of the Indians granted

Esclavo. Slave

Escribano. Secretary or scribe

Españolado. Spanish-speaking Indian

Estacas. Pilings for building

Estancia. Subordinate Indian community; farm

Estancia de ganado mayor. Cattle ranch

Estancia de ganado menor. Sheep or goat ranch

Fanega. Unit of dry measure; about 1.5 bushels

Fanega de sembradura. Area planted with one fanega of seed

Fiador. Bondsman

Fiscal. Fiscal; prosecutor

Frijol. American bean

Gañán. Hacienda laborer

Gobernación. Government

Glossary

Gobernador. Governor
Gobernadoryotl. Gubernatorial rule
Haba. European bean
Hacendado. Hacienda owner
Hacienda. Large landed estate
Hermandad. Sodality
Hermita. Dependent church
Huauhtli. An amaranth
Huehuenches. Type of Indian dance
Hueytlatoani. Great tlatoani
Huictli. Digging stick
Huipil. Woman's shirt
Iglesia de visita. Subordinate church visited by non-resident clergy
Jacal. Hut, generally with a straw roof
Juez (pl. *jueces*). Judge
Juez de residencia. Judge presiding at a residencia
Juez repartidor. Spanish official in charge of labor assignment
Justicia. Justice, or a judge
Labor de pan. Wheat farm
Laborio. Hacienda worker or resident
Labrador. White farmer
Ladino. Spanish-speaking or acculturated Indian
Lagunilla. Small lake
Limosna. Alms
Llamamiento. Summons, usually for labor
Loma. Small hill
Lugar. Place
Macana. Sword-like weapon
Macegual. An Indian commoner
Madrina. Godmother
Maestro de escuela. Schoolteacher
Maguey. Agave, the source of pulque
Mandón. Subordinate town officer
Maravedí. Monetary unit; thirty-four maravedís commonly equalled one real
Marqués. Marquis
Marquesado. Marquisate
Matrícula. List, generally of tributaries
Mayeque(s). Indians of a subordinate or sub-macegual class
Mayoral. Overseer; town officer
Mayordomo. Majordomo; custodian
Medida. Measure
Merced. Grant, generally of land

Merino. Sheepwalk judge; town officer

Mesa central. Central plateau

Mestizo. Person of mixed white and Indian ancestry

Metate (metatl). Grinding stone

Milpa. Land plot or cornfield

Milpero. Field watchman

Molcajete. Stone mortar

Monte. Forest; region of brush or scrub; mountain

Moza. Young woman

Mozo. Young man

Nauhtecuhtli. Four related tecuhtli offices

Obraje. Workshop, especially for woolen cloth

Obras públicas. Public works

Obvención. Obvention; ecclesiastical tax or payment

Ocotl. Torch pine

Oficiales. Officers; skilled workers

Oficio. Office, trade, craft

Ofrenda. Offering

Oidor. Judge of an audiencia

Padrino. Godfather

Papel. Paper; receipt

Parcialidad. Large section of a town

Pardo. Person of mixed white and Negro or Indian and Negro ancestry

Parroquia. Parish

Parte. Part; portion of a town

Partido. Parochial or other jurisdiction

Patronato. Patronage; royal authority in ecclesiastical affairs

Pensión. Pension, annuity

Peón. Unskilled Indian worker; hacienda worker

Peso. Monetary unit of eight reales

Petate. Mat

Pillalli. Land of a pilli

Pilli (pl. pipiltin). Member of the Indian upper class

Plebeyo. Plebeian

Pochtecatl (pl. pochteca). Merchant

Pósito. Municipal storehouse

Potrero. Herdsman for colts

Principal. Member of the Indian upper class

Propios. Public land or property

Próximos a tributar. Persons soon to become tributaries

Pueblo. Town

Pueblo por sí. Independent town; cabecera

Pulque. Liquor obtained from maguey

Pulquería. Tavern for the sale of pulque

Pulquero. Maker or seller of pulque

Quinto. One-fifth; a royal tax on mine products

Rancho. Ranch; small town

Real. Monetary unit; one-eighth of a peso

Realengas. Unappropriated or royal lands

Regatón. Middleman, or economic speculator

Regidor. Councilman in a cabildo

Regimiento. Institution, office, or jurisdiction of regidor rule

Rentero. Lessee; member of the sub-macegual class

Repartidor. Official in charge of a labor repartimiento

Repartimiento. Distribution, forced sale, encomienda, or, most frequently, labor draft

Residencia. Court or trial held at the end of a term in office

Risco. Crag; rocky region

Sementera de trigo. Wheat planting, or field planted in wheat

Sencilla. Seasonal light agricultural labor in repartimiento

Señoría (señorío). Lordship; government

Señor natural. Natural lord; tlatoani

Serape. Blanket or cloak

Servicio. Service, labor, or provision of goods

Sin perjuicio. Without injury

Sirviente. Servant

Sitio. Location; property

Sobras de tributos. Remainder after subtraction of the tribute due from the total amount collected

Soltero. Bachelor

Subdelegado. Late colonial official replacing the corregidor and alcalde mayor

Suerte. Plot of land

Sujeto. Subject town

Tameme (tlamama). Indian carrier

Tasación. Tribute or tribute assessment record

Tecpan. Indian community house

Tecpanpouhque (tecpantlaca). People of the tecpan

Tecpantlalli. Land of the tecpan

Tecuhtlalli. Land of a tecuhtli

Tecuhtli (pl. tetecuhtin). Upper-class Indian of titular rank

Temazcal. Sweat-bath house

Teniente. Deputy or assistant

Teotlalli. Land of the temples or gods

Tepetate. Type of infertile soil

Tepixqui (pl. *tepixque*). Calpulli officer
Tequío. Tax or labor service
Tequisquitl. Soil impregnated with salts
Tequitl. Tax
Tequitlato. Calpulli or town officer; tax collector
Tercio. One-third; one-third of a year or a period of four months
Términos. Limits, boundaries
Terrazguero. Subordinate Indian, especially a lessee of land
Tianquiz. Indian market
Tierra caliente. Hot, tropical, or low lands
Tilma. Cape, mantle
Tlacotli. Slave or slave-like person in Indian society
Tlacuilo. Indian draftsman or scribe
Tlalmaites. Indians of a subordinate or sub-macegual class
Tlalmilli. Land plot in the calpullalli
Tlatoani (pl. *tlatoque*). Indian ruler of a community
Tlatocatlalli (*tlatocamilli*). Land of a tlatoani
Tlaxilacalli. Calpulli
Tochomitl. Rabbit fur textile
Topil. Officer of a calpulli or town
Torta. Small cake
Tortilla. Thin pancake of maize meal
Trajinero. Middleman or carrier
Traza. The central, Spanish portion of Mexico City
Tributo. Tribute
Troje. Bin, granary
Tule. Lake reeds
Tuna. Prickly pear
Vago. Homeless person, vagrant
Vaquero. Cowboy or cattle guard
Vara. Staff of office; unit of measure, usually about thirty-three inches
Viejo. Elder
Visita. Tour of inspection; community or church ministered by non-resident clergy
Visitador. Inspector
Vocales. Persons with voice; electors
Volador. Ceremonial "flying" or swinging from a high pole
Xochiyaotl. War of flowers, or ritual war
Zacate (*zacatl*). Straw, lake reeds, fodder
Zontle. Four hundred

Bibliography

The principal archives used in the preparation of this book are the Archivo General de la Nación (AGN) in Mexico City, the Archivo General de Indias (AGI) in Seville, and the Bibliothèque Nationale (BNP) in Paris.

In the Archivo General de la Nación the ramos of General de parte, Indios, Mercedes, and Tierras furnish a large part of our documentation for the sixteenth and early seventeenth centuries. Tierras also provides data for the later seventeenth and eighteenth centuries, chiefly in the form of legal cases. Other sections of utility for special subjects are Civil, Clero regular y secular, Desagüe, Inquisición, Padrones, Tributos, and Vínculos. Hospital de Jesús contains materials on Coyoacan and Tacubaya for all periods. The ramo of Congregaciones (one volume) was lost when I first worked in this archive, but a microfilm was made available to me through the courtesy of Howard F. Cline. The missing volume has since been recovered. Occasional data are derived from Ordenanzas and a few other ramos. On the whole, this book depends upon materials in the Archivo General de la Nación more than on any other single collection.

In the Archivo General de Indias the most valuable sections for the Indian history of Mexico are, in approximate order of importance, Justicia, Contaduría, (Audiencia de) México, Patronato, Indiferente, and Escribanía de cámara. The early legal cases of Justicia are of great utility in the study of relations between cabeceras and sujetos and in the study of the early encomienda. Contaduría contains unique data on tribute, town status, encomienda, and related topics for the seventeenth and other centuries.

The Bibliothèque Nationale in Paris has the foremost single collection of native pictorial materials as well as the originals and copies of a number of native and Spanish written texts. The Valley of Mexico is rich in pictorial documentation, although it offers no single codex so informative for native life as BNP, no. 387, on sixteenth-century Huejotzingo. The larger part of the Parisian material relates to the sixteenth and early seventeenth centuries.

Other European archives with relevant documentation are the Biblioteca

Nacional (BNMa) in Madrid and the British Museum (BM) in London. Both possess miscellaneous collections relating to all colonial periods. Useful secondary archives in Mexico City are the Archivo Histórico of the Museo Nacional (MNM), the Biblioteca Nacional (BNM), and the Archivo del Antiguo Ayuntamiento (AA). The last is an invaluable source for the history of Mexico City. The Archivo Histórico de Hacienda (AHH), a distinct archive when I examined it but subsequently incorporated in the Archivo General de la Nación, has useful economic data, especially for the late colonial period. Finally, in Mexico City the Centro de Documentación del Museo Nacional (CDMNC), in Chapultepec, houses a collection of microfilm of which not all the originals are readily available elsewhere. I have not systematically examined the parish archives of the Valley, which contain local records of baptisms, deaths, and marriages. Of the parish records examined, those at Huehuetoca (AH), including cofradía records and several series of maize prices, proved most helpful.

Several documentary collections in the United States have materials of value. Worth noting are the library of the University of Texas (UT), the New York Public Library (NYPL), the Ayer Collection of the Newberry Library (NLAC) in Chicago, the Mexican Manuscripts division of the Bancroft Library (BLMM) in the University of California, the Hispanic Society of America (HSA) in New York, the Clements Library (UMCL) of the University of Michigan, and the Sutro Library (SLSF) in San Francisco. Because it is less well known, special mention should be made of the collection of Papeles de los Condes de Regla (PCR) in the library of Washington State University, which has a rich documentation on hacienda and land tenure.

Published guides to these archival materials are in some instances of great value. Carrera Stampa, *Archivalia mexicana,* is the most comprehensive index for the archives of Mexico City. Titles of documents of numerous ramos of the Archivo General de la Nación are published in the Archivo's *Boletín* (BAGN). The *Indice del ramo de Indios,* edited by Chávez Orozco, contains a large number of technical errors and must be used with caution. Ulloa Ortiz, "Catálogo de los fondos," and Zavala, "Catálogo de los fondos," are guides to the collection in Chapultepec. Carrera Stampa, "Guía," has further data on the Archivo del Antiguo Ayuntamiento. There is also a published *Guía del Archivo Histórico de Hacienda.* The depositories in Mexico City that lack published guides ordinarily possess unpublished lists of documentary titles or manuscript indices in various stages of detail and completion.

Tudela, *Los manuscritos de América,* is a survey of American materials in Spanish archives. Several incomplete catalogues exist for the Archivo

General de Indias, the most relevant for the present study being the *Indice de documentos de Nueva España*. Mention may also be made of Torres Lanzas, *Relación descriptiva de los mapas,* a guide to illustrative material in Seville. Paz, *Catálogo de manuscritos de América,* is an index to the Biblioteca Nacional, Madrid. The best catalogue for Mexican documentation in the Bibliothèque Nationale, Paris, is Boban, *Documents pour servir,* essentially a commentary on the Goupil collection. Additional items in the Bibliothèque Nationale are listed in the *Catalogue des manuscrits mexicains* and in other sources. Gayangos, *Catalogue,* is the main guide to Spanish documents in the British Museum.

Of the catalogues of collections in the United States, Castañeda and Dabbs, *Guide to the Latin American Manuscripts in the University of Texas Library,* and Butler, *A Check List of Manuscripts in the Edward E. Ayer Collection,* are detailed and useful. Equivalent or nearly equivalent lists, in published or card-file form, exist for several other United States depositories.

A detailed guide to archives relating to the Indian history of Mexico is currently in preparation by a number of scholars and will appear as part of the forthcoming *Handbook of Middle American Indians.*

The published literature on Indian history in the Valley of Mexico is extensive and it includes works of many types. No comprehensive bibliography exists. The student has at his disposal, however, a number of particular bibliographies on related subjects, such as Romero de Terreros on the chroniclers of Mexico City and Montejano y Aguiñaga on the Guadalupe literature. Many modern studies of Indian or Spanish colonial history likewise contain admirable bibliographies. The most directly related bibliographies are those being compiled for the *Handbook of Middle American Indians,* which is to deal with published as well as with archival sources.

The chroniclers of the conquest, notably Cortés and Díaz del Castillo, provide detailed Spanish accounts of Indian civilization as seen by the first Spaniards. Subsequent lay historians of the sixteenth century, such as Zorita and López de Gómara and Cervantes de Salazar, add details to the early accounts and frequently give information on post-conquest Indian life. The sixteenth-century religious writers offer descriptions of pre-conquest society, and they are especially valuable for the history of conversions to Christianity and for details of early colonial Indian society. The outstanding writers of this class are Motolinía, Las Casas, and Sahagún. In the seventeenth century the tradition of ecclesiastical chronicling continues with Torquemada and Vetancurt. Other religious writers, such as Franco, Grijalva, and Ojea, occasionally have something of interest to say on colonial Indian history.

Indian or derivatively Indian texts of the sixteenth and early seventeenth centuries are rich and important documents. The principal prose sources include the Anales de Cuauhtitlan (*Códice Chimalpopoca*), Chimalpahin, Alvarado Tezozomoc, Durán, and Ixtlilxochitl. A number of other colonial Indian annals have been published, as well as Indian pictorial manuscripts (códices). In this last category, *Codex Mendoza, Códice Kingsborough,* and *Códice Osuna* are outstanding Valley of Mexico examples. But many Indian writings remain in manuscript, including the diaries of Juan Bautista and Chimalpahin, and some of the AAMC series.

Collections of published sources for Mexican colonial history are abundant and most of them bear in one way or another upon the Indian history of the Valley. The great multi-volume collections (CDIHE, CDIAI, and others) repay careful study. The early collection of Ternaux Compans still has some materials not republished elsewhere. Two principal collections of documents gathered by Paso y Troncoso (ENE and PNE), the Zavala volumes of labor documents (FHT), the García Icazbalceta volumes (CDHM, NCDHM), the texts issued in mimeographed form by Chávez Orozco (*Documentos para la historia económica,* and Banco nacional, *Publicaciones*), and the publications of Scholes and Adams are important documentary sources. The Archivo General de la Nación continues to publish documents in its *Boletín* (BAGN); and the records of the Spanish cabildo in Mexico City (AC), while incompletely published, are essential documents for both Spanish and Indian affairs.

Published collections of laws and administrative regulations, if carefully used, yield many relevant data for Indian history. For the early period the chief works are Puga, Encinas, and *El libro de las tasaciones.* Later laws may be studied in the *Recopilación de leyes,* in the *Recopilación sumaria* of Bentura Beleña, and in a large number of other compilations.

Colonial travelers often supply documentation on points that other sources fail to mention. The examples range from Samuel de Champlain, ca. 1600, whose observations are occasionally suspect, to Alexander von Humboldt in the early nineteenth century, one of the most sharp-eyed observers ever to travel in Latin America. Gage, Gemelli Carreri, and Vázquez de Espinosa also provide interesting foreigners' views of Indian life.

A fair number of colonial writings appear in the latter seventeenth and eighteenth centuries. Older Indian traditions are to some extent maintained in the later period by non-Indian writers such as Boturini and Clavigero. The late colonial diarists, Castro Santa-Anna, Gómez, Guijo, and Robles, occasionally record pertinent items for Indian history. In the eighteenth century Villa-señor y Sánchez provides data on the Spanish administrative jurisdictions and the Indian population counts. Finally, a most impressive colonial writer of the eighteenth century is José Antonio Alzate, whose

Gacetas de literatura deal not with literature but with science, agriculture, and other aspects of colonial, including Indian colonial, life. Modern studies of colonial Indian history received their great impetus in the work of Eduard Seler in the late nineteenth and early twentieth centuries, and in the work of Robert Barlow, principally in the 1940's. Outstanding recent contributions are Ricard on religious conversion, Zavala on encomienda, Miranda on tribute, Kubler on architecture, Chevalier on land tenure, and Robertson on manuscript painting. A special feature of the 1950's and 1960's is the detailed demographic and economic work produced by Simpson, Cook, and Borah, who have revolutionized our concept of the size, and the changes in the size, of Indian society. Mention should also be made of the detailed economic studies of Dusenberry, Lee, and Carrera Stampa, and the genealogical and biographical studies of López de Meneses and García Granados.

Colonial maps of the Valley of Mexico are published by Apenas. Plans of Mexico City are published by Carrera Stampa. The *Planos de la ciudad,* of Toussaint, Gómez de Orozco, and Fernández, offers some interesting cartographic commentary; and Alfonso Caso, "Los barrios antiguos," reproduces the eighteenth-century Alzate map, with commentary. A fair number of maps of the modern Valley have been published, and these may be consulted in the American Geographical Society collection in New York, as well as in the Library of Congress and other depositories. A huge three-dimensional model of the Valley, the result of years of painstaking work by Pedro C. Sánchez, is on display in the Instituto Panamericano de Geografía e Historia in Tacubaya.

Acosta, Joseph de. Historia natural y moral de las Indias. Edmundo O'Gorman, ed. Mexico, 1940.

Acosta Saignes, Miguel. Los pochteca, ubicación de los mercaderes en la estructura social tenochca. Mexico, 1945. Acta antropológica, I:1.

———. "Migraciones de los mexica," *Memorias de la Academia mexicana de la historia,* V (1946), 177–87.

Actas de cabildo de la ciudad de México. Title varies. 54 vols. Mexico, 1889–1916.

Advertimientos generales que los virreyes dejaron a sus sucesores para el gobierno de Nueva España 1590–1604. France V. Scholes and Eleanor B. Adams, eds. Mexico, 1956. Documentos para la historia del México colonial, II.

Aguilar, Francisco de. Historia de la Nueva España. Alfonso Teja Zabre, ed. Mexico, 1938.

Aguirre Beltrán, Gonzalo. "Cultura y nutrición," in Estudios antropológicos publicados en homenaje al doctor Manuel Gamio (Mexico, 1956), pp. 227–49.

———. "El gobierno indígena en México y el proceso de aculturación," *América indígena,* XII (1952), 271–97.

———. La población negra de México 1519–1810, estudio etnohistórico. Mexico, 1946.

612   Bibliography

Aiton, Arthur Scott. Antonio de Mendoza, First Viceroy of New Spain. Durham, N.C., 1927.

———. "The Secret Visita Against Viceroy Mendoza," in New Spain and the Anglo-American West (2 vols., Los Angeles, 1932), I, 1–22.

Alamán, Lucas. Disertaciones sobre la historia de la república mejicana, desde la época de la conquista que los españoles hicieron, á fines del siglo XV y principios del XVI, de las islas y continente americano hasta la independencia. 3 vols. Havana, 1873.

———. Historia de México. 5 vols. Mexico, 1883–85.

Albi, Fernando. El corregidor en el municipio español bajo la monarquía absoluta (ensayo histórico-crítico). Madrid, 1943.

Alcocer, Gabriel V. "Catálogo de los frutos comestibles mexicanos," Anales del Museo nacional de arqueología, historia y etnografía, época 2, II (1905), 413–88.

Alcocer, Ignacio. Apuntes sobre la antigua México-Tenochtitlan. Tacubaya, 1935. Instituto panamericano de geografía e historia, Publicación núm. 14.

Alegre, Francisco Javier. Historia de la Compañía de Jesús en Nueva-España. Carlos María Bustamante, ed. 3 vols. Mexico, 1841–42.

Alegría, Ricardo E. "Origin and Diffusion of the Term 'Cacique,'" in Acculturation in the Americas, Proceedings and Selected Papers of the XXIXth International Congress of Americanists (Sol Tax, ed.; Chicago, 1952), pp. 313–15.

"Algunos documentos de la colección Cuevas," Anales del Museo nacional de arqueología, historia y etnografía, época, 3, V (1913), 125–52.

Almonte, Juan Nepomuceno. Guía de forasteros y repertorio de conocimientos utiles. Mexico, 1852.

Al severo tribunal del público, las víctimas de Xuchitepec, por la inquisición de Chalco. Mexico, n.d. (1861).

Alvarado Tezozomoc, Hernando [Fernando]. Crónica mexicana escrita hacia el año de 1598. Manuel Orozco y Berra, ed. Mexico, 1944.

———. Crónica mexicayotl. Adrián León, trans. and ed. Mexico, 1949. Publicaciones del Instituto de historia, ser. 1, no. 10.

Alvarez, Manuel F. Algunos datos sobre cimentación de la ciudad de México y nivel del lago de Texcoco a través de los siglos. Mexico, 1919.

Alvarez del Villar, J., and Leopoldo Navarro G. Los peces del valle de México. Mexico, 1957.

Alzate [y Ramírez], José Antonio. Gacetas de literatura de México. 4 vols. Puebla, 1831.

"Anales de San Gregorio Acapulco 1520–1606" (R. H. Barlow, Byron McAfee, Guillermo Cabrera, trans. and eds.), Tlalocan, III (1949–57), 103–41.

Anales de Tlatelolco, unos annales históricos de la nación mexicana y Códice de Tlatelolco. Salvador Toscano, Heinrich Berlin, and Robert H. Barlow, eds. Mexico, 1948. Fuentes para la historia de México, II.

"Anales de Tula, Hidalgo, 1361–1521" (R. H. Barlow, ed.), Tlalocan, III (1949–57), 2–13.

Anderson, Edgar, and R. H. Barlow. "The Maize Tribute of Moctezuma's Empire," Annals of the Missouri Botanical Garden, XXX (1943), 413–20.

Apenas, Ola. Mapas antiguos del valle de México. Mexico, 1947.

———. "The Pond in Our Backyard," Mexican Life, XIX (1943), 15–18, 60.

———. "The Primitive Salt Production of Lake Texcoco, Mexico," Ethnos, IX (1944), 35–40.

———. "The 'Tlateles' of Lake Texcoco," American Antiquity, IX (1943–44), 29–32.

Aranzel para todos los curas de este arzobispado, fuera de la ciudad de México. Mexico, 1767.

Aranzeles de los tribunales, juzgados, y oficinas de justicia, gobierno, y real hacienda, que comprehende la ciudad de México capital de Nueva-España. Mexico, 1759.

Archivo mexicano. Documentos para la historia de México. 2 vols. Mexico, 1852–53.

Armillas, Pedro. Program of the History of American Indians, Part II: Post-Columbian America. Washington, 1960. Pan American Union Social Science Monographs, VIII.

Aschmann, Homer. "The Subsistence Problem in Mesoamerican History," *Middle American Anthropology*, II. Pan American Union Social Science Monographs, X (Washington, 1960), 1–9.

Aubin, J. M. A. Mémoires sur la peinture didactique et l'écriture figurative des anciens mexicains. Paris, 1885.

Aveleyra Arroyo de Anda, Luis, and Manuel Maldonado-Koerdell, "Association of Artifacts with Mammoth in the Valley of Mexico," *American Antiquity*, XVIII (1952–53), 332–40.

Banco nacional de crédito agrícola y ganadero. Publicaciones. 21 vols. Mexico, 1953–58.

Bancroft, Hubert Howe. History of Mexico. 6 vols. San Francisco, 1886–88. Bancroft, Hubert Howe. Works, IX–XIV.

Bandelier, Ad. F. "On the Art of War and Mode of Warfare of the Ancient Mexicans," in Tenth Annual Report of the Peabody Museum of Archaeology and Ethnology (Salem, Mass., 1877), pp. 95–161.

———. "On the Distribution and Tenure of Lands, and the Customs with Respect to Inheritance, Among the Ancient Mexicans," in Eleventh Annual Report of the Peabody Museum of Archaeology and Ethnology (Salem, Mass., 1878), pp. 385–448.

———. "On the Social Organization and Mode of Government of the Ancient Mexicans," in Twelfth Annual Report of the Trustees of the Peabody Museum of American Archaeology and Ethnology, II (Cambridge, Mass., 1880), 557–699.

Barlow, Robert H. "Dos documentos de principios del siglo XVII, referentes a Tlatelolco," *Memorias de la Academia mexicana de la historia*, IV (1945), 101–10.

———. "El Códice Azcatitlan," *Journal de la Société des américanistes*, n.s., XXXVIII (1949), 101–35.

———. "El Códice de los alfareros de Cuauhtitlán," *Revista mexicana de estudios antropológicos*, XII (1951), 5–8.

———. "El reverso del Códice García Granados," *Memorias de la Academia mexicana de la historia*, V (1946), 422–38.

———. "La crónica 'X,'" *Revista mexicana de estudios antropológicos*, VII (1945), 65–87.

———. "La fundación de la triple alianza (1427–1433)," *Anales del Instituto nacional de antropología e historia*, III (1947–48), 147–55.

———. "Las ocho ermitas de Santiago Tlatelolco," *Memorias de la Academia mexicana de la historia*, VI (1947), 183–88.

———. "Los caciques coloniales de Tlatelolco en un documento de 1561," *Memorias de la Academia mexicana de la historia*, III (1944), 552–56.

———. "Los caciques de Tlatelolco en el Códice Cozcatzin," *Memorias de la Academia mexicana de la historia*, V (1946), 416–21.

———. "Los caciques precortesianos de Tlatelolco en el Códice García Granados (Techialoyan Q)," *Memorias de la Academia mexicana de la historia*, IV (1945), 467–83.

———. "Los tecpaneca después de la caída de Azcapotzalco," *Tlalocan,* III (1949–57), 285–87.

———. "Some Remarks on the Term 'Aztec Empire,'" *The Americas,* I (1944–45), 345–49.

———. The Extent of the Empire of the Culhua Mexica. Berkeley and Los Angeles, 1949. Ibero-Americana: 28.

———. "The Periods of Tribute Collection in Moctezuma's Empire," *Notes on Middle American Archaeology and Ethnology,* no. 23 (1943), pp. 152–54.

———. "Tlatelolco como tributario de la triple alianza," *Memorias de la Academia mexicana de la historia,* IV (1945), 200–215.

Barrio Lorenzot, Francisco del. El trabajo en México durante la época colonial: ordenanzas de gremios de la Nueva España. Genaro Estrada, ed. Mexico, 1921.

Barrios E., P. Miguel. "Tecpanecos y mexicanos," *Tlalocan,* III (1949–57), 287–88.

Basurto, J. Trinidad. El arzobispado de México. Mexico, 1905.

Beltrán, Enrique. El hombre y su ambiente. Ensayo sobre el valle de México. Mexico, 1958.

·———. "Plantas usadas en la alimentación por los antiguos mexicanos," *América indígena,* IX (1949), 195–204.

Benítez, José R. "Toponimia indígena de la ciudad de México," in Vigesimoséptimo congreso internacional de americanistas, actas de la primera sesión celebrada en la ciudad de México en 1939 (2 vols., Mexico, n.d.), II, 511–54.

Bentura Beleña, Eusebio. Recopilación sumaria de todos los autos acordados de la real audiencia y sala del crimen de esta Nueva España, y providencias de su superior gobierno. 2 vols. Mexico, 1787.

Beyer, Hermann. "La tiradera (atlatl) todavía en uso en el valle de México," *El México antiguo,* II (1924–27), 220–22.

Blanchard, Raphaël. "Encore sur les tableaux de métissage du Musée de México," *Journal de la Société des américanistes de Paris,* n.s. VII (1910), 37–60.

———. "Les tableaux de métissage au Mexique," *Journal de la Société des américanistes de Paris,* n.s. V (1908), 59–66.

———. "Survivances ethnographiques au Mexique. Le metatl et le molcajetl. Introduction du metatl en Europe," *Journal de la Société des américanistes de Paris,* n.s. VI (1909), 45–62.

Boban, Eugène. Documents pour servir à l'histoire du Mexique. 2 vols. and Atlas. Paris, 1891.

Boletín del Archivo general de la nación, I (1930) et seq.

Borah, Woodrow. Early Colonial Trade and Navigation Between Mexico and Peru. Berkeley and Los Angeles, 1954. Ibero-Americana: 38.

———. New Spain's Century of Depression. Berkeley and Los Angeles, 1951. Ibero-Americana: 35.

———. Silk Raising in Colonial Mexico. Berkeley and Los Angeles, 1943. Ibero-Americana: 20.

———, and Sherburne F. Cook. Price Trends of Some Basic Commodities in Central Mexico, 1531–1570. Berkeley and Los Angeles, 1958. Ibero-Americana: 40.

———, and Sherburne F. Cook. The Population of Central Mexico in 1548. An Analysis of the Suma de visitas de pueblos. Berkeley and Los Angeles, 1960. Ibero-Americana: 43.

Bosch García, Carlos. La esclavitud prehispánica entre los aztecas. Mexico, 1944.

Boturini Benaduci, Lorenzo. Catálogo del museo histórico indiano del cavallero

Lorenzo Boturini Benaduci. Madrid, 1746. Bound with Idea de una nueva historia general de la América septentrional.

Bowman, J. N. "The Vara de Burgos," *Pacific Historical Review*, XXX (1961), 17–21.

"Brevajes en la colonia," *Memorias de la Academia mexicana de la historia*, XVII (1958), 310–36.

Brinton, Daniel G. The Lineal Measures of the Semi-Civilized Nations of Mexico and Central America. Philadelphia, 1885.

Bruman, Henry. "The Culture History of Mexican Vanilla," *Hispanic American Historical Review*, XXVIII (1948), 360–76.

Butler, Ruth Lapham. A Check List of Manuscripts in the Edward E. Ayer Collection. Chicago, 1937.

Cabrera y Quintero, Cayetano de. Escudo de armas de México. Mexico, 1746.

Cárcer Disdier, M. de. "Los pavos," in Homenaje a Rafael García Granados (Mexico, 1960), pp. 89–110.

Carlson, Fred A. Geography of Latin America. New York, 1952.

Carrasco [Pizana], Pedro. "El barrio y la regulación del matrimonio en un pueblo del valle de México en el siglo XVI," *Revista mexicana de estudios antropológicos*, XVII (1961), 7–26.

———. Los otomíes. Cultura e historia prehispánicas de los pueblos mesoamericanos de habla otomiana. Mexico, 1950. Publicaciones del Instituto de historia, primera serie, núm. 15.

Carreño, Alberto María. "El colegio de Tlaltelolco y la educación indígena en el siglo XVI," *Divulgación histórica*, I (1940), 196–202.

———. Fr. Domingo de Betanzos, fundador en la Nueva España de la venerable orden domínica. Mexico, 1924.

———. "Manuscritos, incunables y libros raros en la Biblioteca nacional de México," *Boletín de la Biblioteca nacional*, época 2, I (1950), núm. 4, 3–74.

———. Un desconocido cedulario del siglo XVI perteneciente a la catedral metropolitana de México. Mexico, 1944.

Carrera Stampa, Manuel. Archivalia mexicana. Mexico, 1952.

———. "El obraje novohispano," *Memorias de la Academia mexicana de la historia*, XX (1961), 148–71.

———. Guía del Archivo del antiguo ayuntamiento de la ciudad de México. Havana, 1949. Publicaciones del Archivo nacional de Cuba, XXIII.

———. Los gremios mexicanos. La organización gremial en Nueva España 1521–1861. Mexico, 1954. Colección de estudios histórico-económicos mexicanos de la Cámara nacional de la industria de transformación, I.

———. "Los obrajes de indígenas en el virreinato de la Nueva España," in Vigesimoséptimo congreso internacional de americanistas, actas de la primera sesión celebrada en la ciudad de México en 1939 (2 vols., Mexico, n.d.), II, 555–62.

———. "Planos de la ciudad de México," *Boletín de la Sociedad mexicana de geografía y estadística*, LXVII (1949), 263–427.

———. "The Evolution of Weights and Measures in New Spain," *Hispanic American Historical Review*, XXIX (1949), 2–24.

Carta de un religioso sobre la rebelión de los indios mexicanos. Vargas Rea, ed. Mexico, 1951.

Cartas de Indias. Madrid, 1877.

Caso, Alfonso. "La tenencia de la tierra entre los antiguos mexicanos," in Memoria de el Colegio nacional, IV (1958–60), 29–54.

————. "Los barrios antiguos de Tenochtitlan y Tlatelolco," *Memorias de la Academia mexicana de la historia*, XV (1956), 7–62.

Castañeda, Carlos Eduardo, and Jack Autrey Dabbs. Guide to the Latin American Manuscripts in the University of Texas Library (Cambridge, Mass., 1939).

Castillo, Cristóbal del. Fragmentos de la obra general sobre historia de los mexicanos. Florencia, 1908. Biblioteca náuatl, V.

Castillo, Ignacio B. del. "La inundación de Acolman," *Boletín de la Sociedad mexicana de geografía y estadística*, LIV (1940–41), 549–62.

Castro Santa-Anna, José Manuel de. Diario de sucesos notables. 3 vols. Mexico, 1854. Documentos para la historia de Méjico, ser. 1, IV–VI.

Catalogue des manuscrits mexicains de la Bibliothèque nationale. Paris, 1899.

Cavo, Andrés. Historia de México. Ernesto J. Burrus, S.J., ed. Mexico, 1949.

Ceballos Novelo, Roque J. "El temazcal o baño mexicano de vapor," *Ethnos*, I (1920–22), 28–36.

Cedulario americano del siglo XVIII. Antonio Muro Orejón, ed. Seville, 1956. Publicaciones de la Escuela de estudios hispano-americanos de Sevilla, XCIX.

Cedulario heráldico de conquistadores de Nueva España. Mexico, 1933.

Cepeda, Fernando de, and Fernando Alfonso Carrillo. Relación universal legítima, y verdadera del sitio en que esta fundada la muy noble, insigne, y muy leal ciudad de México, cabeça de las provincias de toda la Nueva España. Mexico, 1637.

Cervantes de Salazar, Francisco. Crónica de la Nueva España. Madrid, 1914.

————. Life in the Imperial and Loyal City of Mexico in New Spain and the Royal and Pontifical University of Mexico as Described in the Dialogues for the Study of the Latin Language. Minnie Lee Barrett Shepard, trans.; Carlos Eduardo Castañeda, ed. Austin, Texas, 1953.

Chamberlain, Robert S. "Castilian Backgrounds of the Repartimiento-Encomienda," in Carnegie Institution of Washington Publication no. 509 (Washington, 1939), pp. 19–66.

————. "The Concept of the *Señor Natural* as Revealed by Castilian Law and Administrative Documents," *Hispanic American Historical Review*, XIX (1939), 130–37.

————. The Conquest and Colonization of Yucatan 1517–1550. Washington, 1948. Carnegie Institution of Washington Publication no. 582.

Champlain, Samuel de. "Brief discovrs des choses plvs remarqvables qve Sammvel Champlain de Brovage a reconneues aux Indes Occidentalles," in The Works of Samuel de Champlain (6 vols., Toronto, 1922–36), I, 1–80.

Chapa, Sostenes N. San Gregorio Atlapulco, Xochimilco, D.F. Mexico, 1957.

Chapman, Anne M. Raíces y consecuencias de la guerra de los aztecas contra los tepanecas de Azcapotzalco. Mexico, 1959. Acta antropológica, época 2, I, no. 4.

Chappe d'Auteroche, Jean. A Voyage to California, to Observe the Transit of Venus. London, 1778.

Chavero, Alfredo. Pinturas jeroglíficas. 2 vols. Mexico, 1901.

————. "Teotihuacan," *Biblioteca de autores mexicanos*, LII (Mexico, 1904), 431–63.

Chávez Orozco, Luis. Las instituciones democráticas de los indígenas mexicanos en la época colonial. Mexico, 1943.

Chevalier, François. La formation des grands domaines au Mexique. Terre et société aux XVIe–XVIIe siècles. Paris, 1952. Travaux et mémoires de l'Institut d'ethnologie, LVI.

Chimalpahin [Quauhtlehuanitzin], Domingo Francisco de San Antón Muñon. Annales. Sixième et septième relations (1258–1612). Rémi Siméon, trans. and ed. Paris, 1889. Bibliothèque linguistique américaine, XII.

——. Das Memorial breve acerca de la fundación de la ciudad de Culhuacan und weitere ausgewählte Teile aus den "Diferentes historias originales" ("MS. mexicain no. 74," Paris). Walter Lehmann and Gerdt Kutscher, trans. Stuttgart, 1958. Quellenwerke zur alten Geschichte Amerikas aufgezeichnet in den Sprachen der Eingeborenen, VII.

——. Diferentes historias originales de los reynos de Culhuacan, y Mexico, y de otras provincias. Ernst Mengin, trans. and ed. Hamburg, 1950. Mitteilungen aus dem Museum für Völkerkunde in Hamburg, XXII.

Cisneros, Diego de. Sitio, natvraleza y propiedades de la civdad de Mexico. Mexico, 1618.

Clavigero, Francisco Javier. Historia de México. 4 vols. Mexico, 1945. Colección de escritores mexicanos, 7–10.

Cline, Howard F. "Civil Congregations of the Indians in New Spain, 1598–1606," Hispanic American Historical Review, XXIX (1949), 349–69.

Cobo, Bernabé. Obras. Madrid, 1956. Biblioteca de autores españoles desde la formación del lenguaje hasta nuestros días, LXXXXI–XCII.

Codex Magliabecchiano XIII. 3. manuscrit mexicain post-colombien de la Bibliothèque nationale de Florence reproduit en photochromographie aux frais du Duc de Loubat correspondant de l'Institut. Rome, 1904.

Codex Mendoza. The Mexican Manuscript Known as the Collection of Mendoza and Preserved in the Bodleian Library, Oxford. James Cooper Clark, trans. and ed. 3 vols. London, 1938.

Codex Telleriano-Remensis. Manuscrit mexicain du cabinet de Ch.-M. Le Tellier, archevêque de Reims à la Bibliothèque nationale (Ms. Mexicain No. 385). E.-T. Hamy, ed. Paris, 1889.

"Códice Azcatitlan," Journal de la Société des américanistes, n.s., XXXVIII (1949), enclosure.

Códice Chimalpopoca. Anales de Cuauhtitlan y Leyenda de los soles. Primo Feliciano Velázquez, trans. Mexico, 1945.

Códice Kingsborough—Memorial de los indios de Tepetlaoztoc al monarca español contra los encomenderos del pueblo. Francisco del Paso y Troncoso, ed. Madrid, 1912.

Códice Mariano Jiménez. Nómina de tributos de los pueblos Otlazpan y Tepexic en geroglífico azteca y lenguas castellana y náhuatl. 1,549. Nicolás León, ed. Mexico, n.d.

Códice Osuna. Reproducción facsimilar de la obra del mismo título, editada en Madrid, 1878. Luis Chávez Orozco, ed. Mexico, 1947.

Códice Ramírez. Manuscrito del siglo XVI intitulado: Relación del origen de los indios que habitan esta Nueva España, según sus historias. Manuel Orozco y Berra and others, eds. Mexico, 1944.

Códice Xolotl. Charles E. Dibble, ed. Mexico, 1951. Universidad nacional, Instituto de historia, ser. 1, no. 22.

Códices indígenas de algunos pueblos del Marquesado del valle de Oaxaca. Mexico, 1933.

Colección de documentos inéditos para la historia de España. Martín Fernández Navarrete and others, eds. 112 vols. Madrid, 1842–95.

Colección de documentos inéditos para la historia de Ibero-América. Title varies. 14 vols. Madrid, 1927–32.

Colección de documentos inéditos relativos al descubrimiento, conquista y organización de las antiguas posesiones españolas de América y Oceanía, sacados de los archivos del reino, y muy especialmente del de Indias. Title varies. 42 vols. Madrid, 1864–84.

Colección de documentos inéditos relativos al descubrimiento, conquista y organización de las antiguas posesiones españolas de ultramar. 25 vols. Madrid, 1885–1932.

Colección de documentos para la historia de México. Joaquín García Icazbalceta, ed. 2 vols. Mexico, 1858–66.

Compendio histórico del concilio III mexicano, o índices de los tres tomos de la colección del mismo concilio. Fortino Hipólito Vera, ed. 3 vols. Amecameca, 1879.

Concilio III provincial mexicano, celebrado en México el año de 1585, confirmado en Roma por el papa Sixto V, y mandado observar por el gobierno español, en diversas reales órdenes. Mariano Galván Rivera, ed. Mexico, 1859.

Conway, G. R. G., ed. The Last Will and Testament of Hernando Cortés, Marqués del Valle. Mexico, 1939.

Cook, Sherburne F. Soil Erosion and Population in Central Mexico. Berkeley and Los Angeles, 1949. Ibero-Americana: 34.

———. The Historical Demography and Ecology of the Teotlalpan. Berkeley and Los Angeles, 1949. Ibero-Americana: 33.

———. "The Incidence and Significance of Disease Among the Aztecs and Related Tribes," Hispanic American Historical Review, XXVI (1946), 320–35.

———. "The Interrelation of Population, Food Supply, and Building in Pre-Conquest Central Mexico," American Antiquity, XIII (1947–49), 45–52.

———. "The Smallpox Epidemic of 1797 in Mexico," Bulletin of the History of Medicine, VII (1939), 937–69.

———, and Woodrow Borah. The Indian Population of Central Mexico 1531–1610. Berkeley and Los Angeles, 1960. Ibero-Americana: 44.

———, and Lesley Byrd Simpson. The Population of Central Mexico in the Sixteenth Century. Berkeley and Los Angeles, 1948. Ibero-Americana: 31.

Cook de Leonard, Carmen, ed. Esplendor del México antiguo. 2 vols. Mexico, 1959.

———, and Ernesto Lemoine V. "Materiales para la geografía histórica de la región Chalca-Amecameca," Revista mexicana de estudios antropológicos, XIV, Primera Parte (1954–55), 289–95.

Cooper, Donald B. Epidemic Disease in Mexico City: 1761–1813. Dissertation, University of Texas, 1963.

"Copia de una carta," El Museo mexicano, IV (1844–45), 73–80.

Correo seminario político y mercantil del México, I (1809) et seq.

Cortés, Hernán [Fernando]. Cartas de relación de la conquista de Méjico. 2 vols. Madrid, 1942.

———. Cartas y otros documentos de Hernán Cortés novísimamente descubiertos en el Archivo general de Indias de la ciudad de Sevilla. Mariano Cuevas, ed. Seville, 1915.

———. Cartas y relaciones de Hernán Cortés al emperador Carlos V. Pascual de Gayangos, ed. Paris, 1866.

———. Relaciones de Hernán Cortés a Carlos V sobre la invasión de Anahuac. Eulalia Guzmán, ed. Mexico, 1958.

Cosío Villegas, Daniel, and others. Historia moderna de México, la república restaurada, la vida social. Mexico, 1956.

Bibliography 619

Cossío, José Lorenzo, Sr. "Algunas noticias sobre las colonias de esta capital," *Boletín de la Sociedad mexicana de geografía y estadística*, XLVII (1937–38), 5–41.

———. "Las aguas de la ciudad," *Boletín de la Sociedad mexicana de geografía y estadística*, XLV (1935–37), 33–52.

Cravioto, René O., and others. "Nutritive Value of the Mexican Tortilla," *Science*, CII (1945), 91–93.

"Cuadros de mestizos del Museo de México," *Anales del Museo nacional de arqueología, historia y etnografía*, época 3, IV (1912–13), 237–48.

Cuesta, Luisa, and Jaime Delgado. "Pleitos cortesianos en la Biblioteca nacional," *Revista de Indias*, IX (1948), 247–96.

Cuevas, Mariano. Album histórico guadalupano del IV centenario. Mexico, 1930.

———, ed. Documentos inéditos del siglo XVI para la historia de México. Mexico, 1914.

———. Historia de la iglesia en México. 5 vols. El Paso, 1928.

Cuevas Aguirre y Espinosa, Joseph Francisco. Extracto de los autos de diligencias, y reconocimientos de los ríos, lagunas, vertientes, y desagües de la capital México, y su valle. Mexico, 1748.

"Culhuacan," *Revista mexicana de estudios históricos*, I (1927), 171–73.

Dávila, Padilla, Augustín. Historia de la fvndacion y discurso de la prouincia de Santiago de México de la Orden de predicadores, por las vidas de sus varones insignes, y casos notables de Nueua España. Madrid, 1596.

Decorme, Gerard. La obra de los jesuítas mexicanos durante la época colonial 1572–1767. 2 vols. Mexico, 1941.

Deevey, Edward S., Jr. "Limnological Studies in Middle America with a Chapter on Aztec Limnology," *Transactions of the Connecticut Academy of Arts and Sciences*, XXXIX (1957), 213–328.

De Terra, Helmut, Javier Romero, and T. D. Stewart. Tepexpan Man. New York, 1949. Viking Fund Publications in Anthropology, no. 11.

Díaz del Castillo, Bernal. Historia verdadera de la conquista de la Nueva España. 2 vols. Mexico, 1942.

Díaz del Pino, Alfonso. El maíz. Cultivo—fertilización, cosecha. Mexico, 1954.

Diccionario universal de historia y de geografía. 10 vols. Mexico, 1853–56.

Díez de la Calle, Juan. Memorial y noticias sacras y reales de las Indias occidentales. Mexico, 1932.

Diguet, Léon. "Histoire de la cochenille au Mexique," *Journal de la Société des américanistes de Paris*, n.s., VI (1909), 75–99.

Disposiciones complementarias de las leyes de Indias. 3 vols. Madrid, 1930.

Documentos americanos del Archivo de protocolos de Sevilla, siglo XVI. Madrid, 1935.

Documentos inéditos relativos a Hernán Cortés y su familia. Mexico, 1935. Publicaciones del Archivo general de la nación, XXVII.

Documentos para la historia económica de México. Luis Chávez Orozco, ed. 12 vols. Mexico, 1933–38.

Documentos relativos al arrendamiento del impuesto o renta de alcabalas de la ciudad de México y distritos circundantes. Mexico, 1945. Archivo histórico de hacienda. Colección de documentos publicados bajo la dirección de Jesús Silva Herzog, IV.

Documentos relativos al tumulto de 1624, colectados por D. Mariano Fernández de Echeverría y Veitia, caballero del orden de Santiago. 2 vols. Mexico, 1855. Documentos para la historia de México, ser. 2, II–III.

620   Bibliography

Don Vasco de Quiroga. Documentos. Rafael Aguayo Spencer, ed. Mexico, 1939.

Dorantes de Carranza, Baltasar. Sumaria relación de las cosas de la Nueva España con noticia individual de los descendientes legítimos de los conquistadores y primeros pobladores españoles. Mexico, 1902.

Durán, Diego. Historia de las Indias de Nueva-España y islas de tierra firme. 2 vols. and Atlas. Mexico, 1867–80.

Dusenberry, William H. "The Regulation of Meat Supply in Sixteenth-Century Mexico City," Hispanic American Historical Review, XXVIII (1948), 38–52.

———. "Woolen Manufacture in Sixteenth-Century New Spain," The Americas, IV (1947–48), 223–34.

El libro de las tasaciones de pueblos de la Nueva España. Siglo XVI. Mexico, 1952.

El segundo conde de Revilla Gigedo (juicio de residencia). Mexico, 1933. Publicaciones del Archivo general de la nación, XXII.

Encinas, Diego de. Cedulario indiano. 4 vols. Madrid, 1945.

Epistolario de Nueva España 1505–1818. Francisco del Paso y Troncoso, ed. 16 vols. Mexico, 1939–42. Biblioteca histórica mexicana de obras inéditas, ser. 2.

"Estado de las rentas que tenía el gobierno español el año de 1794, época en que el virey, conde de Revilla-Gigedo, entregó el mando a su sucesor el marqués de Branci-forte," El Museo mexicano, III (1844), 407–8.

Fernández, Justino. "El hospital real de los indios de la ciudad de México," Anales del Instituto de investigaciones estéticas, I (1937–39), 25–47.

———, and Hugo Leicht. "Códice del tecpan de Santiago Tlaltelolco (1576–1581)," Investigaciones históricas, I (1938–39), 243–64.

Fernández de Recas, Guillermo S. Cacicazgos y nobilario indígena de la Nueva España. Mexico, 1961.

Fernández del Castillo, Antonio. "Hernán Cortés y el Distrito federal," Boletín de la Sociedad mexicana de geografía y estadística, LX (1945), 525–43.

Fernández del Castillo, Francisco. "Alonso de Estrada, su familia," Memorias de la Academia mexicana de la historia, I (1942), 398–431.

———. Apuntes para la historia de San Angel (San Jacinto Tenanitla) y sus alrede-dores. Mexico, 1913.

———. "Don Pelayo y la virgen de Los Remedios," Anales del Museo nacional de ar-queología, historia y etnografía, época 4, VII (1931–32), 461–72.

Fisher, Lillian Estelle. The Intendant System in Spanish America. Berkeley, 1929.

Florencia, Francisco de. La estrella del norte de México. Madrid, 1785.

Fonseca, Fabián de, and Carlos de Urrutia. Historia general de real hacienda. 6 vols. Mexico, 1845–53.

Foster, George M. Culture and Conquest: America's Spanish Heritage. New York, 1960. Viking Fund Publications in Anthropology, XXVII.

Franco, Alonso. Segunda parte de la historia de la provincia de Santiago de México, Orden de predicadores de la Nueua España. Mexico, 1900.

Freund, Georg. "Agrarrecht und Katasterwesen im alten Mexiko," Ethnos (Stock-holm), XI (1946), 24–48.

Fuentes para la historia del trabajo en Nueva España. Silvio A. Zavala and María Castelo, eds. 8 vols. Mexico, 1939–46.

Gage, Thomas. A New Survey of the West-Indies: Being a Journal of Three Thousand and Three Hundred Miles Within the Main Land of America. London, 1699.

Galván Rivera, Mariano. Ordenanzas de tierras y aguas ó sea formulario geométrico-judicial. Paris, 1868.

Gálvez, José. Informe general que en virtud de real órden instruyó y entregó el excmo. Sr. Marqués de Sonora siendo visitador general de este reyno al excmo. Sr. virrey Frey D. Antonio Bucarely y Ursua con fecha de 31 de diciembre de 1771. Mexico, 1867.

Gamio, Manuel. La población del valle de Teotihuacan. 3 vols. Mexico, 1922.

——. "Restos de la cultura tepaneca," *Anales del Museo nacional de arqueología, historia y etnología,* época 3, I (1909), 233–53.

Garay, Francisco de. El Valle de México. Apuntes históricos sobre su hidrografía. Mexico, 1888.

García, Genaro, and Carlos Pereyra, eds. Documentos inéditos ó muy raros para la historia de México. 36 vols. Mexico, 1905–11.

García Cubas, Antonio. Diccionario geográfico, histórico y biográfico de los estados unidos mexicanos. 5 vols. Mexico, 1889–91.

García Granados, Rafael. Diccionario biográfico de historia antigua de Méjico. 3 vols. Mexico, 1952–53. Publicaciones del Instituto de historia, primera serie, núm. 23.

García Icazbalceta, Joaquín. Bibliografía mexicana del siglo XVI. Agustín Millares Carlo, ed. Mexico, 1954.

——. Carta acerca del origen de la imagen de Nuestra Señora de Guadalupe de México. Mexico, 1896.

——. Carta a José María Vigil aclarando un proceso de la inquisición en el siglo XVI. Mexico, 1939.

——. Don Fray Juan de Zumárraga primer obispo y arzobispo de México. 3 vols. Mexico, 1947. Colección de escritores mexicanos, 41–43.

García Pimentel, Luis, ed. Descripción del arzobispado de México hecha en 1570 y otros documentos. Mexico, 1897.

——. Relación de los obispados de Tlaxcala, Michoacan, Oaxaca y otros lugares en el siglo XVI. Mexico, Paris, Madrid, 1904. Documentos históricos de Méjico, II.

Gardiner, C. Harvey. Martín López Conquistador Citizen of Mexico. Lexington, Kentucky, 1958.

——. Naval Power in the Conquest of Mexico. Austin, Texas, 1956.

Garibay K., Angel M. "Un cuadro real de la infiltración del hispanismo en el alma india en el llamado 'Códice de Juan Bautista,' " *Filosofía y letras,* IX (1945), 213–41.

Gayangos, Pascual de. Catalogue of the Manuscripts in the Spanish Language in the British Museum. 4 vols. London, 1875–93.

Gazetas de México, compendio de noticias de Nueva España desde principios del año de 1784. Manuel Antonio Valdés, ed. 16 vols. Mexico, 1784–1809.

Gemelli Carreri, Juan Francisco. Las cosas más considerables en la Nueva España. José María de Agreda y Sánchez, trans. Mexico, 1946.

Gibson, Charles. "Llamamiento general, Repartimiento, and the Empire of Acolhuacan," *Hispanic American Historical Review,* XXXVI (1956), 1–27.

——. "Rotation of Alcaldes in the Indian Cabildo of Mexico City," *Hispanic American Historical Review,* XXXIII (1953), 212–23.

——. "The Aztec Aristocracy in Colonial Mexico," *Comparative Studies in Society and History,* II (1959–60), 169–96.

——. "The Tepanec Zone and the Labor Drafts of the Sixteenth Century" (in press).

——. Tlaxcala in the Sixteenth Century. New Haven, 1952. Yale Historical Publications, Miscellany, LVI.

Giralt Raventos, Emilio. "En torno al precio del trigo en Barcelona durante el siglo XVI," *Hispania, revista española de historia,* XVIII (1958), 38–61.

622 Bibliography

Gómez, José. Diario curioso de México. Mexico, 1854. Documentos para la historia de Méjico, ser. 1, VII.

Gómez de Cervantes, Gonzalo. La vida económica y social de Nueva España al finalizar el siglo XVI. Alberto María Carreño, ed. Mexico, 1944. Biblioteca histórica mexicana de obras inéditas, ser. 1, XIX.

Gómez de Orozco, Federico. "Apuntes para la historia de la villa de San Angel, D.F.," *Anales del Museo nacional de arqueología, historia y etnografía,* época 4, V (1927), 472–81.

———. "Dos escritores indígenas del siglo XVI," *Universidad de México,* I (1930–31), 126–30.

———. "El mercado de los perros," *Ethnos,* I (1920–22), 152–55.

Gonçalves de Lima, Oswaldo. El maguey y el pulque en los códices mexicanos. Mexico, 1956.

González, Genaro María. "¡ Huehuetoca . . . un pueblo más allá de Cuautitlan!," *Boletín de la Sociedad mexicana de geografía y estadística,* LXXVII (1954), 153–271.

González Navarro, Moisés. La vida social. Daniel Cosío Villegas, ed. Mexico and Buenos Aires, 1957. Historia moderna de México, IV.

———. "México en una laguna," *Historia mexicana,* IV (1954–55), 506–21.

González Rul, Francisco, and Federico Mooser. "La calzada de Iztapalapa," *Anales del Instituto nacional de antropología e historia,* XIV (XLIII) (1961), 113–19.

Grijalva, Juan de. Cronica de la Orden de N.P.S. Agustin en las prouincias de Nueua España. En quatro edades desde el año de 1533 hasta el de 1592. Mexico, 1624.

Guía del Archivo histórico de hacienda. Mexico, 1940.

Guijo, Gregorio Martín de. Diario de sucesos notables. Mexico, 1853. Documentos para la historia de Méjico, ser. 1, I.

Guthrie, Chester L. "Colonial Economy. Trade, Industry, and Labor in Seventeenth Century Mexico City," *Revista de historia de América,* no. 7 (1939), 103–34.

———. "Riots in Seventeenth-Century Mexico City: A Study of Social and Economic Conditions," in Greater America, Essays in Honor of Herbert Eugene Bolton (Berkeley and Los Angeles, 1945), pp. 243–58.

Gutiérrez de Medina, Christoual. Viage de tierra, y mar, feliz por mar, y tierra, qve hizo el excellentissimo señor Marqves de Villena mi señor, yendo por virrey, y capitan general de la Nueua España. Mexico, 1640.

Guzmán, Eulalia. "Un manuscrito de la colección Boturini que trata de los antiguos señores de Teotihuacán," *Ethnos,* III (1938), 89–103.

Hakluyt, Richard. The Principal Navigations Voyages Traffiques & Discoveries of the English Nation. 12 vols. Glasgow and New York, 1903–5.

Hall, Frederic. The Laws of Mexico: A Compilation and Treatise Relating to Real Property, Mines, Water Rights, Personal Rights, Contracts, and Inheritances. San Francisco, 1885.

Hanke, Lewis, and Agustín Millares Carlo, eds. Cuerpo de documentos del siglo XVI sobre los derechos de España en las Indias y Filipinas. Mexico, 1943.

Hay, Guillermo. "Apuntes geográficos, estadísticos e históricos del distrito de Texcoco," *Boletín de la Sociedad mexicana de geografía y estadística,* época 2, II (1870), 541–55; IV (1872), 236–50.

Heizer, Robert F., and Sherburne F. Cook. "New Evidence of Antiquity of Tepexpan and Other Human Remains from the Valley of Mexico," *Southwestern Journal of Anthropology,* XV (1959), 36–42.

Hernández, Francisco. Antigüedades de la Nueva España. Joaquín García Pimentel, trans. and ed. Mexico, 1945.

Hernández Xolocotzi, Efraim. "Maize Granaries in Mexico," *Harvard University Botanical Museum Leaflets,* XIII, no. 7 (1949), 153–92.

Herrera, Antonio de. Historia general de los hechos de los castellanos en las islas y tierra firme del mar oceano. Title varies. 4 vols., 8 decades. Madrid, 1726–40.

Herrera y Pérez, Manuel María. "Tlahuac," *Boletín de la Sociedad mexicana de geografía y estadística,* época 3, I (1873), 294–303.

Histoire de la nation mexicaine depuis le départ d'Aztlan jusqu'à l'arrivée des conquérants espagnols (et au delà 1607). J. M. A. Aubin, trans. Paris, 1893.

Historia tolteca-chichimeca. Anales de Quauhtinchan. Heinrich Berlin, Silvia Rendón, Paul Kirchhoff, and Salvador Toscano, eds. Mexico, 1947. Fuentes para la historia de México, I.

Humboldt, Alexander de. Political Essay on the Kingdom of New Spain. John Black, trans. 4 vols. London, 1822.

Icaza, Francisco A. de. Diccionario autobiográfico de conquistadores y pobladores de Nueva España. 2 vols. Madrid, 1923.

————. "Miscelánea histórica," *Revista mexicana de estudios históricos,* II (1928), Appendix, 5–112.

Il manoscritto messicano vaticano 3738 detto el Codice Rios. Rome, 1900.

Indice de documentos de Nueva España existentes en el Archivo de Indias de Sevilla. 4 vols. Mexico, 1928–31. Monografías bibliográficas mexicanas, 12, 14, 22, 23.

Indice del ramo de Indios del Archivo general de la nación. Luis Chávez Orozco, ed. 2 vols. Mexico, 1951–53.

"Información del señor de Coyoacán," *Anales del Museo nacional de arqueología, historia y etnografía,* época 4, V (1927), 354–59.

Información que el arzobispo de México Don Fray Alonso de Montúfar mandó practicar con motivo de un sermón que en la fiesta de la Natividad de Nuestra Señora (8 de setiembre de 1556) predicó en la capilla de San José de naturales del convento de San Francisco de Méjico, el provincial fray Francisco de Bustamante acerca de la devoción y culto de Nuestra Señora de Guadalupe. Mexico, 1891.

Información sobre los tributos que los indios pagaban a Moctezuma. Año de 1554. France V. Scholes and Eleanor B. Adams, eds. Mexico, 1957. Documentos para la historia del México colonial, IV.

Instrucción del virrey Marqués de Croix que deja a su sucesor Antonio María Bucareli. Norman F. Martin, ed. Mexico, 1960.

Instrucciones que los vireyes de Nueva España dejaron a sus sucesores. Mexico, 1867.

Instrucciones que los vireyes de Nueva España dejaron a sus sucesores. 2 vols. Mexico, 1873. Biblioteca histórica de la Iberia, XIII–XIV.

Ixtlilxochitl, Fernando de Alva. Historia de la nación chichimeca. Alfredo Chavero, ed. Mexico, 1892. Obras históricas, II.

————. Relaciones. Alfredo Chavero, ed. Mexico, 1891. Obras históricas, I.

Jacobs Muller, E. Florencia. "Recursos naturales del lago de Xochimilco, del siglo X al XVI," *Boletín de la Sociedad mexicana de geografía y estadística,* LXXIII (1952), 7–16.

Jiménez Moreno, Wigberto. "Síntesis de la historia precolonial del valle de México," *Revista mexicana de estudios antropológicos,* XIV, Primera Parte (1954–55), 219–36.

Katz, Friedrich. Die sozialökonomischen Verhältnisse bei den Azteken im 15. und

624 Bibliography

16. Jahrhundert. Berlin, 1956. Ethnographisch-archäologische Forschungen, III (2).

Kelly, Isabel, and Angel Palerm. The Tajin Totonac, Part 1. History, Subsistence, Shelter and Technology. Washington, 1952. Smithsonian Institution, Institute of Social Anthropology, Publication no. 13.

Kirchhoff, Paul. "Composición étnica y organización política de Chalco según las Relaciones de Chimalpahin," Revista mexicana de estudios antropológicos, XIV, Primera Parte (1954–55), 297–98.

————. "Land Tenure in Ancient Mexico, A Preliminary Sketch," Revista mexicana de estudios antropológicos, XIV, Primera Parte (1954–55), 351–61.

Krickeberg, Walter. Altmexikanische Kulturen. Berlin, 1956.

Kubler, George. Mexican Architecture of the Sixteenth Century. 2 vols. New Haven, 1948. Yale Historical Publications, History of Art, V.

————, and Charles Gibson. The Tovar Calendar. New Haven, 1951. Memoirs of the Connecticut Academy of Arts & Sciences, XI.

La administración de D. Frey Antonio María de Bucareli y Ursua, cuadragésimo sexto virey de México. 2 vols. Mexico, 1936. Publicaciones del Archivo general de la nación, XXIX–XXX.

La constitución de 1812 en la Nueva España. 2 vols. Mexico, 1912–13. Publicaciones del Archivo general de la nación, IV–V.

Lamb, Ursula. "Religious Conflicts in the Conquest of Mexico," Journal of the History of Ideas, XVII (1956), 526–39.

Larsen, Helga. "Notes on the Volador and Its Associated Ceremonies and Superstitions," Ethnos (Stockholm), II (1937), 179–92.

Las Casas, Bartolomé de. Apologética historia de las Indias. M. Serrano y Sanz, ed. Madrid, 1909. Nueva biblioteca de autores españoles, XIII.

Las siete partidas del rey Alfonso el sabio. 3 vols. Madrid, 1807.

Latorre, Germán, ed. Relaciones geográficas de Indias. Seville, 1920. Biblioteca colonial americana, IV.

Lee, Raymond L. "American Cochineal in European Commerce, 1526–1625," The Journal of Modern History, XXIII (1951), 205–24.

————. "Cochineal Production and Trade in New Spain to 1600," The Americas, IV (1947–48), 449–73.

————. "Grain Legislation in Colonial Mexico, 1575–85," Hispanic American Historical Review, XXVII (1947), 647–60.

Legislación del trabajo en los siglos XVI, XVII y XVIII. Relación entre la economía, las artes y los oficios en la Nueva España. Mexico, 1938.

Leicht, Hugo. "Chinampas y almácigos flotantes," Anales del Instituto de biología, VIII (1937), 375–86.

León, Nicolás. "Bibliografía mexicana del siglo XVIII," Boletín del Instituto bibliográfico mexicano, núms. 1, 4, 5, 7, 8, 10. Mexico, 1902–8.

————, ed. Documentos inéditos referentes al ilustrísimo señor Don Vasco de Quiroga existentes en el Archivo general de Indias. Mexico, 1940. Biblioteca histórica mexicana de obras inéditas, XVII.

————. Las castas del México colonial o Nueva España. Mexico, 1924.

León Pinelo, Antonio de. Tratado de confirmaciones reales de encomiendas, oficios i casos, en que se requieren para las Indias occidentales. Madrid, 1630.

León y Gama, Antonio de. "Descripción de la ciudad de México, antes y despúes de la llegada de los conquistadores españoles," *Revista mexicana de estudios históricos,* I (1927), Appendix, 8–58.

Leonard, Irving A. Don Carlos de Sigüenza y Góngora, A Mexican Savant of the Seventeenth Century. Berkeley, 1929.

Leyes y ordenanzas nvevamente hechas por sv magestad, para la gouernaciō de las Indias, y buen tratamiento y conseruacion de los indios. Valladolid, 1603.

Linné, Sigvald. "Bird Nets of Lake Texcoco, Mexico Valley," *Ethnos* (Stockholm), V (1940), 122–30.

———. El valle y la ciudad de México en 1550. Relación histórica fundada sobre un mapa geográfico, que se conserva en la biblioteca de la Universidad de Uppsala, Swecia. Stockholm, 1948.

Lizardi Ramos, César. "El manantial y el acueducto de Acuecuexco," *Historia mexicana,* IV (1954–55), 218–34.

Llamas, Roberto. "La alimentación de los antiguos mexicanos," *Anales del Instituto de biología,* VI (1935), 245–58.

Lobato, José G. "Meteorología de México," *Boletín de la Sociedad mexicana de geografía y estadística,* época 3, III (1876), 3–131.

López, Patricio Ana. "Inventario de los documentos recogidos a Don Lorenzo Boturini por orden del gobierno virreinal," *Anales del Museo nacional de arqueología, historia y etnografía,* época 4, III (1925), 1–55.

López de Gómara, Francisco. Historia de la conquista de México. Joaquín Ramírez Cabañas, ed. Mexico, 1943.

López de Meneses, Amada. "Dos nietas de Moteczuma, monjas de la Concepción de México," *Revista de Indias,* XII (1952), 81–100.

———. "El primer regreso de Hernán Cortés a España," *Revista de Indias,* XIV (1954), 69–91.

———. "Tecuichpochtzin, hija de Moteczuma (¿1510?–1550)," *Revista de Indias,* IX (1948), 471–95.

López de Velasco, Juan. Geografía y descripción universal de las Indias. Justo Zaragoza, ed. Madrid, 1894.

López Sarrelangue, Delfina. "Los tributos de la parcialidad de Santiago Tlatelolco," *Memorias de la Academia mexicana de la historia,* XV (1956), 129–224.

———. Una villa mexicana en el siglo XVIII. Mexico, 1957. Colección cultura mexicana, 20.

Lorenzana, Francisco Antonio. Cartas pastorales, y edictos. Mexico, 1770.

———. Concilio provinciales primero, y segundo, celebrados en la muy noble, y muy leal ciudad de México, presidiendo el Illmo. y Rmo. Señor D. Fr. Alonso de Montúfar, en los años de 1555, y 1565. Mexico, 1769.

Madsen, William. "Christo-Paganism. A Study of Mexican Religious Syncretism," in Middle American Research Institute, Tulane University, Publication no. 19, pp. 105–80.

———. The Virgin's Children. Life in an Aztec Village Today. Austin, Texas, 1960.

Maniau Torquemada, Joaquín. Compendio de la historia de la real hacienda de Nueva España. Mexico, 1914.

"Mappe de Tepechpan. (Histoire synchronique et seigneuriale de Tepechpan et de Mexico)," *Anales del Museo nacional de arqueología, historia y etnografía,* III (1886), Pl. 3 (fac. p. 368).

Marroquí, José María. La ciudad de México. 3 vols. Mexico, 1909–1903.

Martin, Norman F. Los vagabundos en la Nueva España siglo XVI. Mexico, 1957.

Martín del Campo, Rafael. "El pulque en el México precortesiano," *Anales del Instituto de biología,* IX (1938), 5–23.

———. "Productos biológicos del valle de México," *Revista mexicana de estudios antropológicos,* XIV, Primera Parte (1954–55), 53–77.

Martínez, Henrico. Reportorio de los tiempos e historia natural de Nueva España. Mexico, 1948. Testimonios mexicanos, historiadores, I.

Martínez Cosio, Leopoldo. Los caballeros de las órdenes militares en México. Catálogo biográfico y genealógico. Mexico, 1946.

Maza, Francisco de la. Enrico Martínez, cosmógrafo e impresor de Nueva España. Mexico, 1943.

Maza, Francisco F. de la. Código de colonización y terrenos baldíos de la república mexicana. Mexico, 1893.

McAfee, Byron, and Robert H. Barlow. "Anales de la conquista de Tlatelolco en 1473 y en 1521," *Memorias de la Academia mexicana de la historia,* IV (1945), 326–38.

———. "La segunda parte del Códice Aubin," *Memorias de la Academia mexicana de la historia,* VI (1947), 156–82.

———. "The Titles of Tetzcotzinco (Santa María Nativitas)," *Tlalocan,* II (1945–48), 110–27.

McAlister, Lyle N. The "Fuero militar" in New Spain 1764–1800. Gainesville, Florida, 1957.

McBride, George McCutchen. The Land Systems of Mexico. New York, 1923. American Geographical Society Research Series, no. 12.

Memoria histórica, técnica y administrativa de las obras del desagüe del valle de México. 2 vols. and Atlas. Mexico, 1902.

Mendieta, Gerónimo de. Historia eclesiástica indiana. Joaquín García Icazbalceta, ed. Mexico, 1870.

Mendizábal, Miguel O. de. "El santuario del Señor de Sacromonte, en Amecameca," in Obras completas (6 vols. Mexico, 1946–47), II, 521–27.

———. "Influencia de la sal en la distribución geográfica de los grupos indígenas de México," in Obras completas (6 vols. Mexico, 1946–47), II, 175–340.

———. "Los otomies no fueron los primeros pobladores del valle de México," in Obras completas (6 vols. Mexico, 1946–47), II, 453–74.

Mendoza, Vicente T. "Un barrio prehispánico de la ciudad de México," *Tlalocan,* I (1943–44), 361.

Mercedes y pensiones, limosnas y salarios en la real hacienda de la Nueva España. Mexico, 1945. Archivo histórico de hacienda. Colección de documentos publicados bajo la dirección de Jesús Silva Herzog, V.

Mier, Servando Teresa de. Escritos inéditos. Mexico, 1944.

Millares Carlo, Agustín, and J. I. Mantecón. Indice y extractos de los protocolos del Archivo de notarías de México, D.F. 2 vols. Mexico, 1945–46.

Miranda, José. El tributo indígena en la Nueva España durante el siglo XVI. Mexico, 1952.

———. "La función económica del encomendero en los orígenes del régimen colonial de Nueva España (1525–1531)," *Anales del Instituto nacional de antropología e historia,* II (1941–46), 421–62.

———. "La población indígena de México en el siglo XVII," *Historia mexicana,* XII (1962–63), 182–89.

———. Las ideas y las instituciones políticas mexicanas. Primera parte 1521–1820. Mexico, 1952.

Moderación de doctrinas de la real corona administradas por las órdenes ~ ~idicantes 1623. France V. Scholes and Eleanor B. Adams, eds. Mexic~ ~959. Documentos para la historia de México colonial, VI.

Molina, Alonso de. Vocabulario en lengua castellana y mexicana. Madrid, 1944. Colección de incunables americanos, IV.

Molíns Fábrega, N. "El Códice mendocino y la economía de Tenochtitlan," *Revista mexicana de estudios antropológicos,* XIV, Primera Parte (1954–55), 303–35.

Mols, Roger. Introduction à la démographie historique des villes d'Europe du XIVe au XVIIIe siècle. 3 vols. Louvain, 1954–56. Université de Louvain, Recueil de travaux d'histoire et de philologie, ser. 4, I–III.

Montejano y Aguiñaga, Rafael. "Notas para una bibliografía guadalupana," *Abside,* XIII (1949), 355–402, 497–546.

Montúfar, Alonso de. "Carta del arzobispo de México al Consejo de Indias sobre la necesidad de que los indios pagasen diezmos," *Anales del Museo nacional de arqueología, historia y etnografía,* época 5, I (1934), 339–60.

Monzón, Arturo. El calpulli en la organización social de los tenochca. Mexico, 1949. Publicaciones del Instituto de historia, primera serie, 14.

Mooser, Federico, Sidney E. White, and José L. Lorenzo. La cuenca de México. Consideraciones geológicas y arqueológicas. Mexico, 1956.

Morales Rodríguez, Sergio. "Costumbres y creencias en la Nueva España," in Homenaje a Silvio Zavala. Estudios históricos americanos (Mexico, 1953), pp. 425–76.

Moreno, Manuel M. La organización política y social de los aztecas. Mexico, 1931.

Motolinía (Toribio de Benavente). History of the Indians of New Spain. Elizabeth Andros Foster, trans. and ed. Berkeley, 1950. The Cortés Society, Documents and Narratives Concerning the Discovery & Conquest of Latin America, n.s., no. 4.

———. Memoriales. Luis García Pimentel, ed. Mexico, Paris, Madrid, 1903. Documentos históricos de Méjico, I.

Moxó, Benito María de. Cartas mejicanas. Genoa, 1839.

Muñoz Camargo, Diego. Historia de Tlaxcala. Mexico, 1947.

Muriel, Josefina. "Reflexiones sobre Hernán Cortés," *Revista de Indias,* IX (1948), 229–45.

Navarro de Vargas, Joseph. "Padrón del pueblo de San Mateo Huitzilopochco, inventario de su iglesia y directorio de sus obvenciones parroquiales," *Anales del Museo nacional de arqueología, historia y etnología,* época 3, I (1909), 553–99.

Navarro García, Luis. Intendencias en Indias. Seville, 1959. Publicaciones de la Escuela de estudios hispano-americanos de Sevilla, CXVIII.

Navarro y Noriega, Fernando. Catálogo de los curatos y misiones de la Nueva España seguido de la Memoria sobre la población del reino de Nueva España. Mexico, 1943.

———. "Memoria sobre la población del reino de Nueva-España," *Boletín de la Sociedad de geografía y estadística de la república mexicana,* época 2, I (1869), 281–91.

Nobilario de conquistadores de Indias. Madrid, 1892.

"Noticias de Nueva-España en 1805," *Boletín del Instituto nacional de geografía y estadística de la república mexicana,* época 1, II (1864; ed. 3), 3–41.

Nueva colección de documentos para la historia de México. Joaquín García Icazbalceta, ed. 5 vols. Mexico, 1886–92.

Nueva colección de documentos para la historia de México. Joaquín García Icazbalceta, ed. 3 vols. Mexico, 1941.

Nuevos documentos relativos a los bienes de Hernán Cortés 1547–1947. Mexico, 1946.

Nuttall, Zelia. "Las tres casas en Coyoacán, atribuídas a conquistadores," *Boletín de la Sociedad mexicana de geografía y estadística,* LIV (1940–41), 587–604.

Ocaranza, Fernando. Capítulos de la historia franciscana. 2 vols. Mexico, 1933–34.

——. El imperial colegio de indios de la Santa Cruz de Santiago Tlaltelolco. Mexico, 1934.

Ojea, Hernando. Libro tercero de la historia religiosa de la prouincia de México de la orden de Sto. Domingo. Mexico, 1897.

Olivé N., Julio César, and Beatriz Barba A. "Sobre la disintegración de las culturas clásicas," *Anales del Instituto nacional de antropología e historia,* IX (1955), 57–71.

Olivera Sedano, Alicia. "Cuitlahuac," *Revista mexicana de estudios antropológicos,* XIV, Primera Parte (1954–55), 299–302.

Ordenanzas del trabajo, siglos XVI y XVII. Silvio Zavala, ed. Mexico, 1947.

Oroz, Pedro, Jerónimo [Gerónimo] de Mendieta, and Francisco Suárez. Relación de la descripción de la provincia del Santo Evangelio que es en las Indias occidentales que llaman la Nueva España. Fidel de J. Chauvet, ed. Mexico, 1947. Anales de la provincia del Santo Evangelio de México, año 4, no. 2.

Orozco, Wistano Luis. Legislación y jurisprudencia sobre terrenos baldíos. 2 vols. Mexico, 1895.

Orozco y Berra, Manuel. Historia antigua y de la conquista de México. 4 vols. Mexico, 1880.

——. Historia de la dominación española en México. 4 vols. Mexico, 1938. Biblioteca histórica mexicana de obras inéditas, ser. 1, VIII–XI.

——. Memoria para el plano de la ciudad de México. Mexico, 1867.

——. Memoria para la carta hidrográfica del valle de México. Mexico, 1864.

——. Noticia histórica de la conjuración del Marqués del Valle. Años de 1565–1568. Mexico, 1853.

——. "Tlacopan y Texcoco," *Divulgación histórica,* IV (1942–43), 507–10.

Ortega y Pérez Gallardo, Ricardo. Historia genealógica de las familias más antiguas de México. 3 vols. Mexico, 1908–10.

Osores, Felix de. Historia de todos los colegios de la ciudad de México desde la conquista hasta 1780. Carlos E. Castañeda, ed. Mexico, 1929. Nuevos documentos inéditos o muy raros para la historia de México, II.

Oviedo y Valdés, Gonzalo Fernández de. Historia general y natural de las Indias, islas y tierra-firme del mar océano. 4 vols. Madrid, 1851–55.

Palacios, Enrique Juan. "¿De donde viene la palabra México?," *Anales del Museo nacional de arqueología, historia y etnografía,* época 4, IV (1926), 478–508.

Palafox y Mendoza, Juan de. Virtudes del indio. Madrid, 1893. Colección de libros raros ó curiosos que tratan de América, X.

Palerm, Angel. "La distribución del regadío en el área central de Mesoamérica," *Ciencias sociales,* V (1954), 2–15, 64–74.

——. "The Agricultural Basis of Urban Civilization in Mesoamerica," in Irrigation Civilizations: A Comparative Study (Pan American Union Social Science Monographs, I. Washington, 1955), pp. 28–42.

——, and Eric R. Wolf. "El desarrollo del área clave del imperio texcocano," *Revista mexicana de estudios antropológicos,* XIV, Primera Parte (1954–55), 337–49.

Papeles de Nueva España. Francisco del Paso y Troncoso, ed. 9 vols. Madrid and Mexico, 1905–48.

Paso y Troncoso, Francisco del, and Faustino Chimalpopoca Galicia, eds. "Lista de los pueblos principales que pertenecían antiguamente a Tetzcoco," *Anales del Museo nacional de México,* época 1, IV (1897), 48–56.

Payno, Manuel. "Memoria sobre el maguey mexicano y sus diversos productos," *Boletín de la Sociedad mexicana de geografía y estadística,* época 1, X (1863), 383–451, 485–530.

Paz, Julián. Catálogo de manuscritos de América existentes en la Biblioteca nacional. Madrid, 1933.

Paz, Octavio. "Todos Santos, día de muertos," *Evergreen Review,* no. 7 (1959), 22–37.

Peñafiel, Antonio, ed. Colección de documentos para la historia mexicana. Mexico, 1904.

———. Memoria sobre las aguas potables de la capital. Mexico, 1884.

Pérez de Rivas, Andrés. Corónica y historia religiosa de la provincia de la Compañía de Jesús de México en Nueva España. 2 vols. Mexico, 1896.

Pferdekamp, Wilhelm. "Enrico Martinez oder die Wassersnot von Mexico," *Ibero-Amerikanisches Archiv,* XI (1937–38), 423–34.

Phelan, John Leddy. The Millennial Kingdom of the Franciscans in the New World. A Study of the Writings of Gerónimo de Mendieta (1525–1604). Berkeley and Los Angeles, 1956. University of California Publications in History, LII.

Poumarède, J. A. "Desagüe del valle de México," *Boletín del Instituto nacional de geografía y estadística de la república mexicana,* época 1, VII (1859), 463–89.

Prescott, William Hickling. History of the Conquest of Mexico. John Foster Kirk, ed 3 vols. Philadelphia, 1873.

Proceso inquisitorial del cacique de Tetzcoco. Mexico, 1910. Publicaciones del Archivo general de la nación, I.

Procesos de indios idólatras y hechiceros. Mexico, 1912. Publicaciones del Archivo general de la nación, III.

Procesos de residencia, instruídos contra Pedro de Alvarado y Nuño de Guzmán. J. F. Ramírez, ed. Mexico, 1847.

Puga, Vasco de. Provisiones cédulas instrucciones para el gobierno de la Nueva España. Madrid, 1945. Colección de incunables americanos, III.

Querol y Roso, Luis. Negros y mulatos de Nueva España (historia de su alzamiento en Méjico en 1612). Valencia, 1935. Separado de Anales de la Universidad de Valencia, año XII, cuaderno 90.

Radin, Paul. "The Sources and Authenticity of the History of the Ancient Mexicans," *University of California Publications in American Archaeology and Ethnology,* XVII (Berkeley, 1920), 1–150.

Ramírez, José. La vegetación de México. Mexico, 1899.

Ramírez, José Fernando. Adiciones á la biblioteca de Beristain. 2 vols. Mexico, 1898. Biblioteca de autores mexicanos, XVI–XVII.

Ramírez Cabañas, Joaquín. "Los macehuales," *Filosofía y letras,* II (1941), 119–24.

Real ordenanza para el establecimiento é instrucción de intendentes de exército y provincia en el reino de la Nueva-España. Madrid, 1786.

Recopilación de leyes de los reynos de las Indias. Edición facsimilar de la cuarta impresión hecha en Madrid el año 1791. 3 vols. Madrid, 1943.

Reiche, Carlos. La vegetación en los alrededores de la capital de México. Mexico, 1914.

Relación de las encomiendas de indios hechas en Nueva España a los conquistadores y pobladores de ella, año de 1564. France V. Scholes and Eleanor B. Adams, eds. Mexico, 1955. Documentos para la historia del México colonial, I.

"Relación de Téquisquiac, Citlaltepec y Xilocingo," *Tlalocan,* III (1949–57), 289–308.

"Relación de Zempoala y su partido, 1580," *Tlalocan,* III (1949–57), 29–41.

Rendón, Silvia, ed. "Ordenanza del Señor Cuauhtemoc," in Middle American Research Institute, Tulane University, Publication no. 12 (New Orleans, 1952), pp. 13–40.

Ribadeneyra y Barrientos, Antonio Joachín de. Manual compendio de el regio patronato indiano, para su mas fácil uso en las materias conducentes à la práctica. Madrid, 1755.

Ricard, Robert. "Documents pour l'histoire des franciscains au Mexique," *Revue d'histoire franciscaine,* I (1924), 216–35.

———. La "conquête spirituelle" du Mexique. Paris, 1933. Université de Paris, Travaux et mémoires de l'Institut d'ethnologie, XX.

Rivera, Juan Antonio. "Diario curioso y esacto," *El Museo mexicano,* I (1843), 49–53, 84–87, 99–102, 132–33.

Rivera Cambas, Manuel. México pintoresco artístico y monumental. 3 vols. Mexico, 1880–83.

Robertson, Donald. Mexican Manuscript Painting of the Early Colonial Period, The Metropolitan Schools. New Haven, 1959. Yale Historical Publications, History of Art, XII.

———. "The Techialoyan Codex of Tepotzotlán: Codex X (Rylands Mexican MS. I)," *Bulletin of the John Rylands Library,* XLIII (1960), 109–30.

Robles, Antonio de. Diario de sucesos notables (1665–1703). Antonio Castro Leal, ed. 3 vols. Mexico, 1946.

Román y Zamora, Jerónimo. Repúblicas de Indias: Idolatrías y gobierno en México y Perú antes de la conquista. 2 vols. Madrid, 1897. Colección de libros raros ó curiosos que tratan de América, XIV–XV.

Romero de Terreros, Manuel. Antiguas haciendas de México. Mexico, 1956.

———. Bibliografía de cronistas de la ciudad de México. Mexico, 1926. Monografías bibliográficas mexicanas, núm. 4.

———. "Dos conquistadores," *Historia mexicana,* V (1955–56), 228–32.

———. El conde de Regla, creso de la Nueva España. Mexico, 1943.

———. "Epigrafía de la hacienda de Xalpa," *Anales del Museo nacional de arqueología, historia y etnografía,* época 4, VII (1931–32), 418–21.

———. "Los acueductos de México," *Anales del Museo nacional de arqueología, historia y etnografía,* época 4, III (1925), 131–42.

———. Los acueductos de México en la historia y en el arte. Mexico, 1949.

———. "Los corregidores de México," *Anales del Museo nacional de arqueología, historia y etnografía,* época 4, I (1922), 84–92.

Rosa y Saldívar, Vicente de la. "Un inventario de los documentos de la colección Boturini," *Memorias de la Academia mexicana de la historia,* V (1946), 257–301.

Rosenblat, Angel. La población indígena de América desde 1492 hasta la actualidad. Buenos Aires, 1945.

Rubio Mañé, J. Ignacio. "Apuntes para la biografía de Don Luis de Velasco, el viejo," *Revista de historia de América,* núm. 13 (1941), 41–99.

Ruiz de Alarcón, Hernando. "Tratado de las supersticiones y costumbres gentilicas que oy viuen entre los indios naturales desta Nueua España," *Anales del Museo nacional de arqueología, historia y etnografía,* época 1, VI (1892), 123–223.

Sahagún, Bernardino de. Einige Kapitel aus dem Geschichtswerk des Fray Bernardino de Sahagún. Eduard Seler, trans. Stuttgart, 1927.
———. General History of the Things of New Spain; Florentine Codex. Arthur J. O. Anderson and Charles E. Dibble, trans. and eds. 13 Parts. Santa Fe, 1950 et seq. Monographs of The School of American Research, No. 14.
———. Historia general de las cosas de Nueva España. Miguel Acosta Saignes, ed. 3 vols. Mexico, 1946.
———. "Relación breve de las fiestas de los dioses," Tlalocan, II (1945–48), 289–320.
———. Vida económica de Tenochtitlan. 1. Pochtecayotl (arte de traficar). Angel María Garibay K., trans. and ed. Mexico, 1961. Fuentes indígenas de la cultura náhuatl, Informantes de Sahagún, 3.
San Vicente, Juan Manuel de. "Exacta descripción de la magnífica corte mexicana," Anales del Museo nacional de arqueología, historia y etnografía, época 3, V (1913), 3–40.
Schäfer, Ernesto. El Consejo real y supremo de las Indias, su historia, organización y labor administrativa hasta la terminación de la casa de Austria. 2 vols. Seville, 1935–47.
Scholes, Walter V. The Diego Ramírez Visita. Columbia, Mo., 1946. The University of Missouri Studies, XX, no. 4.
Schottelius, Justus Wolfram. "Wieviel Dämme verbanden die Inselstadt Mexico-Tenochtitlan mit dem Festlande?," Ibero-Amerikanisches Archiv, VIII (1934–35), 173–85.
Sears, Paul B. "El análisis de polén en la investigación arqueológica," Tlatoani, I (1952), nos. 3–4, 29–30.
———. "Palynology in Southern North America. I: Archeological Horizons in the Basins of Mexico," Bulletin of the Geological Society of America, LXIII (1952), 241–54.
———. "Pollen Profiles and Culture Horizons in the Basin of Mexico," in The Civilizations of Ancient America, Selected Papers of the XXIXth International Congress of Americanists (Sol Tax, ed. Chicago, 1951), pp. 57–61.
———. "The Interdependence of Archeology and Ecology, with Examples from Middle America," Transactions of the New York Academy of Sciences, Ser. II, Vol. 15 (1952–53), 113–17.
Sedano, Francisco. Noticias de México. 2 vols. Mexico, 1880.
Segura, José C. El maguey. Memoria sobre el cultivo y beneficio de sus productos. Mexico, 1891.
Seler, Eduard. "Mexican Picture Writing of Alexander von Humboldt," in Mexican and Central American Antiquities, Calendar Systems, and History (Smithsonian Institution, Bureau of American Ethnology, Bulletin 28, Washington, 1904), pp. 127–229.
Serna, Jacinto de la. "Manual de ministros de indios para el conocimiento de sus idolatrías, y extirpación de ellas," Anales del Museo nacional de arqueología, historia y etnografía, época 1, VI (1892–99), 261–480.
Simpson, Lesley Byrd. Exploitation of Land in Central Mexico in the Sixteenth Century. Berkeley and Los Angeles, 1952. Ibero-Americana: 36.
———. Studies in the Administration of the Indians in New Spain. I. The Laws of Burgos of 1512. II. The Civil Congregation. Berkeley, 1934. Ibero-Americana: 7.
———. The Encomienda in New Spain. The Beginning of Spanish Mexico. Berkeley and Los Angeles, 1950.

Smith, Robert Sidney. "Sales Taxes in New Spain, 1575–1770," *Hispanic American Historical Review,* XXVIII (1948), 2–37.

Sobre el modo de tributar los indios de Nueva España a su magestad 1561–1564. France V. Scholes and Eleanor B. Adams, eds. Mexico, 1958. Documentos para la historia del México colonial, V.

Sokoloff, V. P., and José L. Lorenzo. "Modern and Ancient Soils at Some Archaeological Sites in the Valley of Mexico," *American Antiquity,* XIX (1953–54), 50–55.

Solórzano y Pereira, Juan de. *Política indiana.* Amberes, 1703.

Soustelle, Jacques. "Apuntes sobre la psicología y el sistema de valores en México antes de la conquista," in Estudios antropológicos publicados en homenaje al doctor Manuel Gamio (Mexico, 1956), pp. 497–502.

———. La vie quotidienne des Aztèques à la veille de la conquête espagnole. Paris, 1955.

Steck, Francisco Borgia. El primer colegio de América—Santa Cruz de Tlaltelolco. Mexico, 1944.

Sticker, Georg. "Die Einschleppung Europäischer Krankheiten in Amerika während der Entdeckungszeit; ihr Einfluss auf den Rückgang der Bevölkerung," *Ibero-Amerikanisches Archiv,* VI (1932–33), 62–83, 194–224.

Suárez de Peralta, Juan. Noticias históricas de la Nueva España. Madrid, 1878.

Téllez Pizarro, Mariano. Estudio sobre cimientos para los edificios de la ciudad de México. Mexico, 1907.

Ternaux Compans, Henri. Voyages, relations et mémoires originaux pour servir à l'histoire de la découverte de l'Amérique, 20 vols. Paris, 1837–41.

"Testamento de María Alonso, india de Tlatelolco," *Memorias de la Academia mexicana de la historia,* V (1946), 198–204.

The Badianus Manuscript (Codex Barberini, Latin 241) Vatican Library, An Aztec Herbal of 1552. Emily Walcott Emmart, trans. and ed. Baltimore, 1940.

Thompson, J. Eric S. "Notes on the Use of Cacao in Middle America," *Notes on Middle American Archaeology and Ethnology,* no. 128 (1956), pp. 95–116.

Títulos principales del nombre y ejidos del barrio de la Magdalena Mexihuca antes barrio y hermita de Lloalatzinco Anepantla. Mexico, 1915.

Tolstoy, Paul. Surface Survey of the Northern Valley of Mexico: the Classic and Post-Classic Periods. Philadelphia, 1958. Transactions of the American Philosophical Society, n.s., XLVIII, Part 5.

Torquemada, Juan de. Primera (Segunda, Tercera) parte de los veinte i vn libros rituales i monarchia indiana. 3 vols. Madrid, 1723.

Torres Lanzas, Pedro. Relación descriptiva de los mapas, planos, &, de México y Floridas existentes en el Archivo general de Indias. 2 vols. Seville, 1900.

Torres Quintero, Gregorio. México hacia el fin del virreinato español. Antecedentes sociológicos del pueblo mexicano. Paris and Mexico, 1921.

Toussaint, Manuel. La catedral de México. Mexico, 1924. Iglesias de México (Gerardo Murillo, ed. 6 vols.), II.

———, Federico Gómez de Orozco, and Justino Fernández. Planos de la ciudad de México. Siglos XVI y XVII. Estudio histórico, urbanístico y bibliográfico. Mexico, 1938.

Tudela, José. "El 'volador' mejicano," *Revista de Indias,* VII (1946), 71–88.

———. Los manuscritos de América en las bibliotecas de España. Madrid, 1954.

Ulloa Ortiz, Berta. "Catálogo de los fondos del Centro de documentación del Museo nacional de historia, castillo de Chapultepec," *Anales del Instituto nacional de antropología e historia,* IV (1949–50), 289–322.

"Unos anales coloniales de Tlatelolco, 1519–1633," *Memorias de la Academia mexicana de la historia*, VII (1948), 152–87.

Urbina, Manuel. "Plantas comestibles de los antiguos mexicanos," *Anales del Museo nacional de arqueología, historia y etnografía*, época 2, I (1903), 503–91.

———. "Raíces comestibles entre los antiguos mexicanos," *Anales del Museo nacional de arqueología, historia y etnografía*, época 2, III (1906), 117–90.

Vaillant, George C. Aztecs of Mexico. Origin, Rise, and Fall of the Aztec Nation. Garden city, N.Y., 1944.

———. Early Cultures of the Valley of Mexico: Results of the Stratigraphical Project of the American Museum of Natural History in the Valley of Mexico, 1928–1933. New York, 1935. Anthropological Papers of the American Museum of Natural History, XXXV, Part III.

———. Excavations at El Arbolillo. New York, 1935. Anthropological Papers of the American Museum of Natural History, XXXV, Part II.

———. Excavations at Zacatenco. New York, 1930. Anthropological Papers of the American Museum of Natural History, XXXII, Part I.

Valderrama, Jerónimo. Cartas del licenciado Jerónimo Valderrama y otros documentos sobre su visita al gobierno de Nueva España. 1563–1565. France V. Scholes and Eleanor B. Adams, eds. Mexico, 1961. Documentos para la historia del México colonial, VII.

Valdés, Octaviano. El padre Tembleque. Mexico, 1945.

———. "Fray Francisco de Tembleque," *The Americas*, III (1946–47), 223–33.

Vázquez de Espinosa, Antonio. Compendium and Description of the West Indies. Charles Upson Clark, trans. Washington, 1942. Smithsonian Miscellaneous Collections, CII.

Vázquez de Tapia, Bernardino. Relación del conquistador Bernardino Vázquez de Tapia. Manuel Romero de Terreros, ed. Mexico, 1939.

Vera, Fortino Hipólito. Erecciones parroquiales de México y Puebla. Amecameca, 1889.

———. Informaciones sobre la milagrosa aparición de la santísima virgen de Guadalupe, recibidas en 1666 y 1723. Amecameca, 1889.

———. Tesoro guadalupano. Noticia de los libros, documentos, inscripciones &c. que tratan, mencionan ó aluden á la aparición y devoción de Nuestra Señora de Guadalupe. Amecameca, 1887.

Vetancurt, Agustín de. Chronica de la provincia del Santo Evangelio de Mexico. Quarta parte del Teatro mexicano de los successos religiosos. Mexico, 1697.

———. Teatro mexicano. Descripción breve de los svcessos exemplares, historicos, politicos, militares, y religiosos del nuevo mundo occidental de las Indias. 2 vols. Mexico, 1698.

Veytia, Mariano. Historia antigua de Méjico. C. F. Ortega, ed. 3 vols. Mexico, 1836.

Viera, Juan de. Compendiosa narración de la ciudad de México. Mexico, 1952.

Villa R., Bernardo. "Mamíferos silvestres del valle de México," *Anales del Instituto de biología*, XXIII (1952), 269–492.

Villada, Manuel M. "Los anátidos del valle de México," *Anales del Museo nacional de México*, IV (1897), 151–66, 253–60.

Villarroel, Hipólito. México por dentro y fuera bajo el gobierno de los vireyes. ó sea enfermedades políticas que padece la capital de la N. España en casi todos los cuerpos de que se compone, y remedios que se deben aplicar para su curación. Mexico, 1831.

Villa-señor y Sánchez, Joseph Antonio. Theatro americano. Descripción general de los

634 Bibliography

reynos, y provincias de la Nueva España, y sus jurisdicciones. 2 vols. Mexico, 1746–48.

Viñas y Mey, Carmelo, and Ramón Paz. Relaciones histórico-geográfico-estadísticas de los pueblos de España hechas por iniciativa de Felipe II. 2 vols. Madrid, 1949–51.

Walton, William. Present State of the Spanish Colonies. 2 vols. London, 1810.

Waterman, T. T. "Bandelier's Contribution to the Study of Ancient Mexican Social Organization," *University of California Publications in American Archaeology and Ethnology*, XII (Berkeley, 1917), 249–82.

Wauchope, Robert. "Implications of Radiocarbon Dates from Middle and South America," in Middle American Research Institute, Tulane University, Publication no. 18 (New Orleans, 1954), pp. 17–39.

———. Ten Years of Middle American Archaeology. Annotated Bibliography and News Summary, 1948–1957. New Orleans, 1961. Middle American Research Institute, Tulane University, Publication no. 28.

Weismann, Elizabeth Wilder. Mexico in Sculpture 1521–1821. Cambridge, Mass., 1950.

West, Robert C., and Pedro Armillas. "Las chinampas de México. Poesía y realidad de los 'jardines flotantes,' " *Cuadernos americanos*, L (1950), 165–82.

Willey, Norman L., and Carlos García Prada. "El embrujo de las chinampas," *Hispanic American Historical Review*, XIX (1939), 83–96.

Wolf, Eric R. Sons of the Shaking Earth. Chicago, 1959.

———, and Angel Palerm. "Irrigation in the Old Acolhua Domain, Mexico," *Southwestern Journal of Anthropology*, XI (1955), 265–81.

Zahar Vergara, Alfonso. "Fray Juan de Gaona y el colegio de Santa Cruz de Santiago en el barrio de Tlaltelolco," *Filosofía y letras*, XIII (1947), 265–86.

Zamora y Coronado, José María. Biblioteca de legislación ultramarina en forma de diccionario alfabético. 6 vols. Madrid, 1844–46.

Zavala, Silvio. "Catálogo de los fondos del Centro de documentación del Museo nacional de historia, en el castillo de Chapultepec," *Memorias de la Academia mexicana de la historia*, X (1951), 459–95.

———. De encomiendas y propiedad territorial en algunas regiones de la América española. Mexico, 1940.

———. Ideario de Vasco de Quiroga. Mexico, 1941.

———. La encomienda indiana. Madrid, 1935.

———. "La libertad de movimiento de los indios de Nueva España," *Memoria de El Colegio nacional*, II (1947), 103–63.

———. La "Utopía" de Tomás Moro en la Nueva España y otros estudios. Mexico, 1937. Biblioteca histórica mexicana de obras inéditas, ser. 1, IV.

———. "Los esclavos indios de Nueva España," in Homenaje al doctor Alfonso Caso (Mexico, 1951), pp. 427–40.

———. "Orígenes coloniales del peonaje en México," *El trimestre económico*, X (1943–44), 711–48.

Zimmermann, Günter. Das Geschichtswerk des Domingo de Muñon Chimalpahin Quauhtlehuanitzin (Quellenkritische Studien zur frühindianischen Geschichte Mexikos). Hamburg, 1960. Beiträge zur mittelamerikanischen Völkerkunde, V.

Zorita, Alonso de. Historia de la Nueva España. Madrid, 1909. Colección de libros y documentos referentes á la historia de América, IX.

Zúñiga y Ontiveros, Felipe. Calendario manual y guía de forasteros de México para el año de 1791. n.p., n.d.

Index

Index

638

Index

Index

Printed in the United States
1011200002B